CONTENTS.

CONTENTS.

MISCELLANEOUS POEMS.

CONTENTS.

THE BIGLOW PAPERS — FIRST SERIES.

THE BIGLOW PAPERS — SECOND SERIES.

CONTENTS.

JAMES RUSSELL LOWELL.

BIOGRAPHICAL SKETCH.

In the year 1639 ·Percival Lowle, or Lowell, a merchant of Bristol, England, landed at the little seaport town of Newbury, Mass.

We generally speak of a man's descent. In the case of James Russell Lowell's ancestry it was rather an ascent through eight generations. Percival Lowle's son, John Lowell, was a worthy cooper in old Newbury; his great-grandson was a shoemaker, his great-great-grandson was the Rev. John Lowell of Newbury-port, the father of the Hon. John Lowell, who is regarded as the author of the clause in the Massachusetts Constitution abolishing slavery.

Judge Lowell's son, Charles, was a Unitarian minister, "learned, saintly, and discreet." He married Miss Harriet Traill Spence, of Portsmouth, — a woman of superior mind, of great wit, vivacity, and an impetuosity that reached eccentricity. She was of Keltic blood, of a family that came from the Orkneys, and claimed descent from the Sir Patrick Spens of "the grand old ballad." Several of her family were connected with the American navy. Her father was Keith Spence, purser of the frigate "Philadelphia," and a prisoner at Tripoli.

By ancestry on both sides, and by connections with the Russells and other distinguished families, Lowell was a good type of the New England gentleman.

He was born on the 22d of February, 1819, at Elmwood, not far from Brattle Street, Cambridge.

This three-storied colonial mansion of wood was built in 1767 by Thomas Oliver, the last royal Lieutenant-Governor, before the Revolution.[1] Like ·other houses in "Tory Row,"

[1] Thomas Oliver was graduated from Harvard College in the class of 1753. He was a gentleman of fortune, and lived first in Roxbury. He bought the property on

it was abandoned by its owners. Soon afterwards it came into
possession of Elbridge Gerry, Governor of Massachusetts, and
fifth Vice-President of the United States, whose memory and
name are kept alive by the term "*gerrymander.*" It next be-
came the property of Dr. Lowell about a year before the birth
of his youngest child, and it was the home of the poet until his
death.

Lowell's early education was obtained mainly at a school kept
nearly opposite Elmwood by a retired publisher, an English-
man, Mr. William Wells. He also studied in the classical
school of Mr. Danial G. Ingraham in Boston. He was gradu-
ated from Harvard College in the class of 1838. He is reported
as declaring that he read almost everything except the class-
books prescribed by the faculty. Lowell says, in one of his
early poems referring to Harvard, —

> "Tho' lightly prized the ribboned parchments three,
>   Yet *collegisse juvat,* I am glad
>   That here what colleging was mine I had."

He was secretary of the Hasty Pudding Society, and one of
the editors of the college periodical *Harvardiana,* to which he
contributed various articles in prose and verse. His neglect of
prescribed studies, and disregard of college discipline, resulted
in his rustication just before commencement in 1838. He was
sent to Concord, where he resided in the family of Barzillai
Frost, and made the acquaintance of Emerson, then beginning
to rouse the ire of conservative Unitarianism by his transcen-
dental philosophy, of the brilliant but overestimated Margaret
Fuller, who afterwards severely criticised Lowell's verse, and of

---

Elmwood Avenue in 1766. When he accepted the royal commission of Lieutenant-
Governor, he became President of the Council appointed by the King. On Sept. 2,
1774, about four thousand Middlesex freeholders assembled at Cambridge and com-
pelled the mandamus councillors to resign. The President of the Council urged the
propriety of delay, but the Committee would not spare him. He was forced to sign
an agreement, "as a man of honor and a Christian, that he would never hereafter,
upon any terms whatsoever, accept a seat at said Board on the present novel and
oppressive form of government." He immediately quitted Cambridge ; and when
the British troops evacuated Boston he accompanied them. By an odd coincidence
he went to reside at Bristol, England, where he died at the age of eighty-two years,
in 1815, shortly before the Lowells, who were of Bristol origin, took possession of his
former home. In Underwood's sketch of Lowell, Thomas Oliver is confused with
Chief Justice Peter Oliver, a man of a very different type of character.

other well-known residents of the pretty town. He had been elected poet of his class. His removal from college prevented him from delivering the poem which was afterwards published anonymously for private distribution. It contained a satire on abolitionists and reformers. "I know the village," he writes long afterwards in the person of Hosea Biglow, Esquire.

> "I know the village though, was sent there once
> A-schoolin', 'cause to home I played the dunce!"

On his return to Cambridge he took up the study of law, and, in 1840, received the degree of LL.B. He even went so far as to open an office in Boston; but it is a question whether there was any actual basis of fact in a whimsical sketch of his entitled "My First Client," published in the short-lived *Boston Miscellany*, edited by Nathan Hale.

Several things engrossed Lowell's attention to the exclusion of law. Society at Cambridge was particularly attractive at that time. Allston the painter was living at Cambridgeport. Judge Story's pleasant home was on Brattle Street. The Fays then occupied the house which has since become the seat of Radcliffe College. Longfellow, described as "a slender, blond young professor," was established in the Craigie House. The famous names of Dr. Palfrey, Professor Andrews Norton, father of Lowell's friend and biographer, the "saintly" Henry Ware, and others will occur to the reader. He was fond of walking and knew every inch of the beautiful ground then called "Sweet Auburn," now turned by the hand of misguided man into that most distressing of monstrosities — a modern cemetery. He haunted the poetic shades of the Waverley Oaks, heard the charming music of Beaver Brook, and climbed the hills of Belmont and Arlington.

He himself took his turn in establishing a magazine. In January, 1843, he started *The Pioneer*, to which Hawthorne, John Neal, Miss Barrett, Poe, Whittier, Story, Parsons, and others contributed, and which, in spite of such an array of talent, perished untimely during the winds of March.

He had already published, in 1841, a little volume of poems entitled "A Year's Life." They were marked by no great originality, betrayed little promise of future eminence, and Margaret Fuller, who reviewed them, was quite right in asserting that "neither the imagery nor the music of Lowell's verses was his own." The first sonnet in the present volume (page 1) practically acknowledges the force of this criticism. The influence of Wordsworth and Tennyson may be distinctly traced in most of them. But many of the lines were harsh and many of the rhymes were careless. Lowell's later and correcter taste omitted most of them from his collected works.

Not far from Elmwood, but in the adjoining village of Watertown, lived one of Lowell's classmates, whose sister, Maria White, a slender, delicate girl, with a poetic genius in some respects more regulated and lofty than his own, early inspired him with a true and saving love. Speaking of the influences that moulded his life, George William Curtis says : —

"The first and most enduring was an early and happy passion for a lovely and high-minded woman who became his wife — the Egeria who exalted his youth and confirmed his noblest aspirations; a heaven-eyed counsellor of the serener air, who filled his mind with peace and his life with joy."

The young lady's prudent father objected to the marriage until the newly fledged lawyer should be in a position to support a wife.

Shortly after the shipwreck of *The Pioneer*, Lowell was offered a hundred dollars by *Graham's Monthly* for ten poems. When Pegasus is able to earn such princely sums, there seems no reason why Love should be kept waiting at the cottage door. In 1844 Lowell published a new edition of his poems, and married Miss White. It was her influence that decided him to cast in his lot with the abolitionists. It was her refined taste that shaped and tempered his impetuous verse. A volume of her poems was in 1855, in an edition of fifty copies, privately printed, and is now very rare. It is an odd circumstance that in Lowell's library, from which Harvard College was allowed to select any volumes not in Gore Hall, neither this book nor any of Lowell's own early poems was to be found.

The young couple took up their residence at Elmwood, and here were born three daughters and a son. All but one of his children died in infancy. Many of the tenderest of his poems refer with touching pathos to his bereavement : such for instance are " The Changeling " and " The First Snowfall."

In 1845 appeared "The Vision of Sir Launfal," — a genuine inspiration composed in two days in a sort of ecstasy of poetic fervor. That more than anything established his fame. He recognized that he was dedicated to the Muses.

In 1846 he wrote : —

"If I have any vocation, it is the making of verse. When I take my pen for that, the world opens itself ungrudgingly before me : everything seems clear and easy, as it seems sinking to the bottom could be as one leans over the edge of his boat in one of those dear coves at Fresh Pond. . . . My true place is to serve the cause as a poet. Then my heart leaps before me into the conflict."

The same year he began his "Biglow Papers" in the Boston *Courier*. Such *jeux d'esprit* are apt to be ephemeral. Lowell's are immortal. They preserved in literary form a fast-fading dialect; they caught and embalmed the mighty issues of a tremendous world-problem. Their influence was incalculable. He gathered them into a volume in 1848, and became corresponding editor of the *Anti-Slavery Standard*. Fortunate man who throws himself into an unpopular cause which is in harmony with the Right! How different from Wordsworth who attacked the ballot and took sides against reform!

Lowell's penchant for satire was exemplified again the same year in his "Fable for Critics."

In this Lowell with no sparing hand laid on his portraits most droll and amusing colors. It is a comic portrait gallery, a series of caricatures whose greatest value (as in all good caricatures) lies in the accurate presentation of characteristic features. He did not spare himself : —

"There is Lowell, who's striving Parnassus to climb
With a whole bale of *isms* tied together with rhyme.
He might get on alone, spite of troubles and bowlders,
But he can't with that bundle he has on his shoulders.
The top of the hill he will ne'er come nigh reaching
Till he learns the distinctions 'twixt singing and preaching;
His lyre has some chords that would ring pretty well,
But he'd rather by half make a drum of the shell,
And rattle away till he's old as Methusalem
At the head of a march to the last New Jerusalem."

Some of his thrusts left embittered feelings, but in general the tone was so good-natured that only the thin-skinned could object, and it must be confessed many of his judgments have been confirmed by Time.

In 1851 Lowell visited Europe, and spent upwards of a year widening his acquaintance with the polite languages. But it is remarkable that Lowell gave the world almost no metrical translations. Shortly after his return his wife died (Oct. 27, 1853) after a slow decline. In reference to this bereavement Longfellow wrote his beautiful poem, " The Two Angels."

The following year Longfellow resigned the Smith Professorship of the French and Spanish Languages and Literature and Belles Lettres, and Lowell was appointed his successor with two years' leave of absence. He had won his spurs. He had collected his poems in two volumes, not including " A Year's Life," the " Biglow Papers," or the " Fable for Critics." He was known as one of the most brilliant contributors to *Putnam's Monthly* and other magazines.

In 1854 he delivered a series of twelve lectures on English poetry before the Lowell Institute. Ten years before he had published a volume of " Conversations on the Poets." The contrast between the two works is no less pronounced than that between his earlier and later poems.

In both, however, there is a tendency toward a confusing over-elaboration — Metaphors trample on the heels of Similes, and quaint and often grotesque conceits sometimes pall upon the taste, just as in the poems a flash of incongruous wit sometimes disturbs the serenity that is desirable.

On his return from Europe, Mr. Lowell occupied the chair which he adorned by his brilliant attainments and made memorable by his fame. He lectured on Dante, Shakespeare, Chaucer, and Cervantes, and delighted his audiences. At the same time he was editor of the *Atlantic Monthly* for several years. From 1863 until 1872 he was associated with Professor Charles Eliot Norton in the conduct of the *North American Review*.

In 1857 he married Miss Frances Dunlap of Portland, Me., a cultivated lady who had been the governess of his daughter. She had unerring literary taste and sound judgment, and Mr. Lowell soon came to entrust to her the management of his financial affairs. She was enabled to make their comparatively small income more than meet the exigencies of an exacting position.

The second series of the "Biglow Papers," relating to the War of the Rebellion, were first published in the *Atlantic*. They were collected into a volume in 1865. That year was rendered notable by his "Commemoration Ode," the worthy crowning of one of the grandest poetic opportunities ever granted to man. "Under the Willows" appeared in 1869; "The Cathedral" in 1870.

In 1864 he had issued a collection of his early descriptive articles under the title, "Fireside Travels." In 1870 came "Among my Books." The second series followed in 1876. "My Study Windows" was published in 1871. All these prose works were marked by an exuberant, vivid, poetic, impassioned style. The tropical efflorescence of imagery was characteristic of them all. He ought to have remembered his own words, —

"Over-ornament ruins both poem and prose."

In 1876 appeared three memorial poems : that read at Concord, April 19, 1875; that read at Cambridge under the Washington Elm, July 3, 1875; and the Fourth of July Ode of 1876. This year Mr. Lowell was appointed one of the presidential electors; and the following year President Hayes first offered him the Austrian mission, and, on his refusal of that, gave him the honorary post at Madrid, which had been adorned by Everett, Irving, and Prescott. He was there three years, and, on the retirement of Mr. Welsh in 1880, was transferred to the Court of St. James, or, as one of the English papers expressed it, he became "His Excellency the Ambassador of American Literature to the Court of Shakespeare."

He was extremely popular. Known in private as "one of the most marvellous of story-tellers," he became the lion of many public occasions. The *London News* spoke of the "Extraordinary felicity of his occasional speeches." At Birmingham he delivered a noble address on Democracy. He was selected to deliver the oration at the dedication of the Dean Stanley Memorial. He spoke on Fielding at Taunton, on Coleridge at Westminster Abbey, on Gray at Cambridge. He was President of the Wordsworth Society. All sorts of honors were heaped upon him, both at home and abroad.

He returned to America in 1885, and once more occupied the somewhat dilapidated historic mansion at Elmwood. Once more he moved amid his rare and precious books, and heard the birds singing in the elms that his father had planted, or in the clustered bushes back of the house. He took a deep interest in the struggle for international copyright. He was President of the American Copyright League, and wrote the memorable lines : —

> "In vain we call old notions fudge,
>   And bend our conscience to our dealing;
>   The Ten Commandments will not budge;
>   And stealing *will* continue stealing."

He used the leisure of his failing health in revising his works. His last volume of poems was entitled " Heart's Ease and Rue.' One of his latest poems, " My Book," appeared in the Christmas number of the New York *Ledger* in 1890. In the December number of the *Atlantic* his hand was visible in the anonymous " Contributor's Club."

During the last years his health was a matter of grave anxiety to his friends. In the spring of 1891 he seemed better. He was engaged in writing a life of Nathaniel Hawthorne. When the present writer call to see him one beautiful spring day, he found him in his library, at that moment engaged in making suggestions for the inscriptions on the new Boston Public Library. His manner was the perfection of courtesy and high breeding. His keen eyes seemed to read the very soul. Simplicity and beautiful dignity, tempered by evident feebleness of health, made him a memorable figure.

Toward the end of the summer he suddenly grew more seriously ill. He suffered severely, and his last words were, " Oh! why don't you let me die ? "

He drew his last breath in the early morning of Aug. 12, 1891. He was buried at Mount Auburn, in the shadow of Indian Ridge, not far from Longfellow's grave, in a lot unenclosed and marked by no monument.

Memorial services were held in many places. Lord Tennyson cabled a message of sympathy: " England and America will mourn Mr. Lowell's death. They loved him and he loved them." The Queen publicly expressed her respect and sorrow.

Few men have left a deeper impress on their age. Few men have used noble powers more nobly. In private life and public station there is not a shadow to stain the whiteness of his fame.

As a poet he stands in the front rank of those who have yet appeared in America. As a critic he was generous and just; as a humorist he used his shafts of ridicule only to wound wrong; as a statesman and diplomat he was actuated by broad, far-seeing views; as a man he was a type to be upheld and followed. America has just cause to reverence his memory; and the whole English-speaking world, without geographical distinction, claims him as its own.

NATHAN HASKELL DOLE.

EARLY POEMS.

———o○o○o○o○o———

SONNET.

IF some small savor creep into my rhyme
Of the old poets, if some words I use,
Neglected long, which have the lusty thews
Of that gold-haired and earnest-hearted time,
Whose loving joy and sorrow all sublime
Have given our tongue its starry eminence, —
It is not pride, God knows, but reverence
Which hath grown in me since my childhood's prime;
Wherein I feel that my poor lyre is strung
With soul-strings like to theirs, and that I have
No right to muse their holy graves among,
If I can be a custom-fettered slave,
And, in mine own true spirit, am not brave
To speak what rusheth upward to my tongue.

———

HAKON'S LAY.

THEN Thorstein looked at Hakon, where he sate,
Mute as a cloud amid the stormy hall,
And said: "O, Skald, sing now an olden song,
Such as our fathers heard who led great lives;
And, as the bravest on a shield is borne
Along the waving host that shouts him king,
So rode their thrones upon the thronging seas!"

Then the old man arose: white-haired he stood,
White-bearded, and with eyes that looked afar
From their still region of perpetual snow,
Over the little smokes and stirs of men:
His head was bowed with gathered flakes of years,
As winter bends the sea-foreboding pine,
But something triumphed in his brow and eye,
Which whoso saw it, could not see and crouch:

Loud rang the emptied beakers as he mused,
Brooding his eyried thoughts; then, as an eagle
Circles smooth-winged above the wind-vexed woods,
So wheeled his soul into the air of song
High o'er the stormy hall; and thus he sang:

"The fletcher for his arrow-shaft picks out
Wood closest-grained, long-seasoned, straight as light;
And, from a quiver full of such as these,
The wary bow-man, matched against his peers,
Long doubting, singles yet once more the best.
Who is it that can make such shafts as Fate?
What archer of his arrows is so choice,
Or hits the white so surely?   They are men,
The chosen of her quiver; nor for her
Will every reed suffice, or cross-grained stick
At random from life's vulgar fagot plucked:
Such answer household ends; but she will have
Souls straight and clear, of toughest fibre, sound
Down to the heart of heart; from these she strips
All needless stuff, all sapwood, hardens them,
From circumstance untoward feathers plucks
Crumpled and cheap, and barbs with iron will:
The hour that passes is her quiver-boy;
When she draws bow, 't is not across the wind,
Nor 'gainst the sun, her haste-snatched arrow sings,
For sun and wind have plighted faith to her:
Ere men have heard the sinew twang, behold,
In the butt's heart her trembling messenger!

"The song is old and simple that I sing:
Good were the days of yore, when men were tried
By ring of shields, as now by ring of gold;
But, while the gods are left, and hearts of men,
And the free ocean, still the days are good;
Through the broad Earth roams Opportunity
And knocks at every door of hut or hall,
Until she finds the brave soul that she wants."

He ceased, and instantly the frothy tide
Of interrupted wassail roared along;
But Leif, the son of Eric, sate apart
Musing, and, with his eyes upon the fire,
Saw shapes of arrows, lost as soon as seen;

But then with that resolve his heart was bent,
Which, like a humming shaft, through many a strife
Of day and night across the unventured seas,
Shot the brave prow to cut on Vinland sands
The first rune in the Saga of the West.

OUT OF DOORS.

'T is good to be abroad in the sun,
His gifts abide when day is done;
Each thing in nature from his cup
Gathers a several virtue up;
The grace within its being's reach
Becomes the nutriment of each,
And the same life imbibed by all
Makes each most individual:
Here the twig-bending peaches seek
The glow that mantles in their cheek —
Hence comes the Indian-summer bloom
That hazes round the basking plum,
And, from the same impartial light,
The grass sucks green, the lily white.

Like these the soul, for sunshine made,
Grows wan and gracile in the shade,
Her faculties, which God decreed
Various as Summer's dædal breed,
With one sad color are imbued,
Shut from the sun that tints their blood;
The shadow of the poet's roof
Deadens the dyes of warp and woof;
Whate'er of ancient song remains
Has fresh air flowing in its veins,
For Greece and eldest Ind knew well
That out of doors, with world-wide swell
Arches the student's lawful cell.

Away, unfruitful lore of books,
For whose vain idiom we reject
The spirit's mother-dialect,
Aliens among the birds and brooks,
Dull to interpret or believe

What gospels lost the woods retrieve,
Or what the eaves-dropping violet
Reports from God, who walketh yet
His garden in the hush of eve!
Away, ye pedants city-bred,
Unwise of heart, too wise of head,
Who handcuff Art with *thus and so,*
And in each other's footprints tread,
Like those who walk through drifted snow;

Who, from deep study of brick walls
Conjecture of the water-falls,
By six square feet of smoke-stained sky
Compute those deeps that overlie
The still tarn's heaven-anointed eye,
And, in your earthen crucible,
With chemic tests essay to spell
How nature works in field and dell!
Seek we where Shakspeare buried gold?
Such hands no charmed witch-hazel hold;
To beach and rock repeats the sea
The mystic *Open Sesame ;*
Old Greylock's voices not in vain
Comment on Milton's mountain strain,
And cunningly the various wind
Spenser's locked music can unbind.

A REVERIE.

In the twilight deep and silent
Comes thy spirit unto mine,
When the moonlight and the starlight
Over cliff and woodland shine,
And the quiver of the river
Seems a thrill of joy benign.

Then I rise and wander slowly
To the headland by the sea,
When the evening star throbs setting
Through the cloudy cedar tree,
And from under, mellow thunder
Of the surf comes fitfully.

Then within my soul I feel thee
Like a gleam of other years,
Visions of my childhood murmur
Their old madness in my ears,
Till the pleasance of thy presence
Cools my heart with blissful tears.

All the wondrous dreams of boyhood —
All youth's fiery thirst of praise —
All the surer hopes of manhood
Blossoming in sadder days —
Joys that bound me, griefs that crowned me
With a better wreath than bays —

All the longings after freedom —
The vague love of human kind,
Wandering far and near at random
Like a winged seed in the wind —
The dim yearnings and fierce burnings
Of an undirected mind —

All of these, oh best belovèd,
Happiest present dreams and past,
In thy love find safe fulfilment,
Ripened into truths at last;
Faith and beauty, hope and duty
To one centre gather fast.

How my nature, like an ocean,
At the breath of thine awakes,
Leaps its shores in mad exulting
And in foamy thunder breaks,
Then downsinking, lieth shrinking
At the tumult that it makes!

Blazing Hesperus hath sunken
Low within the pale-blue west,
And with golden splendor crowneth
The horizon's piny crest;
Thoughtful quiet stills the riot
Of wild longing in my breast.

Home I loiter through the moonlight,
Underneath the quivering trees,
Which, as if a spirit stirred them,

Sway and bend, till by degrees
The far surge's murmur merges
In the rustle of the breeze.

IN SADNESS.

THERE is not in this life of ours
    One bliss unmixed with fears,
The hope that wakes our deepest powers
    A face of sadness wears,
And the dew that showers our dearest flowers
    Is the bitter dew of tears.

Fame waiteth long, and lingereth
    Through weary nights and morns —
And evermore the shadow Death
    With mocking finger scorns
That underneath the laurel wreath
    Should be a wreath of thorns.

The laurel leaves are cool and green,
    But the thorns are hot and sharp,
Lean Hunger grins and stares between
    The poet and his harp;
Though of Love's sunny sheen his woof have been,
    Grim want thrusts in the warp.

And if beyond this darksome clime
    Some fair star Hope may see,
That keeps unjarred the blissful chime
    Of its golden infancy —
Where the harvest-time of faith sublime
    Not always is to be —

Yet would the true soul rather choose
    Its home where sorrow is,
Than in a sated peace to lose
    Its life's supremest bliss —
The rainbow hues that bend profuse
    O'er cloudy spheres like this —

The want, the sorrow and the pain,
    That are Love's right to cure —

FAREWELL.

The sunshine bursting after rain—
  The gladness insecure
That makes us fain strong hearts to gain,
  To do and to endure.

High natures must be thunder-scarred
  With many a searing wrong;
From mother Sorrow's breasts the hard
  Sucks gifts of deepest song,
Nor all unmarred with struggles hard
  Wax the Soul's sinews strong.

Dear Patience, too, is born of woe,
  Patience that opes the gate
Wherethrough the soul of man must go
  Up to each nobler state,
Whose voice's flow so meek and low
  Smooths the bent brows of Fate.

Though Fame be slow, yet Death is swift,
  And, o'er the spirit's eyes,
Life after life doth change and shift
  With larger destinies:
As on we drift, some wider rift
  Shows us serener skies.

And though naught falleth to us here
  But gains the world counts loss,
Though all we hope of wisdom clear
  When climbed to seems but dross,
Yet all, though ne'er Christ's faith they wear,
  At least may share his cross.

———

FAREWELL.

FAREWELL! as the bee round the blossom
Doth murmur drowsily,
So murmureth round my bosom
The memory of thee;
Lingering, it seems to go,
When the wind more full doth flow,
Waving the flower to and fro,
But still returneth, Marian!

My hope no longer burneth,
Which did so fiercely burn,
My joy to sorrow turneth,
Although loath, loath to turn —
I would forget —
And yet — and yet
My heart to thee still yearneth, Marian!

Fair as a single star thou shinest,
And white as lilies are
The slender hands wherewith thou twinest
Thy heavy auburn hair;
Thou art to me
A memory
Of all that is divinest:
Thou art so fair and tall,
Thy looks so queenly are,
Thy very shadow on the wall,
Thy step upon the stair,
The thought that thou art nigh,
The chance look of thine eye
Are more to me than all, Marian,
And will be till I die!

As the last quiver of a bell
Doth fade into the air,
With a subsiding swell
That dies we know not where,
So my hope melted and was gone:
I raised mine eyes to bless the star
That shared its light with me so far
Below its silver throne,
And gloom and chilling vacancy
Were all was left to me,
In the dark, bleak night I was alone!
Alone in the blessed Earth, Marian,
For what were all to me —
Its love, and light, and mirth, Marian,
If I were not with thee?

My heart will not forget thee
More than the moaning brine
Forgets the moon when she is set;
The gush when first I met thee

That thrilled my brain like wine,
Doth thrill as madly yet;
My heart cannot forget thee,
Though it may droop and pine,
Too deeply it had set thee
In every love of mine;
No new moon ever cometh,
No flower ever bloometh,
No twilight ever gloometh
But I 'm more only thine.
Oh look not on me, Marian,
Thine eyes are wild and deep,
And they have won me, Marian,
From peacefulness and sleep;
The sunlight doth not sun me,
The meek moonshine doth shun me,
All sweetest voices stun me —
There is no rest
Within my breast
And I can only weep, Marian!

As a landbird far at sea
Doth wander through the sleet
And drooping downward wearily
Finds no rest for her feet,
So wandereth my memory
O'er the years when we did meet:
I used to say that everything
Partook a share of thee,
That not a little bird could sing,
Or green leaf flutter on a tree,
That nothing could be beautiful
Save part of thee were there,
That from thy soul so clear and full
All bright and blessèd things did cull
The charm to make them fair;
And now I know
That it was so,
Thy spirit through the earth doth flow
And face me wheresoe'er I go —
What right hath perfectness to give
Such weary weight of woe
Unto the soul which cannot live

On anything more low?
Oh leave me, leave me, Marian,
There's no fair thing I see
But doth deceive me, Marian,
Into sad dreams of thee!

A cold snake gnaws my heart
And crushes round my brain,
And I should glory but to part
So bitterly again,
Feeling the slow tears start
And fall in fiery rain:
There's a wide ring round the moon,
The ghost-like clouds glide by,
And I hear the sad winds croon
A dirge to the lowering sky;
There's nothing soft or mild
In the pale moon's sickly light,
But all looks strange and wild
Through the dim, foreboding night:
I think thou must be dead
In some dark and lonely place,
With candles at thy head,
And a pall above thee spread
To hide thy dead, cold face;
But I can see thee underneath
So pale, and still, and fair,
Thine eyes closed smoothly and a wreath
Of flowers in thy hair;
I never saw thy face so clear
When thou wast with the living,
As now beneath the pall, so drear,
And stiff, and unforgiving;
I cannot flee thee, Marian,
I cannot turn away,
Mine eyes must see thee, Marian,
Through salt tears night and day.

A DIRGE.

POET! lonely is thy bed,
And the turf is overhead —

Cold earth is thy cover;
But thy heart hath found release,
And it slumbers full of peace
'Neath the rustle of green trees
And the warm hum of the bees,
   Mid the drowsy clover;
Through thy chamber, still as death,
A smooth gurgle wandereth,
As the blue stream murmureth
   To the blue sky over.
Three paces from the silver strand,
Gently in the fine, white sand,
With a lily in thy hand,
   Pale as snow, they laid thee;
In no coarse earth wast thou hid,
And no gloomy coffin-lid
   Darkly overweighed thee.
Silently as snow-flakes drift,
The smooth sand did sift and sift
   O'er the bed they made thee;
All sweet birds did come and sing
At thy sunny burying —
   Choristers unbidden,
And, beloved of sun and dew,
Meek forget-me-nots upgrew
Where thine eyes so large and blue
   'Neath the turf were hidden.

Where thy stainless clay doth lie,
Blue and open is the sky,
And the white clouds wander by,
 Dreams of summer silently
   Darkening the river;
Thou hearest the clear water run;
And the ripples every one,
Scattering the golden sun,
   Through thy silence quiver;
Vines trail down upon the stream,
Into its smooth and glassy dream
   A green stillness spreading,
And the shiner, perch, and bream
Through the shadowed waters gleam
   'Gainst the current heading.

White as snow, thy winding sheet
Shelters thee from head to feet,
  Save thy pale face only;
Thy face is turned toward the skies,
The lids lie meekly o'er thine eyes,
And the low-voiced pine-tree sighs
  O'er thy bed so lonely.
All thy life thou lov'dst its shade:
Underneath it thou art laid,
  In an endless shelter;
Thou hearest it forever sigh
As the wind's vague longings die
In its branches dim and high —
Thou hear'st the waters gliding by
  Slumberously welter.

Thou wast full of love and truth,
Of forgiveness and ruth —
Thy great heart with hope and youth
  Tided to o'erflowing.
Thou didst dwell in mysteries,
And there lingered on thine eyes
Shadows of serener skies,
Awfully wild memories,
  That were like foreknowing;
Through the earth thou would'st have gone,
Lighted from within alone,
Seeds from flowers in Heaven grown
  With a free hand sowing.

Thou didst remember well and long
Some fragments of thine angel-song,
And strive, through want of woe and wrong,
  To win the world unto it;
Thy sin it was to see and hear
Beyond To-day's dim hemisphere —
Beyond all mists of hope and fear,
Into a life more true and clear,
  And dearly thou didst rue it;
Light of the new world thou hadst won,
O'erflooded by a purer sun —
Slowly Fate's ship came drifting on,
And through the dark, save thou, not one
  Caught of the land a token.

Thou stood'st upon the farthest prow,
Something within thy soul said "Now!"
And leaping forth with eager brow,
   Thou fell'st on shore heart-broken.

Long time thy brethren stood in fear;
Only the breakers far and near,
White with their anger, they could hear;
The sounds of land, which thy quick ear
   Caught long ago, they heard not.
And, when at last they reached the strand,
They found thee lying on the sand
With some wild flowers in thy hand,
   But thy cold bosom stirred not;
They listened, but they heard no sound
Save from the glad life all around
   A low, contented murmur.
The long grass flowed adown the hill,
A hum rose from a hidden rill,
But thy glad heart, that knew no ill
But too much love, lay dead and still —
The only thing that sent a chill
   Into the heart of summer.

Thou didst not seek the poet's wreath
   But too soon didst win it;
Without 't was green, but underneath
Were scorn and loneliness and death,
Gnawing the brain with burning teeth,
   And making mock within it.
Thou, who wast full of nobleness,
Whose very life-blood 't was to bless,
   Whose soul's one law was giving,
Must bandy words with wickedness,
Haggle with hunger and distress,
To win that death which worldliness
   Calls bitterly a living.

"Thou sow'st no gold, and shalt not reap!"
Muttered earth, turning in her sleep;
"Come home to the Eternal Deep!"
Murmured a voice, and a wide sweep
Of wings through thy soul's hush did creep,
   As of thy doom o'erflying;

It seem'd that thy strong heart would leap
Out of thy breast, and thou didst weep,
    But not with fear of dying;
Men could not fathom thy deep fears,
They could not understand thy tears,
The hoarded agony of years
    Of bitter self-denying.
So once, when high above the spheres
Thy spirit sought its starry peers,
It came not back to face the jeers
    Of brothers who denied it;
Star-crowned, thou dost possess the deeps
Of God, and thy white body sleeps
Where the lone pine forever keeps
    Patient watch beside it.

Poet! underneath the turf,
    Soft thou sleepest, free from morrow,
Thou hast struggled through the surf
    Of wild thoughts and want and sorrow.
Now, beneath the moaning pine,
    Full of rest, thy body lieth,
While far up is clear sunshine,
Underneath a sky divine,
    Her loosed wings thy spirit trieth;
Oft she strove to spread them here,
But they were too white and clear
For our dingy atmosphere.

Thy body findeth ample room
In its still and grassy tomb
    By the silent river;
But thy spirit found the earth
Narrow for the mighty birth
    Which it dreamed of ever;
Thou wast guilty of a rhyme
Learned in a benigner clime,
And of that more grievous crime,
An ideal too sublime
For the low-hung sky of Time.

The calm spot where thy body lies
Gladdens thy soul in Paradise,
    It is so still and holy;

Thy body sleeps serenely there,
And well for it thy soul may care,
It was so beautiful and fair,
   Lily white so wholly.
From so pure and sweet a frame
Thy spirit parted as it came,
   Gentle as a maiden;
Now it lieth full of rest —
Sods are lighter on its breast
Than the great, prophetic guest
   Wherewith it was laden.

FANCIES ABOUT A ROSEBUD,

PRESSED IN AN OLD COPY OF SPENSER.

WHO prest you here?   The Past can tell,
   When summer skies were bright above,
And some full heart did leap and swell
   Beneath the white new moon of love.

Some Poet, haply, when the world
   Showed like a calm sea, grand and blue,
Ere its cold, inky waves had curled
   O'er the numb heart once warm and true;

When, with his soul brimful of morn,
   He looked beyond the vale of Time,
Nor saw therein the dullard scorn
   That made his heavenliness a crime;

When, musing o'er the Poets olden,
   His soul did like a sun upstart
To shoot its arrows, clear and golden,
   Through slavery's cold and darksome heart.

Alas! too soon the veil is lifted
   That hangs between the soul and pain,
Too soon the morning-red hath drifted
   Into dull cloud, or fallen in rain!

Or were you prest by one who nurst
   Bleak memories of love gone by,
Whose heart, like a star fallen, burst
   In dark and erring vacancy?

To him you still were fresh and green
    As when you grew upon the stalk,
And many a breezy summer scene
    Came back — and many a moonlit walk;

And there would be a hum of bees,
    A smell of childhood in the air,
And old, fresh feelings cooled the breeze
    That, like loved fingers, stirred his hair!

Then would you suddenly be blasted
    By the keen wind of one dark thought,
One nameless woe, that had outlasted
    The sudden blow whereby 't was brought.

Or were you prest here by two lovers
    Who seemed to read these verses rare,
But found between the antique covers
    What Spenser could not prison there:

Songs which his glorious soul had heard,
    But his dull pen could never write,
Which flew, like some gold-wingèd bird,
    Through the blue heaven out of sight?

My heart is with them as they sit,
    I see the rosebud in her breast,
I see her small hand taking it
    From out its odorous, snowy nest;

I hear him swear that he will keep it,
    In memory of that blessed day,
To smile on it or over-weep it
    When she and spring are far away.

Ah me!   I needs must droop my head,
    And brush away a happy tear,
For they are gone, and, dry and dead,
    The rosebud lies before me here.

Yet is it in no stranger's hand,
    For I will guard it tenderly,
And it shall be a magic wand
    To bring mine own true love to me.

My heart runs o'er with sweet surmises,
  The while my fancy weaves her rhyme,
Kind hopes and musical surprises
  Throng round me from the olden time.

I do not care to know who prest you: *
  Enough for me to feel and know
That some heart's love and longing blest you,
  Knitting to-day with long-ago.

NEW YEAR'S EVE, 1844.

A FRAGMENT.

THE night is calm and beautiful; the snow
Sparkles beneath the clear and frosty moon
And the cold stars, as if it took delight
In its own silent whiteness; the hushed earth
Sleeps in the soft arms of the embracing blue,
Secure as if angelic squadrons yet
Encamped about her, and each watching star
Gained double brightness from the flashing arms
Of wingèd and unsleeping sentinels.
Upward the calm of infinite silence deepens,
The sea that flows between high heaven and earth,
Musing by whose smooth brink we sometimes find
A stray leaf floated from those happier shores,
And hope, perchance not vainly, that some flower
Which we had watered with our holiest tears,
Pale blooms, and yet our scanty garden's best,
O'er the same ocean piloted by love,
May find a haven at the feet of God,
And be not wholly worthless in his sight.
O, high dependence on a higher Power,
Sole stay for all these restless faculties
That wander, Ishmael-like, the desert bare
Wherein our human knowledge hath its home,
Shifting their light-framed tents from day to day, .
With each new-found oasis, wearied soon,
And only certain of uncertainty !
O, mighty humbleness that feels with awe,
Yet with a vast exulting feels, no less,
That this huge Minster of the Universe,

c

Whose smallest oratories are glorious worlds,
With painted oriels of dawn and sunset;
Whose carvèd ornaments are systems grand,
Orion kneeling in his starry niche,
The Lyre whose strings give music audible
To holy ears, and countless splendors more,
Crowned by the blazing Cross high-hung o'er all;
Whose organ music is the solemn stops
Of endless Change breathed through by endless Good;
Whose choristers are all the morning stars;
Whose altar is the sacred human heart
Whereon Love's candles burn unquenchably,
Trimmed day and night by gentle-handed Peace;
With all its arches and its pinnacles
That stretch forever and forever up,
Is founded on the silent heart of God,
Silent, yet pulsing forth exhaustless life
Through the least veins of all created things.
Fit musings these for the departing year;
And God be thanked for such a crystal night
As fills the spirit with good store of thoughts,
That, like a cheering fire of walnut, crackle
Upon the hearthstone of the heart, and cast
A mild home-glow o'er all Humanity!
Yes, though the poisoned shafts of evil doubts
Assail the skyey panoply of Faith,
Though the great hopes which we have had for man,
Foes in disguise, because they based belief
On man's endeavor, not on God's decree —
Though these proud-visaged hopes, once turned to fly,
Hurl backward many a deadly Parthian dart
That rankles in the soul and makes it sick
With vain regret, nigh verging on despair —
Yet, in such calm and earnest hours as this,
We well can feel how every living heart
That sleeps to-night in palace or in cot,
Or unroofed hovel, or which need hath known
. Of other homestead than the arching sky,
Is circled watchfully with seraph fires;
How our own erring will it is that hangs
The flaming sword o'er Eden's unclosed gate,
Which gives free entrance to the pure in heart,
And with its guarding walls doth fence the meek.

Sleep then, O Earth, in thy blue-vaulted cradle,
Bent over always by thy mother Heaven!
We all are tall enough to reach God's hand,
And angels are no taller: looking back
Upon the smooth wake of a year o'erpast,
We see the black clouds furling, one by one,
From the advancing majesty of Truth,
And something won for Freedom, whose least gain
Is as a firm and rock-built citadel
Wherefrom to launch fresh battle on her foes;
Or, leaning from the time's extremest prow,
If we gaze forward through the blinding spray,
And dimly see how much of ill remains,
How many fetters to be sawn asunder
By the slow toil of individual zeal,
Or haply rusted by salt tears in twain,
We feel, with something of a sadder heart,
Yet bracing up our bruisèd mail the while,
And fronting the old foe with fresher spirit,
How great it is to breathe with human breath,
To be but poor foot-soldiers in the ranks
Of our old exiled king, Humanity;
Encamping after every hard-won field
Nearer and nearer Heaven's happy plains.

Many great souls have gone to rest, and sleep
Under this armor, free and full of peace:
If these have left the earth, yet Truth remains,
Endurance, too, the crowning faculty
Of noble minds, and Love, invincible
By any weapons; and these hem us round
With silence such that all the groaning clank
Of this mad engine men have made of earth
Dulls not some ears for catching purer tones,
That wander from the dim surrounding vast,
Or far more clear melodious prophecies,
The natural music of the heart of man,
Which by kind Sorrow's ministry hath learned
That the true sceptre of all power is love
And humbleness the palace-gate of truth.
What man with soul so blind as sees not here
The first faint tremble of Hope's morning-star,
Foretelling how the God-forged shafts of dawn,

Fitted already on their golden string,
Shall soon leap earthward with exulting flight
To thrid the dark heart of that evil faith
Whose trust is in the clumsy arms of Force,
The ozier hauberk of a ruder age ?
Freedom! thou other name for happy Truth,
Thou warrior-maid, whose steel-clad feet were never
Out of the stirrup, nor thy lance uncouched,
Nor thy fierce eye enticèd from its watch,
Thou hast learned now, by hero-blood in vain
Poured to enrich the soil which tyrants reap;
By wasted lives of prophets, and of those
Who, by the promise in their souls upheld,
Into the red arms of a fiery death
Went blithely as the golden-girdled bee
Sinks in the sleepy poppy's cup of flame
By the long woes of nations set at war,
That so the swollen torrent of their wrath
May find a vent, else sweeping off like straws
The thousand cobweb threads, grown cable-huge
By time's long gathered dust, but cobwebs still,
Which bind the Many that the Few may gain
Leisure to wither by the drought of ease
What heavenly germs in their own souls were sown; —
By all these searching lessons thou hast learned
To throw aside thy blood-stained helm and spear
And with thy bare brow daunt the enemy's front,
Knowing that God will make the lily stalk,
In the soft grasp of naked Gentleness,
Stronger than iron spear to shatter through
The sevenfold toughness of Wrong's idle shield.

A MYSTICAL BALLAD.

I.

THE sunset scarce had dimmed away
Into the twilight's doubtful gray;
One long cloud o'er the horizon lay,
'Neath which, a streak of bluish white,
Wavered between the day and night;
Over the pine trees on the hill
The trembly evening-star did thrill,

And the new moon, with slender rim,
Through the elm arches gleaming dim,
Filled memory's chalice to the brim.

II.

On such an eve the heart doth grow
Full of surmise, and scarce can know
If it be now or long ago,
Or if indeed it doth exist; —
A wonderful enchanted mist
From the new moon doth wander out,
Wrapping all things in mystic doubt,
So that this world doth seem untrue,
And all our fancies to take hue
From some life ages since gone through.

III.

The maiden sat and heard the flow
Of the west wind so soft and low
The leaves scarce quivered to and fro;
Unbound, her heavy golden hair
Rippled across her bosom bare,
Which gleamed with thrilling snowy white
Far through the magical moonlight:
The breeze rose with a rustling swell,
And from afar there came the smell
Of a long-forgotten lily-bell.

IV.

The dim moon rested on the hill,
But silent, without thought or will,
Where sat the dreamy maiden still;
And now the moon's tip, like a star,
Drew down below the horizon's bar;
To her black noon the night hath grown,
Yet still the maiden sits alone,
Pale as a corpse beneath a stream
And her white bosom still doth gleam
Through the deep midnight like a dream.

V.

Cloudless the morning came and fair,
And lavishly the sun doth share

His gold among her golden hair,
Kindling it all, till slowly so
A glory round her head doth glow;
A withered flower is in her hand,
That grew in some far distant land,
And, silently transfigurèd,
With wide calm eyes, and undrooped head,
They found the stranger-maiden dead.

VI.

A youth, that morn, 'neath other skies,
Felt sudden tears burn in his eyes,
And his heart throng with memories;
All things without him seemed to win
Strange brotherhood with things within,
And he forever felt that he
Walked in the midst of mystery,
And thenceforth, why, he could not tell,
His heart would curdle at the smell
Of his once-cherished lily-bell.

VII.

Something from him had passed away;
Some shifting trembles of clear day,
Through starry crannies in his clay,
Grew bright and steadfast, more and more,
Where all had been dull earth before;
And, through these chinks, like him of old,
His spirit converse high did hold
With clearer loves and wider powers,
That brought him dewy fruits and flowers
From far Elysian groves and bowers.

VIII.

Just on the farther bound of sense,
Unproved by outward evidence,
But known by a deep influence
Which through our grosser clay doth shine
With light unwaning and divine,
Beyond where highest thought can fly
Stretcheth the world of Mystery —
And they not greatly overween
Who deem that nothing true hath been
Save the unspeakable Unseen.

IX.

One step beyond life's work-day things,
One more beat of the soul's broad wings,
One deeper sorrow sometimes brings
The spirit into that great Vast
Where neither future is nor past;
None knoweth how he entered there,
But, waking, finds his spirit where
He thought an angel could not soar,
And, what he called false dreams before,
The very air about his door.

X.

These outward seemings are but shows
Whereby the body sees and knows;
Far down beneath, forever flows
A stream of subtlest sympathies
That make our spirits strangely wise
In awe, and fearful bodings dim
Which, from the sense's outer rim,
Stretch forth beyond our thought and sight,
Fine arteries of circling light,
Pulsed outward from the Infinite.

OPENING POEM TO

A YEAR'S LIFE.

Hope first the youthful Poet leads,
And he is glad to follow her;
Kind is she, and to all his needs
With a free hand doth minister.

But, when sweet Hope at last hath fled,
Cometh her sister, Memory;
She wreathes Hope's garlands round her head,
And strives to seem as fair as she.

Then Hope comes back, and by the hand
She leads a child most fair to see,
Who with a joyous face doth stand
Uniting Hope and Memory.

So brighter grew the Earth around,
And bluer grew the sky above;
The Poet now his guide hath found,
And follows in the steps of Love.

DEDICATION

TO VOLUME OF POEMS ENTITLED

A YEAR'S LIFE.

THE gentle Una I have loved,
The snowy maiden, pure and mild,
Since ever by her side I roved,
Through ventures strange, a wondering child,
In fantasy a Red Cross Knight,
Burning for her dear sake to fight.

If there be one who can, like her,
Make sunshine in life's shady places,
One in whose holy bosom stir
As many gentle household graces —
And such I think there needs must be —
Will she accept this book from me?

THE SERENADE.

GENTLE, Lady, be thy sleeping,
Peaceful may thy dreamings be,
•While around thy soul is sweeping,
Dreamy-winged, our melody;
Chant we, Brothers, sad and slow,
Let our song be soft and low
As the voice of other years,
Let our hearts within us melt,
To gentleness, as if we felt
The dropping of our mother's tears.

Lady! now our song is bringing
Back again thy childhood's hours —
Hearest thou the humbee singing
Drowsily among the flowers?
Sleepily, sleepily

In the noontide swayeth he,
Half rested on the slender stalks
That edge those well-known garden walks;
Hearest thou the fitful whirring
Of the humbird's viewless wings —
Feel'st not round thy heart the stirring
Of childhood's half-forgotten things?

Seest thou the dear old dwelling
With the woodbine round the door?
Brothers, soft! her breast is swelling
With the busy thoughts of yore;
Lowly sing ye, sing ye mildly, ·
Rouse her spirit not so wildly,
Lest she sleep not any more.
'T is the pleasant summertide,
Open stands the window wide —
Whose voices, Lady, art thou drinking?
Who sings the best belovèd tune
In a clear note, rising, sinking,
Like a thrush's song in June?
Whose laugh is that which rings so clear
And joyous in thine eager ear?

Lower, Brothers, yet more low
Weave the song in mazy twines;
She heareth now the west wind blow
At evening through the clump of pines;
O! mournful is their tune,
As of a crazèd thing
Who, to herself alone,
Is ever murmuring,
Through the night and through the day,
For something that hath passed away.
Often, Lady, hast thou listened,
Often have thy blue eyes glistened,
Where the summer evening breeze
Moaned sadly through those lonely trees,
Or with the fierce wind from the north
Wrung their mournful music forth.
Ever the river floweth
In an unbroken stream,
Ever the west wind bloweth,
Murmuring as he goeth,

And mingling with her dream;
Onward still the river sweepeth
With a sound of long-agone;
Lowly, Brothers, lo! she weepeth, ·
She is now no more alone;
Long-loved forms and long-loved faces
Round about her pillow throng,
Through her memory's desert places
Flow the waters of our song.
Lady! if thy life be holy
As when thou wert yet a child,
Though our song be melancholy,
It will stir no anguish wild;
For the soul that hath lived well,
For the soul that child-like is,
There is quiet in the spell
That brings back early memories.

SONG.

I.

LIFT up the curtains of thine eyes
    And let their light outshine!
Let me adore the mysteries
    Of those mild orbs of thine,
Which ever queenly calm do roll,
Attunèd to an ordered soul!

II.

Open thy lips yet once again
    And, while my soul doth hush
With awe, pour forth that holy strain
    Which seemeth me to gush,
A fount of music, running o'er
From thy deep spirit's inmost core!

III.

The melody that dwells in thee
    Begets in me as well
A spiritual harmony,
    A mild and blessèd spell;
Far, far above earth's atmosphere
I rise, whene'er thy voice I hear.

THE DEPARTED.

Not they alone are the departed,
Who have laid them down to sleep
In the grave narrow and lonely,
Not for them only do I vigils keep,
Not for them only am I heavy-hearted,
Not for them only!

Many, many, there are many
Who no more are with me here,
As cherished, as beloved as any
Whom I have seen upon the bier.
I weep to think of those old faces,
To see them in their grief or mirth;
I weep — for there are empty places
Around my heart's once crowded hearth;
The cold ground doth not cover them,
The grass hath not grown over them,
Yet are they gone from me on earth; —
O! how more bitter is this weeping,
Than for those lost ones who are sleeping
Where sun will shine and flowers blow,
Where gentle winds will whisper low,
And the stars have them in their keeping!
Wherefore from me who loved you so,
O! wherefore did ye go?
I have shed full many a tear,
I have wrestled oft in prayer —
But ye do not come again;
How could anything so dear,
How could anything so fair,
Vanish like the summer rain?
No, no, it cannot be,
But ye are still with me!

And yet, O! where art thou,
Childhood, with sunny brow
And floating hair?
Where art thou hiding now?
I have sought thee everywhere,
All among the shrubs and flowers
Of those garden-walks of ours —

Thou art not there!
When the shadow of Night's wings
Hath darkened all the Earth,
I listen for thy gambolings
Beside the cheerful hearth —
Thou art not there!
I listen to the far-off bell,
I murmur o'er the little songs
Which thou didst love so well,
Pleasant memories come in throngs
And mine eyes are blurred with tears,
But no glimpse of thee appears:
Lonely am I in the Winter, lonely in the Spring,
Summer and Harvest bring no trace of thee —
Oh! whither, whither art thou wandering,
Thou who didst once so cleave to me?

And Love is gone; —
I have seen him come,
I have seen him, too, depart,
Leaving desolate his home,
His bright home in my heart.
I am alone!
Cold, cold is his hearth-stone,
Wide open stands the door;
The frolic and the gentle one
Shall I see no more, no more?
At the fount the bowl is broken,
I shall drink it not again,
All my longing prayers are spoken,
And felt, ah, woe is me, in vain!
Oh, childish hopes and childish fancies,
Whither have ye fled away?
I long for you in mournful trances,
I long for you by night and day;
Beautiful thoughts that once were mine,
Might I but win you back once more,
Might ye about my being twine
And cluster as ye did of yore!
O! do not let me pray in vain —
How good and happy I should be,
How free from every shade of pain,
If ye would come again to me!

O, come again! come, come again!
Hath the sun forgot its brightness,
Have the stars forgot to shine,
That they bring not their wonted lightness
To this weary heart of mine?
'T is not the sun that shone on thee,
Happy childhood, long ago —
Not the same stars silently
Looking on the same bright snow —
Not the same that Love and I
Together watched in days gone by!
No, not the same, alas for me!

Would God that those who early went
To the house dark and low,
For whom our mourning heads were bent,
For whom our steps were slow;
O, would that these alone had left us,
That Fate of these alone had reft us,
Would God indeed that it were so!
Many leaves too soon must wither,
Many flowers too soon must die,
Many bright ones wandering hither,
We know not whence, we know not why,
Like the leaves and like the flowers,
Vanish, ere the summer hours,
That brought them to us, have gone by.

O for the hopes and for the feelings,
Childhood, that I shared with thee —
The high resolves, the bright revealings
Of the soul's might, which thou gav'st me,
Gentle Love, woe worth the day,
Woe worth the hour when thou wert born,
Woe worth the day thou fled'st away —
A shade across the wind-waved corn —
A dewdrop falling from the leaves
Chance-shaken in a summer's morn!
Woe, woe is me! my sick heart grieves,
Companionless and anguish-worn!
I know it well, our manly years
Must be baptized in bitter tears;
Full many fountains must run dry
That youth has dreamed for long hours by,

Choked by convention's siroc blast.
Or drifting sands of many cares;
Slowly they leave us all at last,
And cease their flowing unawares.

THE BOBOLINK.

ANACREON of the meadow,
Drunk with the joy of spring!
Beneath the tall pine's voiceful shadow.
I lie and drink thy jargoning;
My soul is full with melodies,
One drop would overflow it,
And send the tears into mine eyes —
But what car'st thou to know it?
Thy heart is free as mountain air,
And of thy lays thou hast no care,
Scattering them gayly everywhere,
Happy, unconscious poet!

Upon a tuft of meadow grass,
While thy loved-one tends the nest,
Thou swayest as the breezes pass,
Unburthening thine o'erfull breast
Of the crowded songs that fill it,
Just as joy may choose to will it.
Lord of thy love and liberty,
The blithest bird of merry May,
Thou turnest thy bright eyes on me,
That say as plain as eye can say —
"Here sit we, here in the summer weather,
I and my modest mate together;
Whatever your wise thoughts may be,
Under that gloomy old pine tree,
We do not value them a feather."

Now, leaving earth and me behind,
Thou beatest up against the wind,
Or, floating slowly down before it,
Above thy grass-hid nest thou flutterest
And thy bridal love-song utterest,
Raining showers of music o'er it,
Weary never, still thou trillest,

Spring-gladsome lays,
As of moss-rimmed water-brooks
Murmuring through pebbly nooks
In quiet summer days.
My heart with happiness thou fillest,
I seem again to be a boy
Watching thee, gay, blithesome lover,
O'er the bending grass-tops hover,
Quivering thy wings for joy.
There 's something in the apple-blossom,
The greening grass and bobolink's song,
That wakes again within my bosom
Feelings which have slumbered long.
As long, long years ago I wandered,
I seem to wander even yet,
The hours the idle school-boy squandered,
The man would die ere he 'd forget.
O hours that frosty eld deemed wasted,
Nodding his gray head toward my books,
I dearer prize the lore I tasted
With you, among the trees and brooks,
Than all that I have gained since then
From learnèd books or study-withered men!
Nature, thy soul was one with mine,
And, as a sister by a younger brother
Is loved, each flowing to the other,
Such love for me was thine.
Or wert thou not more like a loving mother
With sympathy and loving power to heal,
Against whose heart my throbbing heart I 'd lay
And moan my childish sorrows all away,
Till calm and holiness would o'er me steal?
Was not the golden sunset a dear friend?
Found I no kindness in the silent moon,
And the green trees, whose tops did sway and bend,
Low singing evermore their pleasant tune?
Felt I no heart in dim and solemn woods —
No loved-one's voice in lonely solitudes?
Yes, yes! unhoodwinked then my spirit's eyes,
Blind leaders had not *taught me* to be wise.

Dear hours! which now again I over-live,
Hearing and seeing with the ears and eyes

Of childhood, ye were bees, that to the hive
Of my young heart came laden with rich prize,
Gathered in fields and woods and sunny dells, to be
My spirit's food in days more wintery.
Yea, yet again ye come! ye come!
And, like a child once more at home
After long sojourning in alien climes,
I lie upon my mother's breast,
Feeling the blessedness of rest,
And dwelling in the light of other times.

O ye whose living is not *Life*,
Whose dying is but death,
Song, empty toil and petty strife,
Rounded with loss of breath!
Go, look on Nature's countenance,
Drink in the blessing of her glance;
Look on the sunset, hear the wind,
The cataract, the awful thunder;
Go, worship by the sea;
Then, and then only, shall ye find,
With ever-growing wonder,
Man is not all in all to ye;
Go with a meek and humble soul,
Then shall the scales of self unroll
From off your eyes — the weary packs
Drop from your heavy-laden backs;
And ye shall see,
With reverent and hopeful eyes,
Glowing with new-born energies,
How great a thing it is to BE!

FORGETFULNESS.

THERE 's a haven of sure rest
  From the loud world's bewildering stress
As a bird dreaming on her nest,
As dew hid in a rose's breast,
As Hesper in the glowing West;
    So the heart sleeps
    In thy calm deeps,
  Serene Forgetfulness!

No sorrow in that place may be,
    The noise of life grows less and less:
As moss far down within the sea,
As, in white lily caves, a bee,
As life in a hazy reverie;
        So the heart's wave
        In thy dim cave,
Hushes, Forgetfulness!

Duty and care fade far. away
    What toil may be we cannot guess:
As a ship anchored in the bay,
As a cloud at summer-noon astray,
As water-blooms in a breezeless day;
        So, 'neath thine eyes,
        The full heart lies,
    And dreams, Forgetfulness!

SONG.

I.

WHAT reck I of the stars, when I
    May gaze into thine eyes,
O'er which the brown hair flowingly
    Is parted maidenwise
From thy pale forehead, calm and bright,
Over thy cheeks so rosy white?

II.

What care I for the red moon-rise?
    Far liefer would I sit
And watch the joy within thine eyes
    Gush up at sight of it;
Thyself my queenly moon shall be,
Ruling my heart's deep tides for me!

III.

What heed I if the sky be blue?
    So are thy holy eyes,
And bright with shadows ever new
    Of changeful sympathies,
Which in thy soul's unruffled deep
Rest evermore, but never sleep.

D

THE POET.

HE who hath felt Life's mystery
    Press on him like thick night,
Whose soul hath known no history
    But struggling after light; —
He who hath seen dim shapes arise
    In the soundless depths of soul,
Which gaze on him with meaning eyes
    Full of the mighty whole,
Yet will no word of healing speak,
    Although he pray night-long,
"O, help me, save me! I am weak,
    And ye are wondrous strong!" —
Who, in the midnight dark and deep,
    Hath felt a voice of might
Come echoing through the halls of sleep
    From the lone heart of Night,
And, starting from his restless bed,
    Hath watched and wept to know
What meant that oracle of dread
    That stirred his being so;
He who hath felt how strong and great
    This Godlike soul of man,
And looked full in the eyes of Fate,
    Since Life and Thought began;
The armor of whose moveless trust
    Knoweth no spot of weakness,
Who hath trod fear into the dust
    Beneath the feet of meekness; —
He who hath calmly borne his cross,
    Knowing himself the king
Of time, nor counted it a loss
    To learn by suffering; —
And who hath worshipped woman still
    With a pure soul and lowly,
Nor ever hath in deed or will
    Profaned her temple holy —
He is the Poet, him unto
    The gift of song is given,
Whose life is lofty, strong, and true,
    Who never fell from Heaven;

He is the Poet, from his lips
To live forevermore,
Majestical as full-sailed ships,
The words of Wisdom pour.

FLOWERS.

" Hail be thou, holie hearbe,
Growing on the ground,
All in the mount Calvary
First wert thou found;
Thou art good for manie a sore,
Thou healest manie a wound,
In the name of sweete Jesus
I take thee from the ground."
— *Ancient Charm-verse.*

I.

When, from a pleasant ramble, home
Fresh-stored with quiet thoughts, I come,
I pluck some wayside flower
And press it in the choicest nook
Of a much-loved and oft-read book;
And, when upon its leaves I look
In a less happy hour,
Dear memory bears me far away
Unto her fairy bower,
And on her breast my head I lay,
While, in a motherly, sweet strain,
She sings me gently back again
To by-gone feelings, until they
Seem children born of yesterday.

II.

Yes, many a story of past hours
I read in these dear withered flowers,
And once again I seem to be
Lying beneath the old oak tree,
And looking up into the sky,
Through thick leaves rifted fitfully,
Lulled by the rustling of the vine,
Or the faint low of far-off kine;

And once again I seem
To watch the whirling bubbles flee,
Through shade and gleam alternately,
Down the vine-bowered stream;
Or 'neath the odorous linden trees,
When summer twilight lingers long,
To hear the flowing of the breeze
And unseen insects' slumberous song,
That mingle into one and seem
Like dim murmurs of a dream ;
Fair faces, too, I seem to see,
Smiling from pleasant eyes at me,
And voices sweet I hear,
That, like remembered melody,
Flow through my spirit's ear.

III.

A poem every flower is,
And every leaf a line,
And with delicious memories
They fill this heart of mine:
No living blossoms are so clear
As these dead relics treasured here;
One tells of Love, of friendship one,
Love's quiet after-sunset time,
When the all-dazzling light is gone,
And, with the soul's low vesper-chime,
O'er half its heaven doth out-flow
A holy calm and steady glow.
Some are gay feast-songs, some are dirges,
In some a joy with sorrow merges;
One sings the shadowed woods, and one the roar
Of ocean's everlasting surges,
Tumbling upon the beach's hard-beat floor,
Or sliding backward from the shore
To meet the landward waves and slowly plunge once more.
O flowers of grace, I bless ye all
By the dear faces ye recall!

IV.

Upon the banks of Life's deep streams
Full many a flower groweth,
Which with a wondrous fragrance teems,

And in the silent water gleams,
And trembles as the water floweth,
Many a one the wave upteareth,
Washing ever the roots away,
And far upon its bosom beareth,
To bloom no more in Youth's glad **May**;
As farther on the river runs,
Flowing more deep and strong,
Only a few pale, scattered ones
Are seen the dreary banks along;
And where those flowers do not grow,
The river floweth dark and chill,
Its voice is sad, and with its flow
Mingles ever a sense of ill;
Then, Poet, thou who gather dost
Of Life's best flowers the brightest,
O, take good heed they be not lost
While with the angry flood thou fightest!

v.

In the cool grottos of the soul,
Whence flows thought's crystal river,
Whence songs of joy forever roll
To Him who is the Giver —
There store thou them, where fresh and green
Their leaves and blossoms may be seen,
A spring of joy that faileth never;
There store thou them, and they shall be
A blessing and a peace to thee,
And in their youth and purity
Thou shalt be young forever!
Then, with their fragrance rich and rare,
Thy living shall be rife,
Strength shall be thine thy cross to bear,
And they shall be a chaplet fair,
Breathing a pure and holy air,
To crown thy holy life.

vi.

O Poet! above all men blest,
Take heed that thus thou store them;
Love, Hope, and Faith shall ever rest,

Sweet birds (upon how sweet a nest!)
Watchfully brooding o'er them.
And from those flowers of Paradise
Scatter thou many a blessèd seed,
Wherefrom an offspring may arise
To cheer the hearts and light the eyes
Of after-voyagers in their need.
They shall not fall on stony ground,
But, yielding all their hundred-fold,
Shall shed a peacefulness around,
Whose strengthening joy may not be told,
So shall thy name be blest of all,
And thy remembrance never die;
For of that seed shall surely fall
In the fair garden of Eternity.
Exult then in the nobleness
Of this thy work so holy,
Yet be not thou one jot the less
Humble and meek and lowly,
But let thine exultation be
The reverence of a bended knee;
And by thy life a poem write,
Built strongly day by day —
And on the rock of Truth and Right
Its deep foundations lay.

VII.

It is thy DUTY! Guard it well!
For unto thee hath much been given,
And thou canst make this life a Hell,
Or Jacob's-ladder up to Heaven.
Let not thy baptism in Life's wave
Make thee like him whom Homer sings —
A sleeper in a living grave,
Callous and hard to outward things,
But open all thy soul and sense
To every blessèd influence
That from the heart of Nature springs:
Then shall thy Life-flowers be to thee,
When thy best years are told,
As much as these have been to me —
Yea, more, a thousand-fold!

THE LOVER.

I.

Go from the world from East to West,
Search every land beneath the sky,
You cannot find a man so blest,
A king so powerful as I,
Though you should seek eternally.

II.

For I a gentle lover be,
Sitting at my loved-one's side;
She giveth her whole soul to me
Without a wish or thought of pride,
And she shall be my cherished bride.

III.

No show of gaudiness hath she,
She doth not flash with jewels rare;
In beautiful simplicity
She weareth leafy garlands fair,
Or modest flowers in her hair.

IV.

Sometimes she dons a robe of green,
Sometimes a robe of snowy white,
But, in whatever garb she's seen,
It seems most beautiful and right,
And is the loveliest to my sight.

V.

Not I her lover am alone,
Yet unto all she doth suffice,
None jealous is, and every one
Reads love and truth within her eyes,
And deemeth her his own dear prize.

VI.

And so thou art, Eternal Nature!
Yes, bride of Heaven, so thou art;
Thou wholly lovest every creature,
Giving to each no stinted part,
But filling every peaceful heart.

TO E. W. G.

"DEAR Child! dear happy Girl! if thou appear
Heedless — untouched with awe or serious thought,
Thy nature is not therefore less divine:
Thou liest in Abraham's bosom all the year;
And worship'st at the Temple's inner shrine,
God being with thee when we know it not."
— Wordsworth.

As through a strip of sunny light
A white dove flashes swiftly on,
So suddenly before my sight
Thou gleamed'st a moment and wert gone;
And yet I long shall bear in mind
The pleasant thoughts thou left'st behind.

Thou mad'st me happy with thine eyes,
And happy with thine open smile,
And, as I write, sweet memories
Come thronging round me all the while;
Thou mad'st me happy with thine eyes —
And gentle feelings long forgot
Looked up and oped their eyes,
Like violets when they see a spot
Of summer in the skies.

Around thy playful lips did glitter
Heat-lightnings of a girlish scorn;
Harmless they were, for nothing bitter
In thy dear heart was ever born —
That merry heart that could not lie
Within its warm nest quietly,
But ever from each full, dark eye
Was looking kindly night and morn.

There was an archness in thine eyes,
Born of the gentlest mockeries,
And thy light laughter rang as clear
As water-drops I loved to hear
In days of boyhood, as they fell
Tinkling far down the dim, still well;
And with its sound come back once more

The feelings of my early years,
And half aloud I murmured o'er —
"Sure I have heard that sound before,
It is so pleasant in mine ears."

Whenever thou didst look on me
I thought of merry birds,
And something of spring's melody
Came to me in thy words;
Thy thoughts did dance and bound along
Like happy children in their play,
Whose hearts run over into song
For gladness of the summer's day;
And mine grew dizzy with the sight,
Still feeling lighter and more light,
Till, joining hands, they whirled away,
As blithe and merrily as they.

I bound a larch-twig round with flowers,
Which thou didst twine among thy hair,
And gladsome were the few, short hours
When I was with thee there;
So now that thou art far away,
Safe-nestled in thy warmer clime,
In memory of a happier day
I twine this simple wreath of rhyme.

Dost mind how she, whom thou dost love
More than in light words may be said,
A coronal of amaranth wove
About thy duly-sobered head,
Which kept itself a moment still
That she might have her gentle will?
Thy childlike grace and purity
O keep forevermore,
And as thou art, still strive to be,
That on the farther shore
Of Time's dark waters ye may meet,
And she may twine around thy brow
A wreath of those bright flowers that grow
Where blessèd angels set their feet!

ISABEL.

As the leaf upon the tree,
Fluttering, gleaming constantly,
Such a lightsome thing was she,
My gay and gentle Isabel!
Her heart was fed with love-springs sweet,
And in her face you'd see it beat
To hear the sound of welcome feet —
And were not mine so, Isabel?

She knew it not, but she was fair,
And like a moonbeam was her hair,
That falls where flowing ripples are
In summer evenings, Isabel!
Her heart and tongue were scarce apart,
Unwittingly her lips would part,
And love came gushing from her heart,
The woman's heart of Isabel.

So pure her flesh-garb, and like dew,
That in her features glimmered through
Each working of her spirit true,
In wondrous beauty, Isabel!
A sunbeam struggling through thick leaves,
A reaper's song mid yellow sheaves,
Less gladsome were; — my spirit grieves
To think of thee, mild Isabel!

I know not when I loved thee first;
Not loving, I had been accurst,
Yet, having loved, my heart will burst,
Longing for thee, dear Isabel!
With silent tears my cheeks are wet,
I would be calm, I would forget,
But thy blue eyes gaze on me yet,
When stars have risen, Isabel.

The winds mourn for thee, Isabel,
The flowers expect thee in the dell,
Thy gentle spirit loved them well,
And I for thy sake, Isabel!
The sunsets seem less lovely now
Than when, leaf checkered, on thy brow

They fell as lovingly as thou
Lingered'st till moon-rise, Isabel!

At dead of night I seem to see
Thy fair, pale features constantly
Upturned in silent prayer for me,
O'er moveless clasped hands, Isabel!
I call thee, thou dost not reply;
The stars gleam coldly on thine eye,
As like a dream thou flittest by,
And leav'st me weeping, Isabel!

MUSIC.

I.

I SEEM to lie with drooping eyes,
  Dreaming sweet dreams,
Half longings and half memories,
  In woods where streams
With trembling shades and whirling gleams,
   Many and bright,
   In song and light,
   Are ever, ever flowing;
While the wind, if we list to the rustling grass,
Which numbers his footsteps as they pass,
   Seems scarcely to be blowing;
And the far-heard voice of Spring,
From sunny slopes comes wandering,
Calling the violets from the sleep,
That bound them under snow-drifts deep,
To open their childlike, asking eyes
On the new summer's paradise,
And mingled with the gurgling waters —
   As the dreamy witchery
Of Acheloüs' silver-voiced daughters
   Rose and fell with the heaving sea,
   Whose great heart swelled with ecstasy —
The song of many a floating bird,
   Winding through the rifted trees,
Is dreamily half-heard —
   A sister stream of melodies

Rippled by the flutterings
Of rapture-quivered wings.

II.

And now beside a cataract
I lie, and through my soul,
From over me and under,
The never-ceasing thunder
Arousingly doth roll;
Through the darkness all compact,
Through the trackless sea of gloom,
Sad and deep I hear it boom;
At intervals the cloud is cracked
And a livid flash doth hiss
   Downward from its floating home,
Lighting up the precipice
   And the never-resting foam
With a dim and ghastly glare,
Which, for a heart-beat, in the air,
   Shows the sweeping shrouds
   Of the midnight clouds
And their wildly-scattered hair.

III.

Now listening to a woman's tone,
In a wood I sit alone —
Alone because our souls are one; —
All around my heart it flows,
Lulling me in deep repose;
I fear to speak, I fear to move,
Lest I should break the spell I love —
Low and gentle, calm and clear,
Into my inmost soul it goes,
   As if my brother dear,
   Who is no longer here,
   Had bended from the sky
   And murmured in my ear
A strain of that high harmony,
   Which they may sing alone
   Who worship round the throne.

IV.

Now in a fairy boat,
   On the bright waves of song,

Full merrily I float,
Merrily float along;
· My helm is veered, I care not how,
My white sail bellies over me,
And bright as gold the ripples be
That plash beneath the bow;
Before, behind,
They feel the wind,
And they are dancing joyously —
While, faintly heard, along the far-off shore
The surf goes plunging with a lingering roar;
Or anchored in a shadowy cove,
Entranced with harmonies,
Slowly I sink and rise
As the slow waves of music move.

v.

Now softly dashing,
Bubbling, plashing,
Mazy, dreamy,
Faint and streamy,
Ripples into ripples melt,
Not so strongly heard as felt;
Now rapid and quick,
While the heart beats thick,
The music silver wavelets crowd,
Distinct and clear, but never loud
And now all solemnly and slow,
In mild, deep tones they warble low,
Like the glad song of angels, when
They sang good will and peace to men;
Now faintly heard and far,
As if the spirit's ears
Had caught the anthem of a star
Chanting with his brother-spheres
In the midnight dark and deep,
When the body is asleep
And wondrous shadows pour in streams
From the twofold gate of dreams;
Now onward roll the billows, swelling
With a tempest-sound of might,
As of voices doom foretelling
To the silent ear of Night;

And now a mingled ecstasy
　　Of all sweet sounds it is; —
O! who may tell the agony
　　Of rapture such as this?

VI.

I have drunk of the drink of immortals,
　　I have drunk of the life-giving wine,
And now I may pass the bright portals
　　That open into a realm divine!
I have drunk it through mine ears
　　In the ecstasy of song,
When mine eyes would fill with tears
　　That its life were not more long;
I have drunk it through mine eyes
　　In beauty's every shape,
And now around my soul it lies,
　　No juice of earthly grape!
Wings! wings are given to me,
　　I can flutter, I can rise,
Like a new life gushing through me
　　Sweep the heavenly harmonies!

SONG.

O! I MUST look on that sweet face once more before I die;
God grant that it may lighten up with joy when I draw
　　nigh;
God grant that she may look on me as kindly as she seems
In the long night, the restless night, i' the sunny land of
　　dreams!

I hoped, I thought, she loved me once, and yet, I know
　　not why,
There is a coldness in her speech, and a coldness in her eye.
Something that in another's look would not seem cold to
　　me,
And yet like ice I feel it chill the heart of memory.

She does not come to greet me so frankly as she did,
And in her utmost openness I feel there's something hid;
She almost seems to shun me, as if she thought that I
Might win her gentle heart again to feelings long gone by.

I sought the first spring-buds for her, the fairest and the
    best,
And she wore them for their loveliness upon her spotless
    breast,
The blood-root and the violet, the frail anemone,
She wore them, and alas! I deemed it was for love of me!

As flowers in a darksome place stretch forward to the
    light,
So to the memory of her I turn by day and night;
As flowers in a darksome place grow thin and pale and
    wan,
So is it with my darkened heart, now that her light is
    gone.

The thousand little things that love doth treasure up for
    aye,
And brood upon with moistened eyes when she that's
    loved's away,
The word, the look, the smile, the blush, the ribbon that
    she wore,
Each day they grow more dear to me, and pain me more
    and more.

My face I cover with my hands, and bitterly I weep,
That the quick-gathering sands of life should choke a
    love so deep,
And that the stream, so pure and bright, must turn it
    from its track,
Or to the heart-springs, whence it rose, roll its full waters
    back!

As calm as doth the lily float close by the lakelet's brim,
So calm and spotless, down time's stream, her peaceful
    days did swim,
And I had longed, and dreamed, and prayed, that closely
    by her side,
Down to a haven still and sure, my happy life might glide.

But now, alas! those golden days of youth and hope are
    o'er,
And I must dream those dreams of joy, those guiltless
    dreams no more;

Yet there is something in my heart that whispers cease-
    lessly,
" Would God that I might see that face once more before
    I die!"

IANTHE.

I.

THERE is a light within her eyes,
Like gleams of wandering fire-flies ;
From light to shade it leaps and moves
Whenever in her soul arise
The holy shapes of things she loves;
Fitful it shines and changes ever,
Like star-lit ripples on a river,
Or summer sunshine on the eaves
Of silver-trembling poplar leaves,
Where the lingering dew-drops quiver.
I may not tell the blessedness
Her mild eyes send to mine,
The sunset-tinted haziness
Of their mysterious shine,
The dim and holy mournfulness
Of their mellow light divine;
The shadow of the lashes lie
Over them so lovingly,
That they seem to melt away
In a doubtful twilight-gray,
While I watch the stars arise
In the evening of her eyes,
I love it, yet I almost dread
To think what it foreshadoweth;
And, when I muse how I have read
That such strange light betokened death —
Instead of fire-fly gleams, I see
Wild corpse-lights gliding waveringly.

II.

With wayward thoughts her eyes are bright,
Like shiftings of the northern-light,
Hither, thither, swiftly glance they,
In a mazy twining dance they,

Like ripply lights the sunshine weaves,
Thrown backward from a shaken nook,
Below some tumbling water-brook,
On the o'erarching platan-leaves,
All through her glowing face they flit,
And rest in their deep dwelling-place,
Those fathomless blue eyes of hers,
Till, from her burning soul re-lit,
While her upheaving bosom stirs,
They stream again across her face
And with such hope and glory fill it,
Death could not have the heart to chill it.
Yet when their wild light fades again,
I feel a sudden sense of pain,
As if, while yet her eyes were gleaming,
And like a shower of sun-lit rain
Bright fancies from her face were streaming,
Her trembling soul might flit away
As swift and suddenly as they.

III.

A wild, inspired earnestness
  Her inmost being fills,
And eager self-forgetfulness,
  That speaks not what it wills,
But what unto her soul is given,
A living oracle from Heaven,
Which scarcely in her breast is born,
When on her trembling lips it thrills,
And, like a burst of golden skies
Through storm-clouds on a sudden torn,
Like a glory of the morn,
Beams marvellously from her eyes.
And then, like a Spring-swollen river,
Roll the deep waves of her full-hearted thought
  Crested with sun-lit spray,
  Her wild lips curve and quiver,
And my rapt soul, on the strong tide upcaught,
  Unwittingly is borne away,
  Lulled by a dreamful music ever,
  Far — through the solemn twilight-gray
Of hoary woods — through valleys green

E

Which the trailing vine embowers,
And where the purple-clustered grapes are seen
Deep-glowing through rich clumps of waving flowers —
   Now over foaming rapids swept
   And with maddening rapture shook —
Now gliding where the water-plants have slept
   For ages in a moss-rimmed nook —
   Enwoven by a wild-eyed band
      Of earth-forgetting dreams,
   I float to a delicious land
   By a sunset heaven spanned,
      And musical with streams; —
   Around, the calm, majestic forms
And god-like eyes of early Greece I see,
   Or listen, till my spirit warms,
   To songs of courtly chivalry,
Or weep, unmindful if my tears be seen,
For the meek, suffering love of poor Undine.

IV.

   Her thoughts are never memories,
   But ever changeful, ever new,
   Fresh and beautiful as dew
   That in a dell at noontide lies,
   Or, at the close of summer day,
   The pleasant breath of new-mown hay:
   Swiftly they come and pass
   As golden birds across the sun,
   As light-gleams on tall meadow-grass
   Which the wind just breathes upon.
   And when she speaks, her eyes I see
Down-gushing through their silken lattices,
   Like stars that quiver tremblingly
   Through leafy branches of the trees,
   And her pale cheeks do flush and glow
   With speaking flashes bright and rare
As crimson North-lights on new-fallen snow,
   From out the veiling of her hair —
Her careless hair that scatters down
   On either side her eyes,
A waterfall leaf-tinged with brown
   And lit with the sunrise.

v.

When first I saw her, not of earth,
But heavenly both in grief and mirth,
I thought her; she did seem
As fair and full of mystery,
As bodiless, as forms we see
In the rememberings of a dream;
A moon-lit mist, a strange, dim light,
Circled her spirit from my sight; —
Each day more beautiful she grew,
  More earthly every day,
Yet that mysterious, moony hue
  Faded not all away;
She has a sister's sympathy
With all the wanderers of the sky,
But most I've seen her bosom stir
  When moonlight round her fell,
For the mild moon it loveth her,
  She loveth it as well,
And of their love perchance this grace
Was born into her wondrous face.
I cannot tell how it may be,
For both, methinks, can scarce be true,
Still, as she earthly grew to me,
She grew more heavenly too;
  She seems one born in Heaven
    With earthly feelings,
  For, while unto her soul are given
    More pure revealings
  Of holiest love and truth,
Yet is the mildness of her eyes
Made up of quickest sympathies,
  Of kindliness and ruth;
So, though some shade of awe doth stir
Our souls for one so far above us,
We feel secure that she will love us,
And cannot keep from loving her.
She is a poem, which to me
In speech and look is written bright,
And to her life's rich harmony
Doth ever sing itself aright;
Dear, glorious creature!

With eyes so dewy bright,
    And tenderest feeling
    Itself revealing
In every look and feature,
Welcome as a homestead light
To one long-wandering in a clouded night;
    O, lovelier for her woman's weakness,
        Which yet is strongly mailed
    In armor of courageous meekness
        And faith that never failed!

VI.

    Early and late, at her soul's gate,
Sits Chastity in warderwise,
No thoughts unchallenged, small or great,
Go thence into her eyes;
Nor may a low, unworthy thought
Beyond that virgin warder win,
Nor one, whose password is not "ought,"
May go without or enter in.
I call her, seeing those pure eyes,
The Eve of a new Paradise,
Which she by gentle word and deed,
And look no less, doth still create
About her, for her great thoughts breed
A calm that lifts us from our fallen state,
And makes us while with her both good and great —
Nor is their memory wanting in our need:
With stronger loving, every hour,
Turneth my heart to this frail flower,
Which, thoughtless of the world, hath grown
To beauty and meek gentleness,
Here in a fair world of its own —
By woman's instinct trained alone —
A lily fair which God did bless,
And which from Nature's heart did draw
Love, wisdom, peace, and Heaven's perfect law.

LOVE'S ALTAR.

I.

I BUILT an altar in my soul,
I builded it to one alone;

And ever silently I stole,
In happy days of long-agone,
To make rich offerings to that ONE.

II.

'T was garlanded with purest thought,
And crowned with fancy's flowers bright,
With choicest gems 't was all inwrought
Of truth and feeling; in my sight
It seemed a spot of cloudless light.

III.

Yet when I made my offering there,
Like Cain's, the incense would not rise;
Back on my heart down-sank the prayer,
And altar-stone and sacrifice
Grew hateful in my tear-dimmed eyes.

IV.

O'er-grown with age's mosses green,
The little altar firmly stands;
It is not, as it once hath been,
A selfish shrine; — these time-taught hands
Bring incense now from many lands.

V.

Knowledge doth only widen love;
The stream, that lone and narrow rose,
Doth, deepening ever, onward move,
And with an even current flows
Calmer and calmer to the close.

VI.

The love, that in those early days
Girt round my spirit like a wall,
Hath faded like a morning haze,
And flames, unpent by self's mean thrall,
Rise clearly to the perfect ALL.

IMPARTIALITY.

I.

I CANNOT say a scene is fair
Because it is beloved of thee,
But I shall love to linger there,
For sake of thy dear memory;
I would not be so coldly just
As to love only what I must.

II.

I cannot say a thought is good
Because thou foundest joy in it;
Each soul must choose its proper food
Which Nature hath decreed most fit;
But I shall ever deem it so
Because it made thy heart o'erflow.

III.

I love thee for that thou art fair;
And that thy spirit joys in aught
Createth a new beauty there,
With thine own dearest image fraught;
And love, for others' sake that springs,
Gives half their charm to lovely things.

BELLEROPHON.

DEDICATED TO MY FRIEND, JOHN F. HEATH.

I.

I FEEL the bandages unroll
That bound my inward seeing;
Freed are the bright wings of my soul,
Types of my god-like being;
High thoughts are swelling in my heart
And rushing through my brain;
May I never more lose part
In my soul's realm again!
All things fair, where'er they be,
In earth or air, in sky or sea,
I have loved them all, and taken
All within my throbbing breast;

No more my spirit can be shaken
From its calm and kingly rest!
Love hath shed its light around me,
Love hath pierced the shades that bound me;
Mine eyes are opened, I can see
The universe's mystery,
  The mighty heart and core
  Of After and Before
I see, and I am weak no more!

II.

  Upward! upward evermore,
To Heaven's open gate I soar!
Little thoughts are far behind me,
Which, when custom weaves together,
All the nobler man can tether —
Cobwebs now no more can bind me!
Now fold thy wings a little while,
  My trancèd soul, and lie
At rest on this Calypso-isle
  That floats in mellow sky,
A thousand isles with gentle motion
Rock upon the sunset ocean;
A thousand isles of thousand hues,
How bright! how beautiful! how rare!
Into my spirit they infuse
A purer, a diviner air;
The earth is growing dimmer,
And now the last faint glimmer
  Hath faded from the hill;
But in my higher atmosphere
The sun-light streameth red and clear,
  Fringing the islets still; —
Love lifts us to the sun-light,
Though the whole world would be dark;
Love, wide Love, is the *one* light,
All else is but a fading spark;
Love is the nectar which doth fill
Our soul's cup even to overflowing,
And, warming heart, and thought, and will,
Doth lie within us mildly glowing,
From its own centre raying out
Beauty and Truth on all without.

III.

Each on his golden throne,
Full royally, alone,
I see the stars above me,
With sceptre and with diadem;
Mildly they look down and love me,
For I have ever yet loved them;
I see their ever-sleepless eyes
Watching the growth of destinies;
Calm, sedate,
The eyes of Fate,
They wink not, nor do roll,
But search the depths of soul —
And in those mighty depths they see
The germs of all Futurity,
Waiting but the fitting time
To burst and ripen into prime,
As in the womb of mother Earth
The seeds of plants and forests lie
Age upon age and never die —
So in the souls of all men wait,
Undyingly the seeds of Fate;
Chance breaks the clod and forth they spring,
Filling blind men with wondering.
Eternal stars! with holy awe,
As if a present God I saw,
I look into those mighty eyes
And see great destinies arise,
As in those of mortal men
Feelings glow and fade again!
All things below, all things above,
Are open to the eyes of Love.

IV.

Of Knowledge Love is master-key,
Knowledge of Beauty; passing dear
Is each to each, and mutually
Each one doth make the other clear;
Beauty is Love, and what we love
Straightway is beautiful,
So is the circle round and full,
And so dear Love doth live and move
And have his being,

Finding his proper food
  By sure inseeing,
In all things pure and good,
Which he at will doth cull,
Like a joyous butterfly
Hiving in the sunny bowers
Of the soul's fairest flowers,
Or, between the earth and sky,
Wandering at liberty
For happy, happy hours!

v.

  The thoughts of Love are Poesy,
As this fair earth and all we see
Are the thoughts of Deity —
And Love is ours by our birthright!
He hath cleared mine inward sight;
Glorious shapes with glorious eyes
Round about my spirit glance,
Shedding a mild and golden light
On the shadowy face of Night;
To unearthly melodies,
Hand in hand, they weave their dance,
While a deep, ambrosial lustre
  From their rounded limbs doth shine,
Through many a rich and golden cluster
Of streaming hair divine.
In our gross and earthly hours
We cannot see the Love-given powers
Which ever round the soul await
  To do its sovereign will,
When, in its moments calm and still,
It re-assumes its royal state,
Nor longer sits with eyes downcast,
A beggar, dreaming of the past,
At its own palace-gate.

VI.

I too am a Maker and a Poet;
Through my whole soul I feel it and know it;
My veins are fired with ecstasy!
  All-mother Earth
  Did ne'er give birth

To one who shall be matched with me;
The lustre of my coronal
Shall cast a dimness over all. —
Alas! alas! what have I spoken?
My strong, my eagle wings are broken,
And back again to earth I fall!

SOMETHING NATURAL.

I.

WHEN first I saw thy soul-deep eyes,
My heart yearned to thee instantly,
Strange longing in my soul did rise;
I cannot tell the reason why,
But I must love thee till I die.

II.

The sight of thee hath well-nigh grown
As needful to me as the light;
I am unrestful when alone,
And my heart doth not beat aright
Except it dwell within thy sight.

III.

And yet — and yet — O selfish love!
I am not happy even with thee;
I see thee in thy brightness move,
And cannot well contented be,
Save thou should'st shine alone for me.

IV.

We should love beauty even as flowers —
For all, 't is said, they bud and blow,
They are the world's as well as ours —
But thou — alas! God made thee grow
So fair, I cannot love thee so!

A FEELING.

THE flowers and the grass to me
Are eloquent reproachfully;
For would they wave so pleasantly

Or look so fresh and fair,
If a man, cunning, hollow, mean,
Or one in anywise unclean,
Were looking on them there?

No; he hath grown so foolish-wise
He cannot see with childhood's eyes;
He hath forgot that purity
And lowliness which are the key
Of Nature's mysteries;
No; he hath wandered off so long
From his own place of birth,
That he hath lost his mother-tongue,
And, like one come from far-off lands,
Forgetting and forgot, he stands
Beside his mother's hearth.

THE LOST CHILD.

I.

I WANDERED down the sunny glade,
And ever mused, my love, of thee;
My thoughts, like little children, played,
As gayly and as guilelessly.

II.

If any chanced to go astray,
Moaning in fear of coming harms,
Hope brought the wanderer back alway,
Safe nestled in her snowy arms.

III.

From that soft nest the happy one
Looked up at me and calmly smiled;
Its hair shone golden in the sun,
And made it seem a heavenly child.

IV.

Dear Hope's blue eyes smiled mildly down,
And blest it with a love so deep,
That, like a nursling of her own,
It clasped her neck and fell asleep.

THE CHURCH.

I.

I LOVE the rites of England's church;
  I love to hear and see
The priest and people reading slow
  The solemn Litany;
I love to hear the glorious swell
  Of chanted psalm and prayer,
And the deep organ's bursting heart,
  Throb through the shivering air.

II.

Chants, that a thousand years have heard,
  I love to hear again,
For visions of the olden time
  Are wakened by the strain;
With gorgeous hues the window-glass
  Seems suddenly to glow,
And rich and red the streams of light
  Down through the chancel flow.

III.

And then I murmur, "Surely God
  Delighteth here to dwell;
This is the temple of his Son
  Whom he doth love so well;"
But, when I hear the creed which saith,
  This church alone is His,
I feel within my soul that He
  Hath purer shrines than this.

IV.

For his is not the builded church,
  Nor organ-shaken dome;
In every thing that lovely is
  He loves and hath his home;
And most in soul that loveth well
  All things which he hath made,
Knowing no creed but simple faith
  That may not be gainsaid.

V.

His church is universal Love,
  And whoso dwells therein
Shall need no customed sacrifice
  To wash away his sin;
And music in its aisles shall swell,
  Of lives upright and true,
Sweet as dreamed sounds of angel-harps
  Down-quivering through the blue.

VI.

They shall not ask a litany,
  The souls that worship there,
But every look shall be a hymn,
  And every word a prayer;
Their service shall be written bright
  In calm and holy eyes,
And every day from fragrant hearts
  Fit incense shall arise.

THE UNLOVELY.

THE pretty things that others wear
Look strange and out of place on me,
I never seem dressed tastefully,
  Because I am not fair;
And, when I would most pleasing seem,
And deck myself with joyful care,
I find it is an idle dream,
  Because I am not fair.

If I put roses in my hair,
They bloom as if in mockery;
Nature denies her sympathy,
  Because I am not fair;
Alas! I have a warm, true heart,
But when I show it people stare;
I must forever dwell apart,
  Because I am not fair.

I am least happy being where
The hearts of others are most light,

And strive to keep me out of sight,
  Because I am not fair;
The glad ones often give a glance,
As I am sitting lonely there,
That asks me why I do not dance —
  Because I am not fair.

And if to smile on them I dare,
For that my heart with love runs o'er,
They say: "What *is* she laughing for?" —
  Because I am not fair;
Love scorned or misinterpreted —
It is the hardest thing to bear;
I often wish that I were dead,
  Because I am not fair.

In joy or grief I must not share,
For neither smiles nor tears on me
Will ever look becomingly,
  Because I am not fair;
Whole days I sit alone and cry,
And in my grave I wish I were —
Yet none will weep me if I die,
  Because I am not fair.

My grave will be so lone and bare,
I fear to think of those dark hours,
For none will plant it o'er with flowers,
  Because I am not fair;
They will not in the summer come
And speak kind words above me there;
To me the grave will be no home,
  Because I am not fair.

LOVE–SONG.

NEARER to thy mother-heart,
Simple Nature, press me,
Let me know thee as thou art,
Fill my soul and bless me!
I have loved thee long and well,
I have loved thee heartily;

Shall I never with thee dwell,
Never be at one with thee?

Inward, inward to thy heart,
Kindly Nature, take me,
Lovely even as thou art,
Full of loving make me!
Thou knowest naught of dead-cold forms,
Knowest naught of littleness,
Lifeful Truth thy being warms,
Majesty and earnestness.

Homeward, homeward to thy heart,
Dearest Nature, call me;
Let no halfness, no mean part,
Any longer thrall me!
I will be thy lover true,
I will be a faithful soul,
Then circle me, then look me through,
Fill me with the mighty Whole.

SONG.

ALL things are sad:—
I go and ask of Memory,
That she tell sweet tales to me
  To make me glad;
And she takes me by the hand,
  Leadeth to old places,
  Showeth the old faces
In her hazy mirage-land;
O, her voice is sweet and low,
And her eyes are fresh to mine
    As the dew
    Gleaming through
The half-unfolded Eglantine,
Long ago, long ago!
But I feel that I am only
Yet more sad, and yet more lonely!

Then I turn to blue-eyed Hope,
And beg of her that she will ope
Her golden gates for me;

She is fair and full of grace,
But she hath the form and face
Of her mother Memory;
Clear as air her glad voice ringeth,
Joyous are the songs she singeth,
Yet I hear them mournfully;—
They are songs her mother taught her,
Crooning to her infant daughter,
As she lay upon her knee.
Many little ones she bore me,
Woe is me! in by-gone hours,
Who danced along and sang before me,
Scattering my way with flowers;
    One by one
      They are gone,
And their silent graves are seen,
Shining fresh with mosses green,
Where the rising sunbeams slope
O'er the dewy land of Hope.

But, when sweet Memory faileth,
And Hope looks strange and cold;
When youth no more availeth,
And Grief grows over bold;—
When softest winds are dreary,
And summer sunlight weary,
And sweetest things uncheery
    We know not why:—
When the crown of our desires
Weighs upon the brow and tires,
    And we would die,
Die for, ah! we know not what,
Something we seem to have forgot,
Something we had, and now have not;—
When the present is a weight
And the future seems our foe,
And with shrinking eyes we wait,
As one who dreads a sudden blow
In the dark, he knows not whence;—
When Love at last his bright eye closes,
And the bloom upon his face,
That lends him such a living grace,
Is a shadow from the roses

Wherewith we have decked his bier,
Because he once was passing dear; —
When we feel a leaden sense
Of nothingness and impotence,
   Till we grow mad —
  Then the body saith,
   "There's but one true faith;
    All things are sad!"

A LOVE-DREAM.

PLEASANT thoughts come wandering,
When thou art far, from thee to me;
On their silver wings they bring
A very peaceful ecstasy,
A feeling of eternal spring;
So that Winter half forgets
Everything, but that thou art,
And, in his bewildered heart,
Dreameth of the violets,
Or those bluer flowers that ope,
Flowers of steadfast love and hope,
Watered by the living wells,
Of memories dear, and dearer prophecies,
When young spring forever dwells
In the sunshine of thine eyes.

I have most holy dreams of thee,
  All night I have such dreams;
And, when I awake, reality
  No whit the darker seems;
Through the twin gates of Hope and Memory
  They pour in crystal streams
From out an angel's calmèd eyes,
Who, from twilight till sunrise,
Far away in the upper deep,
Poised upon his shining wings,
Over us his watch doth keep,
And, as he watcheth, ever sings.

Through the still night I hear him sing,
  Down-looking on our sleep;

I hear his clear, clear harp-strings ring,
And, as the golden notes take wing,
Gently downward hovering,
     For very joy I weep;
He singeth songs of holy Love,
That quiver through the depths afar,
Where the blessèd spirits are,
And lingeringly from above
Shower till the morning star
His silver shield hath buckled on
And sentinels the dawn alone,
Quivering his gleamy spear
Through the dusky atmosphere.

Almost, my love, I fear the morn,
When that blessèd voice shall cease,
Lest it should leave me quite forlorn,
Stript of my snowy robe of peace;
And yet the bright reality
Is fairer than all dreams can be,
For, through my spirit, all day long,
Ring echoes of that angel-song
In melodious thoughts of thee;
And well I know it cannot die
Till eternal morn shall break,
For, through life's slumber, thou and I
Will keep it for each other's sake,
And it shall not be silent when we wake.

FOURTH OF JULY ODE.

I.

OUR fathers fought for Liberty,
     They struggled long and well,
     History of their deeds can tell —
But did they leave us free?

II.

Are we free from vanity,
     Free from pride, and free from self,
     Free from love of power and pelf,
From everything that's beggarly?

III.

Are we free from stubborn will,
From low hate and malice small,
From opinion's tyrant thrall?
Are none of us our own slaves still?

IV.

Are we free to speak our thought,
To be happy, and be poor,
Free to enter Heaven's door,
To live and labor as we ought?

V.

Are we then made free at last
From the fear of what men say,
Free to reverence To-day,
Free from the slavery of the Past?

VI.

Our fathers fought for liberty,
They struggled long and well,
History of their deeds can tell —
But *ourselves* must set us free.

SPHINX.

I.

WHY mourn we for the golden prime
When our young souls *were* kingly, strong, and true?
The soul is greater than all time,
It changes not, but yet is ever new.

II.

But that the soul *is* noble, we
Could never know what nobleness had been;
Be what ye dream! and earth shall see
A greater greatness than she e'er hath seen.

III.

The flower pines not to be fair,
It never asketh to be sweet and dear,
But gives itself to sun and air,
And so is fresh and full from year to year.

IV.

Nothing in Nature weeps its lot,
Nothing, save man, abides in memory,
Forgetful that the Past is what
Ourselves may choose the coming time to be.

V.

All things are circular; the Past
Was given us to make the Future great;
And the void Future shall at last
Be the strong rudder of an after fate.

VI.

We sit beside the Sphinx of Life,
We gaze into its void, unanswering eyes,
And spend ourselves in idle strife
To read the riddle of their mysteries.

VII.

Arise! be earnest and be strong!
The Sphinx's eyes shall suddenly grow clear,
And speak as plain to thee ere long,
As the dear maiden's who holds thee most dear.

VIII.

The meaning of all things in *us* —
Yea, in the lives we give our souls — doth lie;
Make, then, their meaning glorious
By such a life as need not fear to die!

IX.

There is no heart-beat in the day,
Which bears a record of the smallest deed,
But holds within its faith alway
That which in doubt we vainly strive to read.

X.

One seed contains another seed,
And that a third, and so for evermore;
And promise of as great a deed
Lies folded in the deed that went before.

XI.

So ask not fitting space or time,
Yet could not dream of things which could not be;
   Each day shall make the next sublime,
And Time be swallowed in Eternity.

XII.

God bless the Present! it is ALL;
It has been Future, and it shall be Past;
   Awake and live! thy strength recall,
And in one trinity unite them fast.

XIII.

Action and Life — lo! here the key
Of all on earth that seemeth dark and wrong;
   Win this — and, with it, freely ye
May enter that bright realm for which ye long.

XIV.

Then all these bitter questionings
Shall with a full and blessèd answer meet;
   Past worlds, whereof the Poet sings,
Shall be the earth beneath his snow-white fleet.

"GOE, LITTLE BOOKE!"

Go little book! the world is wide,
There's room and verge enough for thee;
For thou hast learned that only pride
Lacketh fit opportunity,
Which comes unbid to modesty.

Go! win thy way with gentleness:
I send thee forth, my first-born child,
Quite, quite alone, to face the stress
Of fickle skies and pathways wild,
Where few can keep them undefiled.

Thou camest from a poet's heart,
A warm, still home, and full of rest;

Far from the pleasant eyes thou art
Of those who know and love thee best,
And by whose hearthstones thou wert blest.

Go ! knock thou softly at the door
Where any gentle spirits bin,
Tell them thy tender feet are sore,
Wandering so far from all thy kin,
And ask if thou may enter in.

Beg thou a cup-full from the spring
Of Charity, in Christ's dear name;
Few will deny so small a thing,
Nor ask unkindly if thou came
Of one whose life might do thee shame.

We all are prone to go astray,
Our hopes are bright, our lives are dim;
But thou art pure, and if they say,
"We know thy father, and our whim
He pleases not," — plead thou for him.

For many are by whom all truth,
That speaks not in their mother-tongue,
Is stoned to death with hands unruth,
Or hath its patient spirit wrung
Cold words and colder looks among.

Yet fear not! for skies are fair
To all whose souls are fair within;
Thou wilt find shelter everywhere
With those to whom a different skin
Is not a damning proof of sin.

But, if all others are unkind,
There's *one* heart whither thou canst fly
For shelter from the biting wind;
And, in that home of purity,
It were no bitter thing to die.

SONNETS.

I.

DISAPPOINTMENT.

I PRAY thee call not this society;
I asked for bread, thou givest me a stone;
I am an hungered, and I find not one
To give me meat, to joy or grieve with me;
I find not here what I went out to see —
Souls of true men, of women who can move
The deeper, better part of us to love,
Souls that can hold with mine communion free.
Alas! must then these hopes, these longings high,
This yearning of the soul for brotherhood,
And all that makes us pure, and wise, and good,
Come broken-hearted, home again to die?
No, Hope is left, and prays with bended head,
"Give us this day, O God, our daily bread!"

II.

Great human nature, whither art thou fled?
Are these things creeping forth and back agen,
These hollow formalists and echoes, men?
Art thou entombèd with the mighty dead?
In God's name, no! not yet hath all been said,
Or done, or longed for, that is truly great;
These pitiful dried crusts will never sate
Natures for which pure Truth is daily bread;
We were not meant to plod along the earth,
Strange to ourselves and to our fellows strange;
We were not meant to struggle from our birth
To skulk and creep, and in mean pathways range;
Act! with stern truth, large faith, and loving will!
Up and be doing! God is with us still.

III.

TO A FRIEND.

One strip of bark may feed the broken tree,
Giving to some few limbs a sickly green;

And one light shower on the hills, I ween,
May keep the spring from drying utterly.
Thus seemeth it with these our hearts to be;
Hope is the strip of bark, the shower of rain,
And so they are not wholly crushed with pain.
But live and linger on, far sadder sight to see;
Much do they err, who tell us that the heart
May not be broken; what, then, can we call
A broken heart, if this may not be so,
This death in life, when, shrouded in its pall,
Shunning and shunned, it dwelleth all apart,
Its power, its love, its sympathy laid low?

IV.

So may it be, but let it not be so,
O, let it not be so with thee, my friend;
Be of good courage, bear up to the end,
And on thine after way rejoicing go!
We all must suffer, if we aught would know;
Life is a teacher stern, and wisdom's crown
Is oft a crown of thorns, whence, trickling down,
Blood, mixed with tears, blinding her eyes doth flow
But Time, a gentle nurse, shall wipe away
This bloody sweat, and thou shalt find on earth,
That woman is not all in all to Love,
But, living by a new and second birth,
Thy soul shall see all things below, above,
Grow bright and brighter to the perfect day.

V.

O child of Nature! O most meek and free,
Most gentle spirit of true nobleness!
Thou doest not a worthy deed the less
Because the world may not its greatness see;
What were a thousand triumphings to thee,
Who, in thyself, art as a perfect sphere
Wrapt in a bright and natural atmosphere
Of mighty-souledness and majesty?
Thy soul is not too high for lowly things,
Feels not its strength seeing its brother weak,
Not for itself unto itself is dear,
But for that it may guide the wanderings

Of fellow-men, and to their spirits speak
The lofty faith of heart that knows no fear.

VI.

TO ——

Deem it no Sodom-fruit of vanity,
Or fickle fantasy of unripe youth
Which ever takes the fairest shows for truth,
That I should wish my verse beloved of thee;
'T is love's deep thirst which may not quenchèd be.
There is a gulf of longing and unrest,
A wild love-craving not to be represt,
Whereto, in all our hearts, as to the sea,
The streams of feeling do forever flow.
Therefore it is that thy well-meted praise
Falleth so shower-like and fresh on me,
Filling those springs which else had sunk full low,
Lost in the dreary desert-sands of woe,
Or parched by passion's fierce and withering blaze.

VII.

Might I but be beloved, and, O most fair
And perfect-ordered soul, beloved of thee,
How should I feel a cloud of earthly care,
If thy blue eyes were ever clear to me?
O woman's love! O flower most bright and rare!
That blossom'st brightest in extremest need,
Woe, woe is me! that thy so precious seed
Is ever sown by Fancy's changeful air,
And grows sometimes in poor and barren hearts,
Who can be little even in the light
Of thy meek holiness — while souls more great
Are left to wander in a starless night,
Praying unheard — and yet the hardest parts
Befit those best who best can cope with Fate.

VIII.

Why should we ever weary of this life?
Our souls should widen ever, not contract,
Grow stronger, and not harder, in the strife,
Filling each moment with a noble act;

If we live thus, of vigor all compact,
Doing our duty to our fellow-men,
And striving rather to exalt our race
Than our poor selves, with earnest hand or pen
We shall erect our names a dwelling-place
Which not all ages shall cast down·agen;
Offspring of Time shall then be born each hour,
Which, as of old, earth lovingly shall guard,
To live forever in youth's perfect flower,
And guide her future children Heavenward.

IX.

GREEN MOUNTAINS.

Ye mountains, that far off lift up your heads,
Seen dimly through their canopies of blue,
The shade of my unrestful spirit sheds
Distance-created beauty over you;
I am not well content with this far view;
How may I know what foot of loved-one treads
Your rocks moss-grown and sun-dried torrent beds?
We should love all things better, if we knew
What claims the meanest have upon our hearts:
Perchance even now some eye, that would be bright
To meet my own, looks on your mist-robed forms;
Perchance your grandeur a deep joy imparts
To souls that have encircled mine with light—
O brother-heart, with thee my spirit warms!

X.

My friend, adown Life's valley, hand in hand,
With grateful change of grave and merry speech
Or song, our hearts unlocking each to each,
We'll journey onward to the silent land;
And when stern Death shall loose that loving band,
Taking in his cold hand a hand of ours,
The one shall strew the other's grave with flowers,
Nor shall his heart a moment be unmanned.
My friend and brother! if thou goest first,
Wilt thou no more re-visit me below?
Yea, when my heart seems happy, causelessly
And swells, not dreaming why, as it would burst

With joy unspeakable — my soul shall know
That thou, unseen, art bending over me.

XI.

Verse cannot say how beautiful thou art,
How glorious the calmness of thine eyes,
Full of unconquerable energies,
Telling that thou hast acted well thy part.
No doubt or fear thy steady faith can start,
No thought of evil dare come nigh to thee,
Who hast the courage meek of purity,
The self-stayed greatness of a loving heart,
Strong with serene, enduring fortitude;
Where'er thou art, that seems thy fitting place,
For not of forms, but Nature, art thou child;
And lowest things put on a noble grace
When touched by ye, O patient, Ruth-like, mild
And spotless hands of earnest womanhood.

XII.

The soul would fain its loving kindness tell,
But custom hangs like lead upon the tongue;
The heart is brimful, hollow crowds among,
When it finds one whose life and thought are well;
Up to the eyes its gushing love doth swell,
The angel cometh and the waters move,
Yet it is fearful still to say "I love,"
And words come grating as a jangled bell.
O might we only speak but what we feel,
Might the tongue pay but what the heart doth owe,
Not Heaven's great thunder, when, deep peal on peal,
It shakes the earth, could rouse our spirits so,
Or to the soul such majesty reveal,
As two short words half-spoken faint and low!

XIII.

I saw a gate : a harsh voice spake and said,
"This is the gate of Life;" above was writ,
"Leave hope behind, all ye who enter it;"
Then shrank my heart within itself for dread;
But, softer than the summer rain is shed,

Words dropt upon my soul, and they did say,
" Fear nothing, Faith shall save thee, watch and pray ! "
So, without fear I lifted up my head,
And lo ! that writing was not, one fair word
Was carven in its stead, and it was " Love."
Then rained once more those sweet tones from above
With healing on their wings : I humbly heard,
" I am the Life, ask and it shall be given !
I am the way, by me ye enter Heaven ! "

XIV.

To the dark, narrow house where loved ones go,
Whence no steps outward turn, whose silent door
None but the sexton knocks at any more,
Are they not sometimes with us yet below ?
The longings of the soul would tell us so;
Although, so pure and fine their being's essence,
Our bodily eyes are witless of their presence,
Yet not within the tomb their spirits glow,
Like wizard lamps pent up, but whensoever
With great thoughts worthy of their high behests
Our souls are filled, those bright ones with us be,
As, in the patriarch's tent, his angel guests ; —
O let us live so worthily, that never
We may be far from that blest company.

XV.

I fain would give to thee the loveliest things,
For lovely things belong to thee of right,
And thou hast been as peaceful to my sight,
As the still thoughts that summer twilight brings;
Beneath the shadow of thine angel wings
O let me live ! O let me rest in thee,
Growing to thee more and more utterly,
Upbearing and upborn, till outward things
Are only as they share in thee a part !
Look kindly on me, let thy holy eyes
Bless me from the deep fulness of thy heart;
So shall my soul in its right strength arise,
And nevermore shall pine and shrink and start,
Safe-sheltered in thy full souled sympathies.

XVI.

Much I had mused of Love, and in my soul
There was one chamber where I dared not look,
So much its dark and dreary voidness shook
My spirit, feeling that I was not whole:
All my deep longings flowed toward one goal
For long, long years, but were not answerèd,
Till Hope was drooping, Faith well-nigh stone-dead,
And I was still a blind, earth-delving mole;
Yet did I know that God was wise and good,
And would fulfil my being late or soon;
Nor was such thought in vain, for, seeing thee,
Great Love rose up, as, o'er a black pine wood,
Round, bright, and clear, upstarteth the full moon,
Filling my soul with glory utterly.

XVII.

Sayest thou, most beautiful, that thou wilt wear
Flowers and leafy crowns when thou art old,
And that thy heart shall never grow so cold
But they shall love to wreath thy silvered hair,
And into age's snows the hope of spring-tide bear?
O, in thy child-like wisdom's moveless hold
Dwell ever! still the blessings manifold
Of purity, of peace, and untaught care
For other's hearts, around thy pathway shed,
And thou shalt have a crown of deathless flowers
To glorify and guard thy blessèd head
And give their freshness to thy life's last hours;
And, when the Bridegroom calleth, they shall be
A wedding-garment white as snow for thee.

XVIII.

Poet! who sittest in thy pleasant room,
Warming thy heart with idle thoughts of love,
And of a holy life that leads above,
Striving to keep life's spring-flowers still in bloom,
And lingering to snuff their fresh perfume,—
O, there were other duties meant for thee,
Than to sit down in peacefulness and Be!
O, there are brother-hearts that dwell in gloom,

Souls loathsome, foul, and black with daily sin,
So crusted o'er with baseness, that no ray
Of heaven's blessed light may enter in!
Come down, then, to the hot and dusty way,
And lead them back to hope and peace again —
For, save in Act, thy Love is all in vain.

XIX.

"NO MORE BUT SO?"

No more but so?   Only with uncold looks,
And with a hand not laggard to clasp mine,
Think'st thou to pay what debt of love is thine?
No more but so?   Like gushing water-brooks,
Freshening and making green the dimmest nooks
Of thy friend's soul thy kindliness should flow;
But, if 't is bounded by not saying "no,"
I can find more of friendship in my books,
All lifeless though they be, and more, far more
In every simplest moss, or flower, or tree;
Open to me thy heart of hearts' deep core,
Or never say that I am dear to thee;
Call me not Friend, if thou keep close the door
That leads into thine inmost sympathy.

XX.

TO A VOICE HEARD IN MOUNT AUBURN.

Like the low warblings of a leaf-hid bird,
Thy voice came to me through the screening trees,
Singing the simplest, long-known melodies;
I had no glimpse of thee, and yet I heard
And blest thee for each clearly-carolled word;
I longed to thank thee, and my heart would frame
Mary or Ruth, some sisterly, sweet name
For thee, yet could I not my lips have stirred;
I knew that thou wert lovely, that thine eyes
Were blue and downcast, and methought large tears,
Unknown to thee, up to their lids must rise
With half-sad memories of other years,
As to thyself alone thou sangest o'er
Words that to childhood seemed to say "No More!"

XXI.

ON READING SPENSER AGAIN.

Dear, gentle Spenser! thou my soul dost lead,
A little child again, through Fairy land,
By many a bower and stream of golden sand,
And many a sunny plain whose light doth breed
A sunshine in my happy heart, and feed
My fancy with sweet visions; I become
A knight, and with my charmèd arms would roam
To seek for fame in many a wondrous deed
Of high emprize — for I have seen the light
Of Una's angel's face, the golden hair
And backward eyes of startled Florimel;
And, for their holy sake, I would outdare
A host of cruel Paynims in the fight,
Or Archimage and all the powers of Hell.

XXII.

Light of mine eyes! with thy so trusting look,
And thy sweet smile of charity and love,
That from a treasure well uplaid above,
And from a hope in Christ its blessing took;
Light of my heart! which, when it could not brook
The coldness of another's sympathy,
Finds ever a deep peace and stay in thee,
Warm as the sunshine of a mossy nook;
Light of my soul! who, by thy saintliness
And faith that acts itself in daily life,
Canst raise me above weakness, and canst bless
The hardest thraldom of my earthly strife —
I dare not say how much thou art to me
Even to myself — and O, far less to thee!

XXIII.

Silent as one who treads on new-fallen snow,
Love came upon me ere I was aware;
Not light of heart, for there was troublous care
Upon his eyelids, drooping them full low,
As with sad memory of a healèd woe;
The cold rain shivered in his golden hair,

As if an outcast lot had been his share,
And he seemed doubtful whither he should go:
Then he fell on my neck, and, in my breast
Hiding his face, awhile sobbed bitterly,
As half in grief to be so long distrest,
And half in joy at his security —
At last, uplooking from his place of rest,
His eyes shone blessedness and hope on me.

XXIV.

A gentleness that grows of steady faith;
A joy that sheds its sunshine everywhere;
A humble strength and readiness to bear
Those burthens which strict duty ever lay'th
Upon our souls; — which unto sorrow saith,
" Here is no soil for thee to strike thy roots,
Here only grow those sweet and precious fruits;
Which ripen for the soul that well obey'th;
A patience which the world can neither give
Nor take away; a courage strong and high,
That dares in simple usefulness to live,
And without one sad look behind to die
When that day comes; — these tell me that our love
Is building for itself a home above.

XXV.

When the glad soul is full to overflow,
Unto the tongue all power it denies,
And only trusts its secret to the eyes;
For, by an inborn wisdom, it doth know
There is no other eloquence but so;
And, when the tongue's weak utterance doth suffice,
Prisoned within the body's cell it lies,
Remembering in tears its exiled woe:
That word which all mankind so long to hear,
Which bears the spirit back to whence it came,
Maketh this sullen clay as crystal clear,
And will not be enclouded in a name;
It is a truth which we can feel and see,
But is as boundless as Eternity.

XXVI.

TO THE EVENING-STAR.

When we have once said lowly " Evening-Star ! "
Words give no more — for, in thy silver pride,
Thou shinest as naught else can shine beside:
The thick smoke, coiling round the sooty bar
Forever, and the customed lamp-light mar
The stillness of my thought — seeing things glide
So samely : — then I ope my windows wide,
And gaze in peace to where thou shin'st afar.
The wind that comes across the faint-white snow
So freshly, and the river dimly seen,
Seem like new things that never had been so
Before; and thou art bright as thou hast been
Since thy white rays put sweetness in the eyes
Of the first souls that loved in Paradise.

XXVII.

READING.

As one who on some well-known landscape looks,
Be it alone, or with some dear friend nigh,
Each day beholdeth fresh variety,
New harmonies of hills, and trees, and brooks —
So is it with the worthiest choice of books,
And oftenest read: if thou no meaning spy,
Deem there is meaning wanting in thine eyes;
We are so lured from judgment by the crooks
And winding ways of covert fantasy,
Or turned unwittingly down beaten tracks
Of our foregone conclusions, that we see,
In our own want, the writer's misdeemed lacks:
It is with true books as with Nature, each
New day of living doth new insight teach.

XXVIII.

TO ——, AFTER A SNOW-STORM.

Blue as thine eyes the river gently flows
Between his banks, which, far as eye can see,
Are whiter than aught else on earth may be, ·

G

Save inmost thoughts that in thy soul repose;
The trees all crystalled by the melted snows,
Sparkle with gems and silver, such as we
In childhood saw 'mong groves of Faërie,
And the dear skies are sunny-blue as those;
Still as thy heart, when next mine own it lies
In love's full safety, is the bracing air;
The earth is all enwrapt with draperies
Snow-white as that pure love might choose to wear —
O for one moment's look into thine eyes,
To share the joy such scene would kindle there!

SONNETS ON NAMES.

EDITH.

A LILY with its frail cup filled with dew,
Down-bending modestly, snow-white and pale,
Shedding faint fragrance round its native vale,
Minds me of thee, Sweet Edith, mild and true,
And of thy eyes so innocent and blue,
Thy heart is fearful as a startled hare,
Yet hath in it a fortitude to bear
For Love's sake, and a gentle faith which grew
Of Love: need of a stay whereon to lean,
Felt in thyself, hath taught thee to uphold
And comfort others, and to give, unseen,
The kindness thy still love cannot withhold:
Maiden, I would my sister thou hadst been,
That round thee I my guarding arms might fold.

ROSE.

My ever-lightsome, ever-laughing Rose,
Who always speakest first and thinkest last,
Thy full voice is as clear as bugle-blast;
Right from the ear down to the heart it goes
And says, " I 'm beautiful! as who but knows? "
Thy name reminds me of old romping days,
Of kisses stolen in dark passage-ways,
Or in the parlor, if the mother-nose
Gave sign of drowsy watch. I wonder where

Are gone thy tokens, given with a glance
So full of everlasting love till morrow,
Or a day's endless grieving for the dance
Last night denied, backed with a lock of hair,
That spake of broken hearts and deadly sorrow.

MARY

DARK hair, dark eyes — not too dark to be deep
And full of feeling, yet enough to glow
With fire when angered; feelings never slow,
But which seem rather watching to forthleap
From her full breast; a gently-flowing sweep
Of words in common talk, a torrent-rush,
Whenever through her soul swift feelings gush,
A heart less ready to be gay than weep,
Yet cheerful ever; a calm matron-smile,
That bids God bless you; a chaste simpleness,
With somewhat, too, of "proper pride," in dress; —
This portrait to my mind's eye came, the while
I thought of thee, the well-grown woman Mary,
Whilome a gold-haired, laughing little fairy.

CAROLINE.

A STAIDNESS sobers o'er her pretty face,
Which something but ill-hidden in her eyes,
And a quaint look about her lips denies;
A lingering love of girlhood you can trace
In her checked laugh and half-restrainèd pace;
And, when she bears herself most womanly,
It seems as if a watchful mother's eye
Kept down with sobering glance her childish grace:
Yet oftentimes her nature gushes free
As water long held back by little hands,
Within a pump, and let forth suddenly,
Until, her task remembering, she stands
A moment silent, smiling doubtfully,
Then laughs aloud and scorns her hated bands.

ANNE.

THERE is a pensiveness in quiet Anne,
A mournful drooping of the full gray eye,
As if she had shook hands with misery,

And known some care since her short life began;
Her cheek is seriously pale, nigh wan,
And, though of cheerfulness there is no lack,
You feel as if she must be dressed in black;
Yet is she not of those who, all they can,
Strive to be gay, and striving, seem most sad —
Hers is not grief, but silent soberness;
You would be startled if you saw her glad,
And startled if you saw her weep, no less;
She walks through life, as, on the Sabbath day,
She decorously glides to church to pray.

MISCELLANEOUS POEMS.

THRENODIA.

GONE, gone from us! and shall we see
These sibyl-leaves of destiny,
Those calm eyes, nevermore?
Those deep, dark eyes so warm and bright,
Wherein the fortunes of the man
Lay slumbering in prophetic light,
In characters a child might scan?
So bright, and gone forth utterly!
O stern word — Nevermore!

The stars of those two gentle eyes
Will shine no more on earth;
Quenched are the hopes that had their birth,
As we watched them slowly rise,
Stars of a mother's fate;
And she would read them o'er and o'er,
Pondering as she sate,
Over their dear astrology,
Which she had conned and conned before,
Deeming she needs must read aright
What was writ so passing bright.
And yet, alas! she knew not why,
Her voice would falter in its song,
And tears would slide from out her eye,
Silent, as they were doing wrong.
O stern word — Nevermore!

The tongue that scarce had learned to claim
An entrance to a mother's heart
By that dear talisman, a mother's name,
Sleeps all forgetful of its art!
I loved to see the infant soul
(How mighty in the weakness
Of its untutored meekness!)

Peep timidly from out its nest,
His lips, the while,
Fluttering with half-fledged words,
Or hushing to a smile
That more than words expressed,
When his glad mother on him stole
And snatched him to her breast!
O, thoughts were brooding in those eyes,
That would have soared like strong-winged birds
Far, far, into the skies,
Gladding the earth with song,
And gushing harmonies,
Had he but tarried with us long!
O stern word — Nevermore!

How peacefully they rest,
Crossfolded there
Upon his little breast,
Those small, white hands that ne'er were still before,
But ever sported with his mother's hair,
Or the plain cross that on her breast she wore!
Her heart no more will beat
To feel the touch of that soft palm,
That ever seemed a new surprise
Sending glad thoughts up to her eyes
To bless him with their holy calm, —
Sweet thoughts! they made her eyes as sweet.
How quiet are the hands
That wove those pleasant bands!
But that they do not rise and sink
With his calm breathing, I should think
That he were dropped asleep.
Alas! too deep, too deep
Is this his slumber!
Time scarce can number
The years ere he will wake again.
O, may we see his eyelids open then!
O stern word — Nevermore!

As the airy gossamere,
Floating in the sunlight clear,
Where'er it toucheth clingeth tightly,
Round glossy leaf or stump unsightly,

So from his spirit wandered out
Tendrils spreading all about,
Knitting all things to its thrall
With a perfect love of all:
O stern word — Nevermore!

He did but float a little way
Adown the stream of time,
With dreamy eyes watching the ripples play,
Or listening their fairy chime;
His slender sail
Ne'er felt the gale;
He did but float a little way,
And, putting to the shore
While yet 't was early day,
Went calmly on his way,
To dwell with us no more!
No jarring did he feel,
No grating on his vessel's keel,
A strip of silver sand
Mingled the waters with the land
Where he was seen no more:
O stern word — Nevermore!

Full short his journey was; no dust
Of earth unto his sandals clave;
The weary weight that old men must,
He bore not to the grave.
He seemed a cherub who had lost his way
And wandered hither, so his stay
With us was short, and 't was most meet
That he should be no delver in earth's clod
Nor need to pause and cleanse his feet
To stand before his God:
O blest word — Evermore!
    1839.

THE SIRENS.

THE sea is lonely, the sea is dreary,
The sea is restless and uneasy;
Thou seekest quiet, thou art weary,

Wandering thou knowest not whither;—
Our little isle is green and breezy,
Come and rest thee! O come hither;
Come to this peaceful home of ours,
    Where evermore
The low west-wind creeps panting up the shore
To be at rest among the flowers;
Full of rest, the green moss lifts,
   As the dark waves of the sea
Draw in and out of rocky rifts,
   Calling solemnly to thee
With voices deep and hollow,—
   "To the shore
   Follow! O, follow!
To be at rest forevermore!
   Forevermore!"

   Look how the gray old Ocean
From the depth of his heart rejoices,
Heaving with a gentle motion,
When he hears our restful voices;
List how he sings in an under-tone,
Chiming with our melody;
And all sweet sounds of earth and air
Melt into one low voice alone,
That murmurs over the weary sea,
And seems to sing from everywhere,—
"Here mayst thou harbor peacefully,
Here mayst thou rest from the aching oar;
   Turn thy curvèd prow ashore,
And in our green isle rest for evermore!
    Forevermore!"
And Echo half wakes in the wooded hill,
  And, to her heart so calm and deep,
  Murmurs over in her sleep,
Doubtfully pausing and murmuring still,
   "Evermore!"
        Thus, on Life's weary sea,
        Heareth the marinere
        Voices sweet, from far and near,
        Ever singing low and clear,
        Ever singing longingly.

Is it not better here to be,
Than to be toiling late and soon?
In the dreary night to see
Nothing but the blood-red moon
Go up and down into the sea;
Or, in the loneliness of day,
　To see the still seals only
Solemnly lift their faces gray,
　Making it yet more lonely?
Is it not better, than to hear
Only the sliding of the wave
Beneath the plank, and feel so near
A cold and lonely grave,
A restless grave, where thou shalt lie
Even in death unquietly?
Look down beneath thy wave-worn bark,
　Lean over the side and see
The leaden eye of the sidelong shark
　　Upturnèd patiently,
　Ever waiting there for thee:
Look down and see those shapeless forms,
　Which ever keep their dreamless sleep
Far down within the gloomy deep,
And only stir themselves in storms,
Rising like islands from beneath,
And snorting through the angry spray,
As the frail vessel perisheth
In the whirls of their unwieldy play;
　　Look down! Look down!
Upon the seaweed, slimy and dark,
That waves its arms so lank and brown,
　Beckoning for thee!
Look down beneath thy wave-worn bark
　Into the cold depth of the sea!
　　Look down! Look down!
　　　Thus on Life's lonely sea,
　　　Heareth the marinere
　　　Voices sad, from far and near,
　　　Ever singing full of fear,
　　　Ever singing drearfully.

　Here all is pleasant as a dream;
The wind scarce shaketh down the dew,

The green grass floweth like a stream
  Into the ocean's blue;
   Listen! O, listen!
Here is a gush of many streams,
 A song of many birds,
And every wish and longing seems
Lulled to a numbered flow of words, —
   Listen! O, listen!
Here ever hum the golden bees
Underneath full-blossomed trees,
At once with glowing fruit and flowers crowned; —
The sand is so smooth, the yellow sand,
That thy keel will not grate as it touches the land
All around with a slumberous sound,
The singing waves slide up the strand,
And there, where the smooth, wet pebbles be,
The waters gurgle longingly,
As if they fain would seek the shore,
To be at rest from the ceaseless roar,
To be at rest forevermore, —
  Forevermore.
    Thus, on Life's gloomy sea,
    Heareth the marinere
    Voices sweet, from far and near,
    Ever singing in his ear,
    "Here is rest and peace for thee."

NANTASKET, *July*, 1840.

IRENÉ.

HERS is a spirit deep, and crystal-clear,
Calmly beneath her earnest face it lies,
Free without boldness, meek without a fear,
Quicker to look than speak its sympathies;
Far down into her large and patient eyes
I gaze, deep-drinking of the infinite,
As, in the mid-watch of a clear, still night,
I look into the fathomless blue skies.

So circled lives she with Love's holy light,
That from the shade of self she walketh free;
The garden of her soul still keepeth she

An Eden where the snake did never enter;
She hath a natural, wise sincerity,
A simple truthfulness, and these have lent her
A dignity as moveless as the centre;
So that no influence of earth can stir
Her steadfast courage, nor can take away
The holy peacefulness, which, night and day,
Unto her queenly soul doth minister.

Most gentle is she; her large charity
(An all unwitting, child-like gift in her)
Not freer is to give than meek to bear;
And, though herself not unacquaint with care,
Hath in her heart wide room for all that be, —
Her heart that hath no secrets of its own,
But open is as eglantine full blown.
Cloudless forever is her brow serene,
Speaking calm hope and trust within her, whence
Welleth a noiseless spring of patience,
That keepeth all her life so fresh, so green
And full of holiness, that every look,
The greatness of her woman's soul revealing,
Unto me bringeth blessing, and a feeling
As when I read in God's own holy book.

A graciousness in giving that doth make
The small'st gift greatest, and a sense most meek
Of worthiness, that doth not fear to take
From others, but which always fears to speak
Its thanks in utterance, for the giver's sake; —
The deep religion of a thankful heart,
Which rests instinctively in Heaven's law
With a full peace, that never can depart
From its own steadfastness; — a holy awe
For holy things, — not those which men call holy,
But such as are revealèd to the eyes
Of a true woman's soul bent down and lowly
Before the face of daily mysteries; —
A love that blossoms soon, but ripens slowly
To the full goldenness of fruitful prime,
Enduring with a firmness that defies
All shallow tricks of circumstance and time,
By a sure insight knowing where to cling,

And where it clingeth never withering; —
These are Irené's dowry, which no fate
Can shake from their serene, deep-builded state.

In-seeing sympathy is hers, which chasteneth
No less than loveth, scorning to be bound
With fear of blame, and yet which ever hasteneth
To pour the balm of kind looks on the wound,
If they be wounds which such sweet teaching makes,
Giving itself a pang for others' sakes;
No want of faith, that chills with sidelong eye,
Hath she; no jealousy, no Levite pride
That passeth by upon the other side;
For in her soul there never dwelt a lie.
Right from the hand of God her spirit came
Unstained, and she hath ne'er forgotten whence
It came, nor wandered far from thence,
But laboreth to keep her still the same,
Near to her place of birth, that she may not
Soil her white raiment with an earthly spot.

Yet sets she not her soul so steadily
Above, that she forgets her ties to earth,
But her whole thought would almost seem to be
How to make glad one lowly human hearth;
For with a gentle courage she doth strive
In thought and word and feeling so to live
As to make earth next heaven; and her heart
Herein doth show its most exceeding worth,
That, bearing in our frailty her just part,
She hath not shrunk from evils of this life,
But hath gone calmly forth into the strife,
And all its sins and sorrows hath withstood
With lofty strength of patient womanhood:
For this I love her great soul more than all,
That, being bound, like us, with earthly thrall,
She walks so bright and heaven-like therein, —
Too wise, too meek, too womanly, to sin.

Like a lone star through riven storm-clouds seen
By sailors, tempest-toss'd upon the sea,
Telling of rest and peaceful heavens nigh,
Unto my soul her star-like soul hath been,

Her sight as full of hope and calm to me; —
For she unto herself hath builded high
A home serene, wherein to lay her head,
Earth's noblest thing, a Woman perfected.
1840.

SERENADE.

FROM the close-shut windows gleams no spark,
The night is chilly, the night is dark,
The poplars shiver, the pine-trees moan,
My hair by the autumn breeze is blown,
Under thy window I sing alone,
Alone, alone, ah woe! alone!

The darkness is pressing coldly around,
The windows shake with a lonely sound,
The stars are hid and the night is drear,
The heart of silence throbs in thine ear,
In thy chamber thou sittest alone,
Alone, alone, ah woe! alone!

The world is happy, the world is wide,
Kind hearts are beating on every side;
Ah, why should we lie so coldly curled
Alone in the shell of this great world?
Why should we any more be alone?
Alone, alone, ah woe! alone!

O, 't is a bitter and dreary word,
The saddest by man's ear ever heard!
We each are young, we each have a heart,
Why stand we ever coldly apart?
Must we forever, then, be alone?
Alone, alone, ah woe! alone!
1840.

WITH A PRESSED FLOWER.

THIS little flower from afar
Hath come from other lands to thine;
For, once, its white and drooping star
Could see its shadow in the Rhine.

Perchance some fair-haired German maid
Hath plucked one from the self-same stalk,
And numbered over, half afraid,
Its petals in her evening walk.

"He loves me, loves me not," she cries;
"He loves me more than earth or heaven!"
And then glad tears have filled her eyes
To find the number was uneven.

And thou must count its petals well,
Because it is a gift from me;
And the last one of all shall tell
Something I 've often told to thee.

But here at home, where we were born,
Thou wilt find flowers just as true,
Down-bending every summer morn
With freshness of New-England dew.

For Nature, ever kind to love,
Hath granted them the same sweet tongue,
Whether with German skies above,
Or here our granite rocks among.

    1840.

THE BEGGAR.

A BEGGAR through the world am I, —
From place to place I wander by.
Fill up my pilgrim's scrip for me,
For Christ's sweet sake and charity!

A little of thy steadfastness,
Rounded with leafy gracefulness,
Old oak, give me, —
That the world's blasts may round me blow,
And I yield gently to and fro,
While my stout-hearted trunk below
And firm-set roots unshaken be.

Some of thy stern, unyielding might,
Enduring still through day and night
Rude tempest-shock and withering blight, —

That I may keep at bay
The changeful April sky of chance
And the strong tide of circumstance, —
Give me, old granite gray.

Some of thy pensiveness serene,
Some of thy never-dying green,
Put in this scrip of mine, —
That griefs may fall like snow-flakes light,
And deck me in a robe of white,
Ready to be an angel bright, —
O sweetly-mournful pine.

A little of thy merriment,
Of thy sparkling, light content,
Give me, my cheerful brook, —
That I may still be full of glee
And gladsomeness, where'er I be,
Though fickle fate hath prisoned me
In some neglected nook.

Ye have been very kind and good
To me, since I 've been in the wood;
Ye have gone nigh to fill my heart;
But good-bye, kind friends, every one,
I 've far to go ere set of sun;
Of all good things I would have part,
The day was high ere I could start,
And so my journey 's scarce begun.

Heaven help me! how could I forget
To beg of thee, dear violet!
Some of thy modesty,
That blossoms here as well, unseen,
As if before the world thou 'dst been,
O, give, to strengthen me.
　1839.

MY LOVE.

I.

NOT as all other women are
Is she that to my soul is dear;
Her glorious fancies come from far,

Beneath the silver evening-star,
And yet her heart is ever near.

II.

Great feelings hath she of her own,
Which lesser souls may never know;
God giveth them to her alone,
And sweet they are as any tone
Wherewith the wind may choose to blow.

III.

Yet in herself she dwelleth not,
Although no home were half so fair;
No simplest duty is forgot,
Life hath no dim and lowly spot
That doth not in her sunshine share.

IV.

She doeth little kindnesses,
Which most leave undone, or despise;
For naught that sets one heart at ease,
And giveth happiness or peace,
Is low-esteemèd in her eyes.

V.

She hath no scorn of common things,
And, though she seem of other birth,
Round us her heart entwines and clings,
And patiently she folds her wings
To tread the humble paths of earth.

VI.

Blessing she is : God made her so,
And deeds of weekday holiness
Fall from her noiseless as the snow,
Nor hath she ever chanced to know
That aught were easier than to bless.

VII.

She is most fair, and thereunto
Her life doth rightly harmonize;
Feeling or thought that was not true
Ne'er made less beautiful the blue
Unclouded heaven of her eyes.

VIII.

She is a woman: one in whom
The spring-time of her childish years
Hath never lost its fresh perfume,
Though knowing well that life hath room
For many blights and many tears.

IX.

I love her with a love as still
As a broad river's peaceful might,
Which, by high tower and lowly mill,
Goes wandering at its own will,
And yet doth ever flow aright.

X.

And, on its full, deep breast serene,
Like quiet isles my duties lie;
It flows around them and between,
And makes them fresh and fair and green,
Sweet homes wherein to live and die.
     1840.

SUMMER STORM.

UNTREMULOUS in the river clear,
Toward the sky's image, hangs the imaged bridge
     So still the air that I can hear
The slender clarion of the unseen midge;
     ·Out of the stillness, with a gathering creep,
Like rising wind in leaves, which now decreases,
Now lulls, now swells, and all the while increases,
     The huddling trample of a drove of sheep
Tilts the loose planks, and then as gradually ceases
     In dust on the other side; life's emblem deep,
A confused noise between two silences,
Finding at last in dust precarious peace.
On the wide marsh the purple-blossomed grasses
     Soak up the sunshine; sleeps the brimming tide
Save when the wedge-shaped wake in silence passes
     Of some slow water-rat, whose sinuous glide
     Wavers the long green sedge's shade from side to side;
But up the west, like a rock-shivered surge,
     Climbs a great cloud edged with sun-whitened spray;

H

Huge whirls of foam boil toppling o'er its verge,
  And falling still it seems, and yet it climbs alway.

      Suddenly all the sky is hid
      As with the shutting of a lid,
    One by one great drops are falling
        Doubtful and slow,
  Down the pane they are crookedly crawling,
        And the wind breathes low;
  Slowly the circles widen on the river,
    Widen and mingle, one and all;
  Here and there the slenderer flowers shiver,
    Struck by an icy rain-drop's fall.

  Now on the hills I hear the thunder mutter,
    The wind is gathering in the west;
  The upturned leaves first whiten and flutter,
    Then droop to a fitful rest;
  Up from the stream with sluggish flap
    Struggles the gull and floats away;
  Nearer and nearer rolls the thunder-clap, —
    We shall not see the sun go down to-day:
  Now leaps the wind on the sleepy marsh,
    And tramples the grass with terrified feet,
  The startled river turns leaden and harsh.
    You can hear the quick heart of the tempest beat.

      Look! look! that livid flash!
  And instantly follows the rattling thunder,
  As if some cloud-crag, split asunder,
      Fell, splintering with a ruinous crash,
  On the Earth, which crouches in silence under;
    And now a solid gray wall of rain
  Shuts off the landscape, mile by mile;
    For a breath's space I see the blue wood again,
  And, ere the next heart-beat, the wind-hurled pile,
    That seemed but now a league aloof,
    Bursts crackling o'er the sun-parched roof;
  Against the windows the storm comes dashing,
  Through tattered foliage the hail tears crashing,
      The blue lightning flashes,
      The rapid hail clashes,

The white waves are tumbling,
And, in one baffled roar,
Like the toothless sea mumbling
A rock-bristled shore,
The thunder is rumbling
And crashing and crumbling, —
Will silence return never more?

Hush! Still as death,
The tempest holds his breath
As from a sudden will;
The rain stops short, but from the eaves
You see it drop, and hear it from the leaves,
All is so bodingly still;
Again, now, now, again
Plashes the rain in heavy gouts,
The crinkled lightning
Seems ever brightening,
And loud and long
Again the thunder shouts
His battle-song, —
One quivering flash,
One wildering crash,
Followed by silence dead and dull,
As if the cloud, let go,
Leapt bodily below
To whelm the earth in one mad overthrow,
And then a total lull.

Gone, gone, so soon!
No more my half-crazed fancy there
Can shape a giant in the air,
No more I see his streaming hair,
The writhing portent of his form; —
The pale and quiet moon
Makes her calm forehead bare,
And the last fragments of the storm,
Like shattered rigging from a fight at sea,
Silent and few, are drifting over me.
1839.

LOVE.

TRUE Love is but a humble, low-born thing,
And hath its food served up in earthen ware;
It is a thing to walk with, hand in hand,
Through the everydayness of this work-day world,
Baring its tender feet to every roughness,
Yet letting not one heart-beat go astray
From Beauty's law of plainness and content.
A simple, fireside thing, whose quiet smile
Can warm earth's poorest hovel to a home;
Which, when our autumn cometh, as it must,
And life in the chill wind shivers bare and leafless,
Shall still be blest with Indian-summer youth
In bleak November, and, with thankful heart,
Smile on its ample stores of garnered fruit,
As full of sunshine to our aged eyes
As when it nursed the blossoms of our spring.
Such is true Love, which steals into the heart
With feet as silent as the lightsome dawn
That kisses smooth the rough brows of the dark,
And hath its will through blissful gentleness, —
Not like a rocket, which, with savage glare,
Whirrs suddenly up, then bursts, and leaves the night
Painfully quivering on the dazèd eyes;
A love that gives and takes, that seeth faults,
Not with flaw-seeking eyes like needle points,
But loving-kindly ever looks them down
With the o'ercoming faith of meek forgiveness;
A love that shall be new and fresh each hour,
As is the golden mystery of sunset,
Or the sweet coming of the evening star,
Alike, and yet most unlike, every day,
And seeming ever best and fairest *now;*
A love that doth not kneel for what it seeks,
But faces Truth and Beauty as their peer,
Showing its worthiness of noble thoughts
By a clear sense of inward nobleness;
A love that in its object findeth not
All grace and beauty, and enough to sate
Its thirst of blessing, but, in all of good
Found there, it sees but Heaven-granted types
Of good and beauty in the soul of man,

And traces, in the simplest heart that beats,
A family-likeness to its chosen one,
That claims of it the rights of brotherhood.
For love is blind but with the fleshly eye,
That so its inner sight may be more clear;
And outward shows of beauty only so
Are needful at the first. as is a hand
To guide and to uphold an infant's steps:
Great spirits need them not: their earnest look
Pierces the body's mask of thin disguise,
And beauty ever is to them revealed,
Behind the unshapeliest, meanest lump of clay,
With arms outstretched and eager face ablaze,
Yearning to be but understood and loved.
    1840.

TO PERDITA, SINGING.

THY voice is like a fountain,
  Leaping up in clear moonshine;
Silver, silver, ever mounting,
    Ever sinking,
    Without thinking,
  To that brimful heart of thine.

Every sad and happy feeling,
Thou hast had in bygone years,
Through thy lips come stealing, stealing,
    Clear and low;
  All thy smiles and all thy tears
    In thy voice awaken,
    And sweetness, wove of joy and woe,
    From their teaching it hath taken
Feeling and music move together,
  Like a swan and shadow ever
Heaving on a sky-blue river
In a day of cloudless weather.

  It hath caught a touch of sadness,
    Yet it is not sad;
  It hath tones of clearest gladness,
    Yet it is not glad;

A dim, sweet, twilight voice it is
    Where to-day's accustomed blue
Is over-grayed with memories,
    With starry feelings quivered through.

    Thy voice is like a fountain
Leaping up in sunshine bright,
    And I never weary counting
Its clear droppings, lone and single,
Or when in one full gush they mingle,
    Shooting in melodious light.

    Thine is music such as yields
Feelings of old brooks and fields,
    And, around this pent-up room,
Sheds a woodland, free perfume;
        O, thus forever sing to me!
        O, thus forever!
The green, bright grass of childhood bring to me,
    Flowing like an emerald river,
And the bright blue skies above!
O, sing them back, as fresh as ever,
Into the bosom of my love, —
The sunshine and the merriment,
The unsought, evergreen content,
    Of that never cold time,
The joy, that, like a clear breeze, went
    Through and through the old time!

    Peace sits within thine eyes,
With white hands crossed in joyful rest,
While, through thy lips and face, arise
The melodies from out thy breast;
        She sits and sings,
        With folded wings
        And white arms crost,
    "Weep not for passed things,
        They are not lost:
The beauty which the summer time
O'er thine opening spirit shed,
The forest oracles sublime
That filled thy soul with joyous dread,
The scent of every smallest flower

That made thy heart sweet for an hour, —
Yea, every holy influence,
Flowing to thee, thou knewest not whence,
In thine eyes to-day is seen,
Fresh as it hath ever been;
Promptings of Nature, beckonings sweet,
Whatever led thy childish feet,
Still will linger unawares
The guiders of thy silver hairs;
Every look and every word
Which thou givest forth to-day,
Tell of the singing of the bird
Whose music stilled thy boyish play."

Thy voice is like a fountain,
Twinkling up in sharp starlight,
When the moon behind the mountain
Dims the low East with faintest white,
  Ever darkling,
  Ever sparkling,
We know not if 't is dark or bright;
But, when the great moon hath rolled round,
 And, sudden-slow, its solemn power
Grows from behind its black, clearedged bound,
 No spot of dark the fountain keepeth,
 But, swift as opening eyelids, leapeth
Into a waving silver flower.
 1841.

THE MOON.

My soul was like the sea,
 Before the moon was made,
Moaning in vague immensity,
 Of its own strength afraid,
 Unrestful and unstaid.

Through every rift it foamed in vain,
 About its earthly prison,
Seeking some unknown thing in pain,
And sinking restless back again,
 For yet no moon had risen:

Its only voice a vast dumb moan,
  Of utterless anguish speaking,
It lay unhopefully alone,
  And lived but in an aimless seeking.

So was my soul; but when 't was full
  Of unrest to o'erloading,
A voice of something beautiful
  Whispered a dim foreboding,
And yet so soft, so sweet, so low,
It had not more of joy than woe;
And, as the sea doth oft lie still,
  Making its waters meet,
As if by an unconscious will,
  For the moon's silver feet,
So lay my soul within mine eyes
When thou, its guardian moon, didst rise.
And now, howe'er its waves above
  May toss and seem uneaseful,
One strong, eternal law of Love,
  With guidance sure and peaceful,
As calm and natural as breath,
Moves its great deeps through life and death.

REMEMBERED MUSIC.

A FRAGMENT.

THICK-RUSHING, like an ocean vast
  Of bisons the far prairie shaking,
The notes crowd heavily and fast
As surfs, one plunging while the last
  Draws seaward from its foamy breaking.

Or in low murmurs they began,
  Rising and rising momently,
As o'er a harp Æolian
A fitful breeze, until they ran
  Up to a sudden ecstasy.

And then, like minute drops of rain
  Ringing in water silvery,

They lingering dropped and dropped again,
Till it was almost like a pain
    To listen when the next would be.
1840.

SONG.

TO M. L.

A LILY thou wast when I saw thee first,
    A lily-bud not opened quite,
    That hourly grew more pure and white,
By morning, and noontide, and evening nursed:
    In all of nature thou hadst thy share;
        Thou wast waited on
        By the wind and sun;
    The rain and the dew for thee took care;
    It seemed thou never couldst be more fair.

A lily thou wast when I saw thee first,
    A lily-bud; but O, how strange,
    How full of wonder was the change,
When, ripe with all sweetness, thy full bloom burst!
    How did the tears to my glad eyes start,
        When the woman-flower
        Reached its blossoming hour,
And I saw the warm deeps of thy golden heart!

Glad death may pluck thee, but never before
    The gold dust of thy bloom divine
    Hath dropped from thy heart into mine,
To quicken its faint germs of heavenly lore;
    For no breeze comes nigh thee but carries away
        Some impulses bright
        Of fragrance and light,
    Which fall upon souls that are lone and astray,
    To plant fruitful hopes of the flower of day.

ALLEGRA.

I WOULD more natures were like thine,
    That never casts a glance before, —
Thou Hebe, who thy heart's bright wine
    So lavishly to all dost pour,

That we who drink forget to pine,
   And can but dream of bliss in store.

Thou canst not see a shade in life;
   With sunward instinct thou dost rise,
And, leaving clouds below at strife,
   Gazest undazzled at the skies,
With all their blazing splendors rife,
   A songful lark with eagle's eyes.

Thou wast some foundling whom the Hours
   Nursed, laughing, with the milk of Mirth;
Some influence more gay than ours
   Hath ruled thy nature from its birth,
As if thy natal stars were flowers
   That shook their seeds round thee on earth.

And thou, to lull thine infant rest,
   Wast cradled like an Indian child;
All pleasant winds from south and west
   With lullabies thine ears beguiled,
Rocking thee in thine oriole's nest,
   Till Nature looked at thee and smiled.

Thine every fancy seems to borrow
   A sunlight from thy childish years,
Making a golden cloud of sorrow,
   A hope-lit rainbow out of tears, —
Thy heart is certain of to-morrow,
   Though 'yond to-day it never peers.

I would more natures were like thine,
   So innocently wild and free,
Whose sad thoughts, even, leap and shine,
   Like sunny wavelets in the sea,
Making us mindless of the brine,
   In gazing on the brilliancy.

THE FOUNTAIN.

INTO the sunshine,
   Full of the light,
Leaping and flashing
   From morn till night!

Into the moonlight,
   Whiter than snow,
Waving so flower-like
   When the winds blow!

Into the starlight,
   Rushing in spray,
Happy at midnight,
   Happy by day!

Ever in motion,
   Blithesome and cheery.
Still climbing heavenward,
   Never aweary;—

Glad of all weathers,
   Still seeming best,
Upward or downward,
   Motion thy rest;—

Full of a nature
   Nothing can tame,
Changed every moment,
   Ever the same;—

Ceaseless aspiring,
   Ceaseless content,
Darkness or sunshine
   Thy element;—

Glorious fountain!
   Let my heart be
Fresh, changeful, constant,
   Upward, like thee!

ODE.

I.

In the old days of awe and keen-eyed wonder,
   The Poet's song with blood-warm truth was rife;
He saw the mysteries which circle under
   The outward shell and skin of daily life.
Nothing to him were fleeting time and fashion,

His soul was led by the eternal law;
There was in him no hope of fame, no passion,
But, with calm, god-like eyes, he only saw.
He did not sigh o'er heroes dead and buried,
Chief-mourner at the Golden Age's hearse,
Nor deem that souls whom Charon grim had ferried
Alone were fitting themes of epic verse:
He could believe the promise of to-morrow,
And feel the wondrous meaning of to-day;
He had a deeper faith in holy sorrow
Than the world's seeming loss could take away.
To know the heart of all things was his duty,
All things did sing to him to make him wise,
And, with a sorrowful and conquering beauty,
The soul of all looked grandly from his eyes.
He gazed on all within him and without him,
He watched the flowing of Time's steady tide,
And shapes of glory floated all about him
And whispered to him, and he prophesied.
Than all men he more fearless was and freer,
And all his brethren cried with one accord, —
"Behold the holy man! Behold the Seer!
Him who hath spoken with the unseen Lord!"
He to his heart with large embrace had taken
The universal sorrow of mankind,
And, from that root, a shelter never shaken,
The tree of wisdom grew with sturdy rind.
He could interpret well the wondrous voices
Which to the calm and silent spirit come;
He knew that the One Soul no more rejoices
In the star's anthem than the insect's hum.
He in his heart was ever meek and humble,
And yet with kingly pomp his numbers ran,
As he foresaw how all things false should crumble
Before the free, uplifted soul of man:
And, when he was made full to overflowing
With all the loveliness of heaven and earth,
Out rushed his song, like molten iron glowing,
To show God sitting by the humblest hearth.
With calmest courage he was ever ready
To teach that action was the truth of thought,
And, with strong arm and purpose firm and steady,
An anchor for the drifting world he wrought.

So did he make the meanest man partaker
   Of all his brother-gods unto him gave ;
All souls did reverence him and name him **Maker,**
   And when he died heaped temples on his grave.
And still his deathless words of light are swimming
   Serene throughout the great, deep infinite
Of human soul, unwaning and undimming,
   To cheer and guide the mariner at night.

II.

But now the Poet is an empty rhymer
   Who lies with idle elbow on the grass,
And fits his singing, like a cunning timer,
   To all men's prides and fancies as they pass.
Not his the song, which, in its metre holy,
   Chimes with the music of the eternal stars,
Humbling the tyrant, lifting up the lowly,
   And sending sun through the soul's prison-bars.
Maker no more, — O, no! unmaker rather,
   For he unmakes who doth not all put forth
The power given by our loving Father
   To show the body's dross, the spirit's worth.
Awake! great spirit of the ages olden!
   Shiver the mists that hide thy starry lyre,
And let man's soul be yet again beholden
   To thee for wings to soar to her desire.
O, prophesy no more to-morrow's splendor,
   Be no more shame-faced to speak out for **Truth,**
Lay on her altar all the gushings tender,
   The hope, the fire, the loving faith of youth !
O, prophesy no more the Maker's coming,
   Say not his onward footsteps thou canst hear
In the dim void, like to the awful humming
   Of the great wings of some new-lighted sphere.
O, prophesy no more, but be the Poet !
   This longing was but granted unto thee
That, when all beauty thou couldst feel and know it,
   That beauty in its highest thou couldst be.
O, thou who moanest tost with sea-like longings,
   Who dimly hearest voices call on thee,
Whose soul is overfilled with mighty throngings
   Of love, and fear, and glorious agony,

Thou of the toil-strung hands and iron sinews
  And soul by Mother-Earth with freedom fed,
In whom the hero-spirit yet continues,
  The old free nature is not chained or dead,
Arouse! let thy soul break in music-thunder,
  Let loose the ocean that is in thee pent,
Pour forth thy hope, thy fear, thy love, thy wonder
  And tell the age what all its signs have meant,
Where'er thy wildered crowd of brethren jostles,
  Where'er there lingers but a shade of wrong,
There still is need of martyrs and apostles,
  There still are texts for never-dying song:
From age to age man's still aspiring spirit
  Finds wider scope and sees with clearer eyes,
And thou in larger measure dost inherit
  What made thy great forerunners free and wise.
Sit thou enthroned where the Poet's mountain
  Above the thunder lifts its silent peak,
And roll thy songs down like a gathering fountain,
  That all may drink and find the rest they seek.
Sing! there shall silence grow in earth and heaven,
  A silence of deep awe and wondering;
For, listening gladly, bend the angels, even,
  To hear a mortal like an angel sing.

III.

Among the toil-worn poor my soul is seeking
  For one to bring the Maker's name to light,
To be the voice of that almighty speaking
  Which every age demands to do it right.
Proprieties our silken bards environ;
  He who would be the tongue of this wide land
Must string his harp with chords of sturdy iron
  And strike it with a toil-embrownèd hand;
One who hath dwelt with Nature well-attended,
  Who hath learnt wisdom from her mystic books,
Whose soul with all her countless lives hath blended,
  So that all beauty awes us in his looks;
Who not with body's waste his soul hath pampered,
  Who as the clear northwestern wind is free,
Who walks with Form's observances unhampered,
  And follows the One Will obediently;

Whose eyes, like windows on a breezy summit,
    Control a lovely prospect every way;
Who doth not sound God's sea with earthly plummet,
    And find a bottom still of worthless clay;
Who heeds not how the lower gusts are working,
    Knowing that one sure wind blows on above,
And sees, beneath the foulest faces lurking,
    One God-built shrine of reverence and love;
Who sees all stars that wheel their shining marches
    Around the centre fixed of Destiny,
Where the encircling soul serene o'erarches
    The moving globe of being like a sky;
Who feels that God and Heaven's great deeps are nearer
    Him to whose heart his fellow-man is nigh,
Who doth not hold his soul's own freedom dearer
    Than that of all his brethren, low or high;
Who to the Right can feel himself the truer
    For being gently patient with the wrong,
Who sees a brother in the evil-doer,
    And finds in Love the heart's-blood of his song; —
This, this is he for whom the world is waiting
    To sing the beatings of its mighty heart,
Too long hath it been patient with the grating
    Of scrannel-pipes, and heard it misnamed Art.
To him the smiling soul of man shall listen,
    Laying awhile its crown of thorns aside,
And once again in every eye shall glisten
    The glory of a nature satisfied.
His verse shall have a great, commanding motion,
    Heaving and swelling with a melody
Learnt of the sky, the river, and the ocean,
    And all the pure, majestic things that be.
Awake, then, thou! we pine for thy great presence
    To make us feel the soul once more sublime,
We are of far too infinite an essence
    To rest contented with the lies of Time.
Speak out! and, lo! a hush of deepest wonder
    Shall sink o'er all this many-voicèd scene,
As when a sudden burst of rattling thunder
    Shatters the blueness of a sky serene.

    1841.

THE FATHERLAND.

Where is the true man's fatherland?
  Is it where he by chance is born?
  Doth not the yearning spirit scorn
In such scant borders to be spanned?
O, yes! his fatherland must be
As the blue heaven wide and free!

Is it alone where freedom is,
  Where God is God and man is man?
  Doth he not claim a broader span
For the soul's love of home than this?
O, yes! his fatherland must be
As the blue heaven wide and free!

Where'er a human heart doth wear
  Joy's myrtle-wreath or sorrow's gyves,
  Where'er a human spirit strives
After a life more true and fair,
There is the true man's birthplace grand,
His is a world-wide fatherland!

Where'er a single slave doth pine,
  Where'er one man may help another, —
  Thank God for such a birthright, brother, —
That spot of earth is thine and mine!
There is the true man's birthplace grand,
His is a world-wide fatherland!

THE FORLORN.

The night is dark, the stinging sleet,
  Swept by the bitter gusts of air,
Drives whistling down the lonely street,
  And stiffens on the pavement bare.

The street-lamps flare and struggle dim
  Through the white sleet-clouds as they pass,
Or, governed by a boisterous whim,
  Drop down and rattle on the glass.

One poor, heart-broken, outcast girl
 Faces the east-wind's searching flaws,
And, as about her heart they whirl,
 Her tattered cloak more tightly draws.

The flat brick walls look cold and bleak,
 Her bare feet to the sidewalk freeze;
Yet dares she not a shelter seek,
 Though faint with hunger and disease.

The sharp storm cuts her forehead bare,
 And, piercing through her garments thin,
Beats on her shrunken breast, and there
 Makes colder the cold heart within.

She lingers where a ruddy glow
 Streams outward through an open shutter,
Adding more bitterness to woe,
 More loneness to desertion utter.

One half the cold she had not felt,
 Until she saw this gush of light
Spread warmly forth, and seem to melt
 Its slow way through the deadening night.

She hears a woman's voice within,
 Singing sweet words her childhood knew,
And years of misery and sin
 Furl off, and leave her heaven blue.

Her freezing heart, like one who sinks
 Outwearied in the drifting snow,
Drowses to deadly sleep and thinks
 No longer of its hopeless woe:

Old fields, and clear blue summer days,
 Old meadows, green with grass and trees
That shimmer through the trembling haze
 And whiten in the western breeze, —

Old faces, — all the friendly past
 Rises within her heart again,
And sunshine from her childhood cast
 Makes summer of the icy rain.

I

Enhaloed by a mild, warm glow,
    From all humanity apart,
She hears old footsteps wandering slow
    Through the lone chambers of her heart.

Outside the porch before the door,
    Her cheek upon the cold, hard stone,
She lies, no longer foul and poor,
    No longer dreary and alone.

Next morning something heavily
    Against the opening door did weigh,
And there, from sin and sorrow free,
    A woman on the threshold lay.

A smile upon the wan lips told
    That she had found a calm release,
And that, from out the want and cold,
    The song had borne her soul in peace.

For, whom the heart of man shuts out,
    Sometimes the heart of God takes in,
And fences them all round about
    With silence mid the world's loud din;

And one of his great charities
    Is Music, and it doth not scorn
To close the lids upon the eyes
    Of the polluted and forlorn;

Far was she from her childhood's home,
    Farther in guilt had wandered thence,
Yet thither it had bid her come
    To die in maiden innocence.
        1842.

MIDNIGHT.

THE moon shines white and silent
    On the mist, which, like a tide
Of some enchanted ocean,
    O'er the wide marsh doth glide,
Spreading its ghost-like billows
    Silently far and wide.

A vague and starry magic
   Makes all things mysteries,
And lures the earth's dumb spirit
   Up to the longing skies, —
I seem to hear dim whispers,
   And tremulous replies.

The fireflies o'er the meadow
   In pulses come and go;
The elm-trees' heavy shadow
   Weighs on the grass below;
And faintly from the distance
   The dreaming cock doth crow.

All things look strange and mystic,
   The very bushes swell
And take wild shapes and motions,
   As if beneath a spell, —
They seem not the same lilacs
   From childhood known so well.

The snow of deepest silence
   O'er everything doth fall,
So beautiful and quiet,
   And yet so like a pall, —
As if all life were ended,
   And rest were come to all.

O wild and wondrous midnight,
   There is a might in thee
To make the charmed body
   Almost like spirit be,
And give it some faint glimpses
   Of immortality!

1842.

A PRAYER.

God! do not let my loved one die,
   But rather wait until the time
That I am grown in purity
   Enough to enter thy pure clime
Then take me, I will gladly go,
   So that my love remain below!

O, let her stay! She is by birth
　　What I through death must learn to be,
We need her more on our poor earth,
　　Than thou canst need in heaven with thee.
She hath her wings already, I
Must burst this earth-shell ere I fly.

Then, God, take me! We shall be near,
　　More near than ever, each to each:
Her angel ears will find more clear
　　My heavenly than my earthly speech;
And still, as I draw nigh to thee,
Her soul and mine shall closer be.
　　1841.

THE HERITAGE.

THE rich man's son inherits lands,
　　And piles of brick, and stone, and gold,
And he inherits soft white hands,
　　And tender flesh that fears the cold,
　　Nor dares to wear a garment old;
A heritage, it seems to me,
One scarce would wish to hold in fee.

The rich man's son inherits cares;
　　The bank may break, the factory burn,
A breath may burst his bubble shares,
　　And soft white hands could hardly earn
　　A living that would serve his turn;
A heritage, it seems to me,
One scarce would wish to hold in fee.

The rich man's son inherits wants,
　　His stomach craves for dainty fare;
With sated heart, he hears the pants
　　Of toiling hinds with brown arms bare,
　　And wearies in his easy chair;
A heritage, it seems to me,
One scarce would wish to hold in fee.

What doth the poor man's son inherit?
　　Stout muscles and a sinewy heart,

A hardy frame, a hardier spirit;
   King of two hands, he does his **part**
   In every useful toil and art;
A heritage, it seems to me,
A king might wish to hold in fee.

What doth the poor man's son inherit?
   Wishes o'erjoyed with humble things,
A rank adjudged by toil-won merit,
   Content that from employment springs,
   A heart that in his labor sings;
A heritage, it seems to me,
A king might wish to hold in fee.

What doth the poor man's son inherit?
   A patience learned of being poor,
Courage, if sorrow come, to bear it,
   A fellow-feeling that is sure
   To make the outcast bless his door;
A heritage, it seems to me,
A king might wish to hold in fee.

O, rich man's son! there is a toil,
   That with all others level stands;
Large charity doth never soil,
   But only whiten, soft white hands, —
   This is the best crop from thy lands;
A heritage, it seems to be,
Worth being rich to hold in fee.

O, poor man's son! scorn not thy state;
   There is worse weariness than thine,
In merely being rich and great;
   Toil only gives the soul to shine,
   And makes rest fragrant and benign,
A heritage, it seems to me,
Worth being poor to hold in fee.

Both, heirs to some six feet of sod,
   Are equal in the earth at last;
Both, children of the same dear God,
   Prove title to your heirship vast
   By record of a well-filled past;
A heritage, it seems to me,
Well worth a life to hold in fee.

THE ROSE: A BALLAD.

I.

In his tower sat the poet
 Gazing on the roaring sea,
"Take this rose," he sighed, "and throw it
 Where there's none that loveth me.
On the rock the billow bursteth
 And sinks back into the seas,
But in vain my spirit thirsteth
 So to burst and be at ease.
Take, O, sea! the tender blossom
 That hath lain against my breast;
On thy black and angry bosom
 It will find a surer rest.
Life is vain, and love is hollow,
 Ugly death stands there behind,
Hate and scorn and hunger follow
 Him that toileth for his kind."
Forth into the night he hurled it,
 And with bitter smile did mark
How the surly tempest whirled it
 Swift into the hungry dark.
Foam and spray drive back to leeward,
 And the gale, with dreary moan,
Drifts the helpless blossom seaward,
 Through the breakers all alone.

II.

Stands a maiden, on the morrow,
 Musing by the wave-beat strand,
Half in hope and half in sorrow,
 Tracing words upon the sand:
"Shall I ever then behold him
 Who hath been my life so long, —
Ever to this sick heart fold him, —
 Be the spirit of his song?
Touch not, sea, the blessed letters
 I have traced upon thy shore,
Spare his name whose spirit fetters
 Mine with love forevermore!"
Swells the tide and overflows it,

But, with omen pure and meet,
   Brings a little rose, and throws it
      Humbly at the maiden's feet.
Full of bliss she takes the token,
      And, upon her snowy breast,
Soothes the ruffled petals broken
      With the ocean's fierce unrest.
"Love is thine, O heart! and surely
      Peace shall also be thine own,
For the heart that trusteth purely
      Never long can pine alone."

III.

In his tower sits the poet,
      Blisses new and strange to him
Fill his heart and overflow it
      With a wonder sweet and dim.
Up the beach the ocean slideth
      With a whisper of delight,
And the noon in silence glideth
      Through the peaceful blue of night.
Rippling o'er the poet's shoulder
      Flows a maiden's golden hair,
Maiden-lips, with love grown bolder,
      Kiss his moon-lit forehead bare.
"Life is joy, and love is power,
      Death all fetters doth unbind,
Strength and wisdom only flower
      When we toil for all our kind.
Hope is truth, — the future giveth
      More than present takes away,
And the soul forever liveth
      Nearer God from day to day."
Not a word the maiden uttered,
      Fullest hearts are slow to speak,
But a withered rose-leaf fluttered
      Down upon the poet's cheek.
1842.

A LEGEND OF BRITTANY.

PART FIRST.

I.

FAIR as a summer dream was Margaret, —
Such dream as in a poet's soul might start,
Musing of old loves while the moon doth set :
Her hair was not more sunny than her heart,
Though like a natural golden coronet
It circled her dear head with careless art,
Mocking the sunshine, that would fain have lent
To its frank grace a richer ornament.

II.

His loved one's eyes could poet ever speak,
So kind, so dewy, and so deep were hers, —
But, while he strives, the choicest phrase, too weak
Their glad reflection in his spirit blurs ;
As one may see a dream dissolve and break
Out of his grasp when he to tell it stirs,
Like that sad Dryad doomed no more to bless
The mortal who revealed her loveliness.

III.

She dwelt forever in a region bright,
Peopled with living fancies of her own,
Where naught could come but visions of delight,
Far, far aloof from earth's eternal moan :
A summer cloud thrilled through with rosy light,
Floating beneath the blue sky all alone,
Her spirit wandered by itself, and won
A golden edge from some unsetting sun.

IV.

The heart grows richer that its lot is poor, —
God blesses want with larger sympathies, —
Love enters gladliest at the humble door,
And makes the cot a palace with his eyes ;
So Margaret's heart a softer beauty wore,
And grew in gentleness and patience wise,
For she was but a simple herdsman's child,
A lily chance-sown in the rugged wild.

v.

There was no beauty of the wood or field
  But she its fragrant bosom-secret knew,
Nor any but to her would freely yield
  Some grace that in her soul took root and grew:
Nature to her glowed ever new-revealed,
  All rosy fresh with innocent morning dew,
And looked into her heart with dim, sweet eyes
That left it full of sylvan memories.

VI.

O, what a face was hers to brighten light,
  And give back sunshine with an added glow,
To wile each moment with a fresh delight,
  And part of memory's best contentment grow!
O, how her voice, as with an inmate's right,
  Into the strangest heart would welcome go,
And make it sweet, and ready to become
Of white and gracious thoughts the chosen home!

VII.

None looked upon her but he straightway thought
  Of all the greenest depths of country cheer,
And into each one's heart was freshly brought
  What was to him the sweetest time of year,
So was her every look and motion fraught
  With out-of-door delights and forest lere:
Not the first violet on a woodland lea
Seemed a more visible gift of Spring than she.

VIII.

Is love learned only out of poets' books?
  Is there not somewhat in the dropping flood,
And in the nunneries of silent nooks,
  And in the murmured longing of the wood,
That could make Margaret dream of lovelorn looks,
  And stir a thrilling mystery in her blood
More trembly secret than Aurora's tear
Shed in the bosom of an eglatere?

IX.

Full many a sweet forewarning hath the mind,
  Full many a whispering of vague desire,

Ere comes the nature destined to unbind
    Its virgin zone, and all its deeps inspire, —
Low stirrings in the leaves, before the wind
    Wakes all the green strings of the forest lyre,
Faint heatings in the calyx, ere the rose
Its warm voluptuous breast doth all unclose.

X.

Long in its dim recesses pines the spirit,
    Wildered and dark, despairingly alone;
Though many a shape of beauty wander near it,
    And many a wild and half-remembered tone
Tremble from the divine abyss to cheer it,
    Yet still it knows that there is only one
Before whom it can kneel and tribute bring,
At once a happy vassal and a king.

XI.

To feel a want, yet scarce know what it is,
    To seek one nature that is always new,
Whose glance is warmer than another's kiss,
    Whom we can bare our inmost beauty to,
Nor feel deserted afterwards, — for this
    But with our destined co-mate we can do, —
Such longing instinct fills the mighty scope
Of the young soul with one mysterious hope.

XII.

So Margaret's heart grew brimming with the lore
    Of love's enticing secrets ; and although
She had found none to cast it down before,
    Yet oft to Fancy's chapel she would go
To pay her vows, and count the rosary o'er
    Of her love's promised graces : — haply so
Miranda's hope had pictured Ferdinand
Long ere the gaunt wave tossed him on the strand.

XIII.

A new-made star that swims the lonely gloom,
    Unwedded yet and longing for the sun,
Whose beams, the bride-gifts of the lavish groom
    Blithely to crown the virgin planet run,
Her being was, watching to see the bloom

Of love's fresh sunrise roofing one by one
Its clouds with gold, a triumph-arch to be
For him who came to hold her heart in fee.

XIV.

Not far from Margaret's cottage dwelt a knight
 Of the proud Templars, a sworn celibate,
Whose heart in secret fed upon the light
 And dew of her ripe beauty, through the grate
Of his close vow catching what gleams he might
 Of the free heaven, and cursing — all too late —
The cruel faith whose black walls hemmed him in,
And turned life's crowning bliss to deadly sin.

XV.

For he had met her in the wood by chance,
 And, having drunk her beauty's wildering spell,
His heart shook like the pennon of a lance
 That quivers in a breeze's sudden swell,
And thenceforth, in a close-enfolded trance,
 From mistily golden deep to deep he fell;
Till earth did waver and fade far away
Beneath the hope in whose warm arms he lay.

XVI.

A dark, proud man he was, whose half-blown youth
 Had shed its blossoms even in opening,
Leaving a few that with more winning ruth
 Trembling around grave manhood's stem might cling,
More sad than cheery, making, in good sooth,
 Like the fringed gentian, a late autumn spring: —
A twilight nature, braided light and gloom,
A youth half-smiling by an open tomb.

XVII.

Fair as an angel, who yet inly wore
 A wrinkled heart foreboding his near fall;
Who saw him always wished to know him more,
 As if he were some fate's defiant thrall
And nursed a dreaded secret at its core;
 Little he loved, but power most of all,
And that he seemed to scorn, as one who knew
By what foul paths men choose to crawl thereto.

XVIII.

He had been noble, but some great deceit
   Had turned his better instinct to a vice:
He strove to think the world was all a cheat,
   That power and fame were cheap at any price,
That the sure way of being shortly great
   Was even to play life's game with loaded dice,
Since he had tried the honest play and found
That vice and virtue differed but in sound.

XIX.

Yet Margaret's sight redeemed him for a space
   From his own thraldom; man could never be
A hypocrite when first such maiden grace
   Smiled in upon his heart; the agony
Of wearing all day long a lying face
   Fell lightly from him, and, a moment free,
Erect with wakened faith his spirit stood
And scorned the weakness of its demon-mood.

XX.

Like a sweet wind-harp to him was her thought,
   Which would not let the common air come near,
Till from its dim enchantment it had caught
   A musical tenderness that brimmed his ear
With sweetness more ethereal than aught
   Save silver-dropping snatches that whilere
Rained down from some sad angel's faithful harp
To cool her fallen lover's anguish sharp.

XXI.

Deep in the forest was a little dell
   High overarchèd with the leafy sweep
Of a broad oak, through whose gnarled roots there fell
   A slender rill that sung itself asleep,
Where its continuous toil had scooped a well
   To please the fairy folk; breathlessly deep
The stillness was, save when the dreaming brook
From its small urn a drizzly murmur shook.

XXII.

The wooded hills sloped upward all around
   With gradual rise, and made an even rim,

So that it seemed a mighty casque unbound
From some huge Titan's brow to lighten him,
Ages ago, and left upon the ground,
Where the slow soil had mossed it to the brim,
Till after countless centuries it grew
Into this dell, the haunt of noontide dew.

XXIII.

Dim vistas, sprinkled o'er with sun-flecked green,
Wound through the thickset trunks on every side,
And, toward the west, in fancy might be seen
A gothic window in its blazing pride,
When the low sun, two arching elms between,
Lit up the leaves beyond, which, autumn-dyed
With lavish hues, would into splendor start,
Shaming the labored panes of richest art.

XXIV.

Here, leaning once against the old oak's trunk,
Mordred, for such was the young Templar's name,
Saw Margaret come; unseen, the falcon shrunk
From the meek dove; sharp thrills of tingling flame
Made him forget that he was vowed a monk,
And all the outworks of his pride o'ercame:
Flooded he seemed with bright delicious pain,
As if a star had burst within his brain.

XXV.

Such power hath beauty and frank innocence:
A flower bloomed forth, that sunshine glad to bless,
Even from his love's long leafless stem; the sense
Of exile from Hope's happy realm grew less,
And thoughts of childish peace, he knew not whence,
Thronged round his heart with many an old caress,
Melting the frost there into pearly dew
That mirrored back his nature's morning-blue.

XXVI.

She turned and saw him, but she felt no dread,
Her purity, like adamantine mail,
Did so encircle her; and yet her head
She drooped, and made her golden hair her veil,

Through which a glow of rosiest lustre spread,
   Then faded, and anon she stood all pale,
As snow o'er which a blush of northern-light
Suddenly reddens, and as soon grows white.

XXVII.

She thought of Tristrem and of Lancilot,
   Of all her dreams, and of kind fairies' might,
And how that dell was deemed a haunted spot,
   Until there grew a mist before her sight,
And where the present was she half forgot,
   Borne backward through the realms of old delight, —
Then, starting up awake, she would have gone,
Yet almost wished it might not be alone.

XXVIII.

How they went home together through the wood,
   And how all life seemed focussed into one
Thought-dazzling spot that set ablaze the blood,
   What need to tell? Fit language there is none
For the heart's deepest things. Who ever wooed
   As in his boyish hope he would have done?
For, when the soul is fullest, the hushed tongue
Voicelessly trembles like a lute unstrung.

XXIX.

But all things carry the heart's messages
   And know it not, nor doth the heart well know,
But nature hath her will; even as the bees,
   Blithe go-betweens, fly singing to and fro
With the fruit-quickening pollen; — hard if these
   Found not some all unthought-of way to show
Their secret each to each; and so they did,
And one heart's flower-dust into the other slid.

XXX.

Young hearts are free; the selfish world it is
   That turns them miserly and cold as stone,
And makes them clutch their fingers on the bliss
   Which but in giving truly is their own; —
She had no dreams of barter, asked not his,
   But gave hers freely as she would have thrown
A rose to him, or as that rose gives forth
Its generous fragrance, thoughtless of its worth.

XXXI.

Her summer nature felt a need to bless,
  And a like longing to be blest again;
So, from her sky-like spirit, gentleness
  Dropt ever like a sunlit fall of rain,
And his beneath drank in the bright caress
  As thirstily as would a parched plain,
That long hath watched the showers of sloping gray
Forever, ever, falling far away.

XXXII.

How should she dream of ill? the heart filled quite
  With sunshine, like the shepherd's-clock at noon,
Closes its leaves around its warm delight;
  Whate'er in life is harsh or out of tune
Is all shut out, no boding shade of light
  Can pierce the opiate ether of its swoon:
Love is but blind as thoughtful justice is,
But naught can be so wanton-blind as bliss.

XXXIII.

All beauty and all life he was to her;
  She questioned not his love, she only knew
That she loved him, and not a pulse could stir
  In her whole frame but quivered through and through
With this glad thought, and was a minister
  To do him fealty and service true,
Like golden ripples hasting to the land
To wreck their freight of sunshine on the strand.

XXXIV.

O dewy dawn of love! O hopes that are
  Hung high, like the cliff-swallow's perilous nest,
Most like to fall when fullest, and that jar
  With every heavier billow! O unrest
Than balmiest deeps of quiet sweeter far!
  How did ye triumph now in Margaret's breast,
Making it readier to shrink and start
Than quivering gold of the pond-lily's heart.

XXXV.

Here let us pause: O, would the soul might ever
  Achieve its immortality in youth,

When nothing yet hath damped its high endeavor
   After the starry energy of truth!
Here let us pause, and for a moment sever
   This gleam of sunshine from the days unruth
That sometime come to all, for it is good
To lengthen to the last a sunny mood.

PART SECOND.

I.

As one who, from the sunshine and the green,
   Enters the solid darkness of a cave,
Nor knows what precipice or pit unseen
   May yawn before him with its sudden grave,
And, with hushed breath, doth often forward lean,
   Dreaming he hears the plashing of a wave
Dimly below, or feels a damper air
From out some dreary chasm, he knows not where; —

II.

So, from the sunshine and the green of love,
   We enter on our story's darker part;
And, though the horror of it well may move
   An impulse of repugnance in the heart,
Yet let us think, that, as there's naught above
   The all-embracing atmosphere of Art,
So also there is naught that falls below
Her generous reach, though grimed with guilt and woe.

III.

Her fittest triumph is to show that good
   Lurks in the heart of evil evermore,
That love, though scorned, and outcast, and withstood,
   Can without end forgive, and yet have store;
God's love and man's are of the self-same blood,
   And He can see that always at the door
Of foulest hearts the angel-nature yet
Knocks to return and cancel all its debt.

IV.

It ever is weak falsehood's destiny
   That her thick mask turns crystal to let through

The unsuspicious eyes of honesty;
  But Margaret's heart was too sincere and true
Aught but plain truth and faithfulness to see,
  And Mordred's for a time a little grew
To be like hers, won by the mild reproof
Of those kind eyes that kept all doubt aloof.

V.

Full oft they met, as dawn and twilight meet
  In northern climes; she full of growing day
As he of darkness, which before her feet
  Shrank gradual, and faded quite away,
Soon to return; for power had made love sweet
  To him, and, when his will had gained full sway,
The taste began to pall; for never power
Can sate the hungry soul beyond an hour.

VI.

He fell as doth the tempter ever fall,
  Even in the gaining of his loathsome end;
God doth not work as man works, but makes all
  The crooked paths of ill to goodness tend;
Let him judge Margaret! If to be the thrall
  Of love, and faith too generous to defend
Its very life from him she loved, be sin,
What hope of grace may the seducer win?

VII.

Grim-hearted world, that look'st with Levite eyes
  On those poor fallen by too much faith in man.
She that upon thy freezing threshold lies,
  Starved to more sinning by thy savage ban, —
Seeking that refuge because foulest vice
  More god-like than thy virtue is, whose span
Shuts out the wretched only, — is more free
To enter Heaven than thou wilt ever be!

VIII.

Thou wilt not let her wash thy dainty feet
  With such salt things as tears, or with rude hair
Dry them, soft Pharisee, that sit'st at meat
  With him who made her such, and speak'st him fair,

K

Leaving God's wandering lamb the while to bleat
  Unheeded, shivering in the pitiless air:
Thou hast made prisoned virtue show more wan
And haggard than a vice to look upon.

IX.

Now many months flew by, and weary grew
  To Margaret the sight of happy things;
Blight fell on all her.flowers, instead of dew;
  Shut round her heart were now the joyous wings
Wherewith it wont to soar; yet not untrue,
  Though tempted much, her woman's nature clings
To its first pure belief, and with sad eyes
Looks backward o'er the gate of Paradise.

X.

And so, though altered Mordred came less oft,
  And winter frowned where spring had laughed before,
In his strange eyes, yet half her sadness doffed,
  And in her silent patience loved him more:
Sorrow had made her soft heart yet more soft,
  And a new life within her own she bore
Which made her tenderer, as she felt it move
Beneath her breast, a refuge for her love.

XI.

This babe, she thought, would surely bring him back,
  And be a bond forever them between;
Before its eyes the sullen tempest-rack
  Would fade, and leave the face of heaven serene;
And love's return doth more than fill the lack,
  Which in his absence withered the heart's green;
And yet a dim foreboding still would flit
Between her and her hope to darken it.

XII.

She could not figure forth a happy fate,
  Even for this life from heaven so newly come;
The earth must needs be doubly desolate
  To him scarce parted from a fairer home:
Such boding heavier on her bosom sate
  One night, as, standing in the twilight gloam,

She strained her eyes beyond that dizzy verge
At whose foot faintly breaks the future's surge.

XIII.

Poor little spirit! naught but shame and woe
   Nurse the sick heart whose lifeblood nurses **thine:**
Yet not those only; love hath triumphed so,
   As for thy sake makes sorrow more divine:
And yet, though thou be pure, the world is foe
   To purity, if born in such a shrine;
And, having trampled it for struggling thence,
Smiles to itself, and calls it Providence.

XIV.

As thus she mused, a shadow seemed to rise
   From out her thought, and turn to dreariness
All blissful hopes and sunny memories,
   And the quick blood doth curdle up and press
About her heart, which seemed to shut its eyes
   And hush itself, as who with shuddering guess
Harks through the gloom and dreads e'en now to **feel**
Through his hot breast the icy slide of steel.

XV.

But, at the heart-beat, while in dread she was,
   In the low wind the honeysuckles gleam,
A dewy thrill flits through the heavy grass,
   And, looking forth, she saw, as in a dream,
Within the wood the moonlight's shadowy mass:
   Night's starry heart yearning to hers doth seem,
And the deep sky, full-hearted with the moon,
Folds round her all the happiness of June.

XVI.

What fear could face a heaven and earth like this?
   What silveriest cloud could hang 'neath such a sky?
A tide of wondrous and unwonted bliss
   Rolls back through all her pulses suddenly,
As if some seraph, who had learned to kiss
   From the fair daughters of the world gone by,
Had wedded so his fallen light with hers,
Such sweet, strange joy through soul and body stirs.

XVII.

Now seek we Mordred: He who did not fear
    The crime, yet fears the latent consequence:
If it should reach a brother Templar's ear,
    It haply might be made a good pretence
To cheat him of the hope he held most dear;
    For he had spared no thought's or deed's expense,
That, by-and-by might help his wish to clip
Its darling bride, — the high grand mastership.

XVIII.

The apathy, ere a crime resolved is done,
    Is scarce less dreadful than remorse for crime;
By no allurement can the soul be won
    From brooding o'er the weary creep of time:
Mordred stole forth into the happy sun,
    Striving to hum a scrap of Breton rhyme,
But the sky struck him speechless, and he tried
In vain to summon up his callous pride.

XIX.

In the court-yard a fountain leaped alway,
    A Triton blowing jewels through his shell
Into the sunshine; Mordred turned away,
    Weary because the stone face did not tell
Of weariness, nor could he bear to-day,
    Heartsick, to hear the patient sink and swell
Of winds among the leaves, or golden bees
Drowsily humming in the orange-trees.

XX.

All happy sights and sounds now came to him
    Like a reproach: he wandered far and wide,
Following the lead of his unquiet whim,
    But still there went a something at his side
That made the cool breeze hot, the sunshine dim;
    It would not flee, it could not be defied,
He could not see it, but he felt it there,
By the damp chill that crept among his hair.

XXI.

Day wore at last; the evening star arose,
    And throbbing in the sky grew red and set;

Then with a guilty, wavering step he goes
  To the hid nook where they so oft had met
In happier season, for his heart well knows
  That he is sure to find poor Margaret
Watching and waiting there with lovelorn breast
Around her young dream's rudely scattered nest.

XXII.

Why follow here that grim old chronicle
  Which counts the dagger-strokes and drops of blood?
Enough that Margaret by his mad steel fell,
  Unmoved by murder from her trusting mood,
Smiling on him as Heaven smiles on Hell,
  With a sad love, remembering when he stood
Not fallen yet, the unsealer of her heart,
Of all her holy dreams the holiest part.

XXIII.

His crime complete, scarce knowing what he did,
  (So goes the tale,) beneath the altar there
In the high church the stiffening corpse he hid,
  And then, to 'scape that suffocating air,
Like a scared ghoul out of the porch he slid;
  But his strained eyes saw bloodspots everywhere,
And ghastly faces thrust themselves between
His soul and hopes of peace with blasting mien.

XXIV.

His heart went out within him, like a spark
  Dropt in the sea; wherever he made bold
To turn his eyes, he saw, all stiff and stark,
  Pale Margaret lying dead; the lavish gold
Of her loose hair seemed in the cloudy dark
  To spread a glory, and a thousandfold
More strangely pale and beautiful she grew:
Her silence stabbed his conscience through and through:

XXV.

Or visions of past days, — a mother's eyes
  That smiled down on the fair boy at her knee,
Whose happy upturned face to hers replies, —
  He saw sometimes: or Margaret mournfully

Gazed on him full of doubt, as one who tries
    To crush belief that does love injury;
Then she would wring her hands, but soon again
Love's patience glimmered out through cloudy pain.

XXVI.

Meanwhile he dared not go and steal away
    The silent, dead-cold witness of his sin;
He had not feared the life, but that dull clay,
    Those open eyes that showed the death within,
Would surely stare him mad; yet all the day
    A dreadful impulse, whence his will could win
No refuge, made him linger in the aisle,
Freezing with his wan look each greeting smile.

XXVII.

Now, on the second day there was to be
    A festival in church: from far and near
Came flocking in the sunburnt peasantry,
    And knights and dames with stately antique cheer,
Blazing with pomp, as if all faërie
    Had emptied her quaint halls, or, as it were,
The illuminated marge of some old book,
While we were gazing, life and motion took.

XXVIII.

When all were entered, and the roving eyes
    Of all were staid, some upon faces bright,
Some on the priests, some on the traceries
    That decked the slumber of a marble knight,
And all the rustlings over that arise
    From recognizing tokens of delight,
When friendly glances meet, — then silent ease
Spread o'er the multitude by slow degrees.

XXIX.

Then swelled the organ: up through choir and nave
    The music trembled with an inward thrill
Of bliss at its own grandeur: wave on wave
    Its flood of mellow thunder rose, until
The hushed air shivered with the throb it gave,
    Then, poising for a moment, it stood still,
And sank and rose again, to burst in spray
That wandered into silence far away.

XXX.

Like to a mighty heart the music seemed,
  That yearns with melodies it cannot speak,
Until, in grand despair of what it dreamed,
  In the agony of effort it doth break,
Yet triumphs breaking; on it rushed and streamed
  And wantoned in its might, as when a lake,
Long pent among the mountains, bursts its walls
And in one crowding gush leaps forth and falls.

XXXI.

Deeper and deeper shudders shook the air,
  As the huge bass kept gathering heavily,
Like thunder when it rouses in its lair,
  And with its hoarse growl shakes the low-hung sky,
It grew up like a darkness everywhere,
  Filling the vast cathedral; — suddenly,
From the dense mass a boy's clear treble broke
Like lightning, and the full-toned choir awoke.

XXXII.

Through gorgeous windows shone the sun aslant,
  Brimming the church with gold and purple mist,
Meet atmosphere to bosom that rich chant,
  Where fifty voices in one strand did twist
Their varicolored tones, and left no want
  To the delighted soul, which sank abyssed
In the warm music cloud, while, far below,
The organ heaved its surges to and fro.

XXXIII.

As if a lark should suddenly drop dead
  While the blue air yet trembled with its song,
So snapped at once that music's golden thread,
  Struck by a nameless fear that leapt along
From heart to heart, and like a shadow spread
  With instantaneous shiver through the throng,
So that some glanced behind, as half aware
A hideous shape of dread were standing there.

XXXIV.

As when a crowd of pale men gather round,
  Watching an eddy in the leaden deep,

From which they deem the body of one drowned
　Will be cast forth, from face to face doth creep
An eager dread that holds all tongues fast bound
　Until the horror, with a ghastly leap,
Starts up, its dead blue arms stretched aimlessly,
Heaved with the swinging of the careless sea, —

XXXV.

So in the faces of all these there grew,
　As by one impulse, a dark, freezing awe,
Which, with a fearful fascination drew
　All eyes toward the altar; damp and raw
The air grew suddenly, and no man knew
　Whether perchance his silent neighbor saw
The dreadful thing which all were sure would rise
To scare the strained lids wider from their eyes.

XXXVI.

The incense trembled as it upward sent
　Its slow, uncertain thread of wandering blue,
As 't were the only living element
　In all the church, so deep the stillness grew,
It seemed one might have heard it, as it went,
　Give out an audible rustle, curling through
The midnight silence of that awe-struck air,
More hushed than death, though so much life was there.

XXXVII.

Nothing they saw, but a low voice was heard
　Threading the ominous silence of that fear,
Gentle and terrorless as if a bird,
　Wakened by some volcano's glare, should cheer
The murk air with his song; yet every word
　In the cathedral's farthest arch seemed near
As if it spoke to every one apart,
Like the clear voice of conscience in each heart.

XXXVIII.

"O Rest, to weary hearts thou art most dear!
　O Silence, after life's bewildering din,
Thou art most welcome, whether in the sear
　Days of our age thou comest, or we win

Thy poppy-wreath in youth! then wherefore here
   Linger I yet, once free to enter in
At that wished gate which gentle Death doth ope,
Into the boundless realm of strength and hope?

XXXIX.

"Think not in death my love could ever cease;
   If thou wast false, more need there is for me
Still to be true; that slumber were not peace,
   If 't were unvisited with dreams of thee:
And thou hadst never heard such words as these,
   Save that in heaven I must ever be
Most comfortless and wretched, seeing this
Our unbaptizèd babe shut out from bliss.

XL.

"This little spirit with imploring eyes
   Wanders alone the dreary wild of space;
The shadow of his pain forever lies
   Upon my soul in this new dwelling-place;
His loneliness makes me in Paradise
   More lonely, and, unless I see his face,
Even here for grief could I lie down and die,
Save for my curse of immortality.

XLI.

"World after world he sees around him swim
   Crowded with happy souls, that take no heed
Of the sad eyes that from the night's faint rim
   Gaze sick with longing on them as they speed
With golden gates, that only shut out him;
   And shapes sometimes from Hell's abysses **freed**
Flap darkly by him, with enormous sweep
Of wings that roughen wide the pitchy deep.

XLII.

"I am a mother, — spirits do not shake
   This much of earth from them, — and I must pine
Till I can feel his little hands, and take
   His weary head upon this heart of mine;
And, might it be, full gladly for his sake
   Would I this solitude of bliss resign,

And be shut out of Heaven to dwell with him
Forever in that silence drear and dim.

XLIII.

"I strove to hush my soul, and would not speak
   At first, for thy dear sake; a woman's love
Is mighty, but a mother's heart is weak,
   And by its weakness overcomes; I strove
To smother bitter thoughts with patience meek,
   But still in the abyss my soul would rove,
Seeking my child, and drove me here to claim
The rite that gives him peace in Christ's dear name.

XLIV.

"I sit and weep while blessed spirits sing;
   I can but long and pine the while they praise,
And, leaning o'er the wall of Heaven, I fling
   My voice to where I deem my infant strays,
Like a robbed bird that cries in vain to bring
   Her nestlings back beneath her wings' embrace;
But still he answers not, and I but know
That Heaven and earth are both alike in woe."

XLV.

Then the pale priests, with ceremony due,
   Baptized the child within its dreadful tomb
Beneath that mother's heart, whose instinct true
   Star-like had battled down the triple gloom
Of sorrow, love, and death: young maidens, too,
   Strewed the pale corpse with many a milkwhite bloom,
And parted the bright hair, and on the breast
Crossed the unconscious hands in sign of rest.

XLVI.

Some said, that, when the priest had sprinkled o'er
   The consecrated drops, they seemed to hear
A sigh, as of some heart from travail sore
   Released, and then two voices singing clear,
Misereatur Deus, more and more
   Fading far upward, and their ghastly fear
Fell from them with that sound, as bodies fall
From souls upspringing to celestial hall.

PROMETHEUS.

ONE after one the stars have risen and set,
Sparkling upon the hoarfrost on my chain:
The Bear, that prowled all night about the fold
Of the North-star, hath shrunk into his den,
Scared by the blithesome footsteps of the Dawn,
Whose blushing smile floods all the Orient;
And now bright Lucifer grows less and less,
Into the heaven's blue quiet deep-withdrawn.
Sunless and starless all, the desert sky
Arches above me, empty as this heart
For ages hath been empty of all joy,
Except to brood upon its silent hope,
As o'er its hope of day the sky doth now.
All night have I heard voices: deeper yet
The deep low breathing of the silence grew,
While all about, muffled in awe, there stood
Shadows, or forms, or both, clear-felt at heart,
But, when I turned to front them, far along
Only a shudder through the midnight ran,
And the dense stillness walled me closer round.
But still I heard them wander up and down
That solitude, and flappings of dusk wings
Did mingle with them, whether of those hags
Let slip upon me once from Hades deep,
Or of yet direr torments, if such be,
I could but guess; and then toward me came
A shape as of a woman: very pale
It was, and calm; its cold eyes did not move,
And mine moved not, but only stared on them.
Their fixed awe went through my brain like ice,
A skeleton hand seemed clutching at my heart,
And a sharp chill, as if a dank night fog
Suddenly closed me in, was all I felt:
And then, methought, I heard a freezing sigh,
A long, deep, shivering sigh, as from blue lips
Stiffening in death, close to mine ear.   I thought
Some doom was close upon me, and I looked
And saw the red moon through the heavy mist,
Just setting, and it seemed as if it were falling,
Or reeling to its fall, so dim and dead

And palsy-struck it looked. Then all sounds merged
Into the rising surges of the pines,
Which, leagues below me, clothing the gaunt loins
Of ancient Caucasus with hairy strength,
Sent up a murmur in the morning wind,
Sad as the wail that from the populous earth
All day and night to high Olympus soars,
Fit incense to thy wicked throne, O Jove!

Thy hated name is tossed once more in scorn
From off my lips, for I will tell thy doom.
And are these tears? Nay, do not triumph, Jove,
They are wrung from me but by the agonies
Of prophecy, like those sparse drops which fall
From clouds in travail of the lightning, when
The great wave of the storm high-curled and black
Rolls steadily onward to its thunderous break.
Why art thou made a god of, thou poor type
Of anger, and revenge, and cunning force?
True Power was never born of brutish Strength,
Nor sweet Truth suckled at the shaggy dugs
Of that old she-wolf. Are thy thunderbolts,
That quell the darkness for a space, so strong
As the prevailing patience of meek Light,
Who, with the invincible tenderness of peace,
Wins it to be a portion of herself?
Why art thou made a god of, thou, who hast
The never-sleeping terror at thy heart,
That birthright of all tyrants, worse to bear
Than this thy ravening bird on which I smile?
Thou swear'st to free me, if I will unfold
What kind of doom it is whose omen flits
Across thy heart, as o'er a troop of doves
The fearful shadow of the kite. What need
To know that truth whose knowledge cannot save?
Evil its errand hath, as well as Good;
When thine is finished, thou art known no more:
There is a higher purity than thou,
And higher purity is greater strength;
Thy nature is thy doom, at which thy heart
Trembles behind the thick wall of thy might.
Let man but hope, and thou art straightway chilled
With thought of that drear silence and deep night

Which, like a dream, shall swallow thee and thine:
Let man but will, and thou art god no more,
More capable of ruin than the gold
And ivory that image thee on earth.
He who hurled down the monstrous Titan-brood
Blinded with lightnings, with rough thunders
    stunned,
Is weaker than a simple human thought.
My slender voice can shake thee, as the breeze,
That seems but apt to stir a maiden's hair,
Sways huge Oceanus from pole to pole:
For I am still Prometheus, and foreknow
In my wise heart the end and doom of all.

    Yes, I am still Prometheus, wiser grown
By years of solitude, — that holds apart
The past and future, giving the soul room
To search into itself, — and long commune
With this eternal silence; — more a god,
In my long-suffering and strength to meet
With equal front the direst shafts of fate,
Than thou in thy faint-hearted despotism,
Girt with thy baby-toys of force and wrath.
Yes, I am that Prometheus who brought down
The light to man, which thou, in selfish fear,
Hadst to thyself usurped, — his by sole right,
For Man hath right to all save Tyranny, —
And which shall free him yet from thy frail throne.
Tyrants are but the spawn of Ignorance,
Begotten by the slaves they trample on,
Who, could they win a glimmer of the light,
And see that Tyranny is always weakness,
Or Fear with its own bosom ill at ease,
Would laugh away in scorn the sand-wove chain
Which their own blindness feigned for adamant.
Wrong ever builds on quicksands, but the Right
To the firm centre lays its moveless base.
The tyrant trembles, if the air but stirs
The innocent ringlets of a child's free hair,
And crouches, when the thought of some great spirit,
With world-wide murmur, like a rising gale,
Over men's hearts, as over standing corn,
Rushes, and bends them to its own strong will.

So shall some thought of mine yet circle earth,
And puff away thy crumbling altars, Jove!

And, wouldst thou know of my supreme revenge
Poor tyrant, even now dethroned in heart,
Realmless in soul, as tyrants ever are,
Listen! and tell me if this bitter peak,
This never-glutted vulture, and these chains
Shrink not before it; for it shall befit
A sorrow-taught, unconquered Titan-heart.
Men, when their death is on them, seem to stand
On a precipitous crag that overhangs
The abyss of doom, and in that depth to see,
As in a glass, the features dim and vast
Of things to come, the shadows, as it seems,
Of what have been.   Death ever fronts the wise;
Not fearfully, but with clear promises
Of larger life, on whose broad vans upborne,
Their out-look widens, and they see beyond
The horizon of the Present and the Past,
Even to the very source and end of things.
Such am I now: immortal woe hath made
My heart a seer, and my soul a judge
Between the substance and the shadow of Truth.
The sure supremeness of the Beautiful,
By all the martyrdoms made doubly sure
Of such as I am, this is my revenge,
Which of my wrongs builds a triumphal arch,
Through which I see a sceptre and a throne.
The pipings of glad shepherds on the hills,
Tending the flocks no more to bleed for thee, —
The songs of maidens pressing with white feet
The vintage on thine altars poured no more, —
The murmurous bliss of lovers, underneath
Dim grape-vine bowers, whose rosy bunches press
Not half so closely their warm cheeks, unpaled
By thoughts of thy brute lust, — the hive-like hum
Of peaceful commonwealths, where sunburnt Toil
Reaps for itself the rich earth made its own
By its own labor, lightened with glad hymns
To an omnipotence which thy mad bolts
Would cope with as a spark with the vast sea, —
Even the spirit of free love and peace,

Duty's sure recompense through life and death, —
These are such harvests as all master-spirits
Reap, haply not on earth, but reap no less
Because the sheaves are bound by hands not theirs
These are the bloodless daggers wherewithal
They stab fallen tyrants, this their high revenge:
For their best part of life on earth is when,
Long after death, prisoned and pent no more,
Their thoughts, their wild dreams even, have become
Part of the necessary air men breathe;
When, like the moon, herself behind a cloud,
They shed down light before us on life's sea,
That cheers us to steer onward still in hope.
Earth with her twining memories ivies o'er
Their holy sepulchres; the chainless sea,
In tempest or wide calm, repeats their thoughts;
The lightning and the thunder, all free things,
Have legends of them for the ears of men.
All other glories are as falling stars,
But universal Nature watches theirs:
Such strength is won by love of human kind.

Not that I feel that hunger after fame,
Which souls of a half-greatness are beset with;
But that the memory of noble deeds
Cries, shame upon the idle and the vile,
And keeps the heart of Man forever up
To the heroic level of old time.
To be forgot at first is little pain
To a heart conscious of such high intent
As must be deathless on the lips of men;
But, having been a name, to sink and be
A something which the world can do without,
Which, having been or not, would never change
The lightest pulse of fate, — this is indeed
A cup of bitterness the worst to taste,
And this thy heart shall empty to the dregs.
Endless despair shall be thy Caucasus,
And memory thy vulture; thou wilt find
Oblivion far lonelier than this peak, —
Behold thy destiny! Thou think'st it much
That I should brave thee, miserable god!
But I have braved a mightier than thou,

Even the tempting of this soaring heart,
Which might have made me, scarcely less than thou,
A god among my brethren weak and blind, —
Scarce less than thou, a pitiable thing
To be down-trodden into darkness soon.
But now I am above thee, for thou art
The bungling workmanship of fear, the block
That awes the swart Barbarian; but I
Am what myself have made, — a nature wise
With finding in itself the types of all, —
With watching from the dim verge of the time
What things to be are visible in the gleams
Thrown forward on them from the luminous past, —
Wise with the history of its own frail heart,
With reverence and sorrow, and with love,
Broad as the world, for freedom and for man.

Thou and all strength shall crumble, except Love,
By whom and for whose glory, ye shall cease:
And, when thou art but a dim moaning heard
From out the pitiless glooms of Chaos, I
Shall be a power and a memory,
A name to fright all tyrants with, a light
Unsetting as the pole-star, a great voice
Heard in the breathless pauses of the fight
By truth and freedom ever waged with wrong,
Clear as a silver trumpet, to awake
Huge echoes that from age to age live on
In kindred spirits, giving them a sense
Of boundless power from boundless suffering wrung:
And many a glazing eye shall smile to see
The memory of my triumph, (for to meet
Wrong with endurance, and to overcome
The present with a heart that looks beyond,.
Are triumph,) like a prophet eagle, perch
Upon the sacred banner of the Right.
Evil springs up, and flowers, and bears no seed,
And feeds the green earth with its swift decay,
Leaving it richer for the growth of truth;
But Good, once put in action or in thought,
Like a strong oak, doth from its boughs shed down
The ripe germs of a forest.   Thou, weak god,
Shalt fade and be forgotten! but this soul,

Fresh-living still in the serene abyss,
In every heaving shall partake, that grows
From heart to heart among the sons of men, —
As the ominous hum before the earthquake runs
Far through the Ægean from roused isle to isle, —
Foreboding wreck to palaces and shrines,
And mighty rents in many a cavernous error
That darkens the free light to man : — This heart,
Unscarred by thy grim vulture, as the truth
Grows but more lovely 'neath the beaks and claws
Of Harpies blind that fain would soil it, shall
In all the throbbing exultations share
That wait on freedom's triumphs, and in all
The glorious agonies of martyr-spirits, —
Sharp lightning-throes to split the jagged clouds
That veil the future, showing them the end, —
Pain's thorny crown for constancy and truth,
Girding the temples like a wreath of stars.
This is a thought, that, like a fabled laurel,
Makes my faith thunder-proof; and thy dread bolts
Fall on me like the silent flakes of snow
On the hoar brows of aged Caucasus:
But, O thought far more blissful, they can rend
This cloud of flesh, and make my soul a star!

Unleash thy crouching thunders now, O Jove!
Free this high heart, which, a poor captive long,
Doth knock to be let forth, this heart which still,
In its invincible manhood, overtops
Thy puny godship, as this mountain doth
The pines that moss its roots. O, even now,
While from my peak of suffering I look down,
Beholding with a far-spread gush of hope
The sunrise of that Beauty, in whose face,
Shone all around with love, no man shall look
But straightway like a god he is uplift
Unto the throne long empty for his sake,
And clearly oft foreshadowed in wide dreams
By his free inward nature, which nor thou,
Nor any anarch after thee, can bind
From working its great doom, — now, now set free
This essence, not to die, but to become
Part of that awful Presence which doth haunt

L

The palaces of tyrants, to hunt off,
With its grim eyes and fearful whisperings
And hideous sense of utter loneliness,
All hope of safety, all desire of peace,
All but the loathed forefeeling of blank death, —
Part of that spirit which doth ever brood
In patient calm on the unpilfered nest
Of man's deep heart, till mighty thoughts grow fledged
To sail with darkening shadow o'er the world,
Filling with dread such souls as dare not trust
In the unfailing energy of Good,
Until they swoop, and their pale quarry make
Of some o'erbloated wrong, — that spirit which
Scatters great hopes in the seed-field of man,
Like acorns among grain, to grow and be
A roof for freedom in all coming time!

But no, this cannot be; for ages yet,
In solitude unbroken, shall I hear
The angry Caspian to the Euxine shout,
And Euxine answer with a muffled roar,
On either side storming the giant walls
Of Caucasus with leagues of climbing foam,
(Less, from my height, than flakes of downy snow,)
That draw back baffled but to hurl again,
Snatched up in wrath and horrible turmoil,
Mountain on mountain, as the Titans erst,
My brethren, scaling the high seat of Jove,
Heaved Pelion upon Ossa's shoulders broad
In vain emprise. The moon will come and go
With her monotonous vicissitude;
Once beautiful, when I was free to walk
Among my fellows, and to interchange
The influence benign of loving eyes,
But now by aged use grown wearisome; —
False thought! most false! for how could I endure
These crawling centuries of lonely woe
Unshamed by weak complaining, but for thee,
Loneliest, save me, of all created things,
Mild-eyed Astarte, my best comforter,
With thy pale smile of sad benignity?

Year after year will pass away and seem
To me, in mine eternal agony,

But as the shadows of dumb summer clouds,
Which I have watched so often darkening o'er
The vast Sarmatian plain, league-wide at first,
But, with still swiftness lessening on and on
Till cloud and shadow meet and mingle where
The gray horizon fades into the sky,
Far, far to the northward. Yes, for ages yet
Must I lie here upon my altar huge,
A sacrifice for man. Sorrow will be,
As it hath been, his portion; endless doom,
While the immortal with the mortal linked
Dreams of its wings and pines for what it dreams,
With upward yearn unceasing. Better so:
For wisdom is meek sorrow's patient child,
And empire over self, and all the deep
Strong charities that make men seem like gods;
And love, that makes them be gods, from her breasts
Sucks in the milk that makes mankind one blood.
Good never comes unmixed, or so it seems,
Having two faces, as some images
Are carved, of foolish gods; one face is ill;
But one heart lies beneath, and that is good,
As are all hearts, when we explore their depths.
Therefore, great heart, bear up! thou art but type
Of what all lofty spirits endure, that fain
Would win men back to strength and peace through love:
Each hath his lonely peak, and on each heart
Envy, or scorn, or hatred, tears lifelong
With vulture beak; yet the high soul is left;
And faith, which is but hope grown wise; and love
And patience, which at last shall overcome.
 1843.

SONG.

  VIOLET! sweet violet!
  Thine eyes are full of tears;
   Are they wet
   Even yet
  With the thought of other years?
  Or with gladness are they full,
  For the night so beautiful,
  And longing for those far-off spheres?

Loved-one of my youth thou wast,
Of my merry youth,
    And I see,
    Tearfully,
All the fair and sunny past,
All its openness and truth,
Ever fresh and green in thee
As the moss is in the sea.

Thy little heart, that hath with love
Grown colored like the sky above,
On which thou lookest ever,
    Can it know
    All the woe
Of hope for what returneth never,
All the sorrow and the longing
To these hearts of ours belonging ?

    Out on it! no foolish pining
      For the sky
      Dims thine eye,
    Or for the stars so calmly shining;
    Like thee let this soul of mine
Take hue from that wherefor I long,
Self-stayed and high, serene and strong,
Not satisfied with hoping — but divine.
    Violet! dear violet!
    Thy blue eyes are only wet
With joy and love of him who sent thee,
And for the fulfilling sense
Of that glad obedience
Which made thee all that Nature meant thee!
    1841.

ROSALINE.

Thou look'dst on me all yesternight,
Thine eyes were blue, thy hair was bright
As when we murmured our troth-plight
Beneath the thick stars, Rosaline!
Thy hair was braided on thy head,
As on the day we two were wed,

Mine eyes scarce knew if thou wert dead,
But my shrunk heart knew, Rosaline!

The death-watch ticked behind the wall,
The blackness rustled like a pall,
The moaning wind did rise and fall
Among the bleak pines, Rosaline!
My heart beat thickly in mine ears;
The lids may shut out fleshly fears,
But still the spirit sees and hears, —
Its eyes are lidless, Rosaline!

A wildness rushing suddenly,
A knowing some ill-shape is nigh,
A wish for death, a fear to die, —
Is not this vengeance, Rosaline?
A loneliness that is not lone,
A love quite withered up and gone,
A strong soul trampled from its throne, —
What wouldst thou further, Rosaline?

'T is drear such moonless nights as these,
Strange sounds are out upon the breeze,
And the leaves shiver in the trees,
And then thou comest, Rosaline!
I seem to hear the mourners go,
With long black garments trailing slow,
And plumes anodding to and fro,
As once I heard them, Rosaline!

Thy shroud is all of snowy white,
And, in the middle of the night,
Thou standest moveless and upright,
Gazing upon me, Rosaline!
There is no sorrow in thine eyes,
But evermore that meek surprise, —
O, God! thy gentle spirit tries
To deem me guiltless, Rosaline!

Above thy grave the robin sings,
And swarms of bright and happy things
Flit all about with sunlit wings, —
But I am cheerless, Rosaline!
The violets on the hillock toss,

The gravestone is o'ergrown with moss;
For nature feels not any loss, —
But I am cheerless, Rosaline!

1 did not know when thou wast dead;
A blackbird whistling overhead
Thrilled through my brain; I would have fled,
But dared not leave thee, Rosaline!
The sun rolled down, and very soon,
Like a great fire, the awful moon
Rose, stained with blood, and then a swoon
Crept chilly o'er me, Rosaline!

The stars came out; and, one by one,
Each angel from his silver throne
Looked down and saw what I had done;
I dared not hide me, Rosaline!
I crouched; I feared thy corpse would cry
Against me to God's quiet sky,
I thought I saw the blue lips try
To utter something, Rosaline!

I waited with a maddened grin
To hear that voice all icy thin
Slide forth and tell my deadly sin
To hell and heaven, Rosaline!
But no voice came, and then it seemed
That, if the very corpse had screamed,
The sound like sunshine glad had streamed
Through that dark stillness, Rosaline!

And then, amid the silent night,
I screamed with horrible delight,
And in my brain an awful light
Did seem to crackle, Rosaline!
It is my curse! sweet memories fall
From me like snow, — and only all
Of that one night, like cold worms crawl
My doomed heart over, Rosaline!

Why wilt thou haunt me with thine eyes,
Wherein such blessed memories,
Such pitying forgiveness lies,
Than hate more bitter, Rosaline?

Woe 's me ! I know that love so high
As thine, true soul, could never die,
And with mean clay in churchyard lie, —
Would it might be so, Rosaline!
1841.

THE SHEPHERD OF KING ADMETUS.

THERE came a youth upon the earth,
  Some thousand years ago,
Whose slender hands were nothing worth,
Whether to plough, or reap, or sow.

Upon an empty tortoise-shell
  He stretched some chords, and drew
Music that made men's bosoms swell
Fearless, or brimmed their eyes with dew.

Then King Admetus, one who had
  Pure taste by right divine,
Decreed his singing not too bad
To hear between the cups of wine:

And so, well-pleased with being soothed
  Into a sweet half-sleep,
Three times his kingly beard he smoothed,
And made him viceroy o'er his sheep.

His words were simple words enough,
  And yet he used them so,
That what in other mouths was rough
In his seemed musical and low.

Men called him but a shiftless youth,
  In whom no good they saw;
And yet, unwittingly, in truth,
They made his careless words their law.

They knew not how he learned at all,
  For idly, hour by hour,
He sat and watched the dead leaves fall,
Or mused upon a common flower.

It seemed the loveliness of things
   Did teach him all their use,
For, in mere weeds, and stones, and springs,
He found a healing power profuse.

Men granted that his speech was wise,
   But, when a glance they caught
Of his slim grace and woman's eyes,
They laughed, and called him good-for-naught.

Yet after he was dead and gone,
   And e'en his memory dim,
Earth seemed more sweet to live upon,
More full of love, because of him.

And day by day more holy grew
   Each spot where he had trod,
Till after-poets only knew
Their first-born brother as a god.
   1842.

THE TOKEN.

It is a mere wild rosebud,
   Quite sallow now, and dry,
Yet there 's something wondrous in it, —
   Some gleams of days gone by, —
Dear sights and sounds that are to me
The very moons of memory,
And stir my heart's blood far below
Its short-lived waves of joy and woe.

Lips must fade and roses wither,
   All sweet times be o'er, —
They only smile, and, murmuring "Thither!"
   Stay with us no more :
And yet ofttimes a look or smile,
Forgotten in a kiss's while,
Years after from the dark will start,
And flash across the trembling heart.

Thou hast given me many roses,
   But never one, like this,

O'erfloods both sense and spirit
    With such a deep, wild bliss;
We must have instincts that glean up
Sparse drops of this life in the cup,
Whose taste shall give us all that we
Can prove of immortality.

Earth's stablest things are shadows,
    And, in the life to come,
Haply some chance-saved trifle
    May tell of this old home:
As now sometimes we seem to find,
In a dark crevice of the mind,
Some relic, which, long pondered o'er,
Hints faintly at a life before.

AN INCIDENT IN A RAILROAD CAR.

HE spoke of Burns: men rude and rough
Pressed round to hear the praise of one
Whose heart was made of manly, simple stuff,
    As homespun as their own.

And, when he read, they forward leaned,
    Drinking, with thirsty hearts and ears,
His brook-like songs whom glory never weaned
    From humble smiles and tears.

Slowly there grew a tender awe,
    Sun-like, o'er faces brown and hard,
As if in him who read they felt and saw
    Some presence of the bard.

It was a sight for sin and wrong
    And slavish tyranny to see,
A sight to make our faith more pure and strong
    In high humanity.

I thought, these men will carry hence
    Promptings their former life above,
And something of a finer reverence
    For beauty, truth, and love.

God scatters love on every side,
Freely among his children all,
And always hearts are lying open wide,
Wherein some grains may fall.

There is no wind but soweth seeds
Of a more true and open life,
Which burst, unlooked-for, into high-souled deeds,
With wayside beauty rife.

We find within these souls of ours
Some wild germs of a higher birth,
Which in the poet's tropic heart bear flowers
Whose fragrance fills the earth.

Within the hearts of all men lie
These promises of wider bliss,
Which blossom into hopes that cannot die,
In sunny hours like this.

All that hath been majestical
In life or death, since time began,
Is native in the simple heart of all,
The angel heart of man.

And thus, among the untaught poor,
Great deeds and feelings find a home,
That cast in shadow all the golden lore
Of classic Greece and Rome.

O, mighty brother-soul of man,
Where'er thou art, in low or high,
Thy skiey arches with exulting span
O'er-roof infinity!

All thoughts that mould the age begin
Deep down within the primitive soul,
And from the many slowly upward win
To one who grasps the whole:

In his wide brain the feeling deep
That struggled on the many's tongue
Swells to a tide of thought, whose surges leap
O'er the weak thrones of wrong.

All thought begins in feeling, — wide
  In the great mass its base is hid,
And, narrowing up to thought, stands glorified,
    A moveless pyramid.

  Nor is he far astray who deems
  That every hope, which rises and grows broad
In the world's heart, by ordered impulse streams
    From the great heart of God.

  God wills, man hopes : in common souls
  Hope is but vague and undefined,
Till from the poet's tongue the message rolls
    A blessing to his kind.

  Never did Poesy appear
  So full of heaven to me, as when
I saw how it would pierce through pride and fear
    To the lives of coarsest men.

  It may be glorious to write
  Thoughts that shall glad the two or three
High souls, like those far stars that come in sight
    Once in a century ; —

  But better far it is to speak
  One simple word, which now and then
Shall waken their free nature in the weak
    And friendless sons of men ;

  To write some earnest verse or line,
  Which, seeking not the praise of art,
Shall make a clearer faith and manhood shine
    In the untutored heart.

  He who doth this, in verse or prose,
  May be forgotten in his day,
But surely shall be crowned at last with those
    Who live and speak for aye.

1842.

RHŒCUS.

GOD sends his teachers unto every age,
To every clime, and every race of men,
With revelations fitted to their growth
And shape of mind, nor gives the realm of Truth
Into the selfish rule of one sole race:
Therefore each form of worship that hath swayed
The life of man, and given it to grasp
The master-key of knowledge, reverence,
Enfolds some germs of goodness and of right;
Else never had the eager soul, which loathes
The slothful down of pampered ignorance,
Found in it even a moment's fitful rest.

There is an instinct in the human heart
Which makes that all the fables it hath coined,
To justify the reign of its belief
And strengthen it by beauty's right divine,
Veil in their inner cells a mystic gift,
Which, like the hazel twig, in faithful hands,
Points surely to the hidden springs of truth.
For, as in nature naught is made in vain,
But all things have within their hull of use
A wisdom and a meaning which may speak
Of spiritual secrets to the ear
Of spirit; so, in whatsoe'er the heart
Hath fashioned for a solace to itself,
To make its inspirations suit its creed,
And from the niggard hands of falsehood wring
Its needful food of truth, there ever is
A sympathy with Nature, which reveals,
Not less than her own works, pure gleams of light
And earnest parables of inward lore.
Hear now this fairy legend of old Greece,
As full of freedom, youth, and beauty still
As the immortal freshness of that grace
Carved for all ages on some Attic frieze.

A youth named Rhœcus, wandering in the wood,
Saw an old oak just trembling to its fall,
And, feeling pity of so fair a tree,
He propped its gray trunk with admiring care,

And with a thoughtless footstep loitered on.
But, as he turned, he heard a voice behind
That murmured "Rhœcus!" 'T was as if the leaves,
Stirred by a passing breath, had murmured it,
And, while he paused bewildered, yet again
It murmured "Rhœcus!" softer than a breeze.
He started and beheld with dizzy eyes
What seemed the substance of a happy dream
Stand there before him, spreading a warm glow
Within the green glooms of the shadowy oak.
It seemed a woman's shape, yet all too fair
To be a woman, and with eyes too meek
For any that were wont to mate with gods.
All naked like a goddess stood she there,
And like a goddess all too beautiful
To feel the guilt-born earthliness of shame.
"Rhœcus, I am the Dryad of this tree,"
Thus she began, dropping her low-toned words
Serene, and full, and clear, as drops of dew,
"And with it I am doomed to live and die;
The rain and sunshine are my caterers,
Nor have I other bliss than simple life;
Now ask me what thou wilt, that I can give,
And with a thankful joy it shall be thine."

Then Rhœcus, with a flutter at the heart,
Yet, by the prompting of such beauty, bold,
Answered: "What is there that can satisfy
The endless craving of the soul but love?
Give me thy love, or but the hope of that
Which must be evermore my spirit's goal."
After a little pause she said again,
But with a glimpse of sadness in her tone,
"I give it, Rhœcus, though a perilous gift;
An hour before the sunset meet me here."
And straightway there was nothing he could see
But the green glooms beneath the shadowy oak,
And not a sound came to his straining ears
But the low trickling rustle of the leaves,
And far away upon an emerald slope
The falter of an idle shepherd's pipe.

Now, in those days of simpleness and faith,
Men did not think that happy things were dreams

Because they overstepped the narrow bourne
Of likelihood, but reverently deemed
Nothing too wondrous or too beautiful
To be the guerdon of a daring heart.
So Rhœcus made no doubt that he was blest,
And all along unto the city's gate
Earth seemed to spring beneath him as he walked,
The clear, broad sky looked bluer than its wont,
And he could scarce believe he had not wings
Such sunshine seemed to glitter through his veins
Instead of blood, so light he felt and strange.

Young Rhœcus had a faithful heart enough,
But one that in the present dwelt too much,
And, taking with blithe welcome whatsoe'er
Chance gave of joy, was wholly bound in that,
Like the contented peasant of a vale,
Deemed it the world, and never looked beyond.
So, haply meeting in the afternoon
Some comrades who were playing at the dice
He joined them and forgot all else beside.

The dice were rattling at the merriest,
And Rhœcus, who had met but sorry luck,
Just laughed in triumph at a happy throw,
When through the room there hummed a yellow bee
That buzzed about his ear with down-dropped legs
As if to light. And Rhœcus laughed and said,
Feeling how red and flushed he was with loss,
"By Venus! does he take me for a rose?"
And brushed him off with rough, impatient hand.
But still the bee came back, and thrice again
Rhœcus did beat him off with growing wrath.
Then through the window flew the wounded bee,
And Rhœcus, tracking him with angry eyes,
Saw a sharp mountain-peak of Thessaly
Against the red disc of the setting sun, —
And instantly the blood sank from his heart,
As if its very walls had caved away.
Without a word he turned, and, rushing forth,
Ran madly through the city and the gate,
And o'er the plain, which now the wood's long shade,
By the low sun thrown forward broad and dim,
Darkened wellnigh unto the city's wall.

Quite spent and out of breath he reached the tree,
And, listening fearfully, he heard once more
The low voice murmur "Rhœcus!" close at hand:
Whereat he looked around him, but could see
Naught but the deepening glooms beneath the oak.
Then sighed the voice, "Oh, Rhœcus! nevermore
Shalt thou behold me or by day or night,
Me, who would fain have blessed thee with a love
More ripe and bounteous than ever yet
Filled up with nectar any mortal heart:
But thou didst scorn my humble messenger,
And sent'st him back to me with bruisèd wings.
We spirits only show to gentle eyes.
We ever ask an undivided love,
And he who scorns the least of Nature's works
Is thenceforth exiled and shut out from all.
Farewell! for thou canst never see me more."

Then Rhœcus beat his breast, and groaned aloud
And cried, "Be pitiful! forgive me yet
This once, and I shall never need it more!"
"Alas!" the voice returned, "'t is thou art blind,
Not I unmerciful; I can forgive,
But have no skill to heal thy spirit's eyes;
Only the soul hath power o'er itself."
With that again there murmured "Nevermore!"
And Rhœcus after heard no other sound,
Except the rattling of the oak's crisp leaves,
Like the long surf upon a distant shore,
Raking the sea-worn pebbles up and down.
The night had gathered round him: o'er the plain
The city sparkled with its thousand lights,
And sounds of revel fell upon his ear
Harshly and like a curse; above, the sky,
With all its bright sublimity of stars,
Deepened, and on his forehead smote the breeze;
Beauty was all around him and delight,
But from that eve he was alone on earth.

THE FALCON.

I KNOW a falcon swift and peerless
 As e'er was cradled in the pine;
No bird had ever eye so fearless,
 Or wings so strong as this of mine.

The winds not better love to pilot
 A cloud with molten gold o'errun,
Than him, a little burning islet,
 A star above the coming sun.

For with a lark's heart he doth tower,
 By a glorious, upward instinct drawn;
No bee nestles deeper in the flower
 Than he in the bursting rose of dawn.

No harmless dove, no bird that singeth,
 Shudders to see him overhead;
The rush of his fierce swooping bringeth
 To innocent hearts no thrill of dread.

Let fraud and wrong and baseness shiver,
 For still between them and the sky
The falcon Truth hangs poised forever
 And marks them with his vengeful eye.

TRIAL.

I.

WHETHER the idle prisoner through his grate
Watches the waving of the grass-tuft small,
Which, having colonized its rift i' the wall,
Takes its free risk of good or evil fate,
And, from the sky's just helmet draws its lot
Daily of shower or sunshine, cold or hot; —
Whether the closer captive of a creed,
Cooped up from birth to grind out endless chaff,
Sees through his treadmill-bars the noonday laugh,
And feels in vain his crumpled pinions breed; —
Whether the Georgian slave look up and mark,
With bellying sails puffed full, the tall cloud-bark

Sink northward slowly, — thou alone seem'st good,
Fair only thou, O Freedom, whose desire
Can light in muddiest souls quick seeds of fire,
And strain life's chords to the old heroic mood.

II.

Yet are there other gifts more fair than thine,
Nor can I count him happiest who has never
Been forced with his own hand his chains to sever,
And for himself find out the way divine;
He never knew the aspirer's glorious pains,
He never earned the struggle's priceless gains.
O, block by block, with sore and sharp endeavor,
Lifelong we build these human natures up
Into a temple fit for freedom's shrine,
And Trial ever consecrates the cup
Wherefrom we pour her sacrificial wine.

A REQUIEM.

Ay, pale and silent maiden,
    Cold as thou liest there,
Thine was the sunniest nature
    That ever drew the air,
The wildest and most wayward,
    And yet so gently kind,
Thou seemedst but to body
    A breath of summer wind.

Into the eternal shadow
    That girds our life around,
Into the infinite silence
    Wherewith Death's shore is bound,
Thou hast gone forth, belovèd!
    And I were mean to weep,
That thou hast left Life's shallows,
    And dost possess the Deep.

Thou liest low and silent,
    Thy heart is cold and still,
Thine eyes are shut forever,
    And Death hath had his will;

M

He loved and would have taken,
　I loved and would have kept,
We strove, — and he was stronger,
　And I have never wept.

Let him possess thy body,
　Thy soul is still with me,
More sunny and more gladsome
　Than it was wont to be:
Thy body was a fetter
　That bound me to the flesh,
Thank God that it is broken,
　And now I live afresh!

Now I can see thee clearly;
　The dusky cloud of clay,
That hid thy starry spirit,
　Is rent and blown away:
To earth I give thy body,
　Thy spirit to the sky,
I saw its bright wings growing,
　And knew that thou must fly.

Now I can love thee truly,
　For nothing comes between
The senses and the spirit,
　The seen and the unseen;
Lifts the eternal shadow,
　The silence bursts apart,
And the soul's boundless future
　Is present in my heart.

A PARABLE.

Worn and footsore was the Prophet,
　When he gained the holy hill;
"God has left the earth," he murmured,
　"Here his presence lingers still.

"God of all the olden prophets,
　Wilt thou speak with men no more?
Have I not as truly served thee,
　As thy chosen ones of yore?

"Hear me, guider of my fathers,
　Lo! a humble heart is mine;
By thy mercy I beseech thee,
　Grant thy servant but a sign!"

Bowing then his head, he listened
　For an answer to his prayer;
No loud burst of thunder followed,
　Not a murmur stirred the air: —

But the tuft of moss before him
　Opened while he waited yet,
And, from out the rock's hard bosom,
　Sprang a tender violet.

"God! I thank thee," said the Prophet
　"Hard of heart and blind was I,
Looking to the holy mountain
　For the gift of prophecy.

"Still thou speakest with thy children
　Freely as in eld sublime;
Humbleness, and love, and patience,
　Still give empire over time.

"Had I trusted in my nature,
　And had faith in lowly things,
Thou thyself wouldst then have sought me,
　And set free my spirit's wings.

"But I looked for signs and wonders,
　That o'er men should give me sway,
Thirsting to be more than mortal,
　I was even less than clay.

"Ere I entered on my journey,
　As I girt my loins to start,
Ran to me my little daughter,
　The beloved of my heart; —

"In her hand she held a flower,
　Like to this as like may be,
Which, beside my very threshold,
　She had plucked and brought to me."
　1842.

A GLANCE BEHIND THE CURTAIN.

WE see but half the causes of our deeds,
Seeking them wholly in the outer life,
And heedless of the encircling spirit-world,
Which, though unseen, is felt, and sows in us
All germs of pure and world-wide purposes.
From one stage of our being to the next
We pass unconscious o'er a slender bridge,
The momentary work of unseen hands,
Which crumbles down behind us; looking back,
We see the other shore, the gulf between,
And, marvelling how we won to where we stand,
Content ourselves to call the builder Chance,
We trace the wisdom to the apple's fall,
Not to the birth-throes of a mighty Truth
Which, for long ages in blank Chaos dumb,
Yet yearned to be incarnate, and had found
At last a spirit meet to be the womb
From which it might be born to bless mankind, —
Not to the soul of Newton, ripe with all
The hoarded thoughtfulness of earnest years,
And waiting but one ray of sunlight more
To blossom fully.

                 But whence came that ray?
We call our sorrows Destiny, but ought
Rather to name our high successes so.
Only the instincts of great souls are Fate,
And have predestined sway: all other things,
Except by leave of us, could never be.
For Destiny is but the breath of God
Still moving in us, the last fragment left
Of our unfallen nature, waking oft
Within our thought, to beckon us beyond
The narrow circle of the seen and known,
And always tending to a noble end,
As all things must that overrule the soul,
And for a space unseat the helmsman, Will.
The fate of England and of freedom once
Seemed wavering in the heart of one plain man,
One step of his and the great dial-hand,
That marks the destined progress of the world

In the eternal round from wisdom on
To higher wisdom, had been made to pause
A hundred years. That step he did not take, —
He knew not why, nor we, but only God, —
And lived to make his simple oaken chair
More terrible and grandly beautiful,
More full of majesty than any throne
Before or after, of a British king.

Upon the pier stood two stern-visaged men,
Looking to where a little craft lay moored,
Swayed by the lazy current of the Thames,
Which weltered by in muddy listlessness.
Grave men they were, and battlings of fierce thought
Had trampled out all softness from their brows,
And ploughed rough furrows there before their time,
For another crop than such as homebred Peace
Sows broadcast in the willing soil of Youth.
Care, not of self, but of the commonweal,
Had robbed their eyes of youth, and left instead
A look of patient power and iron will,
And something fiercer, too, that gave broad hint
Of the plain weapons girded at their sides.
The younger had an aspect of command, —
Not such as trickles down, a slender stream,
In the shrunk channel of a great descent, —
But such as lies entowered in heart and head,
And an arm prompt to do the 'hests of both.
His was a brow where gold were out of place,
And yet it seemed right worthy of a crown,
(Though he despised such,) were it only made
Of iron, or some serviceable stuff
That would have matched his sinewy, brown face.
The elder, although he hardly seemed,
(Care makes so little of some five short years,)
Had a clear, honest face, whose rough-hewn strength
Was mildened by the scholar's wiser heart
To sober courage, such as best befits
The unsullied temper of a well-taught mind,
Yet so remained that one could plainly guess
The hushed volcano smouldering underneath.
He spoke: the other, hearing, kept his gaze
Still fixed, as on some problem in the sky.

"O, Cromwell, we are fallen on evil times!
There was a day when England had wide room
For honest men as well as foolish kings;
But now the uneasy stomach of the time
Turns squeamish at them both. Therefore let us
Seek out that savage clime, where men as yet
Are free: there sleeps the vessel on the tide,
Her languid canvas drooping for the wind;
Give us but that, and what need we to fear
This Order of the Council? The free waves
Will not say, No, to please a wayward king,
Nor will the winds turn traitors at his beck:
All things are fitly cared for, and the Lord
Will watch as kindly o'er the exodus
Of us his servants now, as in old time.
We have no cloud or fire, and haply we
May not pass dry-shod through the ocean-stream;
But, saved or lost, all things are in His hand."
So spake he, and meantime the other stood
With wide gray eyes still reading the blank air,
As if upon the sky's blue wall he saw
Some mystic sentence, written by a hand
Such as of old made pale the Assyrian king,
Girt with his satraps in the blazing feast.

"Hampden! a moment since, my purpose was
To fly with thee, — for I will call it flight,
Nor flatter it with any smoother name, —
But something in me bids me not to go;
And I am one, thou knowest, who, unmoved
By what the weak deem omens, yet give heed
And reverence due to whatsoe'er my soul
Whispers of warning to the inner ear.
Moreover, as I know that God brings round
His purposes in ways undreamed by us,
And makes the wicked but his instruments
To hasten on their swift and sudden fall,
I see the beauty of his providence
In the King's order: blind, he will not let
His doom part from him, but must bid it stay
As 't were a cricket, whose enlivening chirp
He loved to hear beneath his very hearth.
Why should we fly? Nay, why not rather stay

And rear again,our Zion's crumbled walls,
Not, as of old the walls of Thebes were built,
By minstrel twanging, but, if need should be,
With the more potent music of our swords?
Think'st thou that score of men beyond the sea
Claim more God's care than all of England here?
No: when he moves His arm, it is to aid
Whole peoples, heedless if a few be crushed,
As some are ever, when the destiny
Of man takes one stride onward nearer home.
Believe it, 't is the mass of men He loves;
And, where there is most sorrow and most want,
Where the high heart of man is trodden down
The most, 't is not because He hides his face
From them in wrath, as purblind teachers prate:
Not so. there most is He, for there is He
Most needed. Men who seek for Fate abroad
Are not so near his heart as they who dare
Frankly to face her where she faces them,
On their own threshold, where their souls are strong
To grapple with and throw her; as I once,
Being yet a boy, did cast this puny king,
Who now has grown so dotard as to deem
That he can wrestle with an angry realm,
And throw the brawned Antæus of men's rights.
No, Hampden! they have half-way conquered Fate
Who go half-way to meet her, — as will I.
Freedom hath yet a work for me to do;
So speaks that inward voice which never yet
Spake falsely, when it urged the spirit on
To noble deeds for country and mankind.
And, for success, I ask no more than this, —
To bear unflinching witness to the truth.
All true, whole men succeed: for what is worth
Success's name, unless it be the thought,
The inward surety, to have carried out
A noble purpose to a noble end,
Although it be the gallows or the block?
'T is only Falsehood that doth ever need
These outward shows of gain to bolster her.
Be it we prove the weaker with our swords;
Truth only needs to be for once spoke out,
And there's such music in her, such strange rhythm,

As makes men's memories her joyous slaves,
And clings around the soul, as the sky clings
Round the mute earth, forever beautiful,
And, if o'erclouded, only to burst forth
More all-embracingly divine and clear:
Get but the truth once uttered, and 't is like
A star new-born, that drops into its place,
And which, once circling in its placid round,
Not all the tumult of the earth can shake.

" What should we do in that small colony
Of pinched fanatics, who would rather choose
Freedom to clip an inch more from their hair,
Than the great chance of setting England free?
Not there, amid the stormy wilderness,
Should we learn wisdom; or if learned, what room
To put it into act, — else worse than naught?
We learn our souls more, tossing for an hour
Upon this huge and ever-vexèd sea
Of human thought, where kingdoms go to wreck
Like fragile bubbles yonder in the stream,
Than in a cycle of New England sloth,
Broke only by some petty Indian war,
Or quarrel for a letter more or less,
In some hard word, which, spelt in either way
Not their most learned clerks can understand.
New times demand new measures and new men;
The world advances, and in time outgrows
The laws that in our fathers' day were best;
And, doubtless, after us, some purer scheme
Will be shaped out by wiser men than we,
Made wiser by the steady growth of truth.
We cannot bring Utopia by force;
But better, almost, be at work in sin;
Than in a brute inaction browse and sleep.
No man is born into the world, whose work
Is not born with him; there is always work,
And tools to work withal, for those who will;
And blessèd are the horny hands of toil!
The busy world shoves angrily aside
The man who stands with arms akimbo set,
Until occasion tells him what to do;
And he who waits to have his task marked out

Shall die and leave his errand unfulfilled.
Our time is one that calls for earnest deeds:
Reason and Government, like two broad seas,
Yearn for each other with outstretched arms
Across this narrow isthmus of the throne,
And roll their white surf higher every day.
One age moves onward, and the next builds up
Cities and gorgeous palaces, where stood
The rude log huts of those who tamed the wild,
Rearing from out the forests they had felled
The goodly framework of a fairer state;
The builder's trowel and the settler's axe
Are seldom wielded by the selfsame hand;
Ours is the harder task, yet not the less
Shall we receive the blessing for our toil
From the choice spirits of the aftertime.
My soul is not a palace of the past,
Where outworn creeds, like Rome's gray senate quake,
Hearing afar the Vandal's trumpet hoarse,
That shakes old systems with a thunder-fit.
The time is ripe, and rotten-ripe, for change;
Then let it come: I have no dread of what
Is called for by the instinct of mankind;
Nor think I that God's world will fall apart,
Because we tear a parchment more or less.
Truth is eternal, but her effluence,
With endless change is fitted to the hour;
Her mirror is turned forward to reflect
The promise of the future, not the past.
He who would win the name of truly great
Must understand his own age and the next,
And make the present ready to fulfil
Its prophecy, and with the future merge
Gently and peacefully, as wave with wave.
The future works out great men's destinies;
The present is enough for common souls,
Who, never looking forward, are indeed
Mere clay, wherein the footprints of their age
Are petrified forever: better those
Who lead the blind old giant by the hand
From out the pathless desert where he gropes,
And set him onward in his darksome way.
I do not fear to follow out the truth,

Albeit along the precipice's edge.
Let us speak plain: there is more force in names
Than most men dream of; and a lie may keep
Its throne a whole age longer, if it skulk
Behind the shield of some fair-seeming name,
Let us call tyrants, *tyrants*, and maintain,
That only freedom comes by grace of God,
And all that comes not by his grace must fall
For men in earnest have no time to waste
In patching fig-leaves for the naked truth.

" I will have one more grapple with the man
Charles Stuart: whom the boy o'ercame,
The man stands not in awe of. I, perchance,
Am one raised up by the Almighty arm
To witness some great truth to all the world.
Souls destined to o'erleap the vulgar lot,
And mould the world unto the scheme of God,
Have a fore-consciousness of their high doom,
As men are known to shiver at the heart,
When the cold shadow of some coming ill
Creeps slowly o'er their spirits unawares.
Hath Good less power of prophecy than Ill?
How else could men whom God hath called to sway
Earth's rudder, and to steer the bark of Truth,
Beating against the tempest tow'rd her port,
Bear all the mean and buzzing grievances,
The petty martyrdoms, wherewith Sin strives
To weary out the tethered hope of Faith,
The sneers, the unrecognizing look of friends,
Who worship the dead corpse of old king Custom,
Where it doth lie in state within the Church,
Striving to cover up the mighty ocean
With a man's palm, and making even the truth
Lie for them, holding up the glass reversed,
To make the hope of man seem farther off?
My God! when I read o'er the bitter lives
Of men whose eager hearts were quite too great
To beat beneath the cramped mode of the day,
And see them mocked at by the world they love,
Haggling with prejudice for pennyworths
Of that reform which their hard toil will make
The common birthright of the age to come, —

When I see this, spite of my faith in God,
I marvel how their hearts bear up so long;
Nor could they, but for this same prophecy,
This inward feeling of the glorious end.

"Deem me not fond; but in my warmer youth,
Ere my heart's bloom was soiled and brushed away,
I had great dreams of mighty things to come;
Of conquest, whether by the sword or pen
I knew not; but some conquest I would have,
Or else swift death: now wiser grown in years,
I find youth's dreams are but the flutterings
Of those strong wings whereon the soul shall soar
In aftertime to win a starry throne;
And so I cherish them, for they were lots,
Which I, a boy, cast in the helm of Fate.
Now will I draw them, since a man's right hand,
A right hand guided by an earnest soul,
With a true instinct, takes the golden prize
From out a thousand blanks. What men call luck
Is the prerogative of valiant souls,
The fealty life pays its rightful kings.
The helm is shaking now, and I will stay
To pluck my lot forth; it were sin to flee!"

So they two turned together; one to die,
Fighting for freedom on the bloody field;
The other, far more happy, to become
A name earth wears forever next her heart;
One of the few that have a right to rank
With the true Makers: for his spirit wrought
Order from Chaos; proved that right divine
Dwelt only in the excellence of truth;
And far within old Darkness' hostile lines
Advanced and pitched the shining tents of Light,
Nor shall the grateful Muse forget to tell,
That — not the least among his many claims
To deathless honor — he was Milton's friend,
A man not second among those who lived
To show us that the poet's lyre demands
An arm of tougher sinew than the sword.

    1843.

SONG.

O, MOONLIGHT deep and tender,
   A year and more agone,
Your mist of golden splendor
   Round my betrothal shone!

O, elm-leaves dark and dewy,
   The very same ye seem,
The low wind trembles through ye,
   Ye murmur in my dream!

O, river, dim with distance,
   Flow thus forever by:
A part of my existence
   Within your heart doth lie!

O, stars, ye saw our meeting,
   Two beings and one soul,
Two hearts so madly beating
   To mingle and be whole!

O, happy night, deliver
   Her kisses back to me,
Or keep them all, and give her
   A blissful dream of me!

1842.

A CHIPPEWA LEGEND.*

ἀλγεινὰ μέν μοι καὶ λέγειν ἐστὶν τάδε
ἄλγος δὲ σιγᾷν.

Æschylus, Prom. Vinct. 197.

THE old Chief, feeling now well-nigh his end,
Called his two eldest children to his side,
And gave them, in few words, his parting charge: —
"My son and daughter, me ye see no more;
The happy hunting-grounds await me, green
With change of spring and summer through the year.
But, for remembrance, after I am gone,
Be kind to little Sheemah for my sake:

---

* For the leading incidents in this tale, I am indebted to the very valuable
" Algic Researches " of Henry R. Schoolcraft, Esq.

Weakling he is and young, and knows not yet
To set the trap, or draw the seasoned bow;
Therefore of both your loves he hath more need,
And he, who needeth love, to love hath right;
It is not like our furs and stores of corn,
Whereto we claim sole title by our toil,
But the Great Spirit plants it in our hearts,
And waters it, and gives it sun, to be
The common stock and heritage of all:
Therefore be kind to Sheemah, that yourselves
May not be left deserted in your need."

Alone, beside a lake, their wigwam stood,
Far from the other dwellings of their tribe;
And, after many moons, the loneliness
Wearied the elder brother, and he said,
"Why should I dwell here all alone, shut out
From the free, natural joys that fit my age?
Lo, I am tall and strong, well skilled to hunt,
Patient of toil and hunger, and not yet
Have seen the danger which I dared not look
Full in the face; what hinders me to be
A mighty Brave and Chief among my kin?"
So, taking up his arrows and his bow,
As if to hunt, he journeyed swiftly on,
Until he gained the wigwams of his tribe,
Where, choosing out a bride, he soon forgot,
In all the fret and bustle of new life,
The little Sheemah and his father's charge.

Now when the sister found her brother gone,
And that, for many days, he came not back,
She wept for Sheemah more than for herself;
For Love bides longest in a woman's heart,
And flutters many times before he flies,
And then doth perch so nearly, that a word
May lure him back, as swift and glad as light;
And Duty lingers even when Love is gone
Oft looking out in hope of his return;
And, after Duty hath been driven forth,
Then Selfishness creeps in the last of all,
Warming her lean hands at the lonely hearth,
And crouching o'er the embers, to shut out

Whatever paltry warmth and light are left,
With avaricious greed, from all beside.
So, for long months, the sister hunted wide,
And cared for little Sheemah tenderly;
But, daily more and more, the loneliness
Grew wearisome, and to herself she sighed,
" Am I not fair ? at least the glassy pool,
That hath no cause to flatter, tells me so;
But, O, how flat and meaningless the tale,
Unless it tremble on a lover's tongue !
Beauty hath no true glass, except it be
In the sweet privacy of loving eyes."
Thus deemed she idly, and forgot the lore
Which she had learned of nature and the woods,
That beauty's chief reward is to itself,
And that the eyes of Love reflect alone
The inward fairness, which is blurred and lost
Unless kept clear and white by Duty's care
So she went forth and sought the haunts of men,
And, being wedded, in her household cares,
Soon, like the elder brother, quite forgot
The little Sheemah and her father's charge.

But Sheemah, left alone within the lodge,
Waited and waited, with a shrinking heart,
Thinking each rustle was his sister's step,
Till hope grew less and less, and then went out,
And every sound was changed from hope to fear.
Few sounds there were: — the dropping of a nut,
The squirrel's chirrup, and the jay's harsh scream,
Autumn's sad remnants of blithe Summer's cheer,
Heard at long intervals, seemed but to make
The dreadful void of silence silenter.
Soon what small store his sister left was gone,
And, through the Autumn, he made shift to live
On roots and berries, gathered in much fear
Of wolves, whose ghastly howl he heard ofttimes,
Hollow and hungry, at the dead of night.
But Winter came at last, and, when the snow,
Thick-heaped for gleaming leagues o'er hill and plain,
Spread its unbroken silence over all,
Made bold by hunger, he was fain to glean,
(More sick at heart than Ruth, and all alone,)

After the harvest of the merciless wolf,
Grim Boaz, who, sharp-ribbed and gaunt, yet feared
A thing more wild and starving than himself;
Till, by degrees, the wolf and he grew friends,
And shared together all the winter through.

    Late in the Spring, when all the ice was gone,
The elder brother, fishing in the lake,
Upon whose edge his father's wigwam stood,
Heard a low moaning noise upon the shore:
Half like a child it seemed, half like a wolf,
And straightway there was something in his heart
That said, "It is thy brother Sheemah's voice."
So, paddling swiftly to the bank, he saw,
Within a little thicket close at hand,
A child that seemed fast changing to a wolf,
From the neck downward, gray with shaggy hair
That still crept on and upward as he looked.
The face was turned away, but well he knew
That it was Sheemah's, even his brother's face.
Then with his trembling hands he hid his eyes,
And bowed his head, so that he might not see
The first look of his brother's eyes, and cried,
"O, Sheemah! O, my brother, speak to me!
Dost thou not know me, that I am thy brother?
Come to me, little Sheemah, thou shalt dwell
With me henceforth, and know no care or want!"
Sheemah was silent for a space, as if
'T were hard to summon up a human voice,
And, when he spake, the sound was of a wolf's:
"I know thee not, nor art thou what thou say'st;
I have none other brethren than the wolves,
And, till thy heart be changed from what it is,
Thou art not worthy to be called their kin."
Then groaned the other, with a choking tongue,
"Alas! my heart is changed right bitterly;
'T is shrunk and parched within me even now!"
And, looking upward fearfully, he saw
Only a wolf that shrank away and ran,
Ugly and fierce, to hide among the woods.

STANZAS ON FREEDOM.

MEN! whose boast it is that ye
Come of fathers brave and free,
If there breathe on earth a slave,
Are ye truly free and brave?
If ye do not feel the chain,
When it works a brother's pain,
Are ye not base slaves indeed,
Slaves unworthy to be freed?

Women! who shall one day bear
Sons to breathe New England air,
If ye hear, without a blush,
Deeds to make the roused blood rush
Like red lava through your veins,
For your sisters now in chains, —
Answer! are ye fit to be
Mothers of the brave and free?

Is true Freedom but to break
Fetters for our own dear sake,
And, with leathern hearts, forget
That we owe mankind a debt?
No! true freedom is to share
All the chains our brothers wear,
And, with heart and hand, to be
Earnest to make others free!

They are slaves who fear to speak
For the fallen and the weak,
They are slaves who will not choose
Hatred, scoffing, and abuse,
Rather than in silence shrink
From the truth they needs must think;
They are slaves who dare not be
In the right with two or three.

COLUMBUS.

THE cordage creaks and rattles in the wind,
With freaks of sudden hush; the reeling sea
Now thumps like solid rock beneath the stern,

Now leaps with clumsy wrath, strikes short, and, falling
Crumbled to whispery foam, slips rustling down
The broad backs of the waves, which jostle and crowd
To fling themselves upon that unknown shore,
Their used familiar since the dawn of time,
Whither this foredoomed life is guided on
To sway on triumph's hushed, aspiring poise
One glittering moment, then to break fulfilled.

How lonely is the sea's perpetual swing,
The melancholy wash of endless waves,
The sigh of some grim monster undescried,
Fear-painted on the canvas of the dark,
Shifting on his uneasy pillow of brine!
Yet night brings more companions than the day
To this drear waste; new constellations burn,
And fairer stars, with whose calm height my soul
Finds nearer sympathy than with my herd
Of earthen souls, whose vision's scanty ring
Makes me its prisoner to beat my wings
Against the cold bars of their unbelief,
Knowing in vain my own free heaven beyond.
O God! this world, so crammed with eager life,
That comes and goes and wanders back to silence
Like the idle wind, which yet man's shaping mind
Can make his drudge to swell the longing sails
Of highest endeavor, — this mad, unthrift world,
Which, every hour, throws life enough away
To make her deserts kind and hospitable,
Lets her great destinies be waved aside
By smooth, lip-reverent, formal infidels,
Who weigh the God they not believe with gold,
And find no spot in Judas, save that he,
Driving a duller bargain than he ought,
Saddled his guild with too cheap precedent.
O Faith! if thou art strong, thine opposite
Is mighty also, and the dull fool's sneer
Hath ofttimes shot chill palsy through the arm,
Just lifted to achieve its crowning deed,
And made the firm-based heart, that would have quailed
The rack or fagot, shudder like a leaf
Wrinkled with frost, and loose upon its stem.
The wicked and the weak, by some dark law,

N

Have a strange power to shut and rivet down
Their own horizon round us, to unwing
Our heaven-aspiring visions, and to blur
With surly clouds the Future's gleaming peaks,
Far seen across the brine of thankless years.
If the chosen soul could never be alone
In deep mid-silence, open-doored to God,
No greatness ever had been dreamed or done;
Among dull hearts a prophet never grew;
The nurse of full-grown souls is solitude.

The old world is effete; there man with man
Jostles, and, in the brawl for means to live,
Life is trod under-foot, — Life, the one block
Of marble that's vouchsafed wherefrom to carve
Our great thoughts, white and god-like, to shine down
The future, Life, the irredeemable block,
Which one o'er-hasty chisel-dint oft mars,
Scanting our room to cut the features out
Of our full hope, so forcing us to crown
With a mean head the perfect limbs, or leave
The god's face glowing o'er a satyr's trunk,
Failure's brief epitaph.
                         Yes, Europe's world
Reels on to judgment; there the common need,
Losing God's sacred use, to be a bond
'Twixt Me and Thee, sets each one scowlingly
O'er his own selfish hoard at bay; no state,
Knit strongly with eternal fibres up
Of all men's separate and united weals,
Self-poised and sole as stars, yet one as light.
Holds up a shape of large Humanity
To which by natural instinct every man
Pays loyalty exulting, by which all
Mould their own lives, and feel their pulses filled
With the red fiery blood of the general life,
Making them mighty in peace, as now in war
They are, even in the flush of victory, weak,
Conquering that manhood which should them subdue.
And what gift bring I to this untried world?
Shall the same tragedy be played anew,
And the same lurid curtain drop at last
On one dread desolation, one fierce crash

Of that recoil which on its makers God
Lets Ignorance and Sin and Hunger make,
Early or late ?   Or shall that commonwealth
Whose potent unity and concentric force
Can draw these scattered joints and parts of men
Into a whole ideal man once more,
Which sucks not from its limbs the life away,
But sends it flood-tide and creates itself
Over again in every citizen,
Be there built up ?   For me, I have no choice;
I might turn back to other destinies,
For one sincere key opes all Fortune's doors;
But whoso answers not God's earliest call,
Forfeits or dulls that faculty supreme
Of lying open to his genius
Which makes the wise heart certain of its ends.

Here am I; for what end God knows, not I;
Westward still points the inexorable soul:
Here am I, with no friend but the sad sea,
The beating heart of this great enterprise,
Which, without me, would stiffen in swift death;
This have I mused on, since mine eye could first
Among the stars distinguish and with joy
Rest on that God-fed Pharos of the north,
On some blue promontory of heaven lighted
That juts far out into the upper sea;
To this one hope my heart hath clung for years,
As would a foundling to the talisman
Hung round his neck by hands he knew not whose.
A poor, vile thing and dross to all beside,
Yet he therein can feel a virtue left
By the sad pressure of a mother's hand,
And unto him it still is tremulous
With palpitating haste and wet with tears,
The key to him of hope and humanness,
The coarse shell of life's pearl, Expectancy.
This hope hath been to me for love and fame,
Hath made me wholly lonely on the earth,
Building me up as in a thick-ribbed tower,
Wherewith enwalled my watching spirit burned,
Conquering its little island from the Dark,
Sole as a scholar's lamp, and heard men's steps,

In the far hurry of the outward world,
Pass dimly forth and back, sounds heard in dream
As Ganymede by the eagle was snatched up
From the gross sod to be Jove's cupbearer,
So was I lifted by my great design:
And who hath trod Olympus, from his eye
Fades not that broader outlook of the gods;
His life's low valleys overbrow earth's clouds,
And that Olympian spectre of the past
Looms towering up in sovereign memory,
Beckoning his soul from meaner heights of doom.
Had but the shadow of the Thunderer's bird,
Flashing athwart my spirit, made of me
A swift-betraying vision's Ganymede,
Yet to have greatly dreamed precludes low ends
Great days have ever such a morning-red,
On such a base great futures are built up,
And aspiration, though not put in act,
Comes back to ask its plighted troth again,
Still watches round its grave the unlaid ghost
Of a dead virtue, and makes other hopes,
Save that implacable one, seem thin and bleak
As shadows of bare trees upon the snow,
Bound freezing there by the unpitying moon.

While other youths perplexed their mandolins,
Praying that Thetis would her fingers twine
In the loose glories of her lover's hair,
And wile another kiss to keep back day,
I, stretched beneath the many-centuried shade
Of some writhed oak, the wood's Laocoön,
Did of my hope a dryad mistress make,
Whom I would woo to meet me privily,
Or underneath the stars, or when the moon
Flecked all the forest floor with scattered pearls.
O days whose memory tames to fawning down
The surly fell of Ocean's bristled neck!

I know not when this hope enthralled me first,
But from my boyhood up I loved to hear
The tall-pine-forests of the Apennine
Murmur their hoary legends of the sea,
Which hearing, I in vision clear beheld;

The sudden dark of tropic night shut down
O'er the huge whisper of great watery wastes,
The while a pair of herons trailingly
Flapped inland, where some league-wide river hurled
The yellow spoil of unconjectured realms
Far through a gulf's green silence, never scarred
By any but the Northwind's hurrying keels.
And not the pines alone; all sights and sounds
To my world-seeking heart paid fealty,
And catered for it as the Cretan bees
Brought honey to the baby Jupiter,
Who in his soft hand crushed a violet,
God-like foremusing the rough thunder's gripe;
Then did I entertain the poet's song,
My great Idea's guest, and, passing o'er
That iron bridge the Tuscan built to hell,
I heard Ulysses tell of mountain-chains
Whose adamantine links, his manacles,
The western main shook growling, and still **gnawed.**
I brooded on the wise Athenian's tale
Of happy Atlantis, and heard Björne's keel
Crunch the gray pebbles of the Vinland shore:
For I believed the poets; it is they
Who utter wisdom from the central deep,
And, listening to the inner flow of things,
Speak to the age out of eternity.

Ah me! old hermits sought for solitude
In caves and desert places of the earth,
Where their own heart-beat was the only stir
Of living thing that comforted the year;
But the bald pillar-top of Simeon,
In midnight's blankest waste, were populous,
Matched with the isolation drear and deep
Of him who pines among the swarm of men,
At once a new thought's king and prisoner,
Feeling the truer life within his life,
The fountain of his spirit's prophecy,
Sinking away and wasting, drop by drop,
In the ungrateful sands of sceptic ears.
He in the palace-aisles of untrod woods
Doth walk a king; for him the pent-up cell
Widens beyond the circles of the stars,

And all the sceptred spirits of the past
Come thronging in to greet him as their peer;
But in the market-place's glare and throng
He sits apart, an exile, and his brow
Aches with the mocking memory of its crown.
But to the spirit select there is no choice;
He cannot say, This will I do, or that,
For the cheap means putting Heaven's ends in pawn,
And bartering his bleak rocks, the freehold stern
Of destiny's first-born, for smoother fields
That yield no crop of self-denying will;
A hand is stretched to him from out the dark,
Which grasping without question, he is led
Where there is work that he must do for God.
The trial still is the strength's complement,
And the uncertain, dizzy path that scales
The sheer heights of supremest purposes
Is steeper to the angel than the child.
Chances have laws as fixed as planets have,
And disappointment's dry and bitter root,
Envy's harsh berries, and the choking pool
Of the world's scorn, are the right mother-milk
To the tough hearts that pioneer their kind,
And break a pathway to those unknown realms
That in the earth's broad shadow lie enthralled;
Endurance is the crowning quality,
And patience all the passion of great hearts;
These are their stay, and when the leaden world
Sets its hard face against their fateful thought,
And brute strength, like a scornful conqueror,
Clangs his huge mace down in the other scale,
The inspired soul but flings his patience in,
And slowly that outweighs the ponderous globe, —
One faith against a whole earth's unbelief,
One soul against the flesh of all mankind.

Thus ever seems it when my soul can hear
The voice that errs not; then my triumph gleams,
O'er the blank ocean beckoning, and all night
My heart flies on before me as I sail;
Far on I see my lifelong enterprise,
Which rose like Ganges mid the freezing snows
Of a world's sordidness, sweep broadening down,

And, gathering to itself a thousand streams,
Grow sacred ere it mingle with the sea;
I see the ungated wall of chaos old,
With blocks Cyclopean hewn of solid night,
Fade like a wreath of unreturning mist
Before the irreversible feet of light; —
And lo, with what clear omen in the east
On day's gray threshold stands the eager dawn,
Like young Leander rosy from the sea
Glowing at Hero's lattice !

     One day more
These muttering shoalbrains leave the helm to me.
God, let me not in their dull ooze be stranded;
Let not this one frail bark, to hollow which
I have dug out the pith and sinewy heart
Of my aspiring life's fair trunk, be so
Cast up to warp and blacken in the sun,
Just as the opposing wind 'gins whistle off
His cheek-swollen mates, and from the leaning mast
Fortune's full sail strains forward !
      One poor day ! —
Remember whose and not how short it is !
It is God's day, it is Columbus's.
A lavish day ! One day, with life and heart,
Is more than time enough to find a world.
 1844.

AN INCIDENT OF THE FIRE AT HAMBURG.

THE tower of old Saint Nicholas soared upward to the
  skies,
Like some huge piece of Nature's make, the growth of
  centuries;
You could not deem its crowding spires a work of human
  art,
They seemed to struggle lightward from a sturdy living
  heart.

Not Nature's self more freely speaks in crystal or in oak,
Than, through the pious builder's hand, in that gray pile
  she spoke;

And as from acorn springs the oak, so, freely and alone,
Sprang from his heart this hymn to God, sung in obedient
stone.

It seemed a wondrous freak of chance, so perfect, yet so
rough,
A whim of Nature crystallized slowly in granite tough;
The thick spires yearned towards the sky in quaint,
harmonious lines,
And in broad sunlight basked and slept, like a grove of
blasted pines.

Never did rock or stream or tree lay claim with better
right
To all the adorning sympathies of shadow and of light;
And, in that forest petrified, as forester there dwells
Stout Herman, the old sacristan, sole lord of all its bells.

Surge leaping after surge, the fire roared onward red as
blood,
Till half of Hamburg lay engulfed beneath the eddying
flood;
For miles away, the fiery spray poured down its deadly
rain,
And back and forth the billows sucked, and paused, and
burst again.

From square to square with tiger leaps panted the lustful
fire,
The air to leeward shuddered with the gasps of its desire;
And church and palace, which even now stood whelmed
but to the knee,
Lift their black roofs like breakers lone amid the whirl-
ing sea.

Up in his tower old Herman sat and watched with quiet
look;
His soul had trusted God too long to be at last forsook;
He could not fear, for surely God a pathway would unfold
Through this red sea for faithful hearts, as once he did
of old.

But scarcely can he cross himself, or on his good saint
call,

Before the sacrilegious flood o'erleaped the churchyard
    wall;
And, ere a *pater* half was said, mid smoke and crackling
    glare,
His island tower scarce juts its head above the wide
    despair.

Upon the peril's desperate peak his heart stood up sub-
    lime;
His first thought was for God above, his next was for his
    chime;
"Sing now and make your voices heard in hymns of
    praise," cried he,
"As did the Israelites of old, safe walking through the
    sea!

"Through this red sea our God hath made the pathway
    safe to shore;
Our promised land stands full in sight; shout now as
    ne'er before!"
And as the tower came crushing down, the bells, in clear
    accord,
Pealed forth the grand old German hymn, — "All good
    souls, praise the Lord!"

THE SOWER.

I saw a Sower walking slow
    Across the earth, from east to west;
His hair was white as mountain snow,
    His head drooped forward on his breast.

With shrivelled hands he flung his seed,
    Nor ever turned to look behind;
Of sight or sound he took no heed;
    It seemed he was both deaf and blind.

His dim face showed no soul beneath,
    Yet in my heart I felt a stir,
As if I looked upon the sheath
    That once had clasped Excalibur.

I heard, as still the seed he cast,
  How, crooning to himself, he sung, —
"I sow again the holy Past,
  The happy days when I was young.

"Then all was wheat without a tare,
  Then all was righteous, fair, and true;
And I am he whose thoughtful care
  Shall plant the Old World in the New.

"The fruitful germs I scatter free,
  With busy hand, while all men sleep;
In Europe now, from sea to sea,
  The nations bless me as they reap."

Then I looked back along his path,
  And heard the clash of steel on steel,
Where man faced man, in deadly wrath,
  While clanged the tocsin's hurrying peal.

The sky with burning towns flared red,
  Nearer the noise of fighting rolled,
And brothers' blood, by brothers shed,
  Crept, curdling, over pavements cold.

Then marked I how each germ of truth
  Which through the dotard's fingers ran
Was mated with a dragon's tooth
  Whence there sprang up an armed man.

I shouted, but he could not hear;
  Made signs, but these he could not see;
And still, without a doubt or fear,
  Broadcast he scattered anarchy.

Long to my straining ears the blast
  Brought faintly back the words he sung: —
"I sow again the holy Past,
  The happy days when I was young."

HUNGER AND COLD.

SISTERS two, all praise to you,
With your faces pinched and blue;
To the poor man you've been true
      From of old:
You can speak the keenest word,
You are sure of being heard,
From the point you're never stirred,
      Hunger and Cold!

Let sleek statesmen temporize;
Palsied are their shifts and lies
When they meet your bloodshot eyes,
      Grim and bold;
Policy you set at naught,
In their traps you'll not be caught,
You're too honest to be bought,
      Hunger and Cold!

Bolt and bar the palace-door;
While the mass of men are poor,
Naked truth grows more and more
      Uncontrolled;
You had never yet, I guess,
Any praise for bashfulness,
You can visit sans court-dress,
      Hunger and Cold!

While the music fell and rose,
And the dance reeled to its close,
Where her round of costly woes
      Fashion strolled,
I beheld with shuddering fear
Wolves' eyes through the windows peer;
Little dream they you are near,
      Hunger and Cold!

When the toiler's heart you clutch,
Conscience is not valued much,
He recks not a bloody smutch
      On his gold:
Everything to you defers,

You are potent reasoners,
At your whisper Treason stirs,
 Hunger and Cold!

Rude comparisons you draw,
Words refuse to sate your maw,
Your gaunt limbs the cobweb law
 Cannot hold:
You 're not clogged with foolish pride,
But can seize a right denied;
Somehow God is on your side,
 Hunger and Cold!

You respect no hoary wrong
More for having triumphed long;
Its past victims, haggard throng,
 From the mould
You unbury: swords and spears
Weaker are than poor men's tears,
Weaker than your silent years,
 Hunger and Cold!

Let them guard both hall and bower;
Through the window you will glower,
Patient till your reckoning hour
 Shall be tolled:
Cheeks are pale, but hands are red,
Guiltless blood may chance be shed,
But ye must and will be fed,
 Hunger and Cold!

God has plans man must not spoil,
Some were made to starve and toil,
Some to share the wine and oil,
 We are told:
Devil's theories are these,
Stifling hope and love and peace,
Framed your hideous lusts to please,
 Hunger and Cold!

Scatter ashes on thy head,
Tears of burning sorrow shed,
Earth! and be by pity led
 To Love's fold;

Ere they block the very door
With lean corpses of the poor,
And will hush for naught but gore, —
 Hunger and Cold!

1844.

THE LANDLORD.

WHAT boot your houses and your lands?
 In spite of close-drawn deed and fence,
Like water, 'twixt your cheated hands,
They slip into the graveyard's sands
 And mock your ownership's pretence.

How shall you speak to urge your right,
 Choked with that soil for which you lust
The bit of clay, for whose delight
You grasp, is mortgaged, too; Death might
 Foreclose this very day in dust.

Fence as you please, this plain poor man,
 Whose only fields are in his wit,
Who shapes the world, as best he can,
According to God's higher plan,
 Owns you and fences as is fit.

Though yours the rents, his incomes wax
 By right of eminent domain;
From factory tall to woodman's axe,
All things on earth must pay their tax,
 To feed his hungry heart and brain.

He takes you from your easy-chair,
 And what he plans, that you must do.
You sleep in down, eat dainty fare, —
He mounts his crazy garret-stair
 And starves, the landlord over you.

Feeding the clods your idlesse drains,
 You make more green six feet of soil;
His fruitful word, like suns and rains,
Partakes the seasons' bounteous pains,
 And toils to lighten human toil.

Your lands, with force or cunning got,
    Shrink to the measure of the grave;
But Death himself abridges not
The tenures of almighty thought,
    The titles of the wise and brave.

TO A PINE-TREE.

FAR up on Katahdin thou towerest,
    Purple-blue with the distance and vast;
Like a cloud o'er the lowlands thou lowerest,
    That hangs poised on a lull in the blast,
        To its fall leaning awful.

In the storm, like a prophet o'ermaddened,
    Thou singest and tossest thy branches;
Thy heart with the terror is gladdened,
    Thou forebodest the dread avalanches,
        When whole mountains swoop valeward

In the calm thou o'erstretchest the valleys
    With thine arms, as if blessings imploring,
Like an old king led forth from his palace,
    When his people to battle are pouring
        From the city beneath him.

To the lumberer asleep 'neath thy glooming
    Thou dost sing of wild billows in motion,
Till he longs to be swung mid their booming
    In the tents of the Arabs of ocean,
        Whose finned isles are their cattle.

For the gale snatches thee for his lyre,
    With mad hand crashing melody frantic,
While he pours forth his mighty desire
    To leap down on the eager Atlantic,
        Whose arms stretch to his playmate.

The wild storm makes his lair in thy branches,
    Preying thence on the continent under;
Like a lion, crouched close on his haunches,
    There awaiteth his leap the fierce thunder,
        Growling low with impatience.

Spite of winter, thou keep'st thy green **glory,**
  Lusty father of Titans past number!
The snow-flakes alone make thee hoary,
  Nestling close to thy branches in slumber,
    And thee mantling with silence.

Thou alone know'st the splendor of winter,
  Mid thy snow-silvered, hushed precipices,
Hearing crags of green ice groan and splinter,
  And then plunge down the muffled abysses
    In the quiet of midnight.

Thou alone know'st the glory of summer,
  Gazing down on thy broad seas of forest,
On thy subjects that send a proud murmur
  Up to thee, to their sachem, who towerest
    From thy bleak throne to heaven.

SI DESCENDERO IN INFERNUM, ADES.

O, WANDERING dim on the extremest edge
  Of God's bright providence, whose spirits sigh
Drearily in you, like the winter sedge
  That shivers o'er the dead pool stiff and dry,
  A thin, sad voice, when the bold wind roars by
    From the clear North of Duty, —
Still by cracked arch and broken shaft I trace
That here was once a shrine and holy place
    Of the supernal Beauty, —
A child's play-altar reared of stones and moss,
  With wilted flowers for offering laid across,
Mute recognition of the all-ruling Grace.

How far are ye from the innocent, from those
  Whose hearts are as a little lane serene,
Smooth-heaped from wall to wall with unbroke snows,
  Or in the summer blithe with lamb-cropped green,
  Save the one track, where naught more rude is seen
    Than the plump wain at even
Bringing home four months' sunshine bound in sheaves! —
How far are ye from those! yet who believes
    That ye can shut out heaven?

Your souls partake its influence, not in vain
Nor all unconscious, as that silent lane
Its drift of noiseless apple-blooms receives.

Looking within myself, I note how thin
A plank of station, chance, or prosperous fate,
Doth fence me from the clutching waves of sin; —
In my own heart I find the worst man's mate,
And see not dimly the smooth-hingèd gate
That opes to those abysses
Where ye grope darkly, — ye who never knew
On your young hearts love's consecrating dew,
Or felt a mother's kisses,
Or home's restraining tendrils round you curled.
Ah, side by side with heart's-ease in this world
The fatal night-shade grows and bitter rue !

One band ye cannot break, — the force that clips
And grasps your circles to the central light;
Yours is the prodigal comet's long ellipse,
Self-exiled to the farthest verge of night;
Yet strives with you no less that inward might
No sin hath e'er imbruted ;
The god in you the creed-dimmed eye eludes;
The Law brooks not to have its solitudes
By bigot feet polluted ; —
Yet they who watch your god-compelled return
May see your happy perihelion burn
Where the calm sun his unfledged planets broods.

TO THE PAST.

WONDROUS and awful are thy silent halls,
O kingdom of the past !
There lie the bygone ages in their palls,
Guarded by shadows vast, —
There all is hushed and breathless,
Save when some image of old error falls
Earth worshipped once as deathless.

There sits drear Egypt, mid beleaguering sands,
Half woman and half beast,

The burnt-out torch within her mouldering hands
    That once lit all the East;
A dotard bleared and hoary,
There Asser crouches o'er the blackened brands
    Of Asia's long-quenched glory.

Still as a city buried 'neath the sea,
    Thy courts and temples stand;
Idle as forms on wind-waved tapestry
    Of saints and heroes grand,
      Thy phantasms grope and shiver,
Or watch the loose shores crumbling silently
    Into Time's gnawing river.

Titanic shapes with faces blank and dun,
    Of their old godhead lorn,
Gaze on the embers of the sunken sun,
    Which they misdeem for morn;
      And yet the eternal sorrow
In their unmonarched eyes says day is done
    Without the hope of morrow.

O realm of silence and of swart eclipse,
    The shapes that haunt thy gloom
Make signs to us and move their withered lips
    Across the gulf of doom;
      Yet all their sound and motion
Bring no more freight to us than wraiths of ships
    On the mirage's ocean.

And if sometimes a moaning wandereth
    From out thy desolate halls,
If some grim shadow of thy living death
    Across our sunshine falls
      And scares the world to error,
The eternal life sends forth melodious breath
    To chase the misty terror.

Thy mighty clamors, wars, and world-noised deeds
    Are silent now in dust,
Gone like a tremble of the huddling reeds
    Beneath some sudden gust;
      Thy forms and creeds have vanished,

o

Tossed out to wither like unsightly weeds
  From the world's garden banished.

Whatever of true life there was in thee
    Leaps in our age's veins;
Wield still thy bent and wrinkled empery,
    And shake thine idle chains; —
  To thee thy dross is clinging,
For us thy martyrs die, thy prophets see,
    Thy poets still are singing.

Here, mid the bleak waves of our strife and care,
    Float the green Fortunate Isles,
Where all thy hero-spirits dwell, and share
    Our martyrdoms and toils;
  The present moves attended
With all of brave and excellent and fair
    That made the old time splendid.

TO THE FUTURE.

O LAND of Promise! from what Pisgah's height
  Can I behold thy stretch of peaceful bowers,
Thy golden harvests flowing out of sight,
    Thy nestled homes and sun-illumined towers?
    Gazing upon the sunset's high-heaped gold,
Its crags of opal and of chrysolite,
    Its deeps on deeps of glory, that unfold
      Still brightening abysses,
      And blazing precipices,
Whence but a scanty leap it seems to heaven,
    Sometimes a glimpse is given
Of thy more gorgeous realm, thy more unstinted blisses.

O Land of Quiet! to thy shore the surf
    Of the perturbèd Present rolls and sleeps;
Our storms breathe soft as June upon thy turf
    And lure out blossoms; to thy bosom leaps,
As to a mother's, the o'erwearied heart,
Hearing far off and dim the toiling mart,
    The hurrying feet, the curses without number,

And, circled with the glow Elysian,
　　Of thine exulting vision,
Out of its very cares wooes charms for peace and slumber.

To thee the Earth lifts up her fettered hands
　　And cries for vengeance; with a pitying smile
Thou blessest her, and she forgets her hands,
　　And her old woe-worn face a little while
Grows young and noble; unto thee the Oppressor
　　Looks, and is dumb with awe;
　　The eternal law,
Which makes the crime its own blindfold redresser,
Shadows his heart with perilous foreboding,
　　And he can see the grim-eyed Doom
　　From out the trembling gloom
Its silent-footed steeds toward his palace goading.

What promises hast thou for Poets' eyes,
　　Aweary of the turmoil and the wrong!
To all their hopes what overjoyed replies!
　　What undreamed ecstasies for blissful song!
Thy happy plains no war-trump's brawling clangor
　　Disturbs, and fools the poor to hate the poor;
The humble glares not on the high with anger;
　　Love leaves no grudge at less, no greed for more;
　　From the soul's deeps
　　It throbs and leaps;
The noble 'neath foul rags beholds his long-lost brother.

To thee the Martyr looketh, and his fires
　　Unlock their fangs and leave his spirit free;
To thee the Poet mid his toil aspires,
　　And grief and hunger climb about his knee,
Welcome as children; thou upholdest
　　The lone Inventor by his demon haunted;
The Prophet cries to thee when hearts are coldest,
　　And, gazing o'er the midnight's bleak abyss,
　　Sees the drowsed soul awaken at thy kiss,
And stretch its happy arms and leap up disenchanted.

Thou bringest vengeance, but so loving-kindly
　　The guilty thinks it pity; taught by thee,

Fierce tyrants drop the scourges wherewith blindly
　　Their own souls they were scarring; conquerors see
With horror in their hands the accursed spear
　　That tore the meek One's side on Calvary,
And from their trophies shrink with ghastly fear;
　　　　Thou, too, art the Forgiver,
　　The beauty of man's soul to man revealing;
　　　　The arrows from thy quiver
Pierce Error's guilty heart, but only pierce for healing.

O, whither, whither, glory-wingèd dreams,
　　From out Life's sweat and turmoil would ye bear me?
Shut, gates of Fancy, on your golden gleams, —
　　This agony of hopeless contrast spare me!
Fade, cheating glow, and leave me to my night!
　　　　He is a coward, who would borrow
　　　　A charm against the present sorrow
From the vague Future's promise of delight:
　　　　As life's alarums nearer roll,
　　　　The ancestral buckler calls,
　　　　Self-clanging from the walls
　　In the high temple of the soul;
Where are most sorrows, there the poet's sphere is,
　　　　To feed the soul with patience,
　　　　To heal its desolations
With words of unshorn truth, with love that never wearies.

HEBE.

　　I saw the twinkle of white feet,
I saw the flash of robes descending;
　　Before her ran an influence fleet,
That bowed my heart like barley bending.

　　As, in bare fields, the searching bees
Pilot to blooms beyond our finding,
　　It led me on, by sweet degrees,
Joy's simple honey-cells unbinding.

　　Those Graces were that seemed grim Fates;
With nearer love the sky leaned o'er me;
　　The long-sought Secret's golden gates
On musical hinges swung before me.

I saw the brimmed bowl in her grasp
Thrilling with godhood; like a lover
　　I sprang the proffered life to clasp; —
The beaker fell; the luck was over.

　　The Earth has drunk the vintage up;
What boots it patch the goblet's splinters?
　　Can Summer fill the icy cup,
Whose treacherous crystal is but Winter's?

　　O spendthrift, haste! await the Gods;
Their nectar crowns the lips of Patience;
　　Haste scatters on unthankful sods
The immortal gift in vain libations.

　　Coy Hebe flies from those that woo,
And shuns the hands would seize upon her,
　　Follow thy life, and she will sue
To pour for thee the cup of honor.

THE SEARCH.

　　　I went to seek for Christ,
　　　　And Nature seemed so fair
That first the woods and fields my youth enticed,
　　　And I was sure to find him there:
　　　　The temple I forsook,
　　　　And to the solitude
Allegiance paid; but winter came and shook
　　The crown and purple from my wood;
His snows, like desert sands, with scornful drift,
　　Besieged the columned aisle and palace-gate;
My Thebes, cut deep with many a solemn rift,
　　But epitaphed her own sepulchred state:
Then I remembered whom I went to seek,
And blessed blunt Winter for his counsel bleak.

　　　　Back to the world I turned,
　　　　For Christ, I said, is king;
So the cramped alley and the hut I spurned,
　　As far beneath his sojourning:
　　　　Mid power and wealth I sought,
　　　　But found no trace of him,

And all the costly offerings I had brought
    With sudden rust and mould grew dim:
I found his tomb, indeed, where, by their laws,
    All must on stated days themselves imprison,
Mocking with bread a dead creed's grinning jaws,
    Witless how long the life had thence arisen;
Due sacrifice to this they set apart,
Prizing it more than Christ's own living heart.

    So from my feet the dust
      Of the proud World I shook;
Then came dear Love and shared with me his crust,
    And half my sorrow's burden took.
    After the World's soft bed,
      Its rich and dainty fare,
Like down seemed Love's coarse pillow to my head,
    His cheap food seemed as manna rare;
Fresh-trodden prints of bare and bleeding feet,
    Turned to the heedless city whence I came,
Hard by I saw, and springs of worship sweet
    Gushed from my cleft heart smitten by the same;
Love looked me in the face and spake no words,
But straight I knew those foot-prints were the Lord's.

    I followed where they led
      And in a hovel rude,
With naught to fence the weather from his head,
    The King I sought for meekly stood
    A naked, hungry child
      Clung round his gracious knee,
And a poor hunted slave looked up and smiled
    To bless the smile that set him free;
New miracles I saw his presence do, —
    No more I knew the hovel bare and poor,
The gathered chips into a woodpile grew,
    The broken morsel swelled to goodly store;
I knelt and wept: my Christ no more I seek,
His throne is with the outcast and the weak.

THE PRESENT CRISIS.

WHEN a deed is done for Freedom, through the broad
    earth's aching breast
Runs a thrill of joy prophetic, trembling on from east to
    west,
And the slave, where'er he cowers, feels the soul within
    him climb
To the awful verge of manhood, as the energy sublime
Of a century bursts full-blossomed on the thorny stem of
    Time.

Through the walls of hut and palace shoots the instan-
    taneous throe,
When the travail of the Ages wrings earth's systems to
    and fro;
At the birth of each new Era, with a recognizing start,
Nation wildly looks at nation, standing with mute lips
    apart,
And glad Truth's yet mightier man-child leaps beneath
    the Future's heart.

So the Evil's triumph sendeth, with a terror and a chill,
Under continent to continent, the sense of coming ill,
And the slave, where'er he cowers, feels his sympathies
    with God
In hot tear-drops ebbing earthward, to be drunk up by
    the sod,
Till a corpse crawls round unburied, delving in the nobler
    clod.

For mankind are one in spirit, and an instinct bears
    along,
Round the earth's electric circle, the swift flush of right
    or wrong;
Whether conscious or unconscious, yet Humanity's vast
    frame
Through its ocean-sundered fibres feels the gush of joy
    or shame; —
In the gain or loss of one race all the rest have equal
    claim.

Once to every man and nation comes the moment to
 decide,
In the strife of Truth with Falsehood, for the good or
 evil side;
Some great cause, God's new Messiah, offering each the
 bloom or blight,
Parts the goats upon the left hand, and the sheep upon
 the right,
And the choice goes by forever 'twixt that darkness and
 that light.

Hast thou chosen, O my people, on whose party thou
 shalt stand,
Ere the Doom from its worn sandals shakes the dust
 against our land?
Though the cause of Evil prosper, yet 't is Truth alone is
 strong,
And, albeit she wander outcast now, I see around her
 throng
Troops of beautiful, tall angels, to enshield her from all
 wrong.

Backward look across the ages and the beacon-moments
 see,
That, like peaks of some sunk continent, jut through
 Oblivion's sea;
Not an ear in court or market for the low foreboding
 cry
Of those Crises, God's stern winnowers, from whose
 feet earth's chaff must fly;
Never shows the choice momentous till the judgment
 hath passed by.

Careless seems the great Avenger; history's pages but
 record
One death-grapple in the darkness 'twixt old systems
 and the Word;
Truth forever on the scaffold, Wrong forever on the
 throne, —
Yet that scaffold sways the Future, and, behind the dim
 unknown,
Standeth God within the shadow, keeping watch above
 his own.

We see dimly in the Present what is small and what is
    great,
Slow of faith, how weak an arm may turn the iron helm
    of fate,
But the soul is still oracular; amid the market's din,
List the ominous stern whisper from the Delphic cave
    within, —
"They enslave their children's children who make com-
    promise with sin."

Slavery, the earthborn Cyclops, fellest of the giant brood,
Sons of brutish Force and Darkness, who have drenched
    the earth with blood,
Famished in his self-made desert, blinded by our purer
    day,
Gropes in yet unblasted regions for his miserable
    prey; —
Shall we guide his gory fingers where our helpless chil-
    dren play?

Then to side with Truth is noble when we share her
    wretched crust,
Ere her cause bring fame and profit, and 't is prosperous
    to be just;
Then it is the brave man chooses, while the coward
    stands aside,
Doubting in his abject spirit, till his Lord is crucified,
And the multitude make virtue of the faith they had
    denied.

Count me o'er earth's chosen heroes, — they were souls
    that stood alone,
While the men they agonized for hurled the contume-
    lious stone,
Stood serene, and down the future saw the golden beam
    incline
To the side of perfect justice, mastered by their faith
    divine,
By one man's plain truth to manhood and to God's
    supreme design.

By the light of burning heretics Christ's bleeding feet
    I track,

Toiling up new Calvaries ever with the cross that turns
　　not back,
And these mounts of anguish number how each genera-
　　tion learned
One new word of that grand *Credo* which in prophet-
　　hearts hath burned
Since the first man stood God-conquered with his face
　　to heaven upturned.

For Humanity sweeps onward: where to-day the martyr
　　stands,
On the morrow crouches Judas with the silver in his
　　hands;
Far in front the cross stands ready and the crackling
　　fagots burn,
While the hooting mob of yesterday in silent awe return
To glean up the scattered ashes into History's golden
　　urn.

'T is as easy to be heroes as to sit the idle slaves
Of a legendary virtue carved upon our fathers' graves,
Worshippers of light ancestral make the present light
　　a crime; —
Was the Mayflower launched by cowards, steered by
　　men behind their time?
Turn those tracks toward Past or Future, that make
　　Plymouth rock sublime?

They were men of present valor, stalwart old iconoclasts,
Unconvinced by axe or gibbet that all virtue was the
　　Past's;
But we make their truth our falsehood, thinking that
　　hath made us free,
Hoarding it· in mouldy parchments, while our tender
　　spirits flee
The rude grasp of that great Impulse which drove them
　　across the sea.

They have rights who dare maintain them; we are
　　traitors to our sires,
Smothering in their· holy ashes Freedom's new-lit altar-
　　fires;
Shall we make their creed our jailer? Shall we, in our
　　haste to slay,

From the tombs of the old prophets steal the funeral
　　lamps away
To light up the martyr-fagots round the prophets of
　　to-day ?

New occasions teach new duties; Time makes ancient
　　good uncouth;
They must upward still, and onward, who would keep
　　abreast of Truth;
Lo, before us gleam her camp-fires! we ourselves must
　　Pilgrims be,
Launch our Mayflower, and steer boldly through the
　　desperate winter sea,
Nor attempt the Future's portal with the Past's blood-
　　rusted key.

December, 1845.

AN INDIAN-SUMMER REVERIE.

WHAT visionary tints the year puts on,
When falling leaves falter through motionless air
　　Or numbly cling and shiver to be gone!
How shimmer the low flats and pastures bare,
　　As with her nectar Hebe Autumn fills
　　The bowl between me and those distant hills,
And smiles and shakes abroad her misty, tremulous hair!

No more the landscape holds its wealth apart.
Making me poorer in my poverty,
　　But mingles with my senses and my heart;
My own projected spirit seems to me
　　In her own reverie the world to steep;
　　'T is she that waves to sympathetic sleep,
Moving, as she is moved, each field and hill, and tree.

How fuse and mix, with what unfelt degrees,
Clasped by the faint horizon's languid arms,
　　Each into each, the hazy distances!
The softened season all the landscape charms;
　　Those hills, my native village that embay,
　　In waves of dreamier purple roll away,
And floating in mirage seem all the glimmering farms.

Far distant sounds the hidden chickadee
Close at my side; far distant sound the leaves;
　　The fields seem fields of dream, where Memory
Wanders like gleaning Ruth; and as the sheaves
　　Of wheat and barley wavered in the eye
　　Of Boaz as the maiden's glow went by,
So tremble and seem remote all things the sense receives.

The cock's shrill trump that tells of scattered corn,
Passed breezily on by all his flapping mates,
　　Faint and more faint, from barn to barn is borne,
Southward, perhaps to far Magellan's Straits;
　　Dimly I catch the throb of distant flails;
　　Silently overhead the henhawk sails,
With watchful, measuring eye, and for his quarry waits. •

The sobered robin, hunger-silent now,
Seeks cedar-berries blue, his autumn cheer;
　　The squirrel on the shingly shagbark's bough,
Now saws, now lists with downward eye and ear,
　　Then drops his nut, and, with a chipping bound,
　　Whisks to his winding fastness underground;
The clouds like swans drift down the streaming
　　atmosphere.

O'er yon bare knoll the pointed cedar shadows
Drowse on the crisp, gray moss; the ploughman's call
　　Creeps faint as smoke from black, fresh-furrowed
　　　meadows;
　　The single crow a single caw lets fall;　　　'
　　And all around me every bush and tree
　　Says Autumn 's here, and Winter soon will be
Who snows his soft, white sleep and silence over all.

The birch, most shy and lady-like of trees,
Her poverty, as best she may, retrieves,
　　And hints at her foregone gentilities
With some saved relics of her wealth of leaves;
　　The swamp-oak, with his royal purple on,
　　Glares red as blood across the sinking sun,
As one who proudlier to a falling fortune cleaves.

He looks a sachem, in red blanket wrapt,
Who, mid some council of the sad-garbed whites,

Erect and stern, in his own memories lapt,
With distant eye broods over other sights,
   Sees the hushed wood the city's flare replace,
   The wounded turf heal o'er the railway's trace,
And roams the savage Past of his undwindled rights.

   The red-oak, softer-grained, yields all for lost,
And, with his crumpled foliage stiff and dry,
    After the first betrayal of the frost,
Rebuffs the kiss of the relenting sky;
    The chestnuts, lavish of their long-hid gold,
    To the faint Summer, beggared now and old,
Pour back the sunshine hoarded 'neath her favoring eye.

   The ash her purple drops forgivingly
And sadly, breaking not the general hush;
    The maple-swamps glow like a sunset sea,
Each leaf a ripple with its separate flush;
    All round the wood's edge creeps the skirting blaze
    Of bushes low, as when, on cloudy days,
Ere the rain falls, the cautious farmer burns his brush.

   O'er yon low wall, which guards one unkempt zone,
Where vines, and weeds, and scrub-oaks intertwine
    Safe from the plough, whose rough, discordant stone
Is massed to one soft gray by lichens fine,
    The tangled blackberry, crossed and recrossed, weaves
    A prickly network of ensanguined leaves;
Hard by, with coral beads, the prim black-alders shine.

   Pillaring with flame this crumbling boundary,
Whose loose blocks topple 'neath the ploughboy's foot,
    Who, with each sense shut fast except the eye,
Creeps close and scares the jay he hoped to shoot,
    The woodbine up the elm's straight stem aspires.
    Coiling it, harmless, with autumnal fires;
In the ivy's paler blaze the martyr oak stands mute.

   Below, the Charles — a stripe of nether sky,
Now hid by rounded apple-trees between,
    Whose gaps the misplaced sail sweeps bellying by,
Now flickering golden through a woodland screen,
    Then spreading out at his next turn beyond,

A silver circle like an inland pond —
Slips seaward silently through marshes purple and green,

Dear marshes! vain to him the gift of sight
Who cannot in their various incomes share,
From every season drawn, of shade and light,
Who sees in them but levels brown and bare;
Each change of storm or sunshine scatters free
On them its largesse of variety,
For nature with cheap means still works her wonders rare.

In Spring they lie one broad expanse of green,
O'er which the light winds run with glimmering feet;
Here, yellower stripes track out the creek unseen,
There, darker growths o'er hidden ditches meet;
And purpler stains show where the blossoms crowd,
As if the silent shadow of a cloud
Hung there becalmed, with the next breath to fleet.

All round, upon the river's slippery edge,
Witching to deeper calm the drowsy tide,
Whispers and leans the breeze-entangling sedge;
Through emerald glooms the lingering waters slide,
Or, sometimes wavering, throw back the sun,
And the stiff banks in eddies melt and run
Of dimpling light, and with the current seem to glide.

In Summer 't is a blithesome sight to see,
As, step by step, with measured swing, they pass,
The wide-ranked mowers wading to the knee,
Their sharp scythes panting through the thick-set grass;
Then, stretched beneath a rick's shade in a ring,
Their nooning take, while one begins to sing
A stave that droops and dies 'neath the close sky of brass.

Meanwhile the devil-may-care, the bobolink,
Remembering duty, in mid-quaver stops
Just ere he sweeps o'er rapture's tremulous brink,
And 'twixt the winrows most demurely drops,
A decorous bird of business, who provides
For his brown mate and fledglings six besides,
And looks from right to left, a farmer mid his crops.

Another change subdues them in the Fall,
But saddens not; they still show merrier tints,
  Though sober russet seems to cover all;
  When the first sunshine through their dew-drops glints,
    Look how the yellow clearness, streamed across,
    Redeems with rarer hues the season's loss,
As Dawn's feet there had touched and left their rosy
    prints.

Or come when sunset gives its freshened zest,
Lean o'er the bridge and let the ruddy thrill,
  While the shorn sun swells down the hazy west,
  Glow opposite;—the marshes drink their fill
    And swoon with purple veins, then slowly fade
    Through pink to brown, as eastward moves the shade,
Lengthening with stealthy creep, of Simond's darkening
    hill.

Later, and yet ere Winter wholly shuts,
Ere through the first dry snow the runner grates,
  And the loath cart-wheel screams in slippery ruts,
  While firmer ice the eager boy awaits,
    Trying each buckle and strap beside the fire,
    And until bed-time plays with his desire,
Twenty times putting on and off his new-bought skates;—

Then, every morn, the river's banks shine bright
With smooth plate-armor, treacherous and frail,
  By the frost's clinking hammers forged at night,
  'Gainst which the lances of the sun prevail,
    Giving a pretty emblem of the day
    When guiltier arms in light shall melt away,
And states shall move free-limbed, loosed from war's
    cramping mail.

And now those waterfalls the ebbing river
Twice every day creates on either side
  Tinkle, as through their fresh-sparred grots they
    shiver
  In grass-arched channels to the sun denied;
    High flaps in sparkling blue the far-heard crow,
    The silvered flats gleam frostily below,
Suddenly drops the gull and breaks the glassy tide.

But, crowned in turn by vying seasons three,
Their winter halo hath a fuller ring;
This glory seems to rest immovably, —
The others were too fleet and vanishing;
When the hid tide is at its highest flow,
O'er marsh and stream one breathless trance of snow
With brooding fulness awes and hushes everything.

The sunshine seems blown off by the bleak wind,
As pale as formal candles lit by day;
Gropes to the sea the river dumb and blind;
The brown ricks, snow-thatched by the storm in play,
Show pearly breakers combing o'er their lee,
White crests as of some just enchanted sea,
Checked in their maddest leap and hanging poised mid-
way.

But when the eastern blow, with rain aslant,
From mid-sea's prairies green and rolling plains
Drives in his wallowing herds of billows gaunt,
And the roused Charles remembers in his veins
Old Ocean's blood and snaps his gyves of frost,
That tyrannous silence on the shores is tost
In dreary wreck, and crumbling desolation reigns.

Edgewise or flat, in Druid-like device,
With leaden pools between or gullies bare,
The blocks lie strewn, a bleak Stonehenge of ice;
No life, no sound, to break the grim despair,
Save sullen plunge, as through the sedges stiff
Down crackles riverward some thaw-sapped cliff,
Or when the close-wedged fields of ice crunch here and
there.

But let me turn from fancy-pictured scenes
To that whose pastoral calm before me lies:
Here nothing harsh or rugged intervenes;
The early evening with her misty dyes
Smooths off the ravelled edges of the nigh,
Relieves the distant with her cooler sky,
And tones the landscape down, and soothes the wearied
eyes.

There gleams my native village, dear to me,
Though higher change's waves each day are seen,
Whelming fields famed in boyhood's history,
Sanding with houses the diminished green;
There, in red brick, which softening time defies,
Stand square and stiff the Muses' factories; —
How with my life knit up is every well-known scene!

Flow on, dear river! not alone you flow
To outward sight, and through your marshes wind;
Fed from the mystic springs of long-ago,
Your twin flows silent through my world of mind:
Grow dim, dear marshes, in the evening's gray!
Before my inner sight ye stretch away,
And will forever, though these fleshly eyes grow blind.

Beyond that hillock's house-bespotted swell,
Where Gothic chapels house the horse and chaise,
Where quiet cits in Grecian temples dwell,
Where Coptic tombs resound with prayer and praise,
Where dust and mud the equal year divide,
There gentle Allston lived, and wrought, and died,
Transfiguring street and shop with his illumined gaze.

Virgilium vidi tantum, — I have seen
But as a boy, who looks alike on all,
That misty hair, that fine Undine-like mien,
Tremulous as down to feeling's faintest call; —
Ah, dear old homestead! count it to thy fame
That thither many times the Painter came; —
One elm yet bears his name, a feathery tree and tall.

Swiftly the present fades in memory's glow, —
Our only sure possession is the past;
The village blacksmith died a month ago,
And dim to me the forge's roaring blast;
Soon fire-new mediævals we shall see
Oust the black smithy from its chestnut tree,
And that hewn down, perhaps, the beehive green and
vast.

How many times, prouder than king on throne,
Loosed from the village school-dame's A's and B's,
Panting have I the creaky bellows blown,

P

And watched the pent volcano's red increase,
　　Then paused to see the ponderous sledge, brought
　　　down
　By that hard arm voluminous and brown,
From the white iron swarm its golden vanishing bees.

　　Dear native town! whose choking elms each year
　With eddying dust before their time turn gray,
　　Pining for rain, — to me thy dust is dear;
　It glorifies the eve of summer day,
　　And when the westering sun half-sunken burns,
　　The mote-thick air to deepest orange turns,
The westward horseman rides through clouds of gold away,

　　So palpable, I've seen those unshorn few,
　The six old willows at the causey's end,
　　(Such trees Paul Potter never dreamed nor drew,)
　Through this dry mist their checkering shadows send,
　　Striped, here and there, with many a long-drawn
　　　thread,
　　Where streamed through leafy chinks the trembling
　　　red,
Past which. in one bright trail, the hangbird's flashes blend.

　　Yes, dearer far thy dust than all that e'er,
　Beneath the awarded crown of victory,
　　Gilded the blown Olympic charioteer;
　Though lightly prized the ribboned parchments three,
　　Yet *collegisse juvat*, I am glad
　　That here what colleging was mine I had, —
It linked another tie, dear native town, with thee!

　　Nearer art thou than simply native earth,
　My dust with thine concedes a deeper tie;
　　A closer claim thy soil may well put forth,
　Something of kindred more than sympathy;
　　For in thy bounds I reverently laid away
　　That blinding anguish of forsaken clay,
That title I seemed to have in earth and sea and sky,

　　That portion of my life more choice to me
　(Though brief, yet in itself so round and whole)
　　Than all the imperfect residue can be; —

The Artist saw his statue of the soul
  Was perfect; so, with one regretful stroke,
  The earthen model into fragments broke,
And without her the impoverished seasons roll.

THE GROWTH OF THE LEGEND.

A FRAGMENT.

A LEGEND that grew in the forest's hush
Slowly as tear-drops gather and gush,
When a word some poet chanced to say
Ages ago, in his careless way,
Brings our youth back to us out of its shroud
Clearly as under yon thunder-cloud
I see that white sea-gull.   It grew and grew,
From the pine-trees gathering a sombre hue,
Till it seems a mere murmur out of the vast
Norwegian forests of the past;
And it grew itself like a true Northern pine,
First a little slender line,
Like a mermaid's green eyelash, and then anon
A stem that a tower might rest upon,
Standing spear-straight in the waist-deep moss,
Its bony roots clutching around and across,
As if they would tear up earth's heart in their grasp
Ere the storm should uproot them or make them unclasp;
Its cloudy boughs singing, as suiteth the pine,
To shrunk snow-bearded sea-kings old songs of the brine,
Till they straightened and let their staves fall to the floor,
Hearing waves moan again on the perilous shore
Of Vinland, perhaps, while their prow groped its way
'Twixt the frothy gnashed tusks of some ship-crunching
    bay.

So, pine-like, the legend grew, strong-limbed and tall,
As the Gipsy child grows that eats crusts in the hall;
It sucked the whole strength of the earth and the sky,
Spring, Summer, Fall, Winter, all brought it supply;
'T was a natural growth, and stood fearlessly there,
A true part of the landscape as sea, land, and air;
For it grew in good times, ere the fashion it was

To force up these wild births of the woods under glass,
And so, if 't is told as it should be told,
Though 't were sung under Venice's moonlight of gold,
You would hear the old voice of its mother, the pine,
Murmur sea-like and northern through every line,
And the verses should hang, self-sustained and free,
Round the vibrating stem of the melody,
Like the lithe sun-steeped limbs of the parent tree.

Yes, the pine is the mother of legends; what food
For their grim roots is left when the thousand-yeared
　　　　wood —
The dim-aisled cathedral, whose tall arches spring
Light, sinewy, graceful, firm-set as the wing
From Michael's white shoulder — is hewn and defaced
By iconoclast axes in desperate waste,
And its wrecks seek the ocean it prophesied long,
Cassandra-like, crooning its mystical song?
Then the legends go with them, — even yet on the sea
A wild virtue is left in the touch of the tree,
And the sailor's night-watches are thrilled to the core
With the lineal offspring of Odin and Thor.

Yes, wherever the pine-wood has never let in,
Since the day of creation, the light and the din
Of manifold life, but has safely conveyed
From the midnight primeval its armful of shade,
And has kept the weird Past with its sagas alive
Mid the hum and the stir of To-day's busy hive,
There the legend takes root in the age-gathered gloom,
And its murmurous boughs for their tossing find room.

Where Aroostook, far-heard, seems to sob as he goes
Groping down to the sea 'neath his mountainous snows;
Where the lake's frore Sahara of never-tracked white,
When the crack shoots across it, complains to the night
With a long, lonely moan, that leagues northward is lost,
As the ice shrinks away from the tread of the frost;
Where the lumberers sit by the log-fires which throw
Their own threatening shadows far round o'er the snow,
When the wolf howls aloof, and the wavering glare
Flashes out from the blackness the eyes of the bear,
When the wood's huge recesses, half-lighted, supply

A canvas where Fancy her mad brush may try,
Blotting in giant Horrors that venture not down
Through the right-angled streets of the brisk, white-
    washed town,
But skulk in the depths of the measureless wood
Mid the Dark's creeping whispers that curdle the blood,
When the eye, glanced in dread o'er the shoulder, may
    dream,
Ere it shrinks to the camp-fire's companioning gleam,
That it saw the fierce ghost of the Red Man crouch back
To the shroud of the tree-trunk's invincible black; —
There the old shapes crowd thick round the pine-shadowed
    camp,
Which shun the keen gleam of the scholarly lamp,
And the seed of the legend finds true Norland ground,
While the border-tale 's told and the canteen flits round.

A CONTRAST.

THY love thou sentest oft to me,
    And still as oft I thrust it back;
Thy messengers I could not see
    In those who everything did lack, —
    The poor the outcast, and the black.

Pride held his hand before mine eyes,
    The world with flattery stuffed mine ears;
I looked to see a monarch's guise,
    Nor dreamed thy love would knock for years,
    Poor, naked, fettered, full of tears.

Yet, when I sent my love to thee,
    Thou with a smile didst take it in,
And entertain'dst it royally,
    Though grimed with earth, with hunger thin,
    And leprous with the taint of sin.

Now every day thy love I meet,
    As o'er the earth it wanders wide,
With weary step and bleeding feet,
    Still knocking at the heart of pride
    And offering grace, though still denied.

EXTREME UNCTION.

Go! leave me, Priest; my soul would be
  Alone with the consoler, Death;
Far sadder eyes than thine will see
  This crumbling clay yield up its breath;
These shrivelled hands have deeper stains
  Than holy oil can cleanse away, —
Hands that have plucked the world's coarse gains
  As erst they plucked the flowers of May.

Call, if thou canst, to these gray eyes
  Some faith from youth's traditions wrung;
This fruitless husk which dustward dries
  Has been a heart once, has been young;
On this bowed head the awful Past
  Once laid its consecrating hands;
The Future in its purpose vast
  Paused, waiting my supreme commands.

But look! whose shadows block the door?
  Who are those two that stand aloof?
See! on my hands this freshening gore
  Writes o'er again its crimson proof!
My looked-for death-bed guests are met; —
  There my dead Youth doth wring its hands,
And there, with eyes that goad me yet,
  The ghost of my Ideal stands!

God bends from out the deep and says, —
  "I gave thee the great gift of life;
Wast thou not called in many ways?
  Are not my earth and heaven at strife?
I gave thee of my seed to sow,
  Bringest thou me my hundred-fold?"
Can I look up with face aglow,
  And answer, "Father, here is gold?"

I have been innocent; God knows
  When first this wasted life began,
Not grape with grape more kindly grows,
  Than I with every brother-man:
Now here I gasp; what lose my kind,
  When this fast-ebbing breath shall part?

What bands of love and service bind
   This being to the world's sad heart?

Christ still was wandering o'er the earth,
   Without a place to lay his head;
He found free welcome at my hearth,
   He shared my cup and broke my bread:
Now, when I hear those steps sublime,
   That bring the other world to this,
My snake-turned nature, sunk in slime,
   Starts sideway with defiant hiss.

Upon the hour when I was born,
   God said, " Another man shall be,"
And the great Maker did not scorn
   Out of himself to fashion me;
He sunned me with his ripening looks,
   And Heaven's rich instincts in me grew,
As effortless as woodland nooks
   Send violets up and paint them blue.

Yes, I who now, with angry tears,
   Am exiled back to brutish clod,
Have borne unquenched for fourscore years
   A spark of the eternal God;
And to what end? How yield I back
   The trust for such high uses given?
Heaven's light hath but revealed a track
   Whereby to crawl away from heaven.

Men think it is an awful sight
   To see a soul just set adrift
On that drear voyage from whose night
   The ominous shadows never lift;
But 't is more awful to behold
   A helpless infant, newly born,
Whose little hands unconscious hold
   The keys of darkness and of morn.

Mine held them once; I flung away
   Those keys that might have open set
The golden sluices of the day,
   But clutch the keys of darkness yet; —

I hear the reapers singing go
   Into God's harvest; I, that might
With them have chosen, here below
   Grope shuddering at the gates of night.

O glorious Youth, that once wast mine!
   O high ideal! all in vain
Ye enter at this ruined shrine
   Whence worship ne'er shall rise again,
The bat and owl inhabit here,
   The snake nests in the altar-stone,
The sacred vessels moulder near,
   The image of the God is gone.

THE OAK.

WHAT gnarlèd stretch, what depth of shade, is his!
   There needs no crown to mark the forest's king;
How in his leaves outshines full summer's bliss!
   Sun, storm, rain, dew, to him their tribute bring,
Which he with such benignant royalty
   Accepts, as overpayeth what is lent;
All nature seems his vassal proud to be,
   And cunning only for his ornament.

How towers he, too, amid the billowed snows,
   An unquelled exile from the summer's throne,
Whose plain, uncinctured front more kingly shows,
   Now that the obscuring courtier leaves are flown.
His boughs make music of the winter air,
   Jewelled with sleet, like some cathedral front
Where clinging snow-flakes with quaint art repair
   The dints and furrows of time's envious brunt.

How doth his patient strength the rude March wind
   Persuade to seem glad breaths of summer breeze,
And win the soil that fain would be unkind,
   To swell his revenues with proud increase!
He is the gem; and all the landscape wide
   (So doth his grandeur isolate the sense)
Seems but the setting, worthless all beside,
   An empty socket, were he fallen thence.

So, from off converse with life's wintry gales,
   Should man learn how to clasp with tougher roots
The inspiring earth; — how otherwise avails
   The leaf-creating sap that sunward shoots ?
So every year that falls with noiseless flake
   Should fill old scars upon the stormward side,
And make hoar age revered for age's sake,
   Not for traditions of youth's leafy pride.

So from the pinched soil of a churlish fate,
   True hearts compel the sap of sturdier growth,
So between earth and heaven stand simply great,
   That these shall seem but their attendants both;
For nature's forces with obedient zeal
   Wait on the rooted faith and oaken will;
As quickly the pretender's cheat they feel,
   And turn mad Pucks to flout and mock him still.

Lord ! all thy works are lessons, — each contains
   Some emblem of man's all-containing soul;
Shall he make fruitless all thy glorious pains,
   Delving within thy grace an eyeless mole ?
Make me the least of thy Dodona-grove,
   Cause me some message of thy truth to bring,
Speak but a word through me, nor let thy love
   Among my boughs disdain to perch and sing.

AMBROSE.

NEVER, surely, was holier man
Than Ambrose, since the world began;
With diet spare and raiment thin,
He shielded himself from the father of sin;
With bed of iron and scourgings oft,
His heart to God's hand as wax made soft.

Through earnest prayer and watchings long
He sought to know 'twixt right and wrong,
Much wrestling with the blessed Word
To make it yield the sense of the Lord,
That he might build a storm-proof creed
To fold the flock in at their need.

At last he builded a perfect faith,
Fenced round about with *The Lord thus saith*,
To himself he fitted the doorway's size,
Meted the light to the need of his eyes,
And knew, by a sure and inward sign,
That the work of his fingers was divine.

Then Ambrose said, " All those shall die
The eternal death who believe not as I ; "
And some were boiled, some burned in fire,
Some sawn in twain, that his heart's desire,
For the good of men's souls, might be satisfied,
By the drawing of all to the righteous side.

One day, as Ambrose was seeking the truth
In his lonely walk, he saw a youth
Resting himself in the shade of a tree ;
It had never been given him to see
So shining a face, and the good man thought
'T were pity he should not believe as he ought.

So he set himself by the young man's side,
And the state of his soul with questions tried ;
But the heart of the stranger was hardened indeed
Nor received the stamp of the one true creed,
And the spirit of Ambrose waxed sore to find
Such face the porch of so narrow a mind.

" As each beholds in cloud and fire
The shape that answers his own desire,
So each," said the youth, " in the Law shall find
The figure and features of his mind ;
And to each in his mercy hath God allowed
His several pillar of fire and cloud."

The soul of Ambrose burned with zeal
And holy wrath for the young man's weal :
" Believest thou then, most wretched youth,"
Cried he, " a dividual essence in Truth ?
I fear me thy heart is too cramped with sin
To take the Lord in his glory in."

Now there bubbled beside them where they stood,
A fountain of waters sweet and good ;

The youth to the streamlet's brink drew near
Saying, "Ambrose, thou maker of creeds, look here!"
Six vases of crystal then he took,
And set them along the edge of the brook.

"As into these vessels the water I pour,
There shall one hold less, another more,
And the water unchanged, in every case,
Shall put on the figure of the vase;
O thou, who wouldst unity make through strife,
Canst thou fit this sign to the Water of Life?"

When Ambrose looked up, he stood alone,
The youth and the stream and the vases were gone;
But he knew, by a sense of humbled grace,
He had talked with an angel face to face,
And felt his heart change inwardly,
As he fell on his knees beneath the tree.

ABOVE AND BELOW.

I.

O DWELLERS in the valley-land,
    Who in deep twilight grope and cower,
Till the slow mountain's dial-hand
    Shortens to noon's triumphal hour,—
While ye sit idle, do ye think
    The Lord's great work sits idle too?
That light dare not o'erleap the brink
    Of morn, because 't is dark with you?

Though yet your valleys skulk in night,
    In God's ripe fields the day is cried,
And reapers with their sickles bright,
    Troop, singing, down the mountain side.
Come up, and feel what health there is
    In the frank Dawn's delighted eyes,
As, bending with a pitying kiss,
    The night-shed tears of Earth she dries!

The Lord wants reapers: O, mount up,
    Before night comes, and says,—"Too late!"

Stay not for taking scrip or cup,
　The Master hungers while ye wait;
'T is from these heights alone your eyes
　The advancing spears of day can see,
Which o'er the eastern hill-tops rise,
　To break your long captivity.

II.

Lone watcher on the mountain-height!
　It is right precious to behold
The first long surf of climbing light
　Flood all the thirsty east with gold;
But we, who in the shadow sit,
　Know also when the day is nigh,
Seeing thy shining forehead lit
　With his inspiring prophecy.

Thou hast thine office; we have ours;
　God lacks not early service here,
But what are thine eleventh hours
　He counts with us for morning cheer
Our day, for Him, is long enough,
　And when he giveth work to do,
The bruisèd reed is amply tough
　To pierce the shield of error through.

But not the less do thou aspire
　Light's earlier messages to preach;
Keep back no syllable of fire, —
　Plunge deep the rowels of thy speech.
Yet God deems not thine aëried sight
　More worthy than our twilight dim, —
For meek Obedience, too, is Light,
　And following that is finding Him.

THE CAPTIVE.

It was past the hour of trysting,
　But she lingered for him still;
Like a child, the eager streamlet
　Leaped and laughed adown the hill,

Happy to be free at twilight
From its toiling at the mill.

Then the great moon on a sudden
Ominous, and red as blood,
Startling as a new creation,
O'er the eastern hill-top stood,
Casting deep and deeper shadows
Through the mystery of the wood.

Dread closed huge and vague about her,
And her thoughts turned fearfully
To her heart, if there some shelter
From the silence there might be,
Like bare cedars leaning inland
From the blighting of the sea.

Yet he came not, and the stillness
Dampened round her like a tomb;
She could feel cold eyes of spirits
Looking on her through the gloom,
She could hear the groping footsteps
Of some blind, gigantic doom.

Suddenly the silence wavered
Like a light mist in the wind,
For a voice broke gently through it,
Felt like sunshine by the blind,
And the dread, like mist in sunshine,
Furled serenely from her mind.

"Once my love, my love forever, —
Flesh or spirit still the same;
If I missed the hour of trysting,
Do not think my faith to blame.
I, alas, was made a captive,
As from Holy Land I came.

"On a green spot in the desert,
Gleaming like an emerald star,
Where a palm-tree, in lone silence,
Yearning for its mate afar,
Droops above a silver runnel,
Slender as a scimitar, —

"There thou 'lt find the humble postern
  To the castle of my foe;
If thy love burn clear and faithful,
  Strike the gateway, green and low,
Ask to enter, and the warder
  Surely will not say thee no."

Slept again the aspen silence,
  But her loneliness was o'er;
Round her heart a motherly patience
  Wrapt its arms for evermore;
From her soul ebbed back the sorrow,
  Leaving smooth the golden shore.

Donned she now the pilgrim scallop,
  Took the pilgrim staff in hand;
Like a cloud-shade, flitting eastward,
  Wandered she o'er sea and land;
And her footsteps in the desert
  Fell like cool rain on the sand.

Soon, beneath the palm-tree's shadow,
  Knelt she at the postern low;
And thereat she knocketh gently,
  Fearing much the warder's no;
All her heart stood still and listened,
  As the door swung backward slow.

There she saw no surly warder
  With an eye like bolt and bar;
Through her soul a sense of music
  Throbbed, — and, like a guardian Lar,
On the threshold stood an angel,
  Bright and silent as a star.

Fairest seemed he of God's seraphs,
  And her spirit, lily-wise,
Blossomed when he turned upon her
  The deep welcome of his eyes,
Sending upward to that sunlight
  All its dew for sacrifice.

Then she heard a voice come onward
  Singing with a rapture new,

As Eve heard the songs in Eden,
    Dropping earthward with the dew;
Well she knew the happy singer,
    Well the happy song she knew.

Forward leaped she o'er the threshold,
    Eager as a glancing surf;
Fell from her the spirit's languor,
    Fell from her the body's scurf; —
'Neath the palm next day some Arabs
    Found a corpse upon the turf.

THE BIRCH-TREE.

RIPPLING through thy branches goes the sunshine,
Among thy leaves that palpitate forever;
Ovid in thee a pining Nymph had prisoned,
The soul once of some tremulous inland river,
Quivering to tell her woe, but, ah! dumb, dumb forever!

While all the forest, witched with slumberous moonshine,
Holds up its leaves in happy, happy silence,
Waiting the dew, with breath and pulse suspended, —
I hear afar thy whispering, gleamy islands,
And track thee wakeful still amid the wide-hung silence.

Upon the brink of some wood-nestled lakelet,
Thy foliage, like the tresses of a Dryad,
Dripping about thy slim white stem, whose shadow
Slopes quivering down the water's dusky quiet,
Thou shrink'st as on her bath's edge would some startled
    Dryad.

Thou art the go-between of rustic lovers;
Thy white bark has their secrets in its keeping;
Reuben writes here the happy name of Patience,
And thy lithe boughs hang murmuring and weeping
Above her, as she steals the mystery from thy keeping.

Thou art to me like my beloved maiden,
So frankly coy, so full of trembly confidences;
Thy shadow scarce seems shade, thy pattering leaflets

Sprinkle their gathered sunshine o'er my senses,
And Nature gives me all her summer confidences.

Whether my heart with hope or sorrow tremble,
Thou sympathizest still; wild and unquiet,
I fling me down; thy ripple, like a river,
Flows valleyward, where calmness is, and by it
My heart is floated down into the land of quiet.

AN INTERVIEW WITH MILES STANDISH.

I SAT one evening in my room,
 In that sweet hour of twilight
When blended thoughts, half light, half gloom,
 Throng through the spirit's skylight;
The flames by fits curled round the bars,
 Or up the chimney crinkled,
While embers dropped like falling stars,
 And in the ashes tinkled.

I sat and mused; the fire burned low,
 And, o'er my senses stealing,
Crept something of the ruddy glow
 That bloomed on wall and ceiling;
My pictures (they are very few, —
 The heads of ancient wise men)
Smoothed down their knotted fronts, and grew
 As rosy as excisemen.

My antique high-backed Spanish chair
 Felt thrills through wood and leather,
That had been strangers since whilere,
 Mid Andalusian heather,
The oak that made its sturdy frame
 His happy arms stretched over
The ox whose fortunate hide became
 The bottom's polished cover.

It came out in that famous bark
 That brought our sires intrepid,
Capacious as another ark
 For furniture decrepit; —

For, as that saved of bird and beast
    A pair for propagation,
So has the seed of these increased
    And furnished half the nation.

Kings sit, they say, in slippery seats;
    But those slant precipices
Of ice the northern voyager meets
    Less slippery are than this is;
To cling therein would pass the wit
    Of royal man or woman,
And whatsoe'er can stay in it
    Is more or less than human.

I offer to all bores this perch,
    Dear well-intentioned people
With heads as void as week-day church,
    Tongues longer than the steeple;
To folks with missions, whose gaunt eyes
    See golden ages rising, —
Salt of the earth! in what queer Guys
    Thou'rt fond of crystallizing!

My wonder, then, was not unmixed
    With merciful suggestion,
When, as my roving eyes grew fixed
    Upon the chair in question,
I saw its trembling arms enclose
    A figure grim and rusty,
Whose doublet plain and plainer hose
    Were something worn and dusty.

Now even such men as Nature forms
    Merely to fill the street with,
Once turned to ghosts by hungry worms,
    Are serious things to meet with;
Your penitent spirits are no jokes,
    And, though I'm not averse to
A quiet shade, even they are folks
    One cares not to speak first to.

Who knows, thought I, but he has come,
    By Charon kindly ferried,
To tell me of a mighty sum
    Behind my wainscot buried?

Q

There is a buccaneerish air
　　About that garb outlandish ⸺
Just then the ghost drew up his chair
　　And said " My name is Standish.

" I come from Plymouth, deadly bored
　　With toasts, and songs, and speeches,
As long and flat as my old sword,
　　As threadbare as my breeches :
They understand us Pilgrims ! they,
　　Smooth men with rosy faces,
Strength's knots and gnarls all pared away,
　　And varnish in their places !

" We had some toughness in our grain,
　　The eye to rightly see us is
Not just the one that lights the brain
　　Of drawing-room Tyrtæuses :
They talk about their Pilgrim blood,
　　Their birthright high and holy ! ⸺
A mountain-stream that ends in mud
　　Methinks is melancholy.

" He had stiff knees, the Puritan,
　　That were not good at bending ;
The homespun dignity of man
　　He thought was worth defending ;
He did not, with his pinchbeck ore,
　　His country's shame forgotten,
Gild Freedom's coffin o'er and o'er,
　　When all within was rotten.

" These loud ancestral boasts of yours,
　　How can they else than vex us ?
Where were your dinner orators
　　When slavery grasped at Texas ?
Dumb on his knees was every one
　　That now is bold as Cæsar, ⸺
Mere pegs to hang an office on
　　Such stalwart men as these are."

" Good Sir," I said, " you seem much stirred
　　The sacred compromises ⸺ "
" Now God confound the dastard word !
　　My gall thereat arises :

Northward it hath this sense alone,
　　That you, your conscience blinding,
Shall bow your fool's nose to the stone,
　　When slavery feels like grinding.

" 'T is shame to see such painted sticks
　　In Vane's and Winthrop's places,
To see your spirit of Seventy-six
　　Drag humbly in the traces,
With slavery's lash upon her back,
　　And herds of office-holders
To shout applause, as, with a crack,
　　It peels her patient shoulders.

" *We* forefathers to such a rout! —
　　No, by my faith in God's word!"
Half rose the ghost, and half drew out
　　The ghost of his old broadsword,
Then thrust it slowly back again,
　　And said, with reverent gesture,
"No, Freedom, no! blood should not stain
　　The hem of thy white vesture.

" I feel the soul in me draw near
　　The mount of prophesying;
In this bleak wilderness I hear
　　A John the Baptist crying;
Far in the east I see upleap
　　The streaks of first forewarning,
And they who sowed the light shall reap
　　The golden sheaves of morning.

" Child of our travail and our woe,
　　Light in our day of sorrow,
Through my rapt spirit I foreknow
　　The glory of thy morrow;
I hear great steps, that through the shade
　　Draw nigher still and nigher,
And voices call like that which bade
　　The prophet come up higher."

I looked, no form mine eyes could find,
　　I heard the red cock crowing,
And through my window-chinks the wind
　　A dismal tune was blowing;

Thought I, My neighbor Buckingham
  Hath somewhat in him gritty,
Some Pilgrim-stuff that hates all sham,
  And he will print my ditty.

ON THE CAPTURE OF CERTAIN FUGITIVE SLAVES NEAR WASHINGTON.

LOOK on who will in apathy, and stifle they who can,
The sympathies, the hopes, the words, that make man
      truly man;
Let those whose hearts are dungeoned up with interest
      or with ease
Consent to hear with quiet pulse of loathsome deeds
      like these!

I first drew in New England's air, and from her hardy
      breast
Sucked in the tyrant-hating milk that will not let me
      rest;
And if my words seem treason to the dullard and the
      tame,
'T is but my Bay-State dialect, — our fathers spake the
      same!

Shame on the costly mockery of piling stone on stone
To those who won our liberty, the heroes dead and gone,
While we look coldly on, and see law-shielded ruffians
      slay
The men who fain would win their own, the heroes of
      to-day!

Are we pledged to craven silence? O fling it to the
      wind,
The parchment wall that bars us from the least of
      human kind, —
That makes us cringe and temporize, and dumbly stand
      at rest,
While Pity's burning flood of words is red-hot in the
      breast!

Though we break our fathers' promise, we have nobler
      duties first;

The traitor to Humanity is the traitor most accursed;
Man is more than Constitutions; better rot beneath the
    sod,
Than be true to Church and State while we are doubly
    false to God!

We owe allegiance to the State; but deeper, truer, more,
To the sympathies that God hath set within our spirit's
    core; —
Our country claims our fealty; we grant it so, but then
Before Man made us citizens, great Nature made us
    men.

He's true to God who's true to man; wherever wrong is
    done,
To the humblest and the weakest, neath the all-behold-
    ing sun,
That wrong is also done to us; and they are slaves most
    base,
Whose love of right is for themselves, and not for all
    their race.

God works for all. Ye cannot hem the hope of being
    free
With parallels of latitude, with mountain-range or sea.
Put golden padlocks on Truth's lips, be callous as ye
    will,
From soul to soul o'er all the world, leaps one electric
    thrill.

Chain down your slaves with ignorance, ye cannot keep
    apart,
With all your craft of tyranny, the human heart from
    heart:
When first the Pilgrims landed on the Bay-State's iron
    shore,
The word went forth that slavery should one day be no
    more.

Out from the land of bondage 't is decreed our slaves
    shall go,
And signs to us are offered, as erst to Pharaoh;
If we are blind, their exodus, like Israel's of yore,
Through a Red Sea is doomed to be, whose surges are of
    gore.

'T is ours to save our brethren, with peace and love to
    win
Their darkened hearts from error, ere they harden it to
    sin;
But if before his duty man with listless spirit stands,
Ere long the Great Avenger takes the work from out his
    hands.

TO THE DANDELION.

DEAR common flower, that grow'st beside the way,
Fringing the dusty road with harmless gold,
    First pledge of blithesome May,
Which children pluck, and, full of pride, uphold,
  High-hearted buccaneers, o'erjoyed that they
An Eldorado in the grass have found,
    Which not the rich earth's ample round
  May match in wealth, — thou art more dear to me
Than all the prouder summer-blooms may be.

  Gold such as thine ne'er drew the Spanish prow
Through the primeval hush of Indian seas,
    Nor wrinkled the lean brow
Of age, to rob the lover's heart of ease;
  'T is the spring's largess, which she scatters now
To rich and poor alike, with lavish hand,
    Though most hearts never understand
  To take it at God's value, but pass by
The offered wealth with unrewarded eye.

  Thou art my tropics and mine Italy;
To look at thee unlocks a warmer clime;
    The eyes thou givest me
Are in the heart, and heed not space or time:
  Not in mid June the golden-cuirassed bee
Feels a more summer-like warm ravishment
    In the white lily's breezy tent,
  His fragrant Sybaris, than I, when first
From the dark green thy yellow circles burst.

  Then think I of deep shadows on the grass, —
Of meadows where in sun the cattle graze,

Where, as the breezes pass,
The gleaming rushes lean a thousand ways, —
Of leaves that slumber in a cloudy mass,
Or whiten in the wind, — of waters blue
　　That from the distance sparkle through
　Some woodland gap, — and of a sky above,
Where one white cloud like a stray lamb doth move.

My childhood's earliest thoughts are linked with thee;
The sight of thee calls back the robin's song,
　　Who, from the dark old tree
Beside the door, sang clearly all day long,
　And I, secure in childish piety,
Listened as if I heard an angel sing
　　With news from heaven, which he could bring
Fresh every day to my untainted ears,
When birds and flowers and I were happy peers.

How like a prodigal doth nature seem,
When thou, for all thy gold, so common art!
　　Thou teachest me to deem
More sacredly of every human heart,
　Since each reflects in joy its scanty gleam
Of heaven, and could some wondrous secret show
　　Did we but pay the love we owe,
And with a child's undoubting wisdom look
On all these living pages of God's book.

THE GHOST-SEER.

Ye who, passing graves by night,
Glance not to the left or right,
Lest a spirit should arise,
Cold and white, to freeze your eyes,
Some weak phantom, which your doubt
Shapes upon the dark without
From the dark within, a guess
At the spirit's deathlessness,
Which ye entertain with fear
In your self-built dungeon here,
Where ye sell your God-given lives
Just for gold to buy you gyves, —

Ye without a shudder meet
In the city's noonday street,
Spirits sadder and more dread
Than from out the clay have fled,
Buried, beyond hope of light,
In the body's haunted night!

See ye not that woman pale?
There are bloodhounds on her trail!
Bloodhounds two, all gaunt and lean, —
For the soul their scent is keen, --
Want and Sin, and Sin is last, —
They have followed far and fast,
Want gave tongue, and, at her howl,
Sin awakened with a growl.
Ah, poor girl! she had a right
To a blessing from the light,
Title-deeds to sky and earth
God gave to her at her birth,
But, before they were enjoyed,
Poverty had made them void,
And had drunk the sunshine up
From all nature's ample cup,
Leaving her a first-born's share
In the dregs of darkness there.
Often, on the sidewalk bleak,
Hungry, all alone, and weak,
She has seen, in night and storm,
Rooms o'erflow with firelight warm,
Which, outside the window-glass,
Doubled all the cold, alas!
Till each ray that on her fell
Stabbed her like an icicle,
And she almost loved the wail
Of the bloodhounds on her trail.
Till the floor becomes her bier,
She shall feel their pantings near,
Close upon her very heels,
Spite of all the din of wheels;
Shivering on her pallet poor,
She shall hear them at the door
Whine and scratch to be let in,
Sister bloodhounds, Want and Sin!

Hark! that rustle of a dress,
Stiff with lavish costliness!
Here comes one whose cheek would flush
But to have her garment brush
'Gainst the girl whose fingers thin
Wove the weary broidery in,
Bending backward from her toil,
Lest her tears the silk might soil,
And, in midnight's chill and murk,
Stitched her life into the work,
Shaping from her bitter thought
Heart's-ease and forget-me-not,
Satirizing her despair
With the emblems woven there.
Little doth the wearer heed
Of the heart-break in the brede;
A hyena by her side
Skulks, down-looking, — it is Pride.
He digs for her in the earth,
Where lie all her claims of birth,
With his foul paws rooting o'er
Some long-buried ancestor,
Who, perhaps, a statue won
By the ill deeds he had done,
By the innocent blood he shed,
By the desolation spread
Over happy villages,
Blotting out the smile of peace.

There walks Judas, he who sold
Yesterday his Lord for gold,
Sold God's presence in his heart
For a proud step in the mart;
He hath dealt in flesh and blood, —
At the bank his name is good,
At the bank, and only there,
'T is a marketable ware.
In his eyes that stealthy gleam
Was not learned of sky or stream,
But it has the cold, hard glint
Of new dollars from the mint.
Open now your spirit's eyes,
Look through that poor clay disguise

Which has thickened, day by day,
Till it keeps all light at bay,
And his soul in pitchy gloom
Gropes about its narrow tomb,
From whose dank and slimy walls
Drop by drop the horror falls.
Look! a serpent lank and cold
Hugs his spirit fold on fold;
From his heart, all day and night,
It doth suck God's blessed light.
Drink it will, and drink it must,
Till the cup holds naught but dust;
All day long he hears it hiss,
Writhing in its fiendish bliss;
All night long he sees its eyes
Flicker with foul ecstasies,
As the spirit ebbs away
Into the absorbing clay.

Who is he that skulks, afraid
Of the trust he has betrayed,
Shuddering if perchance a gleam
Of old nobleness should stream
Through the pent, unwholesome room,
Where his shrunk soul cowers in gloom,
Spirit sad beyond the rest
By more instinct for the best?
'T is a poet who was sent
For a bad world's punishment,
By compelling it to see
Golden glimpses of To Be,
By compelling it to hear
Songs that prove the angels near;
Who was sent to be the tongue
Of the weak and spirit-wrung,
Whence the fiery-winged Despair
In men's shrinking eyes might flare.
'T is our hope doth fashion us
To base use or glorious:
He who might have been a lark
Of Truth's morning, from the dark
Raining down melodious hope
Of a freer, broader scope,

Aspirations, prophecies,
Of the spirit's full sunrise,
Chose to be a bird of night,
Which with eyes refusing light,
Hooted from some hollow tree
Of the world's idolatry.
'T is his punishment to hear
Flutterings of pinions near,
And his own vain wings to feel
Drooping downward to his heel,
All their grace and import lost,
Burdening his weary ghost:
Ever walking by his side
He must see his angel guide,
Who at intervals doth turn
Looks on him so sadly stern,
With such ever-new surprise
Of hushed anguish in her eyes,
That it seems the light of day
From around him shrinks away,
Or drops blunted from the wall
Built around him by his fall.
Then the mountains, whose white peaks
Catch the morning's earliest streaks,
He must see, where prophets sit,
Turning east their faces lit,
Whence, with footsteps beautiful,
To the earth, yet dim and dull,
They the gladsome tidings bring,
Of the sunlight's hastening:
Never can those hills of bliss
Be o'erclimbed by feet like his!

But enough! O, do not dare
From the next the veil to tear,
Woven of station, trade, or dress,
More obscene than nakedness,
Wherewith plausible culture drapes
Fallen Nature's myriad shapes!
Let us rather love to mark
How the unextinguished spark
Will shine through the thin disguise
Of our customs, pomps, and lies,

And, not seldom blown to flame,
Vindicate its ancient claim.
1844.

STUDIES FOR TWO HEADS.

I.

SOME sort of heart I know is hers, —
  I chanced to feel her pulse one night;
A brain she has that never errs,
  And yet is never nobly right;
It does not leap to great results,
  But in some corner out of sight,
  Suspects a spot of latent blight,
  And, o'er the impatient infinite,
She bargains, haggles, and consults.

Her eye, — it seems a chemic test
  And drops upon you like an acid;
It bites you with unconscious zest,
  So clear and bright, so coldly placid;
It holds you quietly aloof,
  It holds, — and yet it does not win you;
It merely puts you to the proof
  And sorts what qualities are in you;
It smiles, but never brings you nearer,
  It lights, — her nature draws not nigh;
'T is but that yours is growing clearer
  To her assays; — yes, try and try,
  You 'll get no deeper than her eye.

There, you are classified: she 's gone
  Far, far away into herself;
Each with its Latin label on,
Your poor components, one by one,
  Are laid upon their proper shelf
In her compact and ordered mind,
And what of you is left behind
Is no more to her than the wind;
In that clear brain, which, day and night,
  No movement of the heart e'er jostles,
Her friends are ranged on left and right, —

Here, silex, hornblende, sienite;
  There, animal remains and fossils.

And yet, O subtile analyst,
  That canst each property detect
Of mood or grain, that canst untwist
  Each tangled skein of intellect.
And with thy scalpel eyes lay bare
Each mental nerve more fine than air, —
  O brain exact, that in thy scales
Canst weigh the sun and never err,
  For once thy patient science fails,
  One problem still defies thy art; —
Thou never canst compute for her
The distance and diameter
  Of any simple human heart.

II.

HEAR him but speak, and you will feel
  The shadows of the Portico
Over your tranquil spirit steal,
  To modulate all joy and woe
  To one subdued, subduing glow;
Above our squabbling business-hours,
Like Phidian Jove's, his beauty lowers,
His nature satirizes ours;
  A form and front of Attic grace,
  He shames the higgling market-place,
And dwarfs our more mechanic powers.

What throbbing verse can fitly render
That face, — so pure, so trembling-tender?
  Sensation glimmers through its rest,
It speaks unmanacled by words,
  As full of motion as a nest
That palpitates with unfledged birds;
  'T is likest to Bethesda's stream,
Forewarned through all its thrilling springs,
  White with the angel's coming gleam,
And rippled with his fanning wings.

Hear him unfold his plots and plans,
And larger destinies seem man's;

You conjure from his glowing face
The omen of a fairer race;
With one grand trope he boldly spans
   The gulf wherein so many fall,
   'Twixt possible and actual;
His first swift word, talaria-shod,
Exuberant with conscious God,
Out of the choir of planets blots
The present earth with all its spots.

Himself unshaken as the sky,
His words, like whirlwinds, spin on high
   Systems and creeds pellmell together;
'T is strange as to a deaf man's eye,
While trees uprooted splinter by,
   The dumb turmoil of stormy weather;
   Less of iconoclast than shaper,
His spirit, safe behind the reach
Of the tornado of his speech,
   Burns calmly as a glowworm's taper.

So great in speech, but, ah! in act
   So overrun with vermin troubles,
The coarse, sharp-cornered, ugly fact
   Of life collapses all his bubbles:
Had he but lived in Plato's day,
   He might, unless my fancy errs,
Have shared that golden voice's sway
   O'er barefooted philosophers.
Our nipping climate hardly suits
The ripening of ideal fruits:
His theories vanquish us all summer,
But winter makes him dumb and dumber
To see him mid life's needful things
   Is something painfully bewildering;
He seems an angel with clipt wings
   Tied to a mortal wife and children,
And by a brother seraph taken
In the act of eating eggs and bacon.
Like a clear fountain, his desire
   Exults and leaps toward the light,
In every drop it says " Aspire!"
   Striving for more ideal height;

And as the fountain, falling thence,
    Crawls baffled through the common gutter
So, from his speech's eminence,
He shrinks into the present tense,
    Unkinged by foolish bread and butter.

Yet smile not, worldling, for in deeds
    Not all of life that's brave and wise is;
He strews an ampler future's seeds,
    'T is your fault if no harvest rises;
Smooth back the sneer; for is it naught
    That all he is and has is Beauty's?
By soul the soul's gains must be wrought,
The Actual claims our coarser thought,
    The Ideal hath its higher duties.

ON A PORTRAIT OF DANTE BY GIOTTO.

Can this be thou who, lean and pale,
    With such immitigable eye
Didst look upon those writhing souls in bale,
    And note each vengeance, and pass by
Unmoved, save when thy heart by chance
Cast backward one forbidden glance,
    And saw Francesca, with child's glee,
    Subdue and mount thy wild-horse knee
And with proud hands control its fiery prance?

With half-drooped lids, and smooth, round brow,
    And eye remote, that inly sees
Fair Beatrice's spirit wandering now
    In some sea-lulled Hesperides,
Thou movest through the jarring street,
Secluded from the noise of feet
    By her gift-blossom in thy hand,
    Thy branch of palm from Holy Land; —
No trace is here of ruin's fiery sleet.

Yet there is something round thy lips
    That prophesies the coming doom,
The soft, gray herald-shadow ere the eclipse
    Notches the perfect disk with gloom;

A something that would banish thee,
And thine untamed pursuer be,
    From men and their unworthy fates,
    Though Florence had not shut her gates,
And grief had loosed her clutch and let thee free.

Ah! he who follows fearlessly
    The beckonings of a poet-heart
Shall wander, and without the world's decree,
    A banished man in field and mart;
Harder than Florence' walls the bar
Which with deaf sternness holds him far
    From home and friends, till death's release,
    And makes his only prayer for peace,
Like thine, scarred veteran of a lifelong war!

ON THE DEATH OF A FRIEND'S CHILD

DEATH never came so nigh to me before,
Nor showed me his mild face: oft had I mused
Of calm and peace and deep forgetfulness,
Of folded hands, closed eye, and heart at rest,
And slumber sound beneath a flowery turf,
Of faults forgotten, and an inner place
Kept sacred for us in the heart of friends;
But these were idle fancies, satisfied
With the mere husk of this great mystery,
And dwelling in the outward shows of things.
Heaven is not mounted to on wings of dreams,
Nor doth the unthankful happiness of youth
Aim thitherward, but floats from bloom to bloom,
With earth's warm patch of sunshine well content.
'T is sorrow builds the shining ladder up,
Whose golden rounds are our calamities,
Whereon our firm feet planting, nearer God
The spirit climbs, and hath its eyes unsealed.

True is it that Death's face seems stern and cold,
When he is sent to summon those we love,
But all God's angels come to us disguised;
Sorrow and sickness, poverty and death,

One after other lift their frowning masks,
And we behold the seraph's face beneath,
All radiant with the glory and the calm
Of having looked upon the front of God.
With every anguish of our earthly part
The spirit's sight grows clearer; this was meant
When Jesus touched the blind man's lids with clay.
Life is the jailer, Death the angel sent
To draw the unwilling bolts and set us free.
He flings not ope the ivory gate of Rest, —
Only the fallen spirit knocks at that, —
But to benigner regions beckons us,
To destinies of more rewarded toil.
In the hushed chamber, sitting by the dead,
It grates on us to hear the flood of life
Whirl rustling onward, senseless of our loss.
The bee hums on; around the blossomed vine
Whirs the light humming-bird; the cricket chirps;
The locust's shrill alarum stings the ear;
Hard by, the cock shouts lustily; from farm to farm,
His cheery brothers, telling of the sun,
Answer, till far away the joyance dies:
We never knew before how God had filled
The summer air with happy living sounds;
All round us seems an overplus of life,
And yet the one dear heart lies cold and still.
It is most strange, when the great miracle
Hath for our sakes been done, when we have had
Our inwardest experience of God,
When with his presence still the room expands,
And is awed after him, that naught is changed,
That Nature's face looks unacknowledging,
And the mad world still dances heedless on
After its butterflies, and gives no sign.
'T is hard at first to see it all aright;
In vain Faith blows her trump to summon back
Her scattered troop; yet, through the clouded glass
Of our own bitter tears, we learn to look
Undazzled on the kindness of God's face;
Earth is too dark, and Heaven alone shines through.
It is no little thing, when a fresh soul
And a fresh heart, with their unmeasured scope
For good, not gravitating earthward yet,

R

But circling in diviner periods,
Are sent into the world, — no little thing,
When this unbounded possibility
Into the outer silence is withdrawn.
Ah, in this world, where every guiding thread
Ends suddenly in the one sure centre, death,
The visionary hand of Might-have-been
Alone can fill Desire's cup to the brim!

How changed, dear friend, are thy part and thy child's!
He bends above *thy* cradle now, or holds
His warning finger out to be thy guide;
Thou art the nurseling now; he watches thee
Slow learning, one by one, the secret things
Which are to him used sights of every day;
He smiles to see thy wondering glances con
The grass and pebbles of the spirit world,
To thee miraculous; and he will teach
Thy knees their due observances of prayer.
Children are God's apostles, day by day
Sent forth to preach of love, and hope, and peace,
Nor hath thy babe his mission left undone.
To me, at least, his going hence hath given
Serener thoughts and nearer to the skies,
And opened a new fountain in my heart
For thee, my friend, and all: and, O, if Death
More near approaches meditates, and clasps
Even now some dearer, more reluctant hand,
God, strengthen thou my faith, that I may see
That 't is thine angel, who, with loving haste,
Unto the service of the inner shrine
Doth waken thy belovèd with a kiss!
    1844.

EURYDICE.

Heaven's cup held down to me I drain,
The sunshine mounts and spurs my brain;
Bathing in grass, with thirsty eye
I suck the last drop of the sky;
With each hot sense I draw to the lees
The quickening out-door influences,

And empty to each radiant comer
A supernaculum of summer:
Not, Bacchus, all thy grosser juice
Could bring enchantment so profuse,
Though for its press each grape-bunch had
The white feet of an Oread.

Through our coarse art gleam, now and then,
The features of angelic men;
'Neath the lewd Satyr's veiling paint
Glows forth the Sibyl, Muse, or Saint;
The dauber's botch no more obscures
The mighty Master's portraitures.
And who can say what luckier beam
The hidden glory shall redeem,
For what chance clod the soul may wait
To stumble on its nobler fate,
Or why, to his unwarned abode,
Still by surprises comes the God?
Some moment, nailed on sorrow's cross,
May mediate a whole youth's loss,
Some windfall joy, we know not whence,
Redeem a lifetime's rash expense,
And, suddenly wise, the soul may mark,
Stripped of their simulated dark,
Mountains of gold that pierce the sky,
Girdling its valleyed poverty.

I feel ye, childhood's hopes, return,
With olden heats my pulses burn, —
Mine be the self-forgetting sweep,
The torrent impulse swift and wild,
Wherewith Taghkanic's rockborn child
Dares gloriously the dangerous leap,
And, in his sky-descended mood,
Transmutes each drop of sluggish blood,
By touch of bravery's simple wand,
To amethyst and diamond,
Proving himself no bastard slip,
But the true granite-cradled one,
Nursed with the rock's primeval drip,
The cloud-embracing mountain's son!

Prayer breathed in vain! no wish's sway
Rebuilds the vanished yesterday;
For plated wares of Sheffield stamp
We gave the old Aladdin's lamp;
'T is we are changed; ah, whither went
That undesigned abandonment,
That wise, unquestioning content,
Which could erect its microcosm
Out of a weed's neglected blossom,
Could call up Arthur and his peers
By a low moss's clump of spears,
Or, in its shingle trireme launched,
Where Charles in some green inlet branched,
Could venture for the golden fleece
And dragon-watched Hesperides,
Or, from its ripple-shattered fate,
Ulysses' chances recreate?
When, heralding life's every phase,
There glowed a goddess-veiling haze,
A plenteous, forewarning grace,
Like that more tender dawn that flies
Before the full moon's ample rise?
Methinks thy parting glory shines
Through yonder grove of singing pines;
At that elm-vista's end I trace
Dimly thy sad leave-taking face,
Eurydice! Eurydice!
The tremulous leaves repeat to me
Eurydice! Eurydice!
No gloomier Orcus swallows thee
Than the unclouded sunset's glow;
Thine is at least Elysian woe;
Thou hast Good's natural decay,
And fadest like a star away
Into an atmosphere whose shine
With fuller day o'ermasters thine,
Entering defeat as 't were a shrine;
For us, — we turn life's diary o'er
To find but one word, — Nevermore.
1845.

SHE CAME AND WENT.

As a twig trembles, which a bird
  Lights on to sing, then leaves unbent,
So is my memory thrilled and stirred; —
  I only know she came and went.

As clasps some lake, by gusts unriven,
  The blue dome's measureless content,
So my soul held that moment's heaven; —
  I only know she came and went.

As, at one bound, our swift spring heaps
  The orchards full of bloom and scent,
So clove her May my wintry sleeps; —
  I only know she came and went.

An angel stood and met my gaze,
  Through the low doorway of my tent;
The tent is struck, the vision stays; —
  I only know she came and went.

O, when the room grows slowly dim,
  And life's last oil is nearly spent,
One gush of light these eyes will brim,
  Only to think she came and went.

THE CHANGELING.

I HAD a little daughter,
  And she was given to me
To lead me gently backward
  To the Heavenly Father's knee,
That I, by the force of nature,
  Might in some dim wise divine
The depth of his infinite patience
  To this wayward soul of mine.

I know not how others saw her,
  But to me she was wholly fair,
And the light of the heaven she came from
  Still lingered and gleamed in her hair;

For it was as wavy and golden,
    And as many changes took,
As the shadows of sun-gilt ripples
    On the yellow bed of a brook.

To what can I liken her smiling
    Upon me, her kneeling lover,
How it leaped from her lips to her eyelids,
    And dimpled her wholly over,
Till her outstretched hands smiled also,
    And I almost seemed to see
The very heart of her mother
    Sending sun through her veins to me!

She had been with us scarce a twelvemonth,
    And it hardly seemed a day,
When a troop of wandering angels
    Stole my little daughter away;
Or perhaps those heavenly Zingari
    But loosed the hampering strings,
And when they had opened her cage-door
    My little bird used her wings.

But they left in her stead a changeling,
    A little angel child,
That seems like her bud in full blossom,
    And smiles as she never smiled:
When I wake in the morning, I see it
    Where she always used to lie,
And I feel as weak as a violet
    Alone 'neath the awful sky.

As weak, yet as trustful also;
    For the whole year long I see
All the wonders of faithful Nature
    Still worked for the love of me;
Winds wander, and dews drip earthward,
    Rain falls, suns rise and set,
Earth whirls, and all but to prosper
    A poor little violet.

This child is not mine as the first was,
    I cannot sing it to rest,
I cannot lift it up fatherly
    And bliss it upon my breast;

Yet it lies in my little one's cradle
And sits in my little one's chair,
And the light of the heaven she's gone to
Transfigures its golden hair.

THE PIONEER.

WHAT man would live coffined with brick and stone,
Imprisoned from the influences of air,
And cramped with selfish land-marks everywhere,
When all before him stretches, furrowless and lone,
The unmapped prairie none can fence or own?

What man would read and read the selfsame faces,
And, like the marbles which the windmill grinds,
Rub smooth forever with the same smooth minds,
This year retracing last year's, every year's, dull traces,
When there are woods and un-man-stifled places?

What man o'er one old thought would pore and pore,
Shut like a book between its covers thin
For every fool to leave his dog's-ears in,
When solitude is his, and God for evermore,
Just for the opening of a paltry door?

What man would watch life's oozy element
Creep Letheward forever, when he might
Down some great river drift beyond men's sight,
To where the undethronèd forest's royal tent
Broods with its hush o'er half a continent?

What man with men would push and altercate,
Piecing out crooked means for crooked ends,
When he can have the skies and woods for friends,
Snatch back the rudder of his undismantled fate,
And in himself be ruler, church, and state?

Cast leaves and feathers rot in last year's nest,
The wingèd brood, flown thence, new dwellings plan;
The serf of his own Past is not a man;
To change and change is life, to move and never rest;—
Not what we are, but what we hope, is best.

The wild, free woods make no man halt or blind;
  Cities rob men of eyes and hands and feet,
  Patching one whole of many incomplete;
The general preys upon the individual mind,
  And each alone is helpless as the wind.

Each man is some man's servant; every soul
  Is by some other's presence quite discrowned;
  Each owes the next through all the imperfect round,
Yet not with mutual help; each man is his own goal,
  And the whole earth must stop to pay his toll.

Here, life the undiminished man demands;
  New faculties stretch out to meet new wants;
  What Nature asks, that Nature also grants;
Here man is lord, not drudge, of eyes and feet and hands,
  And to his life is knit with hourly bands.

Come out, then, from the old thoughts and old ways,
  Before you harden to a crystal cold
  Which the new life can shatter, but not mould;
Freedom for you still waits, still, looking backward, stays,
  But widens still the irretrievable space.

LONGING.

Of all the myriad moods of mind
  That through the soul come thronging,
Which one was e'er so dear, so kind,
  So beautiful as Longing?
The thing we long for, that we are
  For one transcendent moment,
Before the Present poor and bare
  Can make its sneering comment.

Still, through our paltry stir and strife,
  Glows down the wished Ideal,
And Longing moulds in clay what Life
  Carves in the marble Real;
To let the new life in, we know,
  Desire must ope the portal; —
Perhaps the longing to be so
  Helps make the soul immortal.

Longing is God's fresh heavenward will
　　With our poor earthward striving;
We quench it that we may be still
　　Content with merely living;
But, would we learn that heart's full scope
　　Which we are hourly wronging,
Our lives must climb from hope to hope
　　And realize our longing.

Ah! let us hope that to our praise
　　Good God not only reckons
The moments when we tread his ways,
　　But when the spirit beckons, —
That some slight good is also wrought
　　Beyond self-satisfaction,
When we are simply good in thought,
　　Howe'er we fail in action.

ODE TO FRANCE.

FEBRUARY, 1848.

I.

As, flake by flake, the beetling avalanches
　　Build up their imminent crags of noiseless snow,
Till some chance thrill the loosened ruin launches
　　And the blind havoc leaps unwarned below,
So grew and gathered through the silent years
　　The madness of a People, wrong by wrong.
There seemed no strength in the dumb toiler's tears, —
　　No strength in suffering; — but the Past was strong:
The brute despair of trampled centuries
　　Leaped up with one hoarse yell and snapped its bands,
　　Groped for its right with horny, callous hands,
And stared around for God with bloodshot eyes.
　　What wonder if those palms were all too hard
For nice distinctions, — if that mænad throng —
　　They whose thick atmosphere no bard
Had shivered with the lightning of his song,
　　Brutes with the memories and desires of men,
　　Whose chronicles were writ with iron pen,
　　　In the crooked shoulder and the forehead low —

Set wrong to balance wrong,
And physicked woe with woe ?

II.

They did as they were taught; not theirs the blame,
If men who scattered firebrands reaped the flame:
  They trampled Peace beneath their savage feet,
    And by her golden tresses drew
  Mercy along the pavement of the street.
O, Freedom! Freedom! is thy morning-dew
    So gory red ?   Alas, thy light had ne'er
    Shone in upon the chaos of their lair!
They reared to thee such symbol as they knew,
    And worshipped it with flame and blood,
    A Vengeance, axe in hand, that stood
Holding a tyrant's head up by the clotted hair.

III.

What wrongs the Oppressor suffered, these we know;
  These have found piteous voice in song and prose;
But for the Oppressed, their darkness and their woe,
  Their grinding centuries, — what Muse had those ?
Though hall and palace had nor eyes nor ears,
  Hardening a people's heart to senseless stone,
Thou knowest them, O Earth, that drank their tears,
  O Heaven, that heard their inarticulate moan!
They noted down their fetters, link by link;
Coarse was the hand that scrawled, and red the ink;
  Rude was their score, as suits unlettered men, —
Notched with a headman's axe upon a block:
What marvel if, when came the avenging shock,
  'T was Ate, not Urania, held the pen ?

IV.

With eye averted and an anguished frown,
  Loathingly glides the Muse through scenes of strife,
Where, like the heart of Vengeance up and down,
  Throbs in its framework the blood-muffled knife;
Slow are the steps of Freedom, but her feet
  Turn never backward: hers no bloody glare;
Her light is calm, and innocent, and sweet,
  And where it enters there is no despair:

Not first on palace and cathedral spire
Quivers and gleams that unconsuming fire;
  While these stand black against her morning skies,
The peasant sees it leap from peak to peak
  Along his hills; the craftsman's burning eyes
Own with cool tears its influence mother-meek;
   It lights the poet's heart up like a star; —
   Ah! while the tyrant deemed it still afar,
And twined with golden threads his futile snare,
  That swift, convicting glow all round him ran;
    'T was close beside him there,
Sunrise whose Memnon is the soul of man.

V.

O Broker-King, is this thy wisdom's fruit?
  A dynasty plucked out as 't were a weed
  Grown rankly in a night, that leaves no seed!
Could eighteen years strike down no deeper root?
  But now thy vulture eye was turned on Spain, —
A shout from Paris, and thy crown falls off,
  Thy race has ceased to reign,
And thou become a fugitive and scoff:
  Slippery the feet that mount by stairs of gold,
And weakest of all fences one of steel; —
  Go and keep school again like him of old,
The Syracusan tyrant; — thou mayst feel
Royal amid a birch-swayed commonweal!

VI.

Not long can he be ruler who allows
  His time to run before him; thou wast naught
Soon as the strip of gold about thy brows
  Was no more emblem of the People's thought:
Vain were thy bayonets against the foe
  Thou hadst to cope with; thou didst wage
War not with Frenchmen merely; — no,
  Thy strife was with the Spirit of the Age,
The invisible Spirit whose first breath divine
    Scattered thy frail endeavor,
And, like poor last year's leaves, whirled thee and thine
    Into the Dark forever!

VII.

Is here no triumph ?   Nay, what though
The yellow blood of Trade meanwhile should pour
  Along its arteries a shrunken flow,
And the idle canvas droop around the shore ?
      These do not make a state,
        Nor keep it great;
      I think God made
    The earth for man, not trade;
  And where each humblest human creature
Can stand, no more suspicious or afraid,
Erect and kingly in his right of nature,
To heaven and earth knit with harmonious ties, —
  Where I behold the exultation
Of manhood glowing in those eyes
    That had been dark for ages, —
    Or only lit with bestial loves and rages —
There I behold a Nation:
      The France which lies
    Between the Pyrenees and Rhine
      Is the least part of France;
I see her rather in the soul whose shine
Burns through the craftsman's grimy countenance,
  In the new energy divine
    Of Toil's enfranchised glance.

VIII.

    And if it be a dream, —
If the great Future be the little Past
'Neath a new mask, which drops and shows at last
The same weird, mocking face to balk and blast, —
Yet, Muse, a gladder measure suits the theme,
    And the Tyrtæan harp
    Loves notes more resolute and sharp,
Throbbing, as throbs the bosom, hot and fast:
    Such visions are of morning,
    Theirs is no vague forewarning,
The dreams which nations dream come true,
    And shape the world anew;
      If this be a sleep,
      Make it long, make it deep,
O Father, who sendest the harvests men reap!

While Labor so sleepeth
 His sorrow is gone,
No longer he weepeth,
But smileth and steepeth
 His thoughts in the dawn;
He heareth Hope yonder
 Rain, lark-like, her fancies,
His dreaming hands wander
 Mid heart's-ease and pansies;
"'T is a dream!   'T is a vision!"
 Shrieks Mammon aghast;
"The day's broad derision
 Will chase it at last;
Ye are mad, ye have taken,
A slumbering kraken
 For firm land of the Past!"
Ah! if he awaken,
 God shield us all then,
If this dream rudely shaken
 Shall cheat him again!

IX.

Since first I heard our North wind blow,
Since first I saw Atlantic throw
On our fierce rocks his thunderous snow,
I loved thee, Freedom; as a boy
The rattle of thy shield at Marathon
 Did with a Grecian joy
 Through all my pulses run;
But I have learned to love thee now
Without the helm upon thy gleaming brow,
 A maiden mild and undefiled
Like her who bore the world's redeeming child;
 And surely never did thy altars glance
 With purer fires than now in France;
While, in their bright white flashes,
 Wrong's shadow, backward cast,
 Waves cowering o'er the ashes
 Of the dead, blaspheming Past,
O'er the shapes of fallen giants,
 His own unburied brood,
Whose dead hands clench defiance
 At the overpowering Good:

And down the happy future runs a flood
  Of prophesying light;
It shows an Earth no longer stained with blood,
Blossom and fruit where now we see the bud
  Of Brotherhood and Right.

A PARABLE.

Said Christ our Lord, "I will go and see
How the men, my brethren, believe in me."
He passed not again through the gate of birth,
But made himself known to the children of earth.

Then said the chief priests, and rulers, and kings,
"Behold, now, the Giver of all good things;
Go to, let us welcome with pomp and state
Him who alone is mighty and great."

With carpets of gold the ground they spread
Wherever the Son of Man should tread,
And in palace-chambers lofty and rare
They lodged him, and served him with kingly fare.

Great organs surged through arches dim
Their jubilant floods in praise of him,
And in church and palace, and judgment-hall,
He saw his image high over all.

But still, wherever his steps they led,
The Lord in sorrow bent down his head,
And from under the heavy foundation-stones,
The son of Mary heard bitter groans.

And in church and palace, and judgment-hall,
He marked great fissures that rent the wall,
And opened wider and yet more wide
As the living foundation heaved and sighed.

"Have ye founded your thrones and altars, then,
On the bodies and souls of living men?
And think ye that building shall endure,
Which shelters the noble and crushes the poor?

" With gates of silver and bars of gold,
·Ye have fenced my sheep from their Father's fold:
I have heard the dropping of their tears
In heaven, these eighteen hundred years."

"O Lord and Master, not ours the guilt,
We build but as our fathers built;
Behold thine images, how they stand,
Sovereign and sole, through all our land.

"Our task is hard, — with sword and flame
To hold thy earth forever the same,
And with sharp crooks of steel to keep
Still, as thou leftest them, thy sheep."

Then Christ sought out an artisan,
A low-browed, stunted, haggard man,
And a motherless girl, whose fingers thin
Pushed from her faintly want and sin.

These set he in the midst of them,
And as they drew back their garment-hem,
For fear of defilement, " Lo, here," said he,
"The images ye have made of me!"

ODE

**WRITTEN FOR THE CELEBRATION OF THE INTRODUCTION OF THE
COCHITUATE WATER INTO THE CITY OF BOSTON.**

MY name is Water: I have sped
    Through strange, dark ways, untried before,
By pure desire of friendship led,
    Cochituate's ambassador;
He sends four royal gifts by me:
Long life, health, peace, and purity.

I'm Ceres' cup-bearer; I pour,
    For flowers and fruits and all their kin,
Her crystal vintage, from of yore
    Stored in old Earth's selectest bin,
Flora's Falernian ripe, since God
The wine-press of the deluge trod.

In that far isle whence, iron-willed,
  The New World's sires their bark unmoored,
The fairies' acorn-cups I filled
  Upon the toadstool's silver board,
And, 'neath Herne's oak, for Shakspeare's sight,
Strewed moss and grass with diamonds bright.

No fairies in the Mayflower came,
  And, lightsome as I sparkle here,
For Mother Bay-State, busy dame,
  I've toiled and drudged this many a year,
Throbbed in her engines' iron veins,
Twirled myriad spindles for her gains.

I, too, can weave; the warp I set
  Through which the sun his shuttle throws,
And, bright as Noah saw it, yet
  For you the arching rainbow glows,
A sight in Paradise denied
To unfallen Adam and his bride.

When Winter held me in his grip,
  You seized and sent me o'er the wave,
Ungrateful! in a prison-ship;
  But I forgive, not long a slave,
For, soon as summer south-winds blew,
Homeward I fled, disguised as dew.

For countless services I'm fit,
  Of use, of pleasure, and of gain,
But lightly from all bonds I flit,
  Nor lose my mirth, nor feel a stain;
From mill and wash-tub I escape,
And take in heaven my proper shape.

So, free myself, to-day, elate
  I come from far o'er hill and mead,
And here, Cochituate's envoy, wait
  To be your blithesome Ganymede,
And brim your cups with nectar true
That never will make slaves of you.

LINES

SUGGESTED BY THE GRAVES OF TWO ENGLISH SOLDIERS ON
CONCORD BATTLE-GROUND.

THE same good blood that now refills
The dotard Orient's shrunken veins,
The same whose vigor westward thrills,
Bursting Nevada's silver chains,
Poured here upon the April grass,
Freckled with red the herbage new;
On reeled the battle's trampling mass,
Back to the ash the bluebird flew.

Poured here in vain; — that sturdy blood
Was meant to make the earth more green,
But in a higher, gentler mood
Than broke this April noon serene;
Two graves are here; to mark the place,
At head and foot, an unhewn stone,
O'er which the herald lichens trace
The blazon of Oblivion.

These men were brave enough, and true
To the hired soldier's bull-dog creed;
What brought them here they never knew,
They fought as suits the English breed;
They came three thousand miles, and died,
To keep the Past upon its throne;
Unheard, beyond the ocean tide,
Their English mother made her moan.

The turf that covers them no thrill
Sends up to fire the heart and brain;
No stronger purpose nerves the will,
No hope renews its youth again:
From farm to farm the Concord glides,
And trails my fancy with its flow;
O'erhead the balanced henhawk slides,
Twinned in the river's heaven below.

But go, whose Bay-State bosom stirs,
Proud of thy birth and neighbor's right,
Where sleep the heroic villagers
Borne red and stiff from Concord fight;

Thought Reuben, snatching down his gun,
Or Seth, as ebbed the life away,
What earthquake rifts would shoot and run
World-wide from that short April fray?

What then? With heart and hand they wrought
According to their village light;
'T was for the Future that they fought,
Their rustic faith in what was right.
Upon earth's tragic stage they burst
Unsummoned, in the humble sock;
Theirs the fifth act; the curtain first
Rose long ago on Charles's block.

Their graves have voices; if they threw
Dice charged with fates beyond their ken,
Yet to their instincts they were true,
And had the genius to be men.
Fine privilege of Freedom's host,
Of even foot-soldiers for the Right! —
For centuries dead, ye are not lost,
Your graves send courage forth, and might.

TO ——.

WE, too, have autumns, when our leaves
    Drop loosely through the dampened air,
When all our good seems bound in sheaves,
    And we stand reaped and bare.

Our seasons have no fixed returns,
    Without our will they come and go;
At noon our sudden summer burns,
    Ere sunset all is snow.

But each day brings less summer cheer,
    Crimps more our ineffectual spring,
And something earlier every year
    Our singing birds take wing.

As less the olden glow abides,
    And less the chillier heart aspires,
With drift-wood beached in past spring-tides
    We light our sullen fires.

By the pinched rushlight's starving beam
　We cower and strain our wasted sight,
To stitch youth's shroud up, seam by seam,
　In the long arctic night.

It was not so — we once were young —
　When Spring, to womanly Summer turning,
Her dew-drops on each grass-blade strung,
　In the red sunrise burning.

We trusted then, aspired, believed
　That earth could be remade to-morrow; —
Ah, why be ever undeceived?
　Why give up faith for sorrow?

O thou, whose days are yet all spring,
　Faith, blighted once, is past retrieving;
Experience is a dumb, dead thing;
　The victory's in believing.

FREEDOM.

ARE we, then, wholly fallen? Can it be
That thou, North wind, that from thy mountains
　　　bringest
Their spirit to our plains, and thou, blue sea,
Who on our rocks thy wreaths of freedom flingest,
As on an altar, — can it be that ye
Have wasted inspiration on dead ears,
Dulled with the too familiar clank of chains?
The people's heart is like a harp for years
Hung where some petrifying torrent rains
Its slow-incrusting spray: the stiffened chords
Faint and more faint make answer to the tears
That drip upon them: idle are all words;
Only a silver plectrum wakes the tone
Deep buried 'neath that ever-thickening stone.

We are not free: Freedom doth not consist
In musing with our faces toward the Past,
While petty cares, and crawling interests, twist
Their spider-threads about us, which at last

Grow strong as iron chains, to cramp and bind
In formal narrowness heart, soul, and mind.
Freedom is recreated year by year,
In hearts wide open on the Godward side,
In souls calm-cadenced as the whirling sphere,
In minds that sway the future like a tide.
No broadest creeds can hold her, and no codes;
She chooses men for her august abodes,
Building them fair and fronting to the dawn;
Yet, when we seek her, we but find a few
Light footprints, leading morn-ward through the dew;
Before the day had risen, she was gone.

And we must follow: swiftly runs she on,
And, if our steps should slacken in despair,
Half turns her face, half smiles through golden hair,
Forever yielding, never wholly won:
That is not love which pauses in the race
Two close-linked names on fleeting sand to trace;
Freedom gained yesterday is no more ours;
Men gather but dry seeds of last year's flowers:
Still there 's a charm ungranted, still a grace,
Still rosy Hope, the free, the unattained,
Makes us Possession's languid hand let fall;
'T is but a fragment of ourselves is gained, —
The Future brings us more, but never all.

And, as the finder of some unknown realm,
Mounting a summit whence he thinks to see
On either side of him the imprisoning sea,
Beholds, above the clouds that overwhelm
The valley-land, peak after snowy peak
Stretch out of sight, each like a silver helm
Beneath its plume of smoke, sublime and bleak,
And what he thought an island finds to be
A continent to him first oped, — so we
Can from our height of Freedom look along
A boundless future, ours if we be strong;
Or if we shrink, better remount our ships
And, fleeing God's express design, trace back
The hero-freighted Mayflower's prophet-track
To Europe, entering her blood-red eclipse.

BIBLIOLATRES.

Bowing thyself in dust before a Book,
And thinking the great God is thine alone,
O rash iconoclast, thou wilt not brook
What gods the heathen carves in wood and stone,
As if the Shepherd who from outer cold
Leads all his shivering lambs to one sure fold
Were careful for the fashion of his crook.

There is no broken reed so poor and base,
No rush, the bending tilt of swamp-fly blue,
But he therewith the ravening wolf can chase,
And guide his flock to springs and pastures new;
Through ways unlooked for, and through many lands,
Far from the rich folds built with human hands,
The gracious footprints of his love I trace.

And what art thou, own brother of the clod,
That from his hand the crook wouldst snatch away
And shake instead thy dry and sapless rod,
To scare the sheep out of the wholesome day?
Yea, what art thou, blind, unconverted Jew,
That with thy idol-volume's covers two
Wouldst make a jail to coop the living God?

Thou hear'st not well the mountain organ-tones
By prophet ears from Hor and Sinai caught,
Thinking the cisterns of those Hebrew brains
Drew dry the springs of the All-knower's thought,
Nor shall thy lips be touched with living fire,
Who blow'st old altar-coals with sole desire
To weld anew the spirit's broken chains.

God is not dumb, that he should speak no more;
If thou hast wanderings in the wilderness
And find'st not Sinai, 't is thy soul is poor;
There towers the mountain of the Voice no less,
Which whoso seeks shall find, but he who bends,
Intent on manna still and mortal ends,
Sees it not, neither hears its thundered lore.

Slowly the Bible of the race is writ,
And not on paper leaves nor leaves of stone;

Each age, each kindred adds a verse to it,
Texts of despair or hope, of joy or moan.
While swings the sea, while mists the mountains shroud,
While thunder's surges burst on cliffs of cloud,
Still at the prophets' feet the nations sit.

BEAVER BROOK.

HUSHED with broad sunlight lies the hill,
And, minuting the long day's loss,
The cedar's shadow, slow and still,
Creeps o'er its dial of gray moss.

Warm noon brims full the valley's cup,
The aspen's leaves are scarce astir,
Only the little mill sends up
Its busy, never-ceasing burr.

Climbing the loose-piled wall that hems
The road along the mill-pond's brink,
From 'neath the arching barberry-stems,
My footstep scares the shy chewink.

Beneath a bony buttonwood
The mill's red door lets forth the din;
The whitened miller, dust-imbued,
Flits past the square of dark within.

No mountain torrent's strength is here;
Sweet Beaver, child of forest still,
Heaps its small pitcher to the ear,
And gently waits the miller's will.

Swift slips Undine along the race
Unheard, and then, with flashing bound,
Floods the dull wheel with light and grace,
And, laughing, hunts the loath drudge round.

The miller dreams not at what cost
The quivering mill-stones hum and whirl,
Nor how for every turn, are tost
Armfuls of diamond and of pearl.

But Summer cleared my happier eyes
With drops of some celestial juice,
To see how Beauty underlies
For evermore each form of Use.

And more: methought I saw that flood,
Which now so dull and darkling steals,
Thick, here and there, with human blood,
To turn the world's laborious wheels.

No more than doth the miller there,
Shut in our several cells, do we
Know with what waste of beauty rare
Moves every day's machinery.

Surely the wiser time shall come
When this fine overplus of might,
No longer sullen, slow, and dumb,
Shall leap to music and to light.

In that new childhood of the Earth
Life of itself shall dance and play,
Fresh blood in Time's shrunk veins make mirth,
And labor meet delight half-way.

APPLEDORE.

How looks Appledore in a storm?
  I have seen it when its crags seemed frantic,
  Butting against the maddened Atlantic,
When surge after surge would heap enorme,
  Cliffs of Emerald topped with snow,
  That lifted and lifted and then let go
A great white avalanche of thunder,
  A grinding, blinding, deafening ire
Monadnock might have trembled under;
  And the island, whose rock-roots pierce below
  To where they are warmed with the central fire,
You could feel its granite fibres racked,
  As it seemed to plunge with a shudder and thrill
  Right at the breast of the swooping hill,
And to rise again, snorting a cataract
Of rage-froth from every cranny and ledge,
  While the sea drew its breath in hoarse and deep,

And the next vast breaker curled its edge,
    Gathering itself for a mighty leap.

North, east, and south there are reefs and breakers,
    You would never dream of in smooth weather,
That toss and gore the sea for acres,
    Bellowing and gnashing and snarling together;
Look northward, where Duck Island lies,
And over its crown you will see arise,
Against a background of slaty skies,
    A row of pillars still and white
    That glimmer and then are out of sight,
As if the moon should suddenly kiss,
    While you crossed the gusty desert by night,
The long colonnades of Persepolis,
And then as sudden a darkness should follow
To gulp the whole scene at single swallow,
The city's ghost, the drear, brown waste,
And the string of camels, clumsy-paced: —
Look southward for White Island light,
    The lantern stands ninety feet o'er the tide;
There is first a half-mile of tumult and fight,
Of dash and roar and tumble and fright,
    And surging bewilderment wild and wide,
Where the breakers struggle left and right,
    Then a mile or more of rushing sea,
And then the light-house slim and lone;
And whenever the whole weight of ocean is thrown
Full and fair on White Island head,
    A great mist-jotun you will see
    Lifting himself up silently
High and huge o'er the light-house top,
With hands of wavering spray outspread,
    Groping after the little tower,
    That seems to shrink, and shorten and cower,
Till the monster's arms of a sudden drop,
    And silently and fruitlessly
    He sinks again into the sea.

You, meanwhile, where drenched you stand,
    Awaken once more to the rush and roar
And on the rock-point tighten your hand,
As you turn and see a valley deep,

That was not there a moment before,
Suck rattling down between you and a heap
  Of toppling billow, whose instant fall
  Must sink the whole island once for all —
Or watch the silenter, stealthier seas
  Feeling their way to you more and more;
If they once should clutch you high as the knees
They would whirl you down like a sprig of kelp,
Beyond all reach of hope or help; —
  And such in a storm is Appledore.

DARA.

WHEN Persia's sceptre trembled in a hand
Wilted by harem-heats, and all the land
  Was hovered over by those vulture ills
That snuff decaying empire from afar,
Then, with a nature balanced as a star,
  Dara arose, a shepherd of the hills.

He, who had governed fleecy subjects well,
Made his own village, by the self-same spell,
  Secure and peaceful as a guarded fold,
Till, gathering strength by slow and wise degrees,
Under his sway, to neighbor villages
  Order returned, and faith and justice old. •

Now, when it fortuned that a king more wise
Endued the realm with brain and hands and eyes,
  He sought on every side men brave and just,
And having heard the mountain-shepherd's praise,
How he rendered the mould of elder days,
  To Dara gave a satrapy in trust.

So Dara shepherded a province wide,
Nor in his viceroy's sceptre took more pride
  Than in his crook before; but Envy finds
More soil in cities than on mountains bare,
And the frank sun of spirits clear and rare
  Breeds poisonous fogs in low and marish minds.

Soon it was whispered at the royal ear
That, though wise Dara's province, year by year,
   Like a great sponge, drew wealth and plenty up.
Yet, when he squeezed it at the king's behest,
Some golden drops, more rich than all the rest,
   Went to the filling of his private cup.

For proof, they said that whereso'er he went
A chest, beneath whose weight the camel bent,
   Went guarded, and no other eye had seen
What was therein, save only Dara's own,
Yet, when 't was opened, all his tent was known
   To glow and lighten with heapt jewels' sheen.

The king set forth for Dara's province straight,
Where, as was fit, outside his city's gate
   The viceroy met him with a stately train;
And there, with archers circled, close at hand,
A camel with the chest was seen to stand,
   The king grew red, for thus the guilt was plain.

"Open me now," he cried, "yon treasure-chest!"
'T was done, and only a worn shepherd's vest
   Was found within; some blushed and hung the head,
Not Dara; open as the sky's blue roof
He stood, and "O, my lord, behold the proof
   That I was worthy of my trust!" he said.

"For ruling men, lo! all the charm I had;
My soul, in those coarse vestments ever clad,
   Still to the unstained past kept true and leal,
Still on these plains could breathe her mountain air,
And Fortune's heaviest gifts serenely bear,
   Which bend men from the truth, and make them reel.

"To govern wisely I had shown small skill
Were I not lord of simple Dara still;
   That sceptre kept, I cannot lose my way!"
Strange dew in royal eyes grew round and bright
And thrilled the trembling lids; before 't was night
   Two added provinces blest Dara's sway.

TO J. F. H.

NINE years have slipped like hour-glass sand
    From life's fast-emptying globe away,
Since last, dear friend, I clasped your hand,
And lingered on the impoverished land,
    Watching the steamer down the bay.

I held the keepsake which you gave,
    Until the dim smoke-pennon curled
O'er the vague rim 'tween sky and wave,
And closed the distance like a grave,
    Leaving me to the outer world;

The old worn world of hurry and heat,
    The young, fresh world of thought and scope;
While you, where silent surges fleet
Toward far sky beaches still and sweet,
    Sunk wavering down the ocean-slope.

Come back our ancient walks to tread,
    Old haunts of lost or scattered friends,
Amid the Muses' factories red,
Where song, and smoke, and laughter sped
    The nights to proctor-hunted ends.

Our old familiars are not laid,
    Though snapped our wands and sunk our books,
They beckon, not to be gainsaid,
Where, round broad meads which mowers wade,
    Smooth Charles his steel-blue sickle crooks;

Where, as the cloudbergs eastward blow,
    From glow to gloom the hillside shifts
Its lakes of rye that surge and flow,
Its plumps of orchard-trees arow,
    Its snowy white-weed's summer drifts.

Or let us to Nantasket, there
    To wander idly as we list,
Whether, on rocky hillocks bare,
Sharp cedar-points, like breakers, tear
    The trailing fringes of gray mist.

Or whether, under skies clear-blown,
  The heightening surfs with foamy din,
Their breeze-caught forelocks backward blown
Against old Neptune's yellow zone,
  Curl slow, and plunge forever in.

For years thrice three, wise Horace said,
  A poem rare let silence bind;
And love may ripen in the shade,
Like ours, for nine long seasons laid
  In crypts and arches of the mind.

That right Falernian friendship old
  Will we, to grace our feast, call up,
And freely pour the juice of gold,
That keeps life's pulses warm and bold,
  Till Death shall break the empty cup.

MEMORIAL VERSES.

KOSSUTH.

A RACE of nobles may die out,
A royal line may leave no heir;
Wise Nature sets no guards about
Her pewter plate and wooden ware.

But they fail not, the kinglier breed,
Who starry diadems attain;
To dungeon, axe, and stake succeed
Heirs of the old heroic strain.

The zeal of Nature never cools,
Nor is she thwarted of her ends;
When gapped and dulled her cheaper tools,
Then she a saint and prophet spends.

Land of the Magyars! though it be
The tyrant may relink his chain,
Already thine the victory,
As the just Future measures gain.

Thou hast succeeded, thou hast won
The deathly travail's amplest worth;
A nation's duty thou hast done,
Giving a hero to our earth.

And he, let come what will of woe,
Has saved the land he strove to save;
No Cossack hordes, no traitor's blow,
Can quench the voice shall haunt his grave.

" I Kossuth am : O Future, thou
That clear'st the just and blott'st the vile,
O'er this small dust in reverence bow,
Remembering, what I was erewhile.

" I was the chosen trump wherethrough
Our God sent forth awakening breath;
Came chains ? Came death ? The strain He blew
Sounds on, outliving chains and death."

TO LAMARTINE.

1848.

I DID not praise thee when the crowd,
    'Witched with the moment's inspiration,
Vexed thy still ether with hosannas loud,
    And stamped their dusty adoration;
  I but looked upward with the rest,
And, when they shouted Greatest, whispered Best.

They raised thee not, but rose to thee,
    Their fickle wreaths about thee flinging;
So on some marble Phœbus the high sea
    Might leave his worthless sea-weed clinging,
  But pious hands, with reverent care,
Make the pure limbs once more sublimely bare.

Now thou 'rt thy plain, grand self again,
    Thou art secure from panegyric, —
Thou who gav'st politics an epic strain,
    And actedst Freedom's noblest lyric:
  This side the Blessed Isles, no tree
Grows green enough to make a wreath for thee.

Nor can blame cling to thee; the snow
 From swinish foot-prints takes no staining,
But, leaving the gross soils of earth below,
 Its spirit mounts, the skies regaining,
 And unresenting falls again,
To beautify the world with dews and rain.

The highest duty to mere man vouchsafed
 Was laid on thee, — out of wild chaos,
When the roused popular ocean foamed and chafed,
 And vulture War from his Imaus
 Snuffed blood, to summon homely Peace,
And show that only order is release.

To carve thy fullest thought, what though
 Time was not granted? Aye in history,
Like that Dawn's face which baffled Angelo,
 Left shapeless, grander for its mystery,
 Thy great Design shall stand, and day
Flood its blind front from Orients far away.

Who says thy day is o'er? Control,
 My heart, that bitter first emotion;
While men shall reverence the steadfast soul,
 The heart in silent self-devotion
 Breaking, the mild, heroic mien,
Thou 'lt need no prop of marble, Lamartine.

If France reject thee, 't is not thine,
 But her own, exile that she utters;
Ideal France, the deathless, the divine,
 Will be where thy white pennon flutters,
 As once the nobler Athens went
With Aristides into banishment.

No fitting metewand hath To-day
 For measuring spirits of thy stature, —
Only the Future can reach up to lay
 The laurel on that lofty nature, —
 Bard, who with some diviner art
Has touched the bard's true lyre, a nation's heart.

Swept by thy hand, the gladdened chords,
 Crashed now in discords fierce by others,

Gave forth one note beyond all skill of words,
    And chimed together, We are brothers.
O poem unsurpassed! it ran
All round the world, unlocking man to man.

France is too poor to pay alone
    The service of that ample spirit;
Paltry seem low dictatorship and throne,
    If balanced with thy simple merit.
    They had to thee been rust and loss;
Thy aim was higher, — thou hast climbed a Cross

TO JOHN G. PALFREY.

THERE are who triumph in a losing cause,
Who can put on defeat, as 't were a wreath
Unwithering in the adverse popular breath,
    Safe from the blasting demagogue's applause;
'T is they who stand for Freedom and God's laws.

And so stands Palfrey now, as Marvell stood,
Loyal to Truth dethroned, nor could be wooed
    To trust the playful tiger's velvet paws :
And if the second Charles brought in decay
    Of ancient virtue, if it well might wring
Souls that had broadened 'neath a nobler day,
    To see a losel, marketable king
Fearfully watering with his realm's best blood
    Cromwell's quenched bolts, that erst had cracked and
        flamed,
Scaring, through all their depths of courtier mud,
    Europe's crowned bloodsuckers, — how more ashamed
Ought we to be, who see Corruption's flood
    Still rise o'er last year's mark, to mine away
    Our brazen idols' feet of treacherous clay!

O utter degradation! Freedom turned
    Slavery's vile bawd, to cozen and betray
    To the old lecher's clutch a maiden prey,
If so a loathsome pander's fee be earned!
    And we are silent, — we who daily tread

A soil sublime, at least, with heroes' graves! —
  Beckon no more, shades of the noble dead!
Be dumb, ye heaven-touched lips of winds and waves!
  Or hope to rouse some Coptic dullard, hid
Ages ago, wrapt stiffly, fold on fold,
With cerements close, to wither in the cold
  Forever hushed, and sunless pyramid!
  Beauty and Truth, and all that these contain,
Drop not like ripened fruit about our feet;
  We climb to them through years of sweat and pain;
  Without long struggle, none did e'er attain
The downward look from Quiet's blissful seat:
  Though present loss may be the hero's part,
  Yet none can rob him of the victor heart
Whereby the broad-realmed future is subdued,
  And Wrong, which now insults from triumph's car,
  Sending her vulture hope to raven far,
Is made unwilling tributary of Good.

O Mother State, how quenched thy Sinai fires!
  Is there none left of thy staunch Mayflower breed?
No spark among the ashes of thy sires,
  Of Virtue's altar-flame the kindling seed?
Are these thy great men, these that cringe and creep,
  And writhe through slimy ways to place and power? —
How long, O Lord, before thy wrath shall reap
  Our frail-stemmed summer prosperings in their flower?
O for one hour of that undaunted stock
That went with Vane and Sydney to the block!

O for a whiff of Naseby, that would sweep,
  With its stern Puritan besom, all this chaff
  From the Lord's threshing-floor! Yet more than half
The victory is attained, when one or two,
  Through the fool's laughter and the traitor's scorn,
  Beside thy sepulchre can abide the morn,
Crucified Truth, when thou shalt rise anew.

TO W. L. GARRISON.

"Some time afterward, it was reported to me by the city officers that they had ferreted out the paper and its editor; that his office was an obscure hole, his only visible auxiliary a negro boy, and his supporters a few very insignificant persons of all colors." — *Letter of H. G. Otis.*

In a small chamber, friendless and unseen,
Toiled o'er his types one poor, unlearned young man;
The place was dark, unfurnitured, and mean; —
Yet there the freedom of a race began.

Help came but slowly; surely no man yet
Put lever to the heavy world with less:
What need of help? He knew how types were set,
He had a dauntless spirit, and a press.

Such earnest natures are the fiery pith,
The compact nucleus round which systems grow!
Mass after mass becomes inspired therewith,
And whirls impregnate with the central glow

O Truth! O Freedom! how are ye still born
In the rude stable, in the manger nursed!
What humble hands unbar those gates of morn
Through which the splendors of the New Day burst!

What! shall one monk, scarce known beyond his cell,
Front Rome's far-reaching bolts, and scorn her frown?
Brave Luther answered YES; that thunder's swell
Rocked Europe, and discharmed the triple crown.

Whatever can be known of earth we know,
Sneered Europe's wise men, in their snail-shells curled;
No! said one man in Genoa, and that No
Out of the dark created this New World.

Who is it will not dare himself to trust?
Who is it hath not strength to stand alone?
Who is it thwarts and bilks the inward MUST?
He and his works, like sand, from earth are blown.

T

Men of a thousand shifts and wiles, look here!
    See one straightforward conscience put in pawn
To win a world; see the obedient sphere
    By bravery's simple gravitation drawn!

Shall we not heed the lesson taught of old,
    And by the Present's lips repeated still,
In our own single manhood to be bold,
    Fortressed in conscience and impregnable will?

We stride the river daily at its spring,
    Nor, in our childish thoughtlessness, foresee
What myriad vassal streams shall tribute bring,
    How like an equal it shall greet the sea.

O small beginnings, ye are great and strong,
    Based on a faithful heart and weariless brain!
Ye build the future fair, ye conquer wrong,
    Ye earn the crown, and wear it not in vain.

ON THE DEATH OF C. T. TORREY.

Woe worth the hour when it is crime
    To plead the poor dumb bondman's cause,
When all that makes the heart sublime,
The glorious throbs that conquer time,
    Are traitors to our cruel laws!

He strove among God's suffering poor
    One gleam of brotherhood to send;
The dungeon oped its hungry door
To give the truth one martyr more,
    Then shut,—and here behold the end!

O Mother State! when this was done,
    No pitying throe thy bosom gave;
Silent thou saw'st the death-shroud spun,
And now thou givest to thy son
    The stranger's charity — a grave.

Must it be thus forever? No!
    The hand of God sows not in vain;

Long sleeps the darkling seed below,
The seasons come, and change, and go,
   And all the fields are deep with grain.

Although our brother lie asleep,
   Man's heart still struggles, still aspires;
His grave shall quiver yet, while deep
Through the brave Bay State's pulses leap
   Her ancient energies and fires.

When hours like this the senses' gush
   Have stilled, and left the spirit room,
It hears amid the eternal hush
The swooping pinions' dreadful rush,
   That brings the vengeance and the doom; —

Not man's brute vengeance, such as rends
   What rivets man to man apart, —
God doth not so bring round his ends,
But waits the ripened time, and sends
   His mercy to the oppressor's heart.

ELEGY ON THE DEATH OF DR. CHANNING.

I do not come to weep above thy pall,
   And mourn the dying-out of noble powers;
The poet's clearer eye should see, in all
   Earth's seeming woe, the seed of Heaven's flowers.

Truth needs no champions: in the infinite deep
   Of everlasting Soul her strength abides,
From Nature's heart her mighty pulses leap,
   Through Nature's veins her strength, undying, tides.

Peace is more strong than war, and gentleness,
   Where force were vain, makes conquest o'er the wave;
And love lives on and hath a power to bless,
   When they who loved are hidden in the grave.

The sculptured marble brags of death-strewn fields,
   And Glory's epitaph is writ in blood;
But Alexander now to Plato yields,
   Clarkson will stand where Wellington hath stood.

I watch the circle of the eternal years,
  And read forever in the storied page
One lengthened roll of blood, and wrong, and tears, —-
  One onward step of Truth from age to age.

The poor are crushed; the tyrants link their chain;
  The poet sings through narrow dungeon-grates;
Man's hope lies quenched; — and, lo! with steadfast
      gain
  Freedom doth forge her mail of adverse fates.

Men slay the prophets; fagot, rack, and cross
  Make up the groaning record of the past;
But Evil's triumphs are her endless loss,
  And sovereign Beauty wins the soul at last.

No power can die that ever wrought for Truth;
  Thereby a law of Nature it became,
And lives unwithered in its sinewy youth,
  When he who called it forth is but a name.

Therefore I cannot think thee wholly gone;
  The better part of thee is with us still;
Thy soul its hampering clay aside hath thrown,
  And only freer wrestles with the Ill.

Thou livest in the life of all good things;
  What words thou spak'st for Freedom shall not die;
Thou sleepest not, for now thy Love hath wings
  To soar where hence thy Hope could hardly fly.

And often, from that other world, on this
  Some gleams from great souls gone before may shine,
To shed on struggling hearts a clearer bliss,
  And clothe the Right with lustre more divine.

Thou art not idle: in thy higher sphere
  Thy spirit bends itself to loving tasks,
And strength, to perfect what it dreamed of here
  Is all the crown and glory that it asks.

For sure, in Heaven's wide chambers, there is room
  For love and pity, and for helpful deeds;
Else were our summons thither but a doom
  To life more vain than this in clayey weeds.

From off the starry mountain peak of song,
　Thy spirit shows me, in the coming time,
An earth unwithered by the foot of wrong,
　A race revering its own soul sublime.

What wars, what martyrdoms, what crimes, may come,
　Thou knowest not, nor I; but God will lead
The prodigal soul from want and sorrow home,
　And Eden ope her gates to Adam's seed.

Farewell! good man, good angel now! this hand
　Soon, like thine own, shall lose its cunning, too;
Soon shall this soul, like thine, bewildered stand,
　Then leap to thread the free, unfathomed blue:

When that day comes, O, may this hand grow cold,
　Busy, like thine, for Freedom and the Right;
O, may this soul, like thine, be ever bold
　To face dark Slavery's encroaching blight!

This laurel-leaf I cast upon thy bier;
　Let worthier hands than these thy wreath entwine;
Upon thy hearse I shed no useless tear, —
　For us weep rather thou in calm divine.
1842.

TO THE MEMORY OF HOOD.

ANOTHER star 'neath Time's horizon dropped,
　To gleam o'er unknown lands and seas;
Another heart that beat for freedom stopped, —
　What mournful words are these!

O Love Divine, that claspest our tired earth,
　And lullest it upon thy heart,
Thou knowest how much a gentle soul is worth
　To teach men what thou art!

His was a spirit that to all thy poor
　Was kind as slumber after pain:
Why ope so soon thy heaven-deep Quiet's door
　And call him home again?

Freedom needs all her poets : it is they
   Who give her aspirations wings,
And to the wiser law of music sway
   Her wild imaginings.

Yet thou hast called him, nor art thou unkind,
   O Love Divine, for 't is thy will
That gracious natures leave their love behind
   To work for Freedom still.

Let laurelled marbles weigh on other tombs,
   Let anthems peal for other dead,
Rustling the bannered depth of minster-glooms
   With their exulting spread.

His epitaph shall mock the short-lived stone,
   No lichen shall its lines efface,
He needs these few and simple lines alone
   To mark his resting-place : —

" Here lies a Poet.   Stranger, if to thee
   His claim to memory be obscure,
If thou wouldst learn how truly great was he,
   Go, ask it of the poor."

SONNETS.

I.

TO A. C. L.

THROUGH suffering and sorrow thou hast passed
To show us what a woman true may be :
They have not taken sympathy from thee,
Nor made thee any other than thou wast,
Save as some tree, which, in a sudden blast,
Sheddeth those blossoms, that are weakly grown,
Upon the air, but keepeth every one
Whose strength gives warrant of good fruit at last.
So thou hast shed some blooms of gayety,
But never one of steadfast cheerfulness;
Nor hath thy knowledge of adversity

Robbed thee of any faith in happiness,
But rather cleared thy inner eyes to see
How many simple ways there are to bless.
　1840.

II.

What were I, Love, if I were stripped of thee,
If thine eyes shut me out whereby I live,
Thou, who unto my calmer soul dost give
Knowledge, and Truth, and holy Mystery,
Wherein Truth mainly lies for those who see
Beyond the earthly and the fugitive,
Who in the grandeur of the soul believe,
And only in the Infinite are free?
Without thee I were naked, bleak, and bare
As yon dead cedar on the sea-cliff's brow;
And Nature's teachings, which come to me now,
Common and beautiful as light and air,
Would be as fruitless as a stream which still
Slips through the wheel of some old ruined mill.
　1841.

III.

I would not have this perfect love of ours
Grow from a single root, a single stem,
Bearing no goodly fruit, but only flowers
That idly hide life's iron diadem:
It should grow alway like that eastern tree
Whose limbs take root and spread forth constantly;
That love for one, from which there doth not spring
Wide love for all, it is but a worthless thing.
Not in another world, as poets prate,
Dwell we apart above the tide of things,
High floating o'er earth's clouds on faery wings;
But our pure love doth ever elevate
Into a holy bond of brotherhood
All earthly things, making them pure and good.
　1840.

IV.

"For this true nobleness I seek in vain,
In woman and in man I find it not;
I almost weary of my earthly lot,

My life-springs are dried up with burning pain."
Thou find'st it not? I pray thee look again,
Look *inward* through the depths of thine own soul.
How is it with thee? Art thou sound and whole?
Doth narrow search show thee no earthly stain?
BE NOBLE! and the nobleness that lies
In other men, sleeping, but never dead,
Will rise in majesty to meet thine own:
Then wilt thou see it gleam in many eyes,
Then will pure light around thy path be shed,
And thou wilt never more be sad and lone.

   1840.

V.

TO THE SPIRIT OF KEATS.

Great soul, thou sittest with me in my room,
Uplifting me with thy vast, quiet eyes,
On whose full orbs, with kindly lustre, lies
The twilight warmth of ruddy ember-gloom:
Thy clear, strong tones will oft bring sudden bloom
Of hope secure, to him who lonely cries,
Wrestling with the young poet's agonies,
Neglect and scorn, which seem a certain doom:
Yes! the few words which, like great thunderdrops,
Thy large heart down to earth shook doubtfully,
Thrilled by the inward lightning of its might,
Serene and pure, like gushing joy of light,
Shall track the eternal chords of Destiny,
After the moon-led pulse of ocean stops.

   1841.

VI.

Great Truths are portions of the soul of man;
Great souls are portions of Eternity;
Each drop of blood that e'er through true heart ran
With lofty message, ran for thee and me;
For God's law, since the starry song began,
Hath been, and still for evermore must be,
That every deed which shall outlast Time's span
Must goad the soul to be erect and free;
Slave is no word of deathless lineage sprung, —
Too many noble souls have thought and died,

Too many mighty poets have lived and sung,
And our good Saxon, from lips purified
With martyr-fire, throughout the world hath rung
Too long to have God's holy cause denied.
 1841.

VII.

I ask not for those thoughts, that sudden leap
From being's sea, like the isle-seeming Kraken,
With whose great rise the ocean all is shaken
And a heart-tremble quivers through the deep;
Give me that growth which some perchance deem sleep,
Wherewith the steadfast coral-stems uprise,
Which, by the toil of gathering energies,
Their upward way into clear sunshine keep,
Until, by Heaven's sweetest influences,
Slowly and slowly spreads a speck of green
Into a pleasant island in the seas,
Where, mid tall palms, the cane-roofed home is seen,
And wearied men shall sit at sunset's hour,
Hearing the leaves and loving God's dear power.
 1841.

VIII.

TO M. W. ON HER BIRTHDAY.

Maiden, when such a soul as thine is born,
The morning stars their ancient music make,
And, joyful, once again their song awake,
Long silent now with melancholy scorn;
And thou, not mindless of so blest a morn,
By no least deed its harmony shalt break,
But shalt to that high chime thy footsteps take,
Through life's most darksome passes unforlorn;
Therefore from thy pure faith thou shalt not fall,
Therefore shalt thou be ever fair and free,
And in thine every motion musical
As summer air, majestic as the sea,
A mystery to those who creep and crawl
Through Time, and part it from Eternity.
 1841.

IX.

My Love, I have no fear that thou shouldst die;
Albeit I ask no fairer life than this,
Whose numbering-clock is still thy gentle kiss,
While Time and Peace with hands enlockèd fly, —
Yet care I not where in Eternity
We live and love, well knowing that there is
No backward step for those who feel the bliss
Of Faith as their most lofty yearnings high:
Love hath so purified my being's core,
Meseems I scarcely should be startled, even,
To find, some morn, that thou hadst gone before;
Since, with thy love, this knowledge too was given,
Which each calm day doth strengthen more and more
That they who love are but one step from Heaven.
    1841.

X.

I cannot think that thou shouldst pass away,
Whose life to mine is an eternal law,
A piece of nature that can have no flaw,
A new and certain sunrise every day;
But, if thou art to be another ray
About the Sun of Life, and art to live
Free from all of thee that was fugitive,
The debt of Love I will more fully pay,
Not downcast with the thought of thee so high,
But rather raised to be a nobler man,
And more divine in my humanity,
As knowing that the waiting eyes which scan
My life are lighted by a purer being,
And ask meek, calm-browed deeds, with it agreeing.
    1841.

XI.

There never yet was flower fair in vain,
Let classic poets rhyme it as they will;
The seasons toil that it may blow again,
And summer's heart doth feel its every ill;
Nor is a true soul ever born for naught;
Wherever any such hath lived and died,
There hath been something for true freedom wrought,

Some bulwark levelled on the evil side:
Toil on, then, Greatness! thou art in the right,
However narrow souls may call thee wrong;
Be as thou wouldst be in thine own clear sight,
And so thou wilt in all the world's ere long;
For worldlings cannot, struggle as they may,
From man's great soul one great thought hide away
    1841.

XII.

SUB PONDERE CRESCIT.

The hope of Truth grows stronger, day by day;
I hear the soul of Man around me waking,
Like a great sea, its frozen fetters breaking,
And flinging up to heaven its sunlit spray,
Tossing huge continents in scornful play,
And crushing them, with din of grinding thunder,
That makes old emptinesses stare in wonder;
The memory of a glory passed away
Lingers in every heart, as, in the shell,
Resounds the bygone freedom of the sea,
And, every hour new signs of promise tell
That the great soul shall once again be free,
For high, and yet more high, the murmurs swell
Of inward strife for truth and liberty.
    1841.

XIII.

Belovèd, in the noisy city here,
The thought of thee can make all turmoil cease;
Around my spirit, folds thy spirit clear
Its still, soft arms, and circles it with peace;
There is no room for any doubt or fear
In souls so overfilled with love's increase,
There is no memory of the bygone year
But growth in heart's and spirit's perfect ease;
How hath our love, half nebulous at first,
Rounded itself into a full-orbed sun!
How have our lives and wills (as haply erst
They were, ere this forgetfulness begun,)
Through all their earthly distantness outburst,
And melted, like two rays of light, in one!
    1842.

XIV.

ON READING WORDSWORTH'S SONNETS IN DEFENCE OF CAPITAL PUNISHMENT.

As the broad ocean endlessly upheaveth,
With the majestic beating of his heart,
The mighty tides, whereof its rightful part
Each sea-wide bay and little weed receiveth, –
So, through his soul who earnestly believeth,
Life from the universal Heart doth flow,
Whereby some conquest of the eternal Woe,
By instinct of God's nature, he achieveth:
A fuller pulse of this all-powerful beauty
Into the poet's gulf-like heart doth tide,
And he more keenly feels the glorious duty
Of serving Truth, despised and crucified, —
Happy, unknowing sect or creed, to rest
And feel God flow forever through his breast.
    1842.

XV.

THE SAME CONTINUED.

Once hardly in a cycle blossometh
A flower-like soul ripe with the seeds of song,
A spirit fore-ordained to cope with wrong,
Whose divine thoughts are natural as breath,
Who the old Darkness thickly scattereth
With starry words, that shoot prevailing light
Into the deeps, and wither, with the blight
Of serene Truth, the coward heart of Death:
Woe, if such spirit thwart its errand high,
And mock with lies the longing soul of man!
Yet one age longer must true Culture lie,
Soothing her bitter fetters as she can,
Until new messages of love outstart
At the next beating of the infinite Heart.

XVI.

THE SAME CONTINUED.

The love of all things springs from love of one;
Wider the soul's horizon hourly grows,
And over it with fuller glory flows

The sky-like spirit of God; a hope begun
In doubt and darkness 'neath a fairer sun
Cometh to fruitage, if it be of Truth;
And to the law of meekness, faith, and ruth,
By inward sympathy, shall all be won:
This thou shouldst know, who, from·the painted **feature**
Of shifting Fashion, couldst thy brethren turn
Unto the love of ever-youthful Nature,
And of a beauty fadeless and eterne;
And always 't is the saddest sight to see
An old man faithless in Humanity.

XVII.

THE SAME CONTINUED.

A poet cannot strive for despotism;
His harp falls shattered; for it still must **be**
The instinct of great spirits to be free,
And the sworn foes of cunning barbarism:
He, who has deepest searched the wide **abysm**
Of that life-giving Soul which men call fate,
Knows that to put more faith in lies and hate
Than truth and love is the true atheism:
Upward the soul forever turns her eyes;
The next hour always shames the hour before;
One beauty, at its highest, prophesies
That by whose side it shall seem mean and poor ;
No God-like thing knows aught of less and less,
But widens to the boundless Perfectness.

XVIII.

THE SAME CONTINUED.

Therefore think not the Past is wise alone,
For Yesterday knows nothing of the Best,
And thou shalt love it only as the nest
Whence glory-wingèd things to Heaven have flown:
To the great Soul alone are all things known;
Present and future are to her as past,
While she in glorious madness doth forecast
That perfect bud, which seems a flower full-blown
To each new Prophet, and yet always opes
Fuller and fuller with each day and hour,
Heartening the soul with odor of fresh hopes,

And longings high, and gushings of wide power,
Yet never is or shall be fully blown
Save in the forethought of the Eternal One.

XIX.

THE SAME CONCLUDED.

Far 'yond this narrow parapet of Time,
With eyes uplift, the poet's soul should look
Into the Endless Promise, nor should brook
One prying doubt to shake his faith sublime;
To him the earth is ever in her prime
And dewiness of morning; he can see
Good lying hid, from all eternity,
Within the teeming womb of sin and crime;
His soul should not be cramped by any bar,
His nobleness should be so God-like high,
That his least deed is perfect as a star,
His common look majestic as the sky,
And all o'erflooded with a light from far,
Undimmed by clouds of weak mortality.

XX.

TO M. O. S.

Mary, since first I knew thee, to this hour,
My love hath deepened, with my wiser sense
Of what in Woman is to reverence;
Thy clear heart, fresh as e'er was forest-flower,
Still opens more to me its beauteous dower; —
But let praise hush, — Love asks no evidence
To prove itself well-placed; we know not whence
It gleans the straws that thatch its humble bower:
We can but say we found it in the heart,
Spring of all sweetest thoughts, arch foe of blame,
Sower of flowers in the dusty mart,
Pure vestal of the poet's holy flame, —
This is enough, and we have done our part
If we but keep it spotless as it came.
1842.

XXI.

Our love is not a fading, earthly flower:
Its wingèd seed dropped down from Paradise,

And, nursed by day and night, by sun and shower,
Doth momently to fresher beauty rise:
To us the leafless autumn is not bare,
Nor winter's rattling boughs lack lusty green.
Our summer hearts make summer's fulness, where
No leaf, or bud, or blossom may be seen:
For nature's life in love's deep life doth lie,
Love, — whose forgetfulness is beauty's death,
Whose mystic key these cells of Thou and I
Into the infinite freedom openeth,
And makes the body's dark and narrow grate
The wide-flung leaves of Heaven's palace-gate.
    1842.

XXII.

IN ABSENCE.

These rugged, wintry days I scarce could bear,
Did I not know, that, in the early spring,
When wild March winds upon their errands sing,
Thou wouldst return, bursting on this still air,
Like those same winds, when, startled from their
      lair,
They hunt up violets, and free swift brooks,
From icy cares, even as thy clear looks
Bid my heart bloom, and sing, and break all care·
When drops with welcome rain the April day,
My flowers shall find their April in thine eyes,
Save there the rain in dreamy clouds doth stay,
As loath to fall out of those happy skies;
Yet sure, my love, thou art most like to May,
That comes with steady sun when April dies.
    1843.

XXIII.

WENDELL PHILLIPS.

He stood upon the world's broad threshold; wide
The din of battle and of slaughter rose;
He saw God stand upon the weaker side,
That sank in seeming loss before its foes;
Many there were who made great haste and sold
Unto the cunning enemy their swords,
He scorned their gifts of fame, and power, and gold,

And, underneath their soft and flowery words,
Heard the cold serpent hiss ; therefore he went
And humbly joined him to the weaker part,
Fanatic named, and fool, yet well content
So he could be the nearer to God's heart,
And feel its solemn pulses sending blood
Through all the wide-spread veins of endless good.

XXIV.

THE STREET.

They pass me by like shadows, crowds on crowds,
Dim ghosts of men, that hover to and fro,
Hugging their bodies round them, like thin shrouds
Wherein their souls were buried long ago:
They trampled on their youth, and faith, and love,
They cast their hope of human-kind away,
With Heaven's clear messages they madly strove,
And conquered, — and their spirits turned to clay:
Lo! how they wander round the world, their grave,
Whose ever-gaping maw by such is fed,
Gibbering at living men, and idly rave,
" We, only, truly live, but ye are dead."
Alas! poor fools, the anointed eye may trace
A dead soul's epitaph in every face!

XXV.

I grieve not that ripe Knowledge takes away
The charm that Nature to my childhood wore,
For, with that insight, cometh, day by day,
A greater bliss than wonder was before;
The real doth not clip the poet's wings, —
To win the secret of a weed's plain heart
Reveals some clue to spiritual things,
And stumbling guess becomes firm-footed art:
Flowers are not flowers unto the poet's eyes,
Their beauty thrills him by an inward sense;
He knows that outward seemings are but lies,
Or, at the most, but earthly shadows, whence
The soul that looks within for truth may guess
The presence of some wondrous heavenliness.

XXVI.

TO J. R. GIDDINGS.

Giddings, far rougher names than thine have grown
Smoother than honey on the lips of men;
And thou shalt aye be honorably known,
As one who bravely used his tongue and pen,
As best befits a freeman, — even for those,
To whom our Law's unblushing front denies
A right to plead against the life-long woes
Which are the Negro's glimpse of Freedom's skies.
Fear nothing, and hope all things, as the Right
Alone may do securely; every hour
The thrones of Ignorance and ancient Night
Lose somewhat of their long-usurpèd power,
And Freedom's lightest word can make them shiver
With a base dread that clings to them forever.

XXVII.

I thought our love at full, but I did err;
Joy's wreath drooped o'er mine eyes; I could not see
That sorrow in our happy world must be
Love's deepest spokesman and interpreter;
But, as a mother feels her child first stir
Under her heart, so felt I instantly
Deep in my soul another bond to thee
Thrill with that life we saw depart from her;
O mother of our angel-child! twice dear!
Death knits as well as parts, and still, I wis,
Her tender radiance shall enfold us here,
Even as the light, borne up by inward bliss,
Threads the void glooms of space without a fear,
To print on farthest stars her pitying kiss.

L'ENVOI.

WHETHER my heart hath wiser grown or not,
In these three years, since I to thee inscribed,
Mine own betrothed, the firstlings of my muse, —
Poor windfalls of unripe experience,
Young buds plucked hastily by childish hands

U

Not patient to await more full-blown flowers, —
At least it hath seen more of life and men,
And pondered more, and grown a shade more sad,
Yet with no loss of hope or settled trust
In the benignness of that Providence,
Which shapes from out our elements awry
The grace and order that we wonder at,
The mystic harmony of right and wrong,
Both working out His wisdom and our good:
A trust, Beloved, chiefly learned of thee,
Who hast that gift of patient tenderness,
The instinctive wisdom of a woman's heart.

They tell us that our land was made for song,
With its huge rivers and sky-piercing peaks,
Its sea-like lakes and mighty cataracts,
Its forests vast and hoar, and prairies wide,
And mounds that tell of wondrous tribes extinct.
But Poesy springs not from rocks and woods;
Her womb and cradle are the human heart,
And she can find a nobler theme for song
In the most loathsome man that blasts the sight,
Than in the broad expanse of sea and shore
Between the frozen deserts of the poles.
All nations have their message from on high,
Each the messiah of some central thought,
For the fulfilment and delight of Man:
One has to teach that labor is divine;
Another Freedom; and another Mind;
And all, that God is open-eyed and just,
The happy centre and calm heart of all.

Are, then, our woods, our mountains, and our streams,
Needful to teach our poets how to sing?
O, maiden rare, far other thoughts were ours,
When we have sat by ocean's foaming marge,
And watched the waves leap roaring on the rocks,
Than young Leander and his Hero had,
Gazing from Sestos to the other shore.
The moon looks down and ocean worships her,
Stars rise and set, and seasons come and go
Even as they did in Homer's elder time,
But we behold them not with Grecian eyes:

Then they were types of beauty and of strength,
But now of freedom, unconfined and pure,
Subject alone to Order's higher law.
What cares the Russian serf or Southern slave
Though we should speak as man spake never yet
Of gleaming Hudson's broad magnificence,
Or green Niagara's never-ending roar ?
Our country hath a gospel of her own
To preach and practise before all the world, —
The freedom and divinity of man,
The glorious claims of human brotherhood, —
Which to pay nobly, as a freeman should,
Gains the sole wealth that will not fly away, —
And the soul's fealty to none but God.
These are realities, which make the shows
Of outward Nature, be they ne'er so grand,
Seem small, and worthless, and contemptible.
These are the mountain-summits for our bards,
Which stretch far upward into heaven itself,
And give such wide-spread and exulting view
Of hope, and faith, and onward destiny,
That shrunk Parnassus to a molehill dwindles.
Our new Atlantis, like a morning-star,
Silvers the murk face of slow-yielding Night,
The herald of a fuller truth than yet
Hath gleamed upon the upraisèd face of Man
Since the earth glittered in her stainless prime, —
Of a more glorious sunrise than of old
Drew wondrous melodies from Memnon huge,
Yea, draws them still, though now he sits waist-deep
In the engulfing flood of whirling sand,
And looks across the wastes of endless gray,
Sole wreck, where once his hundred-gated Thebes
Pained with her mighty hum the calm, blue heaven.
Shall the dull stone pay grateful orisons,
And we till noonday bar the splendor out,
Lest it reproach and chide our sluggard hearts,
Warm-nestled in the down of Prejudice,
And be content, though clad with angel-wings,
Close-clipped, to hop about from perch to perch,
In paltry cages of dead men's dead thoughts ?
O, rather like the sky-lark, soar and sing,
And let our gushing songs befit the dawn

And sunrise, and the yet unshaken dew
Brimming the chalice of each full-blown hope,
Whose blithe front turns to greet the growing day
Never had poets such high call before,
Never can poets hope for higher one,
And, if they be but faithful to their trust,
Earth will remember them with love and joy,
And O, far better, God will not forget.
For he who settles Freedom's principles
Writes the death-warrant of all tyranny;
Who speaks the truth stabs Falsehood to the heart,
And his mere word makes despots tremble more
Than ever Brutus with his dagger could.
Wait for no hints from waterfalls or woods,
Nor dream that tales of red men, brute and fierce,
Repay the finding of this Western World,
Or needed half the globe to give them birth:
Spirit supreme of Freedom! not for this
Did great Columbus tame his eagle soul
To jostle with the daws that perch in courts;
Not for this, friendless, on an unknown sea,
Coping with mad waves and more mutinous spirits,
Battled he with the dreadful ache at heart
Which tempts, with devilish subtleties of doubt,
The hermit of that loneliest solitude,
The silent desert of a great New Thought;
Though loud Niagara were to-day struck dumb,
Yet would this cataract of boiling life,
Rush plunging on and on to endless deeps
And utter thunder till the world shall cease, —
A thunder worthy of the poet's song,
And which alone can fill it with true life.
The high evangel to our country granted
Could make apostles, yea, with tongues of fire,
Of hearts half-darkened back again to clay!
'T is the soul only that is national,
And he who pays true loyalty to that
Alone can claim the wreath of patriotism.

Beloved! if I wander far and oft
From that which I believe, and feel, and know,
Thou wilt forgive, not with a sorrowing heart,
But with a strengthened hope of better things;

Knowing that I, though often blind and false
To those I love, and O, more false than all
Unto myself, have been most true to thee,
And that whoso in one thing hath been true
Can be as true in all. Therefore thy hope
May yet not prove unfruitful, and thy love
Meet, day by day, with less unworthy thanks
Whether, as now, we journey hand in hand
Or, parted in the body, yet are one
In spirit and the love of holy things.

THE VISION OF SIR LAUNFAL.

PRELUDE TO PART FIRST.

OVER his keys the musing organist,
    Beginning doubtfully and far away,
First lets his fingers wander as they list,
    And builds a bridge from Dreamland for his lay:
Then, as the touch of his loved instrument
    Gives hope and fervor, nearer draws his theme,
First guessed by faint auroral flushes sent
    Along the wavering vista of his dream.

    Not only around our infancy
    Doth heaven with all its splendors lie,
    Daily, with souls that cringe and plot,
    We Sinais climb and know it not.

Over our manhood bend the skies;
    Against our fallen and traitor lives
The great winds utter prophecies;
    With our faint hearts the mountain strives,
Its arms outstretched, the druid wood
    Waits with its benedicite;
And to our age's drowsy blood
    Still shouts the inspiring sea.

Earth gets its price for what Earth gives us;
    The beggar is taxed for a corner to die in,
The priest hath his fee who comes and shrives us,
    We bargain for the graves we lie in;

At the devil's booth are all things sold,
Each ounce of dross costs its ounce of gold;
　For a cap and bells our lives we pay,
Bubbles we buy with a whole soul's tasking:
　'T is heaven alone that is given away,
　'T is only God may be had for the asking,
No price is set on the lavish summer;
June may be had by the poorest comer.

And what is so rare as a day in June?
　Then, if ever, come perfect days;
Then Heaven tries the earth if it be in tune,
　And over it softly her warm ear lays:
Whether we look, or whether we listen,
We hear life murmur, or see it glisten;
Every clod feels a stir of might,
　An instinct within it that reaches and towers,
And, groping blindly above it for light,
　Climbs to a soul in grass and flowers;
The flush of life may well be seen
　Thrilling back over hills and valleys;
The cowslip startles in meadows green,
　The buttercup catches the sun in its chalice,
And there 's never a leaf nor a blade too mean
　To be some happy creature's palace;
The little bird sits at his door in the sun,
　Atilt like a blossom among the leaves,
And lets his illumined being o'errun
　With the deluge of summer it receives;
His mate feels the eggs beneath her wings,
And the heart in her dumb breast flutters and sings;
He sings to the wide world, and she to her nest,—
In the nice ear of Nature which song is the best?

Now is the high-tide of the year,
　And whatever of life hath ebbed away
Comes flooding back with a ripply cheer,
　Into every bare inlet and creek and bay;
Now the heart is so full that a drop overfills it,
We are happy now because God wills it;
No matter how barren the past may have been,
'T is enough for us now that the leaves are green;
We sit in the warm shade and feel right well

How the sap creeps up and the blossoms swell;
We may shut our eyes but we cannot help knowing
That skies are clear and grass is growing;
The breeze comes whispering in our ear,
That dandelions are blossoming near,
   That maize has sprouted, that streams are flowing,
That the river is bluer than the sky,
That the robin is plastering his house hard by;
And if the breeze kept the good news back,
For other couriers we should not lack;
   We could guess it all by yon heifer's lowing,—
And hark! how clear bold chanticleer,
Warmed with the new wine of the year,
   Tells all in his lusty crowing!

Joy comes, grief goes, we know not how;
Everything is happy now,
   Everything is upward striving;
'T is as easy now for the heart to be true
As for grass to be green or skies to be blue,—
   'T is the natural way of living:
Who knows whither the clouds have fled?
   In the unscarred heaven they leave no wake;
And the eyes forget the tears they have shed,
   The heart forgets its sorrow and ache;
The soul partakes the season's youth,
   And the sulphurous rifts of passion and woe
Lie deep 'neath a silence pure and smooth,
   Like burnt-out craters healed with snow.
What wonder if Sir Launfal now
Remembered the keeping of his vow?

PART FIRST.

I.

"My golden spurs now bring to me,
   And bring to me my richest mail,
For to-morrow I go over land and sea
   In search of the Holy Grail;
Shall never a bed for me be spread,
Nor shall a pillow be under my head,
Till I begin my vow to keep;

Here on the rushes will I sleep,
And perchance there may come a vision true
Ere day create the world anew."
　　Slowly Sir Launfal's eyes grew dim,
　　Slumber fell like a cloud on him,
And into his soul the vision flew.

II.

The crows flapped over by twos and threes,
In the pool drowsed the cattle up to their knees,
　　The little birds sang as if it were
　　The one day of summer in all the year,
And the very leaves seemed to sing on the trees,
The castle alone in the landscape lay
Like an outpost of winter, dull and gray;
'T was the proudest hall in the North Countree,
And never its gates might opened be,
Save to lord or lady of high degree;
Summer besieged it on every side,
But the churlish stone her assaults defied;
She could not scale the chilly wall,
Though round it for leagues her pavilions tall
Stretched left and right,
Over the hills and out of sight;
　　Green and broad was every tent,
　　And out of each a murmur went
Till the breeze fell off at night.

III.

The drawbridge dropped with a surly clang,
And through the dark arch a charger sprang,
Bearing Sir Launfal, the maiden knight,
In his gilded mail, that flamed so bright
It seemed the dark castle had gathered all
Those shafts the fierce sun had shot over its wall
　　In his siege of three hundred summers long,
And, binding them all in one blazing sheaf,
　　Had cast them forth: so, young and strong,
And lightsome as a locust-leaf,
Sir Launfal flashed forth in his unscarred mail,
To seek in all climes for the Holy Grail.

IV.

It was morning on hill and stream and tree,
  And morning in the young knight's heart;
Only the castle moodily
Rebuffed the gifts of the sunshine free,
  And gloomed by itself apart;
The season brimmed all other things up
Full as the rain fills the pitcher-plant's cup.

V.

As Sir Launfal made morn through the darksome gate,
  He was 'ware of a leper, crouched by the same,
Who begged with his hand and moaned as he sate;
  And a loathing over Sir Launfal came;
The sunshine went out of his soul with a thrill,
  The flesh 'neath his armor 'gan shrink and crawl,
And midway its leap his heart stood still
  Like a frozen waterfall;
For this man, so foul and bent of stature,
Rasped harshly against his dainty nature,
And seemed the one blot on the summer morn, —
So he tossed him a piece of gold in scorn.

VI.

The leper raised not the gold from the dust:
"Better to me the poor man's crust,
Better the blessing of the poor,
Though I turn me empty from his door;
That is no true alms which the hand can hold;
He gives nothing but worthless gold
  Who gives from a sense of duty;
But he who gives a slender mite,
And gives to that which is out of sight,
  That thread of the all-sustaining Beauty
Which runs through all and doth all unite, —
The hand cannot clasp the whole of his alms,
The heart outstretches its eager palms,
For a god goes with it and makes it store
To the soul that was starving in darkness before."

PRELUDE TO PART SECOND.

Down swept the chill wind from the mountain peak,
 From the snow five thousand summers old;
On open wold and hill-top bleak
 It had gathered all the cold,
And whirled it like sleet on the wanderer's cheek
It carried a shiver everywhere
From the unleafed boughs and pastures bare;
The little brook heard it and built a roof
'Neath which he could house him, winter-proof;
All night by the white stars' frosty gleams
He groined his arches and matched his beams;
Slender and clear were his crystal spars
As the lashes of light that trim the stars:
He sculptured every summer delight
In his halls and chambers out of sight;
Sometimes his tinkling waters slipt
Down through a frost-leaved forest-crypt,
Long, sparkling aisles of steel-stemmed trees
Bending to counterfeit a breeze;
Sometimes the roof no fretwork knew
But silvery mosses that downward grew;
Sometimes it was carved in sharp relief
With quaint arabesques of ice-fern leaf;
Sometimes it was simply smooth and clear
For the gladness of heaven to shine through, and here
He had caught the nodding bulrush-tops
And hung them thickly with diamond drops,
That crystalled the beams of moon and sun,
And made a star of every one:
No mortal builder's most rare device
Could match this winter-palace of ice;
'T was as if every image that mirrored lay
In his depths serene through the summer day,
Each fleeting shadow of earth and sky,
 Lest the happy model should be lost,
Had been mimicked in fairy masonry
 By the elfin builders of the frost.

Within the hall are song and laughter,
 The cheeks of Christmas glow red and jolly,
And sprouting is every corbel and rafter

With lightsome green of ivy and holly;
Through the deep gulf of the chimney wide
Wallows the Yule-log's roaring tide;
The broad flame-pennons droop and flap
   And belly and tug as a flag in the wind;
Like a locust shrills the imprisoned sap,
   Hunted to death in its galleries blind;
And swift little troops of silent sparks,
   Now pausing, now scattering away as in fear,
Go threading the soot-forest's tangled darks
   Like herds of startled deer.

But the wind without was eager and sharp,
Of Sir Launfal's gray hair it makes a harp,
    And rattles and wrings
    The icy strings,
  Singing, in dreary monotone,
  A Christmas carol of its own,
  Whose burden still, as he might guess,
  Was — "Shelterless, shelterless, shelterless!"

The voice of the seneschal flared like a torch
As he shouted the wanderer away from the porch,
And he sat in the gateway and saw all night
   The great hall-fire, so cheery and bold,
   Through the window-slits of the castle old,
Build out its piers of ruddy light
Against the drift of the cold.

PART SECOND.

I.

There was never a leaf on bush or tree,
The bare boughs rattled shudderingly;
The river was numb and could not speak,
   For the weaver Winter its shroud had spun;
A single crow on the tree-top bleak
   From his shining feathers shed off the cold sun.
Again it was morning, but shrunk and cold,
As if her veins were sapless and old,
And she rose up decrepitly
For a last dim look at earth and sea.

II.

Sir Launfal turned from his own hard gate,
For another heir in his earldom sate;
An old, bent man, worn out and frail,
He came back from seeking the Holy Grail;
Little he recked of his earldom's loss,
No more on his surcoat was blazoned the cross,
But deep in his soul the sign he wore,
The badge of the suffering and the poor.

III.

Sir Launfal's raiment thin and spare
Was idle mail 'gainst the barbèd air,
For it was just at the Christmas time;
So he mused, as he sat, of a sunnier clime,
And sought for a shelter from cold and snow
In the light and warmth of long-ago;
He sees the snake-like caravan crawl
O'er the edge of the desert, black and small,
Then nearer and nearer, till, one by one,
He can count the camels in the sun,
As over the red-hot sands they pass
To where, in its slender necklace of grass,
The little spring laughed and leapt in the shade,
And with its own self like an infant played,
And waved its signal of palms.

IV.

"For Christ's sweet sake, I beg an alms;"—
The happy camels may reach the spring,
But Sir Launfal sees only the grewsome thing,
The leper, lank as the rain-blanched bone,
That cowers beside him, a thing as lone
And white as the ice-isles of Northern seas
In the desolate horror of his disease.

V.

And Sir Launfal said,—"1 behold in thee
An image of Him who died on the tree;
Thou also hast had thy crown of thorns,—
Thou also hast had the world's buffets and scorns,—
And to thy life were not denied
The wounds in the hands and feet and side:

Mild Mary's Son, acknowledge me;
Behold, through him, I give to thee!"

VI.

Then the soul of the leper stood up in his eyes
　　And looked at Sir Launfal, and straightway he
Remembered in what a haughtier guise
　　He had flung an alms to leprosie,
When he girt his young life up in gilded mail
And set forth in search of the Holy Grail.
The heart within him was ashes and dust;
He parted in twain his single crust,
He broke the ice on the streamlet's brink,
And gave the leper to eat and drink,
'T was a mouldy crust of coarse brown bread,
　　'T was water out of a wooden bowl, —
Yet with fine wheaten bread was the leper fed,
　　And 't was red wine he drank with his thirsty soul.

VII.

As Sir Launfal mused with a downcast face,
A light shone round about the place;
The leper no longer crouched at his side,
But stood before him glorified,
Shining and tall and fair and straight
As the pillar that stood by the Beautiful Gate, —
Himself the Gate whereby men can
Enter the temple of God in Man.

VIII.

His words were shed softer than leaves from the pine,
And they fell on Sir Launfal as snows on the brine,
Which mingle their softness and quiet in one
With the shaggy unrest they float down upon;
And the voice that was calmer than silence said,
"Lo, it is I, be not afraid!
In many climes, without avail,
Thou hast spent thy life for the Holy Grail;
Behold it is here, — this cup which thou
Didst fill at the streamlet for me but now;
This crust is my body broken for thee,
This water His blood that died on the tree:
The Holy Supper is kept, indeed,

In whatso we share with another's need;
Not what we give, but what we share, —
For the gift without the giver is bare;
Who gives himself with his alms feeds three, —
Himself, his hungering neighbor, and me."

IX.

Sir Launfal awoke as from a swound: —
"The Grail in my castle here is found!
Hang my idle armor up on the wall,
Let it be the spider's banquet hall;
He must be fenced with stronger mail
Who would seek and find the Holy Grail."

X.

The castle gate stands open now,
    And the wanderer is welcome to the hall
As the hangbird is to the elm-tree bough;
    No longer scowl the turrets tall,
The Summer's long siege at last is o'er;
When the first poor outcast went in at the door,
She entered with him in disguise,
And mastered the fortress by surprise;
There is no spot she loves so well on ground,
She lingers and smiles there the whole year round;
The meanest serf on Sir Launfal's land
Has hall and bower at his command;
And there's no poor man in the North Countree
But is lord of the earldom as much as he.

NOTE. — According to the mythology of the Romancers, the San Greal, or Holy Grail, was the cup out of which Jesus partook of the last supper with his disciples. It was brought into England by Joseph of Arimathea, and remained there, an object of pilgrimage and adoration, for many years in the keeping of his lineal descendants. It was incumbent upon those who had charge of it to be chaste in thought, word, and deed; but one of the keepers having broken this condition, the Holy Grail disappeared. From that time it was a favorite enterprise of the knights of Arthur's court to go in search of it. Sir Galahad was at last successful in finding it, as we may read in the seventeenth book of the Romance of King Arthur. Tennyson has made Sir Galahad the subject of one of the most exquisite of his poems.

The plot (if I may give that name to anything so slight) of the foregoing poem is my own, and, to serve its purposes, I have enlarged the circle of competition in search of the miraculous cup in such a manner as to include, not only other persons than the heroes of the Round Table, but also a period of time subsequent to the date of King Arthur's reign.

Reader ! *walk up at once (it will soon be too late)*
and buy at a perfectly ruinous rate

A

FABLE FOR CRITICS :

OR, BETTER,

(I like, as a thing that the reader's first fancy may strike,
an old-fashioned title-page,
such as presents a tabular view of the volume's contents)

A GLANCE

AT A FEW OF OUR LITERARY PROGENIES

(*Mrs. Malaprop's word*)

FROM

THE TUB OF DIOGENES;

A VOCAL AND MUSICAL MEDLEY,

THAT IS,

A SERIES OF JOKES

By A Wonderful Quiz,

who accompanies himself with a rub-a-dub-dub, full of
spirit and grace, on the top of the tub.

Set forth in October, the 31st day,
In the year '48, G. P. Putnam, Broadway.

It being the commonest mode of procedure, I premise a few candid remarks

To the Reader;

This trifle, begun to please only myself and my own private fancy, was laid on the shelf. But some friends, who had seen it, induced me, by dint of saying they liked it, to put it in print. That is, having come to that very conclusion, I consulted them when it could make no confusion. For, (though in the gentlest of ways,) they had hinted it was scarce worth the while, I should doubtless have printed it.

I began it, intending a Fable, a frail, slender thing, rhyme-ywinged, with a sting in its tail. But, by addings and alterings not previously planned,—digressions chance-hatched, like birds' eggs in the sand,—and dawdlings to suit every whimsy's de·mand, (always freeing the bird which I held in my hand, for the two perched, perhaps out of reach, in the tree,)—it grew by degrees to the size which you see. I was like the old woman that carried the calf, and my neighbors, like hers, no doubt, wonder and laugh, and when, my strained arms with their grown burthen full, I call it my Fable, they call it a bull.

Having scrawled at full gallop (as far as that goes) in a style that is neither good verse nor bad prose, and being a person whom nobody knows, some people will say I am rather more free with my readers than it is becoming to be, that I seem to expect them to wait on my leisure in following wherever I wander at pleasure, that, in short, I take more than a young author's lawful ease, and laugh in a queer way so like Mephistopheles, that the public will doubt, as they grope through my rhythm, if in truth I am making fun *at* them or *with* them.

So the excellent Public is hereby assured that the sale of my book is already secured. For there is not a poet throughout the whole land, but will purchase a copy or two out of hand, in the fond expectation of being amused in it, by seeing his betters cut-up and abused in it. Now, I find, by a pretty exact calculation, there are something like ten thousand bards in the nation, of that special variety whom the Review and Magazine critics call *lofty* and *true*, and about thirty thousand (*this* tribe is increasing) of the kinds who are termed *full of promise* and *pleasing*. The Public will see by a glance at this schedule, that they cannot expect me to be over-sedulous about courting *them*, since it seems I have got enough fuel made sure of for boiling my pot.

As for such of our poets as find not their names mentioned once in my pages, with praises or blames, let them send in their cards, without further delay, to my friend G. P. Putnam, Esquire, in Broadway, where a list will be kept with

x   305

the strictest regard to the day and the hour of receiving the
card.   Then, taking them up as I chance to have time, (that is,
if their names can be twisted in rhyme,) I will honestly give
each his PROPER POSITION, at the rate of ONE AUTHOR to each
NEW EDITION.   Thus a PREMIUM is offered sufficiently HIGH
(as the magazines say when they tell their best lie) to induce
bards to CLUB their resources and buy the balance of every edi-
tion, until they have all of them fairly been run through the
mill.

One word to such readers (judicious and wise) as read books
with something behind the mere eyes, of whom in the country,
perhaps, there are two, including myself, gentle reader, and you.
All the characters sketched in this slight *jeu d'esprit*, though, it
may be, they seem, here and there, rather free, and drawn from
a Mephistophelian stand-point, are *meant* to be faithful, and that
is the grand point, and none but an owl would feel sore at a rub
from a jester who tells you, without any subterfuge, that he sits
in Diogenes' tub.

A PRELIMINARY NOTE TO THE SECOND
EDITION,

though it well may be reckoned, of all composition, the species
at once most delightful and healthy, is a thing which an author,
unless he be wealthy and willing to pay for that kind of delight,
is not, in all instances, called on to write.   Though there are, it
is said, who, their spirits to cheer, slip in a new title-page three
times a year, and in this way snuff up an imaginary savor of
that sweetest of dishes, the popular favor, — much as if a starved
painter should fall to and treat the Ugolino inside to a picture of
meat.

You remember (if not, pray turn over and look) that, in
writing the preface which ushered my book, I treated you,
excellent Public, not merely with a cool disregard, but down-
right cavalierly.   Now I would not take back the least thing I
then said, though I thereby could butter both sides of my bread,
for I never could see that an author owed aught to the people he
solaced, diverted, or taught; and, as for mere fame, I have long
ago learned that the persons by whom it is finally earned, are
those with whom *your* verdict weighed not a pin, unsustained by
the higher court sitting within.

But I wander from what I intended to say — that you have,
namely, shown such a liberal way of thinking, and so much
æsthetic perception of anonymous worth in the handsome
reception you gave to my book, spite of some private piques,
(having bought the first thousand in barely two weeks,) that I

think, past a doubt, if you measured the phiz of your's most devotedly, Wonderful Quiz, you would find that its vertical section was shorter, by an inch and two tenths, or 'twixt that and a quarter.

You have watched a child playing — in those wondrous years when belief is not bound to the eyes and the ears, and the vision divine is so clear and unmarred, that each baker of pies in the dirt is a bard? Give a knife and a shingle, he fits out a fleet, and, on that little mudpuddle over the street, his invention, in purest good faith, will make sail round the globe with a puff of his breath for a gale, will visit, in barely ten minutes, all climes, and find Northwestern passages hundreds of times. Or, suppose the young Poet fresh stored with delights from that Bible of childhood the Arabian Nights, he will turn to a crony and cry, "Jack, let's play that I am a Genius!" Jacky straightway makes Aladdin's lamp out of a stone, and, for hours, they enjoy each his own supernatural powers. This is all very pretty and pleasant, but then suppose our two urchins have grown into men, and both have turned authors, — one says to his brother, "Let's play we're the American somethings or other, (only let them be big enough, no matter what.) Come, you shall be Goethe or Pope, which you choose; I'll be Coleridge, and both shall write mutual reviews." So they both (as mere strangers) before many days, send each other a cord of anonymous bays. Each, in piling his epithets, smiles in his sleeve to see what his friend can be made to believe; each, in reading the other's unbiased review, thinks — Here's pretty high praise, but no more than is true. Well, we laugh at them both, and yet make no great fuss when the same farce is acted to benefit us. Even I, who, if asked, scarce a month since, what Fudge meant, should have answered, the dear Public's critical judgment, begin to think sharpwitted Horace spoke sooth when he said, that the Public *sometimes* hit the truth.

In reading these lines, you perhaps have a vision of a person in pretty good health and condition, and yet, since I put forth my primary edition, I have been crushed, scorched, withered, used up and put down, (by Smith with the cordial assistance of Brown,) in all, if you put any faith in my rhymes, to the number of ninety-five several times, and, while I am writing — I tremble to think of it, for I may at this moment be just on the brink of it — Molybdostom, angry at being omitted, has begun a critique, — am I not to be pitied?*

Now I shall not crush *them* since, indeed, for that matter, no pressure I know of could render them flatter; nor wither, nor scorch them, — no action of fire could make either them or their

---

* The wise Scandinavians probably called their bards by the queer-looking title of Scald, in a delicate way, as it were, just to hint to the world the hot water they always get into.

articles drier; nor waste time in putting them down — I am
thinking not their own self-inflation will keep them from sink-
ing; for there's this contradiction about the whole bevy —
though without the least weight, they are awfully heavy. No,
my dear honest bore, *surdo fabulam narras*, they are no more to
me than a rat in the arras. I can walk with the Doctor, get
facts from the Don, or draw out the Lambish quintessence of
John, and feel nothing more than a half-comic sorrow, to think
that they all will be lying to-morrow tossed carelessly up on the
waste-paper shelves, and forgotten by all but their half-dozen
selves. Once snug in my attic, my fire in a roar, I leave the
whole pack of them outside the door. With Hakluyt or
Purchas I wander away to the black northern seas or barbaric
Cathay; get *fou* with O'Shanter, and sober me then with that
builder of brick-kilnish dramas, rare Ben; snuff Herbert, as
holy as a flower on a grave; with Fletcher wax tender, o'er
Chapman grow brave; with Marlowe or Kyd take a fine poet-
rave; in Very, most Hebrew of Saxons, find peace; with Lyci-
das welter on vext Irish seas; with Webster grow wild, and
climb earthward again, down by mystical Browne's Jacob's-
ladder-like brain, to that spiritual Pepys (Cotton's* version)
Montaigne; find a new depth in Wordsworth, undreamed of
before, — that divinely-inspired, wise, deep, tender, grand, —
bore. Or, out of my study, the scholar thrown off, nature
holds up her shield 'gainst the sneer and the scoff; the land-
scape, forever consoling and kind, pours her wine and her oil
on the smarts of the mind. The waterfall, scattering its vanish-
ing gems; the tall grove of hemlocks, with moss on their stems,
like plashes of sunlight; the pond in the woods, where no foot
but mine and the bittern's intrudes; these are all my kind
neighbors, and leave me no wish to say aught to you all, my
poor critics, but — pish! I have buried the hatchet; I am
twisting an allumette out of one of you now, and relighting
my calumet. In your private capacities, come when you please,
I will give you my hand and a fresh pipe a-piece.

As I ran through the leaves of my poor little book, to take a
fond author's first tremulous look, it was quite an excitement
to hunt the *errata*, sprawled in as birds' tracks are in some
kinds of strata, (only these made things crookeder.) Fancy an
heir, that a father had seen born well-featured and fair, turn-
ing suddenly wry-nosed, club-footed, squint-eyed, hare-lipped,
wapper-jawed, carrot-haired, from a pride become an aversion,
— my case was yet worse. A club-foot (by way of a change)
in a verse. I might have forgiven, an *o*'s being wry, a limp in
an *e*, or a cock in an *i*, — but to have the sweet babe of my brain
served in *pi!* I am not queasy-stomached, but such a Thyes-
tean banquet as that was quite out of the question.

In the edition now issued, no pains are neglected, and my
verses, as orators say, stand corrected. Yet some blunders

remain of the public's own make, which I wish to correct for my personal sake. For instance, a character drawn in pure fun and condensing the traits of a dozen in one, has been, as I hear by some persons applied to a good friend of mine, whom to stab in the side, as we walked along chatting and joking together, would not be *my* way. I can hardly tell whether a question will ever arise in which he and I should by any strange fortune agree, but meanwhile my esteem for him grows as I know him, and, though not the best judge upon earth of a poem, he knows what it is he is saying and why, and is honest and fearless, two good points which I have not found so rife I can easily smother my love for them, whether on my side or t' other.

For my other *anonymi*, you may be sure that I know what is meant by a caricature, and what by a portrait. There *are* those who think it is capital fun to be spattering their ink on quiet unquarrelsome folk, but the minute the game changes sides and the others begin it, they see something savage and horrible in it. As for me I respect neither women nor men for their gender, nor own any sex in a pen. I choose just to hint to some causeless unfriends that, as far as I know, there are always two ends (and one of them heaviest, too) to a staff, and two parties also to every good laugh.

A FABLE FOR CRITICS.

PHŒBUS, sitting one day in a laurel-tree's shade,
Was reminded of Daphne, of whom it was made,
For the god being one day too warm in his wooing,
She took to the tree to escape his pursuing;
Be the cause what it might, from his offers she shrunk,
And, Ginevra-like, shut herself up in a trunk;
And, though 't was a step into which he had driven her,
He somehow or other had never forgiven her;
Her memory he nursed as a kind of a tonic,
Something bitter to chew when he'd play the Byronic,
And I can't count the obstinate nymphs that he brought
       over,
By a strange kind of smile he put on when he thought
       of her.
" My case is like Dido's," he sometimes remark'd,
" When I last saw my love, she was fairly embark'd,
In a laurel, as *she* thought — but (ah how Fate mocks!)
She has found it by this time a very bad box;
Let hunters from me take this saw when they need it,
—You're not always sure of your game when you've
       treed it.
Just conceive such a change taking place in one's mistress!
What romance would be left? — who can flatter or kiss
       trees?
And for mercy's sake, how could one keep up a dialogue
With a dull wooden thing that will live and will die a log,—
Not to say that the thought would forever intrude
That you've less chance to win her the more she is wood?
Ah! it went to my heart, and the memory still grieves,
To see those loved graces all taking their leaves;
Those charms beyond speech, so enchanting but now,
As they left me forever, each making its bough!
If her tongue *had* a tang sometimes more than was right,
Her new bark is worse than ten times her old bite."

Now, Daphne, — before she was happily treeified, —
Over all other blossoms the lily had deified,
And when she expected the god on a visit,

('T was before he had made his intentions explicit,)
Some buds she arranged with a vast deal of care,
To look as if artlessly twined in her hair,
Where they seemed, as he said, when he paid his addresses,
Like the day breaking through the long night of her tresses;
So whenever he wished to be quite irresistible,
Like a man with eight trumps in his hand at a whist-table,
(I feared me at first that the rhyme was untwistable,
Though I might have lugged in an allusion to Cristabel,) —
He would take up a lily, and gloomily look in it,
As I shall at the ——, when they cut up my book in it.

Well, here, after all the bad rhyme I 've been spinning,
I 've got back at last to my story's beginning:
Sitting there, as I say, in the shade of his mistress,
As dull as a volume of old Chester mysteries,
Or as those puzzling specimens, which, in old histories,
We read of his verses — the Oracles, namely, —
(I wonder the Greeks should have swallowed them tamely,
For one might bet safely whatever he has to risk,
They were laid at his door by some ancient Miss Asterisk,
And so dull that the men who retailed them out-doors
Got the ill name of augurs, because they were bores,) —
First, he mused what the animal substance or herb is
Would induce a moustache, for you know he 's *imberbis;*
Then he shuddered to think how his youthful position
Was assailed by the age of his son the physician;
At some poems he glanced, had been sent to him lately,
And the metre and sentiment puzzled him greatly.
" Mehercle !   I 'd make such proceedings felonious, —
Have they all of them slept in the cave of Trophonius ?
Look well to your seat, 't is like taking an airing
On a corduroy road, and that out of repairing;
It leads one, 't is true, through the primitive forest,
Grand natural features — but, then, one has no rest;
You just catch a glimpse of some ravishing distance,
When a jolt puts the whole of it out of existence, —
Why not use their ears, if they happen to have any ? "
— Here the laurel-leaves murmured the name of poor
    Daphne.

"O, weep with me, Daphne," he sighed, "for you know it 's
A terrible thing to be pestered with poets !

But, alas, she is dumb, and the proverb holds good,
She never will cry till she 's out of the wood !
What would n't I give if I never had known of her?
'T were a kind of relief had I something to groan over;
If I had but some letters of hers, now, to toss over,
I might turn for the nonce a Byronic philosopher,
And bewitch all the flats by bemoaning the loss of her.
One needs something tangible, though to begin on —
A loom, as it were, for the fancy to spin on;
What boots all your grist ? it can never be ground
Till a breeze makes the arms of the windmill go round,
(Or, if 't is a water-mill, alter the metaphor,
And say it won't stir, save the wheel be well wet afore,
Or lug in some stuff about water ' so dreamily,' —
It is not a metaphor, though, 't is a simile :)
A lily, perhaps, would set *my* mill agoing,
For just at this season, I think, they are blowing,
Here, somebody, fetch one, not very far hence
They 're in bloom by the score, 't is but climbing a fence;
There 's a poet hard by, who does nothing but fill his
Whole garden, from one end to t' other, with lilies;
A very good plan, were it not for satiety,
One longs for a weed here and there, for variety;
Though a weed is no more than a flower in disguise,
Which is seen through at once, if love give a man eyes."

Now there happened to be among Phœbus's followers,
A gentleman, one of the omnivorous swallowers,
Who bolt every book that comes out of the press,
Without the least question of larger or less,
Whose stomachs are strong at the expense of their head, —
For reading new books is like eating new bread,
One can bear it at first, but by gradual steps he
Is brought to death's door of a mental dyspepsy.
On a previous stage of existence, our Hero
Had ridden outside, with the glass below zero;
He had been, 't is a fact you may safely rely on,
Of a very old stock a most eminent scion, —
A stock all fresh quacks their fierce boluses ply on,
Who stretch the new boots Earth 's unwilling to try on,
Whom humbugs of all shapes and sorts keep their eye on,
Whose hair 's in the mortar of every new Zion,
Who, when whistles are dear, go directly and buy one,

Who think slavery a crime that we must not say fie on,
Who hunt, if they e'er hunt at all, with the lion,
(Though they hunt lions also, whenever they spy one,)
Who contrive to make every good fortune a wry one,
And at last choose the hard bed of honor to die on,
Whose pedigree traced to earth's earliest years,
Is longer than anything else but their ears; —
In short, he was sent into life with the wrong key,
He unlocked the door, and stept forth a poor donkey.
Though kicked and abused by his bipedal betters,
Yet he filled no mean place in the kingdom of letters;
Far happier than many a literary hack,
He bore only paper-mill rags on his back;
(For it makes a vast difference which side the mill
One expends on the paper his labor and skill;)
So, when his soul waited a new transmigration,
And Destiny balanced 'twixt this and that station,
Not having much time to expend upon bothers,
Remembering he'd had some connection with authors,
And considering his four legs had grown paralytic, —
She set him on two, and he came forth a critic.

Through his babyhood no kind of pleasure he took
In any amusement but tearing a book;
For him there was no intermediate stage,
From babyhood up to straight-laced middle age;
There were years when he did n't wear coat-tails behind,
But a boy he could never be rightly defined;
Like the Irish Good Folk, though in length scarce a span,
From the womb he came gravely, a little old man;
While other boys' trousers demanded the toil
Of the motherly fingers on all kinds of soil,
Red, yellow, brown, black, clayey, gravelly, loamy,
He sat in the corner and read Viri Romæ.
He never was known to unbend or to revel once
In base, marbles, hockey, or kick up the devil once;
He was just one of those who excite the benevolence
Of your old prigs who sound the soul's depths with a ledger,
And are on the lookout for some young men to "edger
cate," as they call it, who won't be too costly,
And who'll afterward take to the ministry mostly;
Who always wear spectacles, always look bilious,
Always keep on good terms with each *mater-familias*

Throughout the whole parish, and manage to rear
Ten boys like themselves, on four hundred a year;
Who, fulfilling in turn the same fearful conditions,
Either preach through their noses, or go upon missions.

In this way our hero got safely to college,
Where he bolted alike both his commons and knowledge;
A reading-machine, always wound up and going,
He mastered whatever was not worth the knowing,
Appeared in a gown, and a vest of black satin,
To spout such a Gothic oration in Latin,
That Tully could never have made out a word in it,
(Though himself was the model the author preferred in it,)
And grasping the parchment which gave him in fee,
All the mystic and-so-forths contained in A. B.,
He was launched (life is always compared to a sea,)
With just enough learning, and skill for the using it,
To prove he 'd a brain, by forever confusing it.
So worthy Saint Benedict, piously burning
With the holiest zeal against secular learning,
Nesciensque scienter, as writers express it,
Indoctusque sapienter à Româ recessit.

'T would be endless to tell you the things that he knew,
All separate facts, undeniably true,
But with him or each other they 'd nothing to do;
No power of combining, arranging, discerning,
Digested the masses he learned into learning;
There was one thing in life he had practical knowledge for,
(And this, you will think, he need scarce go to college for,)
Not a deed would he do, nor a word would he utter,
Till he 'd weighed its relations to plain bread and butter.
When he left Alma Mater, he practised his wits
In compiling the journals' historical bits, —
Of shops broken open, men falling in fits,
Great fortunes in England bequeathed to poor printers,
And cold spells, the coldest for many past winters, —
Then, rising by industry, knack, and address,
Got notices up for an unbiassed press,
With a mind so wellpoised, it seemed equally made for
Applause or abuse, just which chanced to be paid for;
From this point his progress was rapid and sure,
To the post of a regular heavy reviewer.

And here I must say he wrote excellent articles
On the Hebraic points, or the force of Greek particles,
They filled up the space nothing else was prepared for;
And nobody read that which nobody cared for;
If any old book reached a fiftieth edition,
He could fill forty pages with safe erudition,
He could gauge the old books by the old set of rules,
And his very old nothings pleased very old fools;
But give him a new book, fresh out of the heart,
And you put him at sea without compass or chart, —
His blunders aspired to the rank of an art;
For his lore was engraft, something foreign that grew in
    him,
Exhausting the sap of the native and true in him,
So that when a man came with a soul that was new in him,
Carving new forms of truth out of Nature's old granite,
New and old at their birth, like Le Verrier's planet,
Which, to get a true judgment, themselves must create
In the soul of their critic the measure and weight,
Being rather themselves a fresh standard of grace,
To compute their own judge, and assign him his place,
Our reviewer would crawl all about it and round it,
And, reporting each circumstance just as he found it,
Without the least malice, — his record would be
Profoundly æsthetic as that of a flea,
Which, supping on Wordsworth, should print, for our
    sakes,
Recollections of nights with the Bard of the Lakes,
Or, borne by an Arab guide, ventured to render a
General view of the ruins of Denderah.

As I said, he was never precisely unkind,
The defect in his brain was just absence of mind;
If he boasted, 't was simply that he was self-made,
A position which I, for one, never gainsaid,
My respect for my Maker supposing a skill
In his works which our hero would answer but ill;
And I trust that the mould which he used may be cracked,
    or he
Made bold by success, may enlarge his phylactery.
And set up a kind of a man-manufactory,
An event which I shudder to think about, seeing
That Man is a moral, accountable being.

He meant well enough, but was still in the way
As a dunce always is, let him be where he may;
Indeed, they appear to come into existence
To impede other folks with their awkward assistance;
If you set up a dunce on the very North pole,
All alone with himself, I believe, on my soul,
He'd manage to get betwixt somebody's shins,
And pitch him down bodily, all in his sins,
To the grave polar bears sitting round on the ice,
All shortening their grace, to be in for a slice;
Or, if he found nobody else there to pother,
Why, one of his legs would just trip up the other,
For there's nothing we read of in torture's inventions,
Like a well-meaning dunce, with the best of intentions.

A terrible fellow to meet in society,
Not the toast that he buttered was ever so dry at tea;
There he'd sit at the table and stir in his sugar,
Crouching close for a spring, all the while, like a cougar;
Be sure of your facts, of your measures and weights,
Of your time — he's as fond as an Arab of dates; —
You'll be telling, perhaps, in your comical way,
Of something you've seen in the course of the day;
And, just as you're tapering out the conclusion,
You venture an ill-fated classic allusion, —
The girls have all got their laughs ready, when, whack!
The cougar comes down on your thunderstruck back!
You had left out a comma, — your Greek's put in joint,
And pointed at cost of your story's whole point.
In the course of the evening, you venture on certain
Soft speeches to Anne, in the shade of the curtain;
You tell her your heart can be likened to *one* flower,
" And that, oh most charming of women, 's the sunflower,
Which turns " — here a clear nasal voice, to your terror,
From outside the curtain, says " that 's all an error."
As for him, he 's — no matter, he never grew tender,
Sitting after a ball, with his feet on the fender,
Shaping somebody's sweet features out of cigar smoke,
(Though he'd willingly grant you that such doings are
     smoke;)
All women he damns with *mutabile semper*,
And if ever he felt something like love's distemper,
'T was towards a young lady who spoke ancient Mexican,

And assisted her father in making a lexicon;
Though I recollect hearing him get quite ferocious
About Mary Clausum, the mistress of Grotius,
Or something of that sort, — but, no more to bore ye
With character-painting, I'll turn to my story.

Now, Apollo, who finds it convenient sometimes
To get his court clear of the makers of rhymes,
The *genus*, I think it is called, *irritabile*,
Every one of whom thinks himself treated most shabbily,
And nurses a — what is it? — *immedicabile*,
Which keeps him at boiling-point, hot for a quarrel,
As bitter as wormwood, and sourer than sorrel,
If any poor devil but look at a laurel; —
Apollo, I say, being sick of their rioting,
(Though he sometimes acknowledged their verse had a
        quieting
Effect after dinner, and seemed to suggest a
Retreat to the shrine of a tranquil siesta,)
Kept our hero at hand, who, by means of a bray,
Which he gave to the life, drove the rabble away;
And if that would n't do, he was sure to succeed,
If he took his review out and offered to read;
Or, failing in plans of this milder description,
He would ask for their aid to get up a subscription,
Considering that authorship was n't a rich craft,
To print the " American drama of Witchcraft."
"Stay, I'll read you a scene," — but he hardly began,
Ere Apollo shrieked " Help! " and the authors all ran:
And once, when these purgatives acted with less spirit,
And the desperate case asked a remedy desperate,
He drew from his pocket a foolscap epistle,
As calmly as if 't were a nine-barrelled pistol,
And threatened them all with the judgment to come,
Of " A wandering Star's first impressions of Rome."
" Stop! stop! " with their hands o'er their ears screamed
        the Muses,
" He may go off and murder himself, if he chooses,
'T was a means self-defence only sanctioned his trying,
'T is mere massacre now that the enemy's flying;
If he's forced to 't again, and we happen to be there,
Give us each a large handkerchief soaked in strong
        ether."

I call this a " Fable for Critics "; you think it's
More like a display of my rhythmical trinkets;
My plot, like an icicle, 's slender and slippery,
Every moment more slender, and likely to slip awry,
And the reader unwilling *in loco desipere,*
Is free to jump over as much of my frippery
As he fancies, and, if he's a provident skipper, he
May have an Odyssean sway of the gales,
And get safe into port, ere his patience all fails;
Moreover, although 't is a slender return
For your toil and expense, yet my paper will burn,
And, if you have manfully struggled thus far with me,
You may e'en twist me up, and just light your cigar with
　　　me:
If too angry for that, you can tear me in pieces,
And my *membra disjecta* consign to the breezes,
A fate like great Ratzau's, whom one of those bores,
Who beflead with bad verses poor Louis Quatorze,
Describes, (the first verse somehow ends with *victoire,*)
As *dispersant partout et ses membres et sa gloire;*
Or, if I were over-desirous of earning
A repute among noodles for classical learning,
I could pick you a score of allusions, I wis,
As new as the jests of *Didaskalos tis;*
Better still, I could make out a good solid list
From recondite authors who do not exist, —
But that would be naughty: at least, I could twist
Something out of Absyrtus, or turn your inquiries
After Milton's prose metaphor, drawn from Osiris; —
But, as Cicero says he won't say this or that,
(A fetch, I must say, most transparent and flat,)
After saying whate'er he could possibly think of, —
I simply will state that I pause on the brink of
A mire, ankle-deep, of deliberate confusion,
Made up of old jumbles of classic allusion,
So, when you were thinking yourselves to be pitied,
Just conceive how much harder your teeth you'd have
　　　gritted,
An 't were not for the dulness I've kindly omitted.

　　I'd apologize here for my many digressions,
Were it not that I 'm certain to trip into fresh ones,
('T is so hard to escape if you get in their mesh once;)

Just reflect, if you please, how 't is said by Horatius,
That Mæonides nods now and then, and, my gracious!
It certainly does look a little bit ominous
When he gets under way with *ton d'apameibomenos.*
(Here a something occurs which I 'll just clap a rhyme to,
And say it myself, ere a Zoilus have time to, —
Any author a nap like Van Winkle's may take,
If he only contrive to keep readers awake,
But he 'll very soon find himself laid on the shelf,
If *they* fall a nodding when he nods himself.)

Once for all, to return, and to stay, will I, nill I —
When Phœbus expressed his desire for a lily,
Our hero, whose homœopathic sagacity
With an ocean of zeal mixed his drop of capacity,
Set off for the garden as fast as the wind,
(Or, to take a comparison more to my mind,
As a sound politician leaves conscience behind,)
And leaped the low fence, as a party hack jumps
O'er his principles, when something else turns up trumps.

He was gone a long time, and Apollo meanwhile,
Went over some sonnets of his with a file,
For of all compositions, he thought that the sonnet
Best repaid all the toil you expended upon it;
It should reach with one impulse the end of its course,
And for one final blow collect all of its force;
Not a verse should be salient, but each one should tend
With a wave-like up-gathering to burst at the end; —
So, condensing the strength here, there smoothing a wry
    kink,
He was killing the time, when up walked Mr. ——;
At a few steps behind him, a small man in glasses,
Went dodging about, muttering "murderers! asses!"
From out of his pocket a paper he 'd take,
With the proud look of martyrdom tied to its stake,
And, reading a squib at himself, he 'd say, " Here I see
'Gainst American letters a bloody conspiracy,
They are all by my personal enemies written:
I must post an anonymous letter to Britain,
And show that this gall is the merest suggestion
Of spite at my zeal on the Copyright question,
For, on this side the water, 't is prudent to pull

O'er the eyes of the public their national veil,
By accusing of slavish respect to John Bull
All American authors who have more or less
Of that anti-American humbug — success,
While in private we 're always embracing the knees
Of some twopenny editor over the seas,
And licking his critical shoes, for you know 't is
The whole aim of our lives to get one English notice;
My American puffs I would willingly burn all,
(They 're all from one source, monthly, weekly, diurnal,)
To get but a kick from a transmarine journal!"

So, culling the gibes of each critical scorner
As if they were plums, and himself were Jack Horner,
He came cautiously on, peeping round every corner,
And into each hole where a weasel might pass in,
Expecting the knife of some critic assassin,
Who stabs to the heart with a caricature,
Not so bad as those daubs of the Sun, to be sure,
Yet done with a dagger-o'-type, whose vile portraits
Disperse all one's good, and condense all one's poor traits.

Apollo looked up, hearing footsteps approaching,
And slipped out of sight the new rhymes he was
        broaching, —
" Good day, Mr. ——, I 'm happy to meet
With a scholar so ripe, and a critic so neat,
Who through Grub-street the soul of a gentleman carries, —
What news from that suburb of London and Paris
Which latterly makes such shrill claims to monopolize
The credit of being the New World's metropolis ? "

" Why, nothing of consequence, save this attack
On my friend there, behind, by some pitiful hack,
Who thinks every national author a poor one,
That is n't a copy of something that 's foreign,
And assaults the American Dick — "
                              " Nay, 't is clear
That your Damon there 's fond of a flea in his ear,
And, if no one else furnished them gratis, on tick
He would buy some himself, just to hear the old click;
Why, I honestly think, if some fool in Japan
Should turn up his nose at the ' Poems on Man,'

Your friend there by some inward instinct would know it,
Would get it translated, reprinted, and show it;
As a man might take off a high stock to exhibit
The autograph round his own neck of the gibbet;
Nor would let it rest so, but fire column after column,
Signed Cato, or Brutus, or something as solemn,
By way of displaying his critical crosses,
And tweaking that poor transatlantic proboscis,
His broadsides resulting (and this there's no doubt of,)
In successively sinking the craft they're fired out of.
Now nobody knows when an author is hit,
If he don't have a public hysterical fit;
Let him only keep close in his snug garret's dim ether,
And nobody'd think of his critics — or him either;
If an author have any least fibre of worth in him,
Abuse would but tickle the organ of mirth in him,
All the critics on earth cannot crush with their ban,
One word that's in tune with the nature of man."

 "Well, perhaps so; meanwhile I have brought you a
   book,
Into which if you'll just have the goodness to look,
You may feel so delighted, (when you have got through it,)
As to think it not unworth your while to review it,
And I think I can promise your thoughts, if you do,
A place in the next Democratic Review."

 "The most thankless of gods you must surely have
   thought me,
For this is the forty-fourth copy you've brought me,
I have given them away, or at least I have tried,
But I've forty-two left, standing all side by side,
(The man who accepted that one copy, died,) —
From one end of a shelf to the other they reach,
'With the author's respects' neatly written in each.
The publisher, sure, will proclaim a Te Deum,
When he hears of that order the British Museum
Has sent for one set of what books were first printed
In America, little or big, — for 't is hinted
That this is the first truly tangible hope he
Has ever had raised for the sale of a copy.
I've thought very often 't would be a good thing
In all public collections of books, if a wing

Y

Were set off by itself, like the seas from the dry lands,
Marked *Literature suited to desolate islands,*
And filled with such books as could never be read
Save by readers of proofs, forced to do it for bread, —
Such books as one's wrecked on in small country-taverns,
Such as hermits might mortify over in caverns,
Such as Satan, if printing had then been invented,
As the climax of woe, would to Job have presented,
Such as Crusoe might dip in, although there are few so
Outrageously cornered by fate as poor Crusoe;
And since the philanthropists just now are banging
And gibbeting all who're in favor of hanging, —
(Though Cheever has proved that the Bible and Altar
Were let down from Heaven at the end of a halter,
And that vital religion would dull and grow callous,
Unrefreshed, now and then, with a sniff of the gallows,) —
And folks are beginning to think it looks odd,
To choke a poor scamp for the glory of God;
And that He who esteems the Virginia reel
A bait to draw saints from their spiritual weal,
And regards the quadrille as a far greater knavery
Than crushing His African children with slavery, —
Since all who take part in a waltz or cotillion
Are mounted for hell on the Devil's own pillion,
Who, as every true orthodox Christian well knows,
Approaches the heart through the door of the toes, —
That He, I was saying, whose judgments are stored
For such as take steps in despite of his word,
Should look with delight on the agonized prancing
Of a wretch who has not the least ground for his dancing,
While the State, standing by, sings a verse from the Psalter
About offering to God on his favorite halter,
And, when the legs droop from their twitching divergence,
Sells the clothes to a Jew, and the corpse to the surgeons; —

"Now, instead of all this, I think I can direct you all
To a criminal code both humane and effectual; —
I propose to shut up every doer of wrong
With these desperate books, for such term, short or long,
As by statute in such cases made and provided,
Shall be by your wise legislators decided;
Thus: — Let murderers be shut, to grow wiser and cooler,
At hard labor for life on the works of Miss —— ;

Petty thieves, kept from flagranter crimes by their **fears,**
Shall peruse Yankee Doodle a blank term of years, —
That American Punch, like the English, no doubt —
Just the sugar and lemons and spirit left out.

" But stay, here comes Tityrus Griswold, and leads on
The flocks whom he first plucks alive, and then feeds
    on, —
A loud-cackling swarm, in whose feathers warm-drest,
He goes for as perfect a — swan, as the rest.

" There comes Emerson first, whose rich words, **every**
    one,
Are like gold nails in temples to hang trophies on,
Whose prose is grand verse, while his verse, the Lord
    knows,
Is some of it pr—— No, 't is not even prose ;
I 'm speaking of metres ; some poems have welled
From those rare depths of soul that have ne'er been
    excelled ;
They 're not epics, but that does n't matter a pin,
In creating, the only hard thing 's to begin ;
A grass-blade 's no easier to make than an oak,
If you 've once found the way, you 've achieved the **grand**
    stroke ;
In the worst of his poems are mines of rich matter,
But thrown in a heap with a crash and a clatter ;
Now it is not one thing nor another alone
Makes a poem, but rather the general tone,
The something pervading, uniting the whole,
The before unconceived, unconceivable soul,
So that just in removing this trifle or that, you
Take away, as it were, a chief limb of the statue ;
Roots, wood, bark, and leaves, singly perfect may be,
But, clapt hodge-podge together, they don't make a tree.

" But, to come back to Emerson, (whom by the way,
I believe we left waiting,) — his is, we may say,
A Greek head on right Yankee shoulders, whose range
Has Olympus for one pole, for t' other the Exchange ;
He seems, to my thinking, (although I 'm afraid
The comparison must, long ere this, have been made,)
A Plotinus-Montaigne, where the Egyptian's gold mist

And the Gascon's shrewd wit cheek-by-jowl coexist;
All admire, and yet scarcely six converts he 's got
To I don't (nor they either) exactly know what;
For though he builds glorious temples, 't is odd
He leaves never a doorway to get in a god.
'T is refreshing to old-fashioned people like me,
To meet such a primitive Pagan as he,
In whose mind all creation is duly respected
As parts of himself — just a little projected;
And who 's willing to worship the stars and the sun,
A convert to — nothing but Emerson.
So perfect a balance there is in his head,
That he talks of things sometimes as if they were dead;
Life, nature, love, God, and affairs of that sort,
He looks at as merely ideas; in short,
As if they were fossils stuck round in a cabinet,
Of such vast extent that our earth 's a mere dab in it;
Composed just as he is inclined to conjecture her,
Namely, one part pure earth, ninety-nine parts pure
        lecturer;
You are filled with delight at his clear demonstration,
Each figure, word, gesture, just fits the occasion,
With the quiet precision of science he 'll sort 'em,
But you can't help suspecting the whole a *post mortem*.

    "There are persons, mole-blind to the soul's make and
        style,
Who insist on a likeness 'twixt him and Carlyle;
To compare him with Plato would be vastly fairer,
Carlyle 's the more burly, but E. is the rarer;
He sees fewer objects, but clearlier, truelier,
If C. 's as original, E. 's more peculiar;
That he 's more of a man you might say of the one,
Of the other he 's more of an Emerson;
C. 's the Titan, as shaggy of mind as of limb, —
E. the clear-eyed Olympian, rapid and slim;
The one 's two-thirds Norseman, the other half Greek,
Where the one 's most abounding, the other 's to seek;
C.'s generals require to be seen in the mass, —
E.'s specialties gain if enlarged by the glass;
C. gives nature and God his own fits of the blues,
And rims common-sense things with mystical hues, —
E. sits in a mystery calm and intense,

And looks coolly around him with sharp common sense;
C. shows you how every-day matters unite
With the dim transdiurnal recesses of night, —
While E., in a plain, preternatural way,
Makes mysteries matters of mere every day;
C. draws all his characters quite à *la* Fuseli, —
He don't sketch their bundles of muscles and thews illy,
But he paints with a brush so untamed and profuse,
They seem nothing but bundles of muscles and thews;
E. is rather like Flaxman, lines strait and severe,
And a color'ess outline, but full, round, and clear; —
To the men he thinks worthy he frankly accords
The design of a white marble statue in words.
C. labors to get at the centre, and then
Take a reckoning from there of his actions and men;
E. calmly assumes the said centre as granted,
And, given himself, has whatever is wanted.

"He has imitators in scores, who omit
No part of the man but his wisdom and wit, —
Who go carefully o'er the sky-blue of his brain,
And when he has skimmed it once, skim it again;
If at all they resemble him, you may be sure it is
Because their shoals mirror his mists and obscurities,
As a mud-puddle seems deep as heaven for a minute,
While a cloud that floats o'er is reflected within it.

"There comes ——, for instance; to see him 's rare
            sport,
Tread in Emerson's tracks with legs painfully short;
How he jumps, how he strains, and gets red in the face,
To keep step with the mystagogue's natural pace
He follows as close as a stick to a rocket,
His fingers exploring the prophet's each pocket.
Fie, for shame, brother bard; with good fruit of your
            own,
Can't you let neighbor Emerson's orchards alone?
Besides, 't is no use, you 'll not find e'en a core, —
—— has picked up all the windfalls before.
They might strip every tree, and E. never would catch 'em,
His Hesperides have no rude dragon to watch 'em;
When they send him a dishfull, and ask him to try 'em,
He never suspects how the sly rogues came by 'em;

He wonders why 't is there are none such his trees on,
And thinks 'em the best he has tasted this season.

"Yonder, calm as a cloud, Alcott stalks in a dream,
And fancies himself in thy groves, Academe,
With the Parthenon nigh, and the olive-trees o'er him,
And never a fact to perplex him or bore him,
With a snug room at Plato's, when night comes, to walk to,
And people from morning till midnight to talk to,
And from midnight till morning, nor snore in their listen-
 ing; —
So he muses, his face with the joy of it glistening,
For his highest conceit of a happiest state is
Where they 'd live upon acorns, and hear him talk gratis;
And indeed, I believe, no man ever talked better —
Each sentence hangs perfectly poised to a letter;
He seems piling words, but there 's royal dust hid
In the heart of each sky-piercing pyramid.
While he talks he is great, but goes out like a taper,
If you shut him up closely with pen, ink, and paper;
Yet his fingers itch for 'em from morning till night,
And he thinks he does wrong if he don't always write;
In this, as in all things, a lamb among men,
He goes to sure death when he goes to his pen.

"Close behind him is Brownson, his mouth very full
With attempting to gulp a Gregorian bull;
Who contrives, spite of that, to pour out as he goes
A stream of transparent and forcible prose;
He shifts quite about, then proceeds to expound
That 't is merely the earth, not himself, that turns round,
And wishes it clearly impressed on your mind,
That the weather-cock rules and not follows the wind;
Proving first, then as deftly confuting each side,
With no doctrine pleased that 's not somewhere denied,
He lays the denier away on the shelf,
And then — down beside him lies gravely himself.
He 's the Salt River boatman, who always stands willing
To convey friend or foe without charging a shilling,
And so fond of the trip that, when leisure 's to spare,
He 'll row himself up, if he can't get a fare.
The worst of it is, that his logic 's so strong,
That of two sides he commonly chooses the wrong;

If there *is* only one, why, he'll split it in two,
And first pummel this half, then that, black and blue.
That white's white needs no proof, but it takes a deep
    fellow
To prove it jet-black, and that jet-black is yellow.
He offers the true faith to drink in a sieve,—
When it reaches your lips there's naught left to believe
But a few silly- (syllo-, I mean,) -gisms that squat 'em
Like tadpoles, o'erjoyed with the mud at the bottom.

  "There is Willis, so *natty* and jaunty and gay,
Who says his best things in so foppish a way,
With conceits and pet phrases so thickly o'erlaying 'em,
That one hardly knows whether to thank him for say
    ing 'em;
Over-ornament ruins both poem and prose,
Just conceive of a Muse with a ring in her nose!
His prose had a natural grace of its own,
And enough of it, too, if he'd let it alone;
But he twitches and jerks so, one fairly gets tired,
And is forced to forgive where he might have admired;
Yet whenever it slips away free and unlaced,
It runs like a stream with a musical waste,
And gurgles along with the liquidest sweep;—
'T is not deep as a river, but who'd have it deep?
In a country where scarcely a village is found
That has not its author sublime and profound,
For some one to be slightly shoal is a duty,
And Willis's shallowness makes half his beauty.
His prose winds along with a blithe, gurgling error,
And reflects all of Heaven it can see in its mirror;
'T is a narrowish strip, but it is not an artifice,—
'T is the true out-of-doors with its genuine hearty phiz;
It is Nature herself, and there's something in that,
Since most brains reflect but the crown of a hat.
No volume I know to read under a tree,
More truly delicious than his A l' Abri,
With the shadows of leaves flowing over your book,
Like ripple-shades netting the bed of a brook;
With June coming softly your shoulder to look over,
Breezes waiting to turn every leaf of your book over
And Nature to criticise still as you read,—
The page that bears that is a rare one indeed.

"He's so innate a cockney, that had he been born
Where plain bare-skin's the only full-dress that is worn,
He'd have given his own such an air that you'd say
'T had been made by a tailor to lounge in Broadway.
His nature's a glass of champagne with the foam on't,
As tender as Fletcher, as witty as Beaumont;
So his best things are done in the flush of the moment,
If he wait, all is spoiled; he may stir it and shake it,
But, the fixed air once gone, he can never re-make it.
He might be a marvel of easy delightfulness,
If he would not sometimes leave the *r* out of spright-
        fulness;
And he ought to let Scripture alone — 't is self-slaughter,
For nobody likes inspiration-and-water.
He'd have been just the fellow to sup at the Mermaid,
Cracking jokes at rare Ben, with an eye to the barmaid,
His wit running up as Canary ran down, —
The topmost bright bubble on the wave of The Town.

"Here comes Parker, the Orson of parsons, a man
Whom the Church undertook to put under her ban, —
(The Church of Socinus, I mean) — his opinions
Being So- (ultra) -cinian, they shocked the Socinians;
They believed — faith I'm puzzled — I think I may call
Their belief a believing in nothing at all,
Or something of that sort; I know they all went
For a general union of total dissent:
He went a step farther; without cough or hem,
He frankly avowed he believed not in them;
And, before he could be jumbled up or prevented
From their orthodox kind of dissent he dissented.
There was heresy here, you perceive, for the right
Of privately judging means simply that light
Has been granted to *me*, for deciding on *you*,
And in happier times, before Atheism grew,
The deed contained clauses for cooking you too.
Now at Xerxes and Knut we all laugh, yet our foot
With the same wave is wet that mocked Xerxes and
        Knut;
And we all entertain a sincere private notion,
That our *Thus far!* will have a great weight with the
        ocean.
'T was so with our liberal Christians: they bore

With sincerest conviction their chairs to the shore;
They brandished their worn theological birches,
Bade natural progress keep out of the Churches,
And expected the lines they had drawn to prevail
With the fast-rising tide to keep out of their pale ;
They had formerly dammed the Pontifical See,
And the same thing, they thought, would do nicely for P. ;
But he turned up his nose at their murmuring and
 shamming,
And cared (shall I say ?) not a d— for their damming;
So they first read him out of their church, and next
 minute
Turned round and declared he had never been in it.
But the ban was too small or the man was too big,
For he recks not their bells, books, and candles a fig;
(He don't look like a man who would *stay* treated shab-
 bily,
Sophroniscus' son's head o'er the features of Rabelais;) —
He bangs and bethwacks them, — their backs he salutes
With the whole tree of knowledge torn up by the roots;
His sermons with satire are plenteously verjuiced,
And he talks in one breath of Confutzee, Cass, Zerduscht,
Jack Robinson, Peter the Hermit, Strap, Dathan,
Cush, Pitt, (not the bottomless, *that* he 's no faith in,)
Pan, Pillicock, Shakspeare, Paul, Toots, Monsieur Tonson,
Aldebaran, Alcander, Ben Khorat, Ben Jonson,
Thoth, Richter, Joe Smith, Father Paul, Judah Monis,
Musæus, Muretus, *hem,* — μ Scorpionis,
Maccabee, Maccaboy, Mac — Mac — ah! Machiavelli,
Condorcet, Count d'Orsay, Conder, Say, Ganganelli,
Orion, O'Connell, the Chevalier D'O,
(See the Memoirs of Sully) τὸ πᾶν, the great toe
Of the statue of Jupiter, now made to pass
For that of Jew Peter by good Romish brass, —
(You may add for yourselves, for I find it a bore,
All the names you have ever, or not, heard before,
And when you 've done that — why, invent a few more.)
His hearers can't tell you on Sunday beforehand,
If in that day's discourse they 'll be Bibled or Koraned,
For he 's seized the idea (by his martyrdom fired,)
That all men (not orthodox) *may be* inspired;
Yet tho' wisdom profane with his creed he may weave in,
He makes it quite clear what he *does n't* believe in,

While some, who decry him, think all Kingdom Come
Is a sort of a, kind of a, species of Hum,
Of which, as it were, so to speak, not a crumb
Would be left, if we did n't keep carefully mum,
And, to make a clean breast, that 't is perfectly plain
That *all* kinds of wisdom are somewhat profane;
Now P.'s creed than this may be lighter or darker,
But in one thing, 't is clear, he has faith, namely —
          Parker;
And this is what makes him the crowd-drawing preacher,
There 's a background of god to each hard-working
          feature,
Every word that he speaks has been fierily furnaced
In the blast of a life that has struggled in earnest:
There he stands, looking more like a ploughman than
          priest,
If not dreadfully awkward, not graceful at least,
His gestures all downright and same, if you will,
As of brown-fisted Hobnail in hoeing a drill,
But his periods fall on you, stroke after stroke,
Like the blows of a lumberer felling an oak,
You forget the man wholly, you 're thankful to meet
With a preacher who smacks of the field and the street,
And to hear, you 're not over-particular whence,
Almost Taylor's profusion, quite Latimer's sense.

  "There is Bryant, as quiet, as cool, and as dignified,
As a smooth, silent iceberg, that never is ignified,
Save when by reflection 't is kindled o' nights
With a semblance of flame by the chill Northern Lights.
He may rank (Griswold says so) first bard of your
          nation,
(There 's no doubt that he stands in supreme iceolation,)
Your topmost Parnassus he may set his heel on,
But no warm applauses come, peal following peal on, —
He 's too smooth and too polished to hang any zeal on:
Unqualified merits, I 'll grant, if you choose, he has 'em,
But he lacks the one merit of kindling enthusiasm;
If he stir you at all, it is just, on my soul,
Like being stirred up with the very North Pole.

  "He is very nice reading in summer, but *inter
Nos*, we don't want *extra* freezing in winter;

Take him up in the depth of July, my advice is,
When you feel an Egyptian devotion to ices.
But, deduct all you can, there 's enough that 's right good
    in him,
He has a true soul for field, river, and wood in him;
And his heart, in the midst of brick walls, or where'er
    it is,
Glows, softens, and thrills with the tenderest charities, —
To you mortals that delve in this trade-ridden planet?
No, to old Berkshire's hills, with their limestone and
    granite.
If you 're one who *in loco* (add *foco* here) *desipis*,
You will get of his outermost heart (as I guess) a piece;
But you 'd get deeper down if you came as a precipice,
And would break the last seal of its inwardest fountain,
If you only could palm yourself off for a mountain.
Mr. Quivis, or somebody quite as discerning,
Some scholar who 's hourly expecting his learning,
Calls B. the American Wordsworth; but Wordsworth
Is worth near as much as your whole tuneful herd 's
    worth.
No, don't be absurd, he 's an excellent Bryant;
But, my friends, you 'll endanger the life of your client,
By attempting to stretch him up into a giant:
If you choose to compare him, I think there are two per-
-sons fit for a parallel — Thomson and Cowper; *
I don't mean exactly, — there 's something of each,
There 's T.'s love of nature, C.'s penchant to preach;
Just mix up their minds so that C.'s spice of craziness
Shall balance and neutralize T.'s turn for laziness,
And it gives you a brain cool, quite frictionless, quiet,
Whose internal police nips the buds of all riot, —
A brain like a permanent strait-jacket put on
The heart which strives vainly to burst off a button, —
A brain which, without being slow or mechanic,
Does more than a larger less drilled, more volcanic;
He 's a Cowper condensed, with no craziness bitten,
And the advantage that Wordsworth before him has
    written.

---

* To demonstrate quickly and easily how per-
-versely absurd 't is to sound this name *Cowper*,
As people in general call him named *super*,
I just add that he rhymes it himself with horse-trooper.

" But, my dear little bardlings, don't prick up your ears,
Nor suppose I would rank you and Bryant as peers;
If I call him an iceberg, I don't mean to say
There is nothing in that which is grand, in its way;
He is almost the one of your poets that knows
How much grace, strength, and dignity lie in Repose;
If he sometimes fall short, he is too wise to mar
His thought's modest fulness by going too far;
'T would be well if your authors should all make a trial
Of what virtue there is in severe self-denial,
And measure their writings by Hesiod's staff,
Which teaches that all have less value than half.

" There is Whittier, whose swelling and vehement heart
Strains the strait-breasted drab of the Quaker apart,
And reveals the live Man, still supreme and erect,
Underneath the bemummying wrappers of sect;
There was ne'er a man born who had more of the swing
Of the true lyric bard and all that kind of thing;
And his failures arise, (though perhaps he don't know it,)
From the very same cause that has made him a poet, —
A fervor of mind which knows no separation
'Twixt simple excitement and pure inspiration,
As my Pythoness erst sometimes erred from not knowing
If 't were I or mere wind through her tripod was blowing;
Let his mind once get head in its favorite direction
And the torrent of verse bursts the dams of reflection,
While, borne with the rush of the metre along,
The poet may chance to go right or go wrong,
Content with the whirl and delirium of song;
Then his grammar's not always correct, nor his rhymes,
And he's prone to repeat his own lyrics sometimes.
Not his best, though, for those are struck off at white
      heats
When the heart in his breast like a trip-hammer beats,
And can ne'er be repeated again any more
Than they could have been carefully plotted before:
Like old what's-his-name there at the battle of Hastings,
(Who, however, gave more than mere rhythmical bastings,)
Our Quaker leads off metaphorical fights
For reform and whatever they call human rights,
Both singing and striking in front of the war
And hitting his foes with the mallet of Thor;

Anne haec, one exclaims, on beholding his knocks,
Vestis filii tui, O, leather-clad Fox?
Can that be thy son, in the battle's mid din,
Preaching brotherly love and then driving it in
To the brain of the tough old Goliah of sin,
With the smoothest of pebbles from Castaly's spring
Impressed on his hard moral sense with a sling?

" All honor and praise to the right-hearted bard
Who was true to The Voice when such service was hard,
Who himself was so free he dared sing for the slave
When to look but a protest in silence was brave;
All honor and praise to the women and men
Who spoke out for the dumb and the down-trodden then!
I need not to name them, already for each
I see History preparing the statue and niche;
They were harsh, but shall *you* be so shocked at hard
     words
Who have beaten your pruning-hooks up into swords,
Whose rewards and hurrahs men are surer to gain
By the reaping of men and of women than grain?
Why should *you* stand aghast at their fierce wordy war, if
You scalp one another for Bank or for Tariff?
Your calling them cut-throats and knaves all day long
Don't prove that the use of hard language is wrong;
While the World's heart beats quicker to think of such
     men
As signed Tyranny's doom with a bloody steel-pen,
While on Fourth-of-Julys beardless orators fright one
With hints at Harmodius and Aristogeiton,
You need not look shy at your sisters and brothers
Who stab with sharp words for the freedom of others; —
No, a wreath, twine a wreath for the loyal and true
Who, for the sake of the many, dared stand with the few,
Not of blood-spattered laurel for enemies braved,
But of broad, peaceful oak-leaves for citizens saved!

" Here comes Dana, abstractedly loitering along
Involved in a paulo-post-future of song,
Who 'll be going to write what 'll never be written
Till the Muse, ere he thinks of it, gives him the mitten, —
Who is so well aware of how things should be done,
That his own works displease him before they 're begun, —

Who so well all that makes up good poetry knows
That the best of his poems is written in prose;
All saddled and bridled stood Pegasus waiting,
He was booted and spurred, but he loitered debating,
In a very grave question his soul was immersed, —
Which foot in the stirrup he ought to put first;
And, while this point and that he judicially dwelt on,
He, somehow or other, had written Paul Felton,
Whose beauties or faults, whichsoever you see there,
You'll allow only genius could hit upon either.
That he once was the Idle Man none will deplore,
But I fear he will never be anything more;
The ocean of song heaves and glitters before him,
The depth and the vastness and longing sweep o'er him,
He knows every breaker and shoal on the chart,
He has the Coast Pilot and so on by heart,
Yet he spends his whole life, like the man in the fable,
In learning to swim on his library-table.

"There swaggers John Neal, who has wasted in Maine
The sinews and chords of his pugilist brain,
Who might have been poet, but that, in its stead, he
Preferred to believe that he was so already;
Too hasty to wait till Art's ripe fruit should drop,
He must pelt down an unripe and colicky crop;
Who took to the law, and had this sterling plea for it,
It required him to quarrel, and paid him a fee for it;
A man who's made less than he might have, because
He always has thought himself more than he was, —
Who, with very good natural gifts as a bard,
Broke the strings of his lyre out by striking too hard,
And cracked half the notes of a truly fine voice,
Because song drew less instant attention than noise.
Ah, men do not know how much strength is in poise,
That he goes the farthest who goes far enough,
And that all beyond that is just bother and stuff.
No vain man matures, he makes too much new wood;
His blooms are too thick for the fruit to be good;
'T is the modest man ripens, 't is he that achieves,
Just what's needed of sunshine and shade he receives;
Grapes, to mellow, require the cool dark of their leaves;
Neal wants balance; he throws his mind always too far,
Whisking out flocks of comets, but never a star;

He has so much muscle, and loves so to show it,
That he strips himself naked to prove he 's a poet,
And, to show he could leap Art's wide ditch, if he tried,
Jumps clean o'er it, and into the hedge t' other side.
He has strength, but there 's nothing about him in keeping;
One gets surelier onward by walking than leaping;
He has used his own sinews himself to distress,
And had done vastly more had he done vastly less;
In letters, too soon is as bad as too late,
Could he only have waited he might have been great,
But he plumped into Helicon up to the waist,
And muddied the stream ere he took his first taste.

"There is Hawthorne, with genius so shrinking and
        rare
That you hardly at first see the strength that is there;
A frame so robust, with a nature so sweet,
So earnest, so graceful, so solid, so fleet,
Is worth a descent from Olympus to meet;
'T is as if a rough oak that for ages had stood,
With his gnarled bony branches like ribs of the wood,
Should bloom, after cycles of struggle and scathe,
With a single anemone trembly and rathe;
His strength is so tender, his wildness so meek,
That a suitable parallel sets one to seek, —
He 's a John Bunyan Fouqué, a Puritan Tieck;
When nature was shaping him, clay was not granted
For making so full-sized a man as she wanted,
So, to fill out her model, a little she spared
From some finer-grained stuff for a woman prepared,
And she could not have hit a more excellent plan
For making him fully and perfectly man.
The success of her scheme gave her so much delight,
That she tried it again, shortly after, in Dwight;
Only, while she was kneading and shaping the clay,
She sang to her work in her sweet childish way,
And found, when she 'd put the last touch to his soul,
That the music had somehow got mixed with the whole.

"Here 's Cooper, who 's written six volumes to show
He 's as good as a lord: well, let 's grant that he 's so;
If a person prefer that description of praise,
Why, a coronet 's certainly cheaper than bays;

But he need take no pains to convince us he's not
(As his enemies say) the American Scott.
Choose any twelve men, and let C. read aloud
That one of his novels of which he's most proud,
'And I'd lay any bet that, without ever quitting
Their box, they'd be all, to a man, for acquitting.
He has drawn you one character, though, that is new,
One wildflower he's plucked that is wet with the dew
Of this fresh Western world, and, the thing not to mince,
He has done naught but copy it ill ever since;
His Indians, with proper respect be it said,
Are just Natty Bumpo daubed over with red,
And his very Long Toms are the same useful Nat,
Rigged up in duck pants and a sou'-wester hat,
(Though once in a Coffin, a good chance was found
To have slipt the old fellow away underground.)
All his other men-figures are clothes upon sticks,
The *dernière chemise* of a man in a fix,
(As a captain besieged, when his garrison's small,
Sets up caps upon poles to be seen o'er the wall;)
And the women he draws from one model don't vary,
All sappy as maples and flat as a prairie.
When a character's wanted, he goes to the task
As a cooper would do in composing a cask;
He picks out the staves, of their qualities heedful,
Just hoops them together as tight as is needful,
And, if the best fortune should crown the attempt, he
Has made at the most something wooden and empty.

" Don't suppose I would underrate Cooper's abilities,
If I thought you'd do that, I should feel very ill at ease;
The men who have given to *one* character life
And objective existence, are not very rife,
You may number them all, both prose-writers and singers,
Without overrunning the bounds of your fingers,
And Natty won't go to oblivion quicker
Than Adams the parson or Primrose the vicar.

"There is one thing in Cooper I like, too, and that is
That on manners he lectures his countrymen gratis,
Not precisely so either, because, for a rarity,
He is paid for his tickets in unpopularity.
Now he may overcharge his American pictures,

But you'll grant there's a good deal of truth in his
    strictures;
And I honor the man who is willing to sink
Half his present repute for the freedom to think,
And, when he has thought, be his cause strong or weak,
Will risk t' other half for the freedom to speak,
Caring naught for what vengeance the mob has in store,
Let that mob be the upper ten thousand or lower.

   "There are truths you Americans need to be told,
And it never'll refute them to swagger and scold;
John Bull, looking o'er the Atlantic, in choler
At your aptness for trade, says you worship the dollar;
But to scorn such i-dollar-try's what very few do,
And John goes to that church as often as you do.
No matter what John says, don't try to outcrow him,
'T is enough to go quietly on and outgrow him;
Like most fathers, Bull hates to see Number one
Displacing himself in the mind of his son,
And detests the same faults in himself he'd neglected
When he sees them again in his child's glass reflected;
To love one another you're too like by half,
If he is a bull, you're a pretty stout calf,
And tear your own pasture for naught but to show
What a nice pair of horns you're beginning to grow.

   "There are one or two things I should just like to hint,
For you don't often get the truth told you in print.
The most of you (this is what strikes all beholders)
Have a mental and physical stoop in the shoulders;
Though you ought to be free as the winds and the waves,
You've the gait and the manners of runaway slaves;
Tho' you brag of your New World, you don't half believe
    in it,
And as much of the Old as is possible weave in it;
Your goddess of freedom, a tight, buxom girl,
With lips like a cherry and teeth like a pearl,
With eyes bold as Herè's, and hair floating free,
And full of the sun as the spray of the sea,
Who can sing at a husking or romp at a shearing,
Who can trip through the forests alone without fearing,
Who can drive home the cows with a song through the
    grass,

Keeps glancing aside into Europe's cracked glass,
Hides her red hands in gloves, pinches up her lithe waist,
And makes herself wretched with transmarine taste;
She loses her fresh country charm when she takes
Any mirror except her own rivers and lakes.

" You steal Englishmen's books and think Englishmen's
thought,
With their salt on her tail your wild eagle is caught;
Your literature suits its each whisper and motion
To what will be thought of it over the ocean;
The cast clothes of Europe your statesmanship tries
And mumbles again the old blarneys and lies; —
Forget Europe wholly, your veins throb with blood,
To which the dull current in hers is but mud;
Let her sneer, let her say your experiment fails,
In her voice there 's a tremble e'en now while she rails,
And your shore will soon be in the nature of things
Covered thick with gilt driftwood of runaway kings,
Where alone, as it were in a Longfellow's Waif,
Her fugitive pieces will find themselves safe.
O, my friends, thank your God, if you have one, that he
'Twixt the Old World and you set the gulf of a sea,
Be strong-backed, brown-handed, upright as your pines,
By the scale of a hemisphere shape your designs,
Be true to yourselves and this new nineteenth age,
As a statue by Powers, or a picture by Page,
Plough, sail, forge, build, carve, paint, all things make
new,
To your own New-World instincts contrive to be true,
Keep your ears open wide to the Future's first call,
Be whatever you will, but yourselves first of all,
Stand fronting the dawn on Toil's heaven-scaling peaks,
And become my new race of more practical Greeks. —
Hem! your likeness at present, I shudder to tell o 't,
Is that you have your slaves, and the Greek had his helot."

Here a gentleman present, who had in his attic
More pepper than brains, shrieked — "The man's a fanatic,
I 'm a capital tailor with warm tar and feathers,
And will make him a suit that 'll serve in all weathers;
But we 'll argue the point first, I 'm willing to reason 't,
Palaver before condemnation 's but decent,

So, through my humble person, Humanity begs
Of the friends of true freedom a loan of bad eggs."
But Apollo let one such a look of his show forth
As when ἤιε νύκτι ἐοικώς, and so forth,
And the gentleman somehow slunk out of the way,
But, as he was going, gained courage to say, —
" At slavery in the abstract my whole soul rebels,
I am as strongly opposed to 't as any one else."
" Ay, no doubt, but whenever I 've happened to meet
With a wrong or a crime, it is always concrete,"
Answered Phœbus severely ; then turning to us,
" The mistake of such fellows as just made the fuss
Is only in taking a great busy nation
For a part of their pitiful cotton-plantation. —
But there comes Miranda, Zeus! where shall I flee to?
She has such a penchant for bothering me too!
She always keeps asking if I don't observe a
Particular likeness 'twixt her and Minerva;
She tells me my efforts in verse are quite clever; —
She 's been travelling now, and will be worse than ever ;
One would think, though, a sharp-sighted noter she 'd be
Of all that 's worth mentioning over the sea,
For a woman must surely see well, if she try,
The whole of whose being 's a capital I :
She will take an old notion, and make it her own,
By saying it o'er in her Sibylline tone,
Or persuade you 't is something tremendously deep,
By repeating it so as to put you to sleep;
And she well may defy any mortal to see through it,
When once she has mixed up her infinite *me* through it.
There is one thing she owns in her own single right,
It is native and genuine — namely, her spite:
Though, when acting as censor, she privately blows
A censer of vanity 'neath her own nose."

Here Miranda came up, and said, " Phœbus, you know
That the infinite Soul has its infinite woe,
As I ought to know, having lived cheek by jowl
Since the day I was born, with the infinite Soul;
I myself introduced, I myself, I alone,
To my Land's better life authors solely my own,
Who the sad heart of earth on their shoulders have taken,
Whose works sound a depth by Life's quiet unshaken,

Such as Shakspeare, for instance, the Bible, and Bacon,
Not to mention my own works; Time's nadir is fleet,
And, as for myself, I'm quite out of conceit "—

"Quite out of conceit! I'm enchanted to hear it,"
Cried Apollo aside, " Who'd have thought she was near it ?
To be sure one is apt to exhaust those commodities
He uses too fast, yet in this case as odd it is
As if Neptune should say to his turbots and whitings,
'I'm as much out of salt as Miranda's own writings,'
(Which, as she in her own happy manner has said,
Sound a depth, for 't is one of the functions of lead.)
She often has asked me if I could not find
A place somewhere near me that suited her mind;
I know but a single one vacant, which she,
With her rare talent that way, would fit to a T.
And it would not imply any pause or cessation
In the work she esteems her peculiar vocation, —
She may enter on duty to-day, if she chooses,
And remain Tiring-woman for life to the Muses."

Miranda meanwhile has succeeded in driving
Up into a corner, in spite of their striving,
A small flock of terrified victims, and there,
With an I-turn-the-crank-of-the-Universe air
And a tone which, at least to *my* fancy, appears
Not so much to be entering as boxing your ears,
Is unfolding a tale (of herself, I surmise,
For 't is dotted as thick as a peacock's with I's.)
Apropos of Miranda, I'll rest on my oars
And drift through a trifling digression on bores,
For, though not wearing ear-rings *in more majorum*,
Our ears are kept bored just as if we still wore 'em.
There was one feudal custom worth keeping, at least,
Roasted bores made a part of each well-ordered feast,
And of all quiet pleasures the very *ne plus*
Was in hunting wild bores as the tame ones hunt us.
Archæologians, I know, who have personal fears
Of this wise application of hounds and of spears,
Have tried to make out, with a zeal more than wonted,
'T was a kind of wild swine that our ancestors hunted;
But I'll never believe that the age which has strewn
Europe o'er with cathedrals, and otherwise shown

That it knew what was what, could by chance not have
    known,
(Spending, too, its chief time with its buff on, no doubt,)
Which beast 't would improve the world most to thin out.
I divide bores myself, in the manner of rifles,
Into two great divisions, regardless of trifles; —
There's your smooth-bore and screw-bore, who do not
    much vary
In the weight of cold lead they respectively carry.
The smooth-bore is one in whose essence the mind
Not a corner nor cranny to cling by can find;
You feel as in nightmares sometimes, when you slip
Down a steep slated roof where there's nothing to grip,
You slide and you slide, the blank horror increases,
You had rather by far be at once smashed to pieces,
You fancy a whirlpool below white and frothing,
And finally drop off and light upon — nothing.
The screw-bore has twists in him, faint predilections
For going just wrong in the tritest directions;
When he's wrong he is flat, when he's right he can't show
    it,
He'll tell you what Snooks said about the new poet,*
Or how Fogrum was outraged by Tennyson's Princess;
He has spent all his spare time and intellect since his
Birth in perusing, on each art and science,
Just the books in which no one puts any reliance,
And though *nemo*, we're told, *horis omnibus sapit,*
The rule will not fit him, however you shape it,   `
For he has a perennial foison of sappiness;
He has just enough force to spoil half your day's happi-
    ness,
And to make him a sort of mosquito to be with,
But just not enough to dispute or agree with.

    These sketches I made (not to be too explicit)
From two honest fellows who made me a visit,
And broke, like the tale of the Bear and the Fiddle,
My reflections on Halleck short off by the middle,
I shall not now go into the subject more deeply,
For I notice that some of my readers look sleep'ly,

* (If you call Snooks an owl, he will show by his looks
That he's morally certain you're jealous of Snooks.)

I will barely remark that, 'mongst civilized nations,
There 's none that displays more exemplary patience
Under all sorts of boring, at all sorts of hours,
From all sorts of desperate persons, than ours.
Not to speak of our papers, our State legislatures,
And other such trials for sensitive natures,
Just look for a moment at Congress, — appalled,
My fancy shrinks back from the phantom it called;
Why, there 's scarcely a member unworthy to frown
'Neath what Fourier nicknames the Boreal crown;
Only think what that infinite bore-pow'r could do
If applied with a utilitarian view;
Suppose, for example, we shipped it with care
To Sahara's great desert and let it bore there,
If they held one short session and did nothing else,
They 'd fill the whole waste with Artesian wells.
But 't is time now with pen phonographic to follow
Through some more of his sketches our laughing Apollo: -

" There comes Harry Franco, and, as he draws near,
You find that 's a smile which you took for a sneer;
One half of him contradicts t' other, his wont
Is to say very sharp things and do very blunt;
His manner 's as hard as his feelings are tender,
And a *sortie* he 'll make when he means to surrender;
He 's in joke half the time when he seems to be sternest
When he seems to be joking, be sure he 's in earnest;
He has common sense in a way that 's uncommon,
Hates humbug and cant, loves his friends like a woman,
Builds his dislikes of cards and his friendships of oak,
Loves a prejudice better than aught but a joke,
Is half upright Quaker, half downright Come-outer,
Loves Freedom too well to go stark mad about her,
Quite artless himself, is a lover of Art,
Shuts you out of his secrets and into his heart,
And though not a poet, yet all must admire
In his letters of Pinto his skill on the liar.

" There comes Poe, with his raven, like Barnaby Rudge
Three-fifths of him genius and two-fifths sheer fudge,
Who talks like a book of iambs and pentameters,
In a way to make people of common-sense damn metres,
Who has written some things quite the best of their kind,

But the heart somehow seems all squeezed out by the mind,
Who — but hey-day! What's this? Messieurs Mathews
     and Poe,
You must n't fling mud-balls at Longfellow so,
Does it make a man worse that his character's such
As to make his friends love him (as you think) too much ?
Why, there is not a bard at this moment alive
More willing than he that his fellows should thrive,
While you are abusing him thus, even now
He would help either one of you out of a slough;
You may say that he's smooth and all that till you're
     hoarse,
But remember that elegance also is force;
After polishing granite as much as you will,
The heart keeps its tough old persistency still;
Deduct all you can that still keeps you at bay, —
Why, he 'll live till men weary of Collins and Gray.
I 'm not over-fond of Greek metres in English,
To me rhyme's a gain, so it be not too jinglish,
And your modern hexameter verses are no more
Like Greek ones than sleek Mr. Pope is like Homer;
As the roar of the sea to the coo of a pigeon is,
So, compared to your moderns, sounds old Melesigenes;
I may be too partial, the reason, perhaps, o't is
That I 've heard the old blind man recite his own rhapso-
     dies,
And my ear with that music impregnate may be,
Like the poor exiled shell with the soul of the sea,
Or as one can't bear Strauss when his nature is cloven
To its deeps within deeps by the stroke of Beethoven;
But, set that aside, and 't is truth that I speak,
Had Theocritus written in English, not Greek,
I believe that his exquisite sense would scarce change a
     line
In that rare, tender, virgin-like pastoral Evangeline.
That 's not ancient nor modern, its place is apart
Where time has no sway, in the realm of pure Art,
'T is a shrine of retreat from Earth's hubbub and strife
As quiet and chaste as the author's own life.

"There comes Philothea, her face all a-glow,
She has just been dividing some poor creature's woe
And can't tell which pleases her most, to relieve

His want, or his story to hear and believe;
No doubt against many deep griefs she prevails,
For her ear is the refuge of destitute tales;
She knows well that silence is sorrow's best food,
And that talking draws off from the heart its black blood,
So she'll listen with patience and let you unfold
Your bundle of rags as 't were pure cloth of gold,
Which, indeed, it all turns to as soon as she's touched it,
And, (to borrow a phrase from the nursery,) *muched* it,
She has such a musical taste, she will go
Any distance to hear one who draws a long bow;
She will swallow a wonder by mere might and main
And thinks it geometry 's fault if she 's fain
To consider things flat, inasmuch as they 're plain;
Facts with her are accomplished, as Frenchmen would say,
They will prove all she wishes them to — either way,
And, as fact lies on this side or that, we must try,
If we 're seeking the truth, to find where it don't lie;
I was telling her once of a marvellous aloe
That for thousands of years had looked spindling and
        sallow,
And, though nursed by the fruitfullest powers of mud,
Had never vouchsafed e'en so much as a bud,
Till its owner remarked, (as a sailor, you know,
Often will in a calm,) that it never would blow,
For he wished to exhibit the plant, and designed
That its blowing should help him in raising the wind;
At last it was told him that if he should water
Its roots with the blood of his unmarried daughter,
(Who was born, as her mother, a Calvinist said,
With a Baxter's effectual caul on her head,)
It would blow as the obstinate breeze did when by a
Like decree of her father died Iphigenia;
At first he declared he himself would be blowed
Ere his conscience with such a foul crime he would load.
But the thought, coming oft, grew less dark than before
And he mused, as each creditor knocked at his door,
If *this* were but done they would dun me no more;
I told Philothea his struggles and doubts,
And how he considered the ins and the outs
Of the visions he had, and the dreadful dyspepsy,
How he went to the seer that lives at Po'keepsie,
How the seer advised him to sleep on it first

And to read his big volume in case of the worst,
And further advised he should pay him five dollars
For writing 𝕯um, 𝕯um, on his wristbands and collars;
Three years and ten days these dark words he had studied
When the daughter was missed, and the aloe had budded;
I told how he watched it grow large and more large,
And wondered how much for the show he should charge, —
She had listened with utter indifference to this, till
I told how it bloomed, and discharging its pistil
With an aim the Eumenides dictated, shot
The botanical filicide dead on the spot;
It had blown, but he reaped not his horrible gains,
For it blew with such force as to blow out his brains,
And the crime was blown also, because on the wad,
Which was paper, was writ 'Visitation of God,'
As well as a thrilling account of the deed
Which the coroner kindly allowed me to read.

"Well, my friend took this story up just, to be sure,
As one might a poor foundling that's laid at one's door;
She combed it and washed it and clothed it and fed it,
And as if 't were her own child most tenderly bred it,
Laid the scene (of the legend, I mean,) far away a-
-mong the green vales underneath Himalaya.
And by artist-like touches, laid on here and there,
Made the whole thing so touching, I frankly declare
I have read it all thrice, and, perhaps I am weak,
But I found every time there were tears on my cheek.

"The pole, science tells us, the magnet controls,
But she is a magnet to emigrant Poles,
And folks with a mission that nobody knows,
Throng thickly about her as bees round a rose;
She can fill up the *carets* in such, make their scope
Converge to some focus of rational hope,
And, with sympathies fresh as the morning, their gall
Can transmute into honey, — but this is not all;
Not only for those she has solace, oh, say,
Vice's desperate nursling adrift in Broadway,
Who clingest, with all that is left of thee human,
To the last slender spar from the wreck of the woman,
Hast thou not found one shore where those tired drooping
    feet

Could reach firm mother-earth, one full heart on whose
    beat
The soothed head in silence reposing could hear
The chimes of far childhood throb back on the ear?
Ah, there's many a beam from the fountain of day
That to reach us unclouded, must pass, on its way,
Through the soul of a woman, and hers is wide ope
To the influence of Heaven as the blue eyes of Hope;
Yes, a great soul is hers, one that dares to go in
To the prison, the slave-hut, the alleys of sin,
And to bring into each, or to find there some line
Of the never completely out-trampled divine;
If her heart at high floods swamps her brain now and
    then,
'T is but richer for that when the tide ebbs agen,
As, after old Nile has subsided, his plain
Overflows with a second broad deluge of grain;
What a wealth would it bring to the narrow and sour
Could they be as a Child but for one little hour!

  "What! Irving? thrice welcome, warm heart and fine
    brain,
You bring back the happiest spirit from Spain,
And the gravest sweet humor, that ever were there
Since Cervantes met death in his gentle despair;
Nay, don't be embarrassed, nor look so beseeching, —
I shan't run directly against my own preaching,
And, having just laughed at their Raphaels and Dantes,
Go to setting you up beside matchless Cervantes;
But allow me to speak what I honestly feel, —
To a true poet-heart add the fun of Dick Steele,
Throw in all of Addison, *minus* the chill,
With the whole of that partnership's stock and good
    will,
Mix well, and while stirring, hum o'er, as a spell,
The fine *old* English Gentleman, simmer it well,
Sweeten just to your own private liking, then strain
That only the finest and clearest remain,
Let it stand out of doors till a soul it receives
From the warm lazy sun loitering down through green
    leaves,
And you'll find a choice nature, not wholly deserving
A name either English or Yankee, — just Irving.

" There goes, — but *stet nominis umbra*, — his name
You 'll be glad enough, some day or other, to claim,
And will all crowd about him and swear that you knew
        him
If some English hack-critic should chance to review him.
The old *porcos ante ne projiciatis*
MARGARITAS, for him you have verified gratis;
What matters his name ?   Why, it may be Sylvester,
Judd, Junior, or Junius, Ulysses, or Nestor,
For aught *I* know or care ; 't is enough that I look
On the author of ' Margaret,' the first Yankee book
With the *soul* of Down East in 't, and things farther East,
As far as the threshold of morning, at least,
.Where awaits the fair dawn of the simple and true,
Of the day that comes slowly to make all things new.
'T has a smack of pine woods, of bare field and bleak hill
Such as only the breed of the Mayflower could till ;
The Puritan 's shown in it, tough to the core,
Such as prayed, smiting Agag on red Marston Moor ;
With an unwilling humor, half-choked by the drouth
In brown hollows about the inhospitable mouth ;
With a soul full of poetry, though it has qualms
About finding a happiness out of the Psalms ;
Full of tenderness, too, though it shrinks in the dark,
Hamadryad-like, under the coarse, shaggy bark ;
That sees visions, knows wrestlings of God with the Will,
And has its own Sinais and thunderings still."

        Here, — " Forgive me, Apollo," I cried, " while I pour
My heart out to my birthplace : O, loved more and more
Dear Baystate, from whose rocky bosom thy sons
Should suck milk, strong-will-giving, brave, such as runs
In the veins of old Graylock, — who is it that dares ·
Call thee peddler, a soul wrapt in bank-books and shares ?
It is false ! She 's a Poet. I see, as I write,
Along the far railroad the steam-snake glide white,
The cataract-throb of her mill-hearts I hear,
The swift strokes of trip-hammers weary my ear,
Sledges ring upon anvils, through logs the saw screams,
Blocks swing to their place, beetles drive home the
        beams : —
It is songs such as these that she croons to the din
Of her fast-flying shuttles, year out and year in,

While from earth's farthest corner there comes not a
    breeze
But wafts her the buzz of her gold-gleaning bees:
What tho' those horn hands have as yet found small time
For painting and sculpture and music and rhyme?
These will come in due order, the need that prest sorest
Was to vanquish the seasons, the ocean, the forest,
To bridle and harness the rivers, the steam,
Making that whirl her mill-wheels, this tug in her team,
To vassalize old tyrant Winter, and make
Him delve surlily for her on river and lake;—
When this New World was parted, she strove not to
    shirk
Her lot in the heirdom, the tough, silent Work,
The hero-share ever, from Herakles down
To Odin, the Earth's iron sceptre and crown;
Yes, thou dear, noble Mother! if ever men's praise
Could be claimed for creating heroical lays,
Thou hast won it; if ever the laurel divine
Crowned the Maker and Builder, that glory is thine!
Thy songs are right epic, they tell how this rude
Rock-rib of our earth here was tamed and subdued;
Thou hast written them plain on the face of the planet
In brave, deathless letters of iron and granite;
Thou hast printed them deep for all time; they are set
From the same runic type-fount and alphabet
With thy stout Berkshire hills and the arms of thy
    Bay,—
They are staves from the burly old Mayflower lay.
If the drones of the Old World, in querulous ease,
Ask thy Art and thy Letters, point proudly to these,
Or, if they deny these are Letters and Art,
Toil on with the same old invincible heart;
Thou art rearing the pedestal broad-based and grand
Whereon the fair shapes of the Artist shall stand,
And creating, through labors undaunted and long,
The theme for all Sculpture and Painting and Song!

   "But my good mother Baystate wants no praise of
    mine,
She learned from *her* mother a precept divine
About something that butters no parsnips, her *forte*
In another direction lies, work is her sport,

(Though she'll curtsey and set her cap straight, that she
      will,
If you talk about Plymouth and one Bunker's hill.)
Dear, notable goodwife! by this time of night,
Her hearth is swept clean, and her fire burning bright,
And she sits in a chair (of home plan and make) rocking,
Musing much, all the while, as she darns on a stocking,
Whether turkeys will come pretty high next Thanks-
      giving,
Whether flour'll be so dear, for, as sure as she's living,
She will use rye-and-injun then, whether the pig
By this time ain't got pretty tolerable big,
And whether to sell it outright will be best,
Or to smoke hams and shoulders and salt down the rest, —
At this minute, she'd swop all my verses, ah, cruel!   .
For the last patent stove that is saving of fuel;
So I'll just let Apollo go on, for his phiz
Shows I've kept him awaiting too long as it is."

  "If our friend, there, who seems a reporter, is done
With his burst of emotion, why, *I* will go on,"
Said Apollo; some smiled, and, indeed, I must own
There was something sarcastic, perhaps, in his tone : —

  "There's Holmes, who is matchless among you for
      wit;
A Leyden-jar always full-charged, from which flit
The electrical tingles of hit after hit;
In long poems 't is painful sometimes and invites
A thought of the way the new Telegraph writes,
Which pricks down its little sharp sentences spitefully
As if you got more than you'd title to rightfully,
And you find yourself hoping its wild father Lightning
Would flame in for a second and give you a fright'ning.
He has perfect sway of what *I* call a sham metre,
But many admire it, the English pentameter,
And Campbell, I think, wrote most commonly worse,
With less nerve, swing, and fire in the same kind of verse,
Nor e'er achieved aught in 't so worthy of praise
As the tribute of Holmes to the grand *Marseillaise.*
You went crazy last year over Bulwer's New Timon; —
Why, if B., to the day of his dying, should rhyme on,
Heaping verses on verses and tomes upon tomes,

He could ne'er reach the best point and vigor of Holmes.
His are just the fine hands, too, to weave you a lyric
Full of fancy, fun, feeling, or spiced with satyric
In a measure so kindly, you doubt if the toes
That are trodden upon are your own or your foes'.

" There is Lowell, who's striving Parnassus to climb
With a whole bale of *isms* tied together with rhyme,
He might get on alone, spite of brambles and boulders,
But he can't with that bundle he has on his shoulders,
The top of the hill he will ne'er come nigh reaching
Till he learns the distinction 'twixt singing and preaching;
His lyre has some chords that would ring pretty well,
But he'd rather by half make a drum of the shell,
And rattle away till he's old as Methusalem,
At the head of a march to the last new Jerusalem.

" There goes Halleck, whose Fanny's a pseudo Don
    Juan,
With the wickedness out that gave salt to the true one,
He's a wit, though, I hear, of the very first order,
And once made a pun on the words soft Recorder;
More than this, he's a very great poet, I'm told,
And has had his works published in crimson and gold,
With something they call 'Illustrations,' to wit,
Like those with which Chapman obscured Holy Writ,*
Which are said to illustrate, because, as I view it,
Like *lucus a non*, they precisely don't do it;
Let a man who can write what himself understands
Keep clear, if he can, of designing men's hands,
Who bury the sense, if there's any worth having,
And then very honestly call it engraving.
But, to quit *badinage*, which there isn't much wit in,
Halleck's better, I doubt not, than all he has written;
In his verse a clear glimpse you will frequently find,
If not of a great, of a fortunate mind,
Which contrives to be true to its natural loves
In a world of back-offices, ledgers, and stoves.
When his heart breaks away from the brokers and banks,
And kneels in its own private shrine to give thanks,
There's a genial manliness in him that earns

* (Cuts rightly called wooden, as all must admit.)

Our sincerest respect, (read, for instance, his ' Burns,')
And we can't but regret (seek excuse where we may)
That so much of a man has been peddled away.

   "But what's that ? a mass-meeting ?   No, there come
       in lots
The American Disraelis, Bulwers, and Scotts,
And in short the American everything-elses,
Each charging the others with envies and jealousies ; —
By the way, 't is a fact that displays what profusions
Of all kinds of greatness bless free institutions,
That while the Old World has produced barely eight
Of such poets as all men agree to call great,
And of other great characters hardly a score,
(One might safely say less than that rather than more,)
With you every year a whole crop is begotten,
They 're as much of a staple as corn is, or cotton ;
Why, there 's scarcely a huddle of log-huts and shanties
That has not brought forth its own Miltons and Dantes ;
I myself know ten Byrons, one Coleridge, three Shelleys,
Two Raphaels, six Titians, (I think) one Apelles,
Leonardos and Rubenses plenty as lichens,
One (but that one is plenty) American Dickens,
A whole flock of Lambs, any number of Tennysons, —
In short, if a man has the luck to have any sons,
He may feel pretty certain that one out of twain
Will be some very great person over again.
There is one inconvenience in all this which lies
In the fact that by contrast we estimate size,*
And, where there are none except Titans, great stature
Is only a simple proceeding of nature.
What puff the strained sails of your praise shall you furl
       at, if
The calmest degree that you know is superlative ?
At Rome, all whom Charon took into his wherry must,
As a matter of course, be well *issimus*ed and *errimus*ed,
A Greek, too, could feel, while in that famous boat he tost,
That his friends would take care he was ιστοςed and
     ωτατοςed,

---

* That is in most cases we do, but not all,
    Past a doubt, there are men who are innately small,
    Such as Blank, who, without being 'minished a tittle,
    Might stand for a type of the Absolute Little.

And formerly we, as through graveyards we past,
Thought the world went from bad to worse fearfully fast
Let us glance for a moment, 't is well worth the pains,
And note what an average graveyard contains.
There lie levellers levelled, duns done up themselves,
There are booksellers finally laid on their shelves,
Horizontally there lie upright politicians,
Dose-a-dose with their patients sleep faultless physicians,
There are slave-drivers quietly whipt underground,
There bookbinders, done up in boards, are fast bound,
There card-players wait till the last trump be played,
There all the choice spirits get finally laid,
There the babe that's unborn is supplied with a berth,
There men without legs get their six feet of earth,
There lawyers repose, each wrapt up in his case,
There seekers of office are sure of a place,
There defendant and plaintiff get equally cast,
There shoemakers quietly stick to the last,
There brokers at length become silent as stocks,
There stage-drivers sleep without quitting their box,
And so forth and so forth and so forth and so on,
With this kind of stuff one might endlessly go on;
To come to the point, I may safely assert you
Will find in each yard every cardinal virtue;*
Each has six truest patriots: four discoverers of ether,
Who never had thought on 't nor mentioned it either:
Ten poets, the greatest who ever wrote rhyme:
Two hundred and forty first men of their time:
One person whose portrait just gave the least hint
Its original had a most horrible squint:
One critic, most (what do they call it?) reflective,
Who never had used the phrase ob- or subjective;
Forty fathers of Freedom, of whom twenty bred
Their sons for the rice-swamps, at so much a head,
And their daughters for — faugh! thirty mothers of
    Gracchi:
Non-resistants who gave many a spiritual black eye:
Eight true friends of their kind, one of whom was a
    jailer:
Four captains almost as astounding as Taylor:

* (And at this just conclusion will surely arrive,
That the goodness of earth is more dead than alive.)

Two dozen of Italy's exiles who shoot us his
Kaisership daily, stern pen-and-ink Brutuses,
Who, in Yankee back-parlors, with crucified smile,*
Mount serenely their country's funereal pile:
Ninety-nine Irish heroes, ferocious rebellers
'Gainst the Saxon in cis-marine garrets and cellars,
Who shake their dread fists o'er the sea and all that, —
As long as a copper drops into the hat:
Nine hundred Teutonic republicans stark
From Vaterland's battles just won — in the Park,
Who the happy profession of martyrdom take
Whenever it gives them a chance at a steak:
Sixty-two second Washingtons: two or three Jacksons:
And so many everythings else that it racks one's
Poor memory too much to continue the list,
Especially now they no longer exist; —
I would merely observe that you 've taken to giving
The puffs that belong to the dead to the living,
And that somehow your trump-of-contemporary-doom's
      tones
Is tuned after old dedications and tombstones." —

  Here the critic came in and a thistle presented † —
From a frown to a smile the god's features relented,
As he stared at his envoy, who, swelling with pride,
To the god's asking look, nothing daunted, replied,
" You 're surprised, I suppose, I was absent so long
But your godship respecting the lilies was wrong;
I hunted the garden from one end to t' other,
And got no reward but vexation and bother,
Till, tossed out with weeds in a corner to wither,
This one lily I found and made haste to bring hither."

  "Did he think I had given him a book to review?
I ought to have known what the fellow would do,"
Muttered Phœbus aside, " for a thistle will pass
Beyond doubt for the queen of all flowers with an ass;
He has chosen in just the same way as he 'd choose
His specimens out of the books he reviews;
And now, as this offers an excellent text,

---

    * Not forgetting their tea and their toast, though, the while.
    † Turn back now to page — goodness only knows what,
      And take a fresh hold on the thread of my plot.

I 'll give 'em some brief hints on criticism next."
So, musing a moment, he turned to the crowd,
And, clearing his voice, spoke as follows aloud : —

"My friends, in the happier days of the muse,
We were luckily free from such things as reviews,
Then naught came between with its fog to make clearer
The heart of the poet to that of his hearer;
Then the poet brought heaven to the people, and they
Felt that they, too, were poets in hearing his lay;
Then the poet was prophet, the past in his soul
Pre-created the future, both parts of one whole;
Then for him there was nothing too great or too small,
For one natural deity sanctified all;
Then the bard owned no clipper and meter of moods
Save the spirit of silence that hovers and broods
O'er the seas and the mountains, the rivers and woods
He asked not earth's verdict, forgetting the clods,
His soul soared and sang to an audience of gods.
'T was for them that he measured the thought and the line
And shaped for their vision the perfect design,
With as glorious a foresight, a balance as true,
As swung out the worlds in the infinite blue ;
Then a glory and greatness invested man's heart,
The universal, which now stands estranged and apart,
In the free individual moulded, was Art;
Then the forms of the Artist seemed thrilled with desire
For something as yet unattained, fuller, higher,
As once with her lips, lifted hands, and eyes listening,
And her whole upward soul in her countenance glistening,
Eurydice stood — like a beacon unfired,
Which, once touch'd with flame, will leap heav'nward in-
　　　　spired —
And waited with answering kindle to mark
The first gleam of Orpheus that pained the red Dark.
Then painting, song, sculpture, did more than relieve
The need that men feel to create and believe,
And as, in all beauty, who listens with love,
Hears these words oft repeated — 'beyond and above,'
So these seemed to be but the visible sign
Of the grasp of the soul after things more divine ;
They were ladders the Artist erected to climb
O'er the narrow horizon of space and of time,

And we see there the footsteps by which men had gained
To the one rapturous glimpse of the never-attained,
As shepherds could erst sometimes trace in the sod
The last spurning print of a sky-cleaving god.

"But now, on the poet's dis-privacied moods
With *do this* and *do that* the pert critic intrudes;
While he thinks he's been barely fulfilling his duty
To interpret 'twixt men and their own sense of beauty,
And has striven, while others sought honor or pelf,
To make his kind happy as he was himself,
He finds he's been guilty of horrid offences
In all kinds of moods, numbers, genders, and tenses;
He's been *ob* and *sub*jective, what Kettle calls Pot,
Precisely, at all events, what he ought not,
You have done this, says one judge; *done that,* says an-
    other;
You should have done this, grumbles one; *that,* says
    t' other;
Never mind what he touches, one shrieks out *Taboo!*
And while he is wondering what he shall do,
Since each suggests opposite topics for song,
They all shout together *you're right!* and *you're wrong!*

"Nature fits all her children with something to do,
He who would write and can't write, can surely review.
Can set up a small booth as critic and sell us his
Petty conceit and his pettier jealousies;
Thus a lawyer's apprentice, just out of his teens,
Will do for the Jeffrey of six magazines;
Having read Johnson's lives of the poets half through,
There's nothing on earth he's not competent to;
He reviews with as much nonchalance as he whistles, —
He goes through a book and just picks out the thistles
It matters not whether he blame or commend,
If he's bad as a foe, he's far worse as a friend;
Let an author but write what's above his poor scope,
And he'll go to work gravely and twist up a rope,
And, inviting the world to see punishment done,
Hang himself up to bleach in the wind and the sun;
'T is delightful to see, when a man comes along
Who has anything in him peculiar and strong,

Every cockboat that swims clear its fierce (pop) gundeck
  at him
And make as he passes its ludicrous Peck at him," —

  Here Miranda came up and began, " As to that," —
Apollo at once seized his gloves, cane, and hat,
And, seeing the place getting rapidly cleared,
I, too, snatched my notes and forthwith disappeared.

THE BIGLOW PAPERS.

NOTICES OF AN INDEPENDENT PRESS.

[I HAVE observed, reader, (bene- or male-volent, as it may happen,)
that it is customary to append to the second editions of books, and to
the second works of authors, short sentences commendatory of the
first, under the title of *Notices of the Press.* These, I have been given
to understand, are procurable at certain established rates, payment
being made either in money or advertising patronage by the publisher,
or by an adequate outlay of servility on the part of the author. Con-
sidering these things with myself, and also that such notices are neither
intended, nor generally believed, to convey any real opinions, being a
purely ceremonial accompaniment of literature, and resembling certifi-
cates to the virtues of various morbiferal panaceas, I conceived that it
would be not only more economical to prepare a sufficient number of such
myself, but also more immediately subservient to the end in view to pre-
fix them to this our primary edition rather than await the contingency
of a second, when they would seem to be of small utility. To delay
attaching the *bobs* until the second attempt at flying the kite, would
indicate but a slender experience in that useful art. Neither has it
escaped my notice, nor failed to afford me matter of reflection, that,
when a circus or a caravan is about to visit Jaalam, the initial step is
to send forward large and highly ornamented bills of performance to
be hung in the bar-room and the post-office. These having been suffi-
ciently gazed at, and beginning to lose their attractiveness except for
the flies, and, truly, the boys also, (in whom I find it impossible to
repress, even during school-hours, certain oral and telegraphic com-
munications concerning the expected show,) upon some fine morning
the band enters in a gayly-painted wagon, or triumphal chariot, and
with noisy advertisement, by means of brass, wood, and sheepskin,
makes the circuit of our startled village-streets. Then, as the exciting
sounds draw nearer and nearer, do I desiderate those eyes of Aristar-
chus, "whose looks were as a breeching to a boy." Then do I per-
ceive, with vain regret of wasted opportunities, the advantage of a
pancratic or pantechnic education, since he is most reverenced by my
little subjects who can throw the cleanest summerset or walk most
securely upon the revolving cask. The story of the Pied Piper becomes
for the first time credible to me, (albeit confirmed by the Hameliners
dating their legal instruments from the period of his exit,) as I behold
how those strains, without pretence of magical potency, bewitch the
pupillary legs, nor leave to the pedagogic an entire self-control. For
these reasons, lest my kingly prerogative should suffer diminution, I
prorogue my restless commons, whom I also follow into the street,
chiefly lest some mischief may chance befall them. After the manner
of such a band, I send forward the following notices of domestic manu-
facture, to make brazen proclamation, not unconscious of the advan-
tage which will accrue, if our little craft, *cymbula sutilis,* shall seem
to leave port with a clipping breeze, and to carry, in nautical phrase,
a bone in her mouth. Nevertheless, I have chosen, as being more
equitable, to prepare some also sufficiently objurgatory, that readers of
every taste may find a dish to their palate. I have modelled them upon

actually existing specimens, preserved in my own cabinet of natural curiosities. One, in particular, I had copied with tolerable exactness from a notice of one of my own discourses, which, from its superior tone and appearance of vast experience, I concluded to have been written by a man at least three hundred years of age, though I recollected no existing instance of such antediluvian longevity. Nevertheless, I afterwards discovered the author to be a young gentleman preparing for the ministry under the direction of one of my brethren in a neighboring town, and whom I had once instinctively corrected in a Latin quantity. But this I have been forced to omit, from its too great length. — H. W.]

From the Universal Littery Universe.

Full of passages which rivet the attention of the reader. . . . Under a rustic garb, sentiments are conveyed which should be committed to the memory and engraven on the heart of every moral and social being. . . . We consider this a *unique* performance. . . . We hope to see it soon introduced into our common schools. . . . Mr. Wilbur has performed his duties as editor with excellent taste and judgment. . . . This is a vein which we hope to see successfully prosecuted. . . . We hail the appearance of this work as a long stride toward the formation of a purely aboriginal, indigenous, native, and American literature. We rejoice to meet with an author national enough to break away from the slavish deference, too common among us, to English grammar and orthography. . . . Where all is so good, we are at a loss how to make extracts. . . . On the whole, we may call it a volume which no library, pretending to entire completeness, should fail to place upon its shelves.

From the Higginbottomopolis Snapping-turtle.

A collection of the merest balderdash and doggerel that it was ever our bad fortune to lay eyes on. The author is a vulgar buffoon, and the editor a talkative, tedious old fool. We use strong language, but should any of our readers peruse the book, (from which calamity Heaven preserve them!) they will find reasons for it thick as the leaves of Vallumbrozer, or, to use a still more expressive comparison, as the combined heads of author and editor. The work is wretchedly got up. . . . We should like to know how much *British gold* was pocketed by this libeller of our country and her purest patriots.

From the Oldfogrumville Mentor.

We have not had time to do more than glance through this handsomely printed volume, but the name of its respectable editor, the Rev. Mr. Wilbur, of Jaalam, will afford a sufficient guaranty for the worth of its contents. . . . The paper is white, the type clear, and the volume of a convenient and attractive size. . . . In reading this elegantly executed work, it has seemed to us that a passage or two might have been retrenched with advantage, and that the general style of diction was susceptible of a higher polish. . . . On the whole, we may safely leave the ungrateful task of criticism to the reader. We will barely suggest, that in volumes intended, as this is, for the illustration of a provincial dialect and turns of expression, a dash of humor or satire

might be thrown in with advantage. . . . The work is admirably got
up. . . . This work will form an appropriate ornament to the centre-
table. It is beautifully printed, on paper of an excellent quality.

From the Dekay Bulwark.

We should be wanting in our duty as the conductor of that tremen-
dous engine, a public press, as an American, and as a man, did we allow
such an opportunity as is presented to us by " The Biglow Papers " to
pass by without entering our earnest protest against such attempts
(now, alas! too common) at demoralizing the public sentiment. Under
a wretched mask of stupid drollery, slavery, war, the social glass, and,
in short, all the valuable and time-honored institutions justly dear to
our common humanity and especially to republicans, are made the
butt of coarse and senseless ribaldry by this low-minded scribbler.
It is time that the respectable and religious portion of our community
should be aroused to the alarming inroads of foreign Jacobinism, sans-
culôttism, and infidelity. It is a fearful proof of the wide-spread
nature of this contagion, that these secret stabs at religion and virtue
are given from under the cloak (*credite, posteri!*) of a clergyman. It
is a mournful spectacle indeed to the patriot and Christian to see liber-
ality and new ideas (falsely so called, — they are as old as Eden) in-
vading the sacred precincts of the pulpit. . . . On the whole, we
consider this volume as one of the first shocking results which we pre-
dicted would spring out of the late French " Revolution " (!).

From the Bungtown Copper and Comprehensive Tocsin (a *try-weakly* family journal).

Altogether an admirable work. . . . Full of humor, boisterous, but
delicate — of wit withering and scorching, yet combined with a pathos
cool as morning dew, — of satire ponderous as the mace of Richard, yet
keen as the scymitar of Saladin. . . . A work full of " mountain-
mirth," mischievous as Puck and lightsome as Ariel. . . . We know
not whether to admire most the genial, fresh, and discursive concinnity
of the author, or his playful fancy, weird imagination, and compass of
style, at once both objective and subjective. . . . We might indulge
in some criticisms, but were the author other than he is, he would be a
different being. As it is, he has a wonderful *pose*, which flits from
flower to flower, and bears the reader irresistibly along on its eagle
pinions (like Ganymede) to the " highest heaven of invention." . . .
We love a book so purely objective. . . . Many of his pictures of
natural scenery have an extraordinary subjective clearness and fidelity.
. . . In fine, we consider this as one of the most extraordinary volumes
of this or any age. We know of no English author who could have
written it. It is a work to which the proud genius of our country,
standing with one foot on the Aroostook and the other on the Rio
Grande, and holding up the star-spangled banner amid the wreck of
matter and the crush of worlds, may point with bewildering scorn of
the punier efforts of enslaved Europe. . . . We hope soon to encoun-
ter our author among those higher walks of literature in which he is
evidently capable of achieving enduring fame. Already we should
be inclined to assign him a high position in the bright galaxy of our
American bards.

From the Saltriver Pilot and Flag of Freedom.

A volume in bad grammar and worse taste. . . . While the pieces here collected were confined to their appropriate sphere in the corners of obscure newspapers, we considered them wholly beneath contempt, but, as the author has chosen to come forward in this public manner, he must expect the lash he so richly merits. . . . Contemptible slanders. . . . Vilest Billingsgate. . . . Has raked all the gutters of our language. . . . The most pure, upright, and consistent politicians not safe from his malignant venom. . . . General Cushing comes in for a share of his vile calumnies. . . . The *Reverend* Homer Wilbur is a disgrace to his cloth. . . .

From the World-Harmonic-Æolian-Attachment.

Speech is silver: silence is golden. No utterance more Orphic than this. While, therefore, as highest author, we reverence him whose works continue heroically unwritten, we have also our hopeful word for those who with pen (from wing of goose loud-cackling, or seraph God-commissioned) record the thing that is revealed. . . . Under mask of quaintest irony, we detect here the deep, storm-tost (nigh shipwracked) soul, thunder-scarred, semiarticulate, but ever climbing hopefully toward the peaceful summits of an Infinite Sorrow. . . Yes, thou poor, forlorn Hosea, with Hebrew fire-flaming soul in thee, for thee also this life of ours has not been without its aspects of heavenliest pity and laughingest mirth. Conceivable enough! Through coarse Thersites-cloak, we have revelation of the heart, wild-glowing, world-clasping, that is in him. Bravely he grapples with the life-problem as it presents itself to him, uncombed, shaggy, careless of the "nicer proprieties," inexpert of "elegant diction," yet with voice audible enough to whoso hath ears, up there on the gravelly side-hills, or down on the splashy, Indiarubber-like salt-marshes of native Jaalam. To this soul also the *Necessity of Creating* somewhat has unveiled its awful front. If not Œdipuses and Electras and Alcestices, then in God's name Birdofredum Sawins! These also shall get born into the world, and filch (if so need) a Zingali subsistence therein, these lank, omnivorous Yankees of his. He shall paint the Seen, since the Unseen will not sit to him. Yet in him also are Nibelungen-lays, and Iliads, and Ulysses-wanderings, and Divine Comedies, — if only once he could come at them! Therein lies much, nay all; for what truly is this which we name *All*, but that which we do *not* possess? . . . Glimpses also are given us of an old father Ezekiel, not without paternal pride, as is the wont of such. A brown, parchment-hided old man of the geoponic or bucolic species, gray-eyed, we fancy, *queued* perhaps, with much weather-cunning and plentiful September-gale memories, bidding fair in good time to become the Oldest Inhabitant. After such hasty apparition, he vanishes and is seen no more. . . . Of "Rev. Homer Wilbur, A. M., Pastor of the First Church in Jaalam," we have small care to speak here. Spare touch in him of his Melesigenes namesake, save, haply, the — blindness! A tolerably caliginose, nephelegeretous elderly gentleman, with infinite faculty of sermonizing, muscularized by long practice, and excellent digestive apparatus, and, for the rest, well-meaning enough, and with small private illuminations (somewhat tallowy, it is to be feared) of his own. To him, there, "Pastor of the First Church in Jaalam," our Hosea presents himself as a quite inexplicable Sphinx-riddle. A rich poverty of Latin and Greek, — so far is clear enough, even to eyes peering myopic through horn-lensed editorial spectacles, — but naught farther? O purblind, well-meaning, altogether fuscous Melesigenes-Wilbur, there are things in him incommunicable by stroke of birch! Did it ever enter that old bewildered head of thine that there was the *Possibility of the Infinite* in him? To thee, quite wingless (and even featherless) biped, has not so much even as a dream of wings ever come? "Talented young parishioner"? Among the Arts whereof thou art *Magister*, does that of *seeing* happen to be one? Unhappy *Artium Magister !* Somehow a Nemean lion, fulvous, torrid-eyed, dry-nursed in broad-howling sand-wildernesses of a sufficiently rare spirit-Libya (it may be supposed) has got whelped among the sheep. Already he stands wild-glaring, with feet clutching the ground as with oak-roots, gathering for a Remus-spring over the walls of thy little fold. In Heaven's name, go not near him with that flybite crook of thine! In good time, thou painful preacher, thou wilt go to the appointed place of departed Artillery-Election Sermons, Right-Hands of Fellowship, and Results of Councils, gathered to thy spiritual fathers with much Latin of the Epitaphial sort; thou, too, shalt have thy reward; but on him the Eumenides have looked, not Xantippes of the pit, snake-tressed, finger-threatening, but radiantly calm as on antique gems; for him paws impatient the winged courser of the gods, champing unwelcome bit; him the starry deeps, the empyrean glooms, and far-flashing splendors await.

From the Onion Grove Phœnix.

A talented young townsman of ours, recently returned from a Continental tour, and who is already favorably known to our readers by his sprightly letters from abroad which have graced our columns, called at our office yesterday. We learn from him, that, having enjoyed the distinguished privilege, while in Germany, of an introduction to the celebrated Von Humbug, he took the opportunity to present that eminent man with a copy of the "Biglow Papers." The next morning he received the following note, which he has kindly furnished us for publication. We prefer to print it *verbatim*, knowing that our readers will readily forgive the few errors into which the illustrious writer has fallen, through ignorance of our language.

"HIGH-WORTHY MISTER!

"I shall also now especially happy starve, because I have more or less a work of one those aboriginal Red-Men seen in which I have so deaf an interest ever taken fullworthy on the self shelf with our Gottsched to be upset.

"Pardon my in the English-speech unpractice!

"VON HUMBUG."

He also sent with the above note a copy of his famous work on "Cosmetics," to be presented to Mr. Biglow; but this was taken from our friend by the English custom-house officers, probably through a petty national spite. No doubt, it has by this time found its way into the British Museum. We trust this outrage will be exposed in all our American papers. We shall do our best to bring it to the notice of the State Department. Our numerous readers will share in the pleasure we experience at seeing our young and vigorous national literature thus encouragingly patted on the head by this venerable and world-renowned German. We love to see these reciprocations of good-feeling between the different branches of the great Anglo-Saxon race.

[The following genuine "notice" having met my eye I gladly insert a portion of it here, the more especially as it contains one of Mr. Biglow's poems not elsewhere printed. — H. W.]

From the Jaalam Independent Blunderbuss.

. . . But, while we lament to see our young townsman thus mingling in the heated contests of party politics, we think we detect in him the presence of talents which, if properly directed, might give an innocent pleasure to many. As a proof that he is competent to the production of other kinds of poetry, we copy for our readers a short fragment of a pastoral by him, the manuscript of which was loaned us by a friend. The title of it is "The Courtin'."

ZEKLE crep' up, quite unbeknown,
 An' peeked in thru the winder,
An' there sot Huldy all alone,
 'ith no one nigh to hender.

Agin' the chimbly crooknecks hung,
 An' in amongst 'em rusted
The ole queen's-arm thet gran'ther Young
 Fetched back frum Concord busted.

The wannut logs shot sparkles out
 Towards the pootiest, bless her!
An' leetle fires danced all about
 The chiny on the dresser.

The very room, coz she wuz in,
 Looked warm frum floor to ceilin',
An' she looked full ez rosy agin
 Ez th' apples she wuz peelin'.

She heerd a foot an' knowed it, tu,
 Araspin' on the scraper, —
All ways to once her feelins flew
 Like sparks in burnt-up paper.

He kin' o' l'itered on the mat,
 Some doubtfle o' the seekle;
His heart kep' goin' pitypat,
 But hern went pity Zekle.

An' yet she gin her cheer a jerk
 Ez though she wished him furder,
An' on her apples kep' to work
 Ez ef a wager spurred her.

"You want to see my Pa, I spose?"
 "Wal, no; I come designin'—"
"To see my Ma? She's sprinklin' clo'es
 Agin tomorrow's i'nin'."

He stood a spell on one foot fust
 Then stood a spell on tother,
An' on which one he felt the wust
 He couldn't ha' told ye, nuther.

Sez he, "I'd better call agin;"
 Sez she, "think likely. *Mister;*"
The last word pricked him like a pin,
 An'--wal, he up and kist her.

When Ma bimeby upon 'em slips,
   Huldy sot pale ez ashes,
All kind o' smily round the lips
   An' teary round the lashes.

Her blood riz quick, though, like the **tide**
   Down to the Bay o' Fundy,
An' all I know is they wuz cried
   In meetin', come nex Sunday.

SATIS multis sese emptores futuros libri professis, Georgius
Nichols, Cantabrigiensis, opus emittet de parte gravi sed adhuc
neglecta historiæ naturalis, cum titulo sequenti, videlicet :

*Conatus ad Delineationem naturalem nonnihil perfectiorem
Scarabœi Bombilatoris, vulgo dicti* HUMBUG, ab HOMERO WIL-
BUR, Artium Magistro, Societatis historico-naturalis Jaalamensis
Præside, (Secretario, Socioque (eheu !) singulo,) multarumque
aliarum Societatum eruditarum (sive ineruditarum) tam do-
mesticarum quam transmarinarum Socio — forsitan futuro.

PROEMIUM.

LECTORI BENEVOLO S.

Toga scholastica nondum deposita, quum systemata varia
entomologica, a viris ejus scientiæ cultoribus studiosissimis
summa diligentia ædificata, penitus indagâssem, non fuit quin
luctuose omnibus in iis, quamvis aliter laude dignissimis, hia-
tum magni momenti perciperem.   Tunc, nescio quo motu
superiore impulsus, aut qua captus dulcedine operis, ad eum
implendum (Curtius alter) me solemniter devovi.   Nec ab isto
labore, δαιμονίως imposito, abstinui antequam tractatulum suffi-
cienter inconcinnum lingua vernacula perfeceram.   Inde, juve-
niliter tumefactus, et barathro ineptiæ τῶν βιβλιοπωλῶν (necnon
"Publici Legentis") nusquam explorato, me composuisse quod
quasi placentas præfervidas (ut sic dicam) homines ingurgita-
rent credidi.   Sed, quum huic et alio bibliopolæ MSS. mea
submisissem et nihil solidius responsione valde negativa in
Musæum meum retulissem, horror ingens atque misericordia,
ob crassitudinem Lambertianam in cerebris homunculorum
istius muneris cœlesti quadam ira infixam, me invasere.
Extemplo mei solius impensis librum edere decrevi, nihil
omnino dubitans quin "Mundus Scientificus" (ut aiunt) cru-
menam meam ampliter repleret.   Nullam, attamen, ex agro illo
meo parvulo segetem demessui, præter gaudium vacuum bene
de Republica merendi.   Iste panis meus pretiosus super aquas
literarias fæculentas præfidenter jactus, quasi Harpyiarum
quarundam (scilicet bibliopolarum istorum facinorosorum
supradictorum) tactu rancidus, intra perpaucos dies mihi
domum rediit.   Et, quum ipse tali victu ali non tolerarem,
primum in mentem venit pistori (typographo nempe) nihilo-
minus solvendum esse.   Animum non idcirco demisi, imo æque
ac pueri naviculas suas penes se lino retinent (eo ut e recto
cursu delapsas ad ripam retrahant), sic ego Argò meam charta-
ceam fluctibus laborantem a quæsitu velleris aurei, ipse potius
tonsus pelleque exutus, mente solida revocavi.   Metaphoram
ut mutem, *boomarangam* meam a scopo aberrantem retraxi, dum

majore vi, occasione ministrante, adversus Fortunam intorquerem. Ast mihi, talia volventi, et, sicut Saturnus ille παιδοβόρος, liberos intellectus mei depascere fidenti, casus miserandus, nec antea inauditus, supervenit. Nam, ut ferunt Scythas pietatis causa et parsimoniæ, parentes suos mortuos devorâsse, sic filius hic meus primogenitus, Scythis ipsis minus mansuetus, patrem vivum totum et calcitrantem exsorbere enixus est. Nec tamen hac de causa sobolem meam esurientem exheredavi. Sed famem istam pro valido testimonio virilitatis roborisque potius habui, cibumque ad eam satiandam, salva paterna mea carne, petii. Et quia bilem illam scaturientem ad æs etiam concoquendum idoneam esse estimabam, unde æs alienum, ut minoris pretii, haberem, circumspexi. Rebus ita se habentibus, ab avunculo meo Johanne Doolittle, Armigero, impetravi ut pecunias necessarias suppeditaret, ne opus esset mihi universitatem relinquendi antequam ad gradum primum in artibus pervenissem. Tunc ego, salvum facere patronum meum munificum maxime cupiens, omnes libros primæ editionis operis mei non venditos una cum privilegio in omne ævum ejusdem imprimendi et edendi avunculo meo dicto pigneravi. Ex illo die, atro lapide notando, curæ vociferantes familiæ singulis annis crescentis eo usque insultabant ut nunquam tam carum pignus e vinculis istis aheneis solvere possem.

Avunculo vero nuper mortuo, quum inter alios consanguineos testamenti ejus lectionem audiendi causa advenissem, erectis auribus verba talia sequentia accepi:—" Quoniam persuasum habeo meum dilectum nepotem Homerum, longa et intima rerum angustarum domi experientia, aptissimum esse qui divitias tueatur, beneficenterque ac prudenter iis divinis creditis utatur, — ergo, motus hisce cogitationibus, exque amore meo in illum magno, do, legoque nepoti caro meo supranominato omnes singularesque istas possessiones nec ponderabiles nec computabiles meas quæ sequuntur, scilicet: quingentos libros quos mihi pigneravit dictus Homerus, anno lucis 1792, cum privilegio edendi et repetendi opus istud 'scientificum' (quod dicunt) suum, si sic elegerit. Tamen D. O. M. precor oculos Homeri nepotis mei ita aperiat eumque moveat, ut libros istos in bibliotheca unius e plurimis castellis suis Hispaniensibus tuto abscondat."

His verbis (vix credibilibus) auditis, cor meum in pectore exsultavit. Deinde, quoniam tractatus Anglice scriptus spem auctoris fefellerat, quippe quum studium Historiæ Naturalis in Republica nostra inter factionis strepitum languescat, Latine versum edere statui, et eo potius quia nescio quomodo disciplina academica et duo diplomata proficiant, nisi quod peritos linguarum omnino mortuarum (et damnandarum, ut dicebat iste πανοῦργος Gulielmus Cobbett) nos faciant.

Et mihi adhuc superstes est tota illa editio prima, quam quasi crepitaculum per quod dentes caninos dentibam retineo.

OPERIS SPECIMEN.

(*Ad exemplum Johannis Physiophili speciminis Monachologiæ.*)

12. S. B.   *Militaris*, WILBUR.   *Carnifex*, JABLONSK.   *Profanus.*
DESFONT.

[Male hancce speciem *Cyclopem* Fabricius vocat, ut qui singulo
oculo ad quod sui interest distinguitur. Melius vero Isaacus Outis
nullum inter S. milit.   S. que Belzebul (Fabric. 152) discrimen esse
defendit.]
Habitat civitat. Americ. austral.
Aureis lineis splendidus ; plerumque tamen sordidus, utpote lanienas
valde frequentans, fœtore sanguinis allectus.   Amat quoque insuper
septa apricari, neque inde, nisi maxima conatione, detruditur.   *Candi-
datus* ergo populariter vocatus.   Caput cristam quasi pennarum osten-
dit. Pro cibo vaccam publicam callide mulget ; abdomen enorme ;
facultas suctus haud facile estimanda. Otiosus, fatuus ; ferox nihilomi-
nus, semperque dimicare paratus. Tortuose repit.
Capite sæpe maxima cum cura dissecto, ne illud rudimentum etiam
cerebri commune omnibus prope insectis detegere poteram.
Unam de hoc S. milit. rem singularem notavi ; Nam S. Guineens.
(Fabric. 143) servos facit, et idcirco a multis summa in reverentia
habitus, quasi scintillas rationis pæne humanæ demonstrans.

24. S. B.   *Criticus*, WILBUR.   *Zoilus*, FABRIC.   *Pigmæus*, CARLSEN.

[Stultissime Johannes Stryx cum S. punctato (Fabric. 64–109) con-
fundit.   Specimina quamplurima scrutationi microscopicæ subjeci,
nunquam tamen unum ulla indicia puncti cujusvis prorsus ostendentem
inveni.]
Præcipue formidolosus, insectatusque, in proxima rima anonyma
sese abscondit, *we, we*, creberrime stridens. Ineptus, segnipes.
Habitat ubique gentium ; in sicco ; nidum suum terebratione
indefessa ædificans.   Cibus.   Libros depascit ; siccos præcipue.

MELIBŒUS–HIPPONAX.

THE

𝕭iglow 𝕻apers,

EDITED

WITH AN INTRODUCTION, NOTES, GLOSSARY, AND
COPIOUS INDEX,

BY

HOMER WILBUR, A.M.,

PASTOR OF THE FIRST CHURCH IN JAALAM, AND (PROSPECTIVE)
MEMBER OF MANY LITERARY, LEARNED AND SCIENTIFIC
SOCIETIES,

(for which see page 372.)

The ploughman's whistle, or the trivial flute,
Finds more respect than great Apollo's lute.
Quarles's Emblems, B. ii. E. 8.

Margaritas, munde porcine, calcâsti : en, siliquas accipe.
Jac. Car. Fil. ad Pub. Leg. § 1.

NOTE TO TITLE–PAGE.

It will not have escaped the attentive eye, that I have, on the title-page, omitted those honorary appendages to the editorial name which not only add greatly to the value of every book, but whet and exacerbate the appetite of the reader. For not only does he surmise that an honorary membership of literary and scientific societies implies a certain amount of necessary distinction on the part of the recipient of such decorations, but he is willing to trust himself more entirely to an author who writes under the fearful responsibility of involving the reputation of such bodies as the *S. Archæl. Dahom.*, or the *Acad. Lit. et Scient. Kamtschat.* I cannot but think that the early editions of Shakspeare and Milton would have met with more rapid and general acceptance, but for the barrenness of their respective title-pages; and I believe, that, even now, a publisher of the works of either of those justly distinguished men would find his account in procuring their admission to the membership of learned bodies on the Continent, — a proceeding no whit more incongruous than the reversal of the judgment against Socrates, when he was already more than twenty centuries beyond the reach of antidotes, and when his memory had acquired a deserved respectability. I conceive that it was a feeling of the importance of this precaution which induced Mr. Locke to style himself "Gent." on the title-page of his Essay, as who should say to his readers that they could receive his metaphysics on the honor of a gentleman.

Nevertheless, finding that, without descending to a smaller size of type than would have been compatible with the dignity of the several societies to be named, I could not compress my intended list within the limits of a single page, and thinking, moreover, that the act would carry with it an air of decorous modesty, I have chosen to take the reader aside, as it were, into my private closet, and there not only exhibit to him the diplomas which I already possess, but also to furnish him with a prophetic vision of those which I may, without undue presumption, hope for, as not beyond the reach of human ambition and attainment. And I am the rather induced to this from the fact, that my name has been unaccountably dropped from the last triennial catalogue of our beloved *Alma Mater.*

370

Whether this is to be attributed to the difficulty of Latinizing any of those honorary adjuncts (with a complete list of which I took care to furnish the proper persons nearly a year beforehand), or whether it had its origin in any more culpable motives, I forbear to consider in this place, the matter being in course of painful investigation. But, however this may be, I felt the omission the more keenly, as I had, in expectation of the new catalogue, enriched the library of the Jaalam Athenæum with the old one then in my possession, by which means it has come about that my children will be deprived of a never-wearying winter evening's amusement in looking out the name of their parent in that distinguished roll. Those harmless innocents had at least committed no — but I forbear, having intrusted my reflections and animadversions on this painful topic to the safe-keeping of my private diary, intended for posthumous publication. I state this fact here, in order that certain nameless individuals, who are, perhaps, overmuch congratulating themselves on my silence, may know that a rod is in pickle which the vigorous hand of a justly incensed posterity will apply to their memories.

The careful reader will note, that, in the list which I have prepared, I have included the names of several Cisatlantic societies to which a place is not commonly assigned in processions of this nature. I have ventured to do this, not only to encourage native ambition and genius, but also because I have never been able to perceive in what way distance (unless we suppose them at the end of a lever) could increase the weight of learned bodies. As far as I have been able to extend my researches among such stuffed specimens as occasionally reach America, I have discovered no generic difference between the antipodal *Fogrum Japonicum* and the *F. Americanum* sufficiently common in our own immediate neighborhood. Yet, with a becoming deference to the popular belief that distinctions of this sort are enhanced in value by every additional mile they travel, I have intermixed the names of some tolerably distant literary and other associations with the rest.

I add here, also, an advertisement, which, that it may be the more readily understood by those persons especially interested therein, I have written in that curtailed and otherwise maltreated canine Latin, to the writing and reading of which they are accustomed.

OMNIB. PER TOT. ORB. TERRAR. CATALOG. ACADEM. EDD.

Minim. gent. diplom. ab inclytiss. acad. vest. orans, vir. honorand. operosiss., at sol. ut sciat. quant. glor. nom. meum (dipl. fort. concess.) catal. vest. temp. futur. affer., ill. subjec., addit. omnib. titul. honorar. qu. adh. non tant. opt. quam probab. put.

⁎⁎⁎ Litt. Uncial. distinx. ut Præs. S. Hist. Nat. Jaal.

HOMERUS WILBUR, Mr., Episc. Jaalam, S. T. D. 1850,
et Yal. 1849, et Neo-Cæs. et Brun. et Gulielm. 1852, et Gul. et
Mar. et Bowd. et Georgiop. et Viridimont. et Columb. Nov.
Ebor. 1853, et Amherst. et Watervill. et S. Jarlath. Hib. et S.
Mar. et S. Joseph. et S. And. Scot. 1854, et Nashvill. et Dart.
et Dickins. et Concord. et Wash. et Columbian. et Charlest. et
Jeff. et Dubl. et Oxon. et Cantab. et cæt. 1855, P. U. N. C. H.
et J. U. D. Gott. et Osnab. et Heidelb. 1860, et Acad. BORE US.
Berolin. Soc., et SS. RR. Lugd. Bat. et Patav. et Lond. et Edinb.
et Ins. Feejee. et Null. Terr. et Pekin. Soc. Hon. et S. H. S. et
S. P. A. et A. A. S. et S. Humb. Univ. et S. Omn. Rer. Quarund.
q. Aliar. Promov. Passamaquod. et H. P. C. et I. O. H. et
Å. Δ. Φ. et II. K. P. et Φ. B. K. et Peucin. et Erosoph. et Phila-
delph. et Frat. in Unit. et Σ. T. et S. Archæolog. Athen. et Acad.
Scient. et Lit. Panorm. et SS. R. H. Matrit. et Beeloochist. et
Caffrar. et Caribb. et M. S. Reg. Paris. et S. Am. Antiserv. Soc.
Hon. et P. D. Gott. et LL.D. 1852, et D. C. L. et Mus. Doc.
Oxon. 1860, et M. M. S. S. et M. D. 1854, et Med. Fac. Univ.
Harv. Soc. et S. pro Convers. Pollywog. Soc. Hon. et Higgl.
Piggl. et LL.B. 1853, et S. pro Christianiz. Moschet. Soc., et
SS. Ante-Diluv. ubiq. Gent. Soc. Hon. et Civit. Cleric. Jaalam.
et S. pro Diffus. General. Tenebr. Secret. Corr.

INTRODUCTION.

WHEN, more than three years ago, my talented young parishioner, Mr. Biglow, came to me and submitted to my animadversions the first of his poems which he intended to commit to the more hazardous trial of a city newspaper, it never so much as entered my imagination to conceive that his productions would ever be gathered into a fair volume, and ushered into the august presence of the reading public by myself. So little are we short-sighted mortals able to predict the event! I confess that there is to me a quite new satisfaction in being associated (though only as sleeping partner) in a book which can stand by itself in an independent unity on the shelves of libraries. For there is always this drawback from the pleasure of printing a sermon, that, whereas the queasy stomach of this generation will not bear a discourse long enough to make a separate volume, those religious and godly-minded children (those Samuels, if I may call them so) of the brain must at first lie buried in an undistinguished heap, and then get such resurrection as is vouchsafed to them, mummy-wrapt with a score of others in a cheap binding, with no other mark of distinction than the word "*Miscellaneous*" printed upon the back. Far be it from me to claim any credit for the quite unexpected popularity which I am pleased to find these bucolic strains have attained unto. If I know myself, I am measurably free from the itch of vanity; yet I may be allowed to say that I was not backward to recognize in them a certain wild, puckery, acidulous (sometimes even verging toward that point which, in our rustic phrase, is termed *shut-eye*) flavor, not wholly unpleasing, nor unwholesome, to palates cloyed with the sugariness of tamed and cultivated fruit. It may be, also, that some touches of my own, here and there, may have led to their wider acceptance, albeit solely from my larger experience of literature and authorship.*

I was, at first, inclined to discourage Mr. Biglow's attempts, as knowing that the desire to poetize is one of the diseases naturally incident to adolescence, which, if the fitting remedies

* The reader curious in such matters may refer (if he can find them) to " A Sermon preached on the Anniversary of the Dark Day," "An Artillery Election Sermon," " A Discourse on the Late Eclipse," " Dorcas, a Funeral Sermon on the Death of Madam Submit Tidd, Relict of the late Experience Tidd, Esq.," &c., &c.

be not at once and with a bold hand applied, may become chronic, and render one, who might else have become in due time an ornament of the social circle, a painful object even to nearest friends and relatives. But thinking, on a further experience, that there was a germ of promise in him which required only culture and the pulling up of weeds from around it, I thought it best to set before him the acknowledged examples of English composition in verse, and leave the rest to natural emulation. With this view, I accordingly lent him some volumes of Pope and Goldsmith, to the assiduous study of which he promised to devote his evenings. Not long afterward, he brought me some verses written upon that model, a specimen of which I subjoin, having changed some phrases of less elegancy, and a few rhymes objectionable to the cultivated ear. The poem consisted of childish reminiscences, and the sketches which follow will not seem destitute of truth to those whose fortunate education began in a country village. And, first, let us hang up his charcoal portrait of the school-dame.

" Propt on the marsh, a dwelling now, I see
The humble school-house of my A, B, C,
Where well-drilled urchins, each behind his tire,
Waited in ranks the wished command to fire,
Then all together, when the signal came,
Discharged their *a-b abs* against the dame.
Daughter of Danaus, who could daily pour
In treacherous pipkins her Pierian store,
She, mid the volleyed learning firm and calm
Patted the furloughed ferule on her palm,
And, to our wonder, could divine at once
Who flashed the pan, and who was downright dunce.

" There young Devotion learned to climb with ease
The gnarly limbs of Scripture family-trees,
And he was most commended and admired
Who soonest to the topmost twig perspired;
Each name was called as many various ways
As pleased the reader's ear on different days,
So that the weather, or the ferule's stings,
Colds in the head, or fifty other things,
Transformed the helpless Hebrew thrice a week
To guttural Pequot or resounding Greek,
The vibrant accent skipping here and there,
Just as it pleased invention or despair;
No controversial Hebraist was the Dame;
With or without the points pleased her the same;
If any tyro found a name too tough,
And looked at her, pride furnished skill enough;
She nerved her larynx for the desperate thing,
And cleared the five-barred syllables at a spring.

" Ah, dear old times! there once it was my hap,
Perched on a stool, to wear the long-eared cap;
From books degraded, there I sat at ease,
A drone, the envy of compulsory bees;

Rewards of merit, too, full many a time,
Each with its woodcut and its moral rhyme,
And pierced half-dollars hung on ribbons gay
About my neck — to be restored next day,
I carried home, rewards as shining then
As those which deck the lifelong pains of men,
More solid than the redemanded praise
With which the world beribbons later days.

" Ah, dear old times! how brightly ye return!
How, rubbed afresh, your phosphor traces burn!
The ramble schoolward through dewsparkling meads;
The willow-wands turned Cinderella steeds,
The impromptu pinbent hook, the deep remorse
O'er the chance-captured minnow's inchlong corse;
The pockets, plethoric with marbles round,
That still a space for ball and pegtop found,
Nor satiate yet, could manage to confine
Horsechestnuts, flagroot, and the kite's wound twine,
And, like the prophet's carpet could take in,
Enlarging still, the popgun's magazine;
The dinner carried in the small tin pail,
Shared with the dog, whose most beseeching tail
And dripping tongue and eager ears belied
The assumed indifference of canine pride;
The caper homeward, shortened if the cart
Of neighbor Pomeroy, trundling from the mart,
O'ertook me, — then, translated to the seat
I praised the steed, how staunch he was and fleet,
While the bluff farmer, with superior grin,
Explained where horses should be thick, where thin,
And warned me (joke he always had in store)
To shun a beast that four white stockings wore.
What a fine natural courtesy was his!
His nod was pleasure, and his full bow bliss;
How did his well-thumbed hat, with ardor rapt,
Its decorous curve to every rank adapt!
How did it graduate with a courtly ease
The whole long scale of social differences,
Yet so gave each his measure running o'er,
None thought his own was less, his neighbor's more;
The squire was flattered, and the pauper knew
Old times acknowledged 'neath the threadbare blue!
Dropped at the corner of the embowered lane,
Whistling I wade the knee-deep leaves again,
While eager Argus, who has missed all day
The sharer of his condescending play,
Comes leaping onward with a bark elate
And boisterous tail to greet me at the gate;
That I was true in absence to our love
Let the thick dog's-ears in my primer prove."

I add only one further extract, which will possess a melancholy interest to all such as have endeavored to glean the materials of revolutionary history from the lips of aged persons, who took a part in the actual making of it, and, finding the manufacture profitable, continued the supply in an adequate proportion to the demand.

" Old Joe is gone, who saw hot Percy goad
His slow artillery up the Concord road,
A tale which grew in wonder, year by year,
As, every time he told it, Joe drew near
To the main fight, till, faded and grown gray,
The original scene to bolder tints gave way;
Then Joe had heard the foe's scared double-quick
Beat on stove drum with one uncaptured stick,
And, ere death came the lengthening tale to lop,
Himself had fired, and seen a red-coat drop;
Had Joe lived long enough, that scrambling fight
Had squared more nearly with his sense of right,
And vanquished Percy, to complete the tale,
Had hammered stone for life in Concord jail."

I do not know that the foregoing extracts ought not to be called my own rather than Mr. Biglow's, as, indeed, he maintained stoutly that my file had left nothing of his in them. I should not, perhaps, have felt entitled to take so great liberties with them, had I not more than suspected an hereditary vein of poetry in myself, a very near ancestor having written a Latin poem in the Harvard *Gratulatio* on the accession of George the Third. Suffice it to say, that, whether not satisfied with such limited approbation as I could conscientiously bestow, or from a sense of natural inaptitude, certain it is that my young friend could never be induced to any further essays in this kind. He affirmed that it was to him like writing in a foreign tongue, — that Mr. Pope's versification was like the regular ticking of one of Willard's clocks, in which one could fancy, after long listening, a certain kind of rhythm or tune, but which yet was only a poverty-stricken *tick, tick*, after all, — and that he had never seen a sweet-water on a trellis growing so fairly, or in forms so pleasing to his eye, as a fox-grape over a scrub-oak in a swamp. He added I know not what, to the effect that the sweet-water would only be the more disfigured by having its leaves starched and ironed out, and that Pegāsus (so he called him) hardly looked right with his mane and tail in curl-papers. These and other such opinions I did not long strive to eradicate, attributing them rather to a defective education and senses untuned by too long familiarity with purely natural objects, than to a perverted moral sense. I was the more inclined to this leniency since sufficient evidence was not to seek, that his verses, wanting as they certainly were in classic polish and point, had somehow taken hold of the public ear in a surprising manner. So, only setting him right as to the quantity of the proper name Pegasus, I left him to follow the bent of his natural genius.

Yet could I not surrender him wholly to the tutelage of the pagan (which, literally interpreted, signifies village) muse without yet a further effort for his conversion, and to this end I resolved that whatever of poetic fire yet burned in myself, aided by the assiduous bellows of correct models, should be put in requisition. Accordingly, when my ingenious young parishioner brought to my study a copy of verses which he had written touching the acquisition of territory resulting from the Mexican war, and the folly of leaving the question of slavery or freedom to the adjudication of chance, I did myself indite a short fable or apologue after the manner of Gay and Prior, to the end that he might see how easily even such subjects as he treated of were capable of a more refined style and more elegant expression. Mr. Biglow's production was as follows: —

THE TWO GUNNERS.

A FABLE.

Two fellers, Isrel named and Joe,
One Sundy mornin' 'greed to go
Agunnin' soon 's the bells wuz done
And meetin' finally begun,
So 'st no one would n't be about
Ther Sabbath-breakin' to spy out.

Joe did n't want to go a mite;
He felt ez though 't warnt skeercely right,
But, when his doubts he went to speak on,
Isrel he up and called him Deacon,
An' kep' apokin' fun like sin
An' then arubbin' on it in,
Till Joe, less skeered o' doin' wrong
Than bein' laughed at, went along.

Past noontime they went trampin' round
An' nary thing to pop at found,
Till, fairly tired o' their spree,
They leaned their guns agin a tree,
An' jest ez they wuz settin' down
To take their noonin', Joe looked roun'
And see (across lots in a pond
That warn't more 'n twenty rod beyond,)
A goose that on the water sot
Ez ef awaitin' to be shot.

Isrel he ups and grabs his gun;
Sez he, " By ginger, here 's some fun! "
" Don't fire," sez Joe, " it aint no use,
Thet 's Deacon Peleg's tame wild-goose; "
Sez Isrel, " I don't care a cent,
I 've sighted an' I 'll let her went; "
Bang! went queen's-arm, ole gander flopped
His wings a spell, an' quorked, an' dropped.

Sez Joe, " I would n't ha' been hired
At that poor critter to ha' fired,
But, sence it 's clean gin up the ghost,
We 'll hev the tallest kind o' roast;
I guess our waistbands 'll be tight
'Fore it comes ten o'clock ternight."

" I won't agree to no such bender,"
Sez Isrel, " keep it tell it 's tender;
'T aint wuth a snap afore it 's ripe."
Sez Joe, " I 'd jest ez lives eat tripe;
You *air* a buster ter suppose
I 'd eat what makes me hol' my nose! "

So they disputed to an' fro
Till cunnin' Isrel sez to Joe,
" Don't less stay here an' play the fool,
Less wait till both on us git cool,
Jest for a day or two less hide it
An' then toss up an' so decide it."
" Agreed! " sez Joe, an' so they did,
An' the ole goose wuz safely hid.

Now 't wuz the hottest kind o' weather,
An' when at last they come together,
It did n't signify which won,
Fer all the mischief hed ben done:
The goose wuz there, but, fer his soul,
Joe would n't ha' tetched it with a pole;
But Isrel kind o' liked the smell on 't
An' made *his* dinner very well on 't.

My own humble attempt was in manner and form following,
and I print it here, I sincerely trust, out of no vainglory, but
solely with the hope of doing good.

LEAVING THE MATTER OPEN.

A TALE.

BY HOMER WILBUR, A.M.

Two brothers once, an ill-matched pair,
Together dwelt (no matter where),
To whom an Uncle Sam, or some one,
Had left a house and farm in common.
The two in principles and habits
Were different as rats from rabbits;
Stout farmer North, with frugal care,
Laid up provision for his heir,
Not scorning with hard sun-browned hands
To scrape acquaintance with his lands;
Whatever thing he had to do
He did, and made it pay him, too;
He sold his waste stone by the pound,
His drains made water-wheels spin round,
His ice in summer-time he sold,
His wood brought profit when 't was cold,
He dug and delved from morn till night,
Strove to make profit square with right,
Lived on his means, cut no great dash,
And paid his debts in honest cash.

On tother hand, his brother South
Lived very much from hand to mouth,

Played gentleman, nursed dainty hands,
Borrowed North's money on his lands,
And culled his morals and his graces
From cock-pits, bar-rooms, fights, and races;
His sole work in the farming line
Was keeping droves of long-legged swine,
Which brought great bothers and expenses
To North in looking after fences,
And, when they happened to break through,
Cost him both time and temper too.
For South insisted it was plain
He ought to drive them home again,
And North consented to the work
Because he loved to buy cheap pork.

Meanwhile, South's swine increasing fast,
His farm became too small at last,
So, having thought the matter over,
And feeling bound to live in clover
And never pay the clover's worth,
He said one day to brother North: —

" Our families are both increasing,
And, though we labor without ceasing,
Our produce soon will be too scant
To keep our children out of want;
They who wish fortune to be lasting
Must be both prudent and forecasting;
We soon shall need more land; a lot
I know, that cheaply can be bo't;
You lend the cash, I 'll buy the acres,
And we 'll be equally partakers.

Poor North, whose Anglo-Saxon blood
Gave him a hankering after mud,
Wavered a moment, then consented,
And, when the cash was paid, repented;
To make the new land worth a pin,
Thought he, it must be all fenced in,
For, if South's swine once get the run on 't
No kind of farming can be done on 't;
If that don't suit the other side,
'T is best we instantly divide.

But somehow South could ne'er incline
This way or that to run the line,
And always found some new pretence
'Gainst setting the division fence;
At last he said: —

                " For peace's sake,
Liberal concessions I will make;
Though I believe, upon my soul,
I 've a just title to the whole,
I 'll make an offer which I call
Gen'rous, — we 'll have no fence at all;
Then both of us, whene'er we choose,

Can take what part we want to use;
If you should chance to need it first,
Pick you the best, I'll take the worst."

"Agreed!" cried North; thought he, this fall
With wheat and rye I'll sow it all,
In that way I shall get the start,
And South may whistle for his part;
So thought, so done, the field was sown,
And, winter having come and gone,
Sly North walked blithely forth to spy,
The progress of his wheat and rye;
Heavens, what a sight! his brother's swine
Had asked themselves all out to dine,
Such grunting, munching, rooting, shoving,
The soil seemed all alive and moving,
As for his grain, such work they'd made on 't,
He couldn't spy a single blade on 't.

Off in a rage he rushed to South,
"My wheat and rye" — grief choked his mouth;
"Pray don't mind me," said South, "but plant
All of the new land that you want;"
"Yes, but your hogs," cried North;

                                           "The grain
Won't hurt them," answered South again;
"But they destroy my grain;"

                                            "No doubt;
'T is fortunate you've found it out;
Misfortunes teach, and only they,
You must not sow it in their way;"
"Nay, you," says North, "must keep them out:"
"Did I create them with a snout?"
Asked South demurely; "as agreed,
The land is open to your seed,
And would you fain prevent my pigs
From running there their harmless rigs?
God knows I view this compromise
With not the most approving eyes;
I gave up my unquestioned rights
For sake of quiet days and nights,
I offered then, you know 't is true,
To cut the piece of land in two."
"Then cut it now," growls North;

                                       "Abate
Your heat," says South, "'t is now too late;
I offered you the rocky corner,
But you, of your own good the scorner,
Refused to take it; I am sorry;
No doubt you might have found a quarry,
Perhaps a gold-mine, for aught I know,
Containing heaps of native rhino;
You can't expect me to resign
My right" —

"But where," quoth North, "are.mine?"
"*Your* rights," says tother, "well, that 's funny.
I bought the land"—

  "*I* paid the money;"
"That," answered South, "is from the point,
The ownership, you 'll grant, is joint;
I 'm sure my only hope and trust is
Not law so much as abstract justice,
Though, you remember, 't was agreed
That so and so—consult the deed;
Objections now are out of date,
They might have answered once, but Fate
Quashes them at the point we 've got to;
Obsta principiis, that 's my motto."
So saying, South began to whistle
And looked as obstinate as gristle,
While North went homeward, each brown paw
Clenched like a knot of natural law,
And all the while, in either ear,
Heard something clicking wondrous clear.

To turn now to other matters, there are two things upon which it would seem fitting to dilate somewhat more largely in this place,—the Yankee character and the Yankee dialect. And, first, of the Yankee character, which has wanted neither open maligners, nor even more dangerous enemies in the persons of those unskilful painters who have given to it that hardness, angularity, and want of proper perspective, which, in truth, belonged, not to their subject, but to their own niggard and unskilful pencil.

New England was not so much the colony of a mother country, as a Hagar driven forth into the wilderness. The little self-exiled band which came hither in 1620 came, not to seek gold, but to found a democracy. They came that they might have the privilege to work and pray, to sit upon hard benches and listen to painful preachers as long as they would, yea, even unto thirty-seventhly, if the spirit so willed it. And surely, if the Greek might boast his Thermopylæ, where three hundred men fell in resisting the Persian, we may well be proud of our Plymouth Rock, where a handful of men, women, and children not merely faced, but vanquished, winter, famine, the wilderness, and the yet more invincible *storge* that drew them back to the green island far away. These found no lotus growing upon the surly shore, the taste of which could make them forget their little native Ithaca; nor were they so wanting to themselves in faith as to burn their ship, but could see the fair west wind belly the homeward sail, and then turn unrepining to grapple with the terrible Unknown.

As Want was the prime foe these hardy exodists had to fortress themselves against, so it is little wonder if that traditional feud is long in wearing out of the stock. The wounds of the old warfare were long ahealing, and an east wind of hard times puts a new ache in every one of them. Thrift was the first lesson in their hornbook, pointed out, letter after letter, by the lean finger of the hard schoolmaster, Necessity. Neither were those plump, rosy-gilled Englishmen that came hither, but a hard-faced, atrabilious, earnest-eyed race, stiff from long wrestling with the Lord in prayer, and who had taught Satan to dread the new Puritan hug. Add two hundred years' influence of soil, climate, and exposure, with its necessary result of idiosyncrasies, and we have the present Yankee, full of expedients, half-master of all trades, inventive in all but the beautiful, full of shifts, not yet capable of comfort, armed at all points against the old enemy Hunger, longanimous, good at patching, not so careful for what is best as for what will *do*, with a clasp to his purse and a button to his pocket, not skilled to build against Time, as in old countries, but against sore-pressing Need, accustomed to move the world with no πού στῶ but his own two feet, and no lever but his own long forecast. A strange hybrid, indeed, did circumstance beget, here in the New World, upon the old Puritan stock, and the earth never before saw such mystic-practicalism, such niggard-geniality, such calculating-fanaticism, such cast-iron-enthusiasm, such sourfaced-humor, such close-fisted-generosity. This new *Græculus esuriens* will make a living out of anything. He will invent new trades as well as tools. His brain is his capital, and he will get education at all risks. Put him on Juan Fernandez, and he would make a spelling-book first, and a salt-pan afterward. *In cœlum, jusseris, ibit,* — or the other way either, — it is all one, so anything is to be got by it. Yet, after all, thin, speculative Jonathan is more like the Englishman of two centuries ago than John Bull himself is. He has lost somewhat in solidity, has become fluent and adaptable, but more of the original groundwork of character remains. He feels more at home with Fulke Greville, Herbert of Cherbury, Quarles, George Herbert, and Browne, than with his modern English cousins. He is nearer than John, by at least a hundred years, to Naseby, Marston Moor, Worcester, and the time when, if ever, there were true Englishmen. John Bull has suffered the idea of the Invisible to be very much fattened out of him. Jonathan is conscious still that he lives in the world of the Unseen as well as of the Seen. To move John, you must make your fulcrum of solid beef and pudding; an abstract idea will do for Jonathan.

⁎⁎ TO THE INDULGENT READER.

My friend, the Reverend Mr. Wilbur, having been seized with a dangerous fit of illness, before this Introduction had passed through the press, and being incapacitated for all literary exertion, sent to me his notes, memoranda, &c., and requested me to fashion them into some shape more fitting for the general eye. This, owing to the fragmentary and disjointed state of his manuscripts, I have felt wholly unable to do; yet, being unwilling that the reader should be deprived of such parts of his lucubrations as seemed more finished, and not well discerning how to segregate these from the rest, I have concluded to send them all to the press precisely as they are.

Columbus Nye,

Pastor of a church in Bungtown Corner.

It remains to speak of the Yankee dialect. And, first, it may be premised, in a general way, that any one much read in the writings of the early colonists need not be told that the far greater share of the words and phrases now esteemed peculiar to New England, and local there, were brought from the mother country. A person familiar with the dialect of certain portions of Massachusetts will not fail to recognize, in ordinary discourse, many words now noted in English vocabularies as archaic, the greater part of which were in common use about the time of the King James translation of the Bible. Shakspeare stands less in need of a glossary to most New Englanders than to many a native of the Old Country. The peculiarities of our speech, however, are rapidly wearing out. As there is no country where reading is so universal and newspapers are so multitudinous, so no phrase remains long local, but is transplanted in the mail-bags to every remotest corner of the land. Consequently our dialect approaches nearer to uniformity than that of any other nation.

The English have complained of us for coining new words. Many of those so stigmatized were old ones by them forgotten, and all make now an unquestioned part of the currency, wherever English is spoken. Undoubtedly, we have a right to make new words, as they are needed by the fresh aspects under which life presents itself here in the New World; and, indeed, wherever a language is alive, it grows. It might be questioned whether we could not establish a stronger title to the ownership of the English tongue than the mother-islanders themselves. Here, past all question, is to be its great home and centre. And not only is it already spoken here by greater numbers, but with a higher popular average of correctness, than in Britain. The great writers of it, too, we might claim as ours, were ownership to be settled by the number of readers and lovers.

As regards the provincialisms to be met with in this volume, I may say that the reader will not find one which is not (as I believe) either native or imported with the early settlers, nor one which I have not, with my own ears, heard in familiar use. In the metrical portion of the book, I have endeavored to adapt the spelling as nearly as possible to the ordinary mode of pronunciation. Let the reader who deems me over-particular remember this caution of Martial: —

> " *Quem recitas, meus est, O Fidentine, libellus;*
> *Sed male cum recitas, incipit esse tuus.*"

A few further explanatory remarks will not be impertinent.

I shall barely lay down a few general rules for the reader's guidance.

1. The genuine Yankee never gives the rough sound to the *r* when he can help it, and often displays considerable ingenuity in avoiding it even before a vowel.

2. He seldom sounds the final *g*, a piece of self-denial, if we consider his partiality for nasals. The same of the final *d*, as *han'* and *stan'* for *hand* and *stand*.

3. The *h* in such words as *while, when, where*, he omits altogether.

4. In regard to *a*, he shows some inconsistency, sometimes giving a close and obscure sound, as *hev* for *have*, *hendy* for *handy*, *ez* for *as*, *thet* for *that*, and again giving it the broad sound it has in *father*, as *hânsome* for *handsome*.

5. To the sound *ou* he prefixes an *e* (hard to exemplify otherwise than orally).

The following passage in Shakspeare he would recite thus:—

> "Neow is the winta uv eour discontent
> Med glorious summa by this sun o' Yock,
> An' all the cleouds thet leowered upun eour heouse
> In the deep buzzum o' the oshin buried;
> Neow air eour breows beound 'ith victorious wreaths;
> Eour breused arms hung up fer monimunce;
> Eour starn alarums changed to merry meetins,
> Eour dreffle marches to delightful measures.
> Grim-visaged war heth smeuthed his wrinkled front,
> An' neow, instid o' mountin' barebid steeds
> To fright the souls o' ferfle edverseries,
> He capers nimly in a lady's châmber,
> To the lascivious pleasin' uv a loot."

6. *Au*, in such words as *daughter* and *slaughter*, he pronounces *ah*.

7. To the dish thus seasoned add a drawl *ad libitum*.

[Mr. Wilbur's notes here become entirely fragmentary. — C. N.]

a. Unable to procure a likeness of Mr. Biglow, I thought the curious reader might be gratified with a sight of the editorial effigies. And here a choice between two was offered,—the one a profile (entirely black) cut by Doyle, the other a portrait painted by a native artist of much promise. The first of these seemed wanting in expression, and in the second a slight obliquity of the visual organs has been heightened (perhaps from an over-desire of force on the part of the artist) into too close an approach to actual *strabismus*. This slight divergence in my optical apparatus from the ordinary model — however I may have been taught to regard it in the light of a mercy rather than a cross, since it enabled me to give as much of directness and personal application to my discourses as met the wants of

my congregation, without risk of offending any by being sup-
posed to have him or her in my eye (as the saying is) — seemed
yet to Mrs. Wilbur a sufficient objection to the engraving of
the aforesaid painting. We read of many who either absolutely
refused to allow the copying of their features, as especially did
Plotinus and Agesilaus among the ancients, not to mention the
more modern instances of Scioppius, Palæottus, Pinellus, Velserus,
Gataker, and others, or were indifferent thereto, as Cromwell.

β. Yet was Cæsar desirous of concealing his baldness. *Per
contra*, my Lord Protector's carefulness in the matter of his wart
might be cited. Men generally more desirous of being *improved*
in their portraits than characters. Shall probably find very un-
flattered likenesses of ourselves in Recording Angel's gallery.

γ. Whether any of our national peculiarities may be traced
to our use of stoves, as a certain closeness of the lips in pro-
nunciation, and a smothered smoulderingness of disposition,
seldom roused to open flame? An unrestrained intercourse with
fire probably conducive to generosity and hospitality of soul.
Ancient Mexicans used stoves, as the friar Augustin Ruiz re-
ports, Hakluyt, III., 468, — but the Popish priests not always
reliable authority.

To-day picked my Isabella grapes. Crop injured by attacks
of rose-bug in the spring. Whether Noah was justifiable in
preserving this class of insects?

δ. Concerning Mr. Biglow's pedigree. Tolerably certain
that there was never a poet among his ancestors. An ordina-
tion hymn attributed to a maternal uncle, but perhaps a sort of
production not demanding the creative faculty.

His grandfather a painter of the grandiose or Michael Angelo
school. Seldom painted objects smaller than houses or barns,
and these with uncommon expression.

ε. Of the Wilburs no complete pedigree. The crest said to
be a *wild boar*, whence, perhaps, the name.(?) A connection
with the Earls of Wilbraham (*quasi* wild boar ham) might be
made out. This suggestion worth following up. In 1677, John
W. m. Expect ——, had issue, 1. John, 2. Haggai, 3. Expect,
4. Ruhamah, 5. Desire.

> "Hear lyes yᵉ bodye of Mrs Expect Wilber,
>   Yᵉ crewell salvages they kil'd her
>   Together wᵗʰ other Christian soles eleaven,
>   October yᵉ ix daye, 1707.
>   Yᵉ stream of Jordan sh' as crost ore
>   And now expeacts me on yᵉ other shore:
>   I live in hope her soon to join;
>   Her earthlye yeeres were forty and nine."
>   *From Gravestone in Pekussett, North Parish.*

2c

This is unquestionably the same John who afterward (1711) married Tabitha Hagg or Ragg.

But if this were the case, she seems to have died early; for only three years after, namely, 1714, we have evidence that he married Winifred, daughter of Lieutenant Tipping.

He seems to have been a man of substance, for we find him in 1696 conveying "one undivided eightieth part of a salt-meadow" in Yabbok, and he commanded a sloop in 1702.

Those who doubt the importance of genealogical studies *fuste potius quam argumento erudiendi.*

I trace him as far as 1723, and there lose him. In that year he was chosen selectman.

No gravestone. Perhaps overthrown when new hearse-house was built, 1802.

He was probably the son of John, who came from Bilham Comit. Salop. circa 1642.

This first John was a man of considerable importance, being twice mentioned with the honorable prefix of *Mr.* in the town records. Name spelt with two *l*-s.

"Here lyeth yᵉ bod [*stone unhappily broken.*]
    Mr. Ihon Willber [Esq.] [*I enclose this in brackets as doubtful.* **To**
        me it seems clear.]
    Ob't die [*illegible; looks like xviii.*] . . . iii [*prob.* 1693.]
    .   .   .   .   .   paynt
    .   .   .   .   deseased seinte:
A friend and [fath]er untoe all yᵉ opreast,
Hee gave yᵉ wicked familists noe reast,
When Sat[an bl]ewe his Antinomian blaste,
Wee clong to [Willber as a steadf]ast maste.
[A]gaynst yᵉ horrid Qua[kers]   . . ."

It is greatly to be lamented that this curious epitaph is mutilated. It is said that the sacrilegious British soldiers made a target of this stone during the war of Independence. How odious an animosity which pauses not at the grave! How brutal that which spares not the monuments of authentic history! This is not improbably from the pen of Rev. Moody Pyram, who is mentioned by Hubbard as having been noted for a silver vein of poetry. If his papers be still extant, a copy might possibly be recovered.

THE BIGLOW PAPERS.

FIRST SERIES.

THE BIGLOW PAPERS.

No. I.

A LETTER

FROM MR. EZEKIEL BIGLOW OF JAALAM TO THE HON. JOSEPH T. BUCKINGHAM, EDITOR OF THE BOSTON COURIER, ENCLOSING A POEM OF HIS SON, MR. HOSEA BIGLOW.

JAYLEM, june 1846.

MISTER EDDYTER:—Our Hosea wuz down to Boston last week, and he see a cruetin Sarjunt a struttin round as popler as a hen with 1 chicking, with 2 fellers a drummin and fifin arter him like all nater. the sarjunt he thout Hosea hed n't gut his i teeth cut cos he looked a kindo 's though he 'd jest com down, so he cal'lated to hook him in, but Hosy wood n't take none o' his sarse for all he hed much as 20 Rooster's tales stuck onto his hat and eenamost enuf brass a bobbin up and down on his shoulders and figureed onto his coat and trousis, let alone wut nater hed sot in his featers, to make a 6 pounder out on.

wal, Hosea he com home considerabal riled, and arter I 'd gone to bed I heern Him a thrashin round like a short-tailed Bull in fli-time. The old Woman ses she to me ses she, Zekle, ses she, our Hosee 's gut the chollery or suthin anuther ses she, don't you Bee skeered, ses I, he 's oney amakin pottery * ses i, he 's ollers on hand at that ere busynes like Da & martin, and shure enuf, cum mornin, Hosy he cum down stares full chizzle, hare on eend and cote tales flyin, and sot rite of to go reed his varses to Parson Wilbur bein he haint aney grate shows o' book larnin himself, bimeby he cum back and sed the parson wuz dreffle tickled with 'em as i hoop you will Be, and said they wuz True grit.

Hosea ses taint hardly fair to call 'em hisn now, cos the parson kind o' slicked off sum o' the last varses, but he told Hosee he did n't want to put his ore in to tetch to the Rest on 'em, bein they wuz verry well As thay wuz, and then Hosy ses he sed suthin a nuther about Simplex Mundishes or sum sech feller, but I guess Hosea kind o' did n't hear him, for I never

* *Aut insanit, aut versos facit.* — H. W.

388

hearn o' nobody o' that name in this villadge, and I've lived
here man and boy 76 year cum next tater diggin, and thair aint
no wheres a kitting spryer 'n I be.

If you print 'em I wish you'd jest let folks know who hosy's
father is, cos my ant Keziah used to say it's nater to be curus
ses she, she aint livin though and he's a likely kind o' lad.

EZEKIEL BIGLOW.

THRASH away, you'll *hev* to rattle
  On them kittle-drums o' yourn, —
'T aint a knowin' kind o' cattle
  Thet is ketched with mouldy corn ;
Put in stiff, you fifer feller,
  Let folks see how spry you be, —
Guess you'll toot till you are yeller
  'Fore you git ahold o' me !

Thet air flag's a leetle rotten,
  Hope it aint your Sunday's best ; —
Fact ! it takes a sight o' cotton
  To stuff out a soger's chest :
Sence we farmers hev to pay fer 't,
  Ef you must wear humps like these,
Sposin' you should try salt hay fer 't,
  It would du ez slick ez grease.

'T would n't suit them Southun fellers,
  They 're a dreffle graspin' set,
We must ollers blow the bellers
  Wen they want their irons het ;
May be it's all right ez preachin',
  But *my* narves it kind o' grates,
Wen I see the overreachin'
  O' them nigger-drivin' States.

Them thet rule us, them slave-traders,
  Haint they cut a thunderin' swarth,
(Helped by Yankee renegaders,)
  Thru the vartu o' the North !
We begin to think it's nater
  To take sarse an' not be riled ; —
Who 'd expect to see a tater
  All on eend at bein' biled ?

Ez fer war, I call it murder, —
   There you hev it plain an' flat;
I don't want to go no furder
   Than my Testyment fer that;
God hez sed so plump an' fairly,
   It 's ez long ez it is broad,
An' you 've gut to git up airly
   Ef you want to take in God.

'T aint your eppyletts an' feathers
   Make the thing a grain more right;
'T aint afollerin' your bell-wethers
   Will excuse ye in His sight;
Ef you take a sword an' dror it,
   An' go stick a feller thru,
Guv'ment aint to answer for it,
   God 'll send the bill to you.

Wut 's the use o' meetin'-goin'
   Every Sabbath, wet or dry,
Ef it 's right to go amowin'
   Feller-men like oats an' rye?
I dunno but wut it 's pooty
   Trainin' round in bobtail coats, —
But it 's curus Christian dooty
   This 'ere cuttin' folks's throats.

They may talk o' Freedom's airy
   Tell they 're pupple in the face, —
It 's a grand gret cemetary
   Fer the barthrights of our race;
They jest want this Californy
   So 's to lug new slave-states in
To abuse ye, an' to scorn ye,
   An' to plunder ye like sin.

Aint it cute to see a Yankee
   Take sech everlastin' pains,
All to git the Devil's thankee,
   Helpin' on 'em weld their chains?
Wy, it 's jest ez clear ez figgers,
   Clear ez one an' one make two,
Chaps thet make black slaves o' niggers
   Want to make wite slaves o' you.

Tell ye jest the eend I 've come to
   Arter cipherin' plaguy smart,
An' it makes a handy sum, tu,
   Any gump could larn by heart;
Laborin' man an' laborin' woman
   Hev one glory an' one shame,
Ev'y thin' thet 's done inhuman
   Injers all on 'em the same.

'T aint by turnin' out to hack folks .
   You 're agoin' to git your right,
Nor by lookin' down on black folks
   Coz you 're put upon by wite;
Slavery aint o' nary color,
   'T.aint the hide thet makes it wus,
All it keers fer in a feller
   'S jest to make him fill its pus.

Want to tackle *me* in, du ye?
   I expect you 'll hev to wait;
Wen cold lead puts daylight thru ye
   You 'll begin to kal'klate;
'Spose the crows wun't fall to pickin'
   All the carkiss from your bones,
Coz you helped to give a lickin'
   To them poor half-Spanish drones?

Jest go home an' ask our Nancy
   Wether I 'd be sech a goose
Ez to jine ye, — guess you 'd fancy
   The etarnal bung wuz loose!
She wants me fer home consumption,
   Let alone the hay 's to mow, —
Ef you 're arter folks o' gumption,
   You 've a darned long row to hoe.

Take them editors thet 's crowin'
   Like a cockerel three months old, —
Don't ketch any on 'em goin',
   Though they *be* so blasted bold;
Aint they a prime lot o' fellers?
   'Fore they think on 't they will sprout,
(Like a peach thet 's got the yellers,)
   With the meanness bustin' out.

Wal, go 'long to help 'em stealin'
  Bigger pens to cram with slaves,
Help the men thet's ollers dealin'
  Insults on your fathers' graves;
Help the strong to grind the feeble,
  Help the many agin the few,
Help the men thet call your people
  Witewashed slaves an' peddlin' crew!

Massachusetts, God forgive her,
  She's akneelin' with the rest,
She, thet ough' to ha' clung fer ever
  In her grand old eagle-nest;
She thet ough' to stand so fearless
  Wile the wracks are round her hurled, .
Holdin' up a beacon peerless
  To the oppressed of all the world!

Haint they sold your colored seamen?
  Haint they made your env'ys wiz?
Wut'll make ye act like freemen?
  Wut'll git your dander 1iz?
Come, I'll tell ye wut I'm thinkin'
  Is our dooty in this fix,
They'd ha' done 't ez quick ez winkin'
  In the days o' seventy-six.

Clang the bells in every steeple,
  Call all true men to disown
The tradoocers of our people,
  The enslavers o' their own;
Let our dear old Bay State proudly
  Put the trumpet to her mouth,
Let her ring this messidge loudly
  In the ears of all the South: —

"I'll return ye good fer evil
  Much ez we frail mortils can,
But I wun't go help the Devil
  Makin' man the cus o' man;
Call me coward, call me traiter,
  Jest ez suits your mean idees, —
Here I stand a tyrant-hater,
  An' the friend o' God an' Peace!"

Ef I 'd *my* way I hed ruther
  We should go to work an' part, —
They take one way, we take t 'other, —
  Guess it would n't break my heart;
Man hed ough' to put asunder
  Them thet God has noways jined;
An' I should n't gretly wonder
  Ef there 's thousands o' my mind.

[The first recruiting sergeant on record I conceive to have been that individual who is mentioned in the Book of Job as *going to and fro in the earth, and walking up and down in it.* Bishop Latimer will have him to have been a bishop, but to me that other calling would appear more congenial. The sect of Cainites is not yet extinct, who esteemed the first-born of Adam to be the most worthy, not only because of that privilege of primogeniture, but inasmuch as he was able to overcome and slay his younger brother. That was a wise saying of the famous Marquis Pescara to the Papal Legate, that *it was impossible for men to serve Mars and Christ at the same time.* Yet in time past the profession of arms was judged to be κατ' ἐξοχήν that of a gentleman, nor does this opinion want for strenuous upholders even in our day. Must we suppose, then, that the profession of Christianity was only intended for losels, or, at best, to afford an opening for plebeian ambition? Or shall we hold with that nicely metaphysical Pomeranian, Captain Vratz, who was Count Königsmark's chief instrument in the murder of Mr. Thynne, that the Scheme of Salvation has been arranged with an especial eye to the necessities of the upper classes, and that "God would consider *a gentleman* and deal with him suitably to the condition and profession he had placed him in"? It may be said of us all, *Exemplo plus quam ratione vivimus.* — H. W.]

No. II.

A LETTER

FROM MR. HOSEA BIGLOW TO THE HON. J. T. BUCKING-HAM, EDITOR OF THE BOSTON COURIER, COVERING A LETTER FROM MR. B. SAWIN, PRIVATE IN THE MASSA-CHUSETTS REGIMENT.

[THIS letter of Mr. Sawin's was not originally written in verse. Mr. Biglow, thinking it peculiarly susceptible of metrical adornment, translated it, so to speak, into his own vernacular tongue. This is not the time to consider the question, whether rhyme be a mode of expression natural to the human race. If leisure from other and more important avocations be granted, I will handle the matter more at large in an appendix to the present volume. In this place I will barely remark, that I have sometimes noticed in the unlanguaged prattlings of infants a fondness for alliteration, assonance, and even rhyme, in which natural predisposition we may trace the three degrees through which our Anglo-Saxon verse rose to its culmination in the poetry of Pope. I would not be understood as questioning in these remarks that pious theory which supposes that children, if left entirely to themselves, would naturally discourse in Hebrew. For this the authority of one experiment is claimed, and I could, with Sir Thomas Browne, desire its establishment, inasmuch as the acquirement of that sacred tongue would thereby be facilitated. I am aware that Herodotus states the conclusion of Psammeticus to have been in favor of a dialect of the Phrygian. But, beside the chance that a trial of this importance would hardly be blessed to a Pagan monarch whose only motive was curiosity, we have on the Hebrew side the comparatively recent investigation of James the Fourth of Scotland. I will add to this prefatory remark, that Mr. Sawin, though a native of Jaalam, has never been a stated attendant on the religious exercises of my congregation. I consider my humble efforts prospered in that not one of my sheep hath ever indued the wolf's clothing of war, save for the comparatively innocent diversion of a militia training. Not that my flock are backward to undergo the hardships of *defensive* warfare. They serve cheerfully in the great army which fights even unto death *pro aris et focis,* accoutred with the spade, the axe, the plane, the sledge, the spelling-book, and other such effectual weapons against want and ignorance and unthrift. I have taught them (under God) to esteem our human institutions as but tents of a night, to be stricken whenever Truth puts the bugle to her lips and sounds a march to the heights of wider-viewed intelligence and more perfect organization. — H. W.]

MISTER BUCKINUM, the follerin Billet was writ hum by a Yung feller of our town that wuz cussed fool enuff to goe atrottin inter Miss Chiff arter a Drum and fife. it ain't Nater for a feller to let on that he 's sick o' any bizness that He went intu off his own free will and a Cord, but I rather cal'late he 's middlin tired o' voluntearin By this Time. I bleeve u may put dependunts on his statemence. For I never heered nothin bad on him let Alone his havin what Parson Wilbur cals a *pongshong* for cocktales, and he ses it wuz a soshiashun of idees sot him agoin arter the Crootin Sargient cos he wore a cocktale onto his hat.

his Folks gin the letter to me and i shew it to parson Wilbur and he ses it oughter Bee printed. send It to mister Buckinum, ses he, i don't ollers agree with him, ses he, but by Time,* ses he, I *du* like a feller that ain't a Feared.

I have intusspussed a Few refleckshuns hear and thair. We 're kind o' prest with Hayin.

Ewers respecfly
HOSEA BIGLOW.

THIS kind o' sogerin' aint a mite like our October trainin',
A chap could clear right out from there ef 't only looked
    like rainin',

---

* In relation to this expression, I cannot but think that Mr. Biglow has been too hasty in attributing it to me. Though Time be a comparatively innocent personage to swear by, and though Longinus in his discourse Περὶ Ὕψους has commended timely oaths as not only a useful but sublime figure of speech, yet I have always kept my lips free from that abomination. *Odi profanum vulgus,* I hate your swearing and hectoring fellows. — H. W.

An˙ th' Cunnles, tu, could kiver up their shappoes with
    bandanners,   ·
An' send the insines skootin' to the bar-room with their
    banners,
(Fear o' gittin' on 'em spotted,) an' a feller could cry
    quarter
Ef he fired away his ramrod arter tu much rum an' water.
Recollect wut fun we hed, you 'n' 1 an' Ezry Hollis,
Up there to Waltham plain last fall, along o' the Corn-
    wallis ? *
This sort o' thing aint *jest* like thet, — I wish thet I wuz
    furder,† —
Nimepunce a day fer killin' folks comes kind o' low fer
    murder,
(Wy I 've worked out to slarterin' some fer Deacon Cephas
    Billins,
An' in the hardest times there wuz I ollers tetched ten
    shillins,)
There 's sutthin' gits into my throat thet makes it hard to
    swaller,
It comes so nateral to think about a hempen collar ;
It 's glory, — but, in spite o' all my tryin' to git callous,
I feel a kind o' in a cart, aridin' to the gallus.
But wen it comes to *bein'* killed, — I tell ye I felt streakèd
The fust time 't ever I found out wy baggonets wuz
    peaked ;
Here 's how it wuz: I started out to go to a fandango,
The sentinul he ups an' sez, " Thet 's furder 'an you can
    go."
" None o' your sarse," sez I ; sez he, " Stan' back ! " " Aint
    you a buster ? "
Sez I, " I 'm up to all thet air, I guess I 've ben to muster ;
I know wy sentinuls air sot ; you aint agoin' to eat us ;
Caleb haint no monopoly to court the seenoreetas ;
My folks to hum air full ez good ez hisn be, by golly ! "
An' so ez I wuz goin' by, not thinkin' wut would folly,
The everlastin' cus he stuck his one-pronged pitchfork in
    me
An' made a hole right thru my close ez ef I wuz an
    in'my.

---

* i hait the Site of a feller with a muskit as I du pizn But their *is* fun to a cor-
wallis I aint agoin' to deny it. — H. B.
† he means Not quite so fur I guess. — H. B.

Wal, it beats all how big I felt hoorawin' in ole Funnel
Wen Mister Bolles he gin the sword to our Leftenant
.....Cunnle,
(It's Mister Secondary Bolles,* thet writ the prize peace
.....essay;
Thet's why he did n't list himself along o' us, I dessay,)
An' Rantoul, tu, talked pooty loud, but don't put *his*
.....foot in it,
Coz human life's so sacred thet he's principled agin it, —
Though I myself can't rightly see it's any wus achokin'
.....on 'em,
Than puttin' bullets thru their lights, or with a bagnet
.....pokin' on 'em;
How dreffle slick he reeled it off, (like Blitz at our lyceum
Ahaulin' ribbins from his chops so quick you skeercely
.....see 'em,)
About the Anglo-Saxon race (an' saxons would be handy
To du the buryin' down here upon the Rio Grandy),
About our patriotic pas an' our star-spangled banner,
Our country's bird alookin' on an' singin' out hosanner,
An' how he (Mister B. himself) wuz happy fer Amer-
.....iky, —
I felt, ez sister Patience sez, a leetle mite histericky.
I felt, I swon, ez though it wuz a dreffle kind o' privilege
Atrampin' round thru Boston streets among the gutter's
.....drivelage;
I act'lly thought it wuz a treat to hear a little drummin',
An' it did bonyfidy seem millanyum wuz acomin'
Wen all on us got suits (darned like them wore in the
.....state prison)
An' every feller felt ez though all Mexico wuz hisn.†

This 'ere's about the meanest place a skunk could wal
.....diskiver
(Saltillo's Mexican, I b'lieve, fer wut we call Salt-river);
The sort o' trash a feller gits to eat doos beat all nater,
I'd give a year's pay fer a smell o' one good blue-nose
.....tater;

* the ignerant creeter means Sekketary; but he ollers stuck to his books like
cobbler's wax to an ile-stone. — H. B.
† it must be aloud that thare 's a streak o' nater in lovin' sho, but it sartinly is 1
of the curusest things in nater to see a rispecktable dri goods dealer (deekon off a
chutch mayby) ariggin' himself out in the Weigh they du and struttin' round in the
Reign aspilin' his trowsis and makin' wet goods of himself. Ef any thin 's foolisher
and moor dicklus than militerry gloary it is milishy gloary. — H. B.

The country here thet Mister Bolles declared to be so
    charmin'
Throughout is swarmin' with the most alarmin' kind o'
    varmin.

He talked about delishis froots, but then it wuz a wopper
    all,
The holl on 't 's mud an' prickly pears, with here an' there
    a chapparal;
You see a feller peekin' out, an', fust you know, a lariat
Is round your throat an' you a copse, 'fore you can say,
    " Wut air ye at ? "*
You never see sech darned gret bugs (it may not be
    irrelevant
To say I 've seen a *scarabœus pilularius* † big ez a year old
    elephant,)
The rigiment come up one day in time to stop a red bug
From runnin' off with Cunnle Wright, — 't wuz jest a
    common *cimex lectularius.*

One night I started up on eend an' thought I wuz to hum
    agin,
I heern a horn, thinks I it 's Sol the fisherman hez come
    agin,
His bellowses is sound enough, — ez I 'm a livin' creeter,
I felt a thing go thru my leg, — 't wuz nothin' more 'n a
    skeeter !
Then there 's the yaller fever, tu, they call it here el
    vomito, —
(Come, thet wun't du, you landcrab there, I tell ye to le'
    go my toe !
My gracious ! it 's a scorpion thet 's took a shine to play
    with 't,
I dars n't skeer the tarnal thing fer fear he 'd run away
    with 't.)

Afore I come away from hum I hed a strong persuasion
Thet Mexicans wor n't human beans, ‡ — an ourang ou-
    tang nation,

* these fellers are verry proppilly called Rank Heroes, and the more tha kill the
ranker and more Herowick tha bekum. — H. B.
   † it wuz " tumblebug " as he Writ it, but the parson put the Latten instid. i sed
tother maid better meeter, but he said tha was eddykated peepl to Boston and tha
would n't stan' it no how. idnow as tha *wood* and idnow *as* tha wood. — H. B.
   ‡ he means human beins, that 's wut he means. i spose he kinder thought tha
wuz human beans ware the Xisle Poles comes from. — H. B.

A sort o' folks a chap could kill an' never dream on 't
    arter,
No more 'n a feller 'd dream o' pigs thet he hed hed to
    slarter;
I 'd an idee thet they were built arter the darkie fashion
    all,
An' kickin' colored folks about, you know, 's a kind o'
    national;
But wen I jined I wor n't so wise ez thet air queen o'
    Sheby,
Fer, come to look at 'em, they aint much diff'rent from
    wut we be,
An' here we air ascrougin' 'em out o' thir own dominions,
Ashelterin' 'em, ez Caleb sez, under our eagle's pinions,
Wich means to take a feller up jest by the slack o' 's
    trowsis
An' walk him Spanish clean right out o' all his homes
    an' houses;
Wal, it doos seem a curus way, but then hooraw fer
    Jackson!
It must be right, fer Caleb sez it 's reg'lar Anglosaxon.
The Mex'cans don't fight fair, they say, they piz'n all the
    water,
An' du amazin' lots o' things thet is n't wut they ough' to;
Bein' they haint no lead, they make their bullets out o'
    copper
An' shoot the darned things at us, tu, wich Caleb sez
    aint proper;
He sez they 'd ough' to stan' right up an' let us pop 'em
    fairly,
(Guess wen he ketches 'em at thet he 'll hev to git up
    airly,)
Thet our nation 's bigger 'n theirn an' so its rights air
    bigger,
An' thet it 's all to make 'em free thet we air pullin'
    trigger,
Thet Anglo Saxondom's idee 's abreakin' 'em to pieces,
An' thet idee 's thet every man doos jest wut he damn
    pleases;
Ef I don't make his meanin' clear, perhaps in some respex
    I can,
I know thet "every man" don't mean a nigger or a
    Mexican;

An' there's another thing I know, an' thet is, ef these
    creeturs,
Thet stick an Anglosaxon mask onto State-prison feeturs,
Should come to Jaalam Centre fer to argify an' spout on 't,
The gals 'ould count the silver spoons the minnit they
    cleared out on 't.

This goin' ware glory waits ye haint one agreeable feetur,
An' ef it wor n't fer wakin' snakes, I'd home agin short
    meter;
O, would n't I be off, quick time, ef 't wor n't thet I wuz
    sartin
They 'd let the daylight into me to pay me fer desartin'!
I don't approve o' tellin' tales, but jest to you I may state
Our ossifers aint wut they wuz afore they left the Bay-
    state;
Then it wuz "Mister Sawin, sir, you're middlin' well
    now, be ye?
Step up an' take a nipper, sir; I'm dreffle glad to see ye";
But now it's "Ware's my eppylet? here, Sawin, step an'
    fetch it!
An' mind your eye, be thund'rin' spry, or, damn ye, you
    shall ketch it!"
Wal, ez the Doctor sez, some pork will bile so, but by
    mighty,
Ef I hed some on 'em to hum, I'd give 'em linkum vity,
I'd play the rogue's march on their hides an' other music
    follerin' —
But I must close my letter here, fer one on 'em's ahol-
    lerin',
These Anglosaxon ossifers, — wal, taint no use ajawin',
I'm safe enlisted fer the war,
                Yourn,
                BIRDOFREDOM SAWIN.

[Those have not been wanting (as, indeed, when hath Satan been
to seek for attorneys?) who have maintained that our late inroad upon
Mexico was undertaken, not so much for the avenging of any national
quarrel, as for the spreading of free institutions and of Protestantism.
Capita vix duabus Anticyris medenda! Verily I admire that no pious
sergeant among these new Crusaders beheld Martin Luther riding at
the front of the host upon a tamed pontifical bull, as, in that former
invasion of Mexico, the zealous Gomara (spawn though he were of the
Scarlet Woman) was favored with a vision of St. James of Compostella,
skewering the infidels upon his apostolical lance. We read, also, that
Richard of the lion heart, having gone to Palestine on a similar errand

of mercy, was divinely encouraged to cut the throats of such Paynims as refused to swallow the bread of life (doubtless that they might be thereafter incapacitated for swallowing the filthy gobbets of Mahound) by angels of heaven, who cried to the king and his knights, — *Seigneurs, tuez! tuez!* providentially using the French tongue, as being the only one understood by their auditors. This would argue for the pantoglottism of these celestial intelligences, while, on the other hand, the Devil, *teste* Cotton Mather, is unversed in certain of the Indian dialects. Yet must he be a semeiologist the most expert, making himself intelligible to every people and kindred by signs; no other discourse, indeed, being needful, than such as the mackerel-fisher holds with his finned quarry, who, if other bait be wanting, can by a bare bit of white rag at the end of a string captivate those foolish fishes. Such piscatorial oratory is Satan cunning in. Before one he trails a hat and feather, or a bare feather without a hat; before another, a Presidential chair, or a tidewaiter's stool, or a pulpit in the city, no matter what. To us, dangling there over our heads, they seem junkets dropped out of the seventh heaven, sops dipped in nectar, but, once in our mouths, they are all one, bits of fuzzy cotton.

This, however, by the way. It is time now *revocare gradum.* While so many miracles of this sort, vouched by eyewitnesses, have encouraged the arms of Papists, not to speak of Echetlæus at Marathon and those *Dioscuri* (whom we must conclude imps of the pit) who sundry times captained the pagan Roman soldiery, it is strange that our first American crusade was not in some such wise also signalized. Yet it is said that the Lord hath manifestly prospered our armies. This opens the question, whether, when our hands are strengthened to make great slaughter of our enemies, it be absolutely and demonstratively certain that this might is added to us from above, or whether some Potentate from an opposite quarter may not have a finger in it, as there are few pies into which his meddling digits are not thrust. Would the Sanctifier and Setter-apart of the seventh day have assisted in a victory gained on the Sabbath, as was one in the late war? Or has that day become less an object of his especial care since the year 1697, when so manifest a providence occurred to Mr. William Trowbridge, in answer to whose prayers, when he and all on shipboard with him were starving, a dolphin was sent daily, "which was enough to serve 'em; only on *Saturdays* they still catched a couple, and on the *Lord's Days* they could catch none at all"? Haply they might have been permitted, by way of mortification, to take some few sculpins (those banes of the salt-water angler), which unseemly fish would, moreover, have conveyed to them a symbolical reproof for their breach of the day, being known in the rude dialect of our mariners as *Cape Cod Clergymen.*

It has been a refreshment to many nice consciences to know that our Chief Magistrate would not regard with eyes of approval the (by many esteemed) sinful pastime of dancing, and I own myself to be so far of that mind, that I could not but set my face against this Mexican Polka, though danced to the Presidential piping with a Gubernatorial second. If ever the country should be seized with another such mania *de propagandâ fide,* I think it would be wise to fill our bombshells with alternate copies of the Cambridge Platform and the Thirty-nine Articles, which would produce a mixture of the highest explosive power, and to wrap every one of our cannon-balls in a leaf of the New Testament, the reading of which is denied to those who sit in the darkness of Popery. Those iron evangelists would thus be able to disseminate vital religion and Gospel truth in quarters inaccessible to the ordinary missionary. I have seen lads, unimpregnate with the more sublimated punctiliousness of Walton, secure pickerel, taking their unwary *siesta* beneath the lily-pads too nigh the surface, with a gun and small shot. Why not, then, since gunpowder was unknown in the time of the Apostles (not to enter here upon the question whether it were discovered before that period by the Chinese), suit our metaphor to the age in which we live, and say *shooters* as well as *fishers* of men?

I do much fear that we shall be seized now and then with a Protestant fervor, as long as we have neighbor Naboths whose wallowings in Papistical mire excite our horror in exact proportion to the size and desirableness of their vineyards. Yet I rejoice that some earnest Protestants have been made by this war, — I mean those who protested against it. Fewer they were than I could wish, for one might imagine America to have been colonized by a tribe of those nondescript African animals the Aye-Ayes, so difficult a word is *No* to us all. There is some malformation or defect of the vocal organs, which either prevents our uttering it at all, or gives it so thick a pronunciation as to be unintelligible. A mouth filled with the national pudding, or watering in expectation thereof, is wholly incompetent to this refractory monosyllable. An abject and herpetic Public Opinion is the Pope, the Anti-Christ, for us to protest against *e corde cordium*. And by what College of Cardinals is this our God's-vicar, our binder and looser, elected? Very like, by the sacred conclave of Tag, Rag, and Bobtail, in the gracious atmosphere of the grog-shop. Yet it is of this that we must all be puppets. This thumps the pulpit-cushion, this guides the editor's pen, this wags the senator's tongue. This decides what Scriptures are canonical, and shuffles Christ away into the Apocrypha. According to that sentence fathered upon Solon, Οὕτω δημόσιον κακὸν ἔρχεται οἴκαδ' ἑκάστῳ. This unclean spirit is skilful to assume various shapes. I have known it to enter my own study and nudge my elbow of a Saturday, under the semblance of a wealthy member of my congregation. It were a great blessing, if every particular of what in the sum we call popular sentiment could carry about the name of its manufacturer stamped legibly upon it. I gave a stab under the fifth rib to that pestilent fallacy, — "Our country, right or wrong," — by tracing its original to a speech of Ensign Cilley at a dinner of the Bungtown Fencibles. · H. W.]

No. III.

WHAT MR. ROBINSON THINKS.

[A FEW remarks on the following verses will not be out of place. The satire in them was not meant to have any personal, but only a general, application Of the gentleman upon whose letter they were intended as a commentary Mr. Biglow had never heard, till he saw the letter itself. The position of the satirist is oftentimes one which he would not have chosen, had the election been left to himself. In attacking bad principles, he is obliged to select some individual who has made himself their exponent, and in whom they are impersonate, to the end that what he says may not, through ambiguity, be dissipated *tenues in auras.* For what says Seneca? *Longum iter per præcepta, breve et efficace per exempla.* A bad principle is comparatively harmless while it continues to be an abstraction, nor can the general mind comprehend it fully till it is printed in that large type which all men can read at sight, namely, the life and character, the sayings and doings, of par-

2 D

ticular persons. It is one of the cunningest fetches of Satan, that he never exposes himself directly to our arrows, but, still dodging behind this neighbor or that acquaintance, compels us to wound him through them, if at all. He holds our affections as hostages, the while he patches up a truce with our conscience.

Meanwhile, let us not forget that the aim of the true satirist is not to be severe upon persons, but only upon falsehood, and, as Truth and Falsehood start from the same point, and sometimes even go along together for a little way, his business is to follow the path of the latter after it diverges, and to show her floundering in the bog at the end of it. Truth is quite beyond the reach of satire. There is so brave a simplicity in her, that she can no more be made ridiculous than an oak or a pine. The danger of the satirist is, that continual use may deaden his sensibility to the force of language. He becomes more and more liable to strike harder than he knows or intends. He may be careful to put on his boxing-gloves, and yet forget, that, the older they grow, the more plainly may the knuckles inside be felt. Moreover, in the heat of contest, the eye is insensibly drawn to the crown of victory, whose tawdry tinsel glitters through that dust of the ring which obscures Truth's wreath of simple leaves. I have sometimes thought that my young friend, Mr. Biglow, needed a monitory hand laid on his arm, —*aliquid sufflaminandus erat.* I have never thought it good husbandry to water the tender plants of reform with *aqua fortis,* yet, where so much is to do in the beds, he were a sorry gardener who should wage a whole day's war with an iron scuffle on those ill weeds that make the garden-walks of life unsightly, when a sprinkle of Attic salt will wither them up. *Est ars etiam maledicendi,* says Scaliger, and truly it is a hard thing to say where the graceful gentleness of the lamb merges in downright sheepishness. We may conclude with worthy and wise Dr. Fuller, that "one may be a lamb in private wrongs, but in hearing general affronts to goodness they are asses which are not lions." — H. W.]

GUVENER B. is a sensible man;
   He stays to his home an' looks arter his folks;
He draws his furrer ez straight ez he can,
   An' into nobody's tater-patch pokes; —
      But John P.
      Robinson he
  Sez he wunt vote fer Guvener B.

My! aint it terrible? Wut shall we du?
   We can't never choose him, o' course, — thet's flat:
Guess we shall hev to come round, (don't you?)
   An' go in fer thunder an' guns, an' all that;
      Fer John P.
      Robinson he
  Sez he wunt vote fer Guvener B.

Gineral C. is a dreffle smart man:
   He's ben on all sides thet give places or pelf;

But consistency still wuz a part of his plan, —
  He's been true to *one* party and thet is himself; —
    So John P.
    Robinson he
  Sez he shall vote fer Gineral C.

Gineral C. he goes in fer the war;
  He don't vally principle more 'n an old cud;
Wut did God make us raytional creeturs fer,
  But glory an' gunpowder, plunder an' blood?
    So John P.
    Robinson he
  Sez he shall vote fer Gineral C.

We were gittin' on nicely up here to our village,
  With good old idees o' wut's right an' wut aint,
We kind o' thought Christ went agin war an' pillage,
  An' thet eppyletts wor n't the best mark of a saint
    But John P.
    Robinson he
  Sez this kind o' thing's an exploded idee.

The side of our country must ollers be took,
  An' Presidunt Polk, you know, *he* is our country.
An' the angel thet writes all our sins in a book
  Puts the *debit* to him, an' to us the *per contry ;*
    An' John P.
    Robinson he
  Sez this is his view o' the thing to a **T.**

Parson Wilbur he calls all these argimunts lies;
  Sez they 're nothin' on airth but jest *fee, faw, fum :*
An' thet all this big talk of our destinies
  Is half on it ignorance, an' t' other half rum,
    But John P.
    Robinson he
  Sez it aint no sech thing; an', of course, so must we.

Parson Wilbur sez *he* never heerd in his life
  Thet th' Apostles rigged out in their swaller-tail coats,
An' marched round in front of a drum an' a fife,
  To git some on 'em office, an' some on 'em votes,

But John P.
Robinson he
Sez they did n't know everythin' down in Judee.

Wal, it's a marcy we've gut folks to tell us
    The rights an' the wrongs o' these matters, I vow, —
God sends country lawyers, an' other wise fellers,
    To start the world's team wen it gits in a slough;
Fer John P.
Robinson he
Sez the world 'll go right, ef he hollers out Gee!

[The attentive reader will doubtless have perceived in the foregoing poem an allusion to that pernicious sentiment, — "Our country, right or wrong." It is an abuse of language to call a certain portion of land, much more, certain personages, elevated for the time being to high station, our country. I would not sever nor loosen a single one of those ties by which we are united to the spot of our birth, nor minish by a tittle the respect due to the Magistrate. I love our own Bay State too well to do the one, and as for the other, I have myself for nigh forty years exercised, however unworthily, the function of Justice of the Peace, having been called thereto by the unsolicited kindness of that most excellent man and upright patriot, Caleb Strong. *Patriæ fumus igne alieno luculentior* is best qualified with this, — *Ubi libertas, ibi patria.* We are inhabitants of two worlds, and owe a double but not a divided, allegiance. In virtue of our clay, this little ball of earth exacts a certain loyalty of us, while, in our capacity as spirits, we are admitted citizens of an invisible and holier fatherland. There is a patriotism of the soul whose claim absolves us from our other and terrene fealty. Our true country is that ideal realm which we represent to ourselves under the names of religion, duty, and the like. Our terrestrial organizations are but far-off approaches to so fair a model, and all they are verily traitors who resist not any attempt to divert them from this their original intendment. When, therefore, one would have us to fling up our caps and shout with the multitude, — "*Our country, however bounded!*" he demands of us that we sacrifice the larger to the less, the higher to the lower, and that we yield to the imaginary claims of a few acres of soil our duty and privilege as liege men of Truth. Our true country is bounded on the north and the south, on the east and the west, by Justice, and when she oversteps that invisible boundary-line by so much as a hair's-breadth, she ceases to be our mother, and chooses rather to be looked upon *quasi noverca.* That is a hard choice, when our earthly love of country calls upon us to tread one path and our duty points us to another. We must make as noble and becoming an election as did Penelope between Icarius and Ulysses. Veiling our faces, we must take silently the hand of Duty to follow her.

Shortly after the publication of the foregoing poem, there appeared some comments upon it in one of the public prints which seemed to call for animadversion. I accordingly addressed to Mr. Buckingham, of the Boston Courier, the following letter.

JAALAM, November 4, 1847.

' *To the Editor of the Courier:*

"RESPECTED SIR, — Calling at the post-office this morning, our worthy and efficient postmaster offered for my perusal a paragraph in the Boston Morning Post of the 3d instant, wherein certain effusions of the pastoral muse are attributed to the pen of Mr. James Russell Lowell. For aught I know or can affirm to the contrary, this Mr. Lowell may be a very deserving person and a youth of parts (though I have seen verses of his which I could never rightly understand) ; and if he be such, he, I am certain, as well as I, would be free from any proclivity to appropriate to himself whatever of credit (or discredit) may honestly belong to another. I am confident, that, in penning these few lines, I am only forestalling a disclaimer from that young gentleman, whose silence hitherto, when rumor pointed to himward, has excited in my bosom mingled emotions of sorrow and surprise. Well may my young parishioner, Mr. Biglow, exclaim with the poet,

'Sic vos non vobis,' &c.;

though, in saying this, I would not convey the impression that he is a proficient in the Latin tongue, — the tongue, I might add, of a Horace and a Tully.

"Mr. B. does not employ his pen, I can safely say, for any lucre of worldly gain, or to be exalted by the carnal plaudits of men *digito monstrari*, &c. He does not wait upon Providence for mercies, and in his heart mean *merces*. But I should esteem myself as verily deficient in my duty (who am his friend and in some unworthy sort his spiritual *fidus Achates*, &c.), if I did not step forward to claim for him whatever measure of applause might be assigned to him by the judicious.

"If this were a fitting occasion, I might venture here a brief dissertation touching the manner and kind of my young friend's poetry. But I dubitate whether this abstruser sort of speculation (though enlivened by some apposite instances from Aristophanes) would sufficiently interest your oppidan readers. As regards their satirical tone, and their plainness of speech, I will only say, that, in my pastoral experience, I have found that the Arch-Enemy loves nothing better than to be treated as a religious, moral, and intellectual being, and that there is no *apage Sathanas!* so potent as ridicule. But it is a kind of weapon that must have a button of good-nature on the point of it.

"The productions of Mr. B. have been stigmatized in some quarters as unpatriotic; but I can vouch that he loves his native soil with that hearty, though discriminating, attachment which springs from an intimate social intercourse of many years' standing. In the ploughing season, no one has a deeper share in the well-being of the country than he. If Dean Swift were right in saying that he who makes two blades of grass grow where one grew before confers a greater benefit on the state than he who taketh a city, Mr. B. might exhibit a fairer claim to the Presidency than General Scott himself. I think that some of those disinterested lovers of the hard-handed democracy, whose fingers have never touched anything rougher than the dollars of our common country, would hesitate to compare palms with him. It would do your heart good, respected Sir, to see that young man mow. He cuts a cleaner and wider swarth than any in this town.

"But it is time for me to be at my Post. It is very clear that my young friend's shot has struck the lintel, for the Post is shaken (Amos ix. 1). The editor of that paper is a strenuous advocate of the Mexican war, and a colonel, as I am given to understand. I presume, that, being necessarily absent in Mexico, he has left his journal in some less judicious hands. At any rate, the Post has been too swift on this occasion. It could hardly have cited a more incontrovertible line from any poem than that which it has selected for animadversion, namely, —

'We kind o' thought Christ went agin war an' pillage.'

"If the Post maintains the converse of this proposition, it can hardly be considered as a safe guide-post for the moral and religious portions of its party, however many other excellent qualities of a post it may be blessed with. There is a sign in London on which is painted, — 'The Green Man.' It would do very well as a portrait of any individual who would support so unscriptural a thesis. As regards the language of the line in question, I am bold to say that He who readeth the hearts of men will not account any dialect unseemly which conveys a sound and pious sentiment. I could wish that such sentiments were more common, however uncouthly expressed. Saint Ambrose affirms, that *veritas a quocunque* (why not, then, *quomodocunque ?*) *dicatur, a spiritu sancto est.* Digest also this of Baxter: — 'The plainest words are the most profitable oratory in the weightiest matters.'

"When the paragraph in question was shown to Mr. Biglow, the only part of it which seemed to give him any dissatisfaction was that which classed him with the Whig party. He says, that, if resolutions are a nourishing kind of diet, that party must be in a very hearty and flourishing condition; for that they have quietly eaten more good ones of their own baking than he could have conceived to be possible without repletion. He has been for some years past (I regret to say) an ardent opponent of those sound doctrines of protective policy which form so prominent a portion of the creed of that party. I confess, that, in some discussions which I have had with him on this point in my study, he has displayed a vein of obstinacy which I had not hitherto detected in his composition. He is also (*horresco referens*) infected in no small measure with the peculiar notions of a print called the Liberator, whose heresies I take every proper opportunity of combating, and of which, I thank God, I have never read a single line.

"I did not see Mr. B.'s verses until they appeared in print, and there *is* certainly one thing in them which I consider highly improper. I allude to the personal references to myself by name. To confer notoriety on an humble individual who is laboring quietly in his vocation, and who keeps his cloth as free as he can from the dust of the political arena (though *væ mihi si non evangelizavero*), is no doubt an indecorum. The sentiments which he attributes to me I will not deny to be mine. They were embodied, though in a different form, in a discourse preached upon the last day of public fasting, and were acceptable to my entire people (of whatever political views), except the postmaster, who dissented *ex officio*. I observe that you sometimes devote a portion of your paper to a religious summary. I should be well pleased to furnish a copy of my discourse for insertion in this department of your instructive journal. By omitting the advertisements, it might easily be got within the limits of a single number, and I venture to insure you the sale of some scores of copies in this town. I will cheerfully render myself responsible for ten. It might possibly be advantageous to issue it as an *extra*. But perhaps you will not esteem it an object, and I will not press it. My offer does not spring from any weak desire of seeing my name in print; for I can enjoy this satisfaction at any time by turning to the Triennial Catalogue of the University, where it also possesses that added emphasis of Italics with which those of my calling are distinguished.

"I would simply add, that I continue to fit ingenuous youth for college, and that I have two spacious and airy sleeping apartments at this moment unoccupied. *Ingenuas didicisse*, &c. Terms, which vary according to the circumstances of the parents, may be known on application to me by letter, post paid. In all cases the lad will be expected to fetch his own towels. This rule, Mrs. W. desires me to add, has no exceptions.

"Respectfully, your obedient servant,
"HOMER WILBUR, A.M.

" P. S. Perhaps the last paragraph may look like an attempt to obtain the insertion of my circular gratuitously. If it should appear to you in that light, I desire that you would erase it, or charge for it at the usual rates, and deduct the amount from the proceeds in your hands from the sale of my discourse, when it shall be printed. My circular is much longer and more explicit, and will be forwarded without charge to any who may desire it. It has been very neatly executed on a letter sheet, by a very deserving printer, who attends upon my ministry, and is a creditable specimen of the typographic art. I have one hung over my mantelpiece in a neat frame, where it makes a beautiful and appropriate ornament, and balances the profile of Mrs. W., cut with her toes by the young lady born without arms. **H. W.**"

I have in the foregoing letter mentioned General Scott in connection with the Presidency, because I have been given to understand that he has blown to pieces and otherwise caused to be destroyed more Mexicans than any other commander. His claim would therefore be deservedly considered the strongest. Until accurate returns of the Mexicans killed, wounded, and maimed be obtained, it will be difficult to settle these nice points of precedence. Should it prove that any other officer has been more meritorious and destructive than General S., and has thereby rendered himself more worthy of the confidence and support of the conservative portion of our community, I shall cheerfully insert his name, instead of that of General S., in a future edition. It may be thought, likewise, that General S. has invalidated his claims by too much attention to the decencies of apparel, and the habits belonging to a gentleman. These abstruser points of statesmanship are beyond my scope. I wonder not that successful military achievement should attract the admiration of the multitude. Rather do I rejoice with wonder to behold how rapidly this sentiment is losing its hold upon the popular mind. It is related of Thomas Warton, the second of that honored name who held the office of Poetry Professor at Oxford, that, when one wished to find him, being absconded, as was his wont, in some obscure alehouse, he was counselled to traverse the city with a drum and fife, the sound of which inspiring music would be sure to draw the Doctor from his retirement into the street. We are all more or less bitten with this martial insanity. *Nescio quâ dulcedine . . . cunctos ducit.* I confess to some infection of that itch myself. When I see a Brigadier-General maintaining his insecure elevation in the saddle under the severe fire of the training-field, and when I remember that some military enthusiasts, through haste, inexperience, or an over-desire to lend reality to those fictitious combats, will sometimes discharge their ramrods, I cannot but admire, while I deplore, the mistaken devotion of those heroic officers. *Semel insanivimus omnes.* I was myself, during the late war with Great Britain, chaplain of a regiment, which was fortunately never called to active military duty. I mention this circumstance with regret rather than pride. Had I been summoned to actual warfare, I trust that I might have been strengthened to bear myself after the manner of that reverend father in our New England Israel, Dr. Benjamin Colman, who, as we are told in Turell's life of him, when the vessel in which he had taken passage for England was attacked by a French privateer, "fought like a philosopher and a Christian, . . . and prayed all the while he charged and fired." As this note is already long, I shall not here enter upon a discussion of the question, whether Christians may lawfully be soldiers. I think it sufficiently evident, that, during the first two centuries of the Christian era, at least, two professions were esteemed incompatible. Consult Jortin on this head.—H. W.]

No. IV.

REMARKS OF INCREASE D. O'PHACE, ESQUIRE, AT AN EX-
TRUMPERY CAUCUS IN STATE STREET, REPORTED BY
MR. H. BIGLOW.

[THE ingenious reader will at once understand that no such speech
as the following was ever *totidem verbis* pronounced. But there are
simpler and less guarded wits, for the satisfying of which such an ex-
planation may be needful. For there are certain invisible lines, which
as Truth successively overpasses, she becomes Untruth to one and
another of us, as a large river, flowing from one kingdom into another,
sometimes takes a new name, albeit the waters undergo no change,
how small soever. There is, moreover, a truth of fiction more vera-
cious than the truth of fact, as that of the Poet, which represents to us
things and events as they ought to be, rather than servilely copies them
as they are imperfectly imaged in the crooked and smoky glass of our
mundane affairs. It is this which makes the speech of Antonius, though
originally spoken in no wider a forum than the brain of Shakspeare,
more historically valuable than that other which Appian has reported,
by as much as the understanding of the Englishman was more compre-
hensive than that of the Alexandrian. Mr. Biglow, in the present in-
stance, has only made use of a license assumed by all the historians of
antiquity, who put into the mouths of various characters such words
as seem to them most fitting to the occasion and to the speaker. If
it be objected that no such oration could ever have been delivered, I
answer, that there are few assemblages for speech-making which do
not better deserve the title of *Parliamentum Indoctorum* than did the
sixth Parliament of Henry the Fourth, and that men still continue to
have as much faith in the Oracle of Fools as ever Pantagruel had.
Howell, in his letters, recounts a merry tale of a certain ambassador
of Queen Elizabeth, who, having written two letters, one to her Majesty
and the other to his wife, directed them at cross-purposes, so that the
Queen was beducked and bedeared and requested to send a change of
hose, and the wife was beprincessed and otherwise unwontedly besuper-
latived, till the one feared for the wits of her ambassador, and the other
for those of her husband. In like manner it may be presumed that our
speaker has misdirected some of his thoughts, and given to the whole
theatre what he would have wished to confide only to a select auditory
at the back of the curtain. For it is seldom that we can get any frank
utterance from men, who address, for the most part, a Buncombe either
in this world or the next. As for their audiences, it may be truly said
of our people, that they enjoy one political institution in common with
the ancient Athenians: I mean a certain profitless kind of *ostracism*,
wherewith, nevertheless, they seem hitherto well enough content. For
in Presidential elections, and other affairs of the sort, whereas I ob-
serve that the *oysters* fall to the lot of comparatively few, the *shells*
(such as the privileges of voting as they are told to do by the *ostrivori*
aforesaid, and of huzzaing at public meetings) are very liberally dis-
tributed among the people, as being their prescriptive and quite suffi-
cient portion.

The occasion of the speech is supposed to be Mr. Palfrey's refusal
to vote for the Whig candidate for the Speakership. — H. W.]

No? Hez he? He haint, though? Wut? Voted agin him?
Ef the bird of our country could ketch him, she 'd skin
      him;

I seem 's though I see her, with wrath in each quill,
Like a chancery lawyer, afilin' her bill,
An' grindin' her talents ez sharp ez all nater,
To pounce like a writ on the back o' the traitor.
Forgive me, my friends, ef I seem to be het,
But a crisis like this must with vigor be met;
Wen an Arnold the star-spangled banner bestains,
Holl Fourth o' Julys seem to bile in my veins.

Who ever 'd ha' thought sech a pisonous rig
Would be run by a chap thet wuz chose fer a Wig?
" We knowed wut his principles wuz 'fore we sent him?'
Wut wuz ther in them from this vote to pervent him?
A marciful Providunce fashioned us holler
O' purpose thet we might our principles swaller;
It can hold any quantity on 'em, the belly can,
An' bring 'em up ready fer use like the pelican,
Or more like the kangaroo, who (wich is stranger)
Puts her family into her pouch wen there 's danger.
Aint principle precious? then, who 's goin' to use it
Wen there 's resk o' some chap's gittin' up to abuse it?
I can't tell the wy on 't, but nothin' is *so* sure
Ez thet principle kind o' gits spiled by exposure; *
A man thet lets all sorts o' folks git a sight on 't
Ough' to hev it all took right away, every mite on 't;
Ef he can't keep it all to himself wen it 's wise to,
He aint one it 's fit to trust nothin' so nice to.

Besides, ther 's a wonderful power in latitude
To shift a man's morril relations an' attitude;
Some flossifers think thet a fakkilty 's granted
The minnit it 's proved to be thoroughly wanted,
Thet a change o' demand makes a change o' condition,
An' thet everythin' 's nothin' except by position,
Ez, fer instance, thet rubber-trees fust begun bearin'
Wen p'litikle conshunces come into wearin', —

---

* The speaker is of a different mind from Tully, who, in his recently discovered tractate *De Republicâ*, tells us, — *Nec vero habere virtutem satis est, quasi artem aliquam, nisi utare*, and from our Milton, who says, — " I cannot praise a fugitive and cloistered virtue, unexercised and unbreathed, that never sallies out and sees her adversary, but slinks out of the race where that immortal garland is to be run for, *not without dust and heat.*" — *Areop.* He had taken the words out of the Roman's mouth, without knowing it, and might well exclaim with Austin (if a saint's name may stand sponsor for a curse,) *Pereant qui ante nos nostra dixerint!* — H. W.

Thet the fears of a monkey, whose holt chanced to fail,
Drawed the vertibry out to a prehensile tail;
So, wen one's chose to Congriss, ez soon ez he's in it,
A collar grows right round his neck in a minnit,
An' sartin it is thet a man cannot be strict
In bein' himself, wen he gits to the Deestrict,
Fer a coat thet sets wal here in ole Massachusetts,
Wen it gits on to Washinton, somehow askew sets.

Resolves, do you say, o' the Springfield Convention?
Thet's percisely the pint I was goin' to mention;
Resolves air a thing we most gen'ally keep ill,
They're a cheap kind o' dust fer the eyes o' the people;
A parcel o' delligits jest git together
An' chat fer a spell o' the crops an' the weather,
Then, comin' to order, they squabble awile
An' let off the speeches they're ferful 'll spile;
Then — Resolve, — Thet we wunt hev an inch o' slave
      territory;
Thet President Polk's holl perceedins air very tory;
Thet the war is a damned war, an' them thet enlist in it
Should hev a cravat with a dreffle tight twist in it;
Thet the war is a war fer the spreadin' o' slavery;
Thet our army desarves our best thanks fer their bravery;
Thet we're the original friends o' the nation,
All the rest air a paltry an' base fabrication;
Thet we highly respect Messrs. A, B, an' C,
An' ez deeply despise Messrs. E, F, an' G.
In this way they go to the eend o' the chapter,
An' then they bust out in a kind of a raptur
About their own vartoo, an' folks's stone-blindness
To the men thet 'ould actilly do 'em a kindness, —
The American eagle, — the Pilgrims thet landed, —
Till on ole Plymouth Rock they git finally stranded.
Wal, the people they listen and say, "Thet's the ticket;
Ez fer Mexico, t'aint no great glory to lick it,
But 't would be a darned shame to go pullin' o' triggers
To extend the aree of abusin' the niggers."

So they march in percessions, an' git up hooraws,
An' tramp thru the mud fer the good o' the cause,
An' think they're a kind o' fulfillin' the prophecies,
Wen they're on'y jest changin' the holders of offices;

Ware A sot afore, B is comf'tably seated,
One humbug 's victor'ous, an' t' other defeated,
Each honnable doughface gits jest wut he axes,
An' the people — their annool soft-sodder an' taxes.

Now, to keep unimpared all these glorious feeturs
Thet characterize morril an' reasonin' creeturs,
Thet give every paytriot all he can cram,
Thet oust the untrustworthy Presidunt Flam,
And stick honest Presidunt Sham in his place,
To the manifest gain o' the holl human race,
An' to some indervidgewals on 't in partickler,
Who love Public Opinion an' know how to tickle her, —
I say thet a party with great aims like these
Must stick jest ez close ez a hive full o' bees.

I 'm willin' a man should go tollable strong
Agin wrong in the abstract, fer thet kind o' wrong
Is ollers unpop'lar an' never gits pitied,
Because it 's a crime no one never committed ;
But he mus' n't be hard on partickler sins,
Coz then he 'll be kickin' the people's own shins ;
On'y look at the Demmercrats, see wut they 've done
Jest simply by stickin' together like fun ;
They 've sucked us right into a mis'able war
Thet no one on airth aint responsible for ;
They 've run us a hundred cool millions in debt,
(An' fer Demmercrat Horners ther 's good plums left
        yet ;)
They talk agin tayriffs, but act fer a high one,
An' so coax all parties to build up their Zion ;
To the people they 're ollers ez slick ez molasses,
An' butter their bread on both sides with The Masses,
Half o' whom they 've persuaded, by way of a joke,
Thet Washinton's mantelpiece fell upon Polk.

Now all o' these blessin's the Wigs might enjoy,
Ef they 'd gumption enough the right means to imploy ; *
Fer the silver spoon born in Dermocracy's mouth
Is a kind of a scringe thet they hev to the South ;
Their masters can cuss 'em an' kick 'em an' wale 'em,

---

* That was a pithy saying of Persius, and fits our politicians without a wrinkle, -
Magister artis, ingeniique largitor venter. — H. W.

An' they notice it less 'an the ass did to Balaam;
In this way they screw into second-rate offices
Wich the slaveholder thinks 'ould substract too much off
    his ease;
The file-leaders, I mean, du, fer they, by their wiles,
Unlike the old viper, grow fat on their files.
Wal, the Wigs hev been tryin' to grab all this prey frum
    'em
An' to hook this nice spoon o' good fortin' away frum
    'em
An' they might ha' succeeded, ez likely ez not,
In lickin' the Demmercrats all round the lot,
Ef it warn't thet, wile all faithful Wigs were their knees
    on,
Some stuffy old codger would holler out, — " Treason !
You must keep a sharp eye on a dog thet hez bit you
    once,
An' *I* aint agoin' to cheat my constitoounts," —
Wen every fool knows thet a man represents
Not the fellers thet sent him, but them on the fence, —
Impartially ready to jump either side
An' make the fust use of a turn o' the tide, —
The waiters on Providunce here in the city,
Who compose wut they call a State Centerl Committy.
Constitoounts air hendy to help a man in,
But arterwards don't weigh the heft of a pin.
Wy, the people can't all live on Uncle Sam's pus,
So they 've nothin' to du with 't fer better or wus;
It 's the folks thet air kind o' brought up to depend on 't
Thet hev any consarn in 't, an' thet is the end on 't.

Now here wuz New England ahevin' the honor
Of a chance at the Speakership showered upon her; —
Do you say, — " She don't want no more Speakers, but
    fewer;
She 's hed plenty o' them, wut she wants is a *doer*" *?*
Fer the matter o' thet it 's notorous in town
Thet her own representatives du her quite brown.
But thet 's nothin' to du with it; wut right hed Palfrey
To mix himself up with fanatical small fry ?
Warn't we gittin' on prime with our hot an' cold blowin',
Acondemnin' the war wilst we kep' it agoin'?
We 'd assumed with gret skill a commandin' position,

On this side or thet, no one could n't tell wich one,
So, wutever side wipped, we 'd a chance at the plunder
An' could sue fer infringin' our paytented thunder;
We were ready to vote fer whoever wuz eligible,
Ef on all pints at issoo he 'd stay unintelligible.
Wal, sposin' we hed to gulp down our perfessions,
We were ready to come out next mornin' with fresh ones;
Besides, ef we did, 't was our business alone,
Fer could n't we du wut we would with our own?
An' ef a man can, wen pervisions hev riz so,
Eat up his own words, it 's a marcy it is so.

Wy, these chaps frum the North, with back-bones to 'em,
    darn 'em,
'Ould be wuth more 'an Gennle Tom Thumb is to Barnum;
Ther 's enough thet to office on this very plan grow,
By exhibitin' how very small a man can grow;
But an M. C. frum here ollers hastens to state he
Belongs to the order called invertebraty,
Wence some gret filologists judge primy fashy
Thet M. C. is M. T. by paronomashy;
An' these few exceptions air *loosus naytury*
Folks 'ould put down their quarters to stare at, like fury.

It 's no use to open the door o' success,
Ef a member can bolt so fer nothin' or less;
Wy, all o' them grand constitootional pillers
Our fore-fathers fetched with 'em over the billers,
Them pillers the people so soundly hev slep' on,
Wile to slav'ry, invasion, an' debt they were swep' on,
Wile our Destiny higher an' higher kep' mountin',
(Though I guess folks 'll stare wen she hends her account
    in,)
Ef members in this way go kickin' agin 'em,
They wunt hev so much ez a feather left in 'em.

An', ez fer this Palfrey,* we thought wen we 'd gut him in,
He 'd go kindly in wutever harness we put him in;
Supposin' we *did* know thet he wuz a peace man?
Doos he think he can be Uncle Sammle's policeman,

---

   * There is truth yet in this of Juvenal, —
       " Dat veniam corvis, vexat censura columbas."
                        H. W.

An' wen Sam gits tipsy an' kicks up a riot,
Lead him off to the lockup to snooze till he 's quiet?
Wy, the war is a war thet true paytriots can bear, ef
It leads to the fat promised land of a tayriff;
We don't go an' fight it, nor aint to be driv on,
Nor Demmercrats nuther, thet hev wut to live on;
Ef it aint jest the thing thet 's well pleasin' to God,
It makes us thought highly on elsewhere abroad;
The Rooshian black eagle looks blue in his eerie
An' shakes both his heads wen he hears o' Monteery;
In the Tower Victory sets, all of a fluster,
An' reads, with locked doors, how we won Cherry Buster;
An' old Philip Lewis — thet come an' kep' school here
Fer the mere sake o' scorin' his ryalist ruler
On the tenderest part of our kings *in futuro* —
Hides his crown underneath an old shut in his bureau,
Breaks off in his brags to a suckle o' merry kings,
How he often hed hided young native Amerrikins,
An', turnin' quite faint in the midst of his fooleries,
Sneaks down stairs to bolt the front door o' the Tooleries.*

You say, — "We 'd ha' scared 'em by growin' in peace,
A plaguy sight more then by bobberies like these"?
Who is it dares say thet "our naytional eagle
Wun't much longer be classed with the birds thet air
        regal,
Coz theirn be hooked beaks, an' she, arter this slaughter,
'll bring back a bill ten times longer 'n she ough' to"?
Wut 's your name? Come, I see ye, you up-country
        feller,
You 've put me out severil times with your beller;
Out with it! Wut? Biglow? I say nothin' furder,

---

* Jortin is willing to allow of other miracles besides those recorded in Holy Writ, and why not of other prophecies? It is granting too much to Satan to suppose him, as divers of the learned have done, the inspirer of the ancient oracles. Wiser, I esteem it, to give chance the credit of the successful ones. What is said here of Louis Philippe was verified in some of its minute particulars within a few months' time. Enough to have made the fortune of Delphi or Hammon, and no thanks to Beelzebub neither! That of Seneca in Medea will suit here: —

> " Rapida fortuna ac levis
> Præcepsque regno eripuit, exsilio dedit."

Let us allow, even to richly deserved misfortune, our commiseration, and be not over-hasty meanwhile in our censure of the French people, left for the first time to govern themselves, remembering that wise sentence of Æschylus, —

> Ἅπας, δὲ τραχὺς ὅστις ἂν νέον κρατῇ.

> H. W.

Thet feller would like nothin' better 'n a murder;
He 's a traiter, blasphemer, an' wut ruther worse is,
He puts all his ath'ism in dreffle bad verses;
Socity aint safe till sech monsters air out on it,
Refer to the Post, ef you hev the least doubt on it;
Wy, he goes agin war, agin indirect taxes,
Agin sellin' wild lands 'cept to settlers with axes,
Agin holdin' o' slaves, though he knows it 's the corner
Our libbaty rests on, the mis'able scorner!
In short, he would wholly upset with his ravages
All thet keeps us above the brute critters an' savages,
An' pitch into all kinds o' briles an' confusions
The holl of our civilized, free institutions;
He writes fer thet ruther unsafe print, the Courier,
An' likely ez not hez a squintin' to Foorier;
I 'll be ——, thet is, I mean I 'll be blest,
Ef I hark to a word frum so noted a pest;
I shan't talk with *him*, my religion 's too fervent. —
Good mornin', my friends, I 'm your most humble servant.

[Into the question, whether the ability to express ourselves in articulate language has been productive of more good or evil, I shall not here enter at large. The two faculties of speech and of speech-making are wholly diverse in their natures. By the first we make ourselves intelligible, by the last unintelligible, to our fellows. It has not seldom occurred to me (noting how in our national legislature every thing runs to talk, as lettuces, if the season or the soil be unpropitious, shoot up lankly to seed, instead of forming handsome heads) that Babel was the first Congress, the earliest mill erected for the manufacture of gabble. In these days, what with Town Meetings, School Committees, Boards (lumber) of one kind and another, Congresses, Parliaments, Diets, Indian Councils, Palavers, and the like, there is scarce a village which has not its factories of this description driven by (milk-and-) water power. I cannot conceive the confusion of tongues to have been the curse of Babel, since I esteem my ignorance of other languages as a kind of Martello-tower, in which I am safe from the furious bombardments of foreign garrulity. For this reason I have ever preferred the study of the dead languages, those primitive formations being Ararats upon whose silent peaks I sit secure and watch this new deluge without fear, though it rain figures (*simulacra*, semblances) of speech forty days and nights together, as it not uncommonly happens. Thus is my coat, as it were, without buttons by which any but a vernacular wild bore can seize me. Is it not possible that the Shakers may intend to convey a quiet reproof and hint, in fastening their outer garments with hooks and eyes?

This reflection concerning Babel, which I find in no Commentary, was first thrown upon my mind when an excellent deacon of my congregation (being infected with the Second Advent delusion) assured me that he had received a first instalment of the gift of tongues as a small earnest of larger possessions in the like kind to follow. For, of a truth, I could not reconcile it with my ideas of the Divine justice and mercy that the single wall which protected people of other languages from the incursions of this otherwise well-meaning propagandist should be broken down.

In reading Congressional debates, I have fancied, that, after the subsidence of those painful buzzings in the brain which result from such exercises, I detected a slender residuum of valuable information. I made the discovery that *nothing* takes longer in the saying than any thing else, for, as *ex nihilo nihil fit*, so from one polypus *nothing* any number of similar ones may be produced. I would recommend to the attention of *vivâ voce* debaters and controversialists the admirable example of the monk Copres, who, in the fourth century, stood for half an hour in the midst of a great fire, and thereby silenced a Manichæan antagonist who had less of the salamander in him. As for those who quarrel in print, I have no concern with them here, since the eyelids are a divinely-granted shield against all such. Moreover, I have observed in many modern books that the printed portion is becoming gradually smaller, and the number of blank or fly-leaves (as they are called) greater. Should this fortunate tendency of literature continue, books will grow more valuable from year to year, and the whole Serbonian bog yield to the advances of firm arable land.

The sagacious Lacedæmonians hearing that Tesephone had bragged that he could talk all day long on any given subject, made no more ado, but forthwith banished him, whereby they supplied him a topic and at the same time took care that his experiment upon it should be tried out of ear-shot.

I have wondered, in the Representatives' Chamber of our own Commonwealth, to mark how little impression seemed to be produced by that emblematic fish suspended over the heads of the members. Our wiser ancestors, no doubt, hung it there as being the animal which the Pythagoreans reverenced for its silence, and which certainly in that particular does not so well merit the epithet *cold-blooded*, by which naturalists distinguish it, as certain bipeds, afflicted with ditchwater on the brain, who take occasion to tap themselves in Fanueil Halls, meeting-houses, and other places of public resort. — H. W.]

No. V.

THE DEBATE IN THE SENNIT.

SOT TO A NUSRY RHYME.

[THE incident which gave rise to the debate satirized in the following verses was the unsuccessful attempt of Drayton and Sayres to give freedom to seventy men and women, fellow-beings and fellow-Christians. Had Tripoli, instead of Washington, been the scene of this undertaking, the unhappy leaders in it would have been as secure of the theoretic as they now are of the practical part of martyrdom. I question whether the Dey of Tripoli is blessed with a District Attorney so benighted as ours at the seat of government. Very fitly is he named Key, who would allow himself to be made the instrument of locking the door of hope against sufferers in such a cause. Not all the waters of the ocean can cleanse the vile smutch of the jailer's fingers from off that little Key. *Ahenea clavis*, a brazen Key indeed!

Mr. Calhoun, who is made the chief speaker in this burlesque, seems to think that the light of the nineteenth century is to be put out as soon as he tinkles his little cow-bell curfew. Whenever slavery is touched, he sets up his scarecrow of dissolving the Union. This may do for the North, but I should conjecture that something more than a pumpkin-lantern is required to scare manifest and irretrievable Destiny out of her path. Mr. Calhoun cannot let go the apron-string of the Past. The Past is a good nurse, but we must be weaned from her sooner or later, even though, like Plotinus, we should run home from school to ask the breast, after we are tolerably well-grown youths. It will not do for us to hide our faces in her lap, whenever the strange Future holds out her arms and asks us to come to her.

But we are all alike. We have all heard it said, often enough, that little boys must not play with fire; and yet, if the matches be taken away from us and put out of reach upon the shelf, we must needs get into our little corner, and scowl and stamp and threaten the dire revenge of going to bed without our supper. The world shall stop till we get our dangerous plaything again. Dame Earth, meanwhile, who has more than enough household matters to mind, goes bustling hither and thither as a hiss or a sputter tells her that this or that kettle of hers is boiling over and before bedtime we are glad to eat our porridge cold, and gulp down our dignity along with it.

Mr. Calhoun has somehow acquired the name of a great statesman, and, if it be great statesmanship to put lance in rest and run a tilt at the Spirit of the Age with the certainty of being next moment hurled neck and heels into the dust amid universal laughter, he deserves the title. He is the Sir Kay of our modern chivalry. He should remember the old Scandinavian mythus. Thor was the strongest of gods, but he could not wrestle with Time, nor so much as lift up a fold of the great snake which knit the universe together; and when he smote the Earth, though with his terrible mallet, it was but as if a leaf had fallen. Yet all the while it seemed to Thor that he had only been wrestling with an old woman, striving to lift a cat, and striking a stupid giant on the head.

And in old times, doubtless, the giants *were* stupid, and there was no better sport for the Sir Launcelots and Sir Gawains than to go about cutting off their great blundering heads with enchanted swords. But things have wonderfully changed. It is the giants, now-a-days, that have the science and the intelligence, while the chivalrous Don Quixotes of Conservatism still cumber themselves with the clumsy armor of a by-gone age. On whirls the restless globe through unsounded time, with its cities and its silences, its births and funerals, half light, half shade, but never wholly dark, and sure to swing round into the happy morning at last. With an involuntary smile, one sees Mr. Calhoun letting slip his pack-thread cable with a crooked pin at the end of it to anchor South Carolina upon the bank and shoal of the Past. — H. W.]

TO MR. BUCKENAM.

MR. EDITER, As i wuz kinder prunin round, in a little nussry sot out a year or 2 a go, the Dbait in the sennit cum inter my mine An so i took & Sot it to wut I call a nussry rime. I hev made sum onnable Gentlemun speak that dident speak in a Kind uv Poetikul lie sense the seeson is dreffle backerd upThis way ewers as ushul

HOSEA BIGLOW.

"HERE we stan' on the Constitution, by thunder!
It 's a fact o' wich ther 's bushils o' proofs;

2 E

Fer how could we trample on 't so, I wonder,
  Ef 't wor n't thet it 's ollers under our hoofs ? "
    Sez John C. Calhoun, sez he ;
      " Human rights haint no more
      Right to come on this floor,
    No more 'n the man in the moon," sez he.

" The North haint no kind o' bisness with nothin',
  An' you 've no idee how much bother it saves ;
We aint none riled by their frettin' an' frothin',
  We 're *used* to layin' the string on our slaves,"
    Sez John C. Calhoun, sez he ; —
      Sez Mister Foote,
      " I should like to shoot
    The holl gang, by the great horn spoon," sez he.

" Freedom's Keystone is Slavery, thet ther 's no doubt on,
  It 's sutthin' thet 's — wha' d' ye call it ? — divine, —
An' the slaves thet we allers *make* the most out on
  Air them north o' Mason an' Dixon's line,"
    Sez John C. Calhoun, sez he ; —
      " Fer all thet," sez Mangum,
      " 'T would be better to hang 'em,
    An' so git red on 'em soon," sez he.

" The mass ough' to labor an' we lay on soffies,
  Thet 's the reason I want to spread Freedom's aree ;
It puts all the cunninest on us in office,
  An' reelises our Maker's orig'nal idee,"
    Sez John C. Calhoun, sez he ; —
      " Thet 's ez plain," sez Cass,
      " Ez thet some one 's an ass,
    It 's ez clear ez the sun is at noon," sez he.

" Now don't go to say I 'm the friend of oppression,
  But keep all your spare breath fer coolin' your broth,
Fer I ollers hev strove (at least thet 's my impression)
  To make cussed free with the rights o' the North."
    Sez John C. Calhoun, sez he ; —
      " Yes," sez Davis o' Miss.,
      " The perfection o' bliss
    Is in skinnin' thet same old coon," sez he.

"Slavery 's a thing thet depends on complexion,
  It 's God's law thet fetters on black skins don't chafe;
Ef brains wuz to settle it (horrid reflection!)
  Wich of our onnable body 'd be safe?"
    Sez John C. Calhoun, sez he; —
      Sez Mister Hannegan,
      Afore he began agin,
  "Thet exception is quite oppertoon," sez he.

"Gen'nle Cass, Sir, you needn't be twitchin' your collar,
  Your merit 's quite clear by the dut on your knees,
At the North we don't make no distinctions o' color,
  You can all take a lick at our shoes wen you please,"
    Sez John C. Calhoun, sez he; —
      Sez Mister Jarnagin,
      "They wunt hev to larn agin,
  They all on 'em know the old toon," sez he.

"The slavery question aint no ways bewilderin',
  North an' South hev one int'rest, it 's plain to a glance;
No'thern men, like us patriarchs, don't sell their childrin,
  But they *du* sell themselves, ef they git a good chance,"
    Sez John C. Calhoun, sez he; —
      Sez Atherton here,
      "This is gittin' severe,
  I wish I could dive like a loon," sez he.

"It 'll break up the Union, this talk about freedom,
  An' your fact'ry gals (soon ez we split) 'll make head.
An' gittin' some Miss chief or other to lead 'em,
  'll go to work raisin' pr'miscoous Ned,"
    Sez John C. Calhoun, sez he; —
      "Yes, the North," sez Colquitt,
      "Ef we Southeners all quit,
  Would go down like a busted balloon," sez he.

"Jest look wut is doin', wut annyky 's brewin'
  In the beautiful clime o' the olive an' vine,
All the wise aristoxy is tumblin' to ruin,
  An' the sankylots drorin' an' drinkin' their wine,"
    Sez John C. Calhoun, sez he; —
      "Yes," sez Johnson, "in France
      They 're beginnin' to dance
  Beelzebub's own rigadoon," sez he.

"The South's safe enough, it don't feel a mite skeery,
  Our slaves in their darkness an' dut air tu blest
Not to welcome with proud hallylugers the ery
  Wen our eagle kicks yourn from the naytional nest,"
    Sez John C. Calhoun, sez he; —
      "O," sez Westcott o' Florida,
      "Wut treason is horrider
    Then our priv'leges tryin' to proon ?" sez he.

"It's 'coz they're so happy, thet, wen crazy sarpints
  Stick their nose in our bizness, we git so darned riled;
We think it's our dooty to give pooty sharp hints,
  Thet the last crumb of Edin on airth shan't be spiled,"
    Sez John C. Calhoun, sez he; —
      "Ah," sez Dixon H. Lewis,
      "It perfectly true is
    Thet slavery's airth's grettest boon," sez he.

[It was said of old time, that riches have wings; and, though this
be not applicable in a literal strictness to the wealth of our patriarchal
brethren of the South, yet it is clear that their possessions have legs,
and an unaccountable propensity for using them in a northerly direc-
tion. I marvel that the grand jury of Washington did not find a true
bill against the North Star for aiding and abetting Drayton and Sayres.
It would have been quite of a piece with the intelligence displayed by
the South on other questions connected with slavery. I think that no
ship of state was ever freighted with a more veritable Jonah than this
same domestic institution of ours. Mephistopheles himself could not
feign so bitterly, so satirically sad a sight as this of three millions of
human beings crushed beyond help or hope by this one mighty argu-
ment, — *Our fathers knew no better!* Nevertheless, it is the unavoid-
able destiny of Jonahs to be cast overboard sooner or later. Or shall
we try the experiment of hiding our Jonah in a safe place, that none
may lay hands on him to make jetsam of him? Let us, then, with
equal forethought and wisdom, lash ourselves to the anchor, and await,
in pious confidence, the certain result. Perhaps our suspicious passen-
ger is no Jonah after all, being black. For it is well known that a
superintending Providence made a kind of sandwich of Ham and his
descendants, to be devoured by the Caucasian race.
    In God's name, let all, who hear nearer and nearer the hungry moan
of the storm and the growl of the breakers, speak out! But, alas! we
have no right to interfere. If a man pluck an apple of mine, he shall be
in danger of the justice; but if he steal my brother, I must be silent.
Who says this? Our Constitution, consecrated by the callous consue-
tude of sixty years, and grasped in triumphant argument by the left
hand of him whose right hand clutches the clotted slave-whip. Justice,
venerable with the undethronable majesty of countless æons, says, —
Speak! The Past, wise with the sorrows and desolations of ages, from
amid her shattered fanes and wolf-housing palaces, echoes, — Speak!
Nature, through her thousand trumpets of freedom, her stars, her sun-
rises, her seas, her winds, her cataracts, her mountains blue with
cloudy pines, blows jubilant encouragement, and cries, — Speak!

From the soul's trembling abysses the still, small voice not vaguely murmurs, — SPEAK! But, alas! the Constitution and the Honorable Mr. Bagowind, M. C., say, — BE DUMB!

It occurs to me to suggest, as a topic of inquiry in this connection, whether, on that momentous occasion when the goats and the sheep shall be parted, the Constitution and the Honorable Mr. Bagowind, M. C., will be expected to take their places on the left as our hircine vicars.

> *Quid sum miser tunc dicturus?*
> *Quem patronum rogaturus?*

There is a point where toleration sinks into sheer baseness and poltroonery. The toleration of the worst leads us to look on what is barely better as good enough, and to worship what is only moderately good. Woe to that man, or that nation, to whom mediocrity has become an ideal!

Has our experiment of self-government succeeded, if it barely manage to *rub and go?* Here, now, is a piece of barbarism which Christ and the nineteenth century say shall cease, and which Messrs. Smith, Brown, and others say shall *not* cease. I would by no means deny the eminent respectability of these gentlemen, but I confess, that, in such a wrestling-match, I cannot help having my fears for them.

> *Discite justitiam, moniti, et non temnere divos.*
>
> H. W.]

No. VI.

THE PIOUS EDITOR'S CREED.

[AT the special instance of Mr. Biglow, I preface the following satire with an extract from a sermon preached during the past summer, from Ezekiel xxxiv. 2 : — "Son of man, prophesy against the shepherds of Israel." Since the Sabbath on which this discourse was delivered, the editor of the "Jaalam Independent Blunderbuss" has unaccountably absented himself from our house of worship.

"I know of no so responsible position as that of the public journalist. The editor of our day bears the same relation to his time that the clerk bore to the age before the invention of printing. Indeed, the position which he holds is that which the clergyman should hold even now. But the clergyman chooses to walk off to the extreme edge of the world, and to throw such seed as he has clear over into that darkness which he calls the Next Life. As if *next* did not mean *nearest*, and as if any life were nearer than that immediately present one which boils and eddies all around him at the caucus, the ratification meeting, and the polls! Who taught him to exhort men to prepare for eternity, as for some future era of which the present forms no integral part? The furrow which Time is even now turning runs through the Everlasting, and in that must he plant, or nowhere. Yet he would fain believe and teach that we are *going* to have more of eternity than we have now. This *going* of his is like that of the auctioneer, on which *gone* follows before we have made up our minds to bid, — in which manner, not three months back, I lost an excellent copy of Chappelow on Job. So it has come to pass that the preacher, instead of being a living force, has faded into an emblematic figure at christenings, weddings, and funerals. Or, if he exercise any other function, it is as keeper and feeder of certain theologic dogmas, which, when occasion offers, he unkennels with a *staboy !* ' to bark and bite as 't is their nature to,' whence that reproach of *odium theologicum* has arisen.

"Meanwhile, see what a pulpit the editor mounts daily, sometimes with a congregation of fifty thousand within reach of his voice, and never so much as a nodder, even, among them! And from what a Bible can he choose his text, — a Bible which needs no translation, and which no priestcraft can shut and clasp from the laity, — the open volume of the world, upon which, with a pen of sunshine or destroying fire, the inspired Present is even now writing the annals of God! Methinks the editor who should understand his calling, and be equal thereto, would truly deserve that title of ποιμὴν λαῶν, which Homer bestows upon princes. He would be the Moses of our nineteenth century; and whereas the old Sinai, silent now, is but a common mountain stared at by the elegant tourist and crawled over by the hammering geologist, he must find his tables of the new law here among factories and cities in this Wilderness of Sin (Numbers xxxiii. 12) called Progress of Civilization, and be the captain of our Exodus into the Canaan of a truer social order.

"Nevertheless, our editor will not come so far within even the shadow of Sinai as Mahomet did, but chooses rather to construe Moses by Joe Smith. He takes up the crook, not that the sheep may be fed, but that he may never want a warm woollen suit and a joint of mutton.

Immemor, O, fidei, pecorumque oblite tuorum !

For which reason I would derive the name *editor* not so much from *edo*, to publish, as from *edo*, to eat, that being the peculiar profession to which he esteems himself called. He blows up the flames of political discord for no other occasion than that he may thereby handily boil his own pot. I believe there are two thousand of these mutton-loving shepherds in the United States, and of these, how many have even the dimmest perception of their immense power, and the duties consequent thereon? Here and there, haply, one. Nine hundred and ninety-nine labor to impress upon the people the great principles of *Tweedledum*, and other nine hundred and ninety-nine preach with equal earnestness the gospel according to *Tweedledee.*" — H. W.]

I DU believe in Freedom's cause,
    Ez fur away ez Payris is;
I love to see her stick her claws
    In them infarnal Phayrisees;
It 's wal enough agin a king
    To dror resolves an' triggers, —
But libbaty's a kind o' thing
    Thet don't agree with niggers.

I du believe the people want
    A tax on teas an' coffees,
Thet nothin' aint extravygunt, —
    Purvidin' I'm in office;
Fer I hev loved my country sence
    My eye-teeth filled their sockets,

An' Uncle Sam I reverence,
  Partic'larly his pockets.

I du believe in *any* plan
  O' levyin' the taxes,
Ez long ez, like a lumberman,
  I git jest wut I axes:
I go free-trade thru thick an' thin,
  Because it kind o' rouses
The folks to vote, — an' keeps us in
  Our quiet custom-houses.

I du believe it 's wise an' good
  To sen' out furrin missions,
Thet is, on sartin understood
  An' orthydox conditions ; —
I mean nine thousan' dolls. per ann.,
  Nine thousan' more fer outfit,
An' me to recommend a man
  The place 'ould jest about fit.

I du believe in special ways
  O' prayin' an' convartin' ;
The bread comes back in many days,
  An' buttered, tu, fer sartin ;
I mean in prayin' till one busts
  On wut the party chooses,
An' in convartin' public trusts
  To very privit uses.

I du believe hard coin the stuff
  Fer 'lectioneers to spout on ;
The people 's ollers soft enough
  To make hard money out on ;
Dear Uncle Sam pervides fer his,
  An' gives a good-sized junk to all, —
I don't care *how* hard money is,
  Ez long ez mine 's paid punctooal.

I du believe with all my soul
  In the gret Press's freedom,
To pint the people to the goal
  An' in the traces lead 'em ;

Palsied the arm thet forges yokes
   At my fat contracts squintin',
An' withered be the nose thet pokes
   Inter the gov'ment printin'!

I du believe thet I should give
   Wut's his'n unto Cæsar,
Fer it's by him I move an' live,
   Frum him my bread an' cheese air;
I du believe thet all o' me
   Doth bear his superscription, —
Will, conscience, honor, honesty,
   An' things o' thet description.

I du believe in prayer an' praise
   To him that hez the grantin'
O' jobs, — in every thin' thet pays,
   But most of all in CANTIN';
This doth my cup with marcies fill,
   This lays all thought o' sin to rest, —
I *don't* believe in princerple,
   But O, I *du* in interest.

I du believe in bein' this
   Or thet, ez it may happen
One way or t' other hendiest is
   To ketch the people nappin';
It aint by princerples nor men
   My preudunt course is steadied, —
I scent which pays the best, an' then
   Go into it baldheaded.

I du believe thet holdin' slaves
   Comes nat'ral tu a Presidunt,
Let 'lone the rowdedow it saves
   To hev a wal-broke precedunt;
Fer any office, small or gret,
   I could n't ax with no face,
Without I'd ben, thru dry an' wet,
   Th' unrizzest kind o' doughface.

I du believe wutever trash
   'll keep the people in blindness, —

Thet we the Mexicuns can thrash
　　Right inter brotherly kindness,
Thet bombshells, grape, an' powder 'n' ball
　　Air good-will's strongest magnets,
Thet peace, to make it stick at all,
　　Must be druv in with bagnets.

In short, I firmly du believe
　　In Humbug generally,
Fer it's a thing thet I perceive
　　To hev a solid vally;
This heth my faithful shepherd ben,
　　In pasturs sweet heth led me,
An' this'll keep the people green
　　To feed ez they hev fed me.

[I subjoin here another passage from my before-mentioned discourse.

" Wonderful, to him that has eyes to see it rightly, is the newspaper. T﹅ me, for example, sitting on the critical front bench of the pit, in my study here in Jaalam, the advent of my weekly journal is as that of a strolling theatre, or rather of a puppet-show, on whose stage, narrow as it is, the tragedy, comedy, and farce of life are played in little. Behold the whole huge earth sent to me hebdomadally in a brown-paper wrapper!

"Hither, to my obscure corner, by wind or steam, on horseback or dromedary-back, in the pouch of the Indian runner, or clicking over the magnetic wires, troop all the famous performers from the four quarters of the globe. Looked at from a point of criticism, tiny puppets they seem all, as the editor sets up his booth upon my desk and officiates as showman. Now I can truly see how little and transitory is life. The earth appears almost as a drop of vinegar, on which the solar microscope of the imagination must be brought to bear in order to make out anything distinctly. That animalcule there, in the pea-jacket, is Louis Philippe, just landed on the coast of England. That other, in the gray surtout and cocked hat, is Napoleon Bonaparte Smith, assuring France that she need apprehend no interference from him in the present alarming juncture. At that spot, where you seem to see a speck of something in motion, is an immense mass-meeting. Look sharper and you will see a mite brandishing his mandibles in an excited manner. That is the great Mr. Soandso, defining his position amid tumultuous and irrepressible cheers. That infinitesimal creature, upon whom some score of others, as minute as he, are gazing in open-mouthed admiration, is a famous philosopher, expounding to a select audience their capacity for the infinite. That scarce discernible pufflet of smoke and dust is a revolution. That speck there is a reformer, just arranging the lever with which he is to move the world. And lo, there creeps forward the shadow of a skeleton that blows one breath between its grinning teeth, and all our distinguished actors are whisked off the slippery stage into the dark Beyond.

"Yes, the little show-box has its solemner suggestions. Now and then we catch a glimpse of a grim old man, who lays down a scythe and hour-glass in the corner while he shifts the scenes. There, too, in the dim background, a weird shape is ever delving. Sometimes he leans upon his mattock, and gazes, as a coach whirls by, bearing the newly married on their wedding jaunt, or glances carelessly at a babe brought home from christening. Suddenly (for the scene grows larger and larger as we look) a bony hand snatches back a performer in the midst of his part, and him, whom yesterday two infinites (past and future) would not suffice, a handful of dust is enough to cover and silence forever. Nay, we see the same fleshless fingers opening to clutch the showman himself, and guess, not without a shudder, that they are lying in wait for spectator also.

"Think of it: for three dollars a year I buy a season-ticket to this great Globe Theatre, for which God would write the dramas (only that we like farces, spectacles, and the tragedies of Apollyon better), whose scene-shifter is Time, and whose curtain is rung down by Death.

"Such thoughts will occur to me sometimes as I am tearing off the wrapper of my newspaper. Then suddenly that otherwise too often vacant sheet becomes invested for me with a strange kind of awe. Look! deaths and marriages, notices of inventions, discoveries, and books, lists of promotions, of killed, wounded, and missing, news of fires, accidents, of sudden wealth and as sudden poverty; — I hold in my hand the ends of myriad invisible electric conductors, along which tremble the joys, sorrows, wrongs, triumphs, hopes, and despairs of as many men and women everywhere. So that upon that mood of mind which seems to isolate me from mankind as a spectator of their puppet-pranks, another supervenes, in which I feel that I, too, unknown and unheard of, am yet of some import to my fellows. For, through my newspaper here, do not families take pains to send me, an entire stranger, news of a death among them? Are not here two who would have me know of their marriage? And, strangest of all, is not this singular person anxious to have me informed that he has received a fresh supply of Dimitry Bruisgins? But to none of us does the President continue miraculous (even if for a moment discerned as such) We glance carelessly at the sunrise, and get used to Orion and the Pleiades. The wonder wears off, and to-morrow this sheet, in which a vision was let down to me from Heaven, shall be the wrappage to a bar of soap or the platter for a beggar's broken victuals." — H. W.]

No. VII.

A LETTER

FROM A CANDIDATE FOR THE PRESIDENCY IN ANSWER TO SUTTIN QUESTIONS PROPOSED BY MR. HOSEA BIGLOW, ENCLOSED IN A NOTE FROM MR. BIGLOW TO S. H. GAY, ESQ., EDITOR OF THE NATIONAL ANTI-SLAVERY STANDARD.

[CURIOSITY may be said to be the quality which pre-eminently distinguishes and segregates man from the lower animals. As we trace the scale of animated nature downward, we find this faculty (as it may truly be called) of the mind diminished in the savage, and quite extinct in the brute. The first object which civilized man proposes to himself I take to be the finding out whatsoever he can concerning his neighbors. *Nihil humanum a me alienum puto;* I am curious about even John

Smith. The desire next in strength to this (an opposite pole, indeed, of the same magnet) is that of communicating the unintelligence we have carefully picked up.

Men in general may be divided into the inquisitive and the communicative. To the first class belong Peeping Toms, eaves-droppers, navel-contemplating Brahmins, metaphysicians, travellers, Empedocleses, spies, the various societies for promoting Rhinothism, Columbuses, Yankees, discoverers, and men of science, who present themselves to the mind as so many marks of interrogation wandering up and down the world. or sitting in studies and laboratories. The second class I should again subdivide into four. In the first subdivision I would rank those who have an itch to tell us about themselves, — as keepers of diaries, insignificant persons generally, Montaignes, Horace Walpoles, autobiographers, poets. The second includes those who are anxious to impart information concerning other people, — as historians, barbers, and such. To the third belong those who labor to give us intelligence about nothing at all, — as novelists, political orators, the large majority of authors, preachers, lecturers, and the like. In the fourth come those who are communicative from motives of public benevolence, — as finders of mares'-nests and bringers of ill news. Each of us two-legged fowls without feathers embraces all these subdivisions in himself to a greater or less degree, for none of us so much as lays an egg, or incubates a chalk one, but straightway the whole barn-yard shall know it by our cackle or our cluck. *Omnibus hoc vitium est.* There are different grades in all these classes. One will turn his telescope toward a back-yard, another toward Uranus; one will tell you that he dined with Smith, another that he supped with Plato. In one particular, all men may be considered as belonging to the first grand division, inasmuch as they all seem equally desirous of discovering the mote in their neighbor's eye.

To one or another of these species every human being may safely be referred. I think it beyond a peradventure that Jonah prosecuted some inquiries into the digestive apparatus of whales, and that Noah sealed up a letter in an empty bottle, that news in regard to him might not be wanting in case of the worst. They had else been super or subter human. I conceive, also, that, as there are certain persons who continually peep and pry at the keyhole of that mysterious door through which, sooner or later, we all make our exits, so there are doubtless ghosts fidgetting and fretting on the other side of it, because they have no means of conveying back to this world the scraps of news they have picked up in that. For there is an answer ready somewhere to every question, the great law of *give and take* runs through all nature, and if we see a hook, we may be sure that an eye is waiting for it. I read in every face I meet a standing advertisement of information wanted in regard to A. B., or that the friends of C. D. can hear something to his disadvantage by application to such a one.

It was to gratify the two great passions of asking and answering that epistolary correspondence was first invented. Letters (for by this usurped title epistles are now commonly known) are of several kinds. First, there are those which are not letters at all, — as letters-patent, letters dismissory, letters enclosing bills, letters of administration, Pliny's letters, letters of diplomacy, of Cato, of Mentor, of Lords Lyttleton, Chesterfield, and Orrery, of Jacob Behmen, Seneca (whom St. Jerome includes in his list of sacred writers), letters from abroad, from sons in college to their fathers, letters of marque, and letters generally, which are in nowise letters of mark. Second, are real letters, such as those of Gray, Cowper, Walpole, Howel, Lamb, D. Y., the first letters from children, (printed in staggering capitals,) Letters from New York, letters of credit, and others, interesting for the sake of the

writer or the thing written. I have read also letters from Europe by a
gentleman named Pinto, containing some curious gossip, and which I
hope to see collected for the benefit of the curious. There are, besides,
letters addressed to posterity, — as epitaphs, for example, written for
their own monuments by monarchs, whereby we have lately become
possessed of the names of several great conquerors and kings of kings,
hitherto unheard of and still unpronounceable, but valuable to the
student of the entirely dark ages. The letter which St. Peter sent to
King Pepin in the year of grace 755, that of the Virgin to the magis-
trates of Messina, that of St. Gregory Thaumaturgus to the D—l, and
that of this last-mentioned active police-magistrate to a nun of Gir-
genti, I would place in a class by themselves, as also the letters of can-
didates, concerning which I shall dilate more fully in a note at the end
of the following poem. At present, *sat prata biberunt.* Only, concern-
ing the shape of letters, they are all either square or oblong, to which
general figures circular letters and round-robins also conform them-
selves.—H. W.]

DEER SIR its gut to be the fashun now to rite letters to the
candid 8s and i wus chose at a publick Meetin in Jaalam to du
wut wus nessary fur that town. i writ to 271 ginerals and gut
answers to 209. tha air called candid 8s but I don't see nothin
candid about em. this here 1 wich I send wus thought satty's
factory. I dunno as it's ushle to print Poscrips, but as all the
ansers I got hed the saim, I sposed it wus best. times has gretly
changed. Formaly to knock a man into a cooked hat wus to
use him up, but now it ony gives him a chance fur the cheef
madgustracy. — H. B.

> DEAR SIR, — You wish to know my notions
>   On sartin pints thet rile the land;
> There's nothin' thet my natur so shuns
>   Ez bein' mum or underhand;
> I'm a straight-spoken kind o' creetur
>   Thet blurts right out wut's in his head,
> An' ef I've one pecooler feetur,
>   It is a nose thet wunt be led.
>
> So, to begin at the beginnin',
>   An' come direcly to the pint,
> I think the country's underpinnin'
>   Is some consid'ble out o' jint;
> I aint agoin' to try your patience
>   By tellin' who done this or thet,
> I don't make no insinooations,
>   I jest let on I smell a rat.
>
> Thet is, I mean, it seems to me so,
>   But, ef the public think I'm wrong,

I wunt deny but wut I be so, —
    An', fact, it don't smell very strong;
My mind's tu fair to lose its balance
    An' say wich party hez most sense;
There may be folks o' greater talence
    Thet can't set stiddier on the fence.

I 'm an eclectic; ez to choosin'
    'Twixt this an' thet, I 'm plaguy lawth;
I leave a side thet looks like losin',
    But (wile there 's doubt) I stick to both;
I stan' upon the Constitution,
    Ez preudunt statesmun say, who 've planned
A way to git the most profusion
    O' chances ez to *ware* they 'll stand.

Ez fer the war, I go agin it, —
    I mean to say I kind o' du, —
Thet is, I mean thet, bein' in it,
    The best way wuz to fight it thru;
Not but wut abstract war is horrid,
    I sign to thet with all my heart, —
But civlyzation *doos* git forrid
    Sometimes upon a powder-cart.

About thet darned Proviso matter
    I never hed a grain o' doubt,
Nor I aint one my sense to scatter
    So 'st no one could n't pick it out;
My love fer North an' South is equil,
    So I 'll jest answer plump an' frank, —
No matter wut may be the sequil, —
    Yes, Sir, I *am* agin a Bank.

Ez to the answerin' o' questions,
    I 'm an off ox at bein' druv,
Though I aint one thet ary test shuns
    'll give our folks a helpin' shove;
Kind o' pr'miscoous I go it
    Fer the holl country, an' the ground
I take, ez nigh ez I can show it,
    Is pooty gen'ally all round.

I don't appruve o' givin' pledges;
  You'd ough' to leave a fellar free,
An' not go knockin' out the wedges
  To ketch his fingers in the tree;
Pledges air awfle breachy cattle
  Thet preudunt farmers don't turn out, —
Ez long 'z the people git their rattle,
  Wut is there fer'm to grout about?

Ez to the slaves, there's no confusion
  In *my* idees consarnin' them, —
I think they air an Institution,
  A sort of — yes, jest so, — ahem:
Do *I* own any? Of my merit
  On thet pint you yourself may jedge.
All is, I never drink no sperit,
  Nor I haint never signed no pledge.

Ez to my princerples, I glory
  In hevin' nothin' o' the sort;
I aint a Wig, I aint a Tory,
  I'm jest a candidate, in short;
Thet's fair an' square an' parpendicler,
  But, ef the Public cares a fig
To hev me an'thin' in particler,
  Wy, I'm a kind o' peri-wig.

P. S.

Ez we're a sort o' privateerin',
  O' course, you know, it's sheer an' sheer,
An' there is sutthin' wuth your hearin'
  I'll mention in *your* privit ear;
Ef you git *me* inside the White House,
  Your head with ile I'll kin' o' 'nint
By gittin' *you* inside the Light-house
  Down to the eend o' Jaalam Pint.

An' ez the North hez took to brustlin'
  At bein' scrouged frum off the roost,
I'll tell ye wut'll save all tusslin'
  An' give our side a harnsome boost, —

> Tell 'em thet on the Slavery question
> I 'm RIGHT, although to speak I 'm lawth;
> This gives you a safe pint to rest on,
> An' leaves me frontin' South by North.

[And now of epistles candidatial, which are of two kinds, — namely, letters of acceptance, and letters definitive of position. Our republic, on the eve of an election, may safely enough be called a republic of letters. Epistolary composition becomes then an epidemic, which seizes one candidate after another, not seldom cutting short the thread of political life. It has come to such a pass, that a party dreads less the attacks of its opponents than a letter from its candidate. *Litera scripta manet*, and it will go hard if something bad can not be made of it. General Harrison, it is well understood, was surrounded, during his candidacy, with the *cordon sanitaire* of a vigilance committee. No prisoner in Spielberg was ever more cautiously deprived of writing materials. The soot was scraped carefully from the chimney-places; outposts of expert rifle-shooters rendered it sure death for any goose (who came clad in feathers) to approach within a certain limited distance of North Bend; and all domestic fowls about the premises were reduced to the condition of Plato's original man. By these precautions the General was saved. *Parva componere magnis*, I remember, that, when party-spirit once ran high among my people, upon occasion of the choice of a new deacon, I, having my preferences, yet not caring too openly to express them, made use of an innocent fraud to bring about that result which I deemed most desirable. My stratagem was no other than the throwing a copy of the Complete Letter-Writer in the way of the candidate whom I wished to defeat. He caught the infection, and addressed a short note to his constituents, in which the opposite party detected so many and so grave improprieties, (he had modelled it upon the letter of a young lady accepting a proposal of marriage,) that he not only lost his election, but, falling under a suspicion of Sabellianism and I know not what, (the widow Endive assured me that he was a Paralipomenon, to her certain knowledge,) was forced to leave the town. Thus it is that the letter killeth.

The object which candidates propose to themselves in writing is to convey no meaning at all. And here is a quite unsuspected pitfall into which they successively plunge headlong. For it is precisely in such cryptographies that mankind are prone to seek for and find a wonderful amount and variety of significance. *Omne ignotum pro mirifico.* How do we admire at the antique world striving to crack those oracular nuts from Delphi, Hammon, and elsewhere, in only one of which can I so much as surmise that any kernel had ever lodged; that, namely, wherein Apollo confessed that he was mortal. One Didymus is, moreover, related to have written six thousand books on the single subject of grammar, a topic rendered only more tenebrific by the labors of his successors, and which seems still to possess an attraction for authors in proportion as they can make nothing of it. A singular loadstone for theologians, also, is the Beast in the Apocalypse, whereof, in the course of my studies, I have noted two hundred and three several interpretations, each lethiferal to all the rest. *Non nostrum est tantas componere lites*, yet I have myself ventured upon a two hundred and fourth, which I embodied in a discourse preached on occasion of the demise of the late usurper, Napoleon Bonaparte, and which quieted, in a large measure, the minds of my people. It is true that my views on this important point were ardently controverted by Mr. Shearjashub Holden, the then preceptor of our academy, and in other particulars a very deserving and sensible young man, though possessing a somewhat limited knowledge of the Greek tongue. But his heresy struck down no deep root, and, he having been lately removed by the hand of Providence, I had the satisfaction of reaffirming my cherished sentiments in a sermon preached upon the Lord's day immediately succeeding his funeral. This might seem like taking an unfair advantage, did I not add that he had made provision in his last will (being celibate) for the publication of a posthumous tractate in support of his own dangerous opinions.

I know of nothing in our modern times which approaches so nearly to the ancient oracle as the letter of a Presidential candidate. Now, among the Greeks, the eating of beans was strictly forbidden to all such as had it in mind to consult those expert amphibologists, and this same prohibition on the part of Pythagoras to his disciples is understood to imply an abstinence from politics, beans having been used as ballots. That other explication, *quod videlicet sensus eo cibo obtundi existimaret*, though supported *pugnis et calcibus* by many of the learned, and not wanting the countenance of Cicero, is confuted by the larger experience of New England. On the whole, I think it safer to apply here the rule of interpretation which now generally obtains in regard to antique cosmogonies, myths, fables, proverbial expressions, and knotty points generally, which is, to find a common-sense meaning, and then select whatever can be imagined the most opposite thereto. In this way we arrive at the conclusion, that the Greeks objected to the questioning of candidates. And very properly, if, as I conceive, the chief point be not to discover what a person in that position is, or what he will do, but whether he can be elected. *Vos exemplaria Græca nocturna versate manu, versate diurna.*

But, since an imitation of the Greeks in this particular (the asking of questions being one chief privilege of freemen) is hardly to be hoped for, and our candidates will answer, whether they are questioned or not, I would recommend that these ante-electionary dialogues should be carried on by symbols, as were the diplomatic correspondences of the Scythians and Macrobii, or confined to the language of signs, like the famous interview of Panurge and Goatsnose. A candidate might then convey a suitable reply to all committees of inquiry by closing one eye, or by presenting them with a phial of Egyptian darkness to be speculated upon by their respective constituencies. These answers would be susceptible of whatever retrospective construction the exigencies of the political campaign might seem to demand, and the candidate could take his position on either side of the fence with entire consistency. Or, if letters must be written, profitable use might be made of the Dighton rock hieroglyphic or the cuneiform script, every fresh decipherer of which is enabled to educe a different meaning, whereby a sculptured stone or two supplies us, and will probably continue to supply posterity, with a very vast and various body of authentic history. For even the briefest epistle in the ordinary chirography is dangerous. There is scarce any style so compressed that superfluous words may not be detected in it. A severe critic might curtail that famous brevity of Cæsar's by two thirds, drawing his pen through the supererogatory *veni* and *vidi*. Perhaps, after all, the surest footing of hope is to be found in the rapidly increasing tendency to demand less and less of qualification in candidates. Already have statesmanship, experience, and the possession (nay, the profession, even) of principles been rejected as superfluous, and may not the patriot reasonably hope that the ability to write will follow? At present, there may be death in pot-hooks as well as pots, the loop of a letter may suffice for a bow-string, and all the dreadful heresies of Anti-slavery may lurk in a flourish. — H. W.]

No. VIII.

A SECOND LETTER FROM B. SAWIN, ESQ.

[IN the following epistle, we behold Mr. Sawin returning, a *miles emeritus*, to the bosom of his family. *Quantum mutatus!* The good Father of us all had doubtless intrusted to the keeping of this child of his certain faculties of a constructive kind. He had put in him a share of that vital force, the nicest economy of every minute atom of which is necessary to the perfect development of Humanity. He had given him a brain and heart, and so had equipped his soul with the two strong wings of knowledge and love, whereby it can mount to hang its nest under the eaves of heaven. And this child, so dowered, he had intrusted to the keeping of his vicar, the State. How stands the account of that stewardship? The State, or Society, (call her by what name you will,) had taken no manner of thought of him till she saw him swept out into the street, the pitiful leavings of last night's debauch, with cigar-ends, lemon-parings, tobacco-quids, slops, vile stenches, and the whole loathsome next-morning of the bar-room, — an own child of the Almighty God! I remember him as he was brought to be christened, a ruddy, rugged babe; and now there he wallows, reeking, seething, — the dead corpse, not of a man, but of a soul, — a putrefying lump, horrible for the life that is in it. Comes the wind of heaven, that good Samaritan, and parts the hair upon his forehead, nor is too nice to kiss those parched, cracked lips; the morning opens upon him her eyes full of pitying sunshine, the sky yearns down to him, — and there he lies fermenting. O sleep! let me not profane thy holy name by calling that stertorous unconsciousness a slumber! By and by comes along the State, God's vicar. Does she say, — "My poor, forlorn foster-child! Behold here a force which I will make dig and plant and build for me?" Not so, but, — "Here is a recruit ready-made to my hand, a piece of destroying energy lying unprofitably idle." So she claps an ugly gray suit on him, puts a musket in his grasp, and sends him off, with Gubernatorial and other godspeeds, to do duty as a destroyer.

I made one of the crowd at the last Mechanics' Fair, and, with the rest, stood gazing in wonder at a perfect machine, with its soul of fire, its boiler-heart that sent the hot blood pulsing along the iron arteries· and its thews of steel. And while I was admiring the adaptation of means to end, the harmonious involutions of contrivance, and the never-bewildered complexity, I saw a grimed and greasy fellow, the imperious engine's lackey and drudge, whose sole·office was to let fall, at intervals, a drop or two of oil upon a certain joint. Then my soul said within me, See there a piece of mechanism to which that other you marvel at is but as the rude first effort of a child, — a force which not merely suffices to set a few wheels in motion, but which can send an impulse all through the infinite future, — a contrivance, not for turning out pins, or stitching button-holes, but for making Hamlets and Lears. And yet this thing of iron shall be housed, waited on, guarded from rust and dust, and it shall be a crime but so much as to scratch it with a pin; while the other with its fire of God in it, shall be buffeted hither and thither, and finally sent carefully a thousand miles to be the target for a Mexican cannon-ball. Unthrifty Mother State! My heart burned within me for pity and indignation, and I renewed this covenant with my own soul, — *In aliis mansuetus ero, at, in blasphemiis contra Christum, non ita.* — H. W.]

2 F

I spose you wonder ware I be; I can't tell, fer the soul
    o' me,
Exacly ware I be myself, — meanin' by thet the holl o'
    me.
Wen I left hum, I hed two legs, an' they wor n't bad ones
    neither,
(The scaliest trick they ever played wuz bringin' on me
    hither,)
Now one on 'm's I dunno ware; — they thought I wuz
    adyin',
An' sawed it off because they said 't wuz kin' o' morti-
    fyin';
I'm willin' to believe it wuz, an' yit I don't see, nuther,
Wy one should take to feelin' cheap a minnit sooner 'n
    t' other,
Sence both wuz equilly to blame; but things is ez they
    be;
It took on so they took it off, an' thet's enough fer me:
There's one good thing, though, to be said about my
    wooden new one, —
The liquor can't git into it ez 't used to in the true one;
So it saves drink; an' then, besides, a feller could n't
    beg
A gretter blessin' then to hev one ollers sober peg;
It's true a chap's in want o' two fer follerin' a drum,
But all the march I'm up to now is jest to Kingdom Come.

I've lost one eye, but thet's a loss it's easy to supply
Out o' the glory that I've gut, fer thet is all my eye;
An' one is big enough, I guess, by diligently usin' it,
To see all I shall ever git by way o' pay fer losin' it;
Off'cers, I notice, who git paid fer all our thumps an'
    kickins,
Du wal by keepin' single eyes arter the fattest pickins;
So, ez the eye's put fairly out, I'll larn to go without it,
An' not allow *myself* to be no gret put out about it.
Now, le' me see, thet is n't all; I used, 'fore leavin' Jaalam,
To count things on my finger-eends, but sutthin' seems to
    ail 'em :
Ware's my left hand? O, darn it, yes, I recollect wut's
    come on 't;
I haint no left arm but my right, an' thet's gut jest a
    thumb on 't;

It aint so hendy ez it wuz to cal'late a sum on 't.
I 've hed some ribs broke, — six (I b'lieve), — I haint kep'
    no account on 'em ;
Wen pensions git to be the talk, I 'll settle the amount
    on 'em.
An' now I 'm speakin' about ribs, it kin' o' brings to mind
One thet I could n't never break, — the one I lef' behind ;
Ef you should see her, jest clear out the spout o' your
    invention
An' pour the longest sweetnin' in about an annooal
    pension,
An' kin' o' hint (in case, you know, the critter should
    refuse to be
Consoled) I aint so 'xpensive now to keep ez wut I used
    to be ;
There 's one arm less, ditto one eye, an' then the leg
    thet 's wooden
Can be took off an' sot away wenever ther 's a puddin'.

I spose you think I 'm comin' back ez opperlunt ez
    thunder,
With shiploads o' gold images an' varus sorts o' plunder ;
Wal, 'fore I vullinteered, I thought this country wuz a
    sort o'
Canaan, a reg'lar Promised Land flowin' with rum an'
    water,
Ware propaty growed up like time, without no culti-
    vation,
An' gold wuz dug ez taters be among our Yankee nation,
Ware nateral advantages were pufficly amazin',
Ware every rock there wuz about with precious stuns wuz
    blazin',
Ware mill-sites filled the country up ez thick ez you could
    cram 'em, ·
An' desput rivers run about abeggin' folks to dam 'em ;
Then there were meetinhouses, tu, chockful o' gold an'
    silver
Thet you could take, an' no one could n't hand ye in no
    bill fer ; —
Thet 's wut I thought afore I went, thet 's wut them fel-
    lers told us
Thet stayed to hum an' speechified an' to the buzzards
    sold us ;

I thought thet gold mines could be gut cheaper than
    Chiny asters,
An' see myself a comin' back like sixty Jacob Astors;
But sech idees soon melted down an' did n't leave a grease-
    spot;
I vow my holl sheer o' the spiles would n't come nigh a
    V spot;
Although, most anywares we 've ben, you need n't break
    no locks,
Nor run no kin' o' risks, to fill your pocket full o' rocks.

I guess I mentioned in my last some o' the nateral feeturs
O' this all-fiered buggy hole in th' way o' awfle creeturs,
But I fergut to name (new things to speak on so
    abounded)
How one day you 'll most die o' thust, an' 'fore the next
    git drownded.
The clymit seems to me jest like a teapot made o' pewter
Our Prudence hed, thet would n't pour (all she could du)
    to suit her;
Fust place the leaves 'ould choke the spout, so 's not a
    drop 'ould dreen out,
Then Prude 'ould tip an' tip an' tip, till the holl kit bust
    clean out,
The kiver-hinge-pin bein' lost, tea-leaves an' tea an' kiver
'ould all come down *kerswosh!* ez though the dam broke
    in a river.
Jest so 't is here; holl months there aint a day o' rainy
    weather,
An' jest ez th' officers 'ould be alayin' heads together
Ez t' how they 'd mix their drink at sech a milingtary
    deepot, —
'T 'ould pour ez though the lid wuz off the everlastin'
    teapot.
The cons'quence is, thet I shall take, wen I 'm allowed
    to leave here,
One piece o' propaty along, — an' thet 's the shakin'
    fever;
It 's reggilar employment, though, an' thet aint thought
    to harm one,
Nor 't aint so tiresome ez it wuz with t' other leg an'
    arm on;
An' it 's a consolation, tu, although it doos n't pay,

To hev it said you 're some gret shakes in any kin' o'
    way.
'T wor n't very long, I tell ye wut, I thought o' fortin-
    makin',—
One day a reg'lar shiver-de-freeze, an' next ez good ez
    bakin',—
One day abrilin' in the sand, then smoth'rin' in the
    mashes,—
Git up all sound, be put to bed a mess o' hacks an' smashes.
But then, thinks I, at any rate there 's glory to be hed,—
Thet 's an investment, arter all, thet may n't turn out so
    bad;
But somehow, wen we 'd fit an' licked, I ollers found the
    thanks
Gut kin' o' lodged afore they come ez low down ez the
    ranks;
The Gin'rals gut the biggest sheer, the Cunnles next, an'
    so on,—
We never gut a blasted mite o' glory ez I know on;
An' spose we hed, I wonder how you 're goin' to contrive
    its
Division so 's to give a piece to twenty thousand privits;
Ef you should multiply by ten the portion o' the brav'st
    one,
You would n't git more 'n half enough to speak of on a
    grave-stun;
We git the licks,—we 're jest the grist thet 's put into
    War's hoppers;
Leftenants is the lowest grade thet helps pick up the
    coppers.
It may suit folks thet go agin a body with a soul in 't,
An' aint contented with a hide without a bagnet hole in 't;
But glory is a kin' o' thing *I* shan't pursue no furder,
Coz thet 's the off'cers parquisite,—yourn 's on'y jest the
    murder.

Wal, arter I gin glory up, thinks I at least there 's one
Thing in the bills we aint hed yit, an' thet 's the GLORIOUS
    FUN;
Ef once we git to Mexico, we fairly may persume we
All day an' night shall revel in the halls o' Montezumy.
I 'll tell ye wut *my* revels wuz, an' see how you would
    like 'em;

We never gut inside the hall: the nighest ever *I* come
Wuz stan'in' sentry in the sun (an', fact, it *seemed* a
　　cent'ry)
A ketchin' smells o' biled an' roast thet come out thru
　　the entry,
An' hearin' ez I sweltered thru my passes an' repasses,
A rat-tat-too o' knives an' forks, a clinkty-clink o' glasses:
I can't tell off the bill o' fare the Gin'rals hed inside;
All I know is, thet out o' doors a pair o' soles wuz fried,
An' not a hunderd miles away frum ware this child wuz
　　posted,
A Massachusetts citizen wuz baked an' biled an' roasted;
The on'y thing like revellin' thet ever come to me
Wuz bein' routed out o' sleep by thet darned revelee.

They say the quarrel's settled now; fer my part I've
　　some doubt on't,
'T'll take more fish-skin than folks think to take the
　　rile clean out on't;
At any rate, I'm so used up I can't do no more fightin',
The on'y chance thet's left to me is politics or writin';
Now, ez the people's gut to hev a milingtary man,
An' I aint nothin' else jest now, I've hit upon a plan;
The can'idatin' line, you know, 'ould suit me to a T,
An' ef I lose, 't wunt hurt my ears to lodge another flea;
So I'll set up ez can'idate fer any kin' o' office,
(I mean fer any thet includes good easy-cheers an' soffies;
Fer ez to runnin' fer a place ware work's the time o' day,
You know thet's wut I never did, — except the other
　　way;)
Ef it's the Presidential cheer fer wich I'd better run,
Wut two legs anywares about could keep up with my one?
There aint no kin' o' quality in can'idates, it's said,
So useful ez a wooden leg, — except a wooden head;
There's nothin' aint so poppylar — (wy, it's a parfect sin
To think wut Mexico hez paid fer Santy Anny's pin;) —
Then I haint gut no princerples, an', sence I wuz knee-high,
I never *did* hev any gret, ez you can testify;
I'm a decided peace man, tu, an' go agin the war, —
Fer now the holl on't's gone an' past, wut is there to go
　　for?
Ef, wile you're 'lectioneerin' round, some curus chaps
　　should beg

To know my views o' state affairs, jest answer WOODEN
    LEG!
Ef they aint settisfied with thet, an' kin' o' pry an' doubt
An' ax fer sutthin' deffynit, jest say ONE EYE PUT OUT!
Thet kin' o' talk I guess you'll find'll answer to a charm,
An' wen you're druv tu nigh the wall, hol' up my missin'
    arm;
Ef they should nose round fer a pledge, put on a vartoous
    look
An' tell 'em thet's percisely wut I never gin nor — took!

Then you can call me "Timbertoes," — thet's wut 'the
    people likes;
Sutthin' combinin' morril truth with phrases sech ez
    strikes;
Some say the people's fond o' this, or thet, or wut you
    please, —
I tell ye wut the people want is jest correct idees;
"Old Timbertoes," you see, 's a creed it's safe to be quite
    bold on,
There's nothin' in 't the other side can any ways git hold
    on;
It's a good tangible idee, a sutthin' to embody
Thet valooable class o' men who look thru brandy-toddy;
It gives a Party Platform, tu, jest level with the mind
Of all right-thinkin', honest folks thet mean to go it
    blind;
Then there air other good hooraws to dror on ez you
    need 'em,
Sech ez the ONE-EYED SLARTERER, the BLOODY BIRDO-
    FREDUM;
Them's wut takes hold o' folks thet think, ez well ez o'
    the masses,
An' makes you sartin o' the aid o' good men of all classes.

There's one thing I'm in doubt about; in order to be
    Presidunt,
It's absolutely ne'ssary to be a Southern residunt;
The Constitution settles thet, an' also thet a feller
Must own a nigger o' some sort, jet black, or brown, or
    yeller.
Now I haint no objections agin particklar climes,
Nor agin ownin' anythin' (except the truth sometimes),

But, ez I haint no capital, up there among ye, maybe,
You migh⸪ raise funds enough fer me to buy a low-priced
    baby,
An' then, to suit the No'thern folks, who feel obleeged
    to say
They hate an' cuss the very thing they vote fer every
    day,
Say you 're assured I go full butt fer Liberty's diffusion
An' made the purchis on'y jest to spite the Institootion ; —
But, golly ! there 's the currier's hoss upon the pavement
    pawin' !
I 'll be more 'xplicit in my next.
Yourn,
BIRDOFREDUM SAWIN.

[We have now a tolerably fair chance of estimating how the balance-sheet stands between our returned volunteer and glory. Supposing the entries to be set down on both sides of the account in fractional parts of one hundred, we shall arrive at something like the following result : —

B. SAWIN, Esq., in account with (BLANK) GLORY.

Cr.				Dr.
By loss of one leg, . . . 20		To one 675th three cheers in		
" do. one arm, . . . 15		Faneuil Hall, . . . 30		
" do. four fingers, . . 5		" do. do. on occasion of		
" do. one eye, . . . 10		presentation of sword to		
" the breaking of six ribs, . 6		Colonel Wright, . . 25		
" having served under Colo-		" one suit of gray clothes (in-		
nel Cushing one month, . 44		geniously unbecoming), . 15		
		" musical entertainments		
		(drum and fife six		
		months), ... 5		
		" one dinner after return, . 1		
		" chance of pension, . . 1		
		" privilege of drawing long-		
		bow during rest of natu-		
		ral life, ... 23		

100   100

E. E.

It would appear that Mr. Sawin found the actual feast curiously the reverse of the bill of fare advertised in Faneuil Hall and other places. His primary object seems to have been the making of his fortune. *Quærenda pecunia primum, virtus post nummos.* He hoisted sail for Eldorado, and shipwrecked on Point Tribulation. *Quid non mortalia pectora cogis, auri sacra fames?* The speculation has sometimes crossed my mind, in that dreary interval of drought which intervenes between quarterly stipendiary showers, that Providence, by the creation of a money-tree, might have simplified wonderfully the sometimes perplexing problem of human life. We read of bread-trees, the butter for which lies ready-churned in Irish bogs. Milk-trees we are assured of in South America, and stout Sir John Hawkins testifies to water-trees in the Canaries. Boot-trees bear abundantly in Lynn and elsewhere; and I have seen, in the entries of the wealthy, hat-trees with a fair show of fruit. A family-tree I once cultivated myself, and found therefrom but a scanty yield, and that quite tasteless and innutritious. Of trees bearing men we are not without examples; as those in the park of Louis the Eleventh of France. Who has forgotten, moreover, that olive-tree, growing in the Athenian's back-garden, with its strange uxorious crop, for the general propagation of which, as of a new and precious variety, the philosopher Diogenes, hitherto uninterested in arboriculture, was so zealous? In the *sylva* of our own Southern States, the females of my family have called my attention to the china-tree. Not to multiply examples, I will barely add to my list the birch-tree, in the smaller branches of which has been implanted so miraculous a virtue for communicating the Latin and Greek languages, and which may well, therefore, be classed among the trees producing necessaries of life, — *venerabile donum fatalis virgæ.* That money-trees existed in the golden age there want not prevalent reasons for our believing. For does not the old proverb, when it asserts that money does not grow on *every* bush, imply *a fortiori* that there were certain bushes which did produce it? Again, there is another ancient saw to the effect that money is the *root* of all evil. From which two adages it may be safe to infer that the aforesaid species of tree first degenerated into a shrub, then absconded underground, and finally, in our iron age, vanished altogether. In favorable exposures it may be conjectured that a specimen or two survived to a great age, as in the garden of the Hesperides; and, indeed, what else could that tree in the Sixth Æneid have been, with a branch whereof the Trojan hero procured admission to a territory, for the entering of which money is a surer passport than to a certain other more profitable (too) foreign kingdom? Whether these speculations of mine have any force in them, or whether they will not rather, by most readers, be deemed impertinent to the matter in hand, is a question which I leave to the determination of an indulgent posterity. That there were, in more primitive and happier times, shops where money was sold, — and that, too, on credit and at a bargain, — I take to be matter of demonstration. For what but a dealer in this article was that Æolus who supplied Ulysses with motive power for his fleet in bags? What that Ericus, king of Sweden, who is said to have kept the winds in his cap? What, in more recent times, those Lapland Nornas who traded in favorable breezes? All which will appear the more clearly when we consider, that, even to this day, *raising the wind* is proverbial for raising money, and that brokers and banks were invented by the Venetians at a later period.

And now for the improvement of this digression. I find a parallel to Mr. Sawin's fortune in an adventure of my own. For, shortly after I had first broached to myself the before-stated natural-historical and archæological theories, as I was passing, *hæc negotia penitus mecum revolvens,* through one of the obscure suburbs of our New England metropolis, my eye was attracted by these words upon a sign-board, — CHEAP CASH-STORE. Here was at once the confirmation of my speculations, and the substance of my hopes. Here lingered the fragment of a happier past, or stretched out the first tremulous organic filament of a more fortunate future. Thus glowed the distant Mexico to the eyes of Sawin, as he looked through the dirty pane of the recruiting-office window, or speculated from the summit of that mirage-Pisgah which the imps of the bottle are so cunning in raising up. Already had my Alnaschar-fancy (even during that first half-believing glance) expended in various useful directions the funds to be obtained by pledging the manuscript of a proposed volume of discourses. Already did a clock ornament the tower of the Jaalam meeting-house, a gift appropriately, but modestly, commemorated in the parish and town records, both, for now many years, kept by myself. Already had my son Seneca completed his course at the University. Whether, for the moment, we may not be considered as actually lording it over those Baratarias with the viceroyalty of which Hope invests us, and whether we are ever so warmly housed as in our Spanish castles, would afford matter of argument. Enough that I found that sign-board to be no other than a bait to the trap of a decayed grocer. Nevertheless, I bought a pound of dates (getting short weight by reason of immense flights of harpy flies who pursued and lighted upon their prey even in the very scales), which purchase I made, not only with an eye to the little ones at home, but also as a figurative reproof of that too frequent habit of my mind, which, forgetting the due order of chronology, will often persuade me that the happy sceptre of Saturn is stretched over this Astræa-forsaken nineteenth century.

Having glanced at the ledger of Glory under the title *Sawin, B.*, let us extend our investigations, and discover if that instructive volume does not contain some charges more personally interesting to ourselves. I think we should be more economical of our resources, did we thoroughly appreciate the fact, that, whenever brother Jonathan seems to be thrusting his hand into his own pocket, he is, in fact, picking ours. I confess that the late *muck* which the country has been running has materially changed my views as to the best method of raising revenue. If, by means of direct taxation, the bills for every extraordinary outlay were brought under our immediate eye, so that, like thrifty housekeepers, we could see where and how fast the money was going, we should be less likely to commit extravagances. At present, these things are managed in such a hugger-mugger way, that we know not what we pay for; the poor man is charged as much as the rich; and, while we are saving and scrimping at the spigot, the government is drawing off at the bung. If we could know that a part of the money we expend for tea and coffee goes to buy powder and balls, and that it is Mexican blood which makes the clothes on our backs more costly, it would set some of us athinking. During the present fall, I have often pictured to myself a government official entering my study and handing me the following bill: —

WASHINGTON, Sept. 30, 1848.

REV. HOMER WILBUR to 𝔘ncle 𝔖amuel,

Dr.

To his share of work done in Mexico on partnership account, sundry jobs, as below.

" killing, maiming, and wounding about 5,000 Mexicans,	$2.00
" slaughtering one woman carrying water to wounded,	.10
" extra work on two different Sabbaths (one bombardment and one assault) whereby the Mexicans were prevented from defiling themselves with the idolatries of high mass,	3.50
" throwing an especially fortunate and Protestant bombshell into the Cathedral at Vera Cruz, whereby several female Papists were slain at the altar,	.50
" his proportion of cash paid for conquered territory,	1.75
" do. do. for conquering do.	1.50
" manuring do. with new superior compost called " American Citizen,"	.50
" extending the area of freedom and Protestantism,	.01
" glory,	.01
	$9.87

Immediate payment is requested.

N. B. Thankful for former favors, U. S. requests a continuance of patronage. Orders executed with neatness and despatch. Terms as low as those of any other contractor for the same kind and style of work.

I can fancy the official answering my look of horror with, — " Yes, Sir, it looks like a high charge, Sir: but in these days slaughtering is slaughtering." Verily, I would that every one understood that it was: for it goes about obtaining money under the false pretence of being glory. For me, I have an imagination which plays me uncomfortable tricks. It happens to me sometimes to see a slaughterer on his way home from his day's work, and forthwith my imagination puts a cocked-hat upon his head and epaulettes upon his shoulders, and sets him up as a candidate for the Presidency. So, also, on a recent public occasion, as the place assigned to the "Reverend Clergy" is just behind that of " Officers of the Army and Navy " in processions, it was my fortune to be seated at the dinner-table over against one of these respectable persons. He was arrayed as (out of his own profession, only kings, court-officers, and footmen are in Europe, and Indians in America. Now what does my over-officious imagination but set to work upon him, strip him of his gay livery, and present him to me coatless, his trowsers thrust into the tops of a pair of boots thick with clotted blood, and a basket on his arm out of which lolled a gore-smeared axe, thereby destroying my relish for the temporal mercies upon the board before me! — H. W.]

No. IX.

A THIRD LETTER FROM B. SAWIN, ESQ.

[UPON the following letter slender comment will be needful. In what river Selemnus has Mr. Sawin bathed, that he has become so swiftly oblivious of his former loves? From an ardent and (as befits a soldier) confident wooer of that coy bride, the popular favor, we see him subside of a sudden into the (I trust not jilted) Cincinnatus, returning to his plough with a goodly-sized branch of willow in his hand; figuratively returning, however, to a figurative plough, and from no profound affection for that honored implement of husbandry, (for which, indeed, Mr. Sawin never displayed any decided predilection,) but in order to be gracefully summoned therefrom to more congenial labors. It would seem that the character of the ancient Dictator had become part of the recognized stock of our modern political comedy, though, as our term of office extends to a quadrennial length, the parallel is not so minutely exact as could be desired. It is sufficiently so, however, for purposes of scenic representation. An humble cottage (if built of logs, the better) forms the Arcadian background of the stage. This rustic paradise is labelled Ashland, Jaalam, North Bend, Marshfield, Kinderhook, or Bâton Rouge, as occasion demands. Before the door stands a something with one handle (the other painted in proper perspective), which represents, in happy ideal vagueness, the plough. To this the defeated candidate rushes with delirous joy, welcomed as a father by appropriate groups of happy laborers, or from it the successful one is torn with difficulty, sustained alone by a noble sense of public duty. Only I have observed, that, if the scene be laid at Bâton Rouge or Ashland, the laborers are kept carefully in the background, and are heard to shout from behind the scenes in a singular tone resembling ululation, and accompanied by a sound not unlike vigorous clapping. This, however, may be artistically in keeping with the habits of the rustic population of those localities. The precise connection between agricultural pursuits and statesmanship I have not been able, after diligent inquiry, to discover. But, that my investigations may not be barren of all fruit, I will mention one curious statistical fact, which I consider thoroughly established, namely, that no real farmer ever attains practically beyond a seat in General Court, however theoretically qualified for more exalted station.

It is probable that some other prospect has been opened to Mr. Sawin, and that he has not made this great sacrifice without some definite understanding in regard to a seat in the cabinet or a foreign mission. It may be supposed that we of Jaalam were not untouched by a feeling of villatic pride in beholding our townsman occupying so large a space in the public eye. And to me, deeply revolving the qualifications necessary to a candidate in these frugal times, those of Mr. S. seemed peculiarly adapted to a successful campaign. The loss of a leg, an arm, an eye, and four fingers, reduced him so nearly to the condition of a *vox et præterea nihil*, that I could think of nothing but the loss of his head by which his chance could have been bettered. But since he has chosen to baulk our suffrages, we must content ourselves with what we can get, remembering *lactucas non esse dandas, dum cardui sufficiant.* — H. W.]

I spose you recollect thet I explained my gennle views
In the last billet thet I writ, 'way down frum Veery
    Cruze,
Jest arter I 'd a kind o' ben spontanously sot up
To run unanimously fer the Presidential cup;
O' course it wor n't no wish o' mine, 't wuz ferflely dis·
    tressin',
But poppiler enthusiasm gut so almighty pressin'
Thet, though like sixty all along I fumed an' fussed an'
    sorrered,
There did n't seem no ways to stop their bringin' on me
    forrerd:
Fact is, they udged the matter so, I could n't help admit-
    tin'
The Father o' his Country's shoes no feet but mine 'ould
    fit in,
Besides the savin' o' the soles fer ages to succeed,
Seein' thet with one wannut foot, a pair 'd be more 'n I
    need;
An', tell ye wut, them shoes 'll want a thund'rin' sight o'
    patchin',
Ef this 'ere fashion is to last we 've gut into o' hatchin'
A pair o' second Washintons fer every new election, —
Though, fur ez number one 's consarned, I don't make no
    objection.

I wuz agoin' on to say thet wen at fust I saw
The masses would stick to 't I wuz the Country's father-
 'n-law,
(They would ha' hed it *Father*, but I told 'em 't would n't
 du,
Coz thet wuz sutthin' of a sort they could n't split in tu,
An' Washinton hed hed the thing laid fairly to his door,
Nor dars n't say 't wor n't his'n, much ez sixty year
 afore,)
But 't aint no matter ez to thet; wen I wuz nomernated,
'T wor n't natur but wut I should feel consid'able elated,
An' wile the hooraw o' the thing wuz kind o' noo an'
 fresh,
I thought our ticket would ha' caird the country with a
 resh.

Sence I 've come hum, though, an' looked round, I think
 I seem to find
Strong argimunts ez thick ez fleas to make me change my
 mind;
It 's clear to any one whose brain ain't fur gone in a
 phthisis,
Thet hail Columby's happy land is goin' thru a crisis,
An' 't would n't noways du to hev the people's mind dis-
 tracted
By bein' all to once by sev'ral pop'lar names attackted;
'T would save holl haycartloads o' fuss an' three four
 months o' jaw,
Ef some illustrous paytriot should back out an' with-
 draw;
So, ez I aint a crooked stick, jest like — like ole (I swow,
I dunno ez I know his name) — I 'll go back to my
 plough.

Wenever an Amerikin distinguished politishin
Begins to try et wut they call definin' his posishin,
Wal, I, fer one, feel sure he aint gut nuthin' to define;
It 's so nine cases out o' ten, but jest that tenth is mine;
An' 'taint no more 'n is proper 'n' right in sech a sitooa-
 tion
To hint the course you think 'll be the savin' o' the nation;
To funk right out o' p'lit'cal strife aint thought to be
 the thing,

Without you deacon off the toon you want your folks
    should sing;
So I edvise the noomrous friends thet's in one boat
    with me
To jest up killock, jam right down their hellum hard
    a lee,
Haul the sheets taut, an', laying out upon the Suthun tack,
Make fer the safest port they can, wich, *I* think, is Ole
    Zack.

Next thing you'll want to know, I spose, wut argimunts
    I seem
To see thet makes me think this ere'll be the strongest
    team;
Fust place, I've ben consid'ble round in bar-rooms an'
    saloons
Agethrin' public sentiment, 'mongst Demmercrats and
    Coons,
An' 'taint ve'y offen thet I meet a chap but wut goes in
Fer Rough an' Ready, fair an' square, hufs, taller, horns,
    an' skin;
I don't deny but wut, fer one, ez fur ez I could see,
I did n't like at fust the Pheladelphy nomernee :
I could ha' pinted to a man thet wuz, I guess, a peg
Higher than him, — a soger, tu, an' with a wooden leg;
But every day with more an' more o' Taylor zeal I'm
    burnin',
Seein' wich way the tide thet sets to office is aturnin';
Wy, into Bellers's we notched the votes down on three
    sticks, —
'T wuz Birdofredum *one,* Cass *aught,* an' Taylor *twenty-six,*
An' bein' the on'y canderdate thet wuz upon the ground,
They said 't wuz no more'n right thet I should pay the
    drinks all round;
Ef I'd expected sech a trick, I would n't ha' cut my foot
By goin' an' votin' fer myself like a consumed coot;
It did n't make no diff'rence, though; I wish I may be
    cust,
Ef Bellers wuz n't slim enough to say he would n't trust!

Another pint thet influences the minds o' sober jedges
Is thet the Gin'ral hez n't gut tied hand an' foot with
    pledges;

He hez n't told ye wut he is, an' so there aint no knowin'
But wut he may turn out to be the best there is agoin';
This, at the on'y spot thet pinched, the shoe directly
    eases,
Coz every one is free to 'xpect percisely what he pleases :
I want free-trade; you don't; the Gin'ral is n't bound to
    neither; —
I vote my way; you, yourn, an' both air sooted to a T
    there.
Ole Rough an' Ready, tu, 's a Wig, but without bein'
    · ultry
(He 's like a holsome hayinday, thet 's warm, but is n't
    sultry);
He 's jest wut I should call myself, a kin' o' *scratch,* ez
    't ware,
Thet ain't exacly all a wig nor wholly your own hair;
I 've ben a Wig three weeks myself, jest o' this mod'rate
    sort,
An' don't find them an' Demmercrats so different ez I
    thought;
They both act pooty much alike, an' push an' scrouge an'
    cus;
They 're like two pickpockets in league fer Uncle Sam-
    well's pus;
Each takes a side, an' then they squeeze the old man in
    between 'em,
Turn all his pockets wrong side out an' quick ez lightnin'
    clean 'em;
To nary one on 'em I 'd trust a secon'-handed rail
No furder off 'an I could sling a bullock by the tail.

Webster sot matters right in thet air Mashfiel' speech o'
    his'n; —
"Taylor," sez he, "aint nary ways the one thet I 'd a
    chizzen,
Nor he aint fittin' fer the place, an' like ez not he aint
No more 'n a tough ole bullethead, an' no gret of a saint;
But then," sez he, "obsarve my pint, he 's jest ez good to
    vote fer
Ez though the greasin' on him wor n't a thing to hire
    Choate fer;
Aint it ez easy done to drop a ballot in a box
Fer one ez 't is fer t 'other, fer the bulldog ez the fox ? "

It takes a mind like Dannel's, fact, ez big ez all ou' doors,
To find out thet it looks like rain arter it fairly pours;
I 'gree with him, it aint so dreffle troublesome to vote
Fer Taylor arter all,—it's jest to go an' change your
    coat;
Wen he's once greased, you 'll swaller him an' never
    know on 't, scurce,
Unless he scratches, goin' down, with them 'ere Gin'ral's
    spurs.
I 've ben a votin' Demmercrat, ez reg'lar ez a clock,
But don't find goin' Taylor gives my narves no gret 'f a
    shock;
Truth is, the cutest leadin' Wigs, ever sence fust they
    found
Wich side the bread gut buttered on, hev kep' a edgin'
    round;
They kin' o' slipt the planks frum out th' ole platform
    one by one
An' made it gradooally noo, 'fore folks know'd wut wuz
    done,
Till, fur 'z I know, there aint an inch thet I could lay my
    han' on,
But I, or any Demmercrat, feels comf'table to stan' on,
An' ole Wig doctrines act'lly look, their occ'pants bein'
    gone,
Lonesome ez staddles on a mash without no hayricks on.
I spose it's time now I should give my thoughts upon
    the plan,
Thet chipped the shell at Buffalo, o' settin' up ole Van.
I used to vote fer Martin, but, I swan, I 'm clean dis-
    gusted,—
He aint the man thet I can say is fittin' to be trusted;
He aint half antislav'ry 'nough, nor I aint sure, ez some be,
He 'd go in fer abolishin' the Deestrick o' Columby;
An', now I come to recollect, it kin' o' makes me sick 'z
A horse, to think o' wut he wuz in eighteen thirty-six.
An' then, another thing;—I guess, though mebby I am
    wrong,
This Buff'lo plaster aint agoin' to dror almighty strong;
Some folks, I know, hev gut th' idee thet No'thun
    dough 'll rise,
Though, 'fore I see it riz an' baked, I wouldn't trust my
    eyes;

'T will take more emptins, a long chalk, than this noo
    party's gut,
To give sech heavy cakes ez them a start, I tell ye wut.
But even ef they caird the day, there would n't be no
    endurin'
To stan' upon a platform with sech critters ez Van
    Buren; —
An' his son John, tu, I can't think how thet 'ere chap
    should dare
To speak ez he doos; wy, they say he used to cuss an'
    swear!
I spose he never read the hymn thet tells how down the
    stairs
A feller with long legs wuz throwed thet would n't say
    his prayers.
This brings me to another pint: the leaders o' the party
Aint jest sech men ez I can act along with free an'
    hearty;
They aint not quite respectable, an' wen a feller's
    morrils
Don't toe the straightest kin' o' mark, wy, him an' me
    jest quarrils.
I went to a free soil meetin' once, an' wut d' ye think I see?
A feller was aspoutin' there thet act'lly come to me,
About two year ago last spring, ez nigh ez I can jedge,
An' axed me ef I did n't want to sign the Temprunce
    pledge!
He 's one o' them that goes about an' sez you hed n't
    ough' ter
Drink nothin', mornin', noon, or night, stronger 'an Taun-
    ton water.
There 's one rule I 've ben guided by, in settlin' how to
    vote, ollers, —
I take the side thet *is n't* took by them consarned tee-
    totallers.
Ez fer the niggers, I 've ben South, an' thet hez changed
    my mind;
A lazier, more ongrateful set you could n't nowers find.
You know I mentioned in my last thet I should buy a
    nigger,
Ef I could make a purchase at a pooty mod'rate figger;
So, ez there 's nothin' in the world I 'm fonder of 'an
    gunnin',

2 G

closed a bargin finally to take a feller runnin'.
I shou'dered queen's-arm an' stumped out, an' wen I
    come t' th' swamp,
'T wor n't very long before I gut upon the nest o' Pomp;
I come acrost a kin' o' hut, an', playin' round the door,
Some little woolly-headed cubs, ez many 'z six or more.
At fust I thought o' firin', but *think twice* is safest ollers;
There aint, thinks I, not one on 'em but 's wuth his twenty
    dollars,
Or would be, ef I had 'em back into a Christian land, —
How temptin' all on 'em would look upon an auction-
    stand!
(Not but wut *I* hate Slavery in th' abstract, stem to
    starn, —
I leave it ware our fathers did, a privit State consarn.)
Soon 'z they see me, they yelled an' run, but Pomp wuz
    out ahoein'
A leetle patch o' corn he hed, or else there aint no
    knowin'
He would n't ha' took a pop at me; but I had gut the
    start,
An' wen he looked, I vow he groaned ez though he 'd
    broke his heart;
He done it like a wite man, tu, ez nat'ral ez a pictur,
The imp'dunt, pis'nous hypocrite! wus 'an a boy con-
    strictur.
"You can't gum *me*, I tell ye now, an' so you need n't
    try,
I 'xpect my eye-teeth every mail, so jest shet up," sez I.
"Don't go to actin' ugly now, or else I 'll jest let strip,
You 'd best draw kindly, seein' 'z how I 've gut ye on the
    hip;
Besides, you darned ole fool, it aint no gret of a disaster
To be benev'lently druv back to a contented master,
Ware you hed Christian priv'ledges you don't seem quite
    aware of,
Or you 'd ha' never run away from bein' well took care of;
Ez fer kin' treatment, wy, he wuz so fond on ye, he sed
He 'd give a fifty spot right out, to git ye, live or dead;
Wite folks aint sot by half ez much; 'member I run away,
Wen I wuz bound to Cap'n Jakes, to Mattysqumscot bay;
Don't know him, likely? Spose not; wal, the mean ole
    codger went

An' offered — wut reward, think? Wal, it wor n't no
  less 'n a cent."

Wal, I jest gut 'em into line, an' druv 'em on afore me,
The pis'nous brutes, I 'd no idee o' the ill-will they bore
  me ;
We walked till som'ers about noon, an' then it grew so
  hot
I thought it best to camp awile, so I chose out a spot
Jest under a magnoly tree, an' there right down I sot;
Then I unstrappped my wooden leg, coz it begun to chafe,
An' laid it down 'long side o' me, supposin' all wuz safe ;
I made my darkies all set down around me in a ring,
An' sot an' kin' o' ciphered up how much the lot would
  bring ;
But, wile I drinked the peaceful cup of a pure heart an'
  mind,
(Mixed with some wiskey, now an' then,) Pomp he snaked
  up behind,
An' creepin' grad'lly close tu, ez quiet ez a mink,
Jest grabbed my leg, and then pulled foot, quicker 'an
  you could wink,
An', come to look, they each on 'em hed gut behin' a tree,
An' Pomp poked out the leg a piece, jest so ez I could
  see,
An' yelled to me to throw away my pistils an' my gun,
Or else thet they 'd cair off the leg, an' fairly cut an'
  run.
I vow I did n't b'lieve there wuz a decent alligatur
Thet hed a heart so destitoot o' common human natur;
However, ez there wor n't no help, I finally give in
An' heft my arms away to git my leg safe back agin.
Pomp gethered all the weapins up, an' then he come an'
  grinned,
He showed his ivory some, I guess, an' sez, "You 're
  fairly pinned ;
Jest buckle on your leg agin, an' git right up an come,
'T wun't du fer fammerly men like me to be so long from
  hum."
At fust I put my foot right down an' swore I would n't
  budge.
"Jest ez you choose," sez he, quite cool, "either be shot
  or trudge."

So this black-hearted monster took an' act'lly druv me
    back
Along the very feetmarks o' my happy mornin' track,
An' kep' me pris'ner 'bout six months, an' worked me, tu,
    like sin,
Till I hed gut his corn an' his Carliny taters in;
He made me larn him readin', tu, (although the crittur
    saw
How much it hut my morril sense to act agin the law,)
So 'st he could read a Bible he 'd gut; an' axed ef I could
    pint   .   .
The North Star out; but there I put his nose some out o'
    jint,
Fer I weeled roun' about sou'west, an', lookin' up a bit,
Picked out a middlin' shiny one an' tole him thet wuz it.
Fin'lly, he took me to the door, an', givin' me a kick,
Sez, — "Ef you know wut 's best fer ye, be off, now,
    double-quick;
The winter-time 's a comin' on, an', though I gut ye
    cheap,
You 're so darned lazy, I don't think you 're hardly wuth
    your keep;
Besides, the childrin 's growin' up, an' you aint jest the
    model
I 'd like to hev 'em immertate, an' so you 'd better tod-
    dle!"

Now is there any thin' on airth 'll ever prove to me
Thet renegader slaves like him air fit for bein' free?
D' you think they 'll suck me in to jine the Buff'lo chaps,
    an' them
Rank infidels thet go agin the Scriptur'l cus o' Shem?
Not by a jugfull! sooner 'n thet, I 'd go thru fire an'
    water;
Wen I hev once made up my mind, a meet'nhus aint
    sotter;
No, not though all the crows thet flies to pick my bones
    wuz cawin', —
I guess we 're in a Christian land, —
                    Yourn,
                        BIRDOFREDUM SAWIN.

[Here, patient reader, we take leave of each other, I trust with some mutual satisfaction. I say *patient*, for I love not that kind which skims dippingly over the surface of the page, as swallows over a pool before rain. By such no pearls shall be gathered. But if no pearls there be (as, indeed, the world is not without example of books wherefrom the longest-winded diver shall bring up no more than his proper handful of mud), yet let us hope that an oyster or two may reward adequate perseverance. If neither pearls nor oysters, yet is patience itself a gem worth diving deeply for.

It may seem to some that too much space has been usurped by my own private lucubrations, and some may be fain to bring against me that old jest of him who preached all his hearers out of the meeting-house save only the sexton, who, remaining for yet a little space, from a sense of official duty, at last gave out also, and, presenting the keys, humbly requested our preacher to lock the doors, when he should have wholly relieved himself of his testimony. I confess to a satisfaction in the self act of preaching, nor do I esteem a discourse to be wholly thrown away even upon a sleeping or unintelligent auditory. I cannot easily believe that the Gospel of Saint John, which Jacques Cartier ordered to be read in the Latin tongue to the Canadian savages, upon his first meeting with them, fell altogether upon stony ground. For the earnestness of the preacher is a sermon appreciable by dullest intellects and most alien ears. In this wise did Episcopius convert many to his opinions, who yet understood not the language in which he discoursed. The chief thing is that the messenger believe that he has an authentic message to deliver. For counterfeit messengers that mode of treatment which Father John de Plano Carpini relates to have prevailed among the Tartars would seem effectual, and, perhaps, deserved enough. For my own part, I may lay claim to so much of the spirit of martyrdom as would have led me to go into banishment with those clergymen whom Alphonso the Sixth of Portugal drave out of his kingdom for refusing to shorten their public eloquence. It is possible, that, having been invited into my brother Biglow's desk, I may have been too little scrupulous in using it for the venting of my own peculiar doctrines to a congregation drawn together in the expectation and with the desire of hearing him.

I am not wholly unconscious of a peculiarity of mental organization which impels me, like the railroad-engine with its train of cars, to run backward for a short distance in order to obtain a fairer start. I may compare myself to one fishing from the rocks when the sea runs high, who, misinterpreting the suction of the undertow for the biting of some larger fish, jerks suddenly, and finds that he has *caught bottom*, hauling in upon the end of his line a trail of various *algæ*, among which, nevertheless, the naturalist may haply find something to repay the disappointment of the angler. Yet have I conscientiously endeavored to adapt myself to the impatient temper of the age, daily degenerating more and more from the high standard of our pristine New England. To the catalogue of lost arts I would mournfully add also that of listening to two-hour sermons. Surely we have been abridged into a race of pigmies. For, truly, in those of the old discourses yet subsisting to us in print, the endless spinal column of divisions and subdivisions can be likened to nothing so exactly as to the vertebræ of the saurians, whence the theorist may conjecture a race of Anakim proportionate to the withstanding of these other monsters. I say Anakim rather than Nephelim, because there seem reasons for supposing that the race of those whose heads (though no giants) are constantly enveloped in clouds (which that name imports) will never become extinct. The attempt to vanquish the innumerable *heads* of one of those aforementioned discourses may supply us with a plausible interpretation of the second labor of Hercules, and his successful experiment with fire affords us a useful precedent.

But while I lament the degeneracy of the age in this regard, I cannot refuse to succumb to its influence. Looking out through my study-window, I see Mr. Biglow at a distance busy in gathering his Baldwins, of which, to judge by the number of barrels lying about under the trees, his crop is more abundant than my own, — by which sight I am admonished to turn to those orchards of the mind wherein my labors may be more prospered, and apply myself diligently to the preparation of my next Sabbath's discourse. — H. W.]

MELIBŒUS-HIPPONAX.

THE

𝔅iglow 𝔓apers.

SECOND SERIES.

Ἔστιν ἄρ' ὁ ἰδιωτισμὸς ἐνίοτε τοῦ κόσμου παραπολὺ ἐμφανιστικώτερον.

LONGINUS.

" J'aimerois mieulx que mon fils apprinst aux tavernes à parler,
qu' aux escholes de la parlerie."

MONTAIGNE.

„Unſer Sprach iſt auch ein Sprach und kan ſo wohl ein Sack nennen
als die Latiner saccus."

FISCHART.

" Vim rebus aliquando ipsa verborum humilitas affert."

QUINTILIANUS.

" O ma lengo,
Plantarèy une estèlo à toun froun encrumit ! "

JASMIN.

TO E. R. HOAR.

"Multos enim, quibus loquendi ratio non desit, invenias, quos curiose potius loqui dixeris quam Latine ; quomodo et illa Attica anus Theophrastum, hominem alioqui disertissimum, annotata unius affectatione verbi, hospitem dixit, nec alio se id deprehendisse interrogata respondit, quam quod nimium Attice loqueretur."

QUINTILIANUS.

"Et Anglice sermonicari solebat populo, sed secundum linguam Norfolchie ubi natus et nutritus erat."

CRONICA JOCELINI.

"La politique est une pierre attachée au cou de la littérature, et qui, en moins de six mois la submerge. . . Cette politique va offenser mortellement une moitié des lecteurs, et ennuyer l'autre qui l'a trouvée bien autrement spéciale et énergique dans le journal du matin."

HENRI BEYLE.

INTRODUCTION.

THOUGH prefaces seem of late to have fallen under some reproach, they have at least this advantage, that they set us again on the feet of our personal consciousness and rescue us from the gregarious mock-modesty or cowardice of that *we* which shrills feebly throughout modern literature like the shrieking of mice in the walls of a house that has past its prime. Having a few words to say to the many friends whom the "Biglow Papers" have won me, I shall accordingly take the freedom of the first person singular of the personal pronoun. Let each of the good-natured unknown who have cheered me by the written communication of their sympathy look upon this Introduction as a private letter to himself.

When, more than twenty years ago, I wrote the first of the series, I had no definite plan and no intention of ever writing another. Thinking the Mexican war, as I think it still, a national crime committed in behoof of Slavery, our common sin, and wishing to put the feeling of those who thought as I did in a way that would tell, I imagined to myself such an upcountry man as I had often seen at antislavery gatherings, capable of district-school English, but always instinctively falling back into the natural stronghold of his homely dialect when heated to the point of self-forgetfulness. When I began to carry out my conception and to write in my assumed character, I found myself in a strait between two perils. On the one hand, I was in danger of being carried beyond the limit of my own opinions, or at least of that temper with which every man should speak his mind in print, and on the other I feared the risk of seeming to vulgarize a deep and sacred conviction. I needed on occasion to rise above the level of mere *patois*, and for this purpose conceived the Reverend Mr. Wilbur who should express the more cautious element of the New England character and

457

its pedantry, as Mr. Biglow should serve for its homely common-sense vivified and heated by conscience. The parson was to be the complement rather than the antithesis of his parishioner, and I felt or fancied a certain humorous element in the real identity of the two under a seeming incongruity. Mr. Wilbur's fondness for scraps of Latin, though drawn from the life, I adopted deliberately to heighten the contrast. Finding soon after that I needed some one as a mouthpiece of the mere drollery, for I conceive that true humor is never divorced from moral conviction, I invented Mr. Sawin for the clown of my little puppet-show. I meant to embody in him that half-conscious *unmorality* which I had noticed as the recoil in gross natures from a puritanism that still strove to keep in its creed the intense savor which had long gone out of its faith and life. In the three I thought I should find room enough to express, as it was my plan to do, the popular feeling and opinion of the time. For the names of two of my characters, since I have received some remonstrances from very worthy persons who happened to bear them, I would say that they were purely fortuitous, probably mere unconscious memories of signboards or directories. Mr. Sawin's sprang from the accident of a rhyme at the end of his first epistle, and I purposely christened him by the impossible surname of Birdofredum not more to stigmatize him as the incarnation of "Manifest Destiny," in other words, of national recklessness as to right and wrong, than to avoid the chance of wounding any private sensitiveness.

The success of my experiment soon began not only to astonish me, but to make me feel the responsibility of knowing that I held in my hand a weapon instead of the mere fencing-stick I had supposed. Very far from being a popular author under my own name, so far, indeed, as to be almost unread, I found the verses of my pseudonym copied everywhere; I saw them pinned up in workshops; I heard them quoted and their authorship debated; I once even, when rumor had at length caught up my name in one of its eddies, had the satisfaction of overhearing it demonstrated, in the pauses of a concert, that *I* was utterly incompetent to have written anything of the kind. I had read too much not to know the utter worthlessness of contemporary reputation, especially as regards satire, but I knew also that by giving a certain amount of influence it also had its worth, if that influence were used on the right side. I had learned, too, that the first requisite of good writing is to have an earnest and definite purpose, whether æsthetic or moral, and that even good writing, to please long, must have more than an average amount either of imagination or common-sense. The first of these falls to the lot of scarcely one in several generations; the last is within the reach of many in every one that passes; and of this an author may fairly hope to become in part the mouthpiece. If I put on the cap and bells and made myself one of the court-fools of King Demos, it was less to make his majesty laugh than to win a passage to his royal ears for certain serious things which I had deeply at heart. I say this because there is no imputation that could be more galling to any man's self-respect than that of being a mere jester. I endeavored, by generalizing my satire, to give it what value I could beyond the passing moment and the immediate application. How far I have succeeded I cannot tell, but I have had better luck than I ever looked for in seeing my verses survive to pass beyond their nonage.

In choosing the Yankee dialect, I did not act without forethought. It had long seemed to me that the great vice of American writing and speaking was a studied want of simplicity, that we were in danger of coming to look on our mother-tongue as a dead language, to be sought in the grammar and dictionary rather than in the heart, and that our only chance of escape was by seeking it at its living sources among those who were, as Scottowe says of Major-General Gibbons, "divinely illiterate." President Lincoln, the only really great public man whom these latter days have seen, was great also in this, that he was master — witness his speech at Gettysburg — of a truly masculine English, classic because it was of no special period, and level at once to the highest and lowest of his countrymen. But whoever should read the debates in Congress might fancy himself present at a meeting of the city council of some city of southern Gaul in the decline of the Empire, where barbarians with a Latin varnish emulated each other in being more than Ciceronian. Whether it be

want of culture, for the highest outcome of that is sim.
plicity, or for whatever reason, it is certain that very few
American writers or speakers wield their native language
with the directness, precision, and force that are common
as the day in the mother country. We use it like Scots-
men, not as if it belonged to us, but as if we wished to
prove that we belong to it, by showing our intimacy with
its written rather than with its spoken dialect. And yet
all the while our popular idiom is racy with life and vigor
and originality, bucksome (as Milton used the word) to
our new occasions, and proves itself no mere graft by
sending up new suckers from the old root in spite of us.
It is only from its roots in the living generations of men
that a language can be reinforced with fresh vigor for its
needs; what may be called a literate dialect grows ever
more and more pedantic and foreign, till it becomes at
last as unfitting a vehicle for living thought as monkish
Latin. That we should all be made to talk like books is
the danger with which we are threatened by the Universal
Schoolmaster, who does his best to enslave the minds and
memories of his victims to what he esteems the best mod-
els of English composition, that is to say, to the writers
whose style is faultily correct and has no blood-warmth
in it. No language after it has faded into *diction*, none
that cannot suck up the feeding juices secreted for it in
the rich mother-earth of common folk, can bring forth a
sound and lusty book. True vigor and heartiness of
phrase do not pass from page to page, but from man to
man, where the brain is kindled and the lips suppled by
downright living interests and by passion in its very throe.
Language is the soil of thought, and our own especially is
a rich leaf-mould, the slow deposit of ages, the shed foliage
of feeling, fancy, and imagination, which has suffered an
earth-change, that the vocal forest, as Howell called it, may
clothe itself anew with living green. There is death in
the dictionary; and, where language is too strictly limited
by convention, the ground for expression to grow in is lim-
ited also; and we get a *potted* literature, Chinese dwarfs
instead of healthy trees.

But while the schoolmaster has been busy starching
our language and smoothing it flat with the mangle of a
supposed classical authority, the newspaper reporter has

been doing even more harm by stretching and swelling it
to suit his occasions. A dozen years ago I began a list,
which I have added to from time to time, of some of the
changes which may be fairly laid at his door. I give a
few of them as showing their tendency, all the more dan-
gerous that their effect, like that of some poisons, is in-
sensibly cumulative, and that they are sure at last of
effect among a people whose chief reading is the daily
paper. I give in two columns the old style and its mod-
ern equivalent.

Old Style.	*New Style.*
Was hanged.	Was launched into eternity.
When the halter was put round his neck.	When the fatal noose was adjusted about the neck of the unfortunate victim of his own unbridled passions.
A great crowd came to see.	A vast concourse was assembled to witness.
Great fire.	Disastrous conflagration.
The fire spread.	The conflagration extended its devastating career.
House burned.	Edifice consumed.
The fire was got under.	The progress of the devouring element was arrested.
Man fell.	Individual was precipitated.
A horse and wagon ran against.	A valuable horse attached to a vehicle driven by J. S., in the employment of J. B., collided with.
The frightened horse.	The infuriated animal.
Sent for the doctor.	Called into requisition the services of the family physician.
The mayor of the city in a short speech welcomed.	The chief magistrate of the metropolis, in well-chosen and eloquent language, frequently interrupted by the plaudits of the surging multitude, officially tendered the hospitalities.
I shall say a few words.	I shall, with your permission, beg leave to offer some brief observations.
Began his answer.	Commenced his rejoinder.
A bystander advised.	One of those omnipresent characters who, as if in pursuance of some previous arrangement, are certain to be encountered in the vicinity when an accident occurs, ventured the suggestion.

He died.

He deceased, he passed out of existence, his spirit quitted its earthly habitation, winged its way to eternity, shook off its burden, &c.

In one sense this is nothing new. The school of Pope in verse ended by wire-drawing its phrase to such thinness that it could bear no weight of meaning whatever. Nor is fine writing by any means confined to America. All writers without imagination fall into it of necessity whenever they attempt the figurative. I take two examples from Mr. Merivale's " History of the Romans under the Empire," which, indeed, is full of such. " The last years of the age familiarly styled the Augustan were singularly barren of the literary glories from which its celebrity was chiefly derived. One by one the stars in its firmament had been lost to the world; Virgil and Horace, &c., had long since died; the charm which the imagination of Livy had thrown over the earlier annals of Rome had ceased to shine on the details of almost contemporary history; and if the flood of his eloquence still continued flowing, we can hardly suppose that the stream was as rapid, as fresh, and as clear as ever." I will not waste time in criticising the bad English or the mixture of metaphor in these sentences, but will simply cite another from the same author which is even worse. " The shadowy phantom of the Republic continued to flit before the eyes of the Cæsar. There was still, he apprehended, a germ of sentiment existing, on which a scion of his own house, or even a stranger, might boldly throw himself and raise the standard of patrician independence." Now a ghost may haunt a murderer, but hardly, I should think, to scare him with the threat of taking a new lease of its old tenement. And fancy the *scion* of a *house* in the act of *throwing itself* upon a *germ of sentiment* to *raise a standard!* I am glad, since we have so much in the same kind to answer for, that this bit of horticultural rhetoric is from beyond sea. I would not be supposed to condemn truly imaginative prose. There is a simplicity of splendor, no less than of plainness, and prose would be poor indeed if it could not find a tongue for that meaning of the mind which is behind the meaning of the words. It has sometimes seemed to me that in England there was a growing tendency to curtail language into a mere convenience, and to defecate it of all emotion as thoroughly as algebraic signs. This has arisen, no doubt, in part from that healthy national contempt of humbug which is characteristic of Englishmen, in part from that sensitiveness to the ludicrous which makes them so shy of expressing feeling, but in part also, it is to be feared, from a growing distrust, one might almost say hatred, of whatever is super-material. There is something sad in the scorn with which their journalists treat the notion of there being such a thing as a national ideal, seeming utterly to have forgotten that even in the affairs of this world the imagination is as much matter-of-fact as the understanding. If we were to trust the impression made on us by some of the cleverest and most characteristic of their periodical literature, we should think England hopelessly stranded on the good-humored cynicism of well-to-do middle-age, and should fancy it an enchanted nation, doomed to sit forever with its feet under the mahogany in that after-dinner mood which follows conscientious repletion, and which it is ill-manners to disturb with any topics more exciting than the quality of the wines. But there are already symptoms that a large class of Englishmen are getting weary of the dominion of consols and divine common-sense, and to believe that eternal three *per cent* is not the chief end of man, nor the highest and only kind of interest to which the powers and opportunities of England are entitled.

The quality of exaggeration has often been remarked on as typical of American character, and especially of American humor. In Dr. Petri's *Gedrängtes Handbuch der Fremdwörter*, we are told that the word *humbug* is commonly used for the exaggerations of the North Americans. To be sure, one would be tempted to think the dream of Columbus half fulfilled, and that Europe had found in the West a nearer way to Orientalism, at least in diction. But it seems to me that a great deal of what is set down as mere extravagance is more fitly to be called intensity and picturesqueness, symptoms of the imaginative faculty in full health and strength, though producing, as yet, only the raw and formless material in which poetry is to work. By and by, perhaps, the world will see it fashioned into poem and picture, and Europe, which will be hard pushed for originality erelong, may have to thank us for a new sensation. The French continue to find Shakespeare exaggerated because he treated English just as our country-folk do when they speak of a " steep price," or say that they " freeze to " a thing. The first postulate of an original literature is that a people should use their language instinctively and unconsciously, as if it were a lively part of their growth and personality, not as the mere torpid boon of education or inheritance. Even Burns contrived to write very poor verse and prose in English. Vulgarisms are often only poetry in the egg. The late Mr. Horace Mann, in one of his public addresses, commented at some length on the beauty and moral significance of the French phrase *s'orienter,* and called on his young friends to practise upon it in life. There was not a Yankee in his audience whose problem had not always been to find out what was *about east,* and to shape his course accordingly. This charm which a familiar expression gains by being commented, as it were, and set in a new light by a foreign language, is curious and instructive. I cannot help thinking that Mr. Matthew Arnold forgets this a little too much sometimes when he writes of the beauties of French style. It would not be hard to find in the works of French Academicians phrases as coarse as those he cites from Burke, only they are veiled by the unfamiliarity of the language. But, however this may be, it is certain that poets and peasants please us in the same way by translating words back again to their primal freshness, and infusing them with a delightful strangeness which is anything but alienation. What, for example, is Milton's " *edge* of battle " but a doing into English of the Latin *acies ? Was die Gans gedacht das der Schwan vollbracht,* what the goose but thought, that the swan full brought (or, to de-Saxonize it a little, what the goose conceived, that the swan achieved), and it may well be that the life, invention, and vigor shown by our popular speech, and the freedom with which it is shaped to the instant want of those who use it, are of the best omen for our having a swan at last.

The part I have taken on myself is that of the humbler bird.

But it is affirmed that there is something innately vulgar in the Yankee dialect. M. Sainte-Beuve says, with his usual neatness: "*Je définis un patois une ancienne langue qui a eu des malheurs, ou encore une langue toute jeune et qui n'a pas faite fortune.*" The first pàrt of his definition applies to a dialect like the Provençal, the last to the Tuscan before Dante had lifted it into a classic, and neither, it seems to me, will quite fit a *patois*, which is not properly a dialect, but rather certain archaisms, proverbial phrases, and modes of pronunciation, which maintain themselves among the uneducated side by side with the finished and universally accepted language. Norman French, for example, or Scotch down to the time of James VI., could hardly be called *patois*, while I should be half inclined to name the Yankee a *lingo* rather than a dialect. It has retained a few words now fallen into disuse in the mother country, like *to tarry, to progress, fleshy, fall,* and some others; it has changed the meaning of some, as in *freshet;* and it has clung to what I suspect to have been the broad Norman pronunciation of *e* (which Molière puts into the mouth of his rustics) in such words as *sarvant, parfect, vartoo,* and the like. It maintains something of the French sound of *a* also in words like *chămber, dănger* (though the latter had certainly begun to take its present sound so early as 1636, when I find it sometimes spelt *dainger*). But in general it may be said that nothing can be found in it which does not still survive in some one or other of the English provincial dialects. I am not speaking now of Americanisms properly so called, that is, of words or phrases which have grown into use here either through necessity, invention, or accident, such as a *carry,* a *one-horse affair,* a *prairie,* to *vamose.* Even these are fewer than is sometimes taken for granted. But I think some fair defence may be made against the charge of vulgarity. Properly speaking, vulgarity is in the thought, and not in the word or the way of pronouncing it. Modern French, the most polite of languages, is barbarously vulgar if compared with the Latin out of which it has been corrupted, or even with Italian. There is a wider

2 H

gap, and one implying greater boorishness, between *min-isterium* and *métier*, or *sapiens* and *sachant*, than between *druv* and *drove*, or *agin* and *against*, which last is plainly an arrant superlative. Our rustic *coverlid* is nearer its French original than the diminutive cover*let*, into which it has been ignorantly corrupted in politer speech. I obtained from three cultivated Englishmen at different times three diverse pronunciations of a single word, — *cowcumber, coocumber*, and *cucumber*. Of these the first, which is Yankee also, comes nearest to the nasality of *concombre*. Lord Ossory assures us that Voltaire saw the best society in England, and Voltaire tells his countrymen that *handkerchief* was pronounced *hanker-cher.* I find it so spelt in Hakluyt and elsewhere. This enormity the Yankee still persists in, and as there is always a reason for such deviations from the sound as represented by the spelling, may we not suspect two sources of derivation, and find an ancestor for *kercher* in *couverture* rather than in *couvrechef ?* And what greater phonetic vagary (which Dryden, by the way, called *fegary*) in our *lingua rustic* than this *ker* for *couvre ?* I copy from the fly-leaves of my books where I have noted them from time to time a few examples of pronunciation and phrase which will show that the Yankee often has antiquity and very respectable literary authority on his side. My list might be largely increased by referring to glossaries, but to them every one can go for himself, and I have gathered enough for my purpose.

I will take first those cases in which something like the French sound has been preserved in certain single letters and diphthongs. And this opens a curious question as to how long this Gallicism maintained itself in England. Sometimes a divergence in pronunciation has given us two words with different meanings, as in *genteel* and *jaunty*, which I find coming in toward the close of the seventeenth century, and wavering between *genteel* and *jantee.* It is usual in America to drop the *u* in words ending in *our*, — a very proper change recommended by Howell two centuries ago, and carried out by him so far as his printers would allow. This and the corresponding changes in *musique, musick*, and the like, which he also advocated, show that in his time the French accent in-

dicated by the superfluous letters (for French had once
nearly as strong an accent as Italian) had gone out of use.
There is plenty of French accent down to the end of Eliz-
abeth's reign. In Daniel we have *riches'* and *counsel'*, in
Bishop Hall *comet'*, *chapëlain*, in Donne *pictures'*, *virtue'*,
presence', *mortal'*, *merit'*, *hainous'*, *giant'*, with many more,
and Marston's satires are full of them. The two latter,
however, are not to be relied on, as they may be suspected
of Chaucerizing. Herrick writes *baptime.* The tendency
to throw the accent backward began early. But the in-
congruities are perplexing, and perhaps mark the period
of transition. In Warner's "Albion's England" we have
creator and *crëature'* side by side with the modern *creator*
and *creature.* *E'nvy* and *e'nvying* occur in Campion (1602),
and yet *envy'* survived Milton. In some cases we have
gone back again nearer to the French, as in *rev'enue* for
reven'ue. I had been so used to hearing *imbecile* pro-
nounced with the accent on the first syllable, which is in
accordance with the general tendency in such matters,
that I was surprised to find *imbec'ile* in a verse of Words-
worth. The dictionaries all give it so. I asked a highly
cultivated Englishman, and he declared for *imbeceel'.*
In general it may be assumed that accent will finally
settle on the syllable dictated by greater ease and there-
fore quickness of utterance. *Blas'phemous*, for example,
is more rapidly pronounced than *blasphem'ous*, to which
our Yankee clings, following in this the usage of many
of the older poets. *Amer'ican* is easier than *Ameri'can*,
and therefore the false quantity has carried the day,
though the true one may be found in George Herbert,
and even so late as Cowley.

To come back to the matter in hand. Our "uplandish
men" retain the soft or thin sound of the *u* in some words,
such as *rule, .truth* (sometimes also pronounced *trüth*,
not *trooth*), while he says *noo* for *new*, and gives to *view*
and *few* so indescribable a mixture of the two sounds with
slight nasal tincture that it may be called the Yankee
shibboleth. In *rule* the least sound of *a* precedes the *u.*
I find *reule* in Pecock's "Repressor." He probably pro-
nounced it *rayoolë*, as the old French word from which it
is derived was very likely to be sounded at first, with
a reminiscence of its original *regula.* Tindal has *rueler,*

and the Coventry Plays have *preudent.* As for *noo,* may it not claim some sanction in its derivation, whether from *nouveau* or *neuf,* the ancient sound of which may well have been *noof,* as nearer *novus ?* *Beef* would seem more like to have come from *buffe* than from *bœuf,* unless the two were mere varieties of spelling. The Saxon *few* may have caught enough from its French cousin *peu* to claim the benefit of the same doubt as to sound; and our slang phrase *a few* (as " I licked him a few ") may well appeal to *un peu* for sense and authority. Nay, might not *lick* itself turn out to be the good old word *lam* in an English disguise, if the latter should claim descent as, perhaps, he fairly might, from the Latin *lambere ?* The New England *ferce* for *fierce,* and *perce* for *pierce* (sometimes heard as *fairce* and *pairce*), are also Norman. For its antiquity I cite the rhyme of *verse* and *pierce* in Chapman and Donne, and in some commendatory verses by a Mr. Berkenhead before the poems of Francis Beaumont. Our *pairlous* for *perilous* is of the same kind, and is nearer Shakespeare's *parlous* than the modern pronunciation. One other Gallicism survives in our pronunciation. Perhaps I should rather càll it a semi-Gallicism, for it is the result of a futile effort to reproduce a French sound with English lips. Thus for *joint, employ, royal,* we have *jynt, emply, rỹle,* the last differing only from *rile* (*roil*) in a prolongation of the *y* sound. In Walter de Biblesworth I find *solives* Englished by *gistes.* This, it is true, may have been pronounced *jeests,* but the pronunciation *jystes* must have preceded the present spelling, which was no doubt adopted after the radical meaning was forgotten, as analogical with other words in *oi.* In the same way after Norman-French influence had softened the *l* out of *would* (we already find *woud* for *veut* in N. F. poems), *should* followed the example, and then an *l* was put into *could,* where it does not belong, to satisfy the logic of the eye, which has affected the pronunciation and even the spelling of English more than is commonly supposed. I meet with *eyster* for *oyster* as early as the fourteenth century. I find *dystrye* for *destroy* in the Coventry Plays, *viage* in Bishop Hall and Middleton the dramatist, *bile* in Donne and Chrononhotonthologos, *line* in Hall, *ryall* and *chyse* (for *choice*) in the Coventry Plays. In Chapman's " All Fools " is the misprint of *employ* for *imply*, fairly inferring an identity of sound in the last syllable. Indeed, this pronunciation was habitual till after Pope, and Rogers tells us that the elegant Gray said *naise* for *noise* just as our rustics still do. Our *cornish* (which I find also in Herrick) remembers the French better than *cornice* does. While, clinging more closely to the Anglo-Saxon in dropping the *g* from the end of the present participle, the Yankee now and then pleases himself with an experiment in French nasality in words ending in *n*. It is not, so far as my experience goes, very common, though it may formerly have been more so. *Capting,* for instance, I never heard · save in jest, the habitual form being *kepp'n.* But at any rate it is no invention of ours. In that delightful old volume, " Ane Compendious Buke of Godly and Spirituall Songs," in which I know not whether the piety itself or the simplicity of its expression be more charming, I find *burding, garding,* and *cousing,* and in the State Trials *uncertin* used by a gentleman. The *n* for *ng* I confess preferring.

Of Yankee preterites I find *risse* and *rize* for *rose* in Middleton and Dryden, *clim* in Spenser, *chees (chose)* in Sir John Mandevil, *give (gave)* in the Coventry Plays, *shet (shut)* in Golding's Ovid,* *het* in Chapman and in Weever's Epitaphs, *thriv* and *smit* in Drayton, *quit* in Ben Jonson and Henry More, and *pled* in the fastidious Landor. *Rid* for *rode* was anciently common. So likewise was *see* for *saw*, but I find it in no writer of authority, unless Chaucer's *seie* was so sounded. *Shew* is used by Hector Boece, Giles Fletcher, and Drummond of Hawthornden. Similar strong preterites, like *snew, thew,* and even *mew,* are not without example. I find *sew* for *sowed* in Piers Ploughman. Indeed, the anomalies in English preterites are perplexing. We have probably transferred *flew* from *flow* (as the preterite of which I have heard it) to *fly* because we had another preterite in *fled*. Of weak preterites the Yankee retains *growed, blowed,* for which he has good authority, and less often *knowed.* His *sot* is merely a broad sounding of *sat*, no more inelegant than the common *got* for *gat*, which he further degrades into *gut.* When he says *darst*, he uses a form as old as Chaucer.

---

* Cited in Warton's Obs. Faery Q.

The Yankee has retained something of the long sound of the *a* in such words as *axe, wax,* pronouncing them *exe, wex* (shortened from *aix, waix*). He also says *hev* and *hed* (*hăve, hăd*) for *have* and *had.* In most cases he follows an Anglo-Saxon usage. In *aix* for *axle* he certainly does. I find *wex* and *aisches* (*ashes*) in Pecock, and *exe* in the Paston Letters. Chaucer wrote *hendy.* Dryden rhymes *can* with *men,* as Mr. Biglow would. Alexander Gill, Milton's teacher, in his "Lagonomia" cites *hez* for *hath* as peculiar to Lincolnshire. I find *hayth* in Collier's "Bibliographical Account of Early English Literature" under the date 1584, and Lord Cromwell so wrote it. Sir Christopher Wren wrote *belcony.* *Thaim* for *them* was common in the sixteenth century. We have an example of the same thing in the double form of the verb *thrash, thresh.* While the New-Englander cannot be brought to say *instead* for *instid* (commonly *'stid* where not the last word in a sentence), he changes the *i* into *e* in *red* for *rid, tell* for *till, hender* for *hinder, rense* for *rinse.* I find *red* in the old interlude of " Thersytes," *tell* in a letter of Daborne to Henslowe, and also, I shudder to mention it, in a letter of the great Duchess of Marlborough, Atossa herself! It occurs twice in a single verse of the Chester Plays, which I copy as containing another Yankeeism : —

" *Tell* the day of dome, *tell* the heames *blow.*"

From this word *blow* is formed *blowth,* which I heard again this summer after a long interval. Mr. Wright[*] explains it as meaning " a blossom." With us a single blossom is a *blow,* while *blowth* means the blossoming in general. A farmer would say that there was a good blowth on his fruit-trees. The word retreats farther inland and away from the railways, year by year. Wither rhymes *hinder* with *slender,* and Lovelace has *renched* for *rinsed.* In " Gammer Gurton" is *sence* for *since;* Marlborough's Duchess so writes it, and Donne rhymes *since* with *Amiens* and *patïence,* Bishop Hall and Otway with *pretence,* Chapman with *citizens,* Dryden with *providence.* Indeed, why should not *sithence* take that form ?

E sometimes takes the place of *u,* as *jedge, tredge, bresh*

---

[*] Dictionary of Obsolete and Provincial English.

I find *tredge* in the interlude of "Jack Jugler," *bresh* in a citation by Collier from "London Cries" of the middle of the seventeenth century, and *resche* for *rush* (fifteenth century) in the very valuable "Volume of Vocabularies" edited by Mr. Wright. *Resce* is one of the Anglo-Saxon forms of the word in Bosworth's A. S. Dictionary. The Yankee always shortens the *u* in the ending *ture*, making *ventur, natur, pictur,* and so on. This was common, also, among the educated of the last generation. I am inclined to think it may have been once universal, and I certainly think it more elegant than the vile *vencher, naycher, pick-cher,* that have taken its place, sounding like the invention of a lexicographer with his mouth full of hot pudding. Nash in his "Pierce Penniless" has *ventur,* and so spells it, and I meet it also in Spenser, Drayton, Ben Jonson, Herrick, and Prior. Spenser has *tort'rest,* which can only be contracted from *tortur* and not from *torcher.* Quarles rhymes *nature* with *creator,* and Dryden with *satire,* which he doubtless pronounced according to its older form of *satyr.*

I shall now give some examples which cannot so easily be ranked under any special head. Gill charges the Eastern counties with *kiver* for *cover,* and *ta* for *to.* The Yankee pronounces both *too* and *to* like *ta* (like the *tou* in *touch*) where they are not emphatic. In that case, both become *tu.* In old spelling, *to* is the common (and indeed correct) form of *too,* which is only *to* with the sense of *in addition.* I suspect that the sound of our *too* has caught something from the French *tout,* and it is possible that the old *too-too* is not a reduplication, but a reminiscence of the feminine form of the same word (*toutes*) as anciently pronounced, with the *e* not yet silenced. Gill gives a Northern origin to *geaun* for *gown* and *waund* for *wound* (*vulnus*). Lovelace has *waund,* but there is something too dreadful in suspecting Spenser (who *borealized* in his pastorals) of having ever been guilty of *geaun!* And yet some delicate mouths even now are careful to observe the Hibernicism of *ge-ard* for *guard,* and *ge-url* for *girl.* Sir Philip Sidney (*credite posteri!*) wrote *furr* for *far.* I would hardly have believed it had I not seen it in *fac-simile.* As some consolation, I find *furder* in Lord Bacon and Donne, and Wither rhymes *far* with *cur.* The Yankee, who omits the final *d* in many words, as do the Scotch, makes up for it by adding one in *qeound.* The purist does not feel the loss of the *d* sensibly in *lawn* and *yon,* from the former of which it has dropped again after a wrongful adoption (retained in *laundry*), while it properly belongs to the latter. But what shall we make of *git, yit,* and *yis* ? I find *yis* and *git* in Warner's "Albion's England," yet rhyming with *wit, admit,* and *fit* in Donne, with *wit* in the "Revenger's Tragedy," Beaumont, and Suckling, with *writ* in Dryden, and latest of all with *wit* in Sir Hanbury Williams. Prior rhymes *fitting* and *begetting.* Worse is to come. Among others, Donne rhymes *again* with *sin,* and Quarles repeatedly with *in.* *Ben* for *been,* of which our dear Whittier is so fond, has the authority of Sackville, "Gammer Gurton" (the work of a bishop), Chapman, Dryden, and many more, though *bin* seems to have been the common form. Whittier's accenting the first syllable of *rom'ance* finds an accomplice in Drayton among others, and though manifestly wrong, is analogous with *Ro'mans.* Of other Yankeeisms, whether of form or pronunciation, which I have met with I add a few at random. Pecock writes *sowdiers* (*sogers, soudoyers*), and Chapman and Gill *sodder.* This absorption of the *l* is common in various dialects, especially in the Scottish. Pecock writes also *biyende,* and the authors of "Jack Jugler" and "Gammer Gurton" *yender.* The Yankee includes "*yon*" in the same category, and says "hither an' yen," for "to and fro." (Cf. German *jenseits.*) Pecock and plenty more have *wrastle.* Tindal has *agynste, gretter, shett, ondone, debytë,* and *scace.* "Jack Jugler" has *scacely,* (which I have often heard, though *skurce* is the common form), and Donne and Dryden make *great* rhyme with *set.* In the inscription on Caxton's tomb I find *ynd* for *end,* which the Yankee more often makes *eend,* still using familiarly the old phrase "right anend" for "continuously." His "*stret* (straight) along," in the same sense which I thought peculiar to him, I find in Pecock. Tindal's *debytë* for *deputy* is so perfectly Yankee that I could almost fancy the brave martyr to have been deacon of the First Parish at Jaalam Centre. "Jack Jugler" further gives us *playsent* and *sartayne.* Dryden rhymes *certain* with *parting,* and Chapman and Ben Jonson use *certain,* as the Yankee always does, for *certainly*. The "Coventry Mysteries" have *occapied*, *massage*, *nateralle*, *materal* (*material*), and *meracles*, all excellent Yankeeisms. In the "Quatre fils" Aymon (1504) * is *vertus* for *virtuous*. Thomas Fuller called *volume vollum*, I suspect, for he spells it *volumne*. However, *per contra*, Yankees habitually say *colume* for *column*. Indeed, to prove that our ancestors brought their pronunciation with them from the Old Country, and have not wantonly debased their mother tongue, I need only to cite the words *scriptur, Israll, athists*, and *cherfulness* from Governor Bradford's "History." Brampton Gurdon writes *shet* in a letter to Winthrop. So the good man wrote them, and so the good descendants of his fellow-exiles still pronounce them. *Purtend* (*pretend*) has crept like a serpent into the "Paradise of Dainty Devices"; *purvide*, which is not so bad, is in Chaucer. These, of course, are universal vulgarisms, and not peculiar to the Yankee. Butler has a Yankee phrase and pronunciation too in "To which these carr'ings-on did tend." Langham or Laneham, who wrote an account of the festivities at Kenilworth in honor of Queen Bess, and who evidently tried to spell phonetically, makes *sorrows* into *sororz*. Herrick writes *hollow* for *halloo*, and perhaps pronounced it (*horresco suggerins!*) *holla*, as Yankees do. Why not, when it comes from *holà?* I find *ffelaschyppe* (fellowship) in the Coventry Plays. Spenser and his queen neither of them scrupled to write *afore*, and the former feels no inelegance even in *chaw*. *'Fore* was common till after Herrick. *Afeared* was once universal. Warner has *ery* for *ever a*, nay, he also has *illy*, with which we were once ignorantly reproached by persons more familiar with Murray's grammar than with English literature. And why not *illy?* Mr. Bartlett says it is "a word used by writers of an inferior class, who do not seem to perceive that *ill* is itself an adverb, without the termination *ly*," and quotes Dr. Messer, President of Brown University, as asking triumphantly, "Why don't you say *welly?*" I should like to have had Dr. Messer answer his own question. It would be truer to say that it was used by people who still remembered that *ill* was an adjective, the shortened form of *evil*, out of which

* Cited in Collier. (I give my authority where I do not quote from the original book.)

Shakespeare ventured to make *evilly.* The objection to
illy is not an etymological one, but simply that it is con-
trary to good usage, a very sufficient reason. *Ill* as an
adverb was at first a vulgarism, precisely like the rustic's
when he says, "I was treated *bad.*" May not the reason
of this exceptional form be looked for in that tendency
to dodge what is hard to pronounce, to which I have
already alluded? If the letters were distinctly uttered,
as they should be, it would take too much time to say
ill-ly, well-ly, and it is to be observed that we have avoided
smally and *tally* in the same way, though we add *ish* to
them without hesitation in *smallish* and *tallish.* We
have, to be sure, *dully* and *fully,* but for the one we pre-
fer *stupidly,* and the other (though this may have come
from eliding the *y* before *as*) is giving way to *full.* The
uneducated, whose utterance is slower, still make ad-
verbs when they will by adding *like* to all manner of
adjectives. We have had *big* charged upon us, because
we use it where an Englishman would now use *great.* I
fully admit that it were better to distinguish between
them, allowing to *big* a certain contemptuous quality,
but as for authority, I want none better than that of
Jeremy Taylor, who, in his noble sermon "On the Return
of Prayer," speaks of "Jesus, whose spirit was meek and
gentle up to the greatness of the *biggest* example." As
for our double negative, I shall waste no time in quoting
instances of it, because it was once as universal in Eng-
lish as it still is in the neo-Latin languages, where it
does not strike us as vulgar. I am not sure that the
loss of it is not to be regretted. But surely I shall ad-
mit the vulgarity of slurring or altogether eliding certain
terminal consonants? I admit that a clear and sharp-
cut enunciation is one of the crowning charms and ele-
gancies of speech. Words so uttered are like coins
fresh from the mint, compared with the worn and dingy
drudges of long service, — I do not mean American
coins, for those look less badly, the more they lose of
their original ugliness. No one is more painfully con-
scious than I of the contrast between the rifle-crack of
an Englishman's *yes* and *no,* and the wet-fuse drawl of
the same monosyllables in the mouths of my countrymen.
But I do not find the dropping of final consonants dis-
agreeable in Allan Ramsay or Burns, nor do I believe

that our literary ancestors were sensible of that inelegance in the fusing them together of which we are conscious. How many educated men pronounce the *t* in *chestnut?* how many say *pentise* for *penthouse,* as they should? When a Yankee skipper says that he is " boun' for Gloster" (not Gloucëster, with the leave of the Universal Schoolmaster), he but speaks like Chaucer or an old ballad-singer, though they would have pronounced it *boon.* This is one of the cases where the *d* is surreptitious, and has been added in compliment to the verb *bind,* with which it has nothing to do. If we consider the root of the word (though of course I grant that every race has a right to do what it will with what is so peculiarly its own as its speech), the *d* has no more right there than at the end of *gone,* where it is often put by children, who are our best guides to the sources of linguistic corruption, and the best teachers of its processes. Cromwell, minister of Henry VIII., writes *worle* for *world.* Chapman has *wan* for *wand,* and *lawn* has rightfully displaced *laund,* though with no thought, I suspect, of etymology. Rogers tells us that Lady Bathurst sent him some letters written to William III. by Queen Mary, in which she addresses him as *"Dear Husban."* The old form *expoun',* which our farmers use, is more correct than the form with a barbarous *d* tacked on which has taken its place. Of the kind opposite to this, like our *gownd* for *gown,* and the London cockney's *wind* for *wine,* I find *drownd* for *drown* in the " Misfortunes of Arthur" (1584) and in Swift. And, by the way, whence came the long sound of *wind* which our poets still retain, and which survives in "wīnding" a horn, a totally different word from " winding" a kite-string? We say *behīnd* and *hīnder* (comparative), and yet *to hinder.* Shakespeare pronounced *kind kīnd,* or what becomes of his play on that word and *kin* in Hamlet? Nay, did he not even (shall I dare to hint it?) drop the final *d* as the Yankee still does? John Lilly plays in the same way on *kindred* and *kindness.* But to come to some other ancient instances. Warner rhymes *bounds* with *crowns, grounds* with *towns, text* with *sex, worst* with *crust, interrupts* with *cups;* Drayton, *defects* with *sex;* Chapman, *amends* with *cleanse;* Webster, *defects* with *checks;* Ben Jonson, *minds* with *combines;* Marston,

trust and *obsequious, clothes* and *shows;* Dryden gives the
same sound to *clothes,* and has also *minds* with *designs.*
Of course, I do not affirm that their ears may not have
told them that these were imperfect rhymes (though I
am by no means sure even of that), but they surely
would never have tolerated any such, had they suspected
the least vulgarity in them.   Prior has the rhyme *first*
and *trust,* but puts it into the mouth of a landlady.
Swift has *stunted* and *burnt it,* an intentionally imperfect
rhyme, no doubt, but which I cite as giving precisely
the Yankee pronunciation of *burned.*   Donne couples in
unhallowed wedlock *after* and *mutter,* thus seeming to
give to both the true Yankee sound, and it is not
uncommon to find *after* and *daughter.*   Worse than
all, in one of Dodsley's Old Plays we have *onions*
rhyming with *minions,* — I have tears in my eyes while
I record it.   And yet what is viler than the univer-
sal *Misses* (*Mrs.*) for *Mistress?*   This was once a vul-
garism, and in "The Miseries of Inforced Marriage"
the rhyme (printed as prose in Dodsley's Old Plays by
Collier),

> " To make my young *mistress,*
>   Delighting in *kisses,*"

is put in the mouth of the clown.   Our people say *Injun*
for *Indian.*   The tendency to make this change where *i*
follows *d* is common.   The Italian *giorno* and French *jour*
from *diurnus* are familiar examples.   And yet *Injun* is one
of those depravations which the taste challenges peremp-
torily, though it have the authority of Charles Cotton,
who rhymes "*Indies*" with "*cringes,*" and four English
lexicographers, beginning with Dr. Sheridan, bid us say
invidgeous.   Yet after all it is no worse than the debase-
ment which all our terminations in *tion* and *tience* have
undergone, which yet we hear with *resignashun* and *pay-
shunce* though it might have aroused both *impat-i-ence*
and *indigna-ti-on* in Shakespeare's time.   When George
Herbert tells us that if the sermon be dull,

> " God takes a text and preacheth *pati-ence,*"

the prolongation of the word seems to convey some hint
at the longanimity of the virtue.   Consider what a poor
curtal we have made of Ocean.   There was something of

his heave and expanse in *o-ce-an*, and Fletcher knew how to use it when he wrote so fine a verse as the second of these, the best deep-sea verse I know, —

> "In desperate storms stem with a little rudder
> The tumbling ruins of the oceän."

Oceanus was not then wholly shorn of his divine proportions, and our modern *oshun* sounds like the gush of small-beer in comparison. Some other contractions of ours have a vulgar air about them. *More 'n* for *more than*, as one of the worst, may stand for a type of such. Yet our old dramatists are full of such obscurations (elisions they can hardly be called) of the *th*, making *wh'r* of *whether*, *bro'r* of *brother*, *smo'r* of *smother*, *mo'r* of *mother*, and so on. Indeed, it is this that explains the word *rare* (which has Dryden's support), and which we say of meat where an Englishman would use *underdone*. I do not believe, with the dictionaries, that it had ever anything to do with the Icelandic *hrár* (*raw*), as it plainly has not in *rareripe*, which means earlier ripe. And I do not believe it for this reason, that the earlier form of the word with us was, and the commoner now in the inland parts still is, so far as I can discover, *raredone*. I find *rather* as a monosyllable in Donne, and still better as giving the sound rhyming with *fair* in Warner. The contraction *more 'n* I find in the old play "Fuimus Troes," in a verse where the measure is so strongly accented as to leave it beyond doubt, —

> "A golden crown whose heirs
> More than half the world subdue."

It may be, however, that the contraction is in "th' orld." Is our *gin* for *given* more violent than *mar'l* for *marvel*, which was once common, and which I find as late as Herrick? Nay, Herrick has *gin* (spelling it *g'en*), too, as do the Scotch, who agree with us likewise in preferring *chimly* to *chimney*.

I will now leave pronunciation and turn to words or phrases which have been supposed peculiar to us, only pausing to pick up a single dropped stitch in the pronunciation of the word *sup'reme*, which I had thought native till I found it in the well-languaged Daniel. I will begin with a word of which I have never met with any ex-

ample in print.   We express the first stage of withering
in a green plant suddenly cut down by the verb *to wilt.*
It is, of course, own cousin of the German *welken,* but I
have never come upon it in print, and my own books of
reference give me faint help.   Graff gives *welhèn, marces-
cere,* and refers to *weih (weak),* and conjecturally to A. S.
hvelan.   The A. S. *wealwian (to wither)* is nearer, but not
so near as two words in the Icelandic, which perhaps put
us on the track of its ancestry, *velgi (tepefacere)* and *velki,*
with the derivative meaning *contaminare.*   *Wilt,* at any
rate, is a good word, filling, as it does, a sensible gap
between drooping and withering, and the imaginative
phrase " he wilted right down," like " he caved right in,"
is a true Americanism.   *Wilt* occurs in English provin-
cial glossaries, but is explained by *wither,* which with us
it does not mean.   We have a few words, such as *cache,
cohog, carry (portage), shoot (chute), timber (forest), bush-
whack* (to pull a boat along by the bushes on the edge
of a stream), *buckeye* (a picturesque word for the horse-
chestnut), but how many can we be said to have fairly
brought into the language, as Alexander Gill, who first
mentions Americanisms, meant it when he said, " *Sed
et ab Americanis nonnulla mutuamur ut* MAIZ et CANOA " ?
Very few, I suspect, and those mostly by borrowing from
the French, German, Spanish, or Indian.   " The Dipper "
for the " Great Bear " strikes me as having a native air.
Bogus, in the sense of *worthless,* is undoubtedly ours, but
is, I more than suspect, a corruption of the French *ba-
gasse* (from low Latin *bagasea*), which travelled up the
Mississippi from New Orleans, where it was used for the
refuse of the sugar-cane.   It is true we have modified
the meaning of some words.   We use *freshet* in the sense
of *flood,* for which I have not chanced upon any author-
ity.   Our New England cross between Ancient Pistol
and Dugald Dalgetty, Captain Underhill, uses the word
(1638) to mean a *current,* and I do not recollect it else-
where in that sense.   I therefore leave it with a ? for
future explorers.   *Crick* for *creek* I find in Captain John
Smith and in the dedication of Fuller's " Holy Warre,"
and *run,* meaning a *small stream,* in Waymouth's " Voy-
age " (1605).   *Humans* for *men,* which Mr. Bartlett
includes in his " Dictionary of Americanisms," is Chap-
man's habitual phrase in his translation of Homer.   I

find it also in the old play of "The Hog hath lost his Pearl." *Dogs* for *andirons* is still current in New England, and in Walter de Biblesworth I find *chiens* glossed in the margin by *andirons*. *Gunning* for *shooting* is in Drayton. We once got credit for the poetical word *fall* for *autumn*, but Mr. Bartlett and the last edition of Webster's Dictionary refer us to Dryden. It is even older, for I find it in Drayton, and Bishop Hall has *autumn fall*. Middleton plays upon the word: "May'st thou have a reasonable good *spring*, for thou art like to have many dangerous foul *falls*." Lord Herbert of Cherbury (more properly perhaps than even Sidney the last *preux chevalier*) has "the Emperor's folks" just as a Yankee would say it. *Loan* for *lend*, with which we have hitherto been blackened, I must retort upon the mother island, for it appears so long ago as in "Albion's England." *Fleshy*, in the sense of *stout*, may claim Ben Jonson's warrant. *Chore* is also Jonson's word, and I am inclined to prefer it to *chare* and *char*, because I think that I see a more natural origin for it in the French *jour*, whence it might come to mean a day's work, and thence a job, than anywhere else. *At onst* for *at once* I thought a corruption of our own, till I found it in the Chester Plays. I am now inclined to suspect it no corruption at all, but only an erratic and obsolete superlative *at onest*. *To progress'* was flung in our teeth till Mr. Pickering retorted with Shakespeare's "doth pro'gress down thy cheeks." I confess that I was never satisfied with this answer, because the accent was different, and because the word might here be reckoned a substantive quite as well as a verb. Mr. Bartlett (in his Dictionary above cited) adds a surrebutter in a verse from Ford's "Broken Heart." Here the word is clearly a verb, but with the accent unhappily still on the first syllable. Mr. Bartlett says that he "cannot say whether the word was used in Bacon's time or not." It certainly was, and with the accent we give to it. Ben Jonson, in the "Alchemist," has this verse, —

"Progress' so from extreme unto extreme."

Surely we may now sleep in peace, and our English cousins will forgive us, since we have cleared ourselves from any suspicion of originality in the matter! *Poor* for *lean*, *thirds* for *dower*, and *dry* for *thirsty* I find in Middleton's plays. *Dry* is also in Skelton and in the "World" (1754). In a note on Middleton, Mr. Dyce thinks it needful to explain the phrase *I can't tell* (universal in America) by the gloss *I could not say.* Middleton also uses *snecked*, which I had believed an Americanism till I saw it there. It is, of course, only another form of *snatch*, analogous to *theek* and *thatch* (cf. the proper names Dekker and Thacher), *break* (*brack*) and *breach*, *make* (still common with us) and *match.* '*Long on* for *occasioned by* ("who is this 'long on?'") occurs likewise in Middleton. '*Cause why* is in Chaucer. *Raising* (an English version of the French *leaven*) for *yeast* is employed by Gayton in his "Festivous Notes on Don Quixote." I have never seen an instance of our New England word *emptins* in the same sense, nor can I divine its original. Gayton has *limekill;* also *shuts* for *shutters*, and the latter is used by Mrs. Hutchinson in her "Life of Colonel Hutchinson." Bishop Hall, and Purchas in his "Pilgrims," have *chist* for *chest*, and it is certainly nearer *cista* as well as to the form in the Teutonic languages, whence we probably got it. We retain the old sound in *cist*, but *chest* is as old as Chaucer. Lovelace says *wropt* for *wrapt.* "Musicianer" I had always associated with the militia-musters of my boyhood, and too hastily concluded it an abomination of our own, but Mr. Wright calls it a Norfolk word, and I find it to be as old as 1642 by an extract in Collier. "Not worth the time of day" had passed with me for native till I saw it in Shakespeare's "Pericles." For *slick* (which is only a shorter sound of *sleek*, like *crick* and the now universal *britches* for *breeches*) I will only call Chapman and Jonson. "That's a sure card!" and "That's a stinger!" both sound like modern slang, but you will find the one in the old interlude of "Thersytes" (1537), and the other in Middleton. "Right here," a favorite phrase with our orators and with a certain class of our editors, turns up *passim* in the Chester and Coventry plays. Mr. Dickens found something very ludicrous in what he considered our neologism *right away.* But I find a phrase very like it, and which I half suspect to be a misprint for it, in "Gammer Gurton":—

"Lyght it and bring it *tite away.*"

After all, what is it but another form of *straightway?* *Cussedness,* meaning *wickedness, malignity,* and *cuss,* a sneaking, ill-natured fellow, in such phrases as "He done it out o' pure cussedness," and "He is a nateral cuss," have been commonly thought Yankeeisms. To vent certain contemptuously-indignant moods they are admirable in their rough-and-ready way. But neither is our own. *Cursydnesse,* in the same sense of malignant wickedness, occurs in the Coventry Plays, and *cuss* may perhaps claim to have come in with the Conqueror. At least the term is also French. Saint Simon uses it and confesses its usefulness. Speaking of the Abbé Dubois he says, "Qui étoit en plein ce qu'un mauvais françois appelle un *sacre,* mais qui ne se peut guère exprimer autrement." "Not worth a cuss," though supported by "not worth a damn," may be a mere corruption, since "not worth a *cress*" is in "Piers Ploughman." "I don't see it" was the popular slang a year or two ago, and seemed to spring from the soil; but no, it is in Cibber's "Careless Husband." "*Green sauce*" for *vegetables* I meet in Beaumont and Fletcher, Gayton, and elsewhere. Our rustic pronunciation *sahce* (for either the diphthong *au* was anciently pronounced *ah,* or else we have followed abundant analogy in changing it to the latter sound, as we have in *chance, dance,* and so many more) may be the older one, and at least gives some hint at its ancestor *salsa.* *Warn,* in the sense of *notify,* is, I believe, now peculiar to us, but Pecock so employs it. *To cotton to* is, I rather think, an Americanism. The nearest approach to it I have found is *cotton together,* in Congreve's "Love for Love." To *cotton* or *cotten,* in another sense, is old and common. Our word means to *cling,* and its origin, possibly, is to be sought in another direction, perhaps in A. S. *cvead,* which means *mud, clay* (both proverbially clinging), or better yet, in the Icelandic *qvoda* (otherwise *kód*), meaning *resin* and *glue,* which are κατ᾽ ἐξοχήν sticky substances. To *spit cotton* is, I think, American, and also, perhaps, *to flax* for *to beat.* *To the halves* still survives among us, though apparently obsolete in England. It means either to let or to hire a piece of land, receiving half the profit in money or in kind (*partibus locare*). I

2 1

mention it because in a note by some English editor, to
which I have lost my reference, I have seen it wrongly
explained. The editors of Nares cite Burton. *To put,* in
the sense of *to go,* as *Put!* for *Begone!* would seem our
own, and yet it is strictly analogous to the French *se
mettre à la voie,* and the Italian *mettersi in via.* Indeed,
Dante has a verse,

> " *Io sarei* [for *mi sarei*] *già messo per lo sentiero,*"

which, but for the indignity, might be translated,

> " I should, ere this, have *put* along the way."

I deprecate in advance any share in General Banks's
notions of international law, but we may all take a just
pride in his exuberant eloquence as something distinc-
tively American. When he spoke a few years ago of
"letting the Union slide," even those who, for political
purposes, reproached him with the sentiment, admired
the indigenous virtue of his phrase. Yet I find " let the
world slide " in Heywood's " Edward IV."; and in Beau-
mont and Fletcher's " Wit without Money " Valentine
says,

> " Will you go drink,
> And let the world slide ? "

In the one case it is put into the mouth of a clown, in
the other, of a gentleman, and was evidently proverbial.
It has even higher sanction, for Chaucer writes,

> " Well nigh all other curës *let he slide.*"

Mr. Bartlett gives "above one's bend" as an American-
ism; but compare Hamlet's " to the top of my bent." *In
his tracks* for *immediately* has acquired an American accent,
and passes where he can for a native, but is an importa-
tion nevertheless; for what is he but the Latin *e vestigio,*
or at best the Norman French *eneslespas,* both which
have the same meaning? *Hotfoot* (provincial also in
England) I find in the old romance of " Tristan,"

> " *Si s'en parti* CHAUT PAS."

Like for *as* is never used in New England, but is universal in the South and West. It has on its side the authority of two kings (*ego sum rex Romanorum et supra grammaticam*), Henry VIII. and Charles I. This were ample, without throwing into the scale the scholar and poet Daniel. *Them* was used as a nominative by the majesty of Edward VI., by Sir P. Hoby, and by Lord Paget (in Froude's "History "). I have never seen any passage adduced where *guess* was used as the Yankee uses it. The word was familiar in the mouths of our ancestors, but with a different shade of meaning from that we have given it, which is something like *rather think,* though the Yankee implies a confident certainty by it when he says, " I guess I *du!*" There are two examples in Otway, one of which (" So in the struggle, I guess the note was lost ") perhaps might serve our purpose, and Coleridge's

" I guess 't was fearful there to see "

certainly comes very near. But I have a higher authority than either in Selden, who, in one of his notes to the "Polyolbion," writes, "The first inventor of them (I *guess* you dislike not the addition) was one Berthold Swartz." Here he must mean by it, " I take it for granted." Another peculiarity almost as prominent is the beginning sentences, especially in answer to questions, with " well." Put before such a phrase as " How d'e do ? " it is commonly short, and has the sound of *wul,* but in reply it is deliberative, and the various shades of meaning which can be conveyed by difference of intonation, and by prolonging or abbreviating, I should vainly attempt to describe. I have heard *ooa-ahl, wahl, ahl, wăl,* and something nearly approaching the sound of the *le* in *able.* Sometimes before " I " it dwindles to a mere *l,* as " 'l I dunno." A friend of mine (why should I not please myself, though I displease him, by brightening my page with the initials of the most exquisite of humorists, J. H.?) told me that he once heard five " wells," like pioneers, precede the answer to an inquiry about the price of land. The first was the ordinary *wul,* in deference to custom; the second, the long, perpending *ooahl,* with a falling inflection of the voice; the third, the

same, but with the voice rising, as if in despair of a con-
clusion, into a plaintively nasal whine; the fourth, *wulh*,
ending in the aspirate of a sigh; and then, fifth, came a
short, sharp *wal*, showing that a conclusion had been
reached. I have used this latter form in the "Biglow
Papers," because, if enough nasality be added, it repre-
sents most nearly the average sound of what I may call
the interjection.

A locution prevails in the Southern and Middle States
which is so curious that, though never heard in New
England, I will give a few lines to its discussion, the
more readily because it is extinct elsewhere. I mean the
use of *allow* in the sense of *affirm*, as "I allow that's a
good horse." I find the word so used in 1558 by Anthony
Jenkinson in Hakluyt: "Corne they sowe not, neither
doe eate any bread, mocking the Christians for the same,
and disabling our strengthe, saying we live by eating the
toppe of a weede, and drinke a drinke made of the same,
allowing theyr great devouring of flesh and drinking of
milke to be the increase of theyr strength." That is,
they undervalued our strength, and affirmed their own to
be the result of a certain diet. In another passage of the
same narrative the word has its more common meaning
of approving or praising: "The said king, much *allowing*
this declaration, said." Ducange quotes Bracton *sub voce*
ADLOCARE for the meaning "to admit as proved," and
the transition from this to "affirm" is by no means
violent. At the same time, when we consider some of
the meanings of *allow* in old English, and of *allouer* in
old French, and also remember that the verbs *prize* and
praise are from one root, I think we must admit *allaudare*
to a share in the paternity of *allow*. The sentence from
Hakluyt would read equally well, "contemning our
strengthe, . . . and praising (or valuing) their great
eating of flesh as the cause of their increase in strength."
After all, if we confine ourselves to *allocare*, it may turn
out that the word was somewhere and somewhen used for
to bet, analogously to *put up*, *put down*, *post* (cf. Spanish
apostar), and the like. I hear boys in the street contin-
ually saying, "I bet that's a good horse," or what not,
meaning by no means to risk anything beyond their
opinion in the matter.

The word *improve*, in the sense of "to occupy, make

use of, employ," as Dr. Pickering defines it, he long ago proved to be no neologism. He would have done better, I think, had he substituted *profit by* for *employ.* He cites Dr. Franklin as saying that the word had never, so far as he knew, been used in New England before he left it in 1723, except in Dr. Mather's "Remarkable Providences," which he oddly calls a "very old book." Franklin, as Dr. Pickering goes on to show, was mistaken. Mr. Bartlett in his "Dictionary" merely abridges Pickering. Both of them should have confined the application of the word to material things, its extension to which is all that is peculiar in the supposed American use of it. For surely "Complete Letter-writers" have been "*improving* this opportunity" time out of mind. I will illustrate the word a little further, because Pickering cites no English authorities. Skelton has a passage in his "Phyllyp Sparowe," which I quote the rather as it contains also the word *allowed,* and as it distinguishes *improve* from *employ:* —

> " His [Chaucer's] Englysh well alowed,
>   So as it is *enprowed,*
>   For as it is enployd,
>   There is no English voyd."

Here the meaning is *to profit by.* In Fuller's "Holy Warre" (1647), we have "The Egyptians standing on the firm ground, were thereby enabled to *improve* and enforce their darts to the utmost." Here the word might certainly mean *to make use of.* Mrs. Hutchinson (Life of Colonel H.) uses the word in the same way, "And therefore did not *emproove* his interest to engage the country in the quarrell." I find it also in "Strength out of Weakness" (1652), and Plutarch's "Morals" (1714), but I know of only one example of its use in the purely American sense, and that is, "a very good *improvement* for a mill" in the "State Trials" (Speech of the Attorney-General in the Lady Ivy's case, 1684). In the sense of *employ,* I could cite a dozen old English authorities.

In running over the fly-leaves of those delightful folios for this reference, I find a note which reminds me of another word, for our abuse of which we have been deservedly ridiculed. I mean *lady.* It is true I might cite the example of the Italian *donna* * (*domina*), which has been

---

* *Dame,* in English, is a decayed gentlewoman of the same family.

treated in the same way by a whole nation, and not, as
lady among us, by the uncultivated only.   It perhaps
grew into use in the half-democratic republics of Italy in
the same way and for the same reasons as with us.   But
I admit that our abuse of the word is villanous.   I know
of an orator who once said in a public meeting where
bonnets preponderated, that "the ladies were last at the
cross and first at the tomb"!   But similar sins were com-
mitted before our day and in the mother country.   In the
" State Trials " I learn of "a *gentlewoman* that lives cook
with " such a one, and I hear the Lord High Steward
speaking of the wife of a waiter at a bagnio as a *gentle-
woman!*   From the same authority, by the way, I can
state that our vile habit of chewing tobacco had the some-
what unsavory example of Titus Oates, and I know by
tradition from an eye-witness that the elegant General
Burgoyne partook of the same vice.   Howell, in one of
his letters (dated 26 Aug., 1623), speaks thus of another
" institution " which many have thought American:
" They speak much of that boisterous Bishop of Halver-
stadt, (for so they term him here,) that, having taken a
place wher ther were two Monasteries of Nuns and Friers,
he caus'd divers feather-beds to be rip'd, and all the feath-
ers to be thrown in a great Hall, whither the Nuns and
Friers were thrust naked with their bodies oil'd and
pitch'd, and to tumble among the feathers."   Howell
speaks as if the thing were new to him, and I know not
if the " boisterous " Bishop was the inventor of it, but I
find it practised in England before our Revolution.

Before leaving the subject, I will add a few comments
made from time to time on the margin of Mr. Bartlett's
excellent " Dictionary," to which I am glad thus publicly
to acknowledge my many obligations.   " Avails " is good
old English, and the *vails* of Sir Joshua Reynolds's porter
are famous.   Averse *from*, averse *to*, and in connection
with them the English vulgarism " different *to.*"   The
corrupt use of *to* in these cases, as well as in the Yankee
" he lives to Salem," " to home," and others, must be a
very old one, for in the one case it plainly arose from
confounding the two French prepositions *à* (from Latin
ad and *ab*), and in the other from translating the first of
them.   I once thought " different to " a modern vulgar-
ism, and Mr. Thackeray, on my pointing it out to him in

"Henry Esmond," confessed it to be an anachronism.
Mr. Bartlett refers to "the old writers quoted in Richard-
son's Dictionary" for "different to," but in my edition
of that work all the examples are with *from*. But I find
to used invariably by Sir R. Hawkins in Hakluyt. *Banjo*
is a negro corruption of O. E. *bandore*. *Bind-weed* can
hardly be modern, for *wood-bind* is old and radically
right, intertwining itself through *bindan* and *windan* with
classic stems. *Bobolink:* is this a contraction for Bob o'
Lincoln? I find *bobolynes* in one of the poems attributed
to Skelton, where it may be rendered *giddy-pate*, a term
very fit for the bird in his ecstasies. *Cruel* for *great* is in
Hakluyt. *Bowling-alley* is in Nash's "Pierce Pennilesse."
Curious, meaning nice, occurs continually in old writers,
and is as old as Pecock's "Repressor." *Droger* is O. E.
drugger. *Educational* is in Burke. *Feeze* is only a
form of *fizz*. To *fix*, in the American sense, I find used
by the Commissioners of the United Colonies so early as
1675, "their arms well *fixed* and fit for service." *To take
the foot in the hand* is German; so is *to go under*. *Gun-
dalow* is old: I find *gundelo* in Hakluyt, and *gundello* in
Booth's reprint of the folio Shakespeare of 1623. *Gonoff*
is O. E. *gnoffe*. *Heap* is in "Piers Ploughman" ("and
other names *an heep*"), and in Hakluyt ("seeing such a
heap of their enemies ready to devour them "). *To liquor*
is in the "Puritan" ("call 'em in, and liquor 'em a little").
To loaf: this, I think, is unquestionably German. *Laufen*
is pronounced *lofen* in some parts of Germany, and I once
heard one German student say to another, *Ich lauf'* (lofe)
hier bis du wiederkehrest, and he began accordingly to
saunter up and down, in short, to *loaf*. To *mull*, Mr. Bart-
lett says, means "to soften, to dispirit," and quotes from
"Margaret,"—"There has been a pretty considerable
mullin going on among the doctors,"—where it surely
cannot mean what he says it does. We have always
heard *mulling* used for *stirring, bustling*, sometimes in an
underhand way. It is a metaphor derived probably from
mulling wine, and the word itself must be a corruption
of *mell*, from O. F. *mesler*. *Pair* of stairs is in Hakluyt.
To pull up stakes is in Curwen's Journal, and therefore
pre-Revolutionary. I think I have met with it earlier.
Raise: under this word Mr. Bartlett omits "to raise a
house," that is, the frame of a wooden one, and also the

substantive formed from it, a *raisin'*. *Setting-poles* cannot be new, for I find "some *set* [the boats] with long *poles*" in Hakluyt. *Shoulder-hitters :* I find that *shoulder-striker* is old, though I have lost the reference to my authority. *Snag* is no new word, though perhaps the Western application of it is so; but I find in Gill the proverb, "A bird in the bag is worth two on the snag." *Trail:* Hakluyt has "many wayes *traled* by the wilde beastes."

I subjoin a few phrases not in Mr. Bartlett's book which I have heard. *Bald-headed :* "to go it bald-headed"; in great haste, as where one rushes out without his hat. *Bogue:* "I don't git much done 'thout I *bogue* right in along 'th my men." *Carry:* a *portage*. *Cat-nap:* a short doze. *Cat-stick:* a small stick. *Chowder-head:* a muddle-brain. *Cling-john:* a soft cake of rye. *Cocoa-nut:* the head. *Cohees':* applied to the people of certain settlements in Western Pennsylvania, from their use of the archaic form *Quo' he*. *Dunnow'z I know:* the nearest your true Yankee ever comes to acknowledging ignorance. *Essence-pedler:* a skunk. *First-rate and a half*. *Fish-flakes*, for drying fish : O. E. *fleck* (*cratis*). *Gander-party:* a social gathering of men only. *Gawnicus:* a dolt. *Hawkins's whetstone:* rum ; in derision of one Hawkins, a well-known temperance-lecturer. *Hyper:* to bustle : "I mus' *hyper* about an' git tea." *Keeler-tub:* one in which dishes are washed. ("And Greasy Joan doth *keel* the pot.") *Laptea:* where the guests are too many to sit at table. *Last of pea-time:* to be hard-up. *Lose-laid* (loose-laid): a weaver's term, and probably English; weak-willed. *Malahack:* to cut up hastily or awkwardly. *Moonglade:* a beautiful word for the track of moonlight on the water. *Off-ox:* an unmanageable, cross-grained fellow. *Old Driver, Old Splitfoot:* the Devil. *Onhitch:* to pull trigger (cf. Spanish *disparar*). *Popular:* conceited. *Rote:* sound of surf before a storm. *Rot-gut:* cheap whiskey ; the word occurs in Heywood's "English Traveller" and Addison's "Drummer," for a poor kind of drink. *Seem:* it is habitual with the New-Englander to put this verb to strange uses, as, "I can't *seem* to be suited," "I couldn't *seem* to know him." *Sidehill*, for *hillside*. *State-house :* this seems an Americanism, whether invented or derived from the Dutch *Stadhuys*, I know not.

Strike and *string:* from the game of ninepins; to make *a strike* is to knock down all the pins with one ball, hence it has come to mean fortunate, successful. *Swampers*: men who break out roads for lumberers. *Tormented:* euphemism for damned, as, "not a tormented cent." *Virginia fence, to make a:* to walk like a drunken man.

It is always worth while to note down the erratic words or phrases which one meets with in any dialect. They may throw light on the meaning of other words, on the relationship of languages, or even on history itself. In so composite a language as ours they often supply a different form to express a different shade of meaning as in *viol* and *fiddle*, *thrid* and *thread*, *smother* and *smoulder*, where the *l* has crept in by a false analogy with *would*. We have given back to England the excellent adjective *lengthy*, formed honestly like *earthy*, *drouthy*, and others, thus enabling their journalists to characterize our President's messages by a word civilly compromising between *long* and *tedious*, so as not to endanger the peace of the two countries by wounding our national sensitiveness to British criticism. Let me give two curious examples of the antiseptic property of dialects at which I have already glanced. Dante has *dindi* as a childish or low word for *danari* (money), and in Shropshire small Roman coins are still dug up which the peasants call *dinders*. This can hardly be a chance coincidence, but seems rather to carry the word back to the Roman soldiery. So our farmers say *chuk, chuk*, to their pigs, and *ciacco* is one of the Italian words for *hog*. When a countryman tells us that he "fell *all of a heap*," I cannot help thinking that he unconsciously points to an affinity between our word *tumble*, and the Latin *tumulus*, that is older than most others. I believe that words, or even the mere intonation of them, have an astonishing vitality and power of propagation by the root, like the gardener's pest, quitch-grass,* while the application or combination of them may be new. It is in these last that my countrymen seem to me full of humor, invention, quickness of wit, and that sense of subtle analogy which needs only refining to become fancy and imagination. Prosaic as American life seems in many of its

---

* Which, whether in that form, or under its aliases *witch*-grass and *cooch*-grass, points us back to its original Saxon *quick*.

aspects to a European, bleak and bare as it is on the
side of tradition, and utterly orphaned of the solemn
inspiration of antiquity, I cannot help thinking that the
ordinary talk of unlettered men among us is fuller of
metaphor and of phrases that suggest lively images than
that of any other people I have seen. Very many such
will be found in Mr. Bartlett's book, though his short
list of proverbs at the end seem to me, with one or two
exceptions, as un-American as possible. Most of them
have no character at all but coarseness, and are quite
too long-skirted for working proverbs, in which language
always "takes off its coat to it," as a Yankee would say.
There are · plenty that have a more native and puckery
flavor, seedlings from the old stock often, and yet new
varieties. One hears such not seldom among us East-
erners, and the West would yield many more. "Mean
enough to steal acorns from a ·blind hog"; "Cold as
the north side of a Jenooary gravestone by starlight";
"Hungry as a graven image"; "Pop'lar as a hen with
one chicken"; "Quicker 'n greased lightnin'"; "Ther's
sech a thing ez bein' *tu*"; "Stingy enough to skim his
milk at both eends"; "Hot as the Devil's kitchen";
"Handy as a pocket in a shirt"; "He's a whole team
and the dog under the wagon "; "All deacons are good,
but there's odds in deacons" (to *deacon* berries is to put
the largest atop); "So thievish they hev to take in their
stone walls nights ";* may serve as specimens. "I take
my tea *barfoot*," said a backwoodsman when askèd if he
would have cream and sugar. (I find *barfoot*, by the
way, in the Coventry Plays.) A man speaking to me
once of a very rocky clearing said, " Stone's got a pretty
heavy mortgage on that land," and I overheard a guide
in the woods say to his companions who were urging
him to sing, " Wal, I *did* sing once, but toons gut in-
vented, an' thet spilt my trade." Whoever has driven
over a stream by a bridge made of *slabs* will feel the pic-
turesque force of the epithet *slab-bridged* applied to a
fellow of shaky character. Almost every county has
some good die-sinker in phrase, whose mintage passes
into the currency of the whole neighborhood. Such a
one described the county jail (the one stone building

---

* And, by the way, the Yankee never says "o' nights," but uses the older ad-
verbial form, analogous to the German *nachts.*

where all the dwellings are of wood) as "the house whose underpinnin' come up to the eaves," and called hell "the place where they did n't rake up their fires nights." I once asked a stage-driver if the other side of a hill were as steep as the one we were climbing: "Steep? chain-lightnin' could n' go down it 'thout puttin' the shoe on!" And this brings me back to the exaggeration of which I spoke before. To me there is something very taking in the negro "so black that charcoal made a chalk-mark on him," and the wooden shingle "painted so like marble that it sank in water," as if its very consciousness or its vanity had been over-persuaded by the cunning of the painter. I heard a man, in order to give a notion of some very cold weather, say to another that a certain Joe, who had been taking mercury, found a lump of quicksilver in each boot, when he went home to dinner. This power of rapidly dramatizing a dry fact into flesh and blood, and the vivid conception of Joe as a human thermometer, strike me as showing a poetic sense that may be refined into faculty. At any rate, there is humor here, and not mere quickness of wit, — the deeper and not the shallower quality. The *tendency* of humor is always towards overplus of expression, while the very essence of wit is its logical precision. Captain Basil Hall denied that our people had any humor, deceived, perhaps, by their gravity of manner. But this very seriousness is often the outward sign of that humorous quality of the mind which delights in finding an element of identity in things seemingly the most incongruous, and then again in forcing an incongruity upon things identical. Perhaps Captain Hall had no humor himself, and if so he would never find it. Did he always feel the point of what was said to himself? I doubt it, because I happen to know a chance he once had given him in vain. The Captain was walking up and down the veranda of a country tavern in Massachusetts while the coach changed horses. A thunder-storm was going on, and, with that pleasant European air of indirect self-compliment in condescending to be surprised by American merit, which we find so conciliating, he said to a countryman lounging against the door, "Pretty heavy thunder you have here." The other, who had divined at a glance his feeling of generous concession to a new country, drawled gravely, "Waal, we *du*, considerin' the number of inhabitants." This, the more I analyze it, the more humorous does it seem. The same man was capable of wit also, when he would. He was a cabinet-maker, and was once employed to make some commandment-tables for the parish meeting-house. The parson, a very old man, annoyed him by looking into his workshop every morning, and cautioning him to be very sure to pick out "clear mahogany without any *knots* in it." At last, wearied out, he retorted one day, "Wal, Dr. B., I guess ef I was to leave the *nots* out o' some o' the c'man'ments, 't 'ould soot you full ez wal!"

If I had taken the pains to write down the proverbial or pithy phrases I have heard, or if I had sooner thought of noting the Yankeeisms I met with in my reading, I might have been able to do more justice to my theme. But I have done all I wished in respect to pronunciation, if I have proved that where we are vulgar, we have the countenance of very good company. For, as to the *jus et norma loquendi*, I agree with Horace and those who have paraphrased or commented him, from Boileau to Gray. I think that a good rule for style is Galiani's definition of sublime oratory, — "l'art de tout dire sans être mis à la Bastille dans un pays où il est défendu de rien dire." I profess myself a fanatical purist, but with a hearty contempt for the speech-gilders who affect purism without any thorough, or even pedagogic, knowledge of the engendure, growth, and affinities of the noble language about whose *mésalliances* they profess (like Dean Alford) to be so solicitous. If *they* had their way —! "Doch es sey," says Lessing, "dass jene gothische Höflichkeit eine unentbehrliche Tugend des heutigen Umganges ist. Soll sie darum unsere Schriften eben so schaal und falsch machen als unsern Umgang?" And Drayton was not far wrong in affirming that

> "'T is possible to climb,
> To kindle, or to slake,
> Although in Skelton's rhyme."

Cumberland in his Memoirs tells us that when, in the midst of Admiral Rodney's great sea-fight, Sir Charles Douglas said to him, "Behold, Sir George, the

Greeks and Trojans contending for the body of Patroclus!" the Admiral answered, peevishly, "Damn the Greeks and damn the Trojans! I have other things to think of." After the battle was won, Rodney thus to Sir Charles, "Now, my dear friend, I am at the service of your Greeks and Trojans, and the whole of Homer's Iliad, or as much of it as you please!" I had some such feeling of the impertinence of our pseudo-classicality when I chose our homely dialect to work in. Should we be nothing, because somebody had contrived to be something (and that perhaps in a provincial dialect) ages ago? and to be nothing by our very attempt to be that something which they had already been, and which therefore nobody could be again without being a bore? Is there no way left, then, I thought, of being natural, of being *naïf*, which means nothing more than native, of belonging to the age and country in which you are born? The Yankee, at least, is a new phenomenon; let us try to be *that*. It is perhaps a *pis aller*, but is not *No Thoroughfare* written up everywhere else? In the literary world, things seemed to me very much as they were in the latter half of the last century. Pope, skimming the cream of good sense and expression wherever he could find it, had made, not exactly poetry, but an honest, salable butter of worldly wisdom which pleasantly lubricated some of the drier morsels of life's daily bread, and seeing this, scores of harmlessly insane people went on for the next fifty years coaxing his buttermilk with the regular up and down of the pentameter churn. And in our day, do we not scent everywhere, and even carry away in our clothes against our will, that faint perfume of musk which Mr. Tennyson has left behind him, or, worse, of Heine's *pachouli?* And might it not be possible to escape them by turning into one of our narrow New England lanes, shut in though it were by bleak stone walls on either hand, and where no better flowers were to be gathered than golden-rod and hardhack?

Beside the advantage of getting out of the beaten track, our dialect offered others hardly inferior. As I was about to make an endeavor to state them, I remembered something which the clear-sighted Goethe had said about Hebel's *Allemannische Gedichte*, which, making proper deduction for special reference to the book under review, expresses what I would have said far better than I could hope to do: "Allen diesen innern guten Eigenschaften kommt die behagliche naive Sprache sehr zu statten. Man findet mehrere sinnlich bedeutende und wohlklingende Worte . . . von einem, zwei Buchstaben, Abbreviationen, Contractionen, viele kurze, leichte Sylben, neue Reime, welches, mehr als man glaubt, ein Vortheil für den Dichter ist. Diese Elemente werden durch glückliche Constructionen und lebhafte Formen zu einem Styl zusammengedrängt der zu diesem Zwecke vor unserer Büchersprache grosse Vorzüge hat." Of course I do not mean to imply that *I* have come near achieving any such success as the great critic here indicates, but I think the success is *there*, and to be plucked by some more fortunate hand.

Nevertheless, I was encouraged by the approval of many whose opinions I valued. With a feeling too tender and grateful to be mixed with any vanity, I mention as one of these the late A. H. Clough, who, more than any one of those I have known (no longer living), except Hawthorne, impressed me with the constant presence of that indefinable thing we call genius. He often suggested that I should try my hand at some Yankee Pastorals, which would admit of more sentiment and a higher tone without foregoing the advantage offered by the dialect. I have never completed anything of the kind, but, in this Second Series, both my remembrance of his counsel and the deeper feeling called up by the great interests at stake, led me to venture some passages nearer to what is called poetical than could have been admitted without incongruity into the former series. The time seemed calling to me, with the old poet, —

> "Leave, then, your wonted prattle,
> The oaten reed forbear;
> For I hear a sound of battle,
> And trumpets rend the air!"

The only attempt I had ever made at anything like a pastoral (if that may be called an attempt which was the result almost of pure accident) was in "The Courtin'." While the introduction to the First Series was going through the press, I received word from the printer that there was a blank page left which must be filled. I sat down at once and improvised another fictitious "notice of the press," in which, because verse would fill up space more cheaply than prose, I inserted an extract from a supposed ballad of Mr. Biglow. I kept no copy of it, and the printer, as directed, cut it off when the gap was filled. Presently I began to receive letters asking for the rest of it, sometimes for the *balance* of it. I had none, but to answer such demands, I patched a conclusion upon it in a later edition. Those who had only the first continued to importune me. Afterward, being asked to write it out as an autograph for the Baltimore Sanitary Commission Fair, I added other verses, into some of which I infused a little more sentiment in a homely way, and after a fashion completed it by sketching in the characters and making a connected story. Most likely I have spoiled it, but I shall put it at the end of this Introduction, to answer once for all those kindly importunings.

As I have seen extracts from what purported to be writings of Mr. Biglow, which were not genuine, I may properly take this opportunity to say, that the two volumes now published contain every line I ever printed under that pseudonyme, and that I have never, so far as I can remember, written an anonymous article (elsewhere than in the *North American Review,* and the *Atlantic Monthly,* during my editorship of it) except a review of Mrs. Stowe's "Minister's Wooing," and, some twenty years ago, a sketch of the anti-slavery movement in America for an English journal.

A word more on pronunciation. I have endeavored to express this so far as I could by the types, taking such pains as, I fear, may sometimes make the reading harder than need be. At the same time, by studying uniformity I have sometimes been obliged to sacrifice minute exactness. The emphasis often modifies the habitual sound. For example, *for* is commonly *fer* (a shorter sound than *fur* for *far*), but when emphatic it always becomes *for*, as "wut *for?*" So *too* is pronounced like *to* (as it was anciently spelt), and *to* like *ta* (the sound as in the *tou* of *touch*), but *too*, when emphatic, changes into *tue* and *to*, sometimes, in similar cases, into *toe*, as, "I did n' hardly know wut *toe* du!" Where vowels come together, or one precedes another following an aspirate, the two melt together, as was common with the older poets who formed their versification on French or Italian models. Drayton is thoroughly Yankee when he says "I 'xpect," and Pope when he says "t' inspire." *With* becomes sometimes *'ith*, *'ŭth*, or *'th*, or even disappears wholly where it comes before *the*, as, "I went along th' Square" (along with the Squire), the *are* sound being an archaism which I have noticed also in *choir*, like the old Scottish *quhair*. (Herrick has, "Of flowers n'er sucked by th' theeving bee.") *Without* becomes *athout* and *'thout*. *Afterwards* always retains its locative *s*, and is pronounced always *ahterwurds'*, with a strong accent on the last syllable. This oddity has some support in the erratic *towards'* instead of *to'wards*, which we find in the poets and sometimes hear. The sound given to the first syllable of *to'wards*, I may remark, sustains the Yankee lengthening of the *o* in *to*. At the beginning of a sentence, *ahterwurds* has the accent on the first syllable; at the end of one, on the last; as "*ah'terwurds* he tol' me," "he tol' me *ahterwurds'*." The Yankee never makes a mistake in his aspirates. *U* changes in many words to *e*, always in *such*, *brush*, *tush*, *hush*, *rush*, *blush*, seldom in *much*, oftener in *trust* and *crust*, never in *mush*, *gust*, *bust*, *tumble*, or (?) *flush*, in the latter case probably to avoid confusion with *flesh*. I have heard *flush* with the *ĕ* sound, however. For the same reason, I suspect, never in *gush*, (at least, I never heard it,) because we have already one *gesh* for *gash*. *A* and *i* short frequently become *e* short. *U* always becomes *o* in the prefix *un* (except *unto*), and *o* in return changes to *u* short in *uv* for *of*, and in some words beginning with *om*. *T* and *d*, *b* and *p*, *v* and *w*, remain intact. So much occurs to me in addition to what I said on this head in the preface to the former volume.

Of course in what I have said I wish to be understood as keeping in mind the difference between provincialisms properly so called and *slang*. *Slang* is always vulgar, because it is not a natural but an affected way of talking, and all mere tricks of speech or writing are offensive. I do not think that Mr. Biglow can be fairly charged with vulgarity, and I should have entirely failed in my design, if I have not made it appear that high and even refined sentiment may coexist with the shrewder and more comio elements of the Yankee character. I believe that what is essentially vulgar and mean-spirited in politics seldom has its source in the body of the people, but much rather among those who are made timid by their wealth or selfish by their love of power. A democracy can *afford* much better than an aristocracy to follow out its convictions, and is perhaps better qualified to build those convictions on plain principles of right and wrong, rather than on the shifting sands of expediency. I had always thought " Sam Slick " a libel on the Yankee character, and a complete falsification of Yankee modes of speech, though, for aught I know, it may be true in both respects so far as the British Provinces are concerned. To me the dialect was native, was spoken all about me when a boy, at a time when an Irish day-laborer was as rare as an American one now. Since then I have made a study of it so far as opportunity allowed. But when I write in it, it is as in a mother tongue, and I am carried back far beyond any studies of it to long-ago noonings in my father's hay-fields, and to the talk of Sam and Job over their jug of *blackstrap* under the shadow of the ash-tree which still dapples the grass whence they have been gone so long.

But life is short, and prefaces should be. And so, my good friends, to whom this introductory epistle is addressed, farewell. Though some of you have remonstrated with me, I shall never write any more " Biglow Papers," however great the temptation, — great especially at the present time, — unless it be to complete the original plan of this Series by bringing out Mr. Sawin as an " original Union man." The very favor with which they have been received is a hindrance to me, by forcing on me a self-consciousness from which I was entirely free when I wrote the First Series. Moreover, I am no longer the same careless youth, with nothing to do but live to myself, my books, and my friends, that I was then. I always hated politics, in the ordinary sense of the word, and I am not likely to grow fonder of them, now that I have learned how rare it is to find a man who can keep principle clear from party and personal prejudice, or can conceive the possibility of another's doing so. I feel as if I could in some sort claim to be an *emeritus*, and I am sure that political satire will have

2 K

full justice done it by that genuine and delightful humorist, the Rev. Petroleum V. Nasby. I regret that I killed off Mr. Wilbur so soon, for he would have enabled me to bring into this preface a number of learned quotations, which must now go a-begging, and would have enabled me to dispersonalize myself into a vicarious egotism. He would have helped me also in clearing myself from a charge which I shall briefly touch on, because my friend Mr. Hughes has found it needful to defend me in his preface to one of the English editions of the "Biglow Papers." I thank Mr. Hughes heartily for his friendly care of my good name, and were his Preface accessible to my readers here, (as I am glad it is not, for its partiality makes me blush,) I should leave the matter where he left it. The charge is of profanity, brought in by persons who proclaimed African slavery of Divine institution, and is based (so far as I have heard) on two passages in the First Series, —

> " An' you 've gut to git up airly,
> Ef you want to take in God,"

and,

> " God 'll send the bill to you," —

and on some Scriptural illustrations by Mr. Sawin.

Now, in the first place, I was writing under an assumed character, and must talk as the person would whose mouthpiece I made myself. Will any one familiar with the New England countryman venture to tell me that he does *not* speak of sacred things familiarly? that Biblical allusions (allusions, that is, to the single book with whose language, from his church-going habits, he is intimate) are *not* frequent on his lips? If so, he cannot have pursued his studies of the character on so many long-ago muster-fields and at so many cattle-shows as I. But I scorn any such line of defence, and will confess at once that one of the things I am proud of in my countrymen is (I am not speaking now of such persons as I have assumed Mr. Sawin to be) that they do not put their Maker away far from them, or interpret the fear of God into being afraid of Him. The Talmudists had conceived a deep truth when they said, that "all things were in the power of God, save the fear of God"; and when

people stand in great dread of an invisible power, I sus-
pect they mistake quite another personage for the Deity.
I might justify myself for the passages criticised by many
parallel ones from Scripture, but I need not. The Rev-
erend Homer Wilbur's note-books supply me with three
apposite quotations. The first is from a Father of the
Roman Church, the second from a Father of the Angli-
can, and the third from a Father of modern English
poetry. The Puritan divines would furnish me with
many more such. St. Bernard says, *Sapiens nummula-
rius est Deus: nummum fictum non recipiet;* "A cunning
money-changer is God: he will take in no base coin."
Latimer says, "You shall perceive that God, by this ex-
ample, shaketh us by the noses and taketh us by the ears."
Familiar enough, both of them, one would say! But I
should think Mr. Biglow had verily stolen the last of the
two maligned passages from Dryden's "Don Sebastian,"
where I find

"And beg of Heaven to charge the bill on me!"

And there I leave the matter, being willing to believe
that the Saint, the Martyr, and even the Poet, were as
careful of God's honor as my critics are ever likely to be.

J. R. L.

THE COURTIN'.

God makes sech nights, all white an' still
　　Fur 'z you can look or listen,
Moonshine an' snow on field an' hill,
　　All silence an' all glisten.

Zekle crep' up quite unbeknown
　　An' peeked in thru' the winder,
An' there sot Huldy all alone,
　　'Ith no one nigh to hender.

A fireplace filled the room's one side
　　With half a cord o' wood in —
There warn't no stoves (tell comfort died)
　　To bake ye to a puddin'.

The wa'nut logs shot sparkles out
　　Towards the pootiest, bless her,
An' leetle flames danced all about
　　The chiny on the dresser.

Agin the chimbley crook-necks hung,
　　An' in amongst 'em rusted
The ole queen's-arm thet gran'ther Young
　　Fetched back from Concord busted.

The very room, coz she was in,
　　Seemed warm from floor to ceilin',
An' she looked full ez rosy agin
　　Ez the apples she was peelin'.

'T was kin' o' kingdom-come to look
　　On sech a blessed cretur,
A dogrose blushin' to a brook
　　Ain't modester nor sweeter.

He was six foot o' man, A 1,
　　Clean grit an' human natur';
None could n't quicker pitch a ton
　　Nor dror a furrer straighter.

He 'd sparked it with full twenty gals,
 He 'd squired 'em, danced 'em, druv 'em,
Fust this one, an' then thet, by spells —
 All is, he could n't love 'em.

But long o' her his veins 'ould run
 All crinkly like curled maple,
The side she breshed felt full o' sun
 Ez a south slope in Ap'il.

She thought no v'ice hed sech a swing
 Ez hisn in the choir;
My ! when he made Ole Hunderd ring,
 She *knowed* the Lord was nigher.

An' she 'd blush scarlit, right in prayer,
 When her new meetin'-bunnet
Felt somehow thru' its crown a pair
 O' blue eyes sot upon it.

Thet night, I tell ye, she looked *some !*
 She seemed to 've gut a new soul,
For she felt sartin-sure he 'd come,
 Down to her very shoe-sole.

She heered a foot, an' knowed it tu,
 A-raspin' on the scraper, —
All ways to once her feelin's flew
 Like sparks in burnt-up paper.

He kin' o' l'itered on the mat
 Some doubtfle o' the sekle,
His heart kep' goin' pity-pat,
 But hern went pity Zekle.

An' yit she gin her cheer a jerk
 Ez though she wished him furder,
An' on her apples kep' to work,
 Parin' away like murder.

" You want to see my Pa, I s'pose ? "
　" Wal . . . no . . . I come dasignin' " —
" To see my Ma ?　She is sprinklin' clo'es
　Agin to-morrer's i'nin'."

To say why gals acts so or so,
　Or don't, 'ould be presumin';
Mebby to mean *yes* an' say *no*
　Comes nateral to women.

He stood a spell on one foot fust,
　Then stood a spell on t'other,
An' on which one he felt the wust
　He could n't ha' told ye nuther.

Says he, " I 'd better call agin " ;
　Says she, " Think likely, Mister " ;
Thet last word pricked him like a pin,
　An' . . . Wal, he up an' kist her.

When Ma bimeby upon 'em slips,
　Huldy sot pale ez ashes,
All kin' o' smily roun' the lips
　An' teary roun' the lashes.

For she was jes' the quiet kind
　Whose naturs never vary,
Like streams that keep a summer mind
　Snowhid in Jenooary.

The blood clost roun' her heart felt glued
　Too tight for all expressin',
Tell mother see how metters stood,
　And gin 'em both her blessin'.

Then her red come back like the tide
　Down to the Bay o' Fundy,
An' all I know is they was cried
　In meetin' come nex' Sunday.

THE BIGLOW PAPERS.

No. I.

BIRDOFREDUM SAWIN, ESQ., TO MR. HOSEA BIGLOW.

LETTER FROM THE REVEREND HOMER WILBUR, M. A., ENCLOSING THE EPISTLE AFORESAID.

JAALAM, 15th Nov., 1861.

*   *   *   *   *

IT is not from any idle wish to obtrude my humble person with undue prominence upon the publick view that I resume my pen upon the present occasion. *Juniores ad labores.* But having been a main instrument in rescuing the talent of my young parishioner from being buried in the ground, by giving it such warrant with the world as could be derived from a name already widely known by several printed discourses (all of which I may be permitted without immodesty to state have been deemed worthy of preservation in the Library of Harvard College by my esteemed friend Mr. Sibley), it seemed becoming that I should not only testify to the genuineness of the following production, but call attention to it, the more as Mr. Biglow had so long been silent as to be in danger of absolute oblivion. I insinuate no claim to any share in the authorship (*vix ea nostra voco*) of the works already published by Mr. Biglow, but merely take to myself the credit of having fulfilled toward them the office of taster (*experto crede*), who, having first tried, could afterward bear witness (*credenzen* it was aptly named by the Germans), an office always arduous, and sometimes even

503

dangerous, as in the case of those devoted persons who
venture their lives in the deglutition of patent medicines
(*dolus latet in generalibus,* there is deceit in the most
of them) and thereafter are wonderfully preserved long
enough to append their signatures to testimonials in the
diurnal and hebdomadal prints. I say not this as cov-
ertly glancing at the authors of certain manuscripts which
have been submitted to my literary judgment (though an
epick in twenty-four books on the "Taking of Jericho"
might, save for the prudent forethought of Mrs. Wilbur
in secreting the same just as I had arrived beneath the
walls and was beginning a catalogue of the various horns
and their blowers, too ambitiously emulous in longanimity
of Homer's list of ships, might, I say, have rendered frus-
trate any hope I could entertain *vacare Musis* for the small
remainder of my days), but only the further to secure my-
self against any imputation of unseemly forthputting.
I will barely subjoin, in this connexion, that, whereas Job
was left to desire, in the soreness of his heart, that his
adversary had written a book, as perchance misanthropi-
cally wishing to indite a review thereof, yet was not Satan
allowed so far to tempt him as to send Bildad, Eliphaz,
and Zophar each with an unprinted work in his wallet to
be submitted to his censure. But of this enough. Were
I in need of other excuse, I might add that I write by the
express desire of Mr. Biglow himself, whose entire winter
leisure is occupied, as he assures me, in answering de-
mands for autographs, a labour exacting enough in itself,
and egregiously so to him, who, being no ready penman,
cannot sign so much as his name without strange contor-
tions of the face (his nose, even, being essential to com-
plete success) and painfully suppressed Saint-Vitus-dance
of every muscle in his body. This, with his having been
put in the Commission of the Peace by our excellent Gov-
ernor (*O, si sic omnes!*) immediately on his accession to
office, keeps him continually employed. *Haud inexpertus
loquor,* having for many years written myself J. P., and
being not seldom applied to for specimens of my chirog-
raphy, a request to which I have sometimes over weakly
assented, believing as I do that nothing written of set
purpose can properly be called an autograph, but only
those unpremeditated sallies and lively runnings which
betray the fireside Man instead of the hunted Notoriety

doubling on his pursuers. But it is time that I should bethink me of St. Austin's prayer, *libera me a meipso*, if I would arrive at the matter in hand.

Moreover, I had yet another reason for taking up the pen myself. I am informed that the *Atlantic Monthly* is mainly indebted for its success to the contributions and editorial supervision of Dr. Holmes, whose excellent "Annals of America" occupy an honoured place upon my shelves. The journal itself I have never seen; but if this be so, it might seem that the recommendation of a brother-clergyman (though *par magis quam similis*) should carry a greater weight. I suppose that you have a department for historical lucubrations, and should be glad, if deemed desirable, to forward for publication my "Collections for the Antiquities of Jaalam," and my (now happily complete) pedigree of the Wilbur family from its *fons et origo*, the Wild Boar of Ardennes. Withdrawn from the active duties of my profession by the settlement of a colleague-pastor, the Reverend Jeduthun Hitchcock, formerly of Brutus Four-Corners, I might find time for further contributions to general literature on similar topicks. I have made large advances towards a completer genealogy of Mrs. Wilbur's family, the Pilcoxes, not, if I know myself, from any idle vanity, but with the sole desire of rendering myself useful in my day and generation. *Nulla dies sine lineâ*. I inclose a meteorological register, a list of the births, deaths, and marriages, and a few *memorabilia* of longevity in Jaalam East Parish for the last half-century. Though spared to the unusual period of more than eighty years, I find no diminution of my faculties or abatement of my natural vigour, except a scarcely sensible decay of memory and a necessity of recurring to younger eyesight or spectacles for the finer print in Cruden. It would gratify me to make some further provision for declining years from the emoluments of my literary labours. I had intended to effect an insurance on my life, but was deterred therefrom by a circular from one of the offices, in which the sudden death of so large a proportion of the insured was set forth as an inducement, that it seemed to me little less than a tempting of Providence. *Neque in summâ inopiâ levis esse senectus potest, ne sapienti quidem.*

Thus far concerning Mr. Biglow; and so much seemed

needful (*brevis esse laboro*) by way of preliminary, after a silence of fourteen years. He greatly fears lest he may in this essay have fallen below himself, well knowing that, if exercise be dangerous on a full stomach, no less so is writing on a full reputation. Beset as he has been on all sides, he could not refrain, and would only imprecate patience till he shall again have " got the hang " (as he calls it) of an accomplishment long disused. The letter of Mr. Sawin was received some time in last June, and others have followed which will in due season be submitted to the publick. How largely his statements are to be depended on, I more than merely dubitate. He was always distinguished for a tendency to exaggeration — it might almost be qualified by a stronger term. *Fortiter mentire, aliquid hœret,* seemed to be his favourite rule of rhetorick. That he is actually where he says he is the post-mark would seem to confirm; that he was received with the publick demonstrations he describes would appear consonant with what we know of the habits of those regions; but further than this I venture not to decide. I have sometimes suspected a vein of humour in him which leads him to speak by contraries; but since, in the unrestrained intercourse of private life, I have never observed in him any striking powers of invention, I am the more willing to put a certain qualified faith in the incidents and the details of life and manners which give to his narratives some portion of the interest and entertainment which characterizes a Century Sermon.

It may be expected of me that I should say something to justify myself with the world for a seeming inconsistency with my well-known principles in allowing my youngest son to raise a company for the war, a fact known to all through the medium of the publick prints. I did reason with the young man, but *expellas naturam furcâ, tamenusque recurrit.* Having myself been a chaplain in 1812, I could the less wonder that a man of war had sprung from my loins. It was, indeed, grievous to send my Benjamin, the child of my old age; but after the discomfiture of Manassas, I with my own hands did buckle on his armour, trusting in the great Comforter and Commander for strength according to my need. For truly the memory of a brave son dead in his shroud were a greater staff of my declining years than a living coward, (if those may be said to have lived who carry all of

themselves into the grave with them,) though his days
might be long in the land, and he should get much goods.
It is not till our earthen vessels are broken that we find
and truly possess the treasure that was laid up in them.
Migravi in animam meam, I have sought refuge in my
own soul ; nor would I be shamed by the heathen come-
dian with his *Nequam illud verbum, bene vult, nisi bene
facit.* During our dark days, I read constantly in the
inspired book of Job, which I believe to contain more
food to maintain the fibre of the soul for right living and
high thinking than all pagan literature together, though
I would by no means vilipend the study of the classicks.
There I read that Job said in his despair, even as the
fool saith in his heart there is no God, — " The taber-
nacles of robbers prosper, and they that provoke God are
secure." (*Job* xii. 6.) But I sought farther till I found
this Scripture also, which I would have those perpend
who have striven to turn our Israel aside to the worship
of strange gods : — " If I did despise the cause of my
man-servant or of my maid-servant when they contended
with me, what then shall I do when God riseth up ? and
when he visiteth, what shall I answer him ? " (*Job* xxxi.
13, 14.) On this text I preached a discourse on the last
day of Fasting and Humiliation with general acceptance,
though there were not wanting one or two Laodiceans
who said that I should have waited till the President
announced his policy. But let us hope and pray, re-
membering this of Saint Gregory, *Vult Deus rogari, vult
cogi, vult quâdam importunitate vinci.*

We had our first fall of snow on Friday last. Frosts
have been unusually backward this fall. A singular cir-
cumstance occurred in this town on the 20th October,
in the family of Deacon Pelatiah Tinkham. On the
previous evening, a few moments before family-prayers,

* * * * *

[The editors of the *Atlantic* find it necessary here to
cut short the letter of their valued correspondent, which
seemed calculated rather on the rates of longevity in
Jaalam than for less favored localities. They have every
encouragement to hope that he will write again.]

With esteem and respect,

Your obedient servant,

Homer Wilbur, A. M.

It 's some consid'ble of a spell sence I hain't writ no
    letters,
An' ther' 's gret changes hez took place in all polit'cle
    metters :
Some canderdates air dead an' gone, an' some hez ben
    defeated,
Which 'mounts to pooty much the same; fer it 's ben
    proved repeated
A betch o' bread thet hain't riz once ain't goin' to rise
    agin,
An' it 's jest money throwed away to put the emptins in :
But thet 's wut folks wun't never larn; they dunno how
    to go,
Arter you want their room, no more 'n a bullet-headed
    beau ;
Ther' 's ollers chaps a-hangin' roun' thet can't see pea-
    time 's past,
Mis'ble as roosters in a rain, heads down an' tails half-
    mast :
It ain't disgraceful bein' beat, when a holl nation doos it,
But Chance is like an amberill, — it don't take twice to
    lose it.

I spose you 're kin' o' cur'ous, now, to know why I hain't
    writ.
Wal, I 've ben where a litt'ry taste don't somehow seem
    to git
Th' encouragement a feller 'd think, thet 's used to public
    schools,
An' where sech things ez paper 'n' ink air clean agin the
    rules :
A kind o' vicyvarsy house, built dreffle strong an' stout,
So 's 't honest people can't git in, ner t' other sort git out,
An' with the winders so contrived, you 'd prob'ly like the
    view
Better alookin' in than out, though it seems sing'lar, tu ;
But then the landlord sets by ye, can't bear ye out o'
    sight,
And locks ye up ez reg'lar ez an outside door at night.

This world is awfle contrary : the rope may stretch your
    neck
Thet mebby kep' another chap frum washin' off a wreck;

An' you may see the taters grow in one poor feller's
    patch,
So small no self-respectin' hen thet vallied time 'ould
    scratch,
So small the rot can't find 'em out, an' then agin, nex'
    · door,
Ez big ez wut hogs dream on when they 're 'most too fat
    to snore.
But groutin' ain't no kin' o' use ; an' ef the fust throw
    fails,
Why, up an' try agin, thet 's all, — the coppers ain't all
    tails ;
Though I *hev* seen 'em when I thought they hed n't no
    more head
Than 'd sarve a nussin' Brigadier thet gits some ink to
    shed.

When I writ last, I 'd ben turned loose by thet blamed
    nigger, Pomp,
Ferlorner than a musquash, ef you 'd took an' dreened his
    swamp :
But I ain't o' the meechin' kind, thet sets an' thinks fer
    weeks
The bottom 's out o' th' univarse coz their own gillpot
    leaks.
I hed to cross bayous an' criks, (wal, it did beat all
    natur',)
Upon a kin' o' corderoy, fust log, then alligator:
Luck'ly the critters warn't sharp-sot ; I guess 't wuz over-
    ruled
They 'd done their mornin's marketin' an' gut their hun-
    ger cooled ;
Fer missionaries to the Creeks an' runaways are viewed
By them an' folks ez sent express to be their reg'lar
    food :
Wutever 't wuz, they laid an' snoozed ez peacefully ez
    sinners,
Meek ez disgestin' deacons be at ordination dinners ;
Ef any on 'em turned an' snapped, I let 'em kin' o' taste
My live-oak leg, an' so, ye see, ther' warn't no gret o'
    waste ;
Fer they found out in quicker time than ef they 'd ben to
    college

T' warn't heartier food than though 't wuz made out o' the
    tree o' knowledge.
But *I* tell *you* my other leg hed larned wut pizon-nettle
    meant,
An' var'ous other usefle things, afore I reached a settle-
    ment,
An' all o' me thet wuz n't sore an' sendin' prickles thru
    me
Wuz jest the leg I parted with in lickin' Montezumy :
A usefle limb it 's ben to me, an' more of a support
Than wut the other hez ben, — coz I dror my pension
    for 't.

Wal, I gut in at last where folks wuz civerlized an'
    white, ·
Ez I diskivered to my cost afore 't warn't hardly night ;
Fer 'z I wuz settin' in the bar a-takin' sunthin' hot,
An' feelin' like a man agin, all over in one spot,
A feller thet sot opposite, arter a squint at me,
Lep up an' drawed his peacemaker, an', " Dash it, Sir,"
    suz he,
" I 'm doubledashed ef you ain't him thet stole my yaller
    chettle,
(You 're all the stranger thet 's around,) so now you 've
    gut to settle ;
It ain't no use to argerfy ner try to cut up frisky,
I know ye ez I know the smell of ole chain-lightnin'
    whiskey ;
We 're lor-abidin' folks down here, we 'll fix ye so 's 't a
    bar
Would n' tech ye with a ten-foot pole ; (Jedge, you jest
    warm the tar ;)
You 'll think you 'd better ha' gut among a tribe o'
    Mongrel Tartars,
'Fore we 've done showin' how we raise our Southun
    prize tar-martyrs ;
A moultin' fallen cherubim, ef he should see ye, 'd
    snicker,
Thinkin' he warn't a suckemstance. Come, genlemun,
    le' 's liquor ;
An', Gin'ral, when you 've mixed the drinks an' chalked
    'em up, tote roun'

An' see ef ther' 's a feather-bed (thet 's borryable) in town.
We 'll try ye fair, ole Grafted-Leg, an' ef the tar wun't
    stick,
Th' ain't not a juror here but wut 'll 'quit ye double-
    quick."
To cut it short, I wun't say sweet, they gi' me a good
    dip,
(They ain't *perfessin'* Bahptists here,) then give the bed
    a rip, —
The jury 'd sot, an' quicker 'n a flash they hetched me
    out, a livin'
Extemp'ry mammoth turkey-chick fer a Fejee Thanks-
    givin'.
Thet I felt some stuck up is wut it 's nat'ral to suppose,
When poppylar enthusiasm hed funnished me sech
    clo'es;
(Ner 't ain't without edvantiges, this kin' o' suit, ye
    see,
It 's water-proof, an' water 's wut I like kep' out o' me;)
But nut content with thet, they took a kerridge from the
    fence
An' rid me roun' to see the place, entirely free 'f ex-
    pense,
With forty-'leven new kines o' sarse without no charge
    acquainted me,
Gi' me three cheers, an' vowed thet I wuz all their
    fahncy painted me;
They treated me to all their eggs; (they keep 'em I
    should think,
Fer sech ovations, pooty long, for they wuz mos' dis-
    tinc';)
They starred me thick 'z the Milky-Way with indiscrim'-
    nit cherity,
Fer wut we call reception eggs air sunthin' of a rerity;
Green ones is plentifle anough, skurce wuth a nigger's
    getherin',
But your dead-ripe ones ranges high fer treatin' Nothun
    bretherin:
A spotteder, ringstreakeder child the' warn't in Uncle
    Sam's
Holl farm, — a cross of stripëd pig an' one o' Jacob's
    lambs;
'T wuz Dannil in the lions' den, new an' enlarged edit*i*on,

An' everythin' fust-rate o' 'ts kind, the' warn't no im-
    persition.
People's impulsiver down here than wut our folks to
    home be,
An' kin' o' go it 'ith a resh in raisin' Hail Columby:
Thet's *so :* an' they swarmed out like bees, for your real
    Southun men's
Time is n't o' much more account than an ole settin' hen's;
(They jest work semioccashnally, or else don't work at all,
An' so their time an' 'tention both air et saci'ty's call.)
Talk about hospatality! wut Nothun town d' ye know
Would take a totle stranger up an' treat him gratis so?
You'd better b'lieve ther''s nothin' like this spendin'
    days an' nights
Along 'ith a dependent race fer civerlizin' whites.

But this wuz all prelim'nary; it's so Gran' Jurors here
Fin' a true bill, a hendier way than ourn, an' nut so dear;
So arter this they sentenced me, to make all tight 'n'
    snug,
Afore a reg'lar court o' law, to ten years in the Jug.
I did n' make no gret defence: you don't feel much like
    speakin',
When, ef you let your clamshells gape, a quart o' tar
    will leak in:
I *hev* hearn tell o' wingëd words, but pint o' fact it
    tethers
The spoutin' gift to hev your words *tu* thick sot on with
    feathers,
An' Choate ner Webster would n't ha' made an A 1 kin'
    o' speech
Astride a Southun chestnut horse sharper 'n a baby's
    screech.
Two year ago they ketched the thief, 'n' seein' I wuz
    innercent,
They jest oncorked an' le' me run, an' in my stid the
    sinner sent
To see how *he* liked pork 'n' pone flavored with wa'nut
    saplin',
An' nary social priv'ledge but a one-hoss, starn-wheel
    chaplin.
When I come out, the folks behaved mos' gen'manly an'
    harnsome;

They 'lowed it would n't be more 'n right, ef I should cuss
 'n' darn some :
The Cunnle he apolergized; suz he, "I'll du wut's
 right,
I'll give ye settisfection now by shootin' ye at sight,
An' give the nigger, (when he's caught,) to pay him fer
 his trickin'
In gittin' the wrong man took up, a most H fired
 lickin',—
It's jest the way with all on 'em, the inconsistent
 critters,
They're 'most enough to make a man blaspheme his
 mornin' bitters;
I'll be your frien' thru thick an' thin an' in all kines
 o' weathers,
An' all you'll hev to pay fer's jest the waste o' tar an'
 feathers :
A lady owned the bed, ye see, a widder, tu, Miss Shen-
 non ;
It wuz her mite; we would ha' took another, ef ther 'd
 ben one :
We don't make *no* charge for the ride an' all the other
 fixins.
Le' 's liquor; Gin'ral, you can chalk our friend for all
 the mixins."
A meetin' then wuz called, where they "RESOLVED, Thet
 we respec'
B. S. Esquire for quallerties o' heart an' intellec'
Peculiar to Columby's sile, an' not to no one else's,
Thet makes Európean tyrans scringe in all their gilded
 pel'ces,
An' doos gret honor to our race an' Southun institoo-
 tions" :
(I give ye jest the substance o' the leadin' resoloo-
 tibns :)
"RESOLVED, Thet we revere in him a soger 'thout a flor,
A martyr to the princerples o' libbaty an' lor :
RESOLVED, Thet other nations all, ef sot 'longside o' us,
For vartoo, larnin', chivverlry, ain't noways wuth a cuss."
They gut up a subscription, tu, but no gret come o' *thet ;*
I 'xpect in cairin' of it roun' they took a leaky hat;
Though Southun genelmun ain't slow at puttin' down
 their name,

2 L

(When they can write,) fer in the eend it comes to jes'
    the same,
Because, ye see, 't 's the fashion here to sign an' not to
    think
A critter 'd be so sordid ez to ax 'em for the chink:
I did n't call but jest on one, an' *he* drawed toothpick on
    me,
An' reckoned he warn't goin' to stan' no sech dog-
    gauned econ'my;
So nothin' more wuz realized, 'ceptin' the good-will
    shown,
Than ef 't had ben from fust to last a reg'lar Cotton
    Loan.
It 's a good way, though; come to think, coz ye enjy the
    sense
O' lendin' lib'rally to the Lord, an' nary red o' 'xpense:
Sence then I 've gut my name up for a gin'rous-hearted
    man
By jes' subscribin' right an' left on this high-minded
    plan;
I 've gin away my thousans so to every Southun sort
O' missions, colleges, an' sech, ner ain't no poorer for 't.

I warn't so bad off, arter all; I need n't hardly mention
That Guv'ment owed me quite a pile for my arrears o'
    pension, —
I mean the poor, weak thing we *hed:* we run a new one
    now,
Thet strings a feller with a claim up ta the nighes' bough,
An' *prectises* the rights o' man, purtects down-trodden
    debtors,
Ner wun't hev creditors about a-scrougin' o' their betters:
Jeff's gut the last idees ther' is, poscrip', fourteenth
    edition,
He knows it takes some enterprise to run an oppersition;
Ourn 's the fust thru-by-daylight train, with all ou'doors
    for deepot,
Yourn goes so slow you 'd think 't wuz drawed by a las'
    cent'ry teapot; —
Wal, I gut all on 't paid in gold afore our State seceded,
An' done wal, for Confed'rit bonds warn't jest the cheese
    I needed:

Nut but wut they 're ez *good* ez gold, but then it 's hard
 a-breakin' on' 'em,
An' ignorant folks is ollers sot an' wun't git used to takin'
 on 'em ;
They 're wuth ez much ez wut they wuz afore ole Mem'n-
 ger signed 'em,
An' go off middlin' wal for drinks, when ther' 's a knife
 behind 'em ;
We *du* miss silver, jes' fer thet an' ridin' in a bus,
Now we 've shook off the desputs thet wuz suckin' at our
 pus ;
An' it 's *because* the South 's so rich ; 't wuz nat'ral to
 expec'
Supplies o' change wuz jes' the things we should n't
 recollec' ;
We 'd ough' to ha' thought aforehan', though, o' thet good
 rule o' Crockett's,
For 't 's tiresome cairin' cotton-bales an' niggers in your
 pockets,
Ner 't ain't quite hendy to pass off one o' your six-foot
 Guineas
An' git your halves an' quarters back in gals an' picka-
 ninnies :
Wal, 't ain't quite all a feller 'd ax, but then ther' 's this
 to say,
It 's on'y jest among ourselves thet we expec' to pay ;
Our system would ha' caird us thru in any Bible cent'ry,
'Fore this onscripterl plan come up o' books by double
 entry ;
We go the patriarkle here out o' all sight an' hearin',
For Jacob warn't a suckemstance to Jeff at financierin' ;
He never 'd thought o' borryin' from Esau like all nater
An' then corfiscatin' all debts to sech a small pertater ;
There 's p'litickle econ'my, now, combined 'ith morril
 beauty
Thet saycrifices privit eends (your in'my's, tu) to dooty !
Wy, Jeff 'd ha' gin him five an' won his eye-teeth 'fore
 he knowed it,
An', stid o' wastin' pottage, he 'd ha' eat it up an' owed
 it.
But I wuz goin' on to say how I come here to dwall ; —
'Nough said, thet, arter lookin' roun', I liked the place so
 wal,

Where niggers doos a double good, with us atop to stiddy
    'em,
By bein' proofs o' prophecy an' suckleatin' medium,
Where a man's sunthin' coz he's white, an' whiskey's
    cheap ez fleas,
An' the financial pollercy jes' sooted my idees,
Thet I friz down right where I wuz, merried the Widder
    Shennon,
(Her thirds wuz part in cotton-land, part in the curse o'
    Canaan,)
An' here I be ez lively ez a chipmunk on a wall,
With nothin' to feel riled about much later 'n Eddam's
    fall.

Ez fur ez human foresight goes, we made an even trade :
She gut an overseer, an' I a fem'ly ready-made,
(The youngest on 'em 's 'mos' growed up,) rugged an' spry
    ez weazles,
So 's 't ther' 's no resk o' doctors' bills fer hoopin'-cough
    an' measles.
Our farm 's at Turkey-Buzzard Roost, Little Big Boosy
    River,
Wal located in all respex, — fer 't ain't the chills 'n' fever
Thet makes my writin' seem to squirm; a Southuner 'd
    allow I 'd
Some call to shake, for I 've jest hed to meller a
    new cowhide.
Miss S. is all 'f a lady; th' ain't no better on Big
    Boosy,
Ner' one with more accomplishmunts 'twixt here an'
    Tuscaloosy;
She 's an F. F., the tallest kind, an' prouder 'n the Gran'
    Turk,
An' never hed a relative thet done a stroke o' work;
Hern ain't a scrimpin' fem'ly sech ez *you* git up Down
    East,
Th' ain't a growed member on 't but owes his thousuns et
    the least :
She *is* some old; but then agin ther' 's drawbacks in
    my sheer :
Wut 's left o' me ain't more' n enough to make a
    Brigadier :

Wust is, thet she hez tantrums; she's like Seth Moody's
    gun
(Him thet wuz nicknamed frum his limp Ole Dot an'
    Kerry One);
He'd left her loaded up a spell, an' hed to git her
    clear,
So he onhitched, — Jeerusalem! the middle o' last year
Wuz right nex' door compared to where she kicked the
    critter tu
(Though *jest* where he brought up wuz wut no human
    never knew);
His brother Asaph picked her up an' tied her to a tree,
An' then she kicked an hour 'n' a half afore she'd let
    it be:
Wal, Miss S. *doos* hev cuttins-up an' pourins-out o' vials,
But then she hez her widder's thirds, an' all on us hez
    trials.
My objec', though, in writin' now warn't to allude to sech,
But to another suckemstance more dellykit to tech, —
I want thet you should grad'lly break my merriage to
    Jerushy,
An' there's a heap of argymunts thet's emple to indooce
    ye:
Fust place, State's Prison, — wal, it's true it warn't fer
    crime, o' course,
But then it's jest the same fer her in gittin' a disvorce;
Nex' place, my State's secedin' out hez leg'lly lef' me
    free
To merry any one I please, pervidin' it's a she;
Fin'lly, I never wun't come back, she need n't hev no
    fear on 't,
But then it's wal to fix things right fer fear Miss S.
    should hear on 't;
Lastly, I've gut religion South, an' Rushy she's a pagan
Thet sets by th' graven imiges o' the gret Nothun Dagon;
(Now I hain't seen one in six munts, for, sence our
    Treashry Loan,
Though yaller boys is thick anough, eagles hez kind o'
    flown;)
An' ef J. wants a stronger pint than them thet I hev
    stated,
Wy, she's an aliun in 'my now, an' I've been cornfis-
    cated, —

For sence we 've entered on th' estate o' the late naysh-
    nul eagle,
She hain't no kin' o' right but jes' wut I allow ez legle:
Wut *doos* Secedin' mean, ef 't ain't thet nat'rul rights
    hez riz, 'n'
Thet wut is mine 's my own, but wut 's another man's
    ain't his'n ?

Besides, I could n't do no else ; Miss S. suz she to me,
" You 've sheered my bed," [thet 's when I paid my
    interduction fee
To Southun rites,] " an' kep' your sheer," [wal, I allow
    it sticked
So 's 't I wuz most six weeks in jail afore I gut me
    picked,]
" Ner never paid no demmiges ; but thet wun't do no
    harm,
Pervidin' thet you 'll ondertake to oversee the farm ;
(My eldes' boy is so took up, wut with the Ringtail
    Rangers
An' settin' in the Jestice-Court for welcomin' o' stran-
    gers " ;)
[He sot on *me ;*] " an' so, ef you 'll jest ondertake the
    care
Upon a mod'rit sellery, we 'll up an' call it square ;
But ef you *can't* conclude," suz she, an' give a kin' o'
    grin,
" Wy, the Gran' Jurymen, I 'xpect, 'll hev to set agin."
Thet 's the way metters stood at fust ; now wut wuz I to
    du,
But jes' to make the best on 't an' off coat an' buckle tu ?
Ther' ain't a livin' man thet finds an income necessarier
Than me, — bimeby I 'll tell ye how I fin'lly come to
    merry her.

She hed another motive, tu : I mention of it here
T' encourage lads thet 's growin' up to study 'n' perse-
    vere,
An' show 'em how much better 't pays to mind their
    winter-schoolin'
Than to go off on benders 'n' sech, an' waste their time
    in foolin';

Ef 't warn't for studyin' evenins, I never 'd ha' been here
An orn'ment o' saciety, in my approprut spear :
She wanted somebody, ye see, o' taste an' cultivation,
To talk along o' preachers when they stopt to the plan-
    tation ;
For folks in Dixie th't read an' rite, onless it is by jarks,
Is skurce ez wut they wuz among th' oridgenle patri-
    archs ;
To fit a feller f' wut they call the soshle higherarchy,
All thet you 've gut to know is jes' beyund an evrage
    darky ;
Schoolin' 's wut they can't seem to stan', they 're tu con-
    sarned high-pressure,
An' knowin' t' much might spile a boy for bein' a Se-
    cesher.
We hain't no settled preachin' here, ner ministeril taxes;
The min'ster's only settlement's the carpet-bag he packs
    his
Razor an' soap-brush intu, with his hymbook an' his
    Bible, —
But they *du* preach, I swan to man, it 's puf'kly inde-
    scrib'le !
They go it like an Ericsson's ten-hoss-power coleric
    ingine,
An' make Ole Split-Foot winch an' squirm, for all he 's
    used to singein' ;
Hawkins's whetstone ain't a pinch o' primin' to the in-
    nards
To hearin' on 'em put free grace t' a lot o' tough old sin-
    hards !
But I must eend this letter now : 'fore long I 'll send a
    fresh un ;
I 've lots o' things to write about, perticklerly Seceshun :
I 'm called off now to mission-work, to let a leetle law in
To Cynthy's hide : an' so, till death,
        Yourn,
                BIRDOFREDUM SAWIN.

No. II.

MASON AND SLIDELL: A YANKEE IDYLL.

TO THE EDITORS OF THE ATLANTIC MONTHLY.

JAALAM, 6th Jan., 1862.

GENTLEMEN, — I was highly gratified by the insertion
of a portion of my letter in the last number of your valu-
able and entertaining Miscellany, though in a type which
rendered its substance inaccessible even to the beautiful
new spectacles presented to me by a Committee of the
Parish on New-Year's Day. I trust that I was able to
bear your very considerable abridgment of my lucubra-
tions with a spirit becoming a Christian. My third
granddaughter, Rebekah, aged fourteen years, and whom
I have trained to read slowly and with proper emphasis
(a practice too much neglected in our modern systems of
education), read aloud to me the excellent essay upon
"Old Age," the authour of which I cannot help suspect-
ing to be a young man who has never yet known what it
was to have snow (*canities morosa*) upon his own roof.
Dissolve frigus, large super foco ligna reponens, is a rule for
the young, whose wood-pile is yet abundant for such
cheerful lenitives. A good life behind him is the best
thing to keep an old man's shoulders from shivering at
every breath of sorrow or ill-fortune. But methinks it
were easier for an old man to feel the disadvantages of
youth than the advantages of age. Of these latter I
reckon one of the chiefest to be this; that we attach a
less inordinate value to our own productions, and, distrust-
ing daily more and more our own wisdom (with the con-
ceit whereof at twenty we wrap ourselves away from
knowledge as with a garment), do reconcile ourselves
with the wisdom of God. I could have wished, indeed,
that room might have been made for the residue of the
anecdote relating to Deacon Tinkham, which would not
only have gratified a natural curiosity on the part of the

publick (as I have reason to know from several letters of inquiry already received), but would also, as I think, have largely increased the circulation of your Magazine in this town. *Nihil humani alienum*, there is a curiosity about the affairs of our neighbours which is not only pardonable, but even commendable. But I shall abide a more fitting season.

As touching the following literary effort of Esquire Biglow, much might be profitably said on the topick of Idyllick and Pastoral Poetry, and concerning the proper distinctions to be made between them, from Theocritus, the inventor of the former, to Collins, the latest authour I know of who has emulated the classicks in the latter style. But in the time of Civil War worthy a Milton to defend and a Lucan to sing, it may be reasonably doubted whether the publick, never too studious of serious instruction, might not consider other objects more deserving of present attention. Concerning the title of Idyll, which Mr. Biglow has adopted at my suggestion, it may not be improper to animadvert, that the name properly signifies a poem somewhat rustick in phrase (for, though the learned are not agreed as to the particular dialect employed by Theocritus, they are universanimous both as to its rusticity and its capacity of rising now and then to the level of more elevated sentiments and expressions), while it is also descriptive of real scenery and manners. Yet it must be admitted that the production now in question (which here and there bears perhaps too plainly the marks of my correcting hand) does partake of the nature of a Pastoral, inasmuch as the interlocutors therein are purely imaginary beings, and the whole is little better than καπνοῦ σκιᾶς ὄναρ. The plot was, as I believe, suggested by the "Twa Briggs" of Robert Burns, a Scottish poet of the last century, as that found its prototype in the "Mutual Complaint of Plainstanes and Causey" by Fergusson, though the metre of this latter be different by a foot in each verse. I reminded my talented young parishioner and friend that Concord Bridge had long since yielded to the edacious tooth of Time. But he answered me to this effect: that there was no greater mistake of an authour than to suppose the reader had no fancy of his own; that, if once that faculty was to be called into activity, it were *better* to be in for the whole

sheep than the shoulder; and that he knew Concord like
a book, — an expression questionable in propriety, since
there are few things with which he is not more familiar
than with the printed page.' In proof of what he affirmed,
he showed me some verses which with others he had
stricken out as too much delaying the action, but which
I communicate in this place because they rightly define
"punkin-seed" (which Mr. Bartlett would have a kind
of perch, — a creature to which I have found a rod or
pole not to be so easily equivalent in our inland waters
as in the books of arithmetic), and because it conveys an
eulogium on the worthy son of an excellent father, with
whose acquaintance (*eheu, fugaces anni!*) I was formerly
honoured.

> "But nowadays the Bridge ain't wut they show,
> So much ez Em'son, Hawthorne, an' Thoreau.
> I know the village, though; was sent there once
> A-schoolin', 'cause to home I played the dunce;
> An' I've ben sence a-visitin' the Jedge,
> Whose garding whispers with the river's edge,
> Where I've sot mornin's lazy as the bream,
> Whose on'y business is to head up-stream,
> (We call 'em punkin-seed,) or else in chat
> Along 'th the Jedge, who covers with his hat
> More wit an' gumption an' shrewd Yankee sense
> Than there is mosses on an ole stone fence."

Concerning the subject-matter of the verses, I have not
the leisure at present to write so fully as I could wish,
my time being occupied with the preparation of a dis-
course for the forthcoming bi-centenary celebration of the
first settlement of Jaalam East Parish. It may gratify
the publick interest to mention the circumstance, that
my investigations to this end have enabled me to verify
the fact (of much historick importance, and hitherto
hotly debated) that Shearjashub Tarbox was the first
child of white parentage born in this town, being named
in his father's will under date August 7th, or 9th, 1662.
It is well known that those who advocate the claims of
Mehetable Goings, are unable to find any trace of her
existence prior to October of that year. As respects the
settlement of the Mason and Slidell question, Mr. Biglow
has not incorrectly stated the popular sentiment, so far
as I can judge by its expression in this locality. For
myself, I feel more sorrow than resentment; for I am old

enough to have heard those talk of England who still, even after the unhappy estrangement, could not unschool their lips from calling her the Mother-Country. But England has insisted on ripping up old wounds, and has undone the healing work of fifty years; for nations do not reason, they only feel, and the *spretæ injuria formæ* rankles in their minds as bitterly as in that of a woman. And because this is so, I feel the more satisfaction that our Government has acted (as all Governments should, standing as they do between the people and their passions) as if it had arrived at years of discretion. There are three short and simple words, the hardest of all to pronounce in any language (and I suspect they were no easier before the confusion of tongues), but which no man or nation that cannot utter can claim to have arrived at manhood. Those words are, *I was wrong;* and I am proud that, while England played the boy, our rulers had strength enough from the People below and wisdom enough from God above to quit themselves like men.

The sore points on both sides have been skilfully exasperated by interested and unscrupulous persons, who saw in a war between the two countries the only hope of profitable return for their investment in Confederate stock, whether political or financial. The always supercilious, often insulting, and sometimes even brutal tone of British journals and publick men, has certainly not tended to soothe whatever resentment might exist in America.

> "Perhaps it was right to dissemble your love,
> But why did you kick me down stairs?"

We have no reason to complain that England, as a necessary consequence of her clubs, has become a great society for the minding of other people's business, and we can smile good-naturedly when she lectures other nations on the sins of arrogance and conceit; but we may justly consider it a breach of the political *convenances* which are expected to regulate the intercourse of one well-bred government with another, when men holding places in the ministry allow themselves to dictate our domestic policy, to instruct us in our duty, and to stigmatize as unholy a war for the rescue of whatever a high-minded people should hold most vital and most

sacred. Was it in good taste, that I may use the mild-
est term, for Earl Russell to expound our own Con-
stitution to President Lincoln, or to make a new and
fallacious application of an old phrase for our benefit,
and tell us that the Rebels were fighting for indepen-
dence and we for empire? As if all wars for indepen-
dence were by nature just and deserving of sympathy,
and all wars for empire ignoble and worthy only of rep-
robation, or as if these easy phrases in any way char-
acterized this terrible struggle, — terrible not so truly
in any superficial sense, as from the essential and deadly
enmity of the principles that underlie it. His Lord-
ship's bit of borrowed rhetoric would justify Smith
O'Brien, Nana Sahib, and the Maori chieftains, while it
would condemn nearly every war in which England has
ever been engaged. Was it so very presumptuous in
us to think that it would be decorous in English states-
men if they spared time enough to acquire some kind
of knowledge, though of the most elementary kind, in
regard to this country and the questions at issue here,
before they pronounced so off-hand a judgment? Or is
political information expected to come Dogberry-fashion
in England, like reading and writing, by nature?

And now all respectable England is wondering at
our irritability, and sees a quite satisfactory explanation
of it in our national vanity. *Suave mari magno*, it is
pleasant, sitting in the easy-chairs of Downing Street, to
sprinkle pepper on the raw wounds of a kindred people
struggling for life, and philosophical to find in self-con-
ceit the cause of our instinctive resentment. Surely we
were of all nations the least liable to any temptation
of vanity at a time when the gravest anxiety and the
keenest sorrow were never absent from our hearts. Nor
is conceit the exclusive attribute of any one nation.
The earliest of English travellers, Sir John Mandeville,
took a less provincial view of the matter when he said,
"For fro what partie of the erthe that men duellen,
other aboven or beneathen, it semethe alweys to hem
that duellen that thei gon more righte than any other
folke." The English have always had their fair share
of this amiable quality. We may say of them still,
as the authour of the *Lettres Cabalistiques* said of them
more than a century ago, "*Ces derniers disent naturelle-*

ment qu'il a'y a qu'eux qui soient estimables." And, as
he also says, "*J'aimerois presque autant tomber entre les
mains d'un Inquisiteur que d'un Anglois qui me fait
sentir sans cesse combien il s'estime plus que moi, et
qui ne daigne me parler que pour injurier ma Nation
et pour m'ennuyer du récit des grandes qualités de la
sienne.*" Of *this* Bull we may safely say with Horace,
habet fœnum in cornu. What we felt to be especially
insulting was the quiet assumption that the descendants
of men who left the Old World for the sake of principle,
and who had made the wilderness into a New World
patterned after an Idea, could not possibly be suscep-
tible of a generous or lofty sentiment, could have no
feeling of nationality deeper than that of a tradesman
for his shop. One would have thought, in listening
to England, that we were presumptuous in fancying
that we were a nation at all, or had any other principle
of union than that of booths at a fair, where there is
no higher notion of government than the constable,
or better image of God than that stamped upon the
current coin.

It is time for Englishmen to consider whether there
was nothing in the spirit of their press and of their
leading publick men calculated to rouse a just indigna-
tion, and to cause a permanent estrangement on the
part of any nation capable of self-respect, and sensitively
jealous, as ours then was, of foreign interference.
Was there nothing in the indecent haste with which
belligerent rights were conceded to the Rebels, nothing
in the abrupt tone assumed in the Trent case, nothing in
the fitting out of Confederate privateers, that might
stir the blood of a people already overcharged with
doubt, suspicion, and terrible responsibility? The la-
ity in any country do not stop to consider points of
law, but they have an instinctive appreciation of the
animus that actuates the policy of a foreign nation;
and in our own case they remembered that the Brit-
ish authorities in Canada did not wait till diplomacy
could send home to England for her slow official tinder-
box to fire the "Caroline." Add to this, what every
sensible American knew, that the moral support of
England was equal to an army of two hundred thou-
sand men to the Rebels, while it insured us another

year or two of exhausting war. It was not so much
the spite of her words (though the time might have
been more tastefully chosen) as the actual power for
evil in them that we felt as a deadly wrong. Perhaps
the most immediate and efficient cause of mere irritation
was the sudden and unaccountable change of manner
on the other side of the water. Only six months be-
fore, the Prince of Wales had come over to call us
cousins; and everywhere it was nothing but "our
American brethren," that great offshoot of British in-
stitutions in the New World, so almost identical with
them in laws, language, and literature, —this last of
the alliterative compliments being so bitterly true, that
perhaps it will not be retracted even now. To this out-
burst of long-repressed affection we responded with gen-
uine warmth, if with something of the awkwardness
of a poor relation bewildered with the sudden tighten-
ing of the ties of consanguinity when it is rumoured that
he has come into a large estate. Then came the Rebel-
lion, and, *presto!* a flaw in our titles was discovered,
the plate we were promised at the family table is flung
at our head, and we were again the scum of creation,
intolerably vulgar, at once cowardly and overbearing, —
no relations of theirs, after all, but a dreggy hybrid of
the basest bloods of Europe. Panurge was not quicker
to call Friar John his *former* friend. I cannot help
thinking of Walter Mapes's jingling paraphrase of
Petronius, —

> "Dummodo sim splendidis vestibus ornatus,
> Et multa familia sim circumvallatus,
> Prudens sum et sapiens et morigeratus,
> Et tuus nepos sum et tu meus cognatus," —

which I may freely render thus : —

> So long as I was prosperous, I'd dinners by the dozen,
> Was well-bred, witty, virtuous, and everybody's cousin :
> If luck should turn, as well she may, her fancy is so flexile,
> Will virtue, cousinship, and all return with her from exile?

There was nothing in all this to exasperate a philoso-
pher, much to make him smile rather; but the earth's
surface is not chiefly inhabited by philosophers, and I
revive the recollection of it now in perfect good humour,
merely by way of suggesting to our *ci-devant* British

cousins, that it would have been easier for them to hold their tongues than for us to keep our tempers under the circumstances.

The English Cabinet made a blunder, unquestionably, in taking it so hastily for granted that the United States had fallen forever from their position as a first-rate power, and it was natural that they should vent a little of their vexation on the people whose inexplicable obstinacy in maintaining freedom and order, and in resisting degradation, was likely to convict them of their mistake. But if bearing a grudge be the sure mark of a small mind in the individual, can it be a proof of high spirit in a nation? If the result of the present estrangement between the two countries shall be to make us more independent of British twaddle, (*Indomito nec dira ferens stipendia Tauro,*) so much the better; but if it is to make us insensible to the value of British opinion, in matters where it gives us the judgment of an impartial and cultivated outsider, if we are to shut ourselves out from the advantages of English culture, the loss will be ours, and not theirs. Because the door of the old homestead has been once slammed in our faces, shall we in a huff reject all future advances of conciliation, and cut ourselves foolishly off from any share in the humanizing influences of the place, with its ineffable riches of association, its heirlooms of immemorial culture, its historic monuments, ours no less than theirs, its noble gallery of ancestral portraits? We have only to succeed, and England will not only respect, but, for the first time, begin to understand us. And let us not, in our justifiable indignation at wanton insult, forget that England is not the England only of snobs who dread the democracy they do not comprehend, but the England of history, of heroes, statesmen, and poets, whose names are dear, and their influence as salutary to us as to her.

Let us strengthen the hands of those in authority over us, and curb our own tongues, remembering that General Wait commonly proves in the end more than a match for General Headlong, and that the Good Book ascribes safety to a multitude, indeed, but not to a mob, of counsellours. Let us remember and perpend the words of Paulus Emilius to the people of Rome; that, "if they judged they could manage the war to more advantage by any other, he would willingly yield up his charge; but if they confided in him, *they were not to make themselves his colleagues in his office, or raise reports, or criticise his actions, but, without talking, supply him with means and assistance necessary to the carrying on of the war; for, if they proposed to command their own commander, they would render this expedition more ridiculous than the former."* (*Vide Plutarchum in Vitâ P. E.*) Let us also not forget what the same excellent authour says concerning Perseus's fear of spending money, and not permit the covetousness of Brother Jonathan to be the good-fortune of Jefferson Davis. For my own part, till I am ready to admit the Commander-in-Chief to my pulpit, I shall abstain from planning his battles. If courage be the sword, yet is patience the armour of a nation; and in our desire for peace, let us never be willing to surrender the Constitution bequeathed us by fathers at least as wise as ourselves (even with Jefferson Davis to help us), and, with those degenerate Romans, *tuta et presentia quam vetera et periculosa malle.*

And not only should we bridle our own tongues, but the pens of others, which are swift to convey useful intelligence to the enemy. This is no new inconvenience; for, under date, 3d June, 1745, General Pepperell wrote thus to Governor Shirley from Louisbourg: — "What your Excellency observes of the *army's being made acquainted with any plans proposed, until ready to be put in execution,* has always been disagreeable to me, and I have given many cautions relating to it. But when your Excellency considers that *our Council of War consists of more than twenty members,* I am persuaded you will think it *impossible for me to hinder it,* if any of them will persist in communicating to inferior officers and soldiers what ought to be kept secret. I am informed that the Boston newspapers are filled with paragraphs from private letters relating to the expedition. Will your Excellency permit me to say I think it may be of ill consequence? Would it not be convenient, if your Excellency should forbid the Printers' inserting such news?" Verily, if *tempora mutantur,* we may question the *et nos mutamur in illis;* and if tongues be leaky, it will need all hands at the pumps to save the Ship of State. Our history dotes and repeats itself. If Sassycus (rather than Alcibiades)

find a parallel in Beauregard, so Weakwash, as he is called
by the brave Lieutenant Lion Gardiner, need not seek far
among our own Sachems for his antitype.

With respect,
Your ob^t humble serv^t,
HOMER WILBUR, A. M.

I LOVE to start out arter night 's begun,
An' all the chores about the farm are done,
The critters milked an' foddered, gates shet fast,
Tools cleaned aginst to-morrer, supper past,
An' Nancy darnin' by her ker'sene lamp, —
I love, I say, to start upon a tramp,
To shake the kinkles out o' back an' legs,
An' kind o' rack my life off from the dregs
Thet 's apt to settle in the buttery-hutch
Of folks thet foller in one rut too much :
Hard work is good an' wholesome, past all doubt;
But 't ain't so, ef the mind gits tuckered out.
Now, bein' born in Middlesex, you know,
There 's certin spots where I like best to go:
The Concord road, for instance, (I, for one,
Most gin'lly ollers call it *John Bull's Run*,)
The field o' Lexin'ton, where England tried
The fastest colors thet she ever dyed,
An' Concord Bridge, thet Davis, when he came,
Found was the bee-line track to heaven an' fame,
Ez all roads be by natur', ef your soul
Don't sneak thru shun-pikes so 's to save the toll.

They 're 'most too fur away, take too much time
To visit of'en, ef it ain't in rhyme;
But the 's a walk thet 's hendier, a sight,
An' suits me fust-rate of a winter's night, —
I mean the round whale's-back o' Prospect Hill.
I love to l'iter there while night grows still,
An' in the twinklin' villages about,
Fust here, then there, the well-saved lights goes out,
An' nary sound but watch-dogs' false alarms,
Or muffled cock-crows from the drowsy farms,
Where some wise rooster (men act jest thet way)

2 M

Stands to 't thet moon-rise is the break o' day:
(So Mister Seward sticks a three-months pin
Where the war 'd oughto eend, then tries agin;
My gran'ther's rule was safer 'n 't is to crow:
Don't never prophesy, — onless ye know.)
I love to muse there till it kind o' seems
Ez ef the world went eddyin' off in dreams;
The Northwest wind thet twitches at my baird
Blows out o' sturdier days not easy scared,
An' the same moon thet this December shines
Starts out the tents an' booths o' Putnam's lines;
The rail-fence posts, acrost the hill thet runs,
Turn ghosts o' sogers should'rin' ghosts o' guns;
Ez wheels the sentry, glints a flash o' light
Along the firelock won at Concord Fight,
An' 'twixt the silences, now fur, now nigh,
Rings the sharp chellenge, hums the low reply.

Ez I was settin' so, it warn't long sence,
Mixin' the puffict with the present tense,
I heerd two voices som'ers in the air,
Though, ef I was to die, I can't tell where:
Voices I call 'em: 't was a kind o' sough
Like pine-trees thet the wind's ageth'rin' through;
An', fact, I thought it *was* the wind a spell,
Then some misdoubted, could n't fairly tell,
Fust sure, then not, jest as you hold an eel,
I knowed, an' did n't, — fin'lly seemed to feel
'T was Concord Bridge a-talkin' off to kill
With the Stone Spike thet's druv thru Bunker Hill:
Whether 't was so, or ef I on'y dreamed,
I could n't say ; I tell it ez it seemed.

THE BRIDGE.

Wal, neighbor, tell us, wut's turned up thet's new ?
You 're younger 'n I be, — nigher Boston, tu :
An' down to Boston, ef you take their showin',
Wut they don't know ain't hardly wuth the knowin'.
There 's *sunthin'* goin' on, I know: las' night
The British sogers killed in our gret fight
(Nigh fifty year they hed n't stirred nor spoke)
Made sech a coil you 'd thought a dam hed broke:

Why, one he up an' beat a revellee
With his own crossbones on a holler tree,
Till all the graveyards swarmed out like a hive
With faces I hain't seen sence Seventy-five.
Wut *is* the news? 'T ain't good, or they 'd be cheerin'.
Speak slow an' clear, for I 'm some hard o' hearin'.

THE MONIMENT.

I don't know hardly ef it 's good or bad, ——

THE BRIDGE.

At wust, it can't be wus than wut we 've had.

THE MONIMENT.

You know them envys thet the Rebbles sent,
An' Cap'n Wilkes he borried o' the Trent?

THE BRIDGE.

Wut! they ha'n't hanged 'em? Then their wits is
    gone !
Thet 's the sure way to make a goose a swan!

THE MONIMENT.

No: England she *would* hev 'em, *Fee, Faw, Fum!*
(Ez though she hed n't fools enough to home,)
So they 've returned 'em ——

THE BRIDGE.

                    Hev they? Wal, by heaven,
Thet 's the wust news I 've heerd sence Seventy-seven!
By George, I meant to say, though I declare
It 's 'most enough to make a deacon swear.

THE MONIMENT.

Now don't go off half-cock: folks never gains
By usin' pepper-sarse instid o' brains.
Come, neighbor, you don't understand ——

THE BRIDGE.

How ? Hey ?
Not understand ?   Why, wut 's to hender, pray ?
Must ɪ go huntin' round to find a chap
To tell me when my face hez hed a slap ?

THE MONIMENT.

See here : the British they found out a flaw
In Cap'n Wilkes's readin' o' the law :
(They *make* all laws, you know, an' so, o' course,
It 's nateral they should understan' their force :)
He 'd oughto took the vessel into port,
An' hed her sot on by a reg'lar court ;
She was a mail-ship, an' a steamer, tu,
An' thet, they say, hez changed the pint o' view,
Coz the old practice, bein' meant for sails,
Ef tried upon a steamer, kind o' fails ;
You *may* take out despatches, but you mus' n't
Take nary man ——

THE BRIDGE.

You mean to say, you dus' n't !
Changed pint o' view !   No, no, — it 's overboard
With law an' gospel, when their ox is gored !
I tell ye,. England's law, on sea an' land,
Hez ollers ben, " *I 've gut the heaviest hand.*"
Take nary man ?   Fine preachin' from *her* lips !
Why, she hez taken hunderds from our ships,
An' would agin, an' swear she had a right to,
Ef we warn't strong enough to be perlite to.
Of all the sarse thet I can call to mind,
England *doos* make the most onpleasant kind :
It 's you 're the sinner ollers, she 's the saint ;
Wut 's good 's all English, all thet is n't ain't ;
Wut profits her is ollers right an' just,
An' ef you don't read Scriptur so, you must ;
She 's praised herself ontil she fairly thinks
There ain't no light in Natur when she winks ;
Hain't she the Ten Comman'ments in her pus ?
Could the world stir 'thout she went, tu, ez nus ?

She ain't like other mortals, thet's a fact:
She never stopped the habus-corpus act,
Nor specie payments, nor she never yet
Cut down the int'rest on her public debt;
She don't put down rebellions, lets 'em breed,
An' 's ollers willin' Ireland should secede;
She 's all thet's honest, honnable, an' fair,
An' when the vartoos died they made her heir.

THE MONIMENT.

Wal, wal, two wrongs don't never make a right;
Ef we 're mistaken, own up, an' don't fight:
For gracious' sake, ha'n't we enough to du
'Thout gettin' up a fight with England, tu?
She thinks we 're rabble-rid ——

THE BRIDGE.

                  An' so we can't
Distinguish 'twixt *You ought n't* an' *You shan't!*
She jedges by herself; she 's no idear
How 't stiddies folks to give 'em their fair sheer:
The odds 'twixt her an' us is plain 's a steeple, —
Her People 's turned to Mob, our Mob 's turned People.

THE MONIMENT.

She 's riled jes' now ——

THE BRIDGE.

              Plain proof her cause ain't strong, —
The one thet fust gits mad 's most ollers wrong.
Why, sence she helped in lickin' Nap the Fust,
An' pricked a bubble jest agoin' to bust,
With Rooshy, Prooshy, Austry, all asistin',
Th' ain't nut a face but wut she 's shook her fist in,
Ez though she done it all, an' ten times more,
An' nothin' never hed gut done afore,
Nor never could agin', 'thout she wuz spliced
On to one eend an' gin th' old airth a hoist.
She *is* some punkins, thet I wun't deny,
(For ain't she some related to you 'n' I?)

But there 's a few small intrists here below
Outside the counter o' John Bull an' Co.,
An', though they can't conceit how 't should be so,
I guess the Lord druv down Creation's spiles
'Thout no *gret* helpin' from the British Isles,
An' could contrive to keep things pooty stiff
Ef they withdrawed from business in a miff;
I ha'n't no patience with sech swellin' fellers ez
Think God can't forge 'thout them to blow the bellerses.

THE MONIMENT.

You 're ollers quick to set your back aridge, —
Though 't suits a tom-cat more 'n a sober bridge:
Don't you git het: they thought the thing was planned;
They 'll cool off when they come to understand.

THE BRIDGE.

Ef *thet* 's wut you expect, you 'll *hev* to wait:
Folks never understand the folks they hate:
She 'll fin' some other grievance jest ez good,
'Fore the month 's out, to git misunderstood.
England cool off! She 'll do it, ef she sees
She 's run her head into a swarm o' bees.
I ain't so prejudiced ez wut you spose:
I hev thought England was the best thet goes;
Remember, (no, you can't,) when *I* was reared,
God save the King was all the tune you heerd:
But it 's enough to turn Wachuset roun',
This stumpin' fellers when you think they 're down.

THE MONIMENT.

But, neighbor, ef they prove their claim at law,
The best way is to settle, an' not jaw.
An' don't le' 's mutter 'bout the awfle bricks
We 'll give 'em, ef we ketch 'em in a fix:
That 'ere 's most frequently the kin' o' talk
Of critters can't be kicked to toe the chalk;
Your " You 'll see *nex'* time ! " an' " Look out bumby ! "
Most ollers ends in eatin' umble-pie.
'T wun't pay to scringe to England: will it pay

To fear thet meaner bully, old "They 'll say"?
Suppose they *du* say : words are dreffle bores,
But they ain't quite so bad ez seventy-fours.
Wut England wants is jest a wedge to fit
Where it 'll help to widen out our split :
She 's found her wedge, an' 't ain't for us to come
An' lend the beetle thet 's to drive it home.
For growed-up folks like us 't would be a scandle,
When we git sarsed, to fly right off the handle.
England ain't *all* bad, coz she thinks us blind :
Ef she can't change her skin, she can her mind ;
An' we shall see her change it double-quick,
Soon ez we 've proved thet we 're a-goin' to lick.
She an' Columby 's gut to be fas' friends ;
For the world prospers by their privit ends :
'T would put the clock back all o' fifty years,
Ef they should fall together by the ears.

THE BRIDGE.

I 'gree to thet; she 's nigh us to wut France is;
But then she 'll hev to make the fust advances;
We 've gut pride, tu, an' gut it by good rights,
An' ketch *me* stoopin' to pick up the mites
O' condescension she 'll be lettin' fall
When she finds out we ain't dead arter all!
I tell ye wut, it takes more 'n one good week
Afore *my* nose forgits it 's hed a tweak.

THE MONIMENT.

She 'll come out right bumby, thet I 'll engage,
Soon ez she gits to seein' we 're of age ;
This talkin' down o' hers ain't wuth a fuss ;
It 's nat'ral ez nut likin' 't is to us ;
Ef we 're agoin' to prove we *be* growed-up,
'T wun't be by barkin' like a tarrier pup,
But turnin' to an' makin' things ez good
Ez wut we 're ollers braggin' that we could ;
We 're bound to be good friends, an' so we 'd oughto,
In spite of all the fools both sides the water.

THE BRIDGE.

I b'lieve thet 's so; but hearken in your ear, —
I 'm older 'n you, — Peace wun't keep house with Fear:
Ef you want peace, the thing you 've gut to du
Is jes' to show you 're up to fightin', tu.
I recollect how sailors' rights was won
Yard locked in yard, hot gun-lip kissin' gun:
Why, afore thet, John Bull sot up thet he
Hed gut a kind o' mortgage on the sea;
You 'd thought he held by Gran'ther Adam's will,
An' ef you knuckle down, *he* 'll think so still.
Better thet all our ships an' all their crews
Should sink to rot in ocean's dreamless ooze,
Each torn flag wavin' chellenge ez it went,
An' each dumb gun a brave man's moniment,
Than seek sech peace ez only cowards crave:
Give *me* the peace of dead men or of brave!

THE MONIMENT.

I say, ole boy, it ain't the Glorious Fourth:
You 'd oughto larned 'fore this wut talk wuz worth.
It ain't *our* nose thet gits put out o' jint;
It 's England thet gives up her dearest pint.
We 've gut, I tell ye now, enough to du
In our own fem'ly fight, afore we 're thru.
I hoped, las' spring, jest arter Sumter's shame,
When every flag-staff flapped its tethered flame,
An' all the people, startled from their doubt,
Come must'rin' to the flag with sech a shout, —
I hoped to see things settled 'fore this fall,
The Rebbles licked, Jeff Davis hanged, an' all;
Then come Bull Run, an' *sence* then I 've ben waitin'
Like boys in Jennooary thaw for skatin',
Nothin' to du but watch my shadder's trace
Swing, like a ship at anchor, roun' my base,
With daylight's flood an' ebb: it 's gittin' slow,
An' I 'most think we 'd better let 'em go.
I tell ye wut, this war 's a-goin' to cost ——

THE BRIDGE.

An' I tell *you* it wun't be money lost;
Taxes milks dry, but, neighbor, you'll allow
Thet havin' things onsettled kills the cow:
We 've gut to fix this thing for good an' all;
It 's no use buildin' wut 's a-goin' to fall.
I 'm older 'n you, an' I 've seen things an' men,
An' *my* experunce, — tell ye wut it 's ben:
Folks thet worked thorough was the ones thet thriv,
But bad work follers ye ez long 's ye live;
You can't git red on 't; jest ez sure ez sin,
It 's ollers askin' to be done agin:
Ef we should part, it would n't be a week
'Fore your soft-soddered peace would spring aleak.
We 've turned our cuffs up, but, to put her thru,
We must git mad an' off with jackets, tu;
'T wun't du to think thet killin' ain't perlite, —
You 've gut to be in airnest, ef you fight;
Why, two-thirds o' the Rebbles 'ould cut dirt,
Ef they once thought thet Guv'ment meant to hurt;
An' I *du* wish our Gin'rals hed in mind
The folks in front more than the folks behind;
You wun't do much ontil you think it 's God,
An' not constitoounts, thet holds the rod;
We want some more o' Gideon's sword, I jedge,
For proclamations ha'n't no gret of edge;
There 's nothin' for a cancer but the knife,
Onless you set by 't more than by your life.
I 've seen hard times; I see a war begun
Thet folks thet love their bellies never 'd won;
Pharo's lean kine hung on for seven long year;
But when 't was done, we did n't count it dear.
Why, law an' order, honor, civil right,
Ef they *ain't* wuth it, wut *is* wuth a fight?
I 'm older 'n you: the plough, the axe, the mill,
All kin's o' labor an' all kin's o' skill,
Would be a rabbit in a wile-cat's claw,
Ef 't warn't for thet slow critter, 'stablished law;
Onsettle *thet*, an' all the world goes whiz,
A screw 's gut loose in everythin' there is:

Good buttresses once settled, don't you fret
An' stir 'em: take a bridge's word for thet!
Young folks are smart, but all ain't good thet 's new;
I guess the gran'thers they knowed sunthin', tu.

THE MONIMENT.

Amen to thet! build sure in the beginnin',
An' then don't never tech the underpinnin':
Th' older a Guv'ment is, the better 't suits;
New ones hunt folks's corns out like new boots:
Change jes' for change, is like them big hotels
Where they shift plates, and let ye live on smells.

THE BRIDGE.

Wal, don't give up afore the ship goes down:
It 's a stiff gale, but Providence wun't drown;
An' God wun't leave us yit to sink or swim,
Ef we don't fail to du wut 's right by Him.
This land o' ourn, I tell ye, 's gut to be
A better country than man ever see.
I feel my sperit swellin' with a cry
Thet seems to say, "Break forth an' prophesy!"
O strange New World, thet yit wast never young,
Whose youth from thee by gripin' need was wrung,
Brown foundlin' o' the woods, whose baby-bed
Was prowled roun' by the Injun's cracklin' tread,
An' who grew'st strong thru shifts an' wants an' pains,
Nussed by stern men with empires in their brains,
Who saw in vision their young Ishmel strain
With each hard hand a vassal ocean's mane,
Thou, skilled by Freedom an' by gret events
To pitch new States ez Old-World men pitch tents,
Thou, taught by Fate to know Jehovah's plan
Thet man's devices can't unmake a man,
An' whose free latch-string never was drawed in
Against the poorest child of Adam's kin, —
The grave 's not dug where traitor hands shall lay
In fearful haste thy murdered corse away!
I see ——

Jest here some dogs begun to bark,
So thet I lost old Concord's last remark:
I listened long, but all I seemed to hear
Was dead leaves goss'pin' on some birch-trees near;
But ez they hed n't no gret things to say,
An' sed 'em often, I come right away,
An', walkin' home'ards, jest to pass the time,
I put some thoughts thet bothered me in rhyme:
I hain't hed time to fairly try 'em on,
But here they be — it 's

JONATHAN TO JOHN.

It don't seem hardly right, John,
    When both my hands was full,
To stump me to a fight, John, —
    Your cousin, tu, John Bull!
        Ole Uncle S. sez he, "I guess
        We know it now," sez he,
    "The lion's paw is all the law,
        Accordin' to J. B.,
        Thet 's fit for you an' me!"

You wonder why we 're hot, John?
    Your mark wuz on the guns,
The neutral guns, thet shot, John,
    Our brothers an' our sons:
        Ole Uncle S. sez he, "I guess
        There 's human blood," sez he,
    "By fits an' starts, in Yankee hearts,
        Though 't may surprise J. B.
        More 'n it would you an' me."

Ef *I* turned mad dogs loose, John,
    On *your* front-parlor stairs,
Would it jest meet your views, John,
    To wait an' sue their heirs?
        Ole Uncle S. sez he, "I guess,
        I on'y guess," sez he,
    "Thet, ef Vattel on *his* toes fell,
        'T would kind o' rile J. B.,
        Ez wal ez you an' me!"

Who made the law thet hurts, John,
  Heads I win, — ditto tails ?
" *J. B.*" was on his shirts, John,
  Onless my memory fails.
    Ole Uncle S. sez he, " I guess,
    (I'm good at thet,) " sez he,
" Thet sauce for goose ain't *jest* the juice
    For ganders with J. B.,
    No more than you or me ! "

When your rights was our wrongs, John,
  You didn't stop for fuss, —
Britanny's trident prongs, John,
  Was good 'nough law for us.
    Ole Uncle S. sez he, " I guess,
    Though physic 's good," sez he,
" It does n't foller thet he can swaller
    Prescriptions signed ' *J. B.*,'
    Put up by you an' me ! "

We own the ocean, tu, John :
  You mus' n' take it hard,
Ef we can't think with you, John,
  It 's jest your own back-yard.
    Ole Uncle S. sez he, " I guess,
    Ef *thet* 's his claim," sez he,
" The fencin'-stuff 'll cost enough
    To bust up friend J. B.,
    Ez wal ez you an' me ! "

Why talk so dreffle big, John,
  Of honor, when it meant
You did n't care a fig, John,
  But jest for *ten per cent?*
    Ole Uncle S. sez he, " I guess,
    He 's like the rest," sez he:
" When all is done, it 's number one
    Thet 's nearest to J. B.,
    Ez wal ez you an' me ! "

We give the critters back, John,
  Cos Abram thought 't was right ;

It warn't your bullyin' clack, John,
   Provokin' us to fight.
      Ole Uncle S. sez he, " I guess
      We 've a hard row," sez he,
"To hoe jest now ; but thet, somehow,
      May happen to J. B.,
      Ez wal ez you an' me! "

We ain't so weak an' poor, John,
   With twenty million people,
An' close to every door, John,
   A school-house an' a steeple.
      Ole Uncle S. sez he, " I guess
      It is a fact," sez he,
"The surest plan to make a Man
      Is, think him so, J. B.,
      Ez much ez you or me! "

Our folks believe in Law, John ;
   An' it 's for her sake, now,
They 've left the axe an' saw, John,
   The anvil an' the plough.
      Ole Uncle S. sez he, " I guess,
      Ef 't warn't for law," sez he,
" There 'd be one shindy from here to Indy;
      An' thet don't suit J. B.
      (When 't ain't 'twixt you an' me !) "

We know we 've gut a cause, John,
   Thet 's honest, just, an' true ;
We thought 't would win applause, John,
   Ef nowheres else, from you.
      Ole Uncle S. sez he, " I guess
      His love of right," sez he,
" Hangs by a rotten fibre o' cotton :
      There 's natur' in J. B.,
      Ez wal ez you an' me! "

The South says, " *Poor folks down !* " John,
   An' " *All men up !* " say we, —
White, yaller, black, an' brown, John :
   Now which is your idee ?

Ole Uncle S. sez he, " I guess,
John preaches wal," sez he ;
" But, sermon thru, an' come to *du*,
Why, there 's the old J. B.
A crowdin' you an' me ! "

Shall it be love, or hate, John ?
It 's you thet 's to decide ;
Ain't *your* bonds held by Fate, John,
Like all the world's beside ?
Ole Uncle S. sez he, " I guess
Wise men forgive," sez he,
" But not forget ; an' some time yet
Thet truth may strike J. B.,
Ez wal ez you an' me ! "

God means to make this land,.John,
Clear thru, from sea to sea,
Believe an' understand, John,
The *wuth* o' bein' free.
Ole Uncle S. sez he, " I guess,
God's price is high," sez he ;
" But nothin' else than wut He sells
Wears long, an' thet J. B.
May larn, like you an' me ! "

No. III.

BIRDOFREDUM SAWIN, ESQ., TO MR. HOSEA BIGLOW.

With the following Letter from the REVEREND
HOMER WILBUR, A. M.

TO THE EDITORS OF THE ATLANTIC MONTHLY.

JAALAM, 7th Feb., 1862.

RESPECTED FRIENDS, — If I know myself, — and surely a man can hardly be supposed to have overpassed the limit of forescore years without attaining to some proficiency in that most useful branch of learning, (*e cœlo descendit*, says the pagan poet,) — I have no great smack of that weakness which would press upon the publick attention any matter pertaining to my private affairs. But since the following letter of Mr. Sawin contains not only a direct allusion to myself, but that in connexion with a topick of interest to all those engaged in the publick ministrations of the sanctuary, I may be pardoned for touching briefly thereupon. Mr. Sawin was never a stated attendant upon my preaching, — never, as I believe, even an occasional one, since the erection of the new house (where we now worship) in 1845. He did, indeed, for a time, supply a not unacceptable bass in the choir; but, whether on some umbrage (*omnibus hoc vitium est cantoribus*) taken against the bass-viol, then, and till his decease in 1850, (*œt.* 77,) under the charge of Mr. Asaph Perley, or, as was reported by others, on account of an imminent subscription for a new bell, he thenceforth absented himself from all outward and visible communion. Yet he seems to have preserved, (*altâ mente repostum,*) as it were, in the pickle of a mind soured by prejudice, a lasting *scunner*, as he would call it, against our staid and decent form of worship; for I would rather in that wise interpret his fling, than suppose that any chance tares sown by my pulpit discourses should survive so long, while good seed too often fails to root itself. I humbly trust that I have no personal feeling in the matter; though I know that, if we sound any man deep enough, our lead shall bring up the mud of human nature at last. The Bretons believe in an evil spirit which they call *ar c'houskezik*, whose office it is to make the congregation drowsy; and though I have never had reason to think that he was specially busy among my flock, yet have I seen enough to make me sometimes regret the hinged seats of the ancient meeting-house, whose lively clatter, not unwillingly intensified by boys beyond eyeshot of the tithing-man, served at intervals as a wholesome *réveil*. It is true, I have numbered among my parishioners some who are proof against the prophylactick fennel, nay, whose gift of somnolence rivalled that of the Cretan Rip Van Winkle, Epimenides, and who, nevertheless, complained not so much of the substance as of the length of my (by them unheard) discourses. Some ingenious persons of a philosophick turn have assured us that our pulpits were set too high, and that the soporifick tendency increased with the ratio of the angle in which the hearer's eye was constrained to seek the preacher. This were a curious topick for investigation. There can be no doubt that some sermons are pitched too high, and I remember many struggles with the drowsy fiend in my youth. Happy Saint Anthony of Padua, whose finny acolytes, however they might profit, could never murmur! *Quare fremuerunt gentes?* Who is he that can twice a week be inspired, or has eloquence (*ut ita dicum*) always on tap? A good man, and, next to David, a sacred poet, (himself, haply, not inexpert of evil in this particular,) has said, —

> "The worst speak something good : if all want sense,
> God takes a text and preacheth patience."

There are one or two other points in Mr. Sawin's letter which I would also briefly animadvert upon. And first, concerning the claim he sets up to a certain superiority of blood and lineage in the people of our Southern States, now unhappily in rebellion against lawful authority

and their own better interests. There is a sort of opinions,
anachronisms at once and anachorisms, foreign both to the
age and the country, that maintain a feeble and buzzing
existence, scarce to be called life, like winter flies, which
in mild weather crawl out from obscure nooks and crannies
to expatiate in the sun, and sometimes acquire vigour
enough to disturb with their enforced familiarity the
studious hours of the scholar. One of the most stupid and
pertinacious of these is the theory that the Southern States
were settled by a class of emigrants from the Old World
socially superior to those who founded the institutions of
New England. The Virginians especially lay claim to
this generosity of lineage, which were of no possible
account, were it not for the fact that such superstitions
are sometimes not without their effect on the course of
human affairs. The early adventurers to Massachusetts
at least paid their passages; no felons were ever shipped
thither; and though it be true that many deboshed younger
brothers of what are called good families may have sought
refuge in Virginia, it is equally certain that a great part
of the early deportations thither were the sweepings of
the London streets and the leavings of the London stews.
It was this my Lord Bacon had in mind when he wrote:
"It is a shameful and unblessed thing to take the scum
of people and wicked condemned men to be the people
with whom you plant." That certain names are found
there is nothing to the purpose, for, even had an *alias*
been beyond the invention of the knaves of that generation,
it is known that servants were often called by their
masters' names, as slaves are now. On what the heralds
call the spindle side, some, at least, of the oldest Vir-
ginian families are descended from matrons who were
exported and sold for so many hogsheads of tobacco the
head. So notorious was this, that it became one of the
jokes of contemporary playwrights, not only that men
bankrupt in purse and character were "food for the Plan-
tations,"(and this before the settlement of New England,)
but also that any drab would suffice to wive such pitiful
adventurers. "Never choose a wife as if you were going
to Virginia," says Middleton in one of his comedies.
The mule is apt to forget all but the equine side of his
pedigree. How early the counterfeit nobility of the Old
Dominion became a topick of ridicule in the Mother

2 N

Country may be learned from a play of Mrs. Behn's, founded on the Rebellion of Bacon: for even these kennels of literature may yield a fact or two to pay the raking. Mrs. Flirt, the keeper of a Virginia ordinary, calls herself the daughter of a baronet "undone in the late rebellion,"—her father having in truth been a tailor,—and three of the Council, assuming to themselves an equal splendour of origin, are shown to have been, one "a broken exciseman who came over a poor servant," another a tinker transported for theft, and the third "a common pickpocket often flogged at the cart's tail." The ancestry of South Carolina will as little pass muster at the Herald's Visitation, though I hold them to have been more reputable, inasmuch as many of them were honest tradesmen and artisans, in some measure exiles for conscience' sake, who would have smiled at the highflying nonsense of their descendants. Some of the more respectable were Jews. The absurdity of supposing a population of eight millions all sprung from gentle loins in the course of a century and a half is too manifest for confutation. But of what use to discuss the matter? An expert genealogist will provide any solvent man with a *genus et proavos* to order. My Lord Burleigh said that "nobility was ancient riches," whence also the Spanish were wont to call their nobles *ricos hombres*, and the aristocracy of America are the descendants of those who first became wealthy, by whatever means. Petroleum will in this wise be the source of much good blood among our posterity. The aristocracy of the South, such as it is, has the shallowest of all foundations, for it is only skin-deep,—the most odious of all, for, while affecting to despise trade, it traces its origin to a successful traffick in men, women, and children, and still draws its chief revenues thence. And though, as Doctor Chamberlayne consolingly says in his *Present State of England*, "to become a Merchant of Foreign Commerce, without serving any Apprentisage, hath been allowed no disparagement to a Gentleman born, especially to a younger Brother," yet I conceive that he would hardly have made a like exception in favour of the particular trade in question. Oddly enough this trade reverses the ordinary standards of social respectability, no less than of morals, for the retail and domestick is as creditable as the wholesale and foreign is degrading to him who follows it. Are our morals, then, no better than *mores* after all? I do not believe that such aristocracy as exists at the South (for I hold with Marius, *fortissimum quemque generosissimum*) will be found an element of anything like persistent strength in war, — thinking the saying of Lord Bacon (whom one quaintly called *inductionis dominus et Verulamii*) as true as it is pithy, that "the more gentlemen, ever the more books of subsidies." It is odd enough as an historical precedent, that, while the fathers of New England were laying deep in religion, education, and freedom the basis of a polity which has substantially outlasted any then existing, the first work of the founders of Virginia, as may be seen in Wingfield's *Memorial*, was conspiracy and rebellion, — odder yet, as showing the changes which are wrought by circumstance, that the first insurrection in South Carolina was against the aristocratical scheme of the Proprietary Government. I do not find that the cuticular aristocracy of the South has added anything to the refinements of civilization except the carrying of bowie-knives and the chewing of tobacco, — a high-toned Southern gentleman being commonly not only *quadrumanous*, but *quidruminant*.

I confess that the present letter of Mr. Sawin increases my doubts as to the sincerity of the convictions which he professes, and I am inclined to think that the triumph of the legitimate Government, sure sooner or later to take place, will find him and a large majority of his newly-adopted fellow-citizens (who hold with Dædalus, the primal sitter-on-the-fence, that *medium tenere tutissimum*) original Union men. The criticisms towards the close of his letter on certain of our failings are worthy to be seriously perpended; for he is not, as I think, without a spice of vulgar shrewdness. *Fas est et ab hoste doceri:* there is no reckoning without your host. As to the good-nature in us which he seems to gird at, while I would not consecrate a chapel, as they have not scrupled to do in France, to *Nôtre Dame de la Haine* (Our Lady of Hate), yet I cannot forget that the corruption of good-nature is the generation of laxity of principle. Good-nature is our national characteristick; and though it be, perhaps, nothing more than a culpable weakness or cowardice, when it leads us to put up tamely with manifold impositions and breaches of implied contracts, (as too frequently in our publick conveyances,) it becomes a positive crime, when it leads us to look unresentfully on peculation, and to regard treason to the best Government that ever existed as something with which a gentleman may shake hands without soiling his fingers. I do not think the gallows-tree the most profitable member of our *Sylva;* but, since it continues to be planted, I would fain see a Northern limb ingrafted on it, that it may bear some other fruit than loyal Tennesseeans.

A relick has recently been discovered on the east bank of Bushy Brook in North Jaalam, which I conceive to be an inscription in Runick characters relating to the early expedition of the Northmen to this continent. I shall make fuller investigations, and communicate the result in due season.

Respectfully,

Your obedient servant,

Homer Wilbur, A. M.

P. S. — I inclose a year's subscription from Deacon Tinkham.

I hed it on my min' las' time, when I to write ye started,
To tech the leadin' featurs o' my gittin' me convarted;
But, ez my letters hez to go clearn roun' by way o' Cuby,
'T wun't seem no staler now than then, by th' time it gits
  where you be.
You know up North, though secs an' things air plenty ez
  you please,
Ther' warn't nut one on 'em thet come jes' square with
  my idees :
They all on 'em wuz too much mixed with Covenants o'
  Works,
An' would hev answered jest ez wal for Afrikins an'
  Turks,
Fer where 's a Christian's privilige an' his rewards en-
  suin',
Ef 't ain't perfessin' right an eend 'thout nary need o'
  doin' ?

I dessay they suit workin'-folks thet ain't noways per-
    tic'lar,
But nut your Southun gen'leman thet keeps his parpen-
    dic'lar ;
I don't blame nary man thet casts his lot along o' *his*
    folks,
But ef you cal'late to save *me*, 't must be with folks thet
    is folks ;
Cov'nants o' works go 'ginst my grain, but down here I've
    found out
The true fus'-fem'ly A 1 plan, — here's how it come
    about.
When I fus' sot up with Miss S., sez she to me, sez she,
" Without you git religion, Sir, the thing can't never be ;
Nut but wut I respeck," sez she, " your intellectle part,
But you wun't noways du for me athout a change o'
    heart :
Nothun religion works wal North, but it's ez soft ez
    spruce,
Compared to ourn, for keepin' sound," sez she, " upon the
    goose ;
A day's experunce 'd prove to ye, ez easy 'z pull a trigger,
It takes the Southun pint o' view to raise ten bales a
    nigger ;
You 'll fin' thet human natur, South, ain't wholesome
    more 'n skin-deep,
An' once 't a darkie 's took with it, he wun't be wuth his
    keep."
" How *shell* I git it, Ma'am ? " sez I. " Attend the nex'
    camp-meetin',"
Sez she, " an' it 'll come to ye ez cheap ez onbleached
    sheetin'."

Wal, so I went along an' hearn most an impressive
    sarmon
About besprinklin' Afriky with fourth-proof dew o'
    Harmon :
He did n't put no weaknin' in, but gin it tu us hot,
'Z ef he an' Satan 'd ben two bulls in one five-acre lot :
I don't purtend to foller him, but give ye jes' the
    heads ;
For pulpit ellerkence, you know, 'most ollers kin' o'
    spreads.

Ham's seed wuz gin to us in chairge, an' should n't we be li'ble
In Kingdom Come, ef we kep' back their priv'lege in the Bible?
The cusses an' the promerses make one gret chain, an' ef
You snake one link out here, one there, how much on 't ud be lef'?
All things wuz gin to man for 's use, his sarvice, an' delight;
An' don't the Greek an' Hebrew words thet mean a Man mean White?
Ain't it belittlin' the Good Book in all its proudes' featurs
To think 't wuz wrote for black an' brown an' 'lasses-colored creaturs,
Thet could n' read it, ef they would, nor ain't by lor allowed to,
But ough' to take wut we think suits their naturs, an' be proud to?
Warn't it more prof'table to bring your raw materil thru
Where you can work it inta grace an' inta cotton, tu,
Than sendin' missionaries out where fevers might defeat 'em,
An' ef the butcher did n' call, their p'rishioners might eat 'em?
An' then, agin, wut airthly use?   Nor 't warn't our fault, in so fur
Ez Yankee skippers would keep on a-totin' on 'em over.
'T improved the whites by savin' 'em from ary need o' wurkin',
An' kep' the blacks from bein' lost thru idleness an' shirkin';
We took to 'em ez nat'ral ez a barn-owl doos to mice,
An' hed our hull time on our hands to keep us out o' vice;
It made us feel ez pop'lar ez a hen doos with one chicken,
An' fill our place in Natur's scale by givin' 'em a lickin':
For why should Cæsar git his dues more 'n Juno, Pomp, an' Cuffy?
It's justifyin' Ham to spare a nigger when he 's stuffy.
Where 'd their soles go tu, like to know, ef we should let 'em ketch
Freeknowledgism an' Fourierism an' Speritoolism an' sech?

When Satan sets himself to work to raise his very bes'
    muss,
He scatters roun' ouscriptur'l views relatin' to Ones'mus.
You 'd ough' to seen, though, how his facs an' argymunce
    an' figgers
Drawed tears o' real conviction from a lot o' pen'tent
    niggers !
It warn't like Wilbur's meetin', where you 're shet up in
    a pew,
Your dickeys sorrin' off your ears, an' bilin' to be thru;
Ther' wuz a tent clost by thet hed a kag o' sunthin' in
    it,
Where you could go, ef you wuz dry, an' damp ye in a
    minute;
An' ef you did dror off a spell, ther' wuz n't no occasion
To lose the thread, because, ye see, he bellered like all
    Bashan.
It 's dry work follerin' argymunce, an' so, 'twix' this an'
    thet,
I felt conviction weighin' down somehow inside my hat;
It growed an' growed like Jonah's gourd, a kin' o' whirlin'
    ketched me,
Ontil I fin'lly clean giv out an' owned up thet he 'd
    fetched me;
An' when nine tenths o' th' perrish took to tumblin' roun'
    an' hollerin',
I did n' fin' no gret in th' way o' turnin' tu an' follerin'.
Soon ez Miss S. see thet, sez she, " *Thet* 's wut I call
    wuth seein' !
Thet 's actin' like a reas'nable an' intellectle bein' ! "
An' so we fin'lly made it up, concluded to hitch hosses,
An' here I be 'n my ellermunt among creation's bosses;
Arter I 'd drawed sech heaps o' blanks, Fortin at last hez
    sent a prize,
An' chose me for a shinin' light o' missionary entaprise.

This leads me to another pint on which I 've changed my
    plan
O' thinkin' so 's 't I might become a straight-out Southun
    man.
Miss S. (her maiden name wuz Higgs, o' the fus' fem'ly
    here)
On her Ma's side 's all Juggernot, on Pa's all Cavileer,

An' sence I 've married into her an' stept into her shoes,
It ain't more 'n nateral thet I should modderfy my
    views:
I 've ben a-readin' in Debow ontil I 've fairly gut
So 'nlightened thet I 'd full ez lives ha' ben a Dook
    ez nut;
An' when we 've laid ye all out stiff, an' Jeff hez gut his
    crown,
An' comes to pick his nobles out, *wun't* this child be in
    town !
We 'll hev an Age o' Chivverlry surpassin' Mister
    Burke's,
Where every fem'ly is fus'-best an' nary white man
    works:
Our system 's sech, the thing 'll root ez easy ez a tater;
For while your lords in furrin parts ain't noways marked
    by natur',
Nor sot apart from ornery folks in featurs nor in figgers,
Ef ourn 'll keep their faces washed, you 'll know 'em from
    their niggers.
Ain't *sech* things wuth secedin' for, an' gittin' red o' you
Thet waller in your low idees, an' will till all is blue ?
Fact is, we *air* a diff'rent race, an' I, for one, don't see,
Sech havin' ollers ben the case, how w' ever *did* agree.
It 's sunthin' thet you lab'rin'-folks up North hed ough'
    to think on,
Thet Higgses can't bemean themselves to rulin' by a
    Lincoln, —
Thet men, (an' guv'nors, tu,) that hez sech Normal names
    ez Pickens,
Accustomed to no-kin' o' work, 'thout 't is to givin' lickins,
Can't masure votes with folks thet git their livin' from
    their farms,
An' prob'ly think thet Law 's ez good ez hevin' coats
    o' arms.
Sence I 've ben here, I 've hired a chap to look about
    for me
To git me a transplantable an' thrifty fem'ly-tree,
An' he tells *me* the Sawins is ez much o' Normal blood
Ez Pickens an' the rest on 'em, an' older 'n Noah's flood.
Your Normal schools wun't turn ye into Normals, for
    it 's clear,
Ef eddykatin' done the thing, they 'd be some skurcer here.

Pickenses, Boggses, Pettuses, Magoffins, Letchers,
    Polks, —
Where can you scare up names like them among your
    mudsill folks?
Ther' 's nothin' to compare with 'em, you 'd fin', ef you
    should glance,
Among the tip-top femerlies in Englan', nor in France:
I 've hearn from 'sponsible men whose word wuz full ez
    good 's their note,
Men thet can run their face for drinks, an' keep a
    Sunday coat,
Thet they wuz all on 'em come down, and come down
    pooty fur,
From folks thet, 'thout their crowns wuz on, ou'doors
    would n' never stir,
Nor thet ther' warn't a Southun man but wut wuz
    primy fashy
O' the bes' blood in Europe, yis, an' Afriky an' Ashy:
Sech bein' the case, is 't likely we should bend like
    cotton-wickin',
Or set down under anythin' so low-lived ez a lickin'?
More 'n this, — hain't we the literatoor an' science, tu,
    by gorry?
Hain't we them intellectle twins, them giants, Simms
    an' Maury,
Each with full twice the ushle brains, like nothin' thet
    I know,
'Thout 't wuz a double-headed calf I see once to a
    show?

For all thet, I warn't jest at fust in favor o' secedin';
I wuz for layin' low a spell to find out where 't wuz
    leadin',
For hevin' South-Carliny try her hand at seprit-
    nationin',
She takin' resks an' findin' funds, an' we co-opera-
    tionin', —
I mean a kin' o' hangin' roun' an' settin' on the fence,
Till Prov'dunce pinted how to jump an' save the most
    expense;
I recollected thet 'ere mine o' lead to Shiraz Centre
Thet bust up Jabez Pettibone, an' did n't want to
    ventur'

'Fore I wuz sartin wut come out ud pay for wut
    went in,
For swappin' silver off for lead ain't the sure way to
    win;
(An'. fact, it *doos* look now ez though — but folks must
    live an' larn —
We should git lead, an' more 'n we want, out o' the Old
    Consarn;)
But when I see a man so wise an' honest ez Buchanan
A-lettin' us hev all the forts an' all the arms an' cannon,
Admittin' we wuz nat'lly right an' you wuz nat'lly
    wrong,
Coz you wuz lab'rin'-folks an' we wuz wut they call
    bong-tong,
An' coz there warn't no fight in ye more 'n in a mashed
    potater,
While two o' *us* can't skurcely meet but wut we fight
    by natur',
An' th' ain't a bar-room here would pay for openin' on 't
    a night,
Without it giv the priverlege o' bein' shot at sight,
Which proves we 're Natur's noblemen, with whom it
    don't surprise
The British aristoxy should feel boun' to sympathize, —
Seein' all this, an' seein', tu, the thing wuz strikin'
    roots
While Uncle Sam sot still in hopes thet some one 'd
    bring his boots,
I thought th' ole Union's hoops wuz off, an' let myself be
    sucked in
To rise a peg an' jine the crowd thet went for recon-
    structin', —
Thet is, to hev the pardnership under th' ole name con-
    tinner
Jest ez it wuz, we drorrin' pay, you findin' bone an'
    sinner, —
On'y to put it in the bond, an' enter 't in the journals,
Thet you 're the nat'ral rank an' file, an' we the nat'ral
    kurnels.

Now this I thought a fees'ble plan, thet 'ud work smooth
    ez grease,
Suitin' the Nineteenth Century an' Upper Ten idees,

An' there I meant to stick, an' so did most o' th' leaders, tu,
Coz we all thought the chance wuz good o' puttin' on it
    thru;
But Jeff he hit upon a way o' helpin' on us forrard
By bein' unannermous, — a trick you ain't quite up to,
    Norrard.
A baldin hain't no more 'f a chance with them new apple-
    corers
Than folks's oppersition views aginst the Ringtail
    Roarers;
They'll take 'em out on him 'bout east, — one canter on
    a rail
Makes a man feel unannermous ez Jonah in the whale;
Or ef he's a slow-moulded cuss thet can't seem quite
    t' agree,
He gits the noose by tellergraph upon the nighes' tree:
Their mission-work with Afrikins hez put 'em up, thet 's
    sartin,
To all the mos' across-lot ways o' preachin' an' con-
    vartin';
I'll bet my hat th' ain't nary priest, nor all on 'em to-
    gether,
Thet cairs conviction to the min' like Reveren' Taran-
    feather;
Why, he sot up with me one night, an' labored to sech
    purpose,
Thet (ez an owl by daylight 'mongst a flock o' teazin'
    chirpers
Sees clearer 'n mud the wickedness o' eatin' little birds)
I see my error an' agreed to shen it arterwurds;
An' I should say, (to jedge our folks by facs in my pos-
    session,)
Thet three 's Unannermous where one 's a 'Riginal Se-
    cession;
So it 's a thing you fellers North may safely bet your
    chink on,
Thet we 're all water-proofed agin th' usurpin' reign o'
    Lincoln.

Jeff 's *some.* He 's gut another plan thet hez pertic'lar
    merits,
In givin' things a cherfle look an' stiffnin' loose-hung
    sperits;

For while your million papers, wut with lyin' an' dis
    cussin',
Keep folks's tempers all on eend a-fumin' an' a-fussin',
A-wondrin' this an' guessin' thet, an' dreadin', every
    night,
The breechin' o' the Univarse 'll break afore it 's light,
Our papers don't purtend to print on'y wut Guv'ment
    choose,
An' thet insures us all to git the very best o' noose:
Jeff hez it of all sorts an' kines, an' sarves it out ez
    wanted
So 's 't every man gits wut he likes an' nobody ain't
    scanted;
Sometimes it 's vict'ries, (they 're 'bout all ther' is that 's
    cheap down here,)
Sometimes it 's France an' England on the jump to in-
    terfere.
Fact is, the less the people know o' wut ther' is a-doin',
The hendier 't is for Guv'ment, sence it henders trouble
    brewin';
An' noose is like a shinplaster, — it 's good, ef you be-
    lieve it,
Or, wut 's all same, the other man thet 's goin' to receive
    it:
Ef you 've a son in th' army, wy, it 's comfortin' to hear
He 'll hev no gretter resk to run than seein' th' in'my's
    rear,
Coz, ef an F. F. looks at 'em, they ollers break an' run,
Or wilt right down ez debtors will thet stumble on a dun,
(An' this, ef an'thin', proves the wuth o' proper fem'ly
    pride,
Fer sech mean shucks ez creditors are all on Lincoln's
    side);
Ef I hev scrip thet wun't go off no more 'n a Belgin rifle,
An' read thet it 's at par on 'Change, it makes me feel
    deli'fle;
It 's cheerin', tu, where every man mus' fortify his bed,
To hear thet Freedom 's the one thing our darkies mos'ly
    dread,
An' thet experunce, time 'n' agin, to Dixie's Land hez
    shown
Ther' 's nothin' like a powder-cask f'r a stiddy corner-
    stone;

Ain't it ez good ez nuts, when salt is sellin' by the ounce
For its own weight in Treash'ry-bons, (ef bought in small
    amounts,)
When even whiskey's gittin' skurce, an' sugar can't be
    found,
To know thet all the ellerments o' luxury abound?
An' don't it glorify sal'-pork, to come to understand
It's wut the Richmon' editors call fatness o' the land?
Nex' thing to knowin' you're well off is *nut* to know
    when y' ain't;
An' ef Jeff says all's goin' wal, who'll ventur' t' say it
    ain't?

This cairn the Constitooshun roun' ez Jeff doos in his
    hat
Is hendier a dreffle sight, an' comes more kin' o' pat.
I tell ye wut, my jedgment is you're pooty sure to fail,
Ez long 'z the head keeps turnin' back for counsel to the
    tail:
Th' advantiges of our consarn for bein' prompt air
    gret,
While, 'long o' Congress, you can't strike, 'f you git an
    iron het;
They bother roun' with argooin', an' var'ous sorts o'
    foolin',
To make sure ef it's leg'lly het, an' all the while it's
    coolin',
So's 't when you come to strike, it ain't no gret to wish
    ye j'y on,
An' hurts the hammer 'z much or more ez wut it doos the
    iron.
Jeff don't allow no jawin'-sprees for three months at a
    stretch,
Knowin' the ears long speeches suits air mostly made to
    metch;
He jes' ropes in your tonguey chaps an' reg'lar ten-inch
    bores
An' lets 'em play at Congress, ef they'll du it with closed
    doors;
So they ain't no more bothersome than ef we'd took an'
    sunk 'em,
An' yit enj'y th' exclusive right to one another's Bun-
    combe

'Thout doin' nobody no hurt, an' 'thout its costin'
　　nothin',
Their pay bein' jes' Confedrit funds, they findin' keep
　　an' clothin';
They taste the sweets o' public life, an' plan their little
　　jobs,
An' suck the Treash'ry, (no gret harm, for it's ez dry ez
　　cobs,)
An' go thru all the motions jest ez safe ez in a prison,
An' hev their business to themselves, while Buregard hez
　　hisn:
Ez long'z he gives the Hessians fits, committees can't
　　make bother
'Bout whether 't's done the legle way or whether 't's
　　done the t'other.
An' *I* tell *you* you've gut to larn thet War ain't one long
　　teeter
Betwixt *I wan' to* an' *'T wun't du*, debatin' like a skeetur
Afore he lights, — all is, to give the other side a millin',
An' arter thet's done, th' ain't no resk but wut the lor'll
　　be willin';
No metter wut the guv'ment is, ez nigh ez I can hit it,
A lickin' 's constitooshunal, pervidin' *We* don't git it.
Jeff don't stan' dilly-dallyin', afore he takes a fort,
(With no one in,) to git the leave o' the nex' Soopreme
　　Court,
Nor don't want forty-'leven weeks o' jawin' an' ex-
　　poundin'
To prove a nigger hez a right to save him, ef he's drown-
　　din';
Whereas ole Abram 'd sink afore he'd let a darkie boost
　　him,
Ef Taney shouldn't come along an' hedn't interdooced
　　him.
It ain't your twenty millions thet'll ever block Jeff's
　　game,
But one Man thet wun't let 'em jog jest ez he's takin' aim:
Your numbers they may strengthen ye or weaken ye, ez 't
　　heppens
They're willin' to be helpin' hands or wuss'n-nothin' cap'ns.
I've chose my side, an' 't ain't no odds ef I wuz drawed
　　with magnets,
Or ef I thought it prudenter to jine the nighes' bagnets;

I 've made my ch'ice, an' ciphered out, from all I see an'
    heard,
Th' ole Constitooshun never 'd git her decks for action
    cleared,
Long 'z you elect for Congressmen poor shotes thet want
    to go
Coz they can't seem to git their grub no otherways than
    so,
An' let your bes' men stay to home coz they wun't show
    ez talkers,
Nor can't be hired to fool ye an' sof'-soap ye at a caucus, —
Long 'z ye set by Rotashun more 'n ye do by folks's merits,
Ez though experunce thriv by change o' sile, like corn an'
    kerrits, —
Long 'z you allow a critter's " claims " coz, spite o' shoves
    an' tippins,
He 's kep' his private pan jest where 't would ketch mos'
    public drippins, —
Long 'z A. 'll turn tu an' grin' B.'s exe, ef B. 'll help him
    grin' hisn,
(An' thet 's the main idee by which your leadin' men hev
    risen,) —
Long 'z you let *ary* exe be groun', 'less 't is to cut the
    weasan'
O' sneaks thet dunno till they 're told wut is an' wut ain't
    Treason, —
Long 'z ye give out commissions to a lot o' peddlin' drones
Thet trade in whiskey with their men an' skin 'em to their
    bones, —
Long 'z ye sift out " safe " canderdates thet no one ain't
    afeared on
Coz they 're so thund'rin' eminent for bein' never heard on,
An' hain't no record, ez it 's called, for folks to pick a hole
    in,
Ez ef it hurt a man to hev a body with a soul in,
An' it wuz ostentashun to be showin' on 't about,
When half his feller-citizens contrive to do without, —
Long 'z you suppose your votes can turn biled kebbage
    into brain,
An' ary man thet 's pop'lar 's fit to drive a lightnin'-train, —
Long 'z you believe democracy means *I 'm ez good ez you be,*
An' that a feller from the ranks can't be a knave or
    booby, —

Long 'z Congress seems purvided, like yer street-cars an'
    yer 'busses,
With ollers room for jes' one more o' your spiled-in-bakin'
    cusses,
Dough 'thout the emptins of a soul, an' yit with means
    about 'em
(Like essence-peddlers ') thet 'll make folks long to be
    without 'em,
Jest heavy 'nough to turn a scale thet 's doubtfle the wrong
    way,
An' make their nat'ral arsenal o' bein' nasty pay, —
Long 'z them things last, (an' *I* don't see no gret signs of
    improvin',)
I sha'n't up stakes, not hardly yit, nor 't would n't pay
    for movin';
For, 'fore you lick us, it 'll be the long'st day ever *you* see.
Yourn, (ez I 'xpec' to be nex' spring,)

B., MARKISS O' BIG BOOSY.

¹ A rustic euphemism for the American variety of the *Mephitis.*

H. W.

No. IV.

A MESSAGE OF JEFF DAVIS IN SECRET SESSION.

Conjecturally reported by H. BIGLOW.

TO THE EDITORS OF THE ATLANTIC MONTHLY.

JAALAM, 10th March, 1862.

GENTLEMEN, — My leisure has been so entirely occupied with the hitherto fruitless endeavour to decipher the Runick inscription whose fortunate discovery I mentioned in my last communication, that I have not found time to discuss, as I had intended, the great problem of what we are to do with slavery, — a topick on which the publick mind in this place is at present more than ever agitated. What my wishes and hopes are I need not say, but for safe conclusions I do not conceive that we are yet in possession of facts enough on which to bottom them with certainty. Acknowledging the hand of Providence, as I do, in all events, I am sometimes inclined to think that they are wiser than we, and am willing to wait till we have made this continent once more a place where freemen can live in security and honour, before assuming any further responsibility. This is the view taken by my neighbour Habakkuk Sloansure, Esq., the president of our bank, whose opinion in the practical affairs of life has great weight with me, as I have generally found it to be justified by the event, and whose counsel, had I followed it, would have saved me from an unfortunate investment of a considerable part of the painful economies of half a century in the Northwest-Passage Tunnel. After a somewhat animated discussion with this gentleman, a few days since, I expanded, on the *audi alteram partem* principle, something which he happened to say by way of illustration, into the following fable.

2 o

FESTINA LENTE.

ONCE on a time there was a pool
Fringed all about with flag-leaves cool
And spotted with cow-lilies garish,
Of frogs and pouts the ancient parish.
Alders the creaking redwings sink on,
Tussocks that house blithe Bob o' Lincoln
Hedged round the unassailed seclusion,
Where muskrats piled their cells Carthusian;
And many a moss-embroidered log,
The watering-place of summer frog,
Slept and decayed with patient skill,
As watering-places sometimes will.

Now in this Abbey of Theleme,
Which realized the fairest dream
That ever dozing bull-frog had,
Sunned on a half-sunk lily-pad,
There rose a party with a mission
To mend the polliwogs' condition,
Who notified the sélectmen
To a call a meeting there and then.
" Some kind of steps," they said, " are needed;
They don't come on so fast as we did:
Let 's dock their tails; if that don't make 'em
Frogs by brevet, the Old One take 'em!
That boy, that came the other day
To dig some flag-root down this way,
His jack-knife left, and 't is a sign
That Heaven approves of our design:
'T were wicked not to urge the step on,
When Providence has sent the weapon."

Old croakers, deacons of the mire,
That led the deep batrachian choir,
Uk! Uk! Caronk! with bass that might
Have left Lablache's out of sight,
Shook nobby heads, and said, " No go!
You 'd better let 'em try to grow:
Old Doctor Time is slow, but still
He does know how to make a pill."

But vain was all their hoarsest bass,
Their old experience out of place,
And spite of croaking and entreating,
The vote was carried in marsh-meeting.
" Lord knows," protest the polliwogs,
" We 're anxious to be grown-up frogs;
But do not undertake the work
Of Nature till she prove a shirk;

'T is not by jumps that she advances,
But wins her way by circumstances:
Pray, wait awhile, until you know
We 're so contrived as not to grow ;
Let Nature take her own direction,
And she 'll absorb our imperfection ;
You might n't like 'em to appear with,
But we must have the things to steer with."

" No," piped the party of reform,
" All great results are ta'en by storm ;
Fate holds her best gifts till we show
We 've strength to make her let them go ;
The Providence that works in history,
And seems to some folks such a mystery,
Does not creep slowly on *incog.*,
But moves by jumps, a mighty frog ;
No more reject the Age's chrism,
Your queues are an anachronism ;
No more the Future's promise mock,
But lay your tails upon the block,
Thankful that we the means have voted
To have you thus to frogs promoted."

The thing was done, the tails were cropped,
And home each philotadpole hopped,
In faith rewarded to exult,
And wait the beautiful result.
Too soon it came ; our pool, so long
The theme of patriot bull-frog's song,
Next day was reeking, fit to smother,
With heads and tails that missed each other,—
Here snoutless tails, there tailless snouts :
The only gainers were the pouts.

MORAL

From lower to the higher next,
Not to the top, is Nature's text ;
And embryo Good, to reach full stature,
Absorbs the Evil in its nature.

I think that nothing will ever give permanent peace
and security to this continent but the extirpation of
Slavery therefrom, and that the occasion is nigh; but I
would do nothing hastily or vindictively, nor presume
to jog the elbow of Providence. No desperate meas-
ures for me till we are sure that all others are hope-
less, — *flectere si nequeo* SUPEROS, *Acheronta movebo.*
To make Emancipation a reform instead of a revolu-

tion is worth a little patience, that we may have the
Border States first, and then the non-slaveholders of
the Cotton States, with us in principle, — a consum-
mation that seems to be nearer than many imagine.
Fiat justitia, ruat cœlum, is not to be taken in a literal
sense by statesmen, whose problem is to get justice
done with as little jar as possible to existing order,
which has at least so much of heaven in it that it is
not chaos. Our first duty toward our enslaved brother
is to educate him, whether he be white or black. The
first need of the free black, is to elevate himself ac-
cording to the standard of this material generation. So
soon as the Ethiopian goes in his chariot, he will find
not only Apostles, but Chief Priests and Scribes and
Pharisees willing to ride with him.

> Nil habet infelix paupertas durius in se
> Quam quod ridiculos homines facit.

I rejoice in the President's late Message, which at last
proclaims the Government on the side of freedom, jus-
tice, and sound policy.

As I write, comes the news of our disaster at
Hampton Roads. I do not understand the supine-
ness which, after fair warning, leaves wood to an un-
equal conflict with iron. It is not enough merely to
have the right on our side, if we stick to the old
flint-lock of tradition. I have observed in my paro-
chial experience (*haud ignarus mali*) that the Devil
is prompt to adopt the latest inventions of destructive
warfare, and may thus take even such a three-decker
as Bishop Butler at an advantage. It is curious,
that, as gunpowder made armour useless on shore, so
armour is having its revenge by baffling its old enemy
at sea, — and that, while gunpowder robbed land war-
fare of nearly all its picturesqueness to give even greater
stateliness and sublimity to a sea-fight, armour bids fair
to degrade the latter into a squabble between two iron-
shelled turtles.

Yours, with esteem and respect,
HOMER WILBUR, A. M.

P. S. — I had wellnigh forgotten to say that the object
of this letter is to inclose a communication from the
gifted pen of Mr. Biglow.

I SENT you a messige, my friens, t' other day,
To tell you I 'd nothin' pertickler to say :
'T wuz the day our new nation gut kin' o' stillborn,
So 't wuz my pleasant dooty t' acknowledge the corn,
An' I see clearly then, ef I did n't before,
Thet the *augur* in inauguration means *bore*.
I need n't tell *you* thet my messige wuz written
To diffuse correc' notions in France an' Gret Britten,
An' agin to impress on the poppylar mind
The comfort an' wisdom o' goin' it blind, —
To say thet I did n't abate not a hooter
O' my faith in a happy an' glorious futur',
Ez rich in each soshle an' p'litickle blessin'
Ez them thet we now hed the joy o' possessin',
With a people united, an' longin' to die
For wut *we* call their country, without askin' why,
An' all the gret things we concluded to slope for
Ez much within reach now ez ever — to hope for.
We 've gut all the ellerments, this very hour,
Thet make up a fus'-class, self-governin' power:
We 've a war, an' a debt, an' a flag; an' ef this
Ain't to be inderpendunt, why, wut on airth is ?
An' nothin' now henders our takin' our station
Ez the freest, enlightenedest, civerlized nation,
Built up on our bran'-new politickle thesis
Thet a Gov'ment's fust right is to tumble to pieces, —
I say nothin' henders our takin' our place
Ez the very fus'-best o' the whole human race,
A-spittin' tobacker ez proud ez you please
On Victory's bes' carpets, or loafin' at ease
In the Tool'ries front-parlor, discussin' affairs
With our heels on the backs o' Napoleon's new chairs,
An' princes a-mixin' our cocktails an' slings, —
Excep', wal, excep' jest a very few things,
Sech ez navies an' armies an' wherewith to pay,
An' gittin' our sogers to run t' other way,
An' not be too over-pertickler in tryin'
To hunt up the very las' ditches to die in.

Ther' are critters so base thet they want it explained
Jes' wut is the totle amount thet we 've gained,
Ez ef we could maysure stupenjious events
By the low Yankee stan'ard o' dollars an' cents:

They seem to forgit, thet, sence last year revolved,
We 've succeeded in gittin' seceshed an' dissolved,
An' thet no one can't hope to git thru dissolootion
'Thout some kin' o' strain on the best Constitootion.
Who asks for a prospec' more flettrin' an' bright,
When from here clean to Texas it's all one free fight?
Hain't we rescued from Seward the gret leadin' featurs
Thet makes it wuth while to be reasonin' creaturs?
Hain't we saved Habus Coppers, improved it in fact,
By suspendin' the Unionists 'stid o' the Act?
Ain't the laws free to all? Where on airth else d' ye see
Every freeman improvin' his own rope an' tree?
Ain't our piety sech (in our speeches an' messiges)
Ez t' astonish ourselves in the bes'-composed pessiges,
An' to make folks that knowed us in th' ole state o' things
Think convarsion ez easy ez drinkin' gin-slings?

It 's ne'ssary to take a good confident tone
With the public; but here, jest amongst us, I own
Things look blacker 'n thunder. Ther' 's no use denyin'
We 're clean out o' money, an' 'most out o' lyin', —
Two things a young nation can't mennage without,
Ef she wants to look wal at her fust comin' out;
For the fust supplies physickle strength, while the second
Gives a morril edvantage thet 's hard to be reckoned:
For this latter I 'm willin' to du wut I can;
For the former you 'll hev to consult on a plan, —
Though our *fust* want (an' this pint I want your best
      views on)
Is plausible paper to print I. O. U.s on.
Some gennlemen think it would cure all our cankers
In the way o' finance, ef we jes' hanged the bankers:
An' I own the proposle 'ud square with my views,
Ef their lives wuz n't all thet we 'd left 'em to lose.
Some say thet more confidence might be inspired,
Ef we voted our cities an' towns to be fired, —
A plan thet 'ud suttenly tax our endurance,
Coz 't would be our own bills we should git for th' insur-
      ance;
But cinders, no metter how sacred we think 'em,
Might n't strike furrin minds ez good sources of income,
Nor the people, perhaps, would n't like the eclaw
O' bein' all turned into paytriots by law.

Some want we should buy all the cotton an' burn it,
On a pledge, when we 've gut thru the war, to return it, —
Then to take the proceeds an' hold *them* ez security
For an issue o' bonds to be met at maturity
With an issue o' notes to be paid in hard cash
On the fus' Monday follerin' the 'tarnal Allsmash:
This hez a safe air, an', once hold o' the gold,
'Ud leave our vile plunderers out in the cold,
An' *might* temp' John Bull, ef it warn't for the dip he
Once gut from the banks o' my own Mississippi.
Some think we could make, by arrangin' the figgers,
A hendy home-currency out of our niggers;
But it wun't du to lean much on ary sech staff,
For they 're gittin' tu current a'ready, by half.
One gennleman says, ef we lef' our loan out
Where Floyd could git hold on 't, *he* 'd take it, no doubt;
But 't ain't jes' the takin', though 't hez a good look,
We mus' git sunthin' out on it arter it 's took,
An' we need now more 'n ever, with sorrer I own,
Thet some one another should let us a loan,
Sence a soger wun't fight, on'y jes' while he draws his
Pay down on the nail, for the best of all causes,
'Thout askin' to know wut the quarrel 's about, —
An' once come to thet, why, our game is played out.
It 's ez true ez though I should n't never hev said it
Thet a hitch hez took place in our system o' credit;
I swear it 's all right in my speeches an' messiges,
But ther' 's idees afloat, ez ther' is about sessiges:
Folks wun't take a bond ez a basis to trade on,
Without nosin' round to find out wut it 's made on,
An' the thought more an' more thru the public min' crosses
Thet our Treshry hez gut 'mos' too many dead hosses.
Wut 's called credit, you see, is some like a balloon,
Thet looks while it 's up 'most ez harnsome 'z a moon,
But once git a leak in 't an' wut looked so grand
Caves righ' down in a jiffy ez flat ez your hand.
Now the world is a dreffle mean place, for our sins,
Where ther' ollus is critters about with long pins
A-prickin' the bubbles we 've blowed with sech care,
An' provin' ther' 's nothin' inside but bad air:
They 're all Stuart Millses, poor-white trash, an' sneaks,
Without no more chivverlry 'n Choctaws or Creeks,
Who think a real gennleman's promise to pay

Is meant to be took in trade's ornery way:
Them fellers an' I could n' never agree;
They 're the nateral foes o' the Southun Idee;
I 'd gladly take all of our other resks on me
To be red o' this low-lived politikle 'con'my!

Now a dastardly notion is gittin' about
Thet our bladder is bust an' the gas oozin' out,
An' onless we can mennage in some way to stop it,
Why, the thing 's a gone coon, an' we might ez wal
    drop it.
Brag works wal at fust, but it ain't jes' the thing
For a stiddy inves'ment the shiners to bring,
An' votin' we 're prosp'rous a hundred times over
Wun't change bein' starved into livin' on clover.
Manassas done sunthin' tow'rds drawin' the wool
O'er the green, anti-slavery eyes o' John Bull:
Oh, *warn't* it a godsend, jes' when sech tight fixes
Wuz crowdin' us mourners, to throw double-sixes!
I wuz tempted to think, an' it wuz n't no wonder,
Ther' wuz reelly a Providence, — over or under, —
When, all packed for Nashville, I fust ascertained
From the papers up North wut a victory we 'd gained.
'T wuz the time for diffusin' correc' views abroad
Of our union an' strength an' relyin' on God;
An', fact, when I 'd gut thru my fust big surprise,
I much ez half b'lieved in my own tallest lies,
An' conveyed the idee thet the whole Southun popperlace
Wuz Spartans all on the keen jump for Thermopperlies,
Thet set on the Lincolnites' bombs till they bust,
An' fight for the priv'lege o' dyin' the fust;
But Roanoke, Bufort, Millspring, an' the rest
Of our recent starn-foremost successes out West,
Hain't left us a foot for our swellin' to stand on, —
We 've showed *too* much o' wut Buregard calls *abandon*,
For all our Thermopperlies (an' it 's a marcy
We hain't hed no more) hev ben clean vicy-varsy,
An' wut Spartans wuz lef' when the battle wuz done
Wuz them thet wuz too unambitious to run.

Oh, ef we hed on'y jes' gut Reecognition,
Things now would ha' ben in a different position!
You 'd ha' hed all you wanted. the paper blockade

Smashed up into toothpicks, — unlimited trade
In the one thing thet's needfle, till niggers, I swow,
Hed ben thicker 'n provisional shinplasters now, —
Quinine by the ton 'ginst the shakes when they seize
    ye, —
Nice paper to coin into C. S. A. specie;
The voice of the driver 'd be heerd in our land,
An' the univarse scringe, ef we lifted our hand:
Would n't *thet* be some like a fulfillin' the prophecies,
With all the fus' fem'lies in all the fust offices?
'T wuz a beautiful dream, an' all sorrer is idle, —
But *ef* Lincoln *would* ha' hanged Mason an' Slidell!
For would n't the Yankees hev found they 'd ketched
    Tartars,
Ef they 'd raised two sech critters as them into martyrs?
Mason *wuz* F. F. V., though a cheap card to win on,
But tother was jes' New York trash to begin on;
They ain't o' no good in Európean pellices,
But think wut a help they 'd ha' ben on their gallowses!
They 'd ha' felt they wuz truly fulfillin' their mission,
An', oh, how dog-cheap we 'd ha' gut Reecognition!

But somehow another, wutever we 've tried,
Though the the'ry 's fust-rate, the facs *wun't* coincide:
Facs are contrary 'z mules, an' ez hard in the mouth,
An' they allus hev showed a mean spite to the South.
Sech bein' the case, we hed best look about
For some kin' o' way to slip *our* necks out:
Le' 's vote our las' dollar, ef one can be found,
(An', at any rate, votin' it hez a good sound,) —
Le' 's swear thet to arms all our people is flyin',
(The critters can't read, an' wun't know how we 're
    lyin',) —
Thet Toombs is advancin' to sack Cincinnater,
With a rovin' commission to pillage an' slahter, —
Thet we 've throwed to the winds all regard for wut 's
    lawfle,
An' gone in for sunthin' promiscu'sly awfle.
Ye see, hitherto, it 's our own knaves an' fools
Thet we 've used, (those for whetstones, an' t' others ez
    tools,)
An' now our las' chance is in puttin' to test
The same kin' o' cattle up North an' out West, —

Your Belmonts, Vallandighaus, Woodses, an' sech,
Poor shotes thet ye could n't persuade us to tech,
Not in ornery times, though we 're willin' to feed 'em
With a nod now an' then, when we happened to need
    'em ;
Why, for my part, I 'd ruther shake hands with a nigger
Than with cusses that load an' don't darst dror a trigger;
They 're the wust wooden nutmegs the Yankees produce,
Shaky everywheres else, an' jes' sound on the goose ;
They ain't wuth a cus, an' I set nothin' by 'em,
But we 're in sech a fix thet I s'pose we mus' try 'em.
I ——— But, Gennlemen, here 's a despatch jes' come in
Which shows thet the tide 's begun turnin' agin, —
Gret Cornfedrit success !   C'lumbus eevacooated !
I mus' run down an' hev the thing properly stated,
An' show wut a triumph it is, an' how lucky
To fin'lly git red o' thet cussed Kentucky, —
An' how, sence Fort Donelson, winnin' the day
Consists in triumphantly gittin' away.

No. V.

SPEECH OF HONOURABLE PRESERVED DOE
IN SECRET CAUCUS.

TO THE EDITORS OF THE ATLANTIC MONTHLY.

JAALAM, 12th April, 1862.

GENTLEMEN, — As I cannot but hope that the ultimate, if not speedy, success of the national arms is now sufficiently ascertained, sure as I am of the righteousness of our cause and its consequent claim on the blessing of God, (for I would not show a faith inferior to that of the pagan historian with his *Facile evenit quod Dis cordi est,*) it seems to me a suitable occasion to withdraw our minds a moment from the confusing din of battle to objects of peaceful and permanent interest. Let us not neglect the monuments of preterite history because what shall be history is so diligently making under our eyes. *Cras ingens iterabimus æquor;* to-morrow will be time enough for that stormy sea; to-day let me engage the attention of your readers with the Runick inscription to whose fortunate discovery I have heretofore alluded. Well may we say with the poet, *Multa renascuntur quæ jam cecidere.* And I would premise, that, although I can no longer resist the evidence of my own senses from the stone before me to the ante-Columbian discovery of this continent by the Northmen, *gens inclytissima,* as they are called in a Palermitan inscription, written fortunately in a less debatable character than that which I am about to decipher, yet I would by no means be understood as wishing to vilipend the merits of the great Genoese, whose name will never be forgotten so long as the inspiring strains of "Hail Columbia" shall continue to be heard. Though he must be stripped also of whatever praise may belong to the experiment of the egg, which I find proverbially attributed by Castilian authors to a certain Juanito or Jack, (perhaps an offshoot of our giant-killing mythus,) his name will still remain one of the most illustrious of modern times. But the impartial historian owes a duty likewise to obscure merit, and my solicitude to render a tardy justice is perhaps quickened by my having known those who, had their own field of labour been less secluded, might have found a readier acceptance with the reading publick. I could give an example, but I forbear: *forsitan nostris ex ossibus oritur ultor.*

Touching Runick inscriptions, I find that they may be classed under three general heads: 1°. Those which are understood by the Danish Royal Society of Northern Antiquaries, and Professor Rafn, their Secretary; 2°. Those which are comprehensible only by Mr. Rafn; and 3°. Those which neither the Society, Mr. Rafn, nor anybody else can be said in any definite sense to understand, and which accordingly offer peculiar temptations to enucleating sagacity. These last are naturally deemed the most valuable by intelligent antiquaries, and to this class the stone now in my possession fortunately belongs. Such give a picturesque variety to ancient events, because susceptible oftentimes of as many interpretations as there are individual archæologists; and since facts are only the pulp in which the Idea or event-seed is softly imbedded till it ripen, it is of little consequence what colour or flavour we attribute to them, provided it be agreeable. Availing myself of the obliging assistance of Mr. Arphaxad Bowers, an ingenious photographick artist, whose house-on-wheels has now stood for three years on our Meeting-House Green, with the somewhat contradictory inscription, — "*our motto is onward*," — I have sent accurate copies of my treasure to many learned men and societies, both native and European. I may hereafter communicate their different and (*me judice*) equally erroneous solutions. I solicit also, Messrs. Editors, your own acceptance of the copy herewith inclosed. I need only premise further, that the stone itself is a goodly block of metamorphick sandstone, and that the Runes resemble very nearly the ornithichnites or fossil bird-tracks of Dr. Hitchcock, but with less regularity or apparent design than is displayed by those remarkable geological monuments. These are rather the *non bene junctarum discordia semina rerum.* Resolved to leave no door open to cavil, I first of all attempted the elucidation of this remarkable example of lithick literature by the ordinary modes, but with no adequate return for my labour. I then considered myself amply justified in resorting to that heroick treatment the felicity of which, as applied by the great Bentley to Milton, had long ago enlisted my admiration. Indeed, I had already made up my mind, that, in case good-fortune should throw any such invaluable record in my way, I would proceed with it in the following simple and satisfactory method. After a cursory examination, merely sufficing for an approximative estimate of its length, I would write down a hypothetical inscription based upon antecedent probabilities, and then proceed to extract from the characters engraven on the stone a meaning as nearly as possible conformed to this *a priori* product of my own ingenuity. The result more than justified my hopes, inasmuch as the two inscriptions were made without any great violence to tally in all essential particulars. I then proceeded, not without some anxiety, to my second test, which was, to read the Runick letters diagonally, and again with the same success. With an excitement pardonable under the circumstances, yet tempered with thankful humility, I now applied my last and severest trial, my *experimentum crucis*. I turned the stone, now doubly precious in my eyes, with scrupulous exactness upside down. The physical exertion so far displaced my spectacles as to derange for a moment the focus of vision. I confess that it was with some tremulousness that I readjusted them upon my nose, and prepared my mind to bear with calmness any disappointment that might ensue. But, *O albo dies notanda lapillo!* what was my delight to find that the change of position had effected none in the sense of the writing, even by so much as a single letter! I was now, and justly, as I think, satisfied of the conscientious exactness of my interpretation. It is as follows:—

HERE

BJARNA GRÍMÓLFSSON

FIRST DRANK CLOUD-BROTHER

THROUGH CHILD-OF-LAND-AND-WATER:

that is, drew smoke through a reed stem. In other words, we have here a record of the first smoking

of the herb *Nicotiana Tabacum* by an European on
this continent. The probable results of this discovery
are so vast as to baffle conjecture. If it be objected,
that the smoking of a pipe would hardly justify the
setting up of a memorial stone, I answer, that even
now the Moquis Indian, ere he takes his first whiff,
bows reverently toward the four quarters of the sky
in succession, and that the loftiest monuments have
been reared to perpetuate fame, which is the dream
of the shadow of smoke. The *Saga*, it will be re-
membered, leaves this Bjarna to a fate something
like that of Sir Humphrey Gilbert, on board a sink-
ing ship in the "wormy sea," having generously given
up his place in the boat to a certain Icelander. It
is doubly pleasant, therefore, to meet with this proof
that the brave old man arrived safely in Vinland, and
that his declining years were cheered by the respect-
ful attentions of the dusky denizens of our then un-
invaded forests. Most of all was I gratified, however,
in thus linking forever the name of my native town
with one of the most momentous occurrences of modern
times. Hitherto Jaalam, though in soil, climate, and
geographical position as highly qualified to be the thea-
tre of remarkable historical incidents as any spot on
the earth's surface, has been, if I may say it without
seeming to question the wisdom of Providence, almost
maliciously neglected, as it might appear, by occur-
rences of world-wide interest in want of a situation.
And in matters of this nature it must be confessed that
adequate events are as necessary as the *vates sacer*
to record them. Jaalam stood always modestly ready,
but circumstances made no fitting response to her gener-
ous intentions. Now, however, she assumes her place
on the historick roll. I have hitherto been a zealous
opponent of the Circean herb, but I shall now re-examine
the question without bias.

I am aware that the Rev. Jonas Tutchel, in a recent
communication to the Bogus Four Corners Weekly Merid-
ian, has endeavoured to show that this is the sepulchral
inscription of Thorwald Eriksson, who, as is well known.
was slain in Vinland by the natives. But I think he has
been misled by a preconceived theory, and cannot but
feel that he has thus made an ungracious return for my

allowing him to inspect the stone with the aid of my own glasses (he having by accident left his at home) and in my own study. The heathen ancients might have instructed this Christian minister in the rites of hospitality; but much is to be pardoned to the spirit of self-love. He must indeed be ingenious who can make out the words *hèr hvílir* from any characters in the inscription in question, which, whatever else it may be, is certainly not mortuary. And even should the reverend gentleman succeed in persuading some fantastical wits of the soundness of his views, I do not see what useful end he will have gained. For if the English Courts of Law hold the testimony of grave-stones from the burial-grounds of Protestant dissenters to be questionable, even where it is essential in proving a descent, I cannot conceive that the epitaphial assertions of heathens should be esteemed of more authority by any man of orthodox sentiments.

At this moment, happening to cast my eyes upon the stone, on which a transverse light from my southern window brings out the characters with singular distinctness, another interpretation has occurred to me, promising even more interesting results. I hasten to close my letter in order to follow at once the clew thus providentially suggested.

I inclose, as usual, a contribution from **Mr. Biglow**, and remain,

> Gentlemen, with esteem and respect,
>> Your Obedient Humble Servant,
>>> Homer Wilbur, A. M.

I THANK ye, my friens, for the warmth o' your greetin':
Ther 's few airthly blessins but wut 's vain an' fleetin';
But et ther' is one thet hain't *no* cracks an' flaws,
An' is wuth goin' in for, it 's pop'lar applause;
It sends up the sperits ez lively ez rockets,
An' I feel it — wal, down to the eend o' my pockets.
Jes' lovin' the people is Canaan in view,
But it 's Canaan paid quarterly t' hev 'em love you;
It 's a blessin' thet 's breakin' out ollus in fresh spots;
It 's a-follerin' Moses 'thout losin' the flesh-pots.
But, Gennlemen, 'scuse me, I ain't sech a raw cus

Ez to go luggin' ellerkence into a caucus,—
Thet is, into one where the call comprehends
Nut the People in person, but on'y their friends;
I'm so kin' o' used to convincin' the masses
Of th' edvantage o' bein' self-governin' asses,
I forgut thet *we* 're all o' the sort thet pull wires
An' arrange for the public their wants an' desires,
An' thet wut we hed met for wuz jes' to agree
Wut the People's opinions in futur' should be.

Now, to come to the nub, we 've ben all disappinted,
An' our leadin' idees are a kind o' disjinted,—
Though, fur ez the nateral man could discern,
Things ough' to ha' took most an oppersite turn.
But The'ry is jes' like a train on the rail,
Thet, weather or no, puts her thru without fail,
While Fac 's the ole stage thet gits sloughed in the ruts,
An' hez to allow for your darned efs an' buts,
An' so, nut intendin' no pers'nal reflections,
They don't — don't nut allus, thet is,—make connec-
      tions :
Sometimes, when it really doos seem thet they 'd oughter
Combine jest ez kindly ez new rum an' water,
Both 'll be jest ez sot in their ways ez a bagnet,
Ez otherwise-minded ez th' eends of a magnet,
An' folks like you 'n me, thet ain't ept to be sold,
Git somehow or 'nother left out in the cold.

I expected 'fore this, 'thout no gret of a row,
Jeff D. would ha' ben where A. Lincoln is now,
With Taney to say 't wuz all legle an' fair,
An' a jury o' Deemocrats ready to swear
Thet the ingin o' State gut throwed into the ditch
By the fault o' the North in misplacin' the switch.
Things wuz ripenin' fust-rate with Buchanan to nuss 'em;
But the People they would n't be Mexicans, cuss 'em !
Ain't the safeguards o' freedom upsot, 'z you may say,
Ef the right o' rev'lution is took clean away ?
An' doos n't the right primy-fashy include
The bein' entitled to nut be subdued ?
The fact is, we 'd gone for the Union so strong,
When Union meant South ollus right an' North wrong,
Thet the people gut fooled into thinkin' it might

Worry on middlin' wal with the North in the right.
We might ha' ben now jest ez prosp'rous ez France,
Where p'litikle enterprise hez a fair chance,
An' the people is heppy an' proud et this hour,
Long ez they hev the votes, to let Nap hev the power;
But *our* folks they went an' believed wut we'd told 'em,
An', the flag once insulted, no mortle could hold' em.
'T wuz pervokin' jest when we wuz cert'in to win, —
An' I, for one, wun't trust the masses agin :
For a people thet knows much ain't fit to be free
In the self-cockin', back-action style o' J. D.

I can't believe now but wut half on 't is lies ;
For who'd thought the North wuz a-goin' to rise,
Or take the pervokin'est kin' of a stump,
'Thout 't wuz sunthin' ez pressin' ez Gabr'el's las' trump ?
Or who'd ha' supposed, arter *sech* swell an' bluster
'Bout the lick-ary-ten-on-ye fighters they'd muster,
Raised by hand on briled lightnin', ez op'lent 'z you please
In a primitive- furrest o' femmily-trees, —
Who'd ha' thought thet them Southuners ever 'ud show
Starns with pedigrees to 'em like theirn to the foe,
Or, when the vamosin' come, ever to find
Nat'ral masters in front an' mean white folks behind ?
By ginger, ef I'd ha' known half I know now,
When I wuz to Congress, I would n't, I swow,
Hev let 'em cair on so high-minded an' sarsy,
'Thout *some* show o' wut you may call vicy-varsy.
To be sure, we wuz under a contrac' jes' then
To be dreffle forbearin' towards Southun men ;
We hed to go sheers in preservin' the bellance :
An' ez they seemed to feel they wuz wastin' their tellents
'Thout some un to kick, 't warn't more 'n proper, you know,
Each should funnish his part ; an' sence they found the
     toe,
An' we wuz n't cherubs — wal, we found the buffer,
For fear thet the Compromise System should suffer.

I wun't say the plan hed n't onpleasant featurs, —
For men are perverse an' onreasonin' creaturs,
An' forgit thet in this life 't ain't likely to heppen
Their own privit fancy should ollus be cappen, —
But it worked jest ez smooth ez the key of a safe,
2 P

An' the gret Union bearins played free from all chafe.
They warn't hard to suit, ef they hed their own way;
An' we (thet is, some on us) made the thing pay :
'T wuz a fair give-an'-take out of Uncle Sam's heap;
Ef they took wut warn't theirn, wut we give come ez
      cheap;
The elect gut the offices down to tidewaiter,
The people took skinnin' ez mild ez a tater,
Seemed to choose who they wanted tu, footed the bills,
An' felt kind o' 'z though they wuz havin' their wills,
Which kep' 'em ez harmless an' cherfle ez crickets,
While all we invested wuz names on the tickets :
Wal, ther' 's nothin', for folks fond o' lib'ral consumption
Free o' charge, like democ'acy tempered with gumption!

Now warn't thet a system wuth pains in presarvin',
Where the people found jints an' their friens done the
      carvin', —
Where the many done all o' their thinkin' by proxy,
An' were proud on 't ez long ez 't wuz christened
      Democ'cy, —
Where the few let us sap all o' Freedom's foundations,
Ef you call it reformin' with prudence an' patience,
An' were willin' Jeff's snake-egg should hetch with the
      rest,
Ef you writ " Constitootional " over the nest ?
But it's all out o' kilter, ('t wuz too good to last,)
An' all jes' by J. D.'s perceedin' too fast;
Ef he 'd on'y hung on for a month or two more,
We 'd ha' gut things fixed nicer 'n they hed ben before:
Afore he drawed off an' lef' all in confusion,
We wuz safely entrenched in the ole Constitootion,
With an outlyin', heavy-gun, casemated fort
To rake all assailants, — I mean th' S. J. Court.
Now I never 'll acknowledge (nut ef you should skin me)
'T wuz wise to abandon sech works to the in'my,
An' let him fin' out thet wut scared him so long,
Our whole line of argyments, lookin' so strong,
All our Scriptur' an' law, every the'ry an' fac',
Wuz Quaker-guns daubed with Pro-slavery black.
Why, ef the Republicans ever should git
Andy Johnson or some one to lend 'em the wit
An' the spunk jes' to mount Constitootion an' Court

With Columbiad guns, your real ekle-rights sort,
Or drill out the spike from the ole Declaration
Thet can kerry a solid shot clearn roun' creation,
We 'd better take maysures for shettin' up shop,
An' put off our stock by a vendoo or swop.

But they wun 't never dare tu; you 'll see 'em in Edom
'Fore they ventur' to go where their doctrines 'ud lead 'em:
They 've ben takin' our princerples up ez we dropt 'em,
An' thought it wuz terrible 'cute to adopt 'em;
But they'll fin' out 'fore long thet their hope 's ben de-
       ceivin' 'em,
An' thet princerples ain't o' no good, ef you b'lieve in 'em;
It makes 'em tu stiff for a party to use,
Where they 'd ough' to be easy 'z an ole pair o' shoes.
If *we* say 'n our pletform thet all men are brothers,
We don't mean thet some folks ain't more so 'n some
       others;
An' it 's wal understood thet we make a selection,
An' thet brotherhood kin' o' subsides arter 'lection.
The fust thing for sound politicians to larn is,
Thet Truth, to dror kindly in all sorts o' harness,
Mus' be kep' in the abstract, — for, come to apply it,
You 're ept to hurt some folks's interists by it.
Wal, these 'ere Republicans (some on 'em) ects
Ez though gineral mexims 'ud suit speshle facts;
An' there 's where we 'll nick 'em, there 's where they 'll
       be lost:
For applyin' your princerple 's wut makes it cost,
An' folks don't want Fourth o' July t' interfere
With the business-consarns o' the rest o' the year,
No more 'n they want Sunday to pry an' to peek
Into wut they are doin' the rest o' the week.

A ginooine statesman should be on his guard,
Ef he *must* hev beliefs, nut to b'lieve 'em tu hard;
For, ez sure ez he does, he 'll be blartin' 'em out
'Thout regardin' the natur' o' man more 'n a spout,
Nor it don't ask much gumption to pick out a flaw
In a party whose leaders are loose in the jaw:
An' so in our own case I ventur' to hint
Thet we 'd better nut air our perceedins in print,
Nor pass resserlootions ez long ez your arm

Thet may, ez things heppen to turn, do us harm;
For when you 've done all your real meanin' to smother,
The darned things 'll up an' mean sunthin' or 'nother.
Jeff'son prob'ly meant wal with his " born free an' ekle,"
But it 's turned out a real crooked stick in the sekle;
It 's taken full eighty-odd year — don't you see ? —
From the pop'lar belief to root out thet idee,
An', arter all, suckers on 't keep buddin' forth
In the nat'lly onprincipled mind o' the North. .
No, never say nothin' without you 're compelled tu,
An' then don't say nothin' thet you can be held tu,
Nor don't leave no friction-idees layin' loose
For the ign'ant to put to incend'ary use.

You know I 'm a feller thet keeps a skinned eye
On the leetle events thet go skurryin' by,
Coz it 's of'ner by them than by gret ones you 'll see
Wut the p'litickle weather is likely to be.
Now I don't think the South's more 'n begun to be
     licked,
But I *du* think, ez Jeff says, the wind-bag 's gut pricked;
It 'll blow for a spell an' keep puffin' an' wheezin',
The tighter our army an' navy keep squeezin', —
For they can't help spread-eaglein' long 'z ther' 's a
     mouth
To blow Enfield's Speaker thru lef' at the South.
But it 's high time for us to be settin' our faces
Towards reconstructin' the national basis,
With an eye to beginnin' agin on the jolly ticks
We used to chalk up 'hind the back-door o' politics;
An' the fus' thing 's to save wut of Slav'ry ther' 's lef'
Arter this (I mus' call it) imprudence o' Jeff:
For a real good Abuse, with its roots fur an' wide,
Is the kin' o' thing *I* like to hev on my side;
A Scriptur' name makes it ez sweet ez a rose,
An' it 's tougher the older an' uglier it grows —
(I ain't speakin' now o' the righteousness of it,
But the p'litickle purchase it gives, an' the profit).

Things look pooty squally, it must be allowed,
An' I don't see much signs of a bow in the cloud:
Ther' 's too many Deemocrats — leaders, wut 's wuss —
Thet go for the Union 'thout carin' a cuss

Ef it helps ary party thet ever wuz heard on,
So our eagle ain't made a split Austrian bird on.
But ther' 's still some consarvative signs to be found
Thet shows the gret heart o' the People is sound:
(Excuse me for usin' a stump-phrase agin,
But, once in the way on 't, they *will* stick like sin :)
There 's Phillips, for instance, hez jes' ketched a Tartar
In the Law-'n'-Order Party of ole Cincinnater;
An' the Compromise System ain't gone out o' reach,
Long 'z you keep the right limits on freedom o' speech.
'T warn't none too late, neither, to put on the gag,
For he 's dangerous now he goes in for the flag.
Nut thet I altogether approve o' bad eggs,
They 're mos' gin'lly argymunt on its las' legs, —
An' their logic is ept to be tu indiscriminate,
Nor don't ollus wait the right objecs to 'liminate;
But there is a variety on 'em, you 'll find,
Jest ez usefle an' more, besides bein' refined, —
I mean o' the sort thet are laid by the dictionary,
Sech ez sophisms an' cant, thet 'll kerry conviction ary
Way thet you want to the right class o' men,
An' are staler than all 't ever come from a hen :
" Disunion " done wal till our resh Southun friends
Took the savor all out-on 't for national ends;
But I guess "Abolition " 'll work a spell yit,
When the war 's done, an' so will " Forgive-an'-forgit."
Times mus' be pooty thoroughly out o' all jint,
Ef we can't make a good constitootional pint;
An' the good time 'll come to be grindin' our exes,
When the war goes to seed in the nettle o' texes :
Ef Jon'than don't squirm, with sech helps to assist him,
I give up my faith in the free-suffrage system;
Democ'cy wun't be nut a mite interestin',
Nor p'litikle capital much wuth investin';
An' my notion is, to keep dark an' lay low
Till we see the right minute to put in our blow. —

But I 've talked longer now 'n I hed any idee,
An' ther' 's others you want to hear more 'n you du me;
So I 'll set down an' give thet 'ere bottle a skrimmage,
For I 've spoke till I 'm dry ez a real graven image.

No. VI.

SUNTHIN' IN THE PASTORAL LINE.

TO THE EDITORS OF THE ATLANTIC MONTHLY.

JAALAM, 17th May, 1862.

GENTLEMEN, — At the special request of Mr. Biglow, I intended to inclose, together with his own contribution, (into which, at my suggestion, he has thrown a little more of pastoral sentiment than usual,) some passages from my sermon on the day of the National Fast, from the text, "Remember them that are in bonds, as bound with them," *Heb.* xiii. *3.* But I have not leisure sufficient at present for the copying of them, even were I altogether satisfied with the production as it stands. I should prefer, I confess, to contribute the entire discourse to the pages of your respectable miscellany, if it should be found acceptable upon perusal, especially as I find the difficulty of selection of greater magnitude than I had anticipated. What passes without challenge in the fervour of oral delivery, cannot always stand the colder criticism of the closet. I am not so great an enemy of Eloquence as my friend Mr. Biglow would appear to be from some passages in his contribution for the current month. I would not, indeed, hastily suspect him of covertly glancing at myself in his somewhat caustick animadversions, albeit some of the phrases he girds at are not entire strangers to my lips. I am a more hearty admirer of the Puritans than seems now to be the fashion, and believe, that, if they Hebraized a little too much in their speech, they showed remarkable practical sagacity as statesmen and founders. But such phenomena as Puritanism are the results rather of great religious than merely social convulsions, and do not long survive them. So soon as an earnest conviction has cooled into a phrase, its work is over, and the best that can be done with it is to bury it. *Ite, missa est.* I am inclined to agree with Mr. Biglow that we cannot settle

the great political questions which are now presenting
themselves to the nation by the opinions of Jeremiah or
Ezekiel as to the wants and duties of the Jews in their
time, nor do I believe that an entire community with
their feelings and views would be practicable or even
agreeable at the present day. At the same time 1 could
wish that their habit of subordinating the actual to the
moral, the flesh to the spirit, and this world to the other,
were more common. They had found out, at least, the
great military secret that soul weighs more than body. —
But I am suddenly called to a sick-bed in the household
of a valued parishioner.

With esteem and respect,

Your obedient servant,

HOMER WILBUR.

Once git a smell o' musk into a draw,
An' it clings hold like precerdents in law:
Your gra'ma'am put it there, — when, goodness knows,—
To jes' this-worldify her Sunday-clo'es;
But the old chist wun't sarve her gran'son's wife,
(For, 'thout new funnitoor, wut good in life?)
An' so ole clawfoot, from the precinks dread
O' the spare chamber, slinks into the shed,
Where, dim with dust, it fust or last subsides
To holdin' seeds an' fifty things besides;
But better days stick fast in heart an' husk,
An' all you keep in 't gits a scent o' musk.

Jes' so with poets: wut they 've airly read
Gits kind o' worked into their heart an' head,
So 's 't they can't seem to write but jest on sheers
With furrin countries or played-out ideers,
Nor hev a feelin', ef it doos n't smack
O' wut some critter chose to feel 'way back:
This makes 'em talk o' daisies, larks, an' things,
Ez though we 'd nothin' here that blows an' sings, —
(Why, I 'd give more for one live bobolink
Than a square mile o' larks in printer's ink,) —
This makes 'em think our fust o' May is May,
Which 't ain't, for all the almanicks can say.

O little city-gals, don't never go it
Blind on the word o' noospaper or poet!
They 're apt to puff, an' May-day seldom looks
Up in the country ez it doos in books;
They 're no more like than hornets'-nests an' hives,
Or printed sarmons be to holy lives.
I, with my trouses perched on cow-hide boots,
Tuggin' my foundered feet out by the roots,
Hev seen ye come to fling on April's hearse
Your muslin nosegays from the milliner's,
Puzzlin' to find dry ground your queen to choose,
An' dance your throats sore in morocker shoes:
I 've seen ye an' felt proud, thet, come wut would,
Our Pilgrim stock wuz pithed with hardihood.
Pleasure doos make us Yankees kind o' winch,
Ez though 't wuz sunthin' paid for by the inch;
But yit we du contrive to worry thru,
Ef Dooty tells us thet the thing 's to du,
An' kerry a hollerday, ef we set out,
Ez stiddily ez though 't wuz a redoubt.

I, country-born an' bred, know where to find
Some blooms thet make the season suit the mind,
An' seem to metch the doubtin' bluebird's notes, —
Half-vent'rin' liverworts in furry coats,
Bloodroots, whose rolled-up leaves ef you oncurl,
Each on 'em 's cradle to a baby-pearl, —
But these are jes' Spring's pickets; sure ez sin,
The rebble frosts 'll try to drive 'em in;
For half our May 's so awfully like May n't,
'T would rile a Shaker or an evrige saint;
Though I own up I like our back'ard springs
Thet kind o' haggle with their greens an' things,
An' when you 'most give up, 'ithout more words
Toss the fields full o' blossoms, leaves, an' birds:
Thet 's Northun natur', slow an' apt to doubt,
But when it *doos* git stirred, ther' 's no gin-out!

Fust come the blackbirds clatt'rin' in tall trees,
An' settlin' things in windy Congresses, —
Queer politicians, though, for I 'll be skinned
Ef all on 'em don't head against the wind.

'Fore long the trees begin to show belief, —
The maple crimsons to a coral-reef,
Then saffern swarms swing off from all the willers
So plump they look like yaller caterpillars,
Then gray hossches'nuts leetle hands unfold
Softer 'n a baby's be at three days old:
Thet 's robin-redbreast's almanick; he knows
Thet arter this ther' 's only blossom-snows;
So, choosin' out a handy crotch an' spouse,
He goes to plast'rin' his adobë house.

Then seems to come a hitch, — things lag behind,
Till some fine mornin' Spring makes up her mind,
An' ez, when snow-swelled rivers cresh their dams
Heaped-up with ice thet dovetails in an' jams,
A leak comes spirtin' thru some pin-hole cleft,
Grows stronger, fercer, tears out right an' left,
Then all the waters bow themselves an' come,
Suddin, in one gret slope o' shedderin' foam,
Jes' so our Spring gits everythin' in tune
An' gives one leap from April into June:
Then all comes crowdin' in; afore you think,
Young oak-leaves mist the side-hill woods with pink;
The catbird in the laylock-bush is loud;
The orchards turn to heaps o' rosy cloud;
Red-cedars blossom tu, though few folks know it,
An' look all dipt in sunshine like a poet;
The lime-trees pile their solid stacks o' shade
An' drows'ly simmer with the bees' sweet trade;
In ellum-shrouds the flashin' hangbird clings
An' for the summer vy'ge his hammock slings;
All down the loose-walled lanes in archin' bowers
The barb'ry droops its strings o' golden flowers,
Whose shrinkin' hearts the school-gals love to try
With pins, — they 'll worry yourn so, boys, bimeby!
But I don't love your cat'logue style, — do you? —
Ez ef to sell off Natur' by vendoo:
One word with blood in 't 's twice ez good ez two:
'Nuff sed, June's bridesman, poet o' the year,
Gladness on wings, the bobolink, is here;
Half-hid in tip-top apple-blooms he swings,
Or climbs aginst the breeze with quiverin' wings,
Or, givin' way to 't in a mock despair,

Runs down, a brook o' laughter, thru the air.
I ollus feels the sap start in my veins
In Spring, with curus heats an' prickly pains,
Thet drive me, when I git a chance, to walk
Off by myself to hev a privit talk
With a queer critter thet can't seem to 'gree
Along o' me like most folks, — Mister Me.
Ther' 's times when I 'm unsoshle ez a stone,
An' sort o' suffocate to be alone, —
I 'm crowded jes' to think thet folks are nigh,
An' can't bear nothin' closer than the sky;
Now the wind 's full ez shifty in the mind
Ez wut it is ou'-doors, ef I ain't blind,
An' sometimes, in the fairest sou'west weather,
My innard vane pints east for weeks together,
My natur' gits all goose-flesh, an' my sins
Come drizzlin' on my conscience sharp ez pins:
Wal, et sech times I jes' slip out o' sight
An' take it out in a fair stan'-up fight
With the one cuss I can't lay on the shelf,
The crook'dest stick in all the heap, — Myself.

'T wuz so las' Sabbath arter meetin'-time:
Findin' my feelin's would n't noways rhyme
With nobody's, but off the hendle flew
An' took things from an east-wind pint o' view,
I started off to lose me in the hills
Where the pines be, up back o' Siah's Mills:
Pines, ef you 're blue, are the best friends I know,
They mope an' sigh an' sheer your feelin's so, —
They hesh the ground beneath so, tu, I swan,
You half-forgit you 've gut a body on.
Ther' 's a small school'us' there where four roads meet,
The door-steps hollered out by little feet,
An' side-posts carved with names whose owners grew
To gret men, some on 'em, an' deacons, tu;
'T ain't used no longer, coz the town hez gut
A high-school, where they teach the Lord knows wut:
Three-story larnin' 's pop'lar now; I guess
We thriv' ez wal on jes' two stories less,
For it strikes me ther' 's sech a thing ez sinnin'
By overloadin' children's underpinnin':
Wal, here it wuz I larned my A B C,

An' it's a kind o' favorite spot with me.
We're curus critters: Now ain't jes' the minute
Thet ever fits us easy while we're in it;
Long ez 't wuz futur', 't would be perfect bliss, —
Soon ez it's past, *thet* time's wuth ten o' this;
An' yit there ain't a man thet need be told
Thet Now's the only bird lays eggs o' gold.
A knee-high lad, I used to plot an' plan
An think 't wuz life's cap-sheaf to be a man;
Now, gittin' gray, there's nothin' I enjoy
Like dreamin' back along into a boy:
So the ole school'us' is a place I choose
Afore all others, ef I want to muse;
I set down where I used to set, an' git
My boyhood back, an' better things with it, —
Faith, Hope, an' sunthin', ef it is n't Cherrity,
It's want o' guile, an' thet's ez gret a rerrity.

Now, 'fore I knowed, thet Sabbath arternoon
Thet I sot out to tramp myself in tune,
I found me in the school'us' on my seat,
Drummin' the march to No-wheres with my feet.
Thinkin' o' nothin', I've heerd ole folks say,
Is a hard kind o' dooty in its way:
It's thinkin' everythin' you ever knew,
Or ever hearn, to make your feelin's blue.
I sot there tryin' thet on for a spell:
I thought o' the Rebellion, then o' Hell,
Which some folks tell ye now is jest a metterfor
(A the'ry, p'raps, it wun't *feel* none the better for);
I thought o' Reconstruction, wut we'd win
Patchin' our patent self-blow-up agin:
I thought ef this 'ere milkin' o' the wits,
So much a month, warn't givin' Natur' fits, —
Ef folks warn't druv, findin' their own milk fail,
To work the cow thet hez an iron tail,
An' ef idees 'thout ripenin' in the pan
Would send up cream to humor ary man:
From this to thet I let my worryin' creep,
Till finally I must ha' fell asleep.

Our lives in sleep are some like streams thet glide
'Twixt flesh an' sperrit boundin' on each side,

Where both shores' shadders kind o' mix an' mingle
In sunthin' thet ain't jes' like either single;
An' when you cast off moorin's from To-day,
An' down towards To-morrer drift away,
The imiges thet tengle on the stream
Make a new upside-down'ard world o' dream :
Sometimes they seem like sunrise-streaks an' warnin's
O' wut 'll be in Heaven on Sabbath-mornin's,
An', mixed right in ez ef jest out o' spite,
Sunthin' thet says your supper ain't gone right.
I 'm gret on dreams, an' often, when I wake,
I 've lived so much it makes my mem'ry ache,
An' can't skurce take a cat-nap in my cheer
'Thout hevin' 'em, some good, some bad, all queer.

Now I wuz settin' where I 'd ben, it seemed,
An' ain't sure yit whether I r'ally dreamed,
Nor, ef I did, how long I might ha' slep',
When I hearn some un stompin' up the step,
An' lookin' round, ef two an' two make four,
I see a Pilgrim Father in the door.
He wore a steeple-hat, tall boots, an' spurs
With rowels to 'em big ez ches'nut-burrs,
An' his gret sword behind him sloped away
Long'z a man's speech thet dunno wut to say. —
"Ef your name 's Biglow, an' your given-name
Hosee," sez he, "it 's arter you I came;
I 'm your gret-gran'ther multiplied by three." —
" My *wut* ?" sez I. — " Your gret-gret-gret," sez he:
" You would n't ha' never ben here but for me.
Two hundred an' three year ago this May
The ship I come in sailed up Boston Bay;
I 'd been a cunnle in our Civil War, —
But wut on airth hev *you* gut up one for ?
Coz we du things in England, 't ain't for you
To git a notion you can du 'em tu :
I 'm told you write in public prints : ef true,
It 's nateral you should know a thing or two." —
" Thet air 's an argymunt I can't endorse, —
'T would prove, coz you wear spurs, you kep' a horse:
For brains," sez I, " wutever you may think,
Ain't boun' to cash the drafs o' pen-an'-ink, —
Though mos' folks write ez ef they hoped jes' quickenin'

The churn would argoo skim-milk into thickenin';
But skim-milk ain't a thing to change its view
O' wut it's meant for more 'n a smoky flue.
But du pray tell me, 'fore we furder go,
How in all Natur' did you come to know
'Bout our affairs," sez I, "in Kingdom-Come?" —
"Wal, I worked round at sperrit-rappin' some,
An' danced the tables till their legs wuz gone,
In hopes o' larnin' wut wuz goin' on,"
Sez he, "but mejums lie so like all-split
Thet I concluded it wuz best to quit.
But, come now, ef you wun't confess to knowin',
You 've some conjectures how the thing 's a-goin'." —
"Gran'ther," sez I, "a vane warn't never known
Nor asked to hev a jedgment of its own;
An' yit, ef 't ain't gut rusty in the jints,
It 's safe to trust its say on certin pints:
It knows the wind's opinions to a T,
An' the wind settles wut the weather 'll be."
"I never thought a scion of our stock
Could grow the wood to make a weathercock;
When I wuz younger 'n you, skurce more 'n a shaver,
No airthly wind," sez he, "could make me waver!"
(Ez he said this, he clinched his jaw an' forehead,
Hitchin' his belt to bring his sword-hilt forrard.) —
"Jes' so it wuz with me," sez I, "I swow,
When *I* wuz younger 'n wut you see me now, —
Nothin' from Adam's fall to Huldy's bonnet,
Thet I warn't full-cocked with my jedgment on it;
But now I 'm gittin' on in life, I find
It 's a sight harder to make up my mind, —
Nor I don't often try tu, when events
Will du it for me free of all expense.
The moral question 's ollus plain enough, —
It 's jes' the human-natur' side thet 's tough;
Wut 's best to think may n't puzzle me nor you, —
The pinch comes in decidin' wut to *du;*
Ef you *read* History, all runs smooth ez grease,
Coz there the men ain't nothin' more 'n idees, —
But come to *make* it, ez we must to-day,
Th' idees hev arms an' legs an' stop the way:
It 's easy fixin' things in facts an' figgers, —
They can't resist, nor warn't brought up with niggers;

But come to try your the'ry on, — why, then
Your facts an' figgers change to ign'ant men
Actin' ez ugly — " — " Smite 'em hip an' thigh ! "
Sez gran'ther, " and let every man-child die !
Oh for three weeks o' Crommle an' the Lord !
Up, Isr'el, to your tents an' grind the sword ! " —
" Thet kind o' thing worked wal in ole Judee,
But you forgit how long it 's ben A. D. ;
You think thet 's ellerkence, — I call it shoddy,
A thing," sez I, " wun't cover soul nor body ;
I like the plain all-wool o' common-sense,
Thet warms ye now, an' will a twelvemonth hence.
You took to follerin' where the Prophets beckoned,
An', fust you knowed on, back come Charles the Second ;
Now wut I want 's to hev all *we* gain stick,
An' not to start Millennium too quick ;
We hain't to punish only, but to keep,
An' the cure 's gut to go a cent'ry deep."
" Wal, milk-an'-water ain't the best o' glue,"
Sez he, " an' so you 'll find before you 're thru ;
Ef reshness venters sunthin', shilly-shally
Loses ez often wut 's ten times the vally.
Thet exe of ourn, when Charles's neck gut split,
Opened a gap thet ain't bridged over yit :
Slav'ry 's your Charles, the Lord hez gin the exe — " —
" Our Charles," sez I, " hez gut eight million necks.
The hardest question ain't the black man's right,
The trouble is to 'mancipate the white ;
One 's chained in body an' can be sot free,
But t'other 's chained in soul to an idee :
It 's a long job, but we shall worry thru it ;
Ef bag'nets fail, the spellin'-book must du it."
" Hosee," sez he, " I think you 're goin' to fail :
The rettlesnake ain't dangerous in the tail ;
This 'ere rebellion 's nothin' but the rettle, —
You 'll stomp on thet an' think you 've won the bettle ;
It 's Slavery thet 's the fangs an' thinkin' head,
An' ef you want selvation, cresh it dead, —
An' cresh it suddin, or you 'll larn by waitin'
Thet Chance wun't stop to listen to debatin' ! " —
" God's truth ! " sez I, — " an' ef *I* held the club,
An' knowed jes' where to strike, — but there 's the
    rub ! " —

" Strike soon," sez he, " or you 'll be deadly ailin', —
Folks thet 's afeared to fail are sure o' failin' ;
God hates your sneakin' creturs thet believe
He 'll settle things they run away an' leave ! "
He brought his foot down fercely, ez he spoke,
An' give me sech a startle thet I woke.

No. VII.

LATEST VIEWS OF MR. BIGLOW.

PRELIMINARY NOTE.

[It is with feelings of the liveliest pain that we inform our readers of the death of the Reverend Homer Wilbur, A. M., which took place suddenly, by an apoplectic stroke, on the afternoon of Christmas day, 1862. Our venerable friend (for so we may venture to call him, though we never enjoyed the high privilege of his personal acquaintance) was in his eighty-fourth year, having been born June 12, 1779, at Pigsgusset Precinct (now West Jerusha) in the then District of Maine. Graduated with distinction at Hubville College in 1805, he pursued his theological studies with the late Reverend Preserved Thacker, D. D., and was called to the charge of the First Society in Jaalam in 1809, where he remained till his death.

" As an antiquary he has probably left no superior, if, indeed, an equal," writes his friend and colleague, the Reverend Jeduthun Hitchcock, to whom we are indebted for the above facts; " in proof of which I need only allude to his 'History of Jaalam, Genealogical, Topographical, and Ecclesiastical,' 1849, which has won him an eminent and enduring place in our more solid and useful literature. It is only to be regretted that his intense application to historical studies should have so entirely withdrawn him from the pursuit of poetical composition, for which he was endowed by Nature with a remarkable aptitude. His well-known hymn, beginning, 'With clouds of care encompassed round,' has been attributed in some collections to the late President Dwight, and it is hardly presumptuous to affirm that the simile of the rainbow in the eighth stanza would do no discredit to that polished pen."

We regret that we have not room at present for the whole of Mr. Hitchcock's exceedingly valuable communication. We hope to lay more liberal extracts from it

before our readers at an early day. A summary of its
contents will give some notion of its importance and
interest. It contains: 1st, A biographical sketch of Mr.
Wilbur, with notices of his predecessors in the pastoral
office, and of eminent clerical contemporaries; 2d, An
obituary of deceased, from the Punkin-Falls "Weekly
Parallel"; 3d, A list of his printed and manuscript pro-
ductions and of projected works; 4th, Personal anecdotes
and recollections, with specimens of table-talk; 5th, A
tribute to his relict, Mrs. Dorcas (Pilcox) Wilbur; 6th, A
list of graduates fitted for different colleges by Mr. Wilbur,
with biographical memoranda touching the more distin-
guished; 7th, Concerning learned, charitable, and other.
societies, of which Mr. Wilbur was a member, and of those
with which, had his life been prolonged, he would doubtless
have been associated, with a complete catalogue of such
Americans as have been Fellows of the Royal Society;
8th, A brief summary of Mr. Wilbur's latest conclusions
concerning the Tenth Horn of the Beast in its special
application to recent events, for which the public, as Mr.
Hitchcock assures us, have been waiting with feelings of
lively anticipation; 10th, Mr. Hitchcock's own views on
the same topic; and, 11th, A brief essay on the impor-
tance of local histories. It will be apparent that the
duty of preparing Mr. Wilbur's biography could not have
fallen into more sympathetic hands.

In a private letter with which the reverend gentleman
has since favored us, he expresses the opinion that Mr.
Wilbur's life was shortened by our unhappy civil war.
It disturbed his studies, dislocated all his habitual asso-
ciations and trains of thought, and unsettled the founda-
tions of a faith, rather the result of habit than conviction,
in the capacity of man for self-government. "Such has
been the felicity of my life," he said to Mr. Hitchcock,
on the very morning of the day he died, "that, through
the divine mercy, I could always say, *Summum nec metuo
diem, nec opto.* It has been my habit, as you know, on
every recurrence of this blessed anniversary, to read Mil-
ton's 'Hymn of the Nativity' till its sublime harmonies so
dilated my soul and quickened its spiritual sense that I
seemed to hear that other song which gave assurance to
the shepherds that there was One who would lead them
also in green pastures and beside the still waters. But

2 Q

to-day I have been unable to think of anything out that mournful text, 'I came not to send peace, but a sword,' and, did it not smack of pagan presumptuousness, could almost wish I had never lived to see this day."

Mr. Hitchcock also informs us that his friend "lies buried in the Jaalam graveyard, under a large red-cedar which he specially admired. A neat and substantial monument is to be erected over his remains, with a Latin epitaph written by himself; for he was accustomed to say, pleasantly, 'that there was at least one occasion in a scholar's life when he might show the advantages of a classical training.'"

The following fragment of a letter addressed to us, and apparently intended to accompany Mr. Biglow's contribution to the present number, was found upon his table after his decease. — EDITORS ATLANTIC MONTHLY.]

TO THE EDITORS OF THE ATLANTIC MONTHLY.

JAALAM, 24tl Dec., 1862.

RESPECTED SIRS, — The infirm state of my bodily health would be a sufficient apology for not taking up the pen at this time, wholesome as I deem it for the mind to apricate in the shelter of epistolary confidence, were it not that a considerable, I might even say a large, number of individuals in this parish expect from their pastor some publick expression of sentiment at this crisis. Moreover, *Qui tacitus ardet magis uritur.* In trying times like these, the besetting sin of undisciplined minds is to seek refuge from inexplicable realities in the dangerous stimulant of angry partisanship or the indolent narcotick of vague and hopeful vaticination: *fortunam-que suo temperat arbitrio.* Both by reason of my age and my natural temperament, I am unfitted for either. Unable to penetrate the inscrutable judgments of God, I am more than ever thankful that my life has been prolonged till I could in some small measure comprehend His mercy. As there is no man who does not at some time render himself amenable to the one, — *quum vix justus sit securus,* — so there is none that does not feel himself in daily need of the other.

I confess, I cannot feel, as some do, a personal consolation for the manifest evils of this war in any remote or contingent advantages that may spring from it. I am old and weak, I can bear little, and can scarce hope to see better days; nor is it any adequate compensation to know that Nature is old and strong and can bear much. Old men philosophize over the past, but the present is only a burthen and a weariness. The one lies before them like a placid evening landscape; the other is full of the vexations and anxieties of housekeeping. It may be true enough that *miscet hœc illis, prohibetque Clotho fortunam stare*, but he who said it was fain at last to call in Atropos with her shears before her time; and I cannot help selfishly mourning that the fortune of our Republick could not at least stand till my days were numbered.

Tibullus would find the origin of wars in the great exaggeration of riches, and does not stick to say that in the days of the beechen trencher there was peace. But averse as I am by nature from all wars, the more as they have been especially fatal to libraries, I would have this one go on till we are reduced to wooden platters again, rather than surrender the principle to defend which it was undertaken. Though I believe Slavery to have been the cause of it, by so thoroughly demoralizing Northern politicks for its own purposes as to give opportunity and hope to treason, yet I would not have our thought and purpose diverted from their true object, — the maintenance of the idea of Government. We are not merely suppressing an enormous riot, but contending for the possibility of permanent order coexisting with democratical fickleness; and while I would not superstitiously venerate form to the sacrifice of substance, neither would I forget that an adherence to precedent and prescription can alone give that continuity and coherence under a democratical constitution which are inherent in the person of a despotick monarch and the selfishness of an aristocratical class. *Stet pro ratione voluntas* is as dangerous in a majority as in a tyrant.

I cannot allow the present production of my young friend to go out without a protest from me against a certain extremeness in his views, more pardonable in the poet than the philosopher. While I agree with him, that the only cure for rebellion is suppression by force, yet I must animadvert upon certain phrases where I seem to see a coincidence with a popular fallacy on the subject of compromise. On the one hand there are those who do not see that the vital principle of Government and the seminal principle of Law cannot properly be made a subject of compromise at all, and on the other those who are equally blind to the truth that without a compromise of individual opinions, interests, and even rights, no society would be possible. *In medio tutissimus.* For my own part, I would gladly ——

—————

Ef I a song or two could make,
　Like rockets druv by their own burnin',
All leap an' light, to leave a wake
　Men's hearts an' faces skyward turnin'! —
But, it strikes me, 't ain't jest the time
　Fer stringin' words with settisfaction :
Wut 's wanted now 's the silent rhyme
　'Twixt upright Will an' downright Action.

Words, ef you keep 'em, pay their keep,
　But gabble 's the short cut to ruin ;
It 's gratis, (gals half-price,) but cheap
　At no rate, ef it henders doin' ;
Ther' 's nothin' wuss, 'less 't is to set
　A martyr-prem'um upon jawrin' :
Teapots git dangerous, ef you shet
　Their lids down on 'em with Fort Warren.

'Bout long enough it 's ben discussed
　Who sot the magazine afire,
An' whether, ef Bob Wickliffe bust,
　'T would scare us more or blow us higher.
D' ye s'pose the Gret Foreseer's plan
　Wuz settled fer him in town-meetin' ?
Or thet ther' 'd ben no Fall o' Man,
　Ef Adam 'd on'y bit a sweetin' ?

Oh, Jon'than, ef you want to be
　A rugged chap agin an' hearty,

Go fer wutever 'll hurt Jeff D.,
  Nut wut 'll boost up ary party.
Here 's hell broke loose, an' we lay flat
  With half the univarse a-singein',
Till Sen'tor This an' Gov'nor Thet
  Stop squabblin' fer the garding-ingin'.

It 's war we 're in, not politics;
  It 's systems wrastlin' now, not parties;
An' victory in the eend 'll fix
  Where longest will an' truest heart is.
An' wut 's the Guv'ment folks about?
  Tryin' to hope ther' 's nothin' doin',
An' look ez though they did n't doubt
  Sunthin' pertickler wuz a-brewin'.

Ther' 's critters yit thet talk an' act
  Fer wut they call Conciliation;
They 'd hand a buff'lo-drove a tract
  When they wuz madder than all Bashan.
Conciliate? it jest means *be kicked,*
  No metter how they phrase an' tone it;
It means thet we 're to set down licked,
  Thet we 're poor shotes an' glad to own it!

A war on tick 's ez dear 'z the deuce,
  But it wun't leave no lastin' traces,
Ez 't would to make a sneakin' truce
  Without no moral specie-basis:
Ef green-backs ain't nut jest the cheese,
  I guess ther' 's evils thet 's extremer, —
Fer instance, — shinplaster idees
  Like them put out by Gov'nor Seymour.

Last year, the Nation, at a word,
  When tremblin' Freedom cried to shield **her,**
Flamed weldin' into one keen sword
  Waitin' an' longin' fer a wielder:
A splendid flash! — but how 'd the grasp
  With sech a chance ez thet wuz tally?
Ther' warn't no meanin' in our clasp, —
  Half this, half thet, all shilly-shally.

More men ?   More Man!   It 's there we fail;
   Weak plans grow weaker yit by lengthenin':
Wut use in addin' to the tail,
   When it 's the head 's in need o' strengthenin'??
We wanted one thet felt all Chief
   From roots o' hair to soul o' stockin',
Square-sot with thousan'-ton belief
   In him an' us, ef earth went rockin'!

Ole Hick'ry would n't ha' stood see-saw
   'Bout doin' things till they wuz done with, —
He 'd smashed the tables o' the Law
   In time o' need to load his gun with;
He could n't see but jest one side, —
   Ef his, 't wuz God's, an' thet wuz plenty;
An' so his *"Forrards!"* multiplied
   An army's fightin' weight by twenty.

But this 'ere histin', creak, creak, creak,
   Your cappen's heart up with a derrick,
This tryin' to coax a lightnin'-streak
   Out of a half-discouraged hay-rick,
This hangin' on mont' arter mont'
   Fer one sharp purpose 'mongst the twitter, —
I tell ye, it doos kind o' stunt
   The peth and sperit of a critter.

In six months where 'll the People be,
   Ef leaders look on revolution
Ez though it wuz a cup o' tea, —
   Jest social el'ments in solution?
This weighin' things doos wal enough
   When war cools down, an' comes to writin';
But while it 's makin', the true stuff
   Is pison-mad, pig-headed fightin'.

Democ'acy gives every man
   A right to be his own oppressor;
But a loose Gov'ment ain't the plan,
   Helpless ez spilled beans on a dresser:
I tell ye one thing we might larn
   From them smart critters, the Seceders, —

Ef bein' right 's the fust consarn,
  The 'fore-the-fust 's cast-iron leaders.

But 'pears to me I see some signs
  Thet we 're a-goin' to use our senses:
Jeff druv us into these hard lines,
  An' ough' to bear his half th' expenses;
Slavery 's Secession's heart an' will,
  South, North, East, West, where'er you find it,
An' ef it drors into War's mill,
  D' ye say them thunder-stones sha'n't grind it?

D' ye s'pose, ef Jeff giv *him* a lick,
  Ole Hick'ry 'd tried his head to sof'n
So 's 't would n't hurt thet ebony stick
  Thet 's made our side see stars so of'n?
"No!" he 'd ha' thundered, "on your knees,
  An' own one flag, one road to glory!
Soft-heartedness, in times like these,
  Shows sof'ness in the upper story!"

An' why should we kick up a muss
  About the Pres'dunt's proclamation?
It ain't a-goin' to lib'rate us,
  Ef we don't like emancipation:
The right to be a cussed fool
  Is safe from all devices human,
It 's common (ez a gin'l rule)
  To every critter born o' woman.

So *we* 're all right, an' I, fer one,
  Don't think our cause 'll lose in vally
By rammin' Scriptur' in our gun
  An' gittin' Natur' fer an ally:
Thank God, say I, fer even a plan
  To lift one human bein's level,
Give one more chance to make a man,
  Or, anyhow, to spile a devil!

Not thet I 'm one thet much expec'
  Millennium by express to-morrer;
They *will* miscarry, — I rec'lec'
  Tu many on 'em to my sorrer:

Men ain't made angels in a day,
   No matter how you mould an' labor 'em, —
Nor 'riginal ones, I guess, don't stay
   With Abe so of'n ez with Abraham.

The'ry thinks Fact a pooty thing,
   An' wants the banns read right ensuin';
But Fact wun't noways wear the ring
   'Thout years o' settin' up an' wooin':
Though, arter all, Time's dial-plate
   Marks cent'ries with the minute-finger,
An' Good can't never come tu late,
   Though it doos seem to try an' linger.

An' come wut will, I think it's grand
   Abe's gut his will et last bloom-furnaced
In trial-flames till it'll stand
   The strain o' bein' in deadly earnest:
Thet's wut we want, — we want to know
   The folks on our side hez the bravery
To b'lieve ez hard, come weal, come woe,
   In Freedom ez Jeff doos in Slavery.

Set the two forces foot to foot,
   An' every man knows who'll be winner,
Whose faith in God hez ary root
   Thet goes down deeper than his dinner:
Then 't will be felt from pole to pole,
   Without no need o' proclamation,
Earth's Biggest Country's gut her soul
   An' risen up Earth's Greatest Nation!

No. VIII.

KETELOPOTOMACHIA.

PRELIMINARY NOTE.

In the month of February, 1866, the editors of the "Atlantic Monthly" received from the Rev. Mr. Hitchcock of Jaalam a letter enclosing the macaronic verses which follow, and promising to send more, if more should be communicated. "They were rapped out on the evening of Thursday last past," he says, "by what claimed to be the spirit of my late predecessor in the ministry here, the Rev. Dr. Wilbur, through the medium of a young man at present domiciled in my family. As to the possibility of such spiritual manifestations, or whether they be properly so entitled, I express no opinion, as there is a division of sentiment on that subject in the parish, and many persons of the highest respectability in social standing entertain opposing views. The young man who was improved as a medium submitted himself to the experiment with manifest reluctance, and is still unprepared to believe in the authenticity of the manifestations. During his residence with me his deportment has always been exemplary; he has been constant in his attendance upon our family devotions and the public ministrations of the Word, and has more than once privately stated to me, that the latter had often brought him under deep concern of mind. The table is an ordinary quadrupedal one, weighing about thirty pounds, three feet seven inches and an half in height, four feet square on the top, and of beech or maple, I am not definitely prepared to say which. It had once belonged to my respected predecessor, and had been, so far as I can learn upon careful inquiry, of perfectly regular and correct habits up to the evening in question. On that occasion the young man previously alluded to had been sitting with his hands resting carelessly upon it, while I read over to him at his request certain portions of my last Sabbath's discourse. On a sudden the rap-

pings, as they are called, commenced to render themselves
audible, at first faintly, but in process of time more dis-
tinctly and with violent agitation of the table. The
young man expressed himself both surprised and pained
by the wholly unexpected, and, so far as he was concerned,
unprecedented occurrence. At the earnest solicitation,
however, of several who happened to be present, he con-
sented to go on with the experiment, and with the assist-
ance of the alphabet commonly employed in similar
emergencies, the following communication was obtained
and written down immediately by myself. Whether any,
and if so, how much weight should be attached to it, I
venture no decision. That Dr. Wilbur had sometimes
employed his leisure in Latin versification I have ascer-
tained to be the case, though all that has been discovered
of that nature among his papers consists of some frag-
mentary passages of a version into hexameters of portions
of the Song of Solomon. These I had communicated
about a week or ten days previous[ly] to the young
gentleman who officiated as medium in the communication
afterwards received. I have thus, I believe, stated all the
material facts that have any elucidative bearing upon
this mysterious occurrence."

So far Mr. Hitchcock, who seems perfectly master of
Webster's unabridged quarto, and whose flowing style
leads him into certain further expatiations for which we
have not room. We have since learned that the young
man he speaks of was a sophomore, put under his care
during a sentence of rustication from —— College, where
he had distinguished himself rather by physical experi-
ments on the comparative power of resistance in window-
glass to various solid substances, than in the more regular
studies of the place. In answer to a letter of inquiry,
the professor of Latin says, "There was no harm in the
boy that I know of beyond his loving mischief more than
Latin, nor can I think of any spirits likely to possess
him except those commonly called animal. He was cer-
tainly not remarkable for his Latinity, but I see nothing
in verses you enclose that would lead me to think them
beyond his capacity, or the result of any special inspira-
tion whether of beech or maple. Had that of *birch* been
tried upon him earlier and more faithfully, the verses
would perhaps have been better in quality and certainly

in quantity." This exact and thorough scholar then goes on to point out many false quantities and barbarisms. It is but fair to say, however, that the author, whoever he was, seems not to have been unaware of some of them himself, as is shown by a great many notes appended to the verses as we received them, and purporting to be by Scaliger, Bentley and others, — among them the *Esprit de Voltaire!* These we have omitted as clearly meant to be humorous and altogether failing therein.

Though entirely satisfied that the verses are altogether unworthy of Mr. Wilbur, who seems to have been a tolerable Latin scholar after the fashion of his day, yet we have determined to print them here partly as belonging to the *res gestæ* of this collection, and partly as a warning to their putative author which may keep him from such indecorous pranks for the future.

KETELOPOTOMACHIA.

P. Ovidii Nasonis carmen heroicum macaronicum perplexametrum, inter Getas getico more compostum, denuo per medium ardentispiritualem, adjuvante mensâ diabolice obsessâ, recuperatum, curâque Jo. Conradi Schwarzii umbræ, aliis necnon plurimis adjuvantibus, restitutum.

LIBER I.

Punctorum garretos colens et cellara Quinque,
Gutteribus quæ et gaudes sundayam abstingere frontem,
Plerumque insidos solita fluitare liquore
Tanglepedem quem homines appellant Di quoque rotgut,
Pimpliidis, rubicundaque, Musa, O, bourbonolensque,   5
Fenianas rixas procul, alma, brogipotentis
Patricii cyathos iterantis at horrida bella,.
Backos dum virides viridis Brigitta remittit,
Linquens, eximios celebrem, da, Virginienses
Rowdes, præcipue et Te, heros alte, Polarde!   10
Insignes juvenesque, illo certamine lictos,
Colemane, Tylere, nec vos oblivióne relinquam.

Ampla aquilæ invictæ fausto est sub tegmine terra,
Backyfer, ooiskeo pollens, ebenoque bipede,
Socors præsidum et altrix (denique quidruminantium), 15
Duplefveorum uberrima; illis et integre cordi est
Deplere assidue et sine proprio incommodo fiscum;
Nunc etiam placidum hoc opus invictique secuti,
Goosam aureos ni eggos voluissent immo necare
Quæ peperit, saltem ac de illis meliora merentem.   20
   Condidit hanc Smithius Dux, Captinus inclytus ille
Regis Ulyssæ instar, docti arcum intendere longum;
Condidit ille Johnsmith, Virginiamque vocavit,
Settledit autem Jacobus rex, nomine primus,
Rascalis implens ruptis, blagardisque deboshtis,   25
Militibusque ex Falstaffi legione fugatis
Wenchisque illi quas poterant seducere nuptas;
Virgineum, ah, littus matronis talibus impar!
Progeniem stirpe ex hoc non sine stigmate ducunt ·
Multi sese qui jactant regum esse nepotes: 30
Haud omnes, Mater, genitos quæ nuper habebas
Bellofortes, consilio cautos, virtute decoros,
Jamque et habes, sparso si patrio in sanguine virtus,
Mostrabisque iterum, antiquis sub astris reducta!
De illis qui upkikitant, dicebam, rumpora tanta,   35
Letcheris et Floydis magnisque Extra ordine Billis;
Est his prisca fides jurare et breakere wordum;
Poppere fellerum a tergo, aut stickere clam bowiknifo,
Haud sane facinus, dignum sed victrice lauro;
Larrupere et nigerum, factum præstantius ullo: 40
Ast chlamydem piciplumatam, Icariam, flito et ineptam,
Yanko gratis induere, illum et valido railo
Insuper acri equitare docere est hospitio uti.
   Nescio an ille Polardus duplefveoribus ortus,
Sed reputo potius de radice poorwitemanorum;   45
Fortuiti proles, ni fallor, Tylerus erat
Præsidis, omnibus ab Whiggis nominatus a poor cuss;
Et nobilem tertium evincit venerabile nomen.
Ast animosi omnes bellique ad tympana ha! ha!
Vociferant læti, procul et si proelia, sive   50
Hostem incautum atsito possunt shootere salvi;
Imperiique capaces, esset si stylus agmen,
Pro dulci spoliabant et sine dangere fito.
Præ ceterisque Polardus: si Secessia licta,
Se nunquam licturum jurat, res et unheardof,   55

Verbo hæsit, similisque audaci roosteri invicto,
Dunghilli solitus rex pullos whoppere molles,
Grantum, hirelingos stripes quique et splendida tollunt
Sidera, et Yankos, territum et omnem sarsuit orbem.
  Usque dabant operam isti omnes, noctesque diesque, 60
Samuelem demulgere avunculum, id vero siccum ;
Uberibus sed ejus, et horum est culpa, remotis,
Parvam domi vaccam, nec mora minima, quærunt,
Lacticarentem autem et droppam vix in die dantem ;
Reddite avunculi, et exclamabant, reddite pappam !   65
Polko ut consule, gemens, Billy immurmurat Extra ;
Echo respondit, thesauro ex vacuo, pappam !
Frustra explorant pocketa, ruber nare repertum ;
Officia expulsi aspiciunt rapta, et Paradisum
Occlusum, viridesque haud illis nascere backos ;   70
Stupent tunc oculis madidis spittantque silenter.
Adhibere usu ast longo vires prorsus inepti,
Si non ut qui grindeàt axve trabemve revolvat,
Virginiam excruciant totis nunc mightibu' matrem :
Non melius, puta, nono panis dimidiumne est ?   75
  Readere ibi non posse est casus commoner ullo ;
Tanto intentius imprimere est opus ergo statuta ;
Nemo propterea pejor, melior, sine doubto,
Obtineat qui contractum, si et postea rhino ;
Ergo Polardus, si quis, inexsuperabilis heros,   80
Colemanus impavidus nondum, atque in purpure natus
Tylerus Iohanides celerisque in flito Nathaniel,
Quisque optans digitos in tantum stickere pium,
Adstant accincti imprimere aut perrumpere leges :
Quales os miserum rabidi tres ægre molossi,   85
Quales aut dubium textum atra in veste ministri,
Tales circumstabant nunc nostri inopes hoc job.
  Hisque Polardus voce canoro talia fatus :
Primum autem, veluti est mos, præceps quisque liquorat,
Quisque et Nicotianum ingens quid inserit atrum,   90
Heroûm nitidum decus et solamèn avitum,
Masticat ac simul altisonans, spittatque profuse :
Quis de Virginia meruit præstantius unquam ?
Quis se pro patria curavit impigre tutum ?
Speechisque articulisque hominum quis fortior ullus,   95
Ingeminans pennæ lickos et vulnera vocis ?
Quisnam putidius (hic) sarsuit Yankinimicos,
Sæpius aut dedit ultro datam et broke his parolam ?

Mente inquassatus solidaque, tyranno minante,
Horrisonis (hic) bombis mœnia et alta quatente,   100
Sese promptum (hic) jactans Yankos lickere centum,
Atque ad lastum invictus non surrendidit unquam ?
Ergo haud meddlite, posco, mique relinquite (hic) hoc
        job,
Si non —— knifumque enormen mostrat spittatque
        tremendus.
   Dixerat: ast alii reliquorant et sine pauso   105
Pluggos incumbunt maxillis, uterque vicissim
Certamine innocuo valde madidam inquinit assem :
Tylerus autem, dumque liquorat aridus hostis,
Mirum aspicit duplumque bibentem, astante Lyæo ;
Ardens impavidusque edidit tamen impia verba ;   110
Duplum quamvis te aspicio, esses atque viginti,
Mendacem dicerem totumque (hic) thrasherem acervum ;
Nempe et thrasham, doggonatus (hic) sim nisi faxem ;
Lambastabo omnes catawompositer-(hic)-que chawam !
Dixit et impulsus Ryeo ruitur bene titus,   115
Illi nam gravidum caput et laterem habet in hatto.
   Hunc inhiat titubansque Polardus, optat et illum
Stickere inermen, protegit autem rite Lyæus,
Et pronos geminos, oculis dubitantibus, heros
Cernit et irritus hostes, dumque excogitat utrum   120
Primum inpitchere, corruit, inter utrosque recumbit,
Magno asino similis nimio sub pondere quassus :
Colemanus hos mœstus, triste ruminansque solamen,
Inspicit hiccans, circumspittat terque cubantes ;
Funereisque his ritibus humidis inde solutis,   125
Sternitur, invalidusque illis superincidit infans ;
Hos sepelit somnus et snorunt cornisonantes,
Watchmanus inscios ast calybooso deinde reponit.

No. IX.

[The Editors of the "Atlantic" have received so many letters of inquiry concerning the literary remains of the late Mr. Wilbur, mentioned by his colleague and successor, Rev. Jeduthan Hitchcock, in a communication from which we made some extracts in our number for February, 1863, and have been so repeatedly urged to print some part of them for the gratification of the public, that they felt it their duty at least to make some effort to satisfy so urgent a demand. They have accordingly carefully examined the papers intrusted to them, but find most of the productions of Mr. Wilbur's pen so fragmentary, and even chaotic, written as they are on the backs of letters in an exceedingly cramped chirography, — here a memorandum for a sermon; there an observation of the weather; now the measurement of an extraordinary head of cabbage, and then of the cerebral capacity of some reverend brother deceased; a calm inquiry into the state of modern literature, ending in a method of detecting if milk be impoverished with water, and the amount thereof; one leaf beginning with a genealogy, to be interrupted half-way down with an entry that the brindle cow had calved, — that any attempts at selection seemed desperate. His only complete work, "An Enquiry concerning the Tenth Horn of the Beast," even in the abstract of it given by Mr. Hitchcock, would, by a rough computation of the printers, fill five entire numbers of our journal, and as he attempts, by a new application of decimal fractions, to identify it with the Emperor Julian, seems hardly of immediate concern to the general reader. Even the Table-Talk, though doubtless originally highly interesting in the domestic circle, is so largely made up of theological discussion and matters of local or preterite interest, that we have found it hard to extract anything that would at all satisfy expectation. But, in order to silence further inquiry, we subjoin a few passages as illustrations of its general character.]

I think I could go near to be a perfect Christian if I were always a visitor, as I have sometimes been, at the house of some hospitable friend. I can show a great deal of self-denial where the best of everything is urged upon me with kindly importunity. It is not so very hard to turn the other cheek for a kiss. And when I meditate upon the pains taken for our entertainment in this life, on the endless variety of seasons, of human character and fortune, on the costliness of the hangings and furniture of our dwelling here, I sometimes feel a singular joy in looking upon myself as God's guest, and cannot but believe that we should all be wiser and happier, because more grateful, if we were always mindful of our privilege in this regard. And should we not rate more cheaply any honor that men could pay us, if we remembered that every day we sat at the table of the Great King? Yet must we not forget that we are in strictest bonds His servants also; for there is no impiety so abject as that which expects to be *dead-headed* (*ut ita dicam*) through life, and which, calling itself trust in Providence, is in reality asking Providence to trust us and taking up all our goods on false pretences. It is a wise rule to take the world as we find it, not always to leave it so.

It has often set me thinking when I find that I can always pick up plenty of empty nuts under my shagbark-tree. The squirrels know them by their lightness, and I have seldom seen one with the marks of their teeth in it. What a school-house is the world, if our wits would only not play truant! For I observe that men set most store by forms and symbols in proportion as they are mere shells. It is the outside they want and not the kernel. What stores of such do not many, who in material things are as shrewd as the squirrels, lay up for the spiritual winter-supply of themselves and their children! I have seen churches that seemed to me garners of these withered nuts, for it is wonderful how prosaic is the apprehension of symbols by the minds of most men. It is not one sect nor another, but all, who, like the dog of the fable, have let drop the spiritual substance of symbols for their material shadow. If one attribute miraculous virtues to mere holy water, that beautiful emblem of inward purification at the door of God's house, another cannot comprehend the significance of baptism without being ducked over head and ears in the liquid vehicle thereof.

[Perhaps a word of historical comment may be permitted here. My late revered predecessor was, I would humbly affirm, as free from prejudice as falls to the lot of the most highly favored individuals of our species. To be sure, I have heard him say that, " what were called strong prejudices, were in fact only the repulsion of sensitive organizations from that moral and even physical effluvium by which some natures by providential appointment, like certain unsavory quadrupeds, gave warning of their neighborhood. Better ten mistaken suspicions of this kind than one close encounter." This he said somewhat in heat, on being questioned as to his motives for always refusing his pulpit to those itinerant professors of vicarious benevolence who end their discourses by taking up a collection. But at another time I remember his saying, " that there was one large thing which small minds always found room for, and that was great prejudices." This, however, by the way. The statement which I purposed to make was simply this. Down to A. D. 1830, Jaalam had consisted of a single parish, with one house set apart for religious services. In that year the foundations of a Baptist Society were laid by the labors of Elder Joash Q. Balcom, 2d. As the members of the new body were drawn from the First Parish, Mr. Wilbur was for a time considerably exercised in mind. He even went so far as on one occasion to follow the reprehensible practice of the earlier Puritan divines in choosing a punning text, and preached from Hebrews xiii. 9 : " Be not carried about with *divers* and strange doctrines." He afterwards, in accordance with one of his own maxims, — " to get a dead injury out of the mind as soon as is decent, bury it, and then ventilate," — in accordance with this maxim, I say, he lived on very friendly terms with Rev. Shearjashub Scrimgour, present pastor of the Baptist Society in Jaalam. Yet I think it was never unpleasing to him that the church edifice of that society (though otherwise a creditable specimen of architecture) remained without a bell, as indeed it does to this day. So much seemed necessary to do away with any appearance of acerbity toward a respectable community of professing Christians, which might be suspected in the conclusion of the above paragraph. J. H.]

In lighter moods he was not averse from an innocent play upon words. Looking up from his newspaper one morning as I entered his study he said, "When I read a debate in Congress, I feel as if I were sitting at the feet of Zeno in the shadow of the Portico." On my expressing a natural surprise, he added, smiling, "Why, at such times the only view which honorable members give me of what goes on in the world is through their intercalumniations." I smiled at this after a moment's reflection, and he added gravely, "The most punctilious refinement of manners is the only salt that will keep a democracy from stinking; and what are we to expect from the people, if their representatives set them such lessons? Mr. Everett's whole life has been a sermon from this text. There was, at least, this advantage in duelling, that it set a certain limit on the tongue." In this connection, I may be permitted to recall a playful remark of his upon another occasion. The painful divisions in the First Parish, A. D. 1844, occasioned by the wild notions in respect to the rights of (what Mr. Wilbur, so far as concerned the reasoning faculty, always called) the unfairer part of creation, put forth by Miss Parthenia Almira Fitz, are too well known to need more than a passing allusion. It was during these heats, long since happily allayed, that Mr. Wilbur remarked that "the Church had more trouble in dealing with one *she*resiarch than with twenty *he*resiarchs," and that the men's *conscia recti*, or certainty of being right, was nothing to the women's.

When I once asked his opinion of a poetical composition on which I had expended no little pains, he read it attentively, and then remarked, "Unless one's thought pack more neatly in verse than in prose, it is wiser to refrain. Commonplace gains nothing by being translated into rhyme, for it is something which no hocus-pocus can transubstantiate with the real presence of living thought. You entitle your piece, 'My Mother's Grave,' and expend four pages of useful paper in detailing your emotions there. But, my dear sir, watering does not improve the quality of ink, even though you should do it with tears. To publish a sorrow to Tom, Dick, and Harry is in some sort to advertise its unreality, for I have observed in my intercourse with the afflicted that the deepest grief instinctively hides its face with its hands and is silent. If your piece were printed, I have no doubt it would be popular, for people like to fancy that they feel much better than the trouble of feeling. I would put all poets on oath whether they have striven to say everything they possibly could think of, or to leave out all they could not help saying. In your own case, my worthy young friend, what you have written is merely a deliberate exercise, the gymnastic of sentiment. For your excellent maternal relative is still alive, and is to take tea with me this evening, D. V. Beware of simulated feeling; it is hypocrisy's first cousin; it is especially dangerous to a preacher; for he who says one day, 'Go to, let me seem to be pathetic,' may be nearer than he thinks to saying, 'Go to, let me seem to be virtuous, or earnest, or under sorrow for sin.' Depend upon it, Sappho loved her verses more sincerely than she did Phaon, and Petrarch his sonnets better than Laura, who was indeed but his poetical stalking-horse. After you shall have once heard that muffled rattle of the clods on the coffin-lid of an irreparable loss, you will grow acquainted with a pathos that will make all elegies hateful. When I was of your age, I also for a time mistook my desire to write verses for an authentic call of my nature in that direction. But one day as I was going forth for a walk, with my head full of an 'Elegy on the death of Flirtilla,' and vainly groping after a rhyme for *lily* that should not be *silly* or *chilly*, I saw my eldest boy Homer busy over the rain-water hogshead, in that childish experiment at parthenogenesis, the changing a horsehair into a water-snake. An immersion of six weeks showed no change in the obstinate filament. Here was a stroke of unintended sarcasm. Had I not been doing in my study precisely what my boy was doing out of doors? Had my thoughts any more chance of coming to life by being submerged in rhyme than his hair by soaking in water? I burned my elegy and took a course of Edwards on the Will. People do not make poetry; it is made out of *them* by a process for which I do not find myself fitted. Nevertheless, the writing of verses is a good rhetorical exercitation, as teaching us

what to shun most carefully in prose. For prose be-
witched is like window-glass with bubbles in it, distorting
what it should show with pellucid veracity."

It is unwise to insist on doctrinal points as vital to
religion. The Bread of Life is wholesome and sufficing
in itself, but gulped down with these kickshaws cooked
up by theologians, it is apt to produce an indigestion,
nay, even at last an incurable dyspepsia of scepticism.

One of the most inexcusable weaknesses of Americans
is in signing their names to what are called credentials.
But for my interposition, a person who shall be nameless
would have taken from this town a recommendation for
an office of trust subscribed by the selectmen and all the
voters of both parties, ascribing to him as many good
qualities as if it had been his tombstone. The excuse
was that it would be well for the town to be rid of him,
as it would erelong be obliged to maintain him. I
would not refuse my name to modest merit, but I would
be as cautious as in signing a bond. [I trust I shall be
subjected to no imputation of unbecoming vanity, if I
mention the fact that Mr. W. indorsed my own qualifica-
tions as teacher of the high-school at Pequash Junction.
J. H.] When I see a certificate of character with every-
body's name to it, I regard it as a letter of introduction
from the Devil. Never give a man your name unless you
are willing to trust him with your reputation.

There seem now-a-days to be two sources of literary
inspiration, — fulness of mind and emptiness of pocket.

I am often struck, especially in reading Montaigne,
with the obviousness and familiarity of a great writer's
thoughts, and the freshness they gain because said by him.
The truth is, we mix their greatness with all they say and
give it our best attention. Johannes Faber sic cogitavit,
would be no enticing preface to a book, but an accredited
name gives credit like the signature of a note of hand.
It is the advantage of fame that it is always privileged to
take the world by the button, and a thing is weightier for
Shakespeare's uttering it by the whole amount of his
personality.

It is singular how impatient men are with overpraise of others, how patient with overpraise of themselves; and yet the one does them no injury, while the other may be their ruin.

People are apt to confound mere alertness of mind with attention. The one is but the flying abroad of all the faculties to the open doors and windows at every passing rumor ; the other is the concentration of every one of them in a single focus, as in the alchemist over his alembic at the moment of expected projection. Attention is the stuff that memory is made of, and memory is accumulated genius.

Do not look for the Millennium as imminent. One generation is apt to get all the wear it can out of the cast clothes of the last, and is always sure to use up every paling of the old fence that will hold a nail in building the new.

You suspect a kind of vanity in my genealogical enthusiasm. Perhaps you are right; but it is a universal foible. Where it does not show itself in a personal and private way, it becomes public and gregarious. We flatter ourselves in the Pilgrim Fathers, and the Virginian offshoot of a transported convict swells with the fancy of a cavalier ancestry. Pride of birth, I have noticed, takes two forms. One complacently traces himself up to a coronet; another, defiantly, to a lapstone. The sentiment is precisely the same in both cases, only that one is the positive and the other the negative pole of it.

Seeing a goat the other day kneeling in order to graze with less trouble, it seemed to me a type of the common notion of prayer. Most people are ready enough to go down on their knees for material blessings, but how few for those spiritual gifts which alone are an answer to our orisons, if we but knew it !

Some people, now-a-days, seem to have hit upon a new moralization of the moth and the candle. They would lock up the light of Truth, lest poor Psyche should put it out in her effort to draw nigh to it.

No. X.

MR. HOSEA BIGLOW TO THE EDITOR OF THE ATLANTIC MONTHLY.

DEAR SIR, — Your letter come to han',
　Requestin' me to please be funny;
But I ain't made upon a plan
　Thet knows wut 's comin', gall or honey:
Ther' 's times the world doos look so queer,
　Odd fancies come afore I call 'em;
An' then agin, for half a year,
　No preacher 'thout a call 's more solemn.

You 're 'n want o' sunthin' light an' cute,
　Rattlin' an' shrewd an' kin' o' jingleish,
An' wish, pervidin' it 'ould suit,
　I 'd take an' citify my English.
I *ken* write long-tailed, ef I please, —
　But when I 'm jokin', no, I thankee;
Then, 'fore I know it, my idees
　Run helter-skelter into Yankee.

Sence I begun to scribble rhyme,
　I tell ye wut, I hain't ben foolin';
The parson's books, life, death, an' time
　Hev took some trouble with my schoolin';
Nor th' airth don't git put out with me,
　Thet love her 'z though she wuz a woman;
Why, th' ain't a bird upon the tree
　But half forgives my bein' human.

An' yit I love th' unhighschooled way
　Ol' farmers hed when I wuz younger;
Their talk wuz meatier, an' 'ould stay,
　While book-froth seems to whet your hunger;
For puttin' in a downright lick
　'Twixt Humbug's eyes, ther' 's few can metch it,
An' then it helves my thoughts ez slick
　Ez stret-grained hickory doos a hetchet.

But when I can't, I can't, thet 's all,
   For Natur' won't put up with gullin';
Idees you hev to shove an' haul
   Like a druv pig ain't wuth a mullein;
Live thoughts ain't sent for; thru all rifts
   O' sense they pour an' resh ye onwards,
Like rivers when south-lyin' drifts
   Feel thet th' old airth 's a-wheelin' sunwards.

Time wuz, the rhymes come crowdin' thick
   Ez office-seekers arter 'lection,
An' into ary place 'ould stick
   Without no bother nor objection;
But sence the war my thoughts hang back
   Ez though I wanted to enlist 'em,
An' subs'tutes, — *they* don't never lack,
   But then they 'll slope afore you 've mist 'em.

Nothin' don't seem like wut it wuz;
   I can't see wut there is to hender,
An' yit my brains jes' go buzz, buzz,
   Like bumblebees agin a winder;
'Fore these times come, in all airth's row,
   Ther' wuz one quiet place, my head in,
Where I could hide an' think, — but now
   It 's all one teeter, hopin', dreadin'.

Where 's Peace? I start, some clear-blown night,
   When gaunt stone walls grow numb an' number,
An', creakin' 'cross the snow-crus' white,
   Walk the col' starlight into summer;
Up grows the moon, an' swell by swell
   Thru the pale pasturs silvers dimmer
Than the last smile thet strives to tell
   O' love gone heavenward in its shimmer.

I hev ben gladder o' sech things
   Than cocks o' spring or bees o' clover,
They filled my heart with livin' springs,
   But now they seem to freeze 'em over;
Sights innercent ez babes on knee,
   Peaceful ez eyes o' pastur'd cattle,
Jes' coz they be so, seem to me
   To rile me more with thoughts o' battle.

In-doors an' out by spells I try;
    Ma'am Natur' keeps her spin-wheel goin',
But leaves my natur' stiff and dry
    Ez fiel's o' clover arter mowin';
An' her jes' keepin' on the same,
    Calmer 'n a clock, an' never carin',
An' findin' nary thing to blame,
    Is wus than ef she took to swearin'.

Snow-flakes come whisperin' on the pane
    The charm makes blazin' logs so pleasant,
But I can't hark to wut they 're say'n',
    With Grant or Sherman ollers present;
The chimbleys shudder in the gale,
    Thet lulls, then suddin takes to flappin'
Like a shot hawk, but all 's ez stale
    To me ez so much sperit-rappin'.

Under the yaller-pines I house,
    When sunshine makes 'em all sweet-scented,
An' hear among their furry boughs
    The baskin' west-wind purr contented,
While 'way o'erhead, ez sweet an' low
    Ez distant bells thet ring for meetin',
The wedged wil' geese their bugles blow,
    Further an' further South retreatin'.

Or up the slippery knob I strain
    An' see a hunderd hills like islan's
Lift their blue woods in broken chain
    Out o' the sea o' snowy silence;
The farm-smokes, sweetes' sight on airth,
    Slow thru the winter air a-shrinkin'
Seem kin' o' sad, an' roun' the hearth
    Of empty places set me thinkin'.

Beaver roars hoarse with meltin' snows,
    An' rattles di'mon's from his granite;
Time wuz, he snatched away my prose,
    An' into psalms or satires ran it;
But he, nor all the rest thet once
    Started my blood to country-dances,
Can't set me goin' more 'n a dunce
    Thet hain't no use for dreams an' fancies.

Rat-tat-tat-tattle thru the street
　　I hear the drummers makin' riot,
An' I set thinkin' o' the feet
　　Thet follered once an' now are quiet, —
White feet ez snowdrops innercent,
　　Thet never knowed the paths o' Satan,
Whose comin' step ther' 's ears thet won't,
　　No, not lifelong, leave off awaitin'.

Why, hain't I held 'em on my knee?
　　Did n't I love to see 'em growin',
Three likely lads ez wal could be,
　　Hahnsome an' brave an' not tu knowin'?
I set an' look into the blaze
　　Whose natur', jes' like theirn, keeps climbin',
Ez long 'z it lives, in shinin' ways,
　　An' half despise myself for rhymin'.

Wut 's words to them whose faith an' truth
　　On War's red techstone rang true metal,
Who ventered life an' love an' youth
　　For the gret prize o' death in battle?
To him who, deadly hurt, agen
　　Flashed on afore the charge's thunder,
Tippin' with fire the bolt of men
　　Thet rived the Rebel line asunder?

'T ain't right to hev the young go fust,
　　All throbbin' full o' gifts an' graces,
Leavin' life's paupers dry ez dust
　　To try an' make b'lieve fill their places:
Nothin' but tells us wut we miss,
　　Ther' 's gaps our lives can't never fay in,
An' *thet* world seems so fur from this
　　Lef' for us loafers to grow gray in!

My eyes cloud up for rain; my mouth
　　Will take to twitchin' roun' the corners;
I pity mothers, tu, down South,
　　For all they sot among the scorners:
I'd sooner take my chance to stan'
　　At Jedgment where your meanest slave is,
Than at God's bar hol' up a han'
　　Ez drippin' red ez yourn, Jeff Davis!

Come, Peace! not like a mourner bowed
    For honor lost an' dear ones wasted,
But proud, to meet a people proud,
    With eyes thet tell o' triumph tasted!
Come, with han' grippin' on the hilt,
    An' step thet proves ye Victory's daughter!
Longin' for you, our sperits wilt
    Like shipwrecked men's on raf's for water.

Come, while our country feels the lift
    Of a gret instinct shoutin' forwards,
An' knows thet freedom ain't a gift
    Thet tarries long in han's o' cowards!
Come, sech ez mothers prayed for, when
    They kissed their cross with lips thet quivered,
An' bring fair wages for brave men,
    A nation saved, a race delivered!

No. XI.

MR. HOSEA BIGLOW'S SPEECH IN MARCH MEETING.

TO THE EDITOR OF THE ATLANTIC MONTHLY.

JAALAM, April 5, 1866.

My dear Sir, —

(an' noticin' by your kiver thet you 're some dearer than wut you wuz, I enclose the deffrence) I dunno ez I know jest how to interdroce this las' perduction of my mews, ez Parson Wilber allus called 'em, which is goin' to *be* the last an' *stay* the last onless sunthin' pertikler sh'd interfear which I don't expec' ner I wun't yield tu ef it wuz ez pressin' ez a deppity Shiriff. Sence Mr. Wilbur's disease I hev n't hed no one thet could dror out my talons. He ust to kind o' wine me up an' set the penderlum agoin' an' then somehow I seemed to go on tick as it wear tell I run down, but the noo minister ain't of the same brewin' nor I can't seem to git ahold of no kine of huming nater in him but sort of slide rite off as you du on the eedge of a mow. Minnysteeril natur is wal enough an' a site better 'n most other kines I know on, but the other sort sech as Welbor hed wuz of the Lord's makin' an' naterally more wonderfle an' sweet tastin' leastways to me so fur as heerd from. He used to interdooce 'em smooth ez ile athout sayin' nothin' in pertickler an' I misdoubt he did n't set so much by the sec'nd Ceres as wut he done by the Fust, fact, he let on onct thet his mine misgive him of a sort of fallin' off in spots. He wuz as outspoken as a norwester *he* wuz, but I tole him I hoped the fall wuz from so high up thet a feller could ketch a good many times fust afore comin' bunt onto the ground as I see Jethro C. Swett from the meetin' house steeple up to th' old perrish, an' took up for dead but he 's alive now an' spry as wut you be. Turnin' of it over I recclected how they ust to put wut they called Argymunce onto the frunts of poymns, like poorches afore housen whare you could rest ye a spell whilst you wuz concludin'.whether you 'd go in or nut espeshully ware tha wuz darters, though I most allus found it the best plen to go in fust an' think afterwards an' the gals likes it best tu. I duo as speechis ever hez any argimunts to 'em, I never see none thet hed an' I guess they never du but tha must allus be a B'ginnin' to everythin' athout it is Etarnity so I'll begin rite away an' anybody may put it afore any of his speeches ef it soots an' welcome. I don't claim no paytent.

THE ARGYMUNT.

Interducshin, w'ich may be skipt. Begins by talkin' about himself : thet 's jest natur an' most gin'ally allus pleasin', I b'leeve I've notist, to *one* of the cumpany, an' thet 's more than wut you can say of most speshes of talkin'. Nex' comes the gittin' the goodwill of the orjunce by lettin' 'em gether from wut you kind of ex'dentally let drop thet they air about East, A one, an' no mistaik, skare 'em up an' take 'em as they rise. Spring interdooced with a fiew approput flours. Speach finally begins witch nobuddy need n't feel obolygated to read as I never read 'em an' never shell this one ag'in. Subjick staited ; expanded ; delayted ; extended. Pump lively. Subjick staited ag'in so 's to avide all mistaiks. Ginnle remarks ; continooed ; kerried on ; pushed furder ; kind o' gin out. Subjick *re*staited ; dielooted ; stirred up permiscoous. Pump ag'in. Gits back to where he sot out. Can't seem to stay thair. Ketches into Mr. Seaward's hair. Breaks loose ag'in an' staits his subjick ; stretches it ; turns it ; folds it ; onfolds it ; folds it ag'in so 's 't no one can't find it. Argoos with an imedginary bean thet ain't aloud to say nothin' in repleye. Gives him a real good dressin' an' is settysfide he 's rite. Gits into Johnson's hair. No use tryin' to git into his head. Gives it up. Hez to stait his subjick ag'in ; doos it back'ards, sideways, eend-ways, criss-cross, bevellin', noways. Gits finally red ▶n it. Concloods. Concloods more. Reads some xtrax. Sees his subjick a-nosin' round arter him ag'in. Tries to avide it. Wun't du. *Mis*states it. Can't conjectur'

no other plawsable way of staytin' on it.   Tries pump.
No fx.   Finely concloods to conclood.   Yeels the flore.

You kin spall an' punctooate thet as you please.   I
allus do, it kind of puts a noo soot of close onto a word,
thisere funattick spellin' doos an' takes 'em out of the
prissen dress they wair in the Dixonary.   Ef I squeeze
the cents out of 'em it 's the main thing, an' wut they
wuz made for; wut 's left 's jest pummis.

Mistur Wilbur sez he to me onct, sez he, " Hosee," sez
he, " in litterytoor the only good thing is Natur.   It 's
amazin' hard to come at," sez he, " but onct git it an'
you 've gut everythin'.   Wut 's the sweetest small on
airth ? " sez he.   " Noomone hay," sez I, pooty bresk,
for he wuz allus hankerin' round in hayin'.   " Nawthin'
of the kine," sez he.   " My leetle Huldy's breath," sez I
ag'in.   " You 're a good lad," sez he, his eyes sort of
ripplin' like, for he lost a babe onct nigh about her age, —
" You 're a good lad; but 't ain't thet nuther," sez he.   " Ef
you want to know," sez he, " open your winder of a
mornin' et ary season, and you 'll larn thet the best of
perfooms is jest fresh air, *fresh air*," sez he, emphysizin',
" athout no mixtur.   Thet 's wut *I* call natur in writin',
and it bathes my lungs and washes 'em sweet whenever I
git a whiff on 't," sez he.   I offen think o' thet when I
set down to write, but the winders air *so* ept to git stuck,
an' breakin' a pane costs sunthin'.

Yourn for the last time,
Nut to be continooed,
HOSEA BIGLOW.

I DON'T much s'pose, hows'ever I should plen it,
I could git boosted into th' House or Sennit, —
Nut while the twolegged gab-machine 's so plenty,
'Nablin' one man to du the talk o' twenty;
I 'm one o' them thet finds it ruther hard
To mannyfactur' wisdom by the yard,
An' maysure off, accordin' to demand,
The piece-goods el'kence that I keep on hand,
The same ole pattern runnin' thru an' thru,
An'. nothin' but the customer thet 's new.
I sometimes think, the furder on I go,
Thet it gits harder to feel sure I know,

An' when I 've settled my idees, I find
'T war n't I sheered most in makin' up my mind;
'T wuz this an' thet an' t' other thing thet done it,
Sunthin' in th' air, I could n' seek nor shun it.
Mos' folks go off so quick now in discussion,
All th' ole flint locks seems altered to percussion,
Whilst I in agin' sometimes git a hint
Thet I 'm percussion changin' back to flint;
Wal, ef it 's so, I ain't agoin' to werrit,
For th' ole Queen's-arm hez this pertickler merit, —
It gives the mind a hahnsome wedth o' margin
To kin' o' make its will afore dischargin':
I can't make out but jest one ginnle rule, —
No man need go an' *make* himself a fool,
Nor jedgment ain't like mutton, thet can't bear
Cookin' tu long, nor be took up tu rare.

Ez I wuz say'n', I hain't no chance to speak
So 's 't all the country dreads me onct a week,
But I 've consid'ble o' thet sort o' head
Thet sets to home an' thinks wut *might* be said,
The sense thet grows an' werrits underneath.
Comin' belated like your wisdom-teeth,
An' git so el'kent, sometimes, to my gardin
Thet I don' vally public life a fardin'.
Our Parson Wilbur (blessin's on his head!)
'Mongst other stories of ole times he hed,
Talked of a feller thet rehearsed his spreads
Beforehan' to his rows o' kebbige-heads,
(Ef 't war n't Demossenes, I guess 't wuz Sisro,)
Appealin' fust to thet an' then to this row,
Accordin' ez he thought thet his idees
Their diff'runt ev'riges o' brains 'ould please;
" An'," sez the Parson, " to hit right, you must
Git used to maysurin' your hearers fust;
For, take my word for 't, when all 's come an' past,
The kebbige-heads 'll cair the day et last;
Th' ain't ben a meetin' sence the worl' begun
But they made (raw or biled ones) ten to one."

I 've allus foun' 'em, I allow, sence then
About ez good for talkin' to ez men;
They 'll take edvice, like other folks, to keep,

(To use it 'ould be holdin' on 't tu cheap,)
They listen wal, don' kick up when you scold 'em,
An' ef they've tongues, hev sense enough to hold 'em;
Though th' ain't no denger we shall lose the breed,
I gin'lly keep a score or so for seed,
An' when my sappiness gits spry in spring,
So 's 't my tongue itches to run on full swing,
I fin' 'em ready-planted in March-meetin',
Warm ez a lýceum-audience in their greetin',
An' pleased to hear my spoutin' frum the fence, —

Comin', ez 't doos, entirely free 'f expense.
This year I made the follerin' observations
Extrump'ry, like most other tri'ls o' patience,
An', no reporters bein' sent express
To work their abstrac's up into a mess
Ez like th' oridg'nal ez a woodcut pictur'
Thet chokes the life out like a boy-constrictor,
I 've writ 'em out, an' so avide all jeal'sies
'Twixt nonsense o' my own an' some one's else's.

(N. B. Reporters gin'lly git a hint
To make dull orjunces seem 'live in print,
An', ez I hev t' report myself, I vum,
I 'll put th' applauses where they'd *ough'* *to* **come** l)

My FELLER KEBBIGE-HEADS, who look so green,
I vow to gracious thet ef I could dreen
The world of all its hearers but jest you,
'T would leave 'bout all tha' is wuth talkin' to,
An' you, my ven'able ol' frien's, thet show
Upon your crowns a sprinklin' o' March snow,
Ez ef mild Time had christened every sense
For wisdom's church o' second innocence,
Nut Age's winter, no, no sech a thing,
But jest a kin' o' slippin'-back o' spring, —
[Sev'ril noses blowed.]
We 've gathered here, ez ushle, to decide
Which is the Lord's an' which is Satan's side,
Coz all the good or evil thet can heppen
Is 'long o' which on 'em you choose for Cappen.
[Cries o' " Thet 's so l "]

Aprul 's come back; the swellin' buds of oak
Dim the fur hillsides with a purplish smoke;
The brooks are loose an', singing to be seen,
(Like gals,) make all the hollers soft an' green.
The birds are here, for all the season 's late;
They take the sun's height an' don' never wait;
Soon 'z he officially declares it 's spring
Their light hearts lift 'em on a north'ard wing,
An' th' ain't an acre, fur ez you can hear,
Can't by the music tell the time o' year;
But thet white dove Carliny scared away,
Five year ago, jes' sech an Aprul day;
Peace, that we hoped 'ould come an' build last year
An' coo by every housedoor, is n't here, —
No, nor wun't never be, for all our jaw,
Till we 're ez brave in pol'tics ez in war !
O Lord, ef folks wuz made so 's 't they could see
The begnet-pint there is to an idee!   [Sensation.]
Ten times the danger in 'em th' is in steel;
They run your soul thru an' you never feel,
But crawl about an' seem to think you 're livin',
Poor shells o' men, nut wuth the Lord's forgivin',
Till you come bunt ag'in a real live fect,
An' go to pieces when you 'd ough' to eet !
Thet kin' o' begnet 's wut we 're crossin' now,
An' no man, fit to nevvigate a scow,
'Ould stan' expectin' help from Kingdom Come,
While t' other side druv their cold iron home.

My frien's, you never gethered from my mouth,
No, nut one word ag'in the South ez South,
Nor th' ain't a livin' man, white, brown, nor black,
Gladder 'n wut I should be to take 'em back;
But all I ask of Uncle Sam is fust
To write up on his door, " No goods on trust ";
                    [Cries of " Thet 's the ticket! "]
Give us cash down in ekle laws for all,
An' they 'll be snug inside afore nex' fall.
Give wut they ask, an' we shell hev Jamaker,
Wuth minus some consid'able an acre ;
Give wut they need, an' we shell git 'fore long
A nation all one piece, rich, peacefle, strong;
Make 'em Amerikin, an' they 'll begin

To love their country ez they loved their sin;
Let 'em stay Southun, an' you 've kep' a sore
Ready to fester ez it done afore.
No mortle man can boast of perfic' vision,
But the one moleblin' thing is Indecision,
An' th' ain't no futur' for the man nor state
Thet out of j-u-s-t can't spell great.
Some folks 'ould call thet reddikle; do you ?
'T was commonsense afore the war wuz thru;
Thet loaded all our guns an' made 'em speak
So 's 't Europe heared 'em clearn acrost the creek :
" They 're drivin' o' their spiles down now," sez she,
" To the hard grennit o' God's fust idee ;
Ef they reach thet, Democ'cy need n't fear
The tallest airthquakes *we* can git up here."
Some call 't insultin' to ask *ary* pledge,
An' say 't will only set their teeth on edge,
But folks you 've jest licked, fur 'z I ever see,
Are 'bout ez mad 'z they wal know how to be ;
It 's better than the Rebs themselves expected
'Fore they see Uncle Sam wilt down henpected ;
Be kind 'z you please, but fustly make things fast,
For plain Truth 's all the kindness thet 'll last ;
Ef treason is a crime, ez *some* folks say,
How could we punish it a milder way
Than sayin' to 'em, " Brethren, lookee here,
We 'll jes' divide things with ye, sheer an' sheer,
An sence both come o' pooty strongbacked daddies,
You take the Darkies, ez we 've took the Paddies ;
Ign'ant an' poor we took 'em by the hand,
An' they 're the bones an' sinners o' the land."
I ain't o' them thet fancy there 's a loss on
Every inves'ment thet don't start from Bos'on ;
But I know this : our money 's safest trusted
In sunthin', come wut will, thet *can't* be busted,
An' thet 's the old Amerikin idee
To make a man a Man an' let him be.   [Gret applause.]
Ez for their l'yalty, don't take a goad to 't,
But I do' want to block their only road to 't
By lettin' 'em believe thet they can git
Mor 'n wut they lost, out of our little wit :
I tell ye wut, I 'm 'fraid we 'll drif' to leeward
'Thout we can put more stiffenin' into Seward ;

2 s

He seems to think Columby 'd better ect
Like a scared widder with a boy stiff-necked
Thet stomps an' swears he wun't come in to supper;
She mus' set up for him, ez weak ez Tupper,
Keepin' the Constitootion on to warm,
Tell he 'll eccept her 'pologies in form :
The neighbors tell her he 's a cross-grained cuss
Thet needs a hidin' 'fore he comes to wus;
" No," sez Ma Seward, " he 's ez good 'z the best,
All he wants now is sugar-plums an' rest " ;
" He sarsed my Pa," sez one ; " He stoned my son,"
Another edds.   " O, wal, 't wuz jest his fun."
" He tried to shoot our Uncle Samwell dead."
" 'T wuz only tryin' a noo gun he hed."
" Wal, all we ask 's to hev it understood
You 'll take his gun away from him for good;
We don't, wal, nut exac'ly, like his play,
Seein' he allus kin' o' shoots our way.
You kill your fatted calves to no good eend,
'Thout his fust sayin', ' Mother, I hev sinned ! ' "
[" Amen ! " frum Deac'n Greenleaf.]

The Pres'dunt *he* thinks thet the slickest plan
'Ould be t' allow thet he 's our on'y man,
An' thet we fit thru all thet dreffle war
Jes' for his private glory an' eclor ;
" Nobody ain't a Union man," sez he,
" 'Thout he agrees, thru thick an' thin, with me ;
War n't Andrew Jackson's 'nitials jes' like mine ?
An' ain't thet sunthin' like a right divine
To cut up ez kentenkerous ez I please,
An' treat your Congress like a nest o' fleas ? "
Wal, I expec' the People would n' care, if
The question now wuz techin' bank or tariff,
But I conclude they 've 'bout made up their mind
This ain't the fittest time to go it blind,
Nor these ain't metters thet with pol'tics swings,
But goes 'way down amongst the roots o' things ;
Coz Sumner talked o' whitewashin' one day
They wun't let four years' war be throwed away.
" Let the South hev her rights ? "   They say, " Thet 's you !
But nut greb hold of other folks's tu."

Who owns this country, is it they or Andy ?
Leastways it ough' to be the People *and* he ;
Let him be senior pardner, ef he 's so,
But let them kin' o' smuggle in ez Co ;   [Laughter.]
Did he diskiver it ?   Consid'ble numbers
Think thet the job wuz taken by Columbus.
Did he set tu an' make it wut it is ?
Ef so, I guess the One-Man-power *hez* riz.
Did he put thru the rebbles, clear the docket,
An' pay th' expenses out of his own pocket ?
Ef thet 's the case, then everythin' I exes
Is t' hev him come an' pay my ennooal texes.
[Profound sensation.]

Was 't he thet shou'dered all them million guns ?
Did he lose all the fathers, brothers, sons ?
Is this ere pop'lar gov'ment thet we run
A kin' o' sulky, made to kerry one ?
An' is the country goin' to knuckle down
To hev Smith sort their letters 'stid o' Brown ?
Who wuz the 'Nited States 'fore Richmon' fell ?
Wuz the South needfle their full name to spell ?
An' can't we spell it in thet short-han' way
Till th' underpinnin' 's settled so 's to stay ?
Who cares for the Resolves of '61,
Thet tried to coax an airthquake with a bun ? ⋅
Hez act'ly nothin' taken place sence then
To larn folks they must hendle fects like men ?
Ain't *this* the true p'int ?   Did the Rebs accep' 'em ?
Ef nut, whose fault is 't thet we hev n't kep' 'em ?
War n't there *two* sides ? an' don't it stend to reason
Thet this week's 'Nited States ain't las' week's treason?
When all these sums is done, with nothin' missed,
An' nut afore, this school 'll be dismissed.

I knowed ez wal ez though I 'd seen 't with eyes
Thet when the war wuz over copper 'd rise,
An' thet we 'd hev a rile-up in our kettle
'T would need Leviathan's whole skin to settle ;
I thought 't would take about a generation
'Fore we could wal begin to be a nation,
But I allow I never did imegine
'T would be our Pres'dunt thet 'ould drive a wedge in
To keep the split from closin' ef it could,

An' healin' over with new wholesome wood;
For th' ain't no chance o' healin' while they think
Thet law an' gov'ment 's only printer's ink;
I mus' confess I thank him for discoverin'
The curus way in which the States are sovereign;
They ain't nut *quite* enough so to rebel,
But, when they fin' it 's costly to raise h—,

[A groan from Deac'n G.]

Why, then, for jes' the same superl'tive reason,
They 're most too much so to be tetched for treason;
They *can't* go out, but ef they somehow *du,*
Their sovereignty don't noways go out tu;
The State goes out, the sovereignty don't stir,
But stays to keep the door ajar for her.
He thinks secession never took 'em out,
An' mebby he 's correc', but I misdoubt;
Ef they war n't out, then why, 'n the name o' sin,
Make all this row 'bout lettin' of 'em in?
In law, p'r'aps nut; but there 's a diffurence, ruther,
Betwixt your mother-'n-law an' real mother,

[Derisive cheers.]

An' I, for one, shall wish they 'd all been *som'eres,*
Long 'z U. S. Texes are sech reg'lar comers.
But, O my patience! must we wriggle back
Into th' ole crooked, pettyfoggin' track,
When our artil'ry-wheels a road hev cut
Stret to our purpose ef we keep the rut?
War 's jes' dead waste excep' to wipe the slate
Clean for the cyph'rin' of some nobler fate.   [Applause.]

Ez for dependin' on their oaths an' thet,
'T wun't bind 'em more 'n the ribbin roun' my het;
I heared a fable once from Othniel Starns,
That pints it slick ez weathercocks do barns:
Onct on a time the wolves hed certing rights
Inside the fold; they used to sleep there nights,
An', bein' cousins o' the dogs, they took
Their turns et watchin', reg'lar ez a book;
But somehow, when the dogs hed gut asleep,
Their love o' mutton beat their love o' sheep,
Till gradilly the shepherds come to see
Things war n't agoin' ez they 'd ough' to be;

So they sent off a deacon to remonstrate
Along 'th the wolves an' urge 'em to go on straight;
They did n' seem to set much by the deacon,
Nor preachin' did n' cow 'em, nut to speak on;
Fin'ly they swore thet they 'd go out an' stay,
An' hev their fill o' mutton every day;
Then dogs an' shepherds, after much hard dammin',

                    [Groan from Deac'n G.]

Turned tu an' give 'em a tormented lammin',
An' sez, " Ye sha'n't go out, the murrain rot ye,
To keep us wastin' half our time to watch ye ! ".
But then the question come, How live together
'Thout losin' sleep, nor nary yew nor wether ?
Now there wuz some dogs (noways wuth their keep)
Thet sheered their cousins' tastes an' sheered the sheep;
They sez, " Be gin'rous, let 'em swear right in,
An', ef they backslide, let 'em swear ag'in;
Jes' let 'em put on sheep-skins whilst they 're swearin';
To ask for more 'ould be beyond all bearin'."
" Be gin'rous for yourselves, where *you* 're to pay,
Thet 's the best prectice," sez a shepherd gray;
" Ez for their oaths they wun't be wuth a button
Long 'z you don't cure 'em o' their taste for mutton;
Th' ain't but one solid way, howe'er you puzzle:
Tell they 're converted, let 'em wear a muzzle."

                    [Cries of " Bully for you ! "]

I 've noticed thet each half-baked scheme's abetters
Are in the hebbit o' producin' letters
Writ by all sorts o' never-heared-on fellers,
'Bout ez oridge'nal ez the wind in bellers;
I 've noticed, tu, it 's the quack med'cines gits
(An' needs) the grettest heaps o' stiffykits;

                    [Two apothekeries goes out]

Now, sence I lef' off creepin' on all fours,
I hain't ast no man to endorse my course;
It 's full ez cheap to be your own endorser,
An' ef I 've made a cup, I 'll fin' the saucer;
But I 've some letters here from t' other side,
An' them 's the sort thet helps me to decide;
Tell me for wut the copper-comp'nies hanker,
An' I 'll tell you jest where it 's safe to anchor.

                    [Faint hiss.]

Fus'ly the Hon'ble B. O. Sawin writes

Thet for a spell he could n' sleep o' nights,
Puzzlin' which side wuz preudentest to pin to,
Which wuz th' ole homestead, which the temp'ry leanto ;
Et fust he jedged 't would right-side-up his pan
To come out ez a 'ridge'nal Union man,
" But now," he sez, " I ain't nut quite so fresh ;
The winnin' horse is goin' to be Secesh ;
You might, las' spring, hev eas'ly walked the course,
'Fore we contrived to doctor th' Union horse ;
Now *we*'re the ones to walk aroun' the nex' track :
Jest you take hold an' read the follerin' extrac',
Out of a letter I received last week
From an ole frien' thet never sprung a leak,
A Nothun Dem'crat o' th' ole Jarsey blue,
Born coppersheathed an' copperfastened tu."

  " These four years past it hez been tough
   To say which side a feller went for ;
  Guideposts all gone, roads muddy 'n' rough,
   An' nothin' duin' wut 't wuz meant for ;
  Pickets a-firin' left an' right,
  Both sides a lettin' rip et sight, —
  Life war n't wuth hardly payin' rent for.

  " Columby gut her back up so,
   It war n't no use a-tryin' to stop her, —
  War's emptin's riled her very dough
   An' made it rise an' act improper ;
  'T wuz full ez much ez I could du
  To jes' lay low an' worry thru',
  'Thout hevin' to sell out my copper.

  " Afore the war your mod'rit men
   Could set an' sun 'em on the fences,
  Cyph'rin' the chances up, an' then
   Jump off which way bes' paid expenses ;
  Sence, 't wus so resky ary way,
  I did n't hardly darst to say
  I 'greed with Paley's Evidences.
        [Groan from Deac'n G.]

  " Ask Mac ef tryin' to set the fence
   War n't like bein' rid upon a rail on 't,

Headin' your party with a sense
O' bein' tipjint in the tail on 't,
And tryin' to think thet, on the whole,
You kin' o' quasi own your soul
When Belmont's gut a bill o' sale on 't?
[Three cheers for Grant and **Sherman.**]

" Come peace, I sposed thet folks 'ould like
Their pol'tics done ag'in by proxy,
Give their noo loves the bag an' strike
A fresh trade with their reg'lar doxy;
But the drag's broke, now slavery's gone,
An' there's gret resk they'll blunder on,
Ef they ain't stopped, to real Democ'cy.

" We've gut an awful row to hoe
In this 'ere job o' reconstructin';
Folks dunno skurce which way to go,
Where th' ain't some boghole to be ducked in;
But one thing's clear; there *is* a crack,
Ef we pry hard, 'twixt white an' black,
Where the old makebate can be tucked in.

" No white man sets in airth's broad aisle
Thet I ain't willin' t' own ez brother,
An' ef he's heppened to strike ile,
I dunno, fin'ly, but I'd ruther;
An' Paddies, long 'z they vote all right,
Though they ain't jest a nat'ral white,
I hold one on 'em good 'z another.   [Applause.]

Wut *is* there lef' I'd like to know,
Ef 't ain't the difference o' color,
To keep up self-respec' an' show
The human natur' of a fullah?
Wut good in bein' white, onless
It's fixed by law, nut lef' to guess,
That we are smarter an' they duller?

"Ef we're to hev our ekle rights,
'T wun't du to 'low no competition;
Th' ole debt doo us for bein' whites
Ain't safe onless we stop th' emission

O' these noo notes, whose specie base
Is human natur', 'thout no trace
O' shape, nor color, nor condition.

[Continood applause.]

"So fur I 'd writ an' could n' jedge
Aboard wut boat I'd best take pessige,
My brains all mincemeat, 'thout no edge
Upon 'em more than tu a sessige,
But now it seems ez though I see
Sunthin' resemblin' an idee,
Sence Johnson's speech an' veto message.

"I like the speech best, I confess,
The logic, preudence, an' good taste on 't,
An' it's so mad, I ruther guess
There's some dependence to be placed on 't;

[Laughter.]

It's narrer, but 'twixt you an' me,
Out o' the allies o' J. D.
A temp'ry party can be based on 't.

"Jes' to hold on till Johnson's thru
An' dug his Presidential grave is,
An' *then!*—who knows but we could slew
The country roun' to put in——?
Wun't some folks rare up when we pull
Out o' their eyes our Union wool
An' larn 'em wut a p'lit'cle shave is!

"O, did it seem 'z ef Providunce
Could ever send a second Tyler?
To see the South all back to once,
Reapin' the spiles o' the Freesiler,
Is cute ez though an ingineer
Should claim th' old iron for his sheer
Coz 't was himself that bust the biler!"

[Gret laughter.]

Thet tells the story! Thet's wut we shall git
By tryin' squirtguns on the burnin' Pit;
For the day never comes when it 'll du
To kick off Dooty like a worn-out shoe

I seem to hear a whisperin' in the air,
A sighin' like, of unconsoled despair,
Thet comes from nowhere an' from everywhere,
An' seems to say, "Why died we? war n't it, then,
To settle, once for all, thet men wuz men?
O, airth's sweet cup snetched from us barely tasted,
The grave's real chill is feelin' life wuz wasted!
O, you we lef', long-lingerin' et the door,
Lovin' you best, coz we loved Her the more,
Thet Death, not we, had conquered, we should feel
Ef she upon our memory turned her heel,
An' unregretful throwed us all away
To flaunt it in a Blind Man's Holiday!"

My frien's, I've talked nigh on to long enough.
I hain't no call to bore ye coz ye're tough;
My lungs are sound, an' our own v'ice delights
Our ears, but even kebbige-heads hez rights.
It's the las' time thet I shell e'er address ye,
But you'll soon fin' some new tormentor: bless ye!

[Tumult'ous applause and cries of "Go on!" "Don't stop!"]

THE UNHAPPY LOT OF MR. KNOTT.

1850.

THE UNHAPPY LOT OF MR. KNOTT.

PART I.

SHOWING HOW HE BUILT HIS HOUSE AND HIS WIFE MOVED INTO IT.

My worthy friend, A. Gordon Knott,
 From business snug withdrawn,
Was much contented with a lot
That would contain a Tudor cot
'Twixt twelve feet square of garden-plot,
 And twelve feet more of lawn.

He had laid business on the shelf
 To give his taste expansion,
And, since no man, retired with pelf
 The building mania can shun,
Knott, being middle-aged himself,
Resolved to build (unhappy elf!)
 A mediæval mansion.

He called an architect in counsel;
 "I want," said he, "a — you know what
(You are a builder, I am Knott,)
 A thing complete from chimney-pot
Down to the very grounsel;
 Here's a half-acre of good land;
 Just have it nicely mapped and planned
And make your workmen drive on;.
 Meadow there is, and upland too,
 And I should like a water-view,
D' you think you could contrive one?
 (Perhaps the pump and trough would do.
 If painted a judicious blue?)
 The woodland I 've attended to;"
 (He meant three pines stuck up askew,
Two dead ones and a live one.)

" A pocket-full of rocks 't would take
To build a house of free-stone,
　But then it is not hard to make
What now-a-days is *the* stone;
　The cunning painter in a trice
　Your house's outside petrifies,
　And people think it very gneiss
Without inquiring deeper;
　My money never shall be thrown
　Away on such a deal of stone,
When stone of deal is cheaper."

And so the greenest of antiques
　Was reared for Knott to dwell in;
The architect worked hard for weeks
In venting all his private peaks
Upon the roof, whose crop of leaks
　Had satisfied Fluellen;
Whatever any body had
Out of the common, good or bad,
　Knott had it all worked well in,
A donjon-keep, where clothes might dry,
A porter's lodge that was a sty,
A campanile slim and high,
　Too small to hang a bell in;
All up and down and here and there,
With Lord-knows-whats of round and square
Stuck on at random every where, —
It was a house to make one stare,
　All corners and all gables;
Like dogs let loose upon a bear,
Ten emulous styles *staboyed* with care,
The whole among them seemed to tear,
And all the oddities to spare
　Were set upon the stables.

Knott was delighted with a pile
　Approved by fashion's leaders;
(Only he made the builder smile,
By asking, every little while,
Why that was called the Twodoor style,
　Which certainly had *three* doors?)
Yet better for this luckless man

If he had put a downright ban
   Upon the thing *in limine ;*
For, though to quit affairs his plan,
Ere many days, poor Knott began
Perforce, accepting draughts that ran
   All ways — except up chimney ;
The house, though painted stone to mock,
With nice white lines round every block,
   Some trepidation stood in,
When tempests (with petrific shock,
So to speak,) made it really rock,
   Though not a whit less wooden ;
And painted stone, howe'er well done,
Will not take in the prodigal sun
Whose beams are never quite at one
   With our terrestrial lumber ;
So the wood shrank around the knots,
And gaped in disconcerting spots,
And there were lots of dots and rots
   And crannies without number,
Wherethrough, as you may well presume,
The wind, like water through a flume,
   Came rushing in ecstatic,
Leaving, in all three floors, no room
   That was not a rheumatic ;
And, what with points and squares and rounds
   Grown shaky on their poises,
The house at night was full of pounds,
Thumps, bumps, creaks, scratchings, raps — till
    — " Zounds ! "
Cried Knott, " this goes beyond all bounds.
I do not deal in tongues and sounds,
Nor have I let my house and grounds
   To a family of Noyeses ! "

But, though Knott's house was full of airs,
   He had but one — a daughter ;
And, as he owned much stocks and shares,
Many who wished to render theirs
Such vain, unsatisfying cares,
And needed wives to sew their tears,
   In matrimony sought her ;
They vowed her gold they wanted not,

Their faith would never falter,
They longed to tie this single Knott
  In the Hymenæal halter;
So daily at the door they rang,
  Cards for the belle delivering,
Or in the choir at her they sang,
Achieving such a rapturous twang
  As set her nerves a-shivering.

Now Knott had quite made up his mind
  That Colonel Jones should have her;
No beauty he, but oft we find
Sweet kernels 'neath a roughish rind,
So hoped his Jenny 'd be resigned
  And make no more palaver;
Glanced at the fact that love was blind,
That girls were ratherish inclined
  To pet their little crosses,
Then nosologically defined
The rate at which the system pined
In those unfortunates who dined
Upon that metaphoric kind
  Of dish — their own proboscis.

But she, with many tears and moans,
  Besought him not to mock her,
Said 't was too much for flesh and bones
To marry mortgages and loans,
That fathers' hearts were stocks and stones
And that she 'd go, when Mrs. Jones,
  To Davy Jones's locker;
Then gave her head a little toss
That said as plain as ever was,
If men are always at a loss
  Mere womankind to bridle —
To try the thing on woman cross,
  Were fifty times as idle;
For she a strict resolve had made
  And registered in private,
That either she would die a maid,
Or else be Mrs. Doctor Slade,
  If woman could contrive it;
And, though the wedding-day was set,

Jenny was more so, rather,
Declaring, in a pretty pet,
That, howsoe'er they spread their net,
She would out-Jennyral them yet,
    The colonel and her father.

Just at this time the Public's eyes
    Were keenly on the watch, a stir
Beginning slowly to arise
About those questions and replies,
Those raps that unwrapped mysteries
    So rapidly at Rochester,
And Knott, already nervous grown
By lying much awake alone,
And listening, sometimes to a moan,
    And sometimes to a clatter,
Whene'er the wind at night would rouse
The gingerbread-work on his house,
Or when some hasty-tempered mouse,
Behind the plastering, made a towse
    About a family matter,
Began to wonder if his wife,
A paralytic half her life,
    Which made it more surprising,
Might not to rule him from her urn,
Have taken a peripatetic turn
    For want of exorcising.

This thought, once nestled in his head,
Ere long contagious grew, and spread
Infecting all his mind with dread,
Until at last he lay in bed
And heard his wife, with well-known tread,
Entering the kitchen through the shed,
    (Or was 't his fancy, mocking?)
Opening the pantry, cutting bread,
And then (she 'd been some ten years dead)
    Closets and drawers unlocking;
Or, in his room (his breath grew thick)
He heard the long-familiar click
Of slender needles flying quick,
    As if she knit a stocking;
For whom? — he prayed that years might flit

2 T

With pains rheumatic shooting,
Before those ghostly things she knit
Upon his unfleshed sole might fit,
He did not fancy it a bit,
　To stand upon that footing;
At other times, his frightened hairs
　Above the bedclothes trusting,
He heard her, full of household cares,
(No dream entrapped in supper's snares,
The foal of horrible nightmares,
But broad awake, as he declares,)
Go bustling up and down the stairs,
Or setting back last evening's chairs,
　Or with the poker thrusting
The raked-up sea-coal's hardened crust —
And — what! impossible! it must!
He knew she had returned to dust,
And yet could scarce his senses trust,
Hearing her as she poked and fussed
　About the parlor, dusting!

Night after night he strove to sleep
　And take his ease in spite of it;
But still his flesh would chill and creep,
And, though two night-lamps he might keep,
　He could not so make light of it.
At last, quite desperate, he goes
And tells his neighbors all his woes,
　Which did but their amount enhance;
They made such mockery of his fears
That soon his days were of all jeers,
　His nights of the rueful countenance;
"I thought most folks," one neighbor said,
"Gave up the ghost when they were dead,"
Another gravely shook his head,
　Adding, "from all we hear, it 's
Quite plain poor Knott is going mad —
For how can he at once be sad
　And think he 's full of spirits?"
A third declared he knew a knife
　Would cut this Knott much quicker,
"The surest way to end all strife,
And lay the spirit of a wife,

Is just to take and lick her!"
A temperance man caught up the word,
"Ah, yes," he groaned, "I've always heard
   Our poor friend somewhat slanted
Tow'rd taking liquor over-much;
I fear these spirits may be Dutch,
(A sort of gins, or something such,)
   With which his house is haunted;
I see the thing as clear as light —
If Knott would give up getting tight,
   Naught farther would be wanted:"
So all his neighbors stood aloof
And, that the spirits 'neath his roof
Were not entirely up to proof,
   Unanimously granted.

Knott knew that cocks and sprites were foes,
And so bought up, Heaven only knows
How many, though he wanted crows
To give ghosts caws, as I suppose,
   To think that day was breaking;
Moreover what he called his park,
He turned into a kind of ark
For dogs, because a little bark
Is a good tonic in the dark,
   If one is given to waking;
But things went on from bad to worse,
His curs were nothing but a curse,
   And, what was still more shocking,
Foul ghosts of living fowl made scoff
And would not think of going off
   In spite of all his cocking.

Shanghais, Bucks-counties, Dominiques,
Malays (that did n't lay for weeks),
   Polanders, Bantams, Dorkings,
(Waiving the cost, no trifling ill,
Since each brought in his little bill,)
By day or night were never still,
But every thought of rest would kill
   With cacklings and with quorkings;
Henry the Eighth of wives got free
   By a way he had of axing;

But poor Knott's Tudor henery
Was not so fortunate, and he
   Still found his trouble waxing;
As for the dogs, the rows they made,
And how they howled, snarled, barked and bayed,
   Beyond all human knowledge is;
All night, as wide awake as gnats,
The terriers rumpused after rats,
Or, just for practice, taught their brats
To worry cast-off shoes and hats,
The bull-dogs settled private spats,
All chased imaginary cats,
Or raved behind the fence's slats
At real ones, or, from their mats,
With friends, miles off, held pleasant chats,
Or, like some folks in white cravats,
Contemptuous of sharps and flats,
   Sat up and sang dogsologies.
Meanwhile the cats set up a squall,
And, safe upon the garden-wall,
   All night kept cat-a-walling,
As if the feline race were all,
In one wild cataleptic sprawl,
   Into love's tortures falling.

PART II.

SHOWING WHAT IS MEANT BY A FLOW OF SPIRITS.

At first the ghosts were somewhat shy,
Coming when none but Knott was nigh,
And people said 't was all their eye,
(Or rather his) a flam, the sly
   Digestion's machination;
Some recommended a wet sheet,
Some a nice broth of pounded peat,
Some a cold flat-iron to the feet,
Some a decoction of lamb's-bleat,
Some a southwesterly grain of wheat;
Meat was by some pronounced unmeet,
Others thought fish most indiscreet,
And that 't was worse than all to eat
Of vegetables, sour or sweet,

(Except, perhaps, the skin of beat,)
  In such a concatenation:
One quack his button gently plucks
And murmurs "biliary ducks!"
  Says Knott, "I never ate one;"
But all, though brimming full of wrath,
Homœo, Allo, Hydropath,
Concurred in this — that t' other's path .
  To death's door was the straight one
Still, spite of medical advice,
The ghosts came thicker, and a spice
  Of mischief grew apparent;
Nor did they only come at night,
But seemed to fancy broad daylight,
Till Knott, in horror and affright,
  His unoffending hair rent;
Whene'er with handkerchief on lap,
He made his elbow-chair a trap,
To catch an after-dinner nap,
The spirits, always on the tap,
Would make a sudden *rap, rap, rap,*
The half-spun cord of sleep to snap,
(And what is life without its nap
But threadbareness and mere mishap?)
As 't were with a percussion cap
  The trouble's climax capping;
It seemed a party dried and grim
Of mummies had come to visit him,
Each getting off from every limb
  Its multitudinous wrapping;
Scratchings sometimes the walls ran round,
The merest penny-weights of sound;
Sometimes 't was only by the pound
  They carried on their dealing,
A thumping 'neath the parlor floor,
Thump-bump-thump-bumping o'er and o'er,
As if the vegetables in store,
(Quiet and orderly before,)
  Were all together pealing;
You would have thought the thing was done
By the spirit of some son of a gun,
  And that a forty-two pounder,
Or that the ghost which made such sounds

Could be none other than John Pounds,
Of Ragged Schools the founder.

Through three gradations of affright,
The awful noises reached their height;
    At first they knocked nocturnally,
Then, for some reason, changing quite,
(As mourners, after six months' flight,
Turn suddenly from dark to light,)
    Began to knock diurnally,
And last, combining all their stocks,
(Scotland was ne'er so full of Knox,)
Into one Chaos (father of Nox,)
Nocte pluit — they showered knocks,
    And knocked, knocked, knocked eternally
Ever upon the go, like buoys,
(Wooden sea-urchins,) all Knott's joys,
They turned to troubles and a noise
    That preyed on him internally.

Soon they grew wider in their scope;
Whenever Knott a door would ope,
It would ope not, or else elope
And fly back (curbless as a trope
Once started down a stanza's slope
By a bard that gave it too much rope —)
    Like a clap of thunder slamming;
And, when kind Jenny brought his hat,
(She always, when he walked, did that,)
Just as upon his head it sat,
Submitting to his settling pat —
Some unseen hand would jam it flat,
Or give it such a furious bat
    That eyes and nose went cramming
Up out of sight, and consequently,
As when in life it paddled free,
    His beaver caused much damning;
If these things seemed o'erstrained to be,
Read the account of Docter Dee,
'T is in our college library;
Read Wesley's circumstantial plea,
And Mrs. Crowe, more like a bee,
Sucking the nightshade's honeyed fee,

And Stilling's Pneumatology;
Consult Scot, Glanvil, and grave Wie-
rus, and both Mathers; further, see
Webster, Casaubon, James First's trea-
tise, a right royal Q. E. D.
Writ with the moon in perigee,
Bodin de Demonomanie —
(Accent that last line gingerly)
All full of learning as the sea
Of fishes, and all disagree,
Save in *Sathanas apage!*
Or, what will surely put a flea
In unbelieving ears — with glee,
Out of a paper (sent to me
By some friend who forgot to P...
A...Y..., — I use cryptography
Lest I his vengeful pen should dree —
His P...O...S...T...A...G...E...)
    Things to the same effect I cut,
About the tantrums of a ghost,
Not more than three weeks since, at most,
    Near Stratford, in Connecticut.

Knott's Upas daily spread its roots,
Sent up on all sides livelier shoots,
And bore more pestilential fruits;
The ghosts behaved like downright brutes,
They snipped holes in his Sunday suits,
Practised all night on octave flutes,
Put peas (not peace) into his boots,
    Whereof grew corns in season,
They scotched his sheets, and, what was worse,
Stuck his silk night-cap full of burs,
Till he, in language plain and terse,
(But much unlike a Bible verse,)
    Swore he should lose his reason.

The tables took to spinning, too,
Perpetual yarns, and arm-chairs grew
    To prophets and apostles;
One footstool vowed that only he
Of law and gospel held the key,
That teachers of whate'er degree

To whom opinion bows the knee
Were n't fit to teach Truth's a. b. c.
And were (the whole lot) to a T.
　　Mere fogies all and fossils;
A teapoy, late the property
　　Of Knox's Aunt Keziah,
(Whom Jenny most irreverently
Had nicknamed her aunt-tipathy)
With tips emphatic claimed to be
　　The prophet Jeremiah;
The tins upon the kitchen-wall,
Turned tintinnabulators all,
And things that used to come at call
　　For simple household services,
Began to hop and whirl and prance,
Fit to put out of countenance
The *Commis* and *Grisettes* of France
　　Or Turkey's dancing Dervises.

Of course such doings, far and wide,
With rumors filled the country-side,
And (as it is our nation's pride
To think a Truth not verified
Till with majorities allied,)
Parties sprang up, affirmed, denied,
And candidates with questions plied
Who, like the circus-riders, tried
At once both hobbies to bestride,
And each with his opponent vied
　　In being inexplicit.
Earnest inquirers multiplied;
Folks, whose tenth cousins lately died,
Wrote letters long, and Knott replied.
All who could either walk or ride,
Gathered to wonder or deride,
　　And paid the house a visit;
Horses were at his pine-trees tied,
Mourners in every corner sighed,
Widows brought children there that cried,
Swarms of lean Seekers, eager-eyed,
(People Knott never could abide,)
Into each hole and cranny pried
With strings of questions cut and dried

From the Devout Inquirer's Guide,
For the wise spirits to decide —
  As, for example, is it
True that the damned are fried or boiled?
Was the Earth's axis greased or oiled?
Who cleaned the moon when it was soiled?
How baldness might be cured or foiled?
  How heal diseased potatoes?
Did spirits have the sense of smell?
Where would departed spinsters dwell?
If the late Zenas Smith were well?
If Earth were solid or a shell?
Were spirits fond of Doctor Fell?
Did the bull toll Cock-Robin's knell?
What remedy would bugs expel?
If Paine's invention were a sell?
Did spirits by Webster's system spell?
Was it a sin to be a belle?
Did dancing sentence folks to hell?
If so, then where most torture fell —
  On little toes or great toes?
If life's true seat were in the brain?
Did Ensign mean to marry Jane?
By whom, in fact, was Morgan slain?
Could matter ever suffer pain?
What would take out a cherry-stain?
Who picked the pocket of Seth Crane,
Of Waldo precinct, State of Maine?
Was Sir John Franklin sought in vain?
Did primitive Christians ever train?
What was the family-name of Cain?
Them spoons, were they by Betty ta'en?
Would earth-worm poultice cure a sprain?
Was Socrates so dreadful plain?
What teamster guided Charles's wain?
Was Uncle Ethan mad or sane,
And could his will in force remain?
If not, what counsel to retain?
Did Le Sage steal Gil Blas from Spain?
Was Junius writ by Thomas Paine?
Were ducks discomforted by rain?
How did Britannia rule the main?
Was Jonas coming back again?

Was vital truth upon the wane?
Did ghosts, to scare folks, drag a chain?
Who was our Huldah's chosen swain?
Did none have teeth pulled without payin'
　　Ere ether was invented?
Whether mankind would not agree,
If the universe were tuned in C.?
What was it ailed Lucindy's knee?
Whether folks eat folks in Feejee?
Whether *his* name would end with T.?
If Saturn's rings were two or three,
And what bump in Phrenology
　　They truly represented?
These problems dark, wherein they groped,
Wherewith man's reason vainly coped,
Now that the spirit-world was oped,
In all humility they hoped
　　Would be resolved *instanter;*
Each of the miscellaneous rout .
Brought his, or her, own little doubt,
And wished to pump the spirits out,
Through his, or her, own private spout,
　　Into his, or her, decanter.

PART III.

WHEREIN IT IS SHOWN THAT THE MOST ARDENT SPIRITS ARE MORE ORNAMENTAL THAN USEFUL.

Many a speculating wight
Came by express-trains, day and night,
To see if Knott would "sell his right,"
Meaning to make the ghosts a sight —
　　What they call a "meenaygerie;"
One threatened, if he would not "trade,"
His run of custom to invade,
(He could not these sharp folks persuade
That he was not, in some way, paid,)
　　And stamp him as a plagiary,
By coming down at one fell swoop,
With THE ORIGINAL KNOCKING TROUPE,
　　Come recently from Hades,

Who (for a quarter-dollar heard)
Would ne'er rap out a hasty word
Whence any blame might be incurred
  From the most fastidious ladies;
The late lamented Jesse Soule
To stir the ghosts up with a pole
And be director of the whole,
  Who was engaged the rather
For the rare merits he 'd combine,
Having been in the spirit line,
Which trade he only did resign,
With general applause, to shine,
Awful in mail of cotton fine,
  As ghost of Hamlet's father!
Another a fair plan reveals
Never yet hit on, which, he feels,
To Knott's religious sense appeals —
" We 'll have your house set up on wheels,
  A speculation pious;
For music, we can shortly find
A barrel-organ that will grind
Psalm-tunes — an instrument designed
For the New England tour — refined
From secular drosses, and inclined
To an unworldly turn, (combined
  With no sectarian bias;)
Then, travelling by stages slow,
Under the style of Knott & Co.,
I would accompany the show
As moral lecturer, the foe
Of Rationalism; you could throw
The rappings in, and make them go
Strict Puritan principles, you know,
(How *do* you make 'em? with your toe?)
And the receipts which thence might flow,
  We could divide between us;
Still more attractions to combine,
Beside these services of mine,
I will throw in a very fine
(It would do nicely for a sign)
  Original Titian's Venus."
Another offered handsome fees
If Knott would get Demosthenes,

(Nay, his mere knuckles, for more ease,)
To rap a few short sentences ;
Or if, for want of proper keys,
  His Greek might make confusion,
Then just to get a rap from Burke,
To recommend a little work
  On Public Elocution.
Meanwhile, the spirits made replies
To all the reverent *whats* and *whys*
Resolving doubts of every size,
And giving seekers grave and wise,
Who came to know their destinies,
  A rap-turous reception ;
When unbelievers void of grace
Came to investigate the place,
(Creatures of Sadducistic race,
With grovelling intellects and base),
They could not find the slightest trace
  To indicate deception;
Indeed, it is declared by some
That spirits (of this sort) are glum,
Almost, or wholly, deaf and dumb,
And (out of self-respect) quite mum
To sceptic natures cold and numb,
Who of *this* kind of Kingdom Come
  Have not a just conception ;
True, there were people who demurred
That, though the raps no doubt were heard
  Both under them and o'er them,
Yet, somehow, when a search they made,
They found Miss Jenny sore afraid,
Or Jenny's lover, Doctor Slade,
Equally awe-struck and dismayed,
Or Deborah, the chamber-maid,
Whose terrors, not to be gainsaid,
In laughs hysteric were displayed,
  Was always there before them ;
This had its due effect with some
Who straight departed, muttering, Hum !
  Transparent hoax ! and Gammon !
But these were few : believing souls
Came, day by day, in larger shoals,
As the ancients to the windy holes

'Neath Delphi's tripod brought their doles,
    Or to the shrine of Ammon.

The spirits seemed exceeding tame,
Call whom you fancied, and he came;
The shades august of eldest fame
    You summoned with an awful ease;
As grosser spirits gurgled out
From chair and table with a spout,
In Auerbach's cellar once, to flout
The senses of the rabble rout,
Where'er the gimlet twirled about
    Of cunning Mephistophiles —
So did these spirits seem in store,
Behind the wainscot or the door,
Ready to thrill the being's core
Of every enterprising bore
    With their astounding glamour;
Whatever ghost one wished to hear,
By strange coincidence, was near
To make the past or future clear,
    (Sometimes in shocking grammar,)
By raps and taps, now there, now here—
It seemed as if the spirit queer
Of some departed auctioneer
Were doomed to practise by the year
    With the spirit of his hammer;
Whate'er you asked was answered, yet
One could not very deeply get
Into the obliging spirits' debt,
Because they used the alphabet
    In all communications,
And new revealings (though sublime)
Rapped out, one letter at a time,
    With boggles, hesitations,
Stoppings, beginnings o'er again,
And getting matters into train,
Could hardly overload the brain
    With too excessive rations,
Since just to ask *if two and two
Really make four?* or, *How d' ye do?*
And get the fit replies thereto

In the tramundane rat-tat-too,
   Might ask a whole day's patience.

'T was strange ('mongst other things) to find
In what odd sets the ghosts combined,
   Happy forthwith to thump any
Piece of intelligence inspired,
The truth whereof had been inquired
   By some one of the company;
For instance, Fielding, Mirabeau,
Orator Henley, Cicero,
Paley, John Zisca, Marivaux,
Melancthon, Robertson, Junot,
Scaliger, Chesterfield, Rousseau,
Hakluyt, Boccaccio, South, De Foe,
Diaz, Josephus, Richard Roe,
Odin, Arminius, Charles *le gros,*
Tiresias, the late James Crow,
Casabianca, Grose, Prideaux,
Old Grimes, Young Norval, Swift, Brissot,
Maimonides, the Chevalier D'O,
Socrates, Fénelon, Job, Stow,
The inventor of *Elixir pro,*
Euripides, Spinoza, Poe,
Confucius, Hiram Smith, and Fo,
Came (as it seemed, somewhat *de trop*)
With a disembodied Esquimaux,
To say that it was so and so,
   With Franklin's expedition;
One testified to ice and snow,
One that the mercury was low,
One that his progress was quite slow,
One that he much desired to go,
One that the cook had frozen his toe,
(Dissented from by Dandolo,
Wordsworth, Cynaegirus, Boileau,
La Hontan, and Sir Thomas Roe,)
One saw twelve white bears in a row,
One saw eleven and a crow,
With other things we could not know
(Of great statistic value, though)
   By our mere mortal vision.

Sometimes the spirits made mistakes,
And seemed to play at ducks and drakes
With bold inquiry's heaviest stakes
   In science or in mystery;
They knew so little (and that wrong)
Yet rapped it out so bold and strong,
One would have said the entire throng
   Had been Professors of History;
What made it odder was, that those
Who, you would naturally suppose,
Could solve a question, if they chose,
As easily as count their toes,
   Were just the ones that blundered;
One day, Ulysses, happening down,
A reader of Sir Thomas Browne
   And who (with him) had wondered
What song it was the Sirens sang,
Asked the shrewd Ithacan — *bang! bang!*
With this response the chamber rang,
   " I guess it was Old Hundred."
And Franklin, being asked to name
The reason why the lightning came,
   Replied, " Because it thundered."

On one sole point the ghosts agreed,
One fearful point, than which, indeed,
   Nothing could seem absurder;
Poor Colonel Jones they all abused,
And finally downright accused
   The poor old man of murder;
'T was thus; by dreadful raps was shown
Some spirit's longing to make known
A bloody fact, which he alone
Was privy to, (such ghosts more prone
   In Earth's affairs to meddle are;)
Who are you? with awe-stricken looks,
All ask: his airy knuckles he crooks,
And raps, " I *was* Eliab Snooks,
   That used to be a peddler;
Some on ye still are on my books!"
Whereat, to inconspicuous nooks,
(More fearing this than common spooks,)
   Shrank each indebted meddler;

Further the vengeful ghost declared
That while his earthly life was spared,
About the country he had fared,
   A duly licensed follower
Of that much-wandering trade that wins
Slow profit from the sale of tins
   And various kinds of hollow-ware;
That Colonel Jones enticed him in,
Pretending that he wanted tin,
There slew him with a rolling-pin,
Hid him in a potatoe-bin,
   And (the same night) him ferried
Across Great Pond to t' other shore,
And there, on land of Widow Moore,
Just where you turn to Larkin's store,
   Under a rock him buried;
Some friends (who happened to be by)
He called upon to testify
That what he said was not a lie,
   And that he did not stir this
Foul matter, out of any spite
But from a simple love of right; —
   Which statements the Nine Worthies,
Rabbi Akiba, Charlemagne,
Seth, Colley Cibber, General Wayne,
Cambyses, Tasso, Tubal-Cain,
The owner of a castle in Spain,
Jehanghire, and the Widow of Nain,
(The friends aforesaid) made more plain
   And by loud raps attested;
To the same purport testified
Plato, John Wilkes, and Colonel Pride
Who knew said Snooks before he died,
   Had in his wares invested,
Thought him entitled to belief
And freely could concur, in brief,
   In everything the rest did.

Eliab this occasion seized,
(Distinctly here the spirit sneezed,)
To say that he should ne'er be eased
Till Jenny married whom she pleased,
   Free from all checks and urgin's,

(This spirit dropt his final g's)
And that, unless Knott quickly sees
This done, the spirits to appease,
They would come back his life to tease,
As thick as mites in ancient cheese,
And let his house on an endless lease
To the ghosts (terrific rappers these
And veritable Eumenides)
    Of the Eleven Thousand Virgins!

Knott was perplexed and shook his head.
He did not wish his child to wed
    With a suspected murderer,
(For, true or false, the rumor spread)
But as for this roiled life he led,
"It would not answer," so he said,
    "To have it go no furderer."

At last, scarce knowing what it meant,
Reluctantly he gave consent
That Jenny, since 't was evident
That she *would* follow her own bent,
    Should make her own election.
For that appeared the only way
These frightful noises to allay
Which had already turned him gray
    And plunged him in dejection.

Accordingly, this artless maid
Her father's ordinance obeyed,
And, all in whitest crape arrayed,
(Miss Pulsifer the dresses made
And wishes here the fact displayed
That she still carries on the trade,
The third door south from Bagg's Arcade,)
A very faint "I do" essayed
And gave her hand to Hiram Slade,
From which time forth, the ghosts were laid,
    And ne'er gave trouble after;
But the Selectmen, be it known,
Dug underneath the aforesaid stone,
Where the poor peddler's corpse was thrown,
And found thereunder a jaw-bone,

2 u

Though, when the crowner sat thereon,
He nothing hatched, except alone
   Successive broods of laughter;
It was a frail and dingy thing,
In which a grinder or two did cling,
   In color like molasses,
Which surgeons, called from far and wide,
Upon the horror to decide,
   Having put on their glasses,
Reported thus — " To judge by looks,
These bones, by some queer hooks or crooks,
May have belonged to Mr. Snooks,
But, as men deepest-read in books
   Are perfectly aware, bones,
If buried, fifty years or so,
Lose their identity and grow
   From human bones to bare bones."

Still, if to Jaalam you go down,
You 'll find two parties in the town,
One headed by Benaiah Brown,
   And one by Perez Tinkham;
The first believe the ghosts all through
And vow that they shall never rue
The happy chance by which they knew
That people in Jupiter are blue,
And very fond of Irish stew,
Two curious facts which Prince Lee Boo
Rapped clearly to a chosen few —
   Whereas the others think 'em
A trick got up by Doctor Slade
With Deborah the chamber-maid
   And that sly cretur Jinny,
That all the revelations wise,
At which the Brownites made big eyes,
Might have been given by Jared Keyes,
   A natural fool and ninny,
And, last week, did n't Eliab Snooks
Come back with never better looks,
As sharp as new-bought mackerel hooks,
   And bright as a new pin, eh ?
Good Parson Wilbur, too, avers
(Though to be mixed in parish stirs

Is worse than handling chestnut-burs)
That no case to his mind occurs
Where spirits ever did converse
Save in a kind of guttural Erse.
　(So say the best authorities;)
And that a charge by raps conveyed,
Should be most scrupulously weighed
　And searched into, before it is
Made public, since it may give pain
That cannot soon be cured again,
And one word may infix a stain
　Which ten cannot gloss over,
Though speaking for his private part,
He is rejoiced with all his heart
　Miss Knott missed not her lover.

AN ORIENTAL APOLOGUE.

I.

SOMEWHERE in India, upon a time,
(Read it not Injah, or you spoil the verse)
    There dwelt two saints whose privilege sublime
It was to sit and watch the world grow worse,
    Their only care (in that delicious clime)
At proper intervals to pray and curse;
    Pracrit the dialect each prudent brother
    Used for himself, Damnonian for the other.

II.

One half the time of each was spent in praying
For blessings on his own unworthy head,
    The other half in fearfully portraying
Where certain folks would go when they were dead;
    This system of exchanges — there's no saying
To what more solid barter 'twould have led,
    But that a river, vext with boils and swellings
    At rainy times, kept peace between their dwellings.

III.

So they two played at wordy battledore
And kept a curse forever in the air,
    Flying this way or that from shore to shore;
No other labor did this holy pair,
    Clothed and supported from the lavish store
Which crowds lanigerous brought with daily care;
    They toiled not neither did they spin; their bias
    Was tow'rd the harder task of being pious.

IV.

Each from his hut rushed six score times a day,
Like a great canon of the Church full-rammed
    With cartridge theologic, (so to say,)
Touched himself off, and then, recoiling, slammed
    His hovel's door behind him in a way
That to his foe said plainly — *you'll* be damned;
    And so like Potts and Wainwright, shrill and strong
    The two D—D'd each other all day long.

V.

One was a dancing Dervise, a Mohammedan,
The other was a Hindoo, a gymnosophist;
  One kept his whatd'yecallit and his Ramadan,
Laughing to scorn the sacred rites and laws of his
    Transfluvial rival, who, in turn, called Ahmed an
Old top, and, as a clincher, shook across a fist
  With nails six inches long, yet lifted not
  His eyes from off his navel's mystic knot.

VI.

"Who whirls not round six thousand times an hour
Will go," screamed Ahmed, "to the evil place;
  May he eat dirt, and may the dog and Giaour
Defile the graves of him and all his race;
  Allah loves faithful souls and gives them power
To spin till they are purple in the face;
    Some folks get you know what, but he that pure is
    Earns Paradise and ninety thousand houries."

VII.

"Upon the silver mountain, South by East,
Sits Brahma fed upon the sacred bean;
  He loves those men whose nails are still increased,
Who all their lives keep ugly, foul and lean;
  'Tis of his grace that not a bird or beast
Adorned with claws like mine was ever seen;
    The suns and stars are Brahma's thoughts divine
    Even as these trees I seem to see are mine."

VIII.

"Thou seem'st to see, indeed!" roared Ahmed back.
"Were I but once across this plaguy stream,
  With a stout sapling in my hand, one whack
On those lank ribs would rid thee of that Dream!
  Thy Brahma-blasphemy is ipecac
To my soul's stomach; could'st thou grasp the scheme
    Of true redemption, thou would'st know that Deity
    Whirls by a kind of blessed spontaneity.

IX.

" And this it is which keeps our earth here going
With all the stars." — " O, vile ! but there's a place
   Prepared for such ; to think of Brahma throwing
Worlds like a juggler's balls up into Space !
   Why, not so much as a smooth lotos blowing
Is e'er allowed that silence to efface
    Which broods around Brahma, and our earth, 'tis
      known,
    Rests on a tortoise, moveless as this stone."

X.

So they kept up their banning amebean,
When suddenly came floating down the stream
   A youth whose face like an incarnate pæan
Glowed, 'twas so full of grandeur and of gleam ;
   " If there *be* gods, then, doubtless, this must be one."
Thought both at once, and then began to scream,
    " Surely, whate'er immortals know, thou knowest,
Decide between us twain before thou goest ! "

XI.

The youth was drifting in a slim canoe
Most like a huge white waterlily's petal,
   But neither of our theologians knew
Whereof 'twas made ; whether of heavenly metal
   Unknown, or of a vast pearl split in two
And hollowed, was a point they could not settle ;
    'Twas good debate-seed, though, and bore large fruit
In after years of many a tart dispute.

XII.

There were no wings upon the stranger's shoulders
And yet he seemed so capable of rising
   That, had he soared like thistledown, beholders
Had thought the circumstance noways surprising ;
   Enough that he remained, and, when the scolders
Hailed him as umpire in their vocal prize-ring,
    The painter of his boat he lightly threw
Around a lotos-stem, and brought her to

XIII.

The strange youth had a look as if he might
Have trod far planets where the atmosphere,
   (Of nobler temper) steeps the face with light,
Just as our skins are tanned and freckled here;
   His air was that of a cosmopolite
In the wide universe from sphere to sphere;
   Perhaps he was (his face had such grave beauty)
   An officer of Saturn's guards off duty.

XIV.

Both saints began to unfold their tales at once,
Both wished their tales, like simial ones, prehensile,
   That they might seize his ear; *fool! knave!* and *dunce!*
Flew zigzag back and forth, like strokes of pencil
   In a child's fingers; voluble as duns,
They jabbered like the stones on that immense hill
   In the Arabian Nights; until the stranger
   Began to think his ear-drum in some danger.

XV.

In general those who nothing have to say
Contrive to spend the longest time in doing it;
   They turn and vary it in every way,
Hashing it, stewing it, mincing it, *ragouting* it;
   Sometimes they keep it purposely at bay,
Then let it slip to be again pursuing it;
   They drone it, groan it, whisper it and shout it,
   Refute it, flout it, swear to't, prove it, doubt it.

XVI.

Our saints had practised for some thirty years;
Their talk, beginning with a single stem,
   Spread like a banyan, sending down live piers,
Colonies of digression, and, in them,
   Germs of yet new migrations; once by the ears,
They could convey damnation in a hem,
   And blow the pitch of premise-priming off
   Long syllogistic batteries, with a cough.

XVII.

Each had a theory that the human ear
A providential tunnel was, which led
　To a huge vacuüm, (and surely here
They showed some knowledge of the general head,)
　For cant to be decanted through, a mere
Auricular canal or raceway to be fed
　　All day and night, in sunshine and in shower,
　　From their vast heads of milk-and-water-power.

XVIII.

The present being a peculiar case,
Each with unwonted zeal the other scouted,
　Put his spurred hobby through its very pace,
Pished, pshawed, poohed, horribled, bahed, jeered,
　　sneered, flouted,
　Sniffed, nonsensed, infideled, fudged, with his face
Looked scorn too nicely shaded to be shouted,
　　And, with each inch of person and of vesture,
　　Contrived to hint some most disdainful gesture.

XIX.

At length, when their breath's end was come about,
And both could, now and then, just gasp "impostor!"
　Holding their heads thrust menacingly out,
As staggering cocks keep up their fighting posture,
　The stranger smiled and said, "Beyond a doubt
'Tis fortunate, my friends, that you have lost your
　　United parts of speech, or it had been
　　Impossible for me to get between.

XX.

"Produce! says Nature, — what have you produced ;
A new straitwaistcoat for the human mind;
　Are you not limbed, nerved, jointed, arteried, juiced
As other men? yet, faithless to your kind,
　Rather like noxious insects you are used
To puncture life's fair fruit, beneath the rind
　　Laying your creed-eggs whence in time there spring
　　Consumers new to eat and buzz and sting.

XXI.

"Work! you have no conception how 'twill sweeten
Your views of Life and Nature, God and Man;
   Had you been forced to earn what you have eaten,
Your heaven had shown a less dyspeptic plan;
   At present your whole function is to eat ten
And talk ten times as rapidly as you can;
     Were your shape true to cosmogonic laws,
     You would be nothing but a pair of jaws.

XXII.

"Of all the useless beings in creation
The earth could spare most easily you bakers
   Of little clay gods, formed in shape and fashion
Precisely in the image of their makers;
   Why, it would almost move a saint to passion,
To see these blind and deaf, the hourly breakers
     Of God's own image in their brother men,
     Set themselves up to tell the how, where, when,

XXIII.

"Of God's existence; one's digestion's worse —
So makes a god of vengeance and of blood;
   Another — but no matter, they reverse
Creation's plan, out of their own vile mud
   Pat up a god, and burn, drown, hang, or curse
Whoever worships not; each keeps his stud
     Of texts which wait with saddle on and bridle
     To hunt down atheists to their ugly idol.

XXIV.

"This, I perceive, has been your occupation;
You should have been more usefully employed;
   All men are bound to earn their daily ration,
Where States make not that primal contract void
   By cramps and limits; simple devastation
Is the worm's task, and what he has destroyed
     His monument; creating is man's work
     And that, too, something more than mist and murk."

XXV.

So having said, the youth was seen no more,
And straightway our sage Brahmin, the philosopher,
   Cried, "That was aimed at thee, thou endless bore,
Idle and useless as the growth of moss over
   A rotting tree-trunk!" "I would square that score
Full soon," replied the Dervise, "could I cross over
   And catch thee by the beard! Thy nails I'd trim
   And make thee work, as was advised by him."

XXVI.

   "Work? Am I not at work from morn till night
Sounding the deeps of oracles umbilical
   Which for man's guidance never come to light,
With all their various aptitudes, until I call?"
   "And I, do I not twirl from left to right
For conscience' sake? Is that no work? Thou silly gull,
   He had thee in his eye; 'twas Gabriel
   Sent to reward my faith, I know him well."

XXVII.

   "'Twas Vishnu, thou vile whirligig!" and so
The good old quarrel was begun anew;
   One would have sworn the sky was black as sloe,
Had but the other dared to call it blue;   .
   Nor were the followers who fed them slow
To treat each other with their curses, too,
   Each hating t'other (moves it tears or laughter?)
   Because he thought him sure of hell hereafter.

XXVIII.

   At last some genius built a bridge of boats
Over the stream, and Ahmed's zealots filed
   Across, upon a mission to (cut throats
And) spread religion pure and undefiled;
   They sowed the propagandist's wildest oats,
Cutting off all, down to the smallest child,
   And came back, giving thanks for such fat mercies,
   To find their harvest gone past prayers or curses.

XXIX.

All gone except their saint's religious hops,
Which he kept up with more than common flourish;
But these, however satisfying crops
For the inner man, were not enough to nourish
The body politic, which quickly drops
Reserve in such sad juncture, and turns currish;
So Ahmed soon got cursed for all the famine
Where'er the popular voice could edge a damn in.

XXX.

At first he pledged a miracle quite boldly,
And, for a day or two, they growled and waited:
But, finding that this kind of manna coldly
Sat on their stomachs, they ere long berated
The saint for still persisting in that old lie,
Till soon the whole machine of saintship grated,
Ran slow, creaked, stopped, and, wishing him in
    Tophet,
They gathered strength enough to stone the prophet.

XXXI.

Some stronger ones contrived, (by eating leather,
Their weaker friends, and one thing or another,)
The winter months of scarcity to weather;
Among these was the late saint's younger brother,
Who, in the spring, collecting them together,
Persuaded them that Ahmed's holy pother
Had wrought in their behalf, and that the place
Of Saint should be continued to his race.

XXXII.

Accordingly 'twas settled on the spot
That Allah favored that peculiar breed;
Beside, as all were satisfied, 'twould not
Be quite respectable to have the need
Of public spiritual food forgot;
And so the tribe, with proper forms decreed
That he, and, failing him, his next of kin,
Forever for the people's good should spin.

INDEX OF TITLES.

INDEX OF FIRST LINES.

2 x

Printed in the United States
49853LVS00003B/19